THE INDIAN CIVIL RIGHTS ACT AT FORTY

THE INDIAN CIVIL RIGHTS ACT AT FORTY

EDITED BY KRISTEN A. CARPENTER,
MATTHEW L. M. FLETCHER, AND ANGELA R. RILEY

UCLA American Indian Studies Center
3220 Campbell Hall
Box 951548
Los Angeles, California 90095-1548
http://www.books.aisc.ucla.edu

Cover artwork: *Them Two, the First Americans,* © Sam English

Library of Congress Control Number: 2011933108

ISBN 0-935626-67-0
ISBN-13: 978-0-935626-67-4

Printed in the United States of America
Printed on recycled paper by McNaughton & Gunn, Inc. ♻

Dedication

─────

We dedicate this book to the memory of David H. Getches who devoted his career to seeking justice for American Indian people. His abiding belief in the foundational principles of federal Indian law and his determination to see those principles realized remain an inspiration to scholars and advocates in the field.

CONTENTS

CONTENTS

Part IV – Criminal Law in Indian Country

Part V – The Power and Limits of the Indian Civil Rights Act

Acknowledgments

We wish to recognize the many people who made this book possible.

At the University of Colorado Law School, Kristen Carpenter would like to acknowledge colleagues Cynthia Carter, Rick Collins, David Getches (in memoriam), Sarah Krakoff, Jill Tompkins, and Charles Wilkinson; and student research assistants Anna Dronzek and John Hoelle. Thank you to Dean Phil Weiser for his support of the Indian Law Program at CU Law.

At Michigan State University College of Law, Matthew Fletcher would like to thank Wenona Singel, Kate Fort, and Emily Petoskey. Special thanks go to Dean Joan Howarth for her unwavering support of the Indigenous Law and Policy Center, and to the MSU Law Library.

At the University of California, Los Angeles, Angela Riley would like to thank the School of Law for its support of her work with Indian nations and Carole Goldberg for her unparalleled leadership and vision in the field. Special thanks go to student research assistant, Mack Eason, and to the staff and colleagues at the American Indian Studies Center.

We extend our deep appreciation to Pamela Grieman, publications manager, UCLA American Indian Studies Center, for her expertise in assembling the book, and to all of the authors for their contributions.

We also thank the speakers, moderators, and other participants at the 2008 Indigenous Law Conference at Michigan State University College of Law, including Sharon Avery, Lawrence Baca, Hannah Bobee, Trent Crable, Marty Curry, Zeke Fletcher, Francine Hatch, Gordon Henry, Alicia Ivory, Sonia Katyal, Elizabeth Kronk, Stacy Leeds, Dan Lewerenz, Catharine MacKinnon, Rebecca Miles, Sheena Oxendine, Eva Petoskey, Frank Pommersheim, Frank Ravitch, Wenona Singel, Paul Spruhan, Rina Swentzell, Melissa Tatum, Ann Tweedy, and Gloria Valencia-Weber.

Finally, we acknowledge the University of Colorado Law School, Michigan State University College of Law, University of California, Los Angeles School of Law, and the UCLA American Indian Studies Center for generously supporting this project.

Introduction

KRISTEN A. CARPENTER, MATTHEW L. M. FLETCHER,
AND ANGELA R. RILEY

During the height of the Civil Rights era, certain members of Congress became concerned about the particular situation of American Indian civil rights in Indian country. Consequently, the Senate's Constitutional Rights Committee conducted hearings over the course of several years (1961–1968). While many witnesses focused on abuses of Indian individuals committed by state and federal officials, others complained of tribal government practices, including the failure to provide counsel in criminal cases, police brutality, election irregularities, absence of impartial tribunals, and other civil rights issues. These reports were particularly concerning to Congress in light of growing discomfort with the anomalous nature of tribal governments. Indian nations, whose sovereignty predates the United States and is acknowledged by the Constitution, were not invited to the Constitutional Convention and never ratified the document. Thus, the Constitution's protections for individual liberties, embodied in the Bill of Rights and elsewhere, do not restrict the activities of tribal governments. Consequently, pursuant to its broad legislative powers over Indian tribes, Congress passed the Indian Civil Rights Act of 1968 (ICRA) to address civil rights in Indian country.

ICRA extended select, tailored provisions of the Bill of Rights—including equal protection, due process, free speech and religious exercise, criminal procedure, and property rights—to tribal governments. In these and other provisions, Congress sought to ensure that those under the jurisdiction of tribal governments would be guaranteed individual rights comparable to those enjoyed by all citizens vis à vis the state and federal governments. In doing so, Congress attempted to balance individual rights with the rights of tribes to continue to exist as distinct cultural and governmental entities.

But, as subsequent Supreme Court litigation bore out, with the exception of the writ of habeas corpus, Congress did not establish a federal enforcement mechanism for violations of the Act, nor did it abrogate tribal sovereign immunity. Thus,

ICRA strikes a delicate, and often controversial, balance between tribal sovereignty and individual liberties. Indeed, the Act and judicial decisions interpreting it, namely the Supreme Court's 1978 decision in *Santa Clara Pueblo v. Martinez*, have inspired wide-ranging debates. Indian nations' freedom to govern themselves—especially when evaluated against the core tenets of liberalism—remains highly controversial. On the one hand, safeguarding tribal court decisions from federal court review protects tribal sovereignty and the internal development of tribal law consistent with community values and traditions. On the other hand, insulating tribal regimes from external judicial scrutiny has been criticized as privileging the interests of tribes over individual liberties. And the question of ICRA's potentially assimilative effect was, and remains, a core concern.

As a practical matter, pursuant to *Martinez*, ICRA has been interpreted and enforced almost exclusively by Indian tribes and their courts. Our collection of essays, gathered on the fortieth anniversary of ICRA, provides for the first time a summary and critical analysis of how Indian tribes interpret and apply these important civil rights provisions in our contemporary world. What we found in the process of creating this book was a theme of tribal renewal in matters involving civil rights. Rather than approaching ICRA from a dichotomous vantage point—individual versus collective, traditional versus modern, or separate versus assimilative—we found that many Indian people and tribal governments have taken, in the words of renowned legal philosopher Roger Cover, a decidedly "jurisgenerative" approach to civil rights provisions. While informed by ICRA and the dominant society's conception of individual rights, Indian nations are ultimately adapting and interpreting ICRA in ways consistent with their own tribal traditions and beliefs. In this regard, our reflection on ICRA parallels, in some respects, the broader experiences of tribes over the past forty years—a period of growth, revitalization, and self-determination for many Indian nations.

This book owes its inspiration to a recent conference entitled "Forty Years of the Indian Civil Rights Act—History, Tribal Law, and Modern Challenges," organized by Matthew L. M. Fletcher, Wenona T. Singel, and Kathryn E. Fort at Michigan State University College of Law. That conference incorporated a wide array of perspectives and viewpoints by attorneys, scholars, and community members. This book draws on conference proceedings and scholarly works subsequently submitted to highlight some of the greatest impacts of the Indian Civil Rights Act on American Indian tribes.

The first chapter is an introduction and retrospective by Lawrence Baca, a retired Department of Justice, Civil Rights Division attorney who was the first American Indian ever hired through the Department of Justice's Honor Law Program. Ultimately, Baca's piece is a cautionary tale of race and government. It is followed by Part I, which focuses on equal protection issues raised by ICRA and was inspired by conference presentations on *Santa Clara Pueblo v. Martinez*. These included a plenary address by feminist theorist Catharine MacKinnon and panel presentations by indigenous leaders and scholars including Gloria Valencia-Weber (Mexican Indian heritage and University of New Mexico professor), Rina Swentzell

(Santa Clara Pueblo member and anthropologist), Eva Petoskey (Grand Traverse Band of Ottawa and Chippewa Indians member and former tribal council vice chair), Francine Hatch (Isleta Pueblo member and tribal judge), and Rebecca Miles (Nez Perce Tribe member and tribal council member), several of whom provided their remarks for publication in this book. Part I also features chapters by Professors Ann Tweedy and Kevin Noble Maillard, which contrast divergent perspectives on issues of gender, race, and other issues of equality in tribal communities.

Part II turns to questions of due process in tribal court practice, with chapters by leading Indian law scholar Frank Pommersheim and practitioner Paul Spruhan, an associate attorney general at the Navajo Nation Department of Justice. Part III focuses on questions of free speech and religious freedom, respectively, with chapters by two of this book's editors, Matthew Fletcher and Kristen Carpenter. Part IV covers criminal law under the ICRA with chapters by Elizabeth Kronk, regarding criminal justice on the ground in Indian country, and a coauthored chapter by Duane Champagne and Carole Goldberg, who examine ICRA's retrocession processes for Public Law 280 states. The book concludes in Part V with Mark Rosen's empirical analysis of past tribal court ICRA decisions.

We hope you enjoy reading this collection as much as we enjoyed putting it together for you.

KRISTEN A. CARPENTER, Associate Professor and Associate Dean for Faculty Development, University of Colorado Law School

MATTHEW L. M. FLETCHER, Professor of Law and Director of Indigenous Law and Policy Center, Michigan State University College of Law

ANGELA R. RILEY, Professor of Law and Director of the American Indian Studies Center, University of California, Los Angeles

Reflections on the Role of the United States Department of Justice in Enforcing the Indian Civil Rights Act

≡≡≡

LAWRENCE R. BACA

INTRODUCTION

I am very pleased to have been invited to write an essay for inclusion in this work. The perspective I bring to the Indian Civil Rights Act[1] (ICRA) is unique in that I was an attorney at the United States Department of Justice (the Department) while the Department was still enforcing the ICRA and when *Santa Clara Pueblo v. Martinez*[2] was decided.

I do not intend here to make a solid academic argument for or against enforcement of the ICRA. What I intend to do is tell a story, a cautionary tale about the United States Department of Justice and what I assert were misguided attempts to sue tribes under the ICRA both before and after the Court's decision in *Martinez*. The Department has gone from filing direct actions against tribes to enforce the ICRA between 1973 and 1978, to using other statutes to enforce the ICRA through the back door in a post-*Martinez* world. There were efforts from within the Department to amend the ICRA in order to waive tribal immunity from suit, grant the Attorney General Authority pattern or practice jurisdiction to sue tribes, and give the federal courts authority to accept those cases.

I am a major critic of the Civil Rights Division (CRD or the Division) of the Department of Justice and its historic failure to think of American Indians when it thinks enforcement of the civil rights laws. It is in that vein that I think of the Department of Justice and the Division. The Office of Indian Rights was established to bring cases under all of the civil rights acts on behalf of American Indians, yet its leadership seemed overly obsessed with suing tribes under the ICRA. The CRD is supposed to be the leading proponent of the civil rights of American Indians, but it's not. The late Tim Joranko, a deputy director of the Office of Tribal Justice, accused the Civil Rights Division of being more interested in bringing cases against Indians under the ICRA than enforcing the other civil rights laws on behalf of American Indians.

PROLOGUE: THE OFFICE OF INDIAN RIGHTS

The Indian Civil Rights Act was enacted in 1968 when I was a senior in high school. I remember that the buzz of the time was that American Indians had been citizens since 1934 but still didn't have constitutional rights. When you are eighteen and you hear this, you believe it. When you do "angry young Indian" speeches as a college student, you repeat it. And because no one in the audience is a lawyer or a lawyer that practices federal Indian law, they believe it too. That was, of course, as a matter of law, incorrect. And equally incorrect was the belief that passage of the ICRA would have granted constitutional rights to Indians had the assertion been true. The codifiers of Title II of the Civil Rights Act of 1968 called that section in Title 25 of the United States Code, Constitutional Rights of Indians.[3] To many courts and commentators, calling these statutory rights "constitutional rights" colored their thinking about the meaning of those rights in a tribal context. I think that the choice of language prevented some from ever thinking about those rights in a tribe-by-tribe legal and cultural setting. When one reflects on that choice of language one is reminded of Abraham Lincoln's dog story. Confronted with a self-defined "man of intelligence and education" who wanted to be the president's adviser, President Lincoln asked the man, "If you have an ordinary dog and you call its tail a leg, how many legs does the dog have?" The man answered, "Well five, of course." Lincoln responded, "No, four, because calling a dog's tail a leg doesn't make it a leg."[4]

That's how I feel about the claim that ICRA created constitutional rights of Indians. It neither created constitutional rights nor did it ensure the enforcement of any constitutional or civil rights of American Indians. Attorneys at the Department of Justice used to refer to the ICRA as the Indian Bill of Rights and that label colored their thinking in every matter that they reviewed. For most of its history, the Civil Rights Division had ignored the civil rights of Indians. Between 1957 when it was created and 1973, the Civil Rights Division filed thousands of cases on behalf of African American victims of civil rights violations while filing two on behalf of American Indians.[5] Interestingly, neither of those cases was an enforcement of the ICRA.

The Division itself came to grips with the fact that it had been ignoring Indians in 1973. The Civil Rights Division had sent several attorneys to Wounded Knee, South Dakota, following the events involving the occupation of the Village of Wounded Knee on the Pine Ridge Indian reservation by nonresidents of the village, which then brought about the massive influx of federal visitors to the reservation with helicopters, badges, and guns.[6] When the smoke cleared, the Department of Justice concluded that a great deal of civil unrest on Indian reservations was caused by what it believed were bad tribal governments and their failures to adhere to the strictures of the Indian Civil Right Act. In addition, the CRD also concluded that the Civil Rights Division had rarely enforced the other civil rights acts on behalf of American Indians. An Indian Rights Task Force was created, which further discovered that American Indians were victims of race discrimination at a very significant rate. There were major denials of rights—like the right to vote or run for state and county elected office, get a loan from a bank, or rent a home in the neighborhood of your choice—that were completely unchecked by the Division. Everything from the right to walk into the restaurant of your choice without being assaulted to equal educational opportunities had been left unprotected by the Division where American Indians were concerned. In point of fact, the Division had filed one public accommodations case and one case involving equal credit opportunity under the Fair Housing Act on behalf of American Indian victims between 1957 and 1973.[7]

So with the combined notion that someone ought to be enforcing the Indian Civil Rights Act against tribal governments, and that in order to enforce the other civil rights laws where Indians were concerned you needed some expertise in federal Indian law and Indian culture, the task force became the Office of Indian Rights. It is important not to confuse the Office of Indian Rights with the Office of Tribal Justice. The Office of Indian Rights was a litigating unit in the Civil Rights Division between 1973 and 1980.[8] The Office of Tribal Justice was created by Attorney General Janet Reno during the Clinton administration[9] to be the liaison between the 563 federally recognized tribes and the Department of Justice and to advise the attorney general on matters of federal Indian law and policy.

Prior to 1973, the Indian Civil Rights Act had not been enforced by any unit in the Civil Rights Division or anywhere else in the Department of Justice (DOJ). Think about that fact for a moment. A new civil rights law was passed in 1968, and by 1973—five years later—not a single action had been filed by the DOJ to enforce one section of it, nor had any investigation been conducted. Title VIII of the 1968 Civil Rights Act is the Fair Housing Act. The Civil Rights Division filed its first Fair Housing Act complaint the day after the act was signed by the president. Yet not a single investigation was conducted concerning any violation of the ICRA, Title II of the same civil rights act before 1973. It is doubtful that anyone in the Civil Rights Division had even thought about whether or not the authority existed to enforce the act. More importantly, that fact was because no one thought of Indians as a victim class under any of the civil rights statutes at all. In 1976, the year that I was hired, every new attorney in the Civil Rights Division was given a pamphlet, printed by the Government Printing Office (GPO), containing the language of all of the civil rights laws that the Civil Rights Division enforces. It was printed in 1976, and it starts with the 1957 Civil Rights Act and goes forward to the Voting Rights Act of 1975. The ICRA is not one of the statutes included in the pamphlet. It had simply been ignored. Either the GPO ignored it or it didn't believe the federal government had the authority to enforce it.

What this set of facts means is that in 1973 there was no one in the Civil Rights Division with any experience or expertise in federal Indian law. When they formed the Office of Indian Rights, the attorneys were going to learn it as they went. In

1976, I was offered a position in the Civil Rights Division and specifically in the Office of Indian Rights. There are few in life more full of themselves than a third-year Harvard law student with more than one job offer. So I asked the Office of Indian Rights to fly me to Washington, D.C. to interview them and they did. The Division had announced in 1973 that it wanted to staff the Office in part with American Indian lawyers and that interviews would be conducted at the Universities of New Mexico and Arizona, so it was only natural that they found their first Indian lawyer at Harvard. They were so desperate to get an Indian lawyer in the Office of Indian Rights that they flew me to Washington, D.C. as a "consultant" so that I could interview them.

Mind-set Is Everything

When I arrived at the offices of the OIR, the first question after "how was the flight" was "As an Indian do you think ..." It has been my experience that when someone starts a question with "As an Indian," whatever comes next is going to be something really stupid and offensive. The deputy director asked me, "Do you think that, as an Indian, you would have any qualms about suing an Indian tribe?" Many thoughts came to mind. First among them was, "Does this man think I didn't read their brochure and know that they believe they have the authority to sue tribes under the Indian Civil Rights Act?" That thought was followed by, "Does he ask white lawyers, "Do you think that, as a white person, you would have any qualms about suing a white government for violating the law." The man asking the question was a white man who had spent the majority of his legal career suing other white men. I do not know if he had qualms about it; I never asked. But I do know this: If his presumption is that his race is the color of neutrality and the rest of us are biased by our racial background, then his question made perfect sense.

In January 1976, when my visit took place, *Santa Clara Pueblo v. Martinez*[10] was before the Tenth Circuit. The only opinion out was the trial court opinion. The attorneys in the Office of Indian Rights didn't know that my third-year paper was about the Indian Civil Rights Act because I'd originally been interviewed for the Attorney General's Honor Law Graduate Program by an attorney in the Anti-Trust Division.[11] But I was an Indian, so under the assumption that I must have studied Indian law even though my law school didn't have a course, the interviewers asked, "What do you think of the *Martinez* case?" I opined that since the act didn't specifically waive the tribe's immunity from suit, the federal court had no jurisdiction to hear the case. I took the framework for that argument from a really good law review article that I'd read. The office director said with a straight face, "Well, you think that way because you are an Indian."

Martinez, of course, was an Indian woman suing an Indian tribe.[12] I'd call that Indian versus Indian. Call me a "tribal sovereigntist" and I'll plead guilty as charged. But don't tell me that my legal analysis is solely based on my being an Indian unless, of course, you are prepared to say that you think the way you do because you are whatever your race is, and then we don't need to talk anymore because we both always know what the other races think.

Our conflict was, however, what I think is the classic conflict of having the Civil Rights Division as the leading proponent of Indian rights under the ICRA. The attorneys in the Civil Rights Division were individual rightists who simply couldn't understand collective tribal rights when confronted with a conflict between the two. The OIR attorneys used to accuse the rest of the Division of being racist because those attorneys didn't think that "Indian cases" were of equal importance to other cases, and yet when the right case came along, the Office of Indian Rights leadership was capable of saying that a given tribe didn't have a written tribal code because the tribal leaders were "petty dictators" who could then hide the laws from tribal members.[13] The OIR director and deputy director were big proponents of oral tradition except when it didn't serve their argument.

In our Santa Clara Pueblo debate, the director was a classic civil libertarian who believed in individual rights over government restraints on those rights and I was a tribal sovereigntist who believed that Indian tribes have the right to govern in the manner allowed by their members. In the case of tribal immunity from suit, the tribe had not waived its immunity and the Congress had not specifically removed it in the Indian Civil Rights Act. Further, the Supreme Court still had not developed the concept that certain powers may be inconsistent with an Indian tribe's status as a domestic dependent nation, so the Court hadn't revoked tribal sovereignty either.[14] Payback for my heresy came in the summer of 1977 when the draft of the solicitor general's brief recommending certiorari was being circulated to all of the attorneys in the Office of Indian Rights for review. I was the only lawyer in the Office who wasn't given a copy of the draft. Likewise, I did not see the solicitor's brief recommending that the Court find federal jurisdiction. No dissenters allowed.

The Court did accept the case for review and in 1978 the decision was rendered in favor of the tribe. I was in Arizona on an investigation when the decision came down. Back in those days, Civil Rights Division attorneys called in twice a day to let their supervisors know they were alive. In the early days, working in the Deep South, some DOJ attorneys would be followed to their motels. They might see the same people in the parking lot after supper no matter which restaurant they ate at. So when I called in to the office, my boss says with great regret in his voice, "I guess you heard that we lost *Martinez*." I could not help myself; when my supervisor said to me, "We lost *Martinez*," I responded, "What do you mean *we*, white man?"

What litigating direction any unit takes is in fact greatly influenced by the person in charge. Under the first director of the Office of Indian Rights, the emphasis was on traditional civil rights violations, such as voting, housing, and public accommodations. When the second director took over, the emphasis shifted to investigating tribal governments under the ICRA. Under the third Office director in three years, there was more of a balance between the two, but there remained an implicit mandate to go after tribes and enforce the ICRA.[15]

At the time, when a complaint came in to the Office, the attorney assigned to the matter would write a memorandum to the assistant attorney general (AAG) for the CRD and obtain permission to have the Federal Bureau of Investigation (FBI) conduct a preliminary investigation.[16] The attorney then wrote a memorandum to the FBI stating what information he or she wanted agents to collect. The FBI conducted interviews and, where appropriate, copied documents. Using that information and any necessary individual follow-up, the attorney would write a Memorandum of Justification to File Suit (J-memo) which was presented to the AAG who then authorized a lawsuit. The attorney handling the case notified the violator and offered to engage in a negotiated settlement so the parties could present the court with a consent decree at the time the complaint was filed. The CRD settled 90 percent of its civil cases by consent decree.

I've heard stories from some tribal attorneys that some of the Office of Indian Rights attorneys would tell tribes that the United States had an unlimited budget whereas the tribe didn't, so if the tribe didn't settle the United States would run up its litigation costs until the tribe was bankrupt. That is not the way I was trained to negotiate. But I've heard the stories.

What these facts mean is that the Office of Indian Rights had been pursuing actions against tribes under the ICRA with some success for three years without ever having to fire a litigative shot. No case in which the Department was a party had determined whether the ICRA could be enforced in federal court or whether the attorney general had authority to enforce it in any of the CRD actions. These are, in fact, different questions. By contrast, the Civil Rights Act of 1968, specifically the Fair Housing Act (Title VIII), for example, grants specific authority to the attorney general of the United States to bring an action in the appropriate federal district court. An intricate set of enforcement provisions—42 U.S.C. §§ 3612, 3613, and 3614—include enforcement by the secretary of Housing and Urban Development, by private parties, and by the attorney general. These sections are so detailed that they take up eight typed pages. There is no such language in the ICRA. In fact, there had been an enforcement provision in one of the early drafts of the bill, but it was removed. The working theory in the Office of Indian Rights was that the attorney general had authority to sue under the general trust relationship because suing tribes for violations of the ICRA was for the benefit of Indians. This means that either the federal government can enforce the federal trust relationship on behalf of individual Indians or that suing an Indian tribe to enforce the ICRA is for the benefit of the tribe.

The first of these theories would come back to haunt tribes and the second was a return to the *Kagama v. United States*[17] logic from the 1880s. In *Kagama*, the Supreme Court was called on to examine Congress' power to enact a criminal statute covering crimes by Indians against other Indians within Indian country. Remember that the setup for the passage of the Indian Major Crimes Act,[18] the statute being tested in *Kagama*, was that the Indian Country Crimes Act[19] exempted crimes by an Indian against another Indian, and the tribe involved in *Ex parte Crow Dog*[20] didn't hang tribal members for killing other tribal members. The court in *Kagama* struggled to find the constitutional power to pass a criminal law that regulated the dealing of Indians with Indians in Indian country and ultimately concluded the following:

> It seems to us that this is within the competency of congress. These Indian tribes *are* the wards of the nation. They are communities *dependent* on the United States,—dependent largely for their daily food; dependent for their political rights. They owe no allegiance to the states, and receive from them no protection. Because of the local ill feeling, the people of the states where they are found are often their deadliest enemies. From their very weakness and helplessness, so largely due to the course of dealing of the federal government with them, and the treaties in which it has been promised, there arises the duty of protection, and with it the power. This has always been recognized by the executive, and by congress, and by this court, whenever the question has arisen.
> ... The power of the general government over these remnants of a race once powerful, now weak and diminished in numbers, is necessary to their protection, as well as to the safety of those among whom they dwell.[21]

The Court in *Kagama* created a fictional need for protection to find the authority for a protection that wasn't needed. The states had no authority over Indians in Indian country so their "ill feelings" as the tribes' "deadliest enemies" was irrelevant to the passage of the Major Crimes Act. The "protection" the Major Crimes Act provided to tribes was protection from their own improvidence in not having a death penalty. So it would not be illogical for the United States Department of Justice to use the same logic in enforcing the ICRA and argue that it must have the authority to protect tribal members from tribal governments by enforcing the ICRA.[22]

At the time the *Martinez* case was being argued before the Supreme Court, the Office of Indian Rights was in the process of developing a suit against a large western tribe for violating the due process and equal protection clauses of the ICRA for the way it apportioned its legislative body. In this case, the tribal lands were divided into chapters and each chapter had a representative in the tribal council. Some of the chapters are far more populous than others. In Anglo election terms, this is vote dilution and violates the principle of one person one vote in the drawing of electoral districts. The United States' proposed action was a clear application of Anglo equal protection and due process norms to a tribal setting.

After the *Martinez* decision, the question arose whether the Department could go forward with the case. Did immunity from suit in federal court mean immunity from suit by the United States, or was the case limited to its facts and stood only for the proposition that a member of the tribe could not sue the tribe in federal court? The leadership of the OIR developed a legal theory that the United States as trustee could do what a private Indian citizen could not. The theory begins with the proposition that the trust relationship provides a right in the United States government to sue on behalf of individual Indians. No one in the Department of Justice but the OIR section chief and his deputy chief believed that the trust relationship allowed the federal government to sue on behalf of individual Indians.

An alternative theory posited that the United States could bring suit to enforce the ICRA under the authority granted by 25 U.S.C. § 175: "In all States and Territories where there are reservations or allotted Indians the United States attorney shall represent them in all suits at law and in equity."[23] The argument was that the holding of *Martinez* did not apply to the United States because tribes can't hold their immunity from suit up against the superior sovereign.[24] The Civil Division did not accept that legal argument and the matter was closed without litigation.[25]

AFTER THE OFFICE OF INDIAN RIGHTS

On October 10, 1980, Drew Saunders Days III, the first African American assistant attorney general for the Civil Rights Division, terminated the Office of Indian Rights. He created the position of special counsel to the assistant attorney general for Indian Issues (special counsel) and appointed the former director of the Office of Indian Rights to the position.[26]

The Midnight Rider

The man who was supposed to be the adviser to the assistant attorney general for Indian Issues spent most of his time focused on schemes to amend the Indian Civil Rights Act. In November of 1980 there was a political change, and when William Bradford Reynolds became assistant attorney general for Civil Rights he retained the position of special counsel for Indian Issues.

The former OIR director, now special counsel, was firmly of the belief that the Office of Indian Rights would be reinstituted if the ICRA were amended to grant authority to the attorney general to enforce it.[27] Having been unable to develop a legal theory to allow the attorney general to enforce the ICRA, he now engaged in a series of attempts to amend the ICRA. Sometime in the early 1980s, I received a telephone call at about two o'clock in the morning from the general counsel to the Senate Select Committee for Indian Affairs. He was working late because he was searching for riders to the federal budget, which would be voted on the following morning. He spotted a rider attached to the annual appropriations bill that would amend the ICRA by specifically waiving tribal immunity from suit in federal court and granting the attorney general pattern and practice jurisdiction to enforce the

ICRA.[28] He called a House staff member for the congressman who had inserted it. According to the staff member, the special counsel for Indian Affairs in the Civil Rights Division had convinced the House staffer, and presumably his principal, that because he was the adviser to the assistant attorney general for Indian Issues, he spoke for the AAG. The special counsel had further convinced the staffer that the AAG wanted the Indian Civil Rights Act amended to grant jurisdiction to the attorney general to bring pattern and practice cases and specifically to waive tribal sovereign immunity. At the time, Assistant Attorney General Reynolds had very close ties to the attorney general, which led the staff member to assume that the AAG spoke for the attorney general.[29]

When the general counsel for the Senate Select Committee found that the source of this rider language was the Civil Rights Division's special counsel for Indian Issues, a man whom he knew, he then called the one other person working in the Civil Rights Division he knew to ask what authority the special counsel had to speak for the assistant attorney general. He also asked me if amending the ICRA was an official position of the Civil Rights Division or a desire of the attorney general. The answer to both questions was "No," and I reminded the general counsel that the Department of Justice speaks to Congress on legislative matters through the Office of Legislative Affairs not through any individual assistant attorney general.

The Senate Select Committee general counsel then had a discussion with the House staff member, and the rider was cut from the budget bill. What the general counsel told me later was that little one- or two-line riders are slipped into the annual appropriations bill all the time in the wee hours of the morning and because all of the big issues have been agreed upon no one reads the bill the next day before it is voted on. The amendment to the ICRA would have become law and, according to the general counsel, had it been enacted Congress simply wouldn't have gone back and eliminated it.

Manipulating the Commission on Civil Rights

The United States Commission on Civil Rights (the Commission) has the authority to conduct studies, hold hearings, and write reports with recommendations to Congress and/or individual agencies on issue of civil rights. It has done some excellent work in Indian country. The Farmington Report, issued in 1975, led to several investigations and suits by the Department of Justice against the City of Farmington, New Mexico and its police department for discrimination against Indians.

Having failed on his own, the special counsel to the AAG for Civil Rights decided that the Commission may be the conduit to his desired amendment to the ICRA. He convinced the general counsel to the Commission that violations of the ICRA were rampant, that tribal courts were ineffective to file suit in, and that tribal governments that are ruled against will simply fire the judges and appoint new ones who will rule in their favor.[30] The special counsel proposed that the Commission conduct a study of the post-*Martinez* enforcement of the ICRA. Most importantly, he convinced the Commission's general counsel to bring the former deputy director of the Office of Indian Rights to the Commission on a detail from DOJ to assist in the study. What this achieved was the opportunity to skew the study, by having the Commission visit only those tribes with a high number of complaints and those whose tribal government and courts had the poorest response record. The Office of Indian Rights had a ten-year collection of complaints to draw on and use for surgical targeting.[31] We all know how statistics work. As Mark Twain wrote, attributing the quote to Disraeli, "[T]here are only three kinds of lies ... lies, damned lies and statistics."[32] If you control the statistical sample, you can control the outcome of the study.

The study itself wasn't a bad idea. There had been seventeen years of tribal and federal court decisions and experience with the ICRA since its passage, seventeen years of scholarship and growth in tribal courts and governments, and seven years since *Martinez* had passed. The Federal Bar Association's Indian Law Section had recommended that the Commission seize the opportunity to conduct a meaningful study. The Section suggested that the Commission select tribes randomly by size and divide them into three groups based on population, land base, or a combination of both; then select two or three tribes by lottery from each of the pools. The Section suggested cutting the country into three parts at the Mississippi River and the Rocky Mountains and choosing some tribes by lot from each region.[33] The DOJ seemed to gain control of the study from its inception, setting it up to be slanted. However, the study took so long that the administration changed and the new chairman of the Commission replaced the general counsel and some other key staff members. The new general counsel asked a few neutral organizations to review the draft report that the previous group had written. The Federal Bar Association's Indian Law Section was one of those groups. While I am unable to reveal the contents of the original draft report because I signed a statement saying that I wouldn't, I assure you that the attempt to manipulate the outcome of the study had been successful. The reviewers from the Indian Law Section made recommendations to the Commission that eventually helped to bring the report back into some realm of neutrality.

One of the commissioners said it best when the final report was presented to the Commission for approval:

> The temptation to approve this report is great despite its manifest errors of legal and historical interpretation. The reason for this is that the Commission's study has finally been freed from its unhealthy and collusive connection with the Department of Justice's efforts to build a case for legislation previously introduced as S. 517. During that earlier phase the Commission actually had less control over its own study than did certain staff from the Department of Justice. The sheer scope and importance of the inquiry, however, had the effect of producing a

record of far greater weight than the collusion intended. Despite the passage of time and changes in staff, the record remains to support a broader effort, and the Commission's study is now free from those prior suspicions. Nevertheless, some aspects of the prior analysis remain in the final product, and these convey erroneous conclusions even while no longer supporting their pre-determined end.[34]

This is a rather powerful condemnation of the Civil Rights Division.

The Commission's·final report was issued and nothing happened. Congress had held its own hearings while the Commission was floundering. Commissioner Allen notes in his statement about the final report that the congressional hearing and report are more effective than the Commission's. Congress still took no action.

THAT WHICH COMES AFTER THE PROLOGUE

Internal Debates Over 18 U.S.C. § 242

In fact, another legal theory of the Office of Indian Rights arose before the *Martinez* decision. I had been assigned an investigation of a tribal police officer who had struck a young man on the side of the head with a three-cell flashlight while placing him under arrest. The young man had been drinking and had led several officers in a chase across the Navajo Reservation before ultimately bottoming out his vehicle in an arroyo. When the officers pulled the young man out of his vehicle, he made a remark to which the officer responded with a flashlight. That classically is a violation of 18 U.S.C. § 242, known in the Division as the police brutality statute. The operative language of the statute is:

> Whoever, under color of any law, statute, ordinance, regulation, or custom, willfully subjects any person in any State, Territory, Commonwealth, Possession, or District to the deprivation of any rights, privileges, or immunities secured or protected by the Constitution or laws of the United States, or to different punishments, pains, or penalties, on account of such person being an alien, or by reason of his color, or race, than are prescribed for the punishment of citizens, shall be fined under this title or imprisoned not more than one year, or both; and if bodily injury results from the acts committed in violation of this section or if such acts include the use, attempted use, or threatened use of a dangerous weapon, explosives, or fire, shall be fined under this title or imprisoned not more than ten years, or both; and if death results from the acts committed in violation of this section or if such acts include kidnapping or an attempt to kidnap, aggravated sexual abuse, or an attempt to commit aggravated sexual abuse, or an attempt

to kill, shall be fined under this title, or imprisoned for any term of years or for life, or both, or may be sentenced to death.[35]

This was 1979, well before the plethora of cases that have taken dicta out of *Federal Power Commission v. Tuscarora Indian Nation*[36] and developed the line of cases saying that laws of general jurisdiction apply to Indians. So I made the argument at the time that because the act was never intended to remove sovereignty or to apply to an officer acting under color of tribal law that the § 242 did not apply. The act's preamble says that it was enacted pursuant to Congress' power under the Fourteenth Amendment, so I also argued that since the amendment didn't reach the actions of an Indian tribal government, a statute to enforce it couldn't either.[37] Under modern constitutional holdings, however, the Court doesn't focus on which part of the Constitution the Congress cites as giving it power to do something, but rather whether the power exists within the Constitution for Congress to do it. In other words, the Court will not find a statute unconstitutional simply because Congress incorrectly identified where its power for a given piece of legislation arises, as long as the Court can identify a grant of the authority somewhere in the Constitution. The Supreme Court could find that the power to apply the statute to an Indian tribe existed in the Thirteenth Amendment[38] or by the logic of *Kagama*.[39]

This internal debate at the Department of Justice as to the application of § 242 to Indians never really got anywhere. The injury to the victim wasn't that severe and the Navajo Nation fined and suspended the officer. My recommendation that the federal government need not take action was accepted. Had it been a police officer acting under state authority, that's what the Department would have done in light of similar state action.

The greatest internal war, however, came soon thereafter. Shortly after the *Martinez* decision, a man from one of the pueblos was hitchhiking back to his home from Albuquerque, New Mexico and was picked up by some tribal officials on Pueblo territory. They smelled alcohol on his breath and took him to the BIA jail facility to be housed until his trial for having alcohol in his system while on the tribe's lands. The BIA jailer wrote the arrest up as "drunk and disorderly conduct" because that was the only crime he could find in the CFR code comparable to the actual offense. As I understood the offense from the Pueblo official's perspective, it was neither being "drunk and disorderly" nor drinking alcohol on the pueblo's lands, but rather the offense was having alcohol in his body while on the pueblo's lands.

According to FBI interview reports, the man was brought before a tribunal alleged to be closed to the public, where he was required to be on his knees during the proceeding. The tribunal was conducted entirely in the tribal language. At the end of the process, he was sentenced to two weeks in jail and was struck four times with a whip. His wife, who was not a member of that tribe, was outraged, and she filed the complaint with the Federal Bureau of Investigation. That his wife is not a member of the pueblo is key to understanding the final outcome.

The Office of Indian Rights section chief and deputy chief were adamant that the tribal court's actions violated several sections of the ICRA including the right to counsel, the right to a public trial, the right to have the trial in English, and the cruel-and-unusual-punishment clause.[40] They further concluded that the ICRA violations also triggered a violation of 18 U.S.C. § 242. They proposed to have the FBI enter the reservation and interview the tribe's religious leaders because it was the cacique who had called for the four lashes with the whip. The deputy chief kept the case for himself because the matter had been the subject of heavy debate within the unit, with me leading the opposition forces. I was promised an opportunity to write a memorandum opposing the investigation so the assistant attorney general would have two different analyses of the law.

I did some very quick research on the practice of whipping at this particular pueblo and discovered that whipping was not used as criminal punishment, but rather was a purification ritual to bring the individual back into the fold of the people. Section leadership responded that the tribe couldn't call something that was inherently a criminal punishment religious just to avoid prosecution. What is fascinating about their argument is that I was citing an Anglo anthropologist, not any member of the tribe. Therefore, unless tribal members fifty years earlier had anticipated an FBI investigation and lied to the anthropologist or the anthropologist had lied to cover up a violation of the ICRA thirty years before its passage, their argument didn't hold water. At this point in the debate, we were arguing whether or not it was appropriate to have the FBI attempt to interview the cacique. No one had yet spoken to the alleged victim or any other member of the tribe. The complainant to the FBI was the victim's wife, who was Navajo. So the section chief's assumption had to be that the scholar was misrepresenting tribal religion and culture as part of a grand conspiracy to avoid prosecution under the Indian Civil Rights Act, which didn't exist at the time of her research.

The deputy section chief wrote in his memorandum that the tribal leaders didn't write the tribal code down because it allowed them to be petty dictators. Had any other attorney in the Civil Rights Division challenged the right of tribes to have an oral tradition rather than a written code, he would have said that they were racist and just didn't understand Indian culture. But his analysis depended on whose ox was gored; in this case, the Bill of Rights was his sacred cow and he assumed that the ICRA was its equivalent.

I made seven arguments in my memorandum:[41]

(1) The act of striking the man with a whip was not a punishment in the first instance, but a purification ritual that had been a part of the tribe's norms for at least three hundred years.[42]

(2) The appropriate norms for the interpretation of due process were the tribal norms, not Anglo constitutional norms, and therefore this action was neither cruel nor unusual under the ICRA.

(3) 18 U.S.C. § 242 does not apply to the tribal government's actions because it was never intended to reach the actions of someone acting under color of tribal law.

(4) 18 U.S.C. § 242 was written after the Civil War and five years before the federal government stopped dealing with tribes primarily by treaty, and so there was no intent to interfere with the tribe's right to punish its own members, that removal of tribal sovereignty must be done with specificity.

(5) Application of § 242 was inconsistent with congressional thinking at the time; in 1875, nine years after the enactment of § 242, Congress noted that the Indian-against-Indian exemption from the Indian Country Crimes Act had been dropped by the revisers of the criminal code and specifically restored it. That action was inconsistent with a desire to apply § 242 to Indian tribes, and since ambiguities in the law are to be read in favor of the Indians, § 242 did not apply.

(6) 18 U.S.C. § 242 was enacted under the authority of the Fourteenth Amendment, which on its face does not apply to Indian tribes; therefore, statutes to enforce the Amendment also could not control the actions of a tribe.

(7) The ICRA is a civil statute that cannot be enforced through a criminal proceeding.

The assistant attorney general took a central position that the FBI could contact the victim to ascertain exactly what had happened, but that no tribal leaders, either secular or religious, would be contacted. This is where the thunder went out of the OIR leadership's arguments. The alleged victim said that the closed forum was a non-issue because his trial was no one else's business and which, in fact, had been held in a small, close community everybody already knew. His complaint was that he'd only had two beers while in Albuquerque and that he wasn't drunk or disorderly. He said he spoke the tribal language and was familiar with the tribe's prohibition against alcohol. The victim said that being struck four times with the whip was neither cruel nor unusual. In fact, he didn't view it as punishment at all and said the federal government had no business interfering with the religious purification rituals of his tribe. He also stated to the FBI that the man who had struck him with the whip had himself been struck four times so that he was purified to enable him to perform the purification ritual. But the victim was adamant that he should not have been charged as drunk and disorderly. The Division took no other action.

What was fascinating about this particular legal debate is how confused other people in the Civil Rights Division became. Several years later, an American Indian who was an Albuquerque City police officer seriously beat someone he had arrested and the Criminal Section of the Division thought that I had argued that § 242 didn't apply to Indians as a race as opposed to any officer who was acting under the authority of an Indian tribe. I had to explain that my challenge had been to the "color of law" language of § 242, not the color of the police officer. The Criminal

Section has gone back and forth over the years about the efficacy of my argument. There have been three different final memos on the subject during the past twenty-five years. The first one agrees with me, the second says that § 242 applies to tribal officers, and the third says that it does not.[43]

If Not § 242 What About § 241

If color of law doesn't include tribal law and you can't enforce the ICRA through 18 U.S.C. § 242, a clever government prosecutor will ask, "What about 18 U.S.C. § 241? There is no requirement that someone act under color of law in § 241."

Again, 18 U.S.C. § 241 is an 1860s post–Civil War statute designed to protect the rights of former slaves from the people in the states that made up the Confederacy. Its operative language is:

> If two or more persons conspire to injure, oppress, threaten, or intimidate any person in any State, Territory, Commonwealth, Possession, or District in the free exercise or enjoyment of any right or privilege secured to him by the Constitution or laws of the United States, or because of his having so exercised the same; or

> If two or more persons go in disguise on the highway, or on the premises of another, with intent to prevent or hinder his free exercise or enjoyment of any right or privilege so secured—

> They shall be fined under this title or imprisoned not more than ten years, or both; and if death results from the acts committed in violation of this section or if such acts include kidnapping or an attempt to kidnap, aggravated sexual abuse or an attempt to commit aggravated sexual abuse, or an attempt to kill, they shall be fined under this title or imprisoned for any term of years or for life, or both, or may be sentenced to death.[44]

This statute is known in civil rights circles as "The Highwayman Statute."

In 1998, in *United States v. Clark, Rawley and Wadena,*[45] the United States prosecuted three tribal officials on a series of charges and, in what can only be deemed an effort to pile on everything possible, the US attorney also charged the defendants with "conspiracy to oppress free exercise of election rights, in violation of 18 U.S.C. § 241" and violation of 25 U.S.C. § 1302 (the ICRA). Wadena was tribal chairman, and Clark and Rawley were councilmen. On the count of voting fraud, the defendants admitted that they had engaged in stuffing the ballot box but challenged the prosecution for it on the grounds that § 241 didn't apply to tribal elections violations and the ICRA couldn't be enforced in federal court after *Martinez.* On appeal the Eighth Circuit's analysis of this argument is as follows:

The specific question we must then address is whether the ICRA, as a law of the United States, contains a prohibition which allows enforcement of § 241 under general principles of conspiracy law.

The ICRA specifically proscribes a violation of the Tribe's equal protection laws, as well as other constitutional rights of the Tribe.... Article XIII of the Constitution of the Minnesota Chippewa Tribe reads: no member shall be denied any of the constitutional rights or guarantees enjoyed by other citizens of the United States....

By direct incorporation, these rights are now explicitly protected by the ICRA. We hold they are enforceable under § 241, as a general federal law....

There are several reasons why the *Santa Clara* ruling does not control this case. First, in the case at hand, the government is asserting jurisdiction under § 241, *not* under the ICRA. The only reason the ICRA needs to be referenced at all in this case is to establish that a right to be free from fraud in a tribal election does indeed exist under the laws of the United States. There is *nothing* in the language of *Santa Clara* to indicate that the rights under the ICRA are non-existent or in any way invalid. Instead, *Santa Clara* dealt with how those rights may be enforced, and concluded they could not be enforced through a *private* right of action, in a *civil* lawsuit. Nothing in *Santa Clara* addresses the U.S. government's right or obligation to assume *criminal* jurisdiction when one of its laws of generally [*sic*] applicability is violated....

Second,... unlike *Santa Clara*, there is no challenge to the legitimate actions of the tribe or its representatives.... In fact, the Band's right to free and open elections is vindicated by the present criminal action.

Third, in *Santa Clara*, the Court stressed that tribal courts are available to vindicate rights created by the ICRA and are the appropriate forums to do so.... But again, this is stated in the context of a *civil* action. In a *criminal* context—when the entire tribal system allegedly is controlled by a few corrupt individuals—there is no effective tribal forum available to protect an individual tribal member's civil rights.

Finally, even if jurisdiction in this case was asserted under the ICRA, *Santa Clara* would not be dispositive, because the absence of a private right of action does *not* mean absence of *criminal* jurisdiction....

No ... treaty right [exempting the plaintiffs from the statutes in question]—[such as the right] to be free to conduct fraudulent elections against their people—is asserted here by the defendants.

…We find there is no reason why federal criminal jurisdiction over election fraud would work to undermine the sovereignty of the tribe or its political integrity. First, no tribal custom or tradition is being threatened by the enforcement of criminal conspiracy laws. There is no tribal custom or tradition of the Band of fraudulently using the election system to maintain positions of power for a few corrupt individuals.

Second,… no purpose of tribal autonomy is served by allowing a corrupt, unrepresentative system to continue unabated.

Finally, it is relevant to note that tribal governments are dependent sovereigns—not independent foreign ones. As part of this dependent status, the U.S. government serves as a trustee and has a direct responsibility as a trustee to protect the civil rights granted by Congress to the Native Americans living on the reservations. We believe failure of the United States to assert criminal jurisdiction over activity on a reservation when the tribal government no longer operates legitimately would be an abrogation of the U.S. government's trustee relationship with tribes such as the Chippewa.[46]

Let me see if I can sum that argument up in its component parts.
1. 18 U.S.C. § 241 necessitates there be a violation of federal law.
2. The ICRA is a federal law.
3. The ICRA guarantees equal protection under the tribe's laws.
4. The tribal constitution guarantees equal protection and constitutional rights
5. Therefore, the ICRA rights are like constitutional rights.
6. The United States is not asserting jurisdiction under the ICRA.
7. The United States asserts jurisdiction under § 241.
8. *Santa Clara Pueblo v. Martinez* stands for the proposition that no private right of action can be filed in a civil lawsuit, not that the federal government can't bring criminal actions.
9. Because § 241 is a law of general applicability, it applies to Indian tribes.
10. And the federal trust responsibility requires that it be enforced against bad tribal leaders.

This argument is simply dizzying. As I read through the court's fashioning of its § 241 violation, I was reminded of the scene in *The Princess Bride* where Vizzini and the man in black engage in a battle of wits to the death. As you recall, the man in black (MIB) offers up two glasses of wine telling Vizzini that one of them has poison in it. Vizzini's debate about which glass he should drink from has a comparable logical framework.

> MIB: What you do not smell is called iocane powder. It is odorless, tasteless, dissolves instantly in liquid, and is among the more deadlier [*sic*] poisons known to man… All right: where is the poison? The battle of wits has begun. It ends when you decide and we both drink, and find out who is right and who is dead.
>
> Vizzini: But it's so simple. All I have to do is divine from what I know of you. Are you the sort of man who would put the poison into his own goblet, or his enemy's? Now, a clever man would put the poison into his own goblet, because he would know that only a great fool would reach for what he was given. I'm not a great fool, so I can clearly not choose the wine in front of you. But you must have known I was not a great fool; you would have counted on it, so I can clearly not choose the wine in front of me.
>
> MIB: You've made your decision then?
>
> Vizzini: Not remotely. Because iocane comes from Australia, as everyone knows. And Australia is entirely peopled with criminals. And criminals are used to having people not trust them, as you are not trusted by me. So I can clearly not choose the wine in front of you….
>
> …You must have suspected I would have known the powder's origin, so I can clearly not choose the wine in front of me.
>
> …You've beaten my giant, which means you're exceptionally strong. So, you could have put the poison in your own goblet, trusting on your strength to save you. So I can clearly not choose the wine in front of you. But, you've also bested my Spaniard which means you must have studied. And in studying, you must have learned that man is mortal so you would have put the poison as far from yourself as possible, so I can clearly not choose the wine in front of me.[47]

As we all know, there was poison in both glasses; Vizzini drinks and dies, but the man in black is immune to iocane poison. Tribes are not immune from the poison in either of these glasses labeled § 241 and § 242.

In reality, the conspiracy at issue in *Wadena* is to violate tribal law. But because the Court finds that the violation of tribal law is a violation of the ICRA, it is also a denial of a right granted by a federal law, which then also makes it a violation of § 241; it never asks the question, "What does the tribe's court say about the violation?" There is no tribal court that is going to say that ballot-box stuffing is a tribal tradition. However, I think as a matter of law the federal court should have asked whether it was the intent of the tribe's governing body to adopt federal constitutional rights.

Article XIII of the Constitution of the Minnesota Chippewa Tribe reads:

> All members of the Minnesota Chippewa Tribe shall be accorded by the governing body equal rights, equal protection, and equal opportunities to participate in the economic resources and activities of the Tribe, and *no member shall be denied any of the constitutional rights or guarantees enjoyed by other citizens of the United States,* including but not limited to freedom of religion and conscience, freedom of speech, the right to orderly association or assembly, the right to petition for action or the redress of grievances, and due process of law.[48]

Does the tribe really mean that it is providing federal constitutional guarantees to its members in this language? I think that as a matter of comity it is required that the federal court ask the tribe what the tribe's highest court thinks. Maybe this case seems easy because they were stuffing the ballot box, but what about the next case that isn't so easy?

What of the federal government's corruption of the tribal court question? Is the argument claiming that all you have to do is allege that the tribal court is corrupt to get federal court jurisdiction, or do you file the federal action alleging that the court is corrupted and only get jurisdiction to hear all of your other complaints if you win on the first count? Under the Eighth Circuit's analysis, whose judgment is it that the tribal forum is unavailable and, therefore, federal court jurisdiction exists under § 241? While I believe the Eighth Circuit is wrong as a matter of law, I believe the federal government was wrong as a matter of policy to pursue the case in this manner or to support it after the fact.

Let's say the US attorney brings the case without asking Main Justice if this is a sound legal theory. Is it necessary for the attorney general and solicitor general to ratify it in later filings? It is appalling to find that the United States in its cert petition brief told the Court that it didn't need to address whether or not voting rights under the equal protection clause of the ICRA could be enforced through a § 241 prosecution, "given that we don't do it very often."[49] The United States also says in its brief that the Supreme Court doesn't need to look at this issue because the defendants received concurrent sentences on the sixteen other charges and are going to prison for fifty-seven months anyway.

What you have after *Wadena* is a notion that even though the ICRA can't be enforced in federal court on its own, you can enforce it through § 241. But the greater outrage is that the federal government is making a criminal prosecution out of what is inherently a civil violation. Maybe the Department of Justice hasn't done it very often in the past, but, as Mr. Shakespeare wrote, "[W]hat's past is prologue."[50] Now the Department has done it and the Eighth Circuit has approved it. This legal Pandora is out of her box.

Let me end with the words of Mr. Justice Jackson from his dissent in *Korematsu v. United States*,[51] in which the Supreme Court was approving the removal of American citizens of Japanese ancestry to internment camps:

> Much is said of the danger to liberty from the Army program for deporting and detaining these citizens of Japanese extraction. But a judicial construction of the due process clause that will sustain this order is a far more subtle blow to liberty than the promulgation of the order itself. A military order, however unconstitutional, is not apt to last longer than the military emergency. Even during that period a succeeding commander may revoke it all. But once a judicial opinion rationalizes such an order to show that it conforms to the Constitution, or rather rationalizes the Constitution to show that the Constitution sanctions such an order, the Court for all time has validated the principle of racial discrimination in criminal procedure and of transplanting American citizens. *The principle then lies about like a loaded weapon ready for the hand of any authority that can bring forward a plausible claim of an urgent need.* Every repetition imbeds that principle more deeply in our law and thinking and expands it to new purposes. All who observe the work of courts are familiar with what Judge Cardozo described as "the tendency of a principle to expand itself to the limit of its logic." A military commander may overstep the bounds of constitutionality, and it is an incident. But if we review and approve, that passing incident becomes the doctrine of the Constitution. There it has a generative power of its own, and all that it creates will be in its own image. Nothing better illustrates this danger than does the Court's opinion in this case.[52]

I ask my students to look at federal Indian law cases for the IEDs of federal Indian law, improvised explosive declarations of the courts that will come back to haunt Indian tribes, words that lay by the roadside for tribal sovereignty to drive over—or, in the words of Mr. Justice Jackson, legal principles that lay on the table like a loaded weapon. The problem with allowing the ICRA to be enforced through § 241 and § 242 begins with the person who picks the weapon up off the table. Whoever's finger is on the trigger dictates its use.

A § 241 prosecution calls for a conspiracy, and tribal governments by their very nature act in concert. A § 242 prosecution can be brought against one who acts under color of law, and tribal governments by their very nature act under color of law. Thus, future prosecutors will always be able to meet these standards. The court in *Wadena* accepted without proof that the tribe's government was corrupt and the tribe's courts were without the ability to respond. Does the mere allegation of a corrupt tribal government trigger the federal "trust responsibility" to which the court makes reference?

After *Wadena*, § 241 and § 242 are the Little Boy and Fat Man[53] of the US government's Indian law arsenal. For those who think tribal governments need greater federal intervention, these weapons may be seen as a means to achieve that end. For those who fear the use of these nuclear options of prosecutorial discretion in the hands of the attorney general and your local United States attorney, they may be more of a threat than a tool. Be afraid my friends; be very afraid.

NOTES

1. Indian Civil Rights Act, 25 U.S.C. §§ 1301-03 (2006) [hereinafter ICRA].
2. Santa Clara Pueblo v. Martinez, 436 U.S. 49 (1978).
3. ICRA, *supra* note 1.
4. Reminiscences of Abraham Lincoln by Distinguished Men of His Time (Alan Thorndike Rice ed., 1909 [1886]).
5. I was told this when I first went to work at the Department of Justice in 1976, and this figure is supported by a number of accounts of this period. See, e.g., *Hearing on Authorization Request for the Civil Rights Division of the Department of Justice Before the Subcomm On Civil and Const'l Rights of the H. Comm. on the Judiciary*, 97th Cong. 5 (1981): "Prior to the creation of the Office of Indian Rights in 1973, the Justice Department's Civil Rights Division participated in few, if any cases, where Indians were the principal victims of civil rights violations" (testimony of Ronald Andrade, executive director, National Congress of American Indians).
6. Fact and myth collide far too often in the discussions of what happened during the 1973 occupation and siege of the village of Wounded Knee, South Dakota. Suffice it to say that a group of individuals associating themselves with the American Indian Movement moved in to the village, which was then surrounded by United States marshals, Federal Bureau of Investigation agents, and other law enforcement personnel. Gunshots were exchanged for seventy-one days before the standoff ended. For more information about the events, see Stanley David Lyman, Floyd A. O'Neil, June K. Lyman, and Susan McKay, Wounded Knee 1973: A Personal Account (1993); and Joseph H. Trimbach, American Indian Mafia: An FBI Agent's True Story About Wounded Knee, Leonard Peltier, and the American Indian Movement (AIM) (2008).
7. See note 6 *supra*. Neither of those cases is reported. Both were settled by consent decree. The credit and housing case was against the HFC Corporation at one of its offices in Illinois, and the public accommodations case was against a Trails West Motel in Florida.
8. The Office of Indian Rights was terminated October 10, 1980 by Drew S. Days III, the first African American to serve as assistant attorney general for the Civil Rights Division.
9. *See supra* note 9.
10. Santa Clara Pueblo v. Martinez, 436 U.S. 49 (1978).
11. The Attorney General's Employment Program for Honor Law Graduates was instituted in 1954. I was the first American Indian hired under the Honor Law Program.
12. *See* Martinez v. Santa Clara Pueblo, 402 F. Supp. 5, 6 (D.N.M. 1975).
13. *See infra*, at 21.
14. *See* Kiowa Tribe of Oklahoma v. Manufacturing Technologies, 523 U.S. 751 (1998).
15. The names of these individuals are easy to find out but I chose to not give them here. Their names are not relevant to the facts of the Department's actions.

16. The FBI no longer conducts investigations of civil rights violations unless they are criminal in nature.
17. Kagama v. United States, 118 U.S. 375 (1886) [hereinafter *Kagama*].
18. Indian Country Crimes Act, 18 U.S.C. §§ 1151–53, 3242 (2006).
19. *Id.*, at § 1152.
20. Ex Parte Crow Dog, 109 U.S. 556 (1883).
21. *Kagama*, 118 U.S. at 383–384.
22. *Id.*, at 384.
23. Personally, I have always thought 25 U.S.C. § 175 was an omnibus grant of authority to the United States to sue on behalf of American Indians. See FELIX S. COHEN, HANDBOOK OF FEDERAL INDIAN LAW 253 (Government Printing Office 1942).
24. In 1999, in *Florida Paraplegic Association v. Miccosukee Tribe of Indians*, the Eleventh Circuit held that the Americans with Disabilities Act does apply to the tribe's casino and hotel but that the private plaintiffs cannot bring suit because the tribe is immune and the act didn't specifically waive the tribe's immunity. The court also says that the victims are not, however, without relief because the United States can bring suit to enforce the act and the tribe cannot hold its immunity up against the superior sovereign. However, if you read the underlying cases back to the origin of that legal principle it was probably shredded by the Supreme Court's opinion concerning state sovereign immunity in *Florida v. Seminole Tribe of Florida*. Further discussion of that proposition is unnecessary here.
25. In internal discussions of this kind the CRD would normally ask for a position from the Appellate Section and possibly guidance from the Solicitor General's Office. I have made a Freedom of Information Act request for these documents but, as of this writing, I have neither received copies of the documents nor confirmation that they do not exist.
26. AAG Days claimed that there would be an improvement in services to American Indian victims of civil rights violations because now all 225 of the division's attorneys could bring cases on behalf of Indians instead of just the seven OIR attorneys. It was a disaster for the rights of Indians. During the next decade only three cases were filed on behalf of Indian victims by attorneys not formerly with the OIR.
27. He was equally convinced that he would get to be an office director again if that were to occur. How much that guided his actions over the next five years is unknown.
28. Pattern and practice jurisdiction means that suit could not be filed for a single violation of the ICRA. The attorney general would have to demonstrate a pattern of violations of the act.
29. This is all based on a conversation between two staff members as related to me in a telephone call almost thirty years ago.
30. In fact, some tribal courts have held that *Santa Clara Pueblo* stands for the proposition that the tribe is immune from suit in tribal court as well.
31. See Statement of Commissioner William Allen *infra* note 35.
32. Mark Twain, *Chapters from My Autobiography*, NORTH AMERICAN REVIEW (Sept. 7, 1906). Twain's attribution of this quote to Disraeli was actually inaccurate, as it does not appear in any of Disraeli's works.
33. I went so far as to make the absurd suggestion to the commission that selecting tribes to survey by the tribal chairman's height and weight would be more effective than letting DOJ officials dictate where the commission looked.
34. U.S. Commission on Civil Rights, The Indian Civil Rights Act, No. 005-908-00021-3 (June 1991) (Statement by Commissioner William B. Allen on the Indian Civil Rights Act), available at http://williambarclayallen.com/reports.html.
35. Deprivation of Rights Under Color of Law, 18 U.S.C. § 242 (2006).
36. Federal Power Commission v. Tuscarora Indian Nation, 362 U.S. 99 (1960)
37. Today, of course, the so-called "Tuscarora Rule," stipulating that laws of general jurisdiction apply to Indians, would be the primary argument against my proposition. First, a most thorough debunking of the rule has already been done by Professor Judith Royster, so I don't need to do it here. Second, the Supreme Court itself has never cited *Tuscarora* for the Tuscarora Rule. At last check, it had cited Tuscarora nine times, twice for the proposition that the Federal Power Act allows condemnation of reservation lands and seven times for the language of Justice Black's dissent that "Great nations like great men should keep their word."

38. *See In re* Sah Quah, 31 Fed. Rep. 329 (1886).

39. *Kagama id.* at 10.

40. 25 U.S.C. §§ 1302.6, 1302.7.

41. I have a pending Freedom of Information Act Request before the Civil Rights Division for official copies of all of the documents associated with this case. Until I receive them the details of the specific legal arguments are from memory.

42. I was on pretty good ground from ethnological studies of the tribe by outsiders. See, for example, ELSIE CLEWS PARSONS, PUEBLO INDIAN RELIGION, 2 vols. (1939).

43. I have requested copies of these memoranda from the Department of Justice through the Freedom of Information Act and, as of this writing, have not received a response.

44. 18 U.S.C. § 241 (2006).

45. United States v. Wadena, 152 F.3d 831 (8th Cir. 1998), (amended opinion) [hereinafter *Wadena*].

46. *Wadena* at 845–47 (italic emphasis in original, underlined emphasis added).

47. THE PRINCESS BRIDE (Twentieth Century Fox 1987) (shooting script pp. 44–46, available at http://www.imsdb.com/scripts/Princess-Bride,-The.html).

48. MINNESOTA CHIPPEWA CONST. art. XIII, available at http://www.mnchippewatribe.org/constitution_revised.pdf.

49. Brief of the United States in opposition to Writ of Certiorari in Clark v. United States, Docket No. 98-876 with Wadena, Darrell C. v. United States, Docket No. 98-7027 and Rawley, Jerry J. v. United States, Docket No. 98-7069.

50. WILLIAM SHAKESPEARE, THE TEMPEST, Act 2, sc. 1.

51. Korematsu v. United States, 323 U.S. 214 (1944), [hereinafter *Korematsu*].

52. *Korematsu*, 323 U.S. at 245–46 (Jackson, J., dissenting) (emphasis added).

53. The names given the atomic bombs dropped to end World War II. Two weapon designs were used—the gun assembly Little Boy bomb that used uranium highly enriched in U-235, and the implosion assembly Fat Man that used plutonium.

PART I
EQUAL PROTECTION

CHAPTER 2

Martinez Revisited

===

CATHARINE A. MACKINNON

A s litigated, *Santa Clara Pueblo v. Martinez*[1] presented a conflict between two inequalities, two hierarchies. One was visible as such, the other not. The conflict between the United States government and the governments of Native peoples was built into Julia Martinez's choice of forum. This hierarchy—full sovereign over qualified one—was not recognized as an inequality, but was fundamental to the politics of the case and to commentaries on it since. The case was litigated through the question, presented as technical, of whether a private right of action could be implied by Native peoples against their nations for violations of the Indian Civil Rights Act (ICRA).[2] The other hierarchy in the case—men over women—was squarely posed by Julia Martinez's substantive claim of sex discrimination. This inequality was recognized as such when the court of appeals held for Julia Martinez on this question.[3] The United States Supreme Court necessarily ignored it in resolving the case on sovereignty grounds for Santa Clara, finding that the issue was not its to decide. But although the issue of sovereignty prevailed over the issue of sex, the hierarchy of sovereigns was no more explicitly faced than was the hierarchy of the sexes.

When the federal courts left Indian Civil Rights Act claims against Indian nations to their own courts, indigenous tribunals, in an important outpost of sovereignty upon which all Native peoples can build, won power over Native women's equality claims. But the resolution of this case by the United States Supreme Court, recognizing the sovereignty of Santa Clara over Julia Martinez, was itself an exercise of sovereignty by the United States over Native peoples. If someone else can decide whether you are sovereign, in a very real sense you are not. If the US Supreme Court had decided this case the other way, as it could have, sovereignty is not really what Santa Clara won, although Native peoples emerged from the case with more of it than they had before. If Julia Martinez was excoriated for her choice of forum in going to the United States government for a justice her tribe had not given her, when that same forum granted Santa Clara sovereignty over her, no one seemed to think that the power the tribe won was tainted by the forum in which they won it.

My initial engagement with the *Martinez* case, soon after it was decided, was at a talk in Red Earth, Minnesota that the women there requested.[4] The piece took no position on the outcome of the case; among other things, it pointed out that the decision won an advance in sovereignty for Native peoples on the backs of Native women—which it did. For this finding, the analysis has been mischaracterized as "essentialist,"[5] which means (to specify a slippery academic swear word) it presumes that women share the same universal essential identity simply by virtue of being biologically female. Having conceived the analysis that sexuality, in particular, is a social construct, definitive of women's status, and having practiced that analysis since the early 1970s, I found this error surprising. Looking always to the social reality of the situation of women across history and culture, time, and space, my approach has been that if male dominance, however varied, is found there, it is an empirical generalization of social fact, not an assumption of any kind, and certainly not a biological one. Whenever this theory is not accurate, it is not valid. As a matter of fact, among the places where this widespread fact is demonstrably less acute, cultures indigenous to what is now called North America number prominently.[6] To repeat the obvious, the fact that male dominance over women can be found to be socially real in most places at most times does not mean that a universal essential gender or sex identity is being assumed, or that those social relations are considered naturally or necessarily predetermined to be structured in that way. In such a world, social equality—my life's work—would be science fiction.

For clarity, note that a blood quantum definition of what constitutes a tribal member is an essentialist definition of who an Indian is.[7] A social membership definition is cultural, hence nonessentialist. Essentialism is not some politically correct line one has to stay on the right side of, necessarily, although being against it seems to be among the latest academic credentialing postures. Perhaps some find blood to be a proxy for culture; maybe one is assigned and treated as one is socially in substantial part because of who one is genetically. But to illustrate by example, a cultural definition—say, Julia Martinez's children being arguably Santa Claran because they were raised Santa Claran traditionally and speak Tewa—is a nonessentialist definition of the tribal membership that they met. If one is comfortable with essentialist definitions of Indians and critical of essentialist definitions of women, an explanation is in order.

Another widespread misunderstanding and mischaracterization of my work in this area—unlike the first, neither an outright lie nor a careerist distortion—is the notion that my work on sex discrimination, and sex discrimination as a claim generally, is anchored in an individual rights framework. In this critique, sex equality rights are presumed to be individual rights, whereas indigenous people's rights are presumed to be collective rights. This criticism can accurately be leveled at conventional approaches to discrimination, but it does not apply to mine. In all of my work on sex equality, indeed in the approach I originated,[8] whenever a woman is discriminated against as a woman, she is discriminated against as a member of a social group. To be a woman, in this view, is to be a member of a group with a social designation and a social experience, a group made up of a multitude of social designations and experiences, including race and ethnicity and heritage. The same is true for men as such. Whatever or whoever one is as a woman is not who one is as an individual in the one-at-a-time sense. Womanhood is intrinsically a collective and group-based designation, attribution, and experience. This designation is indelibly true in situations of discrimination. If you are not hired for a job because you are a woman, for example, that treatment has nothing to do with who you are as an individual and everything to do with the fact that you are a member of the group "women." I would claim the same for being raped. The meaning of these experiences of discrimination as a woman is an intrinsically collective social meaning. Every individual who is harmed as a woman is harmed as a member of this group, even if the damage is done to her alone at this time. This approach applies a collective rights concept even in individual cases. Women are my people. This belief, not an individual rights legal framework, is the ground of my work.[9]

The third idea in the literature that, by its attention, honors my early work on Julia Martinez's case is the view that to criticize male dominance is a Western or white idea. I have been waiting for evidence of this contention for some time. What Western country is actually critical of male dominance? Where is it acceptable to criticize it? Where does it no longer exist? Though the critique of male dominance has more traction in some places than in others, the few people who make it unapologetically—some in the West, some in the East, some in the North, some in the South—are not mainstream in any place of which I am aware. Nowhere does the criticism of male supremacy predominate *as* culture—far less does sex equality exist. In reality, although some Western countries and cultures purport to favor equality or even to have attained it, there is nothing Western about criticizing male dominance or about the vision of equality as an end to status hierarchies based on group membership. Women originated this critique from their own lives. It is indigenous to women everywhere. Nor is it outdated (don't we wish). Some women resist and resent being kept down and out; some connect with others who are on the same wavelength elsewhere; together we support each other and organize for change with all workable tools at our disposal. What we see and, crucially, how we approach change is defined by everything about who and where we are, which includes our cultures and systems in each particularity. Approached this way, women globally form a culture.[10]

These three erroneous notions cover up, and stand in for, something real. Closer to what may be their underlying impulse is the view that it is important to talk about women's issues, but never to forget the larger context,[11] with the related view that individual rights like those sought by Julia Martinez are valuable, but not when asserted against the whole.[12] These views generate real questions: What is the larger context? What is the whole? Unlike the prior criticisms, these questions frame a conversation worth having.

Shall we agree that no context is whole simply because it includes men? And that it is not necessarily larger just because it is more numerous? That no unit is too small because it is not as big as the group of all women, nor is it whole simply because men are in it? Suppose women bring every specificity with them. We do not speak of Native women as women as if they are not also Indians. If "women" has a collective definition, women's identifications with all groups can inclusively comprise their membership in the group "women," rather than contradict or qualify it. Down this path, with common forms of subordination identified, women become a kind of whole.

No one says that it is irrelevant to the question in *Martinez* that Julia Martinez is Santa Claran. The fact that the people who created the rule challenged in the case were Native people operating under particular conditions that included conquest and expropriation, minimally, is not ignored. But the case is often discussed as if it is not relevant that Julia and her daughter, Audrey, are women in the social sense: women among women who, when treated in these particular ways familiar to male-dominant systems—namely, having families they form not treated as families of their communities when the men's are—connect with other women in other places and times who have long been and are still being treated in similar, sometimes identical, interconnected ways. Instead of being neither part of a community nor constituting one, each woman, seen as a woman, is, in some sense, every woman, and "women" can form a larger context.

Consider now Eva Petoskey's moving response to my criticism of the *Martinez* case that sovereignty was gained on the backs of women. She said, "I would pay that price."[13] Let us honor how many women have paid the price for the survival of their communities, their generosity of body and spirit in doing so. So much is given, so much is taken, yet they stand undiminished. Julia and Audrey Martinez apparently made a different kind of choice, raising not only the question of whether others can make their choice for them, but also whether each choice does not do a great deal for women in women's larger context, as well as for Native peoples as a whole. As a separate matter, it is worth noting that some of us work so that women don't have to pay that price, asking who has set things up, and why, so that it is so often the women who pay. This is not to criticize the willingness to pay, but to point out that some of us make it our life's work to ensure that *women* will not always be the ones who, again and again, over and over, are on the line to sacrifice their sovereignty as women for the sovereignty of their community among what are, in a larger sense, communities dominated by men. This dimension of the problem is obscured entirely when the *Martinez* loss is described as "[t]heir individual loss . . . sustained to protect the Pueblo and its authority."[14] The women's loss is framed as individual rather than as group-based, as the Pueblo's authority to discriminate based on sex is affirmed with no sign of concern, raising a further question about the substance of the sovereignty that indigenous peoples win in communities built on defending a right to women's inequality within them. Who will pay or is paying the price for women's sovereignty? When, where, and by whom is that fight being joined, if not by women like the Martinez women? Who will stand with them to share the price they pay?

Be all that as it may, *Martinez* gave Indian nations in the United States the chance to be worthy of the price paid. Tribal courts can redeem what it cost them, giving to the women of their communities whatever the US government might have, if Native women had won the right to sue their tribes for sex discrimination, and more. So, now accountable only to themselves on questions of civil rights, what women's rights are tribes protecting? Not all the information necessary to answer this question is available. More rights and protections may exist in reality than on paper; the best remedies are often not written down. Without assuming by any means that the tribes are the primary oppressors of Native women, asking what remedies are available against them if they discriminate, as Santa Clara did against Julia Martinez,[15] is still valid. Remembering that not everything needed to assess this issue is accessible by any means, inquiry into the meaning that tribal courts are giving to sex equality can begin.

From the cases I have seen, the approach being taken basically tracks Aristotle, a Greek man whose writings have been foundational to Western culture and whose approach has dominated equality law and theory in most places.[16] The standard sameness/difference approach predicated on his philosophy in the West considers equality a matter of treating likes alike, unlikes unalike. Jurisdictions that know better are Canada, South Africa building on the Canadian approach, and some international forums.[17] To the extent that this approach prevails,[18] tribal courts are dispensing justice on sex equality in a very similar way to the US federal courts, with all its disappointing and unnecessary limitations. We see a good deal of the familiar "similarly situated" language, approaches to sexual harassment as an individual issue, and selective enforcement in a statutory rape case treated in the conventional way.[19] A real opportunity is missed here: to go beyond the US federal courts' approach to equality. Perhaps unavailable cases in tribal courts see through the "likes alike, unlikes unalike" notion that supported racial segregation, permitted the Holocaust, and continues to obstruct needed claims and remedies toward real equality worldwide.[20] Perhaps the tribal courts know that difference is not the problem of inequality and that sameness is not its solution. Navajo cases are staking out an innovative and path-breaking approach, complete with the equal rights amendment US law lacks.[21] Perhaps they do not ignore dominance and subordination, the real dynamic of inequality, as Native peoples well know from direct experience.

This critique of the Aristotelian approach is not academic or abstract at its base, but grounded in the concrete, lived experience of what women need and do not have, inspired by the black civil rights movement's path to social equality through legal equality. The dominant concept of legal equality permits people who are seen as socially different to get less, when typically the lines of difference are lines inscribed by social forces of hierarchy. So long as dominant groups set the standard, subordinated groups are seen as different from that standard, and so can be treated worse, given less, kept down and out—all the way from unequal pay to genocide— and the conventional approach sees no inequality problem. This logic, outmoded at best, is still being used in courts in the United States legal system. Asking whether tribal courts post-*Martinez* are giving women what US federal courts would have given them may thus be asking the wrong question. The right one is: are tribal courts giving Native women equality? From what little is available, tribal courts appear, on the whole, to be using the same approach to equality as US federal courts, which have not delivered equality to women. Nothing says that Indian nations have to follow them. That is what sovereignty means.

An alternate approach to equality inspires a paragraph in the preamble to the Declaration on Indigenous Peoples' rights,[22] paralleling the Convention on the Elimination of All Forms of Racial Discrimination (CERD).[23] It embodies an anti-hierarchical approach, opposing the superiority of people based on race, religion, ethnicity, or national origin as "racist, scientifically false, legally invalid, morally condemnable and socially unjust."[24] The superiority of some peoples, the inferiority of others, is rejected. The Convention on the Elimination of all Forms of Discrimination Against Women,[25] largely modeled on CERD, has no such prefatory paragraph. It does not say that male domination and female subordination is the real name for sex inequality, of which discrimination is the central practice. Women remain stuck having to be the same as men, when men almost never have to be the same as women to get or keep what men have. If we realize that equality is not about sameness, and inequality is not about difference—no more or less with women than with racial and ethnic groups—then we can see that inequality is about more and less, higher and lower, better and worse, superior and inferior, and that equality is about an end to the social order predicated on such status and treatment.

A real equality approach would oppose the superiority of men over women as false, there being no relation between being biologically male and having more resources, more voice, more power, more credibility, more access, or more dignity— except in the discriminatory societies that make it so. Is this arrangement legally invalid? Let's hope, and work to make it so. Is it morally condemnable? Condemning something morally is a soapbox you stand on to elevate yourself to declare, "I say this is wrong." Be my guest. Socially unjust? Demonstrably. This anti-hierarchical approach to equality, tribal courts, with long experience in its opposite, could consider and use.

As a key example, one issue notable for its absence in the conventional view of equality, both in tribal courts and generally, is sexual assault. Being the one who is sexually abused is paradigmatic of being the unequal. A primary way to make a group subordinate is to rape its members. Men do this to other men as well as to women. Native governments, through their work on battering, have begun to recognize that violence against women needs to be addressed within the community.[26] Rape, incest, and prostitution need more attention. If the US government says that the rate of rape of Native women is one in three,[27] and the real data for all women is closer to one in two;[28] if the reported rape figure for Native women is 70 percent, and Native women are far less likely than other women to report a rape to US authorities;[29] what do you suppose the real rape rate of Native women and girls is? We need to know. We also need to know how many Native men and boys are sexually violated and by whom.

Apart from the staggering numbers, the other stunning feature of rape of Native women appears to be the dramatic percentage of sexual assaults perpetrated by nonmembers of the women's own community. Most women are raped most often by men of their own racial and ethnic group.[30] The rate of reported rape shows the interracial rape of Native women to be two to three times more frequent than for other groups.[31] Maybe Native men are not raping Native women in substantial numbers; maybe Native women are not reporting Native men raping them in substantial numbers. Either way, the numbers taken together support what I have heard Native women say, which is that almost none of them knows a Native woman who has not been sexually violated.[32] If you listen to most women you know that this situation is very often the case for women in general. The situation of Native women combines massive underreporting of a problem of monumental proportions with little federal, state, or tribal response. In particular, Native women in Indian country appear to be a free-fire zone for non-Indian men, who can go there, rape Indian women, and get away with it largely because the jurisdictional divide rarely results in criminal prosecution.[33] Reversing this jurisdictional arrangement for sexual assaults at the very least, as the Tribal Law & Order Act of 2010 took some constructive steps toward but did not accomplish,[34] would give tribal justice systems a problem on the other side of *Martinez* to solve: prosecuting non-Native men for raping Native women in Indian country. Standing with Native women in this respect would be an exercise of sovereignty, not a challenge to it.

But query sovereignty. Sovereignty is a Western idea deriving from feudal Europe, meaning a man's home is his castle, his castle his domain.[35] The sovereign has dominion over whatever is within his sphere, equal to others with entitlement to dominate whatever is within theirs—which is not to say that indigenous peoples necessarily should not have or want sovereignty. It is to say that sovereignty is neither an Indian idea nor a woman's idea. Internationally, sovereignty supported the Holocaust; nobody was supposed to intervene in Germany's internal affairs. Not until Germany invaded other countries was anything done because, until then, murdering Jews was an internal matter. Sovereignty means that what is done at home need not be accounted for outside of home. That does not mean this insulation is not worth having or fighting for under certain circumstances or that it may not be used for positive ends. But sovereignty's wholesale rejection of outside recourse has kept women under the domination of men. Sovereign authority, whether as head of household or of government, is insulated from accountability, including for abuse at home, which is where women are violated by men most.

To put this issue into context, few, if any, cultures or governments provide equality for women anywhere. Sex inequality is maintained partly by the tacit deal among men to let other men do what they want with "their women" there, so those other men will let them do what they want with "their women" here. Jurisdictionally, this deal is termed sovereignty, specified as federalism or state's rights or margin of appreciation, or whatever tolerance for local discrimination is termed. Substantively, its content is called culture.

When Bosnian Serbs exterminated and raped Bosnian Muslim and Croat women in Bosnia, they said it was their own internal business. Outside intervention violated their sovereignty. When my Bosnian Muslim and Croat women clients sued Radovan Karadzic, the Bosnian Serb fascist leader, in United States federal court under the Alien Tort Act, implementing customary international law for rape as an act of genocide in this conflict,[36] Karadzic said the case violated his country's sovereignty. Karadzic fought the case for seven years—not saying that what he led was not genocide, not saying that he did not lead it, not saying that the rapes did not happen, not even saying that he was not responsible for them. Rather, he argued we had no jurisdiction to hold him to account *in the United States* for whatever was done to women back home. In essence, he argued that those women should go back to Bosnia and deal with his (genocidal) regime. Many people supported him—not because they thought genocidal rape was a good idea or a practice of Serbian culture. Partly they thought he was going to win, and they recognized how nations are made. Mainly, they thought Bosnian problems should be dealt with in Bosnia.

Our view was, you raped her, she's us. We do not respect the line drawn at the national border under these circumstances. Here, being a woman is global citizenship. We argued, in this instance of genocidal rape, that raping her destroys her community because she is her community, and rape shatters communities, which are built on identifications and relationships, as well as, and through, women themselves. Substantively, this case conceived and established rape as an act of genocide under law for the first time. Jurisdictionally, jurisdiction was established over this rogue regime leader in another country, securing an award to his victims of $745 million from a New York jury.[37] The US federal court held that international law prohibited those violations as, among other things, acts of sex discrimination. In the process, Karadzic was delegitimized, had to flee, was eventually hunted down, and is being prosecuted internationally as well.[38] In the meantime, Bosnian women established jurisdiction over him in another country and held him accountable to the women he hurt outside of Bosnia. And they used US federal courts to do it.

It helps, to say the least, that the United States never conducted genocide in Bosnia, nor colonized it, nor dispossessed its peoples, nor destroyed its culture. So there was no precise *Martinez* problem with the forum. My clients wanted to sue in the United States courts because they sensed they would get a fair hearing, and they did. It is exactly because US federal courts offered accountability by men to women outside their national borders that these women wanted to use this forum. What they sought—and what they got—was exactly justice that is not indigenous. Bosnian sovereignty was not respected because it was in the hands of the women's violators. The law that was applied was international, but the Karadzic case was not brought into an international forum, but into another national one.

Also worth recalling in this connection is the Sandra Lovelace case, in which Canada was held to account by the U.N. for imposing on First Nations the same rule that Santa Clara had imposed on Julia Martinez.[39] After *Lovelace*, the rule was changed.[40] Most indigenous people with whom I have discussed this issue have no problem with Santa Clara being answerable in an international forum for the rule Julia Martinez challenged. Because their nationhood is not yet internationally recognized nor is an analogous process available, such a forum is not yet possible.

Forum was fatal to the legitimacy of Julia Martinez's claim as well as to its legality. What she possibly perceived as her only recourse may not only have doomed her claim but also have generated a durable dynamic of resistance to changing the rule when she lost. Santa Clara apparently has yet to equalize the marrying-out rule,[41] although many people—including me and some members of the Santa Clara Pueblo— think it should go.[42] Had it applied existing equal protection standards, the US Supreme Court would likely have found the rule to be sex discriminatory on the merits. Doubtless, whatever sex equality results are achieved through tribal courts are likely perceived as immeasurably more legitimate than any imposed by US courts. But whatever the benefits of the existing decision, having sovereignty achieved at the price of equality is disheartening, as is having the plaintiff derided for disloyalty and worse as a result of her choice of forum, as if the problem was who she asked, not what she asked for, and then to this day not to have had her own people grant the simple equality she sought. An international approach offers an external forum that can provide sex equality that is not imposed on a subordinated culture by a dominant one, but rather is predicated upon recognition of equal sovereignty. International fora can overcome both hierarchies at once, offering Native women sovereignty and equality too.[43]

NOTES

This work was supported in part by time provided by The Diane Middlebrook and Carl Djerassi Visiting Professorship in Gender Studies, Cambridge University, the superb and resourceful research assistance of Lisa Cardyn, and the incomparable and ever-responsive staff of the University of Michigan Law Library.

  1.   436 U.S. 49 (1978).
  2.   Indian Civil Rights Act of 1968, 25 U.S.C. §§ 1301–03 (2010).
  3.   Martinez v. Santa Clara Pueblo, 540 F.2d 1039, 1047–48 (10th Cir. 1976).
  4.   It was later published as Catharine A. MacKinnon, *Whose Culture? A Case Note on* Martinez v. Santa Clara Pueblo (1983), in FEMINISM UNMODIFIED: DISCOURSES ON LIFE AND LAW 63 (1987).

5. *See, e.g.*, Angela P. Harris, *Race and Essentialism in Feminist Legal Theory*, 42 STAN. L. REV. 581, 593–95 (1990) (identifying *Whose Culture?* as demonstrative of "MacKinnon's refusal to move beyond essentialism"); Gloria Valencia-Weber, Santa Clara Pueblo v. Martinez: *Twenty-five Years of Disparate Cultural Visions*, 14 KAN. J. L. & PUB. POL'Y 49, 53–54, 63 n.44 (2004) (presenting without critique "Angela Harris' response to MacKinnon's gender essentialism"). Angela Harris's description of my work in this respect is factually false. For documentation, *see* Catharine A. MacKinnon, *Keeping It Real: On Anti-"Essentialism,"* in WOMEN'S LIVES, MEN'S LAWS 84 (2005). Equally false is Valencia-Weber's charge that I do not reference voices of American Indian feminists. The entire 1983 article is epigraphed with a quotation from Beth Brant of the Mohawk nation. MacKinnon, *Whose Culture?, supra* note 4, at 63.

6. *See, e.g.,* PAULA GUNN ALLEN, THE SACRED HOOP: RECOVERING THE FEMININE IN AMERICAN INDIAN TRADITIONS (1st ed. 1986); Lillian A. Ackerman, *Complementary But Equal: Gender Status in the Plateau, in* GENDER AND POWER IN NATIVE NORTH AMERICA 75 (Laura F. Klein & Lillian A. Ackerman eds., 1995); Evelyn Blackwood, *Sexuality and Gender in Certain Native American Tribes: The Case of Cross-Gender Females*, 10 SIGNS 27 (1984).

7. *See* Russell Thornton, *Tribal Membership Requirements and the Demography of 'Old' and 'New' Native Americans*, 16 POPULATION RES. & POL'Y REV. 33, 35–38 (1997) (discussing the origins and persistence of blood quantum requirements for tribal membership); *see also* Paul Spruhan, *A Legal History of Blood Quantum in Federal Indian Law to 1935*, 51 S.D. L. REV. 1 (2006) (providing an historical analysis of this practice).

8. This analysis was foundational to sexual harassment as a legal claim as well as accepted as an approach to equality in Canada. (*See* Andrews v. Law Society of British Columbia, [1989] 1 S.C.R. 143 (establishing that laws must promote equality to be nondiscriminatory), and *R. v. Keegstra*, [1990] 3 S.C.R. 697 (holding a race hate propaganda law constitutional on equality grounds)). Long after, it was articulated in Catharine A. MacKinnon, *Toward a New Theory of Equality*, in WOMEN'S LIVES, MEN'S LAWS, *supra* note 5, at 44 (2005).

9. Possibly because the *Martinez* lawsuit "was perceived as an individual rights campaign, counter to the communal values and interests of the community" (Gloria Valencia-Weber, *Three Stories in One: The Story of Martinez Revisited v. Santa Clara Pueblo*, in INDIAN LAW STORIES 482 (Carole Goldberg et al. eds., 2011)), this conceptual framework seems to have been attached to anyone seen as sympathetic to her position.

10. Robin Morgan's well-known collection, SISTERHOOD IS GLOBAL (1st ed. 1984), can be seen to be animated by this spirit.

11. *See, e.g.*, Valencia-Weber, *Three Stories in One, supra* note 9, at 486 n.114.

12. For one notion of "the whole," see Rina Swentzell, *Testimony of a Santa Clara Woman*, 14 KAN. J.L. & PUB. POL'Y 97, 98 (2004).

13. Eva Petoskey is a member of the Grand Traverse Band of Ottawa and Chippewa Indians. Petoskey's comments were delivered in a discussion on "Indigenous Women Assess the Indian Civil Rights Act," at the 5th Annual MSU Indigenous Law Conference, held at Michigan State University College of Law on October 10–11, 2008. *See* Gloria Valencia-Weber, Rina Swentzell, and Eva Petsokey, *40 Years of the Indian Civil Rights Act: Indigenous Women's Reflections*, in THE INDIAN CIVIL RIGHTS ACT AT FORTY (2012).

14. Valencia-Weber, *Three Stories in One, supra* note 9, at 488.

15. It is worth noting that advocates of Santa Clara's position typically do not deny that the rule challenged in *Martinez* is sex discriminatory. *See, e.g., id.*

16. *See* CATHARINE A. MACKINNON, SEX EQUALITY 3–5 (2d ed. 2007) tracing this.

17. *See* Andrews v. Law Society, *supra* note 8; S. AFR. CONST. 1996; Human Rights Committee, General Comment 24 (54), U.N. Doc. CCPR/C/21/Rev.1/Add.6 (1994); Committee on the Elimination of All Forms of Discrimination Against Women (CEDAW), *General Recommendation No. 19*, U.N. Doc. A/47/38 (Feb. 1, 1992).

18. Although I had read these cases and others before the conference presentation on which this paper is based, all are discussed accessibly in the competent survey by Ann E. Tweedy, *Sex Discrimination Under Tribal Law*, 36 WM. MITCHELL L. REV. 392 (2010).

19. *See* Tweedy, *id.* at 403 n.43, 409, 410, 412–15, 428, 429 n.133, 430 n.136.

20. *See* MACKINNON, SEX EQUALITY, *supra* note 16, at 7–8.

21. *See* Tweedy, *supra* note 18, at 418–22.

22. Declaration on the Rights of Indigenous Peoples, G.A. Res. 61/295, U.N. Doc. A/RES/61/295 (Sept. 13, 2007) (hereinafter DRIP).

23. International Convention on the Elimination of All Forms of Racial Discrimination, G.A. Res. 2106 (XX), (Dec. 21, 1965).

24. DRIP, *supra* note 22, at 2.

25. Convention on the Elimination of All Forms of Discrimination against Women, U.N. Doc. A/RES/34/180 (Dec. 18, 1979)

26. *See* SARAH DEER ET AL., A VICTIM-CENTERED APPROACH TO DOMESTIC VIOLENCE AGAINST NATIVE WOMEN: RESOURCE GUIDE FOR DRAFTING OR REVISING TRIBAL LAWS AGAINST DOMESTIC VIOLENCE (2008). For additional information on programs and other resources being developed to address the pervasive problem of violence against women in Indian country, see the websites of the Tribal Law and Policy Institute, , and the Indian Law Resource Center's "Safe Women, Strong Nations" project, http://www.indianlaw.org/en/safewomen.

27. PATRICIA TJADEN & NANCY THOENNES, FULL REPORT OF THE PREVALENCE, INCIDENCE, AND CONSEQUENCES OF VIOLENCE AGAINST WOMEN: FINDINGS FROM THE NATIONAL VIOLENCE AGAINST WOMEN SURVEY 22 (2000) (reporting a lifetime rape victimization rate of 34.1 percent for American Indian and Alaska Native women).

28. DIANA E.H. RUSSELL, SEXUAL EXPLOITATION: RAPE, CHILD SEXUAL ABUSE, AND WORKPLACE HARASSMENT 35 (1984) (discussing results of a San Francisco study in which 44 percent of respondents reported being victims of rape or attempted rape at least once in their lives).

29. According to a recent study undertaken by Amnesty International, "interviews with survivors, activists and support workers across the USA suggest that available statistics greatly underestimate the severity of the problem." AMNESTY INTERNATIONAL, MAZE OF INJUSTICE. THE FAILURE TO PROTECT INDIGENOUS WOMEN FROM SEXUAL VIOLENCE IN THE USA 2 AMR 51/035/2007 (Apr. 24, 2007).

30. *See, e.g.*, MENACHEM AMIR, PATTERNS IN FORCIBLE RAPE 44 (1971) (concluding that approximately 93 percent of rapes are intraracial); NAT'L COMM'N ON THE CAUSES & PREVENTION OF VIOLENCE, FINAL REPORT OF THE NATIONAL COMMISSION ON THE CAUSES AND PREVENTION OF VIOLENCE 210 (1969) (finding a rate of 90 percent).

31. An analysis of data collected by the Bureau of Justice Statistics noted that, while "[v]iolent crime against white and black victims was primarily intraracial," the same did not hold true for Native Americans, particularly in the case of rape and sexual assault, where approximately 80 percent of assailants were described as white and another 10 percent as black. STEVEN W. PERRY, AMERICAN INDIANS AND CRIME: A BJS STATISTICAL PROFILE, 1992–2002, at 9 (2004).

32. This is further borne out in the Amnesty International report. *See* MAZE OF INJUSTICE, *supra* note 29, at 2 ("In the Standing Rock Sioux Reservation, for example, many of the women who agreed to be interviewed could not think of any Native women within their community who had not been subjected to sexual violence"); *see also* Sarah Deer, *Sovereignty of the Soul: Exploring the Intersection of Rape Law Reform and Federal Indian Law*, 38 SUFFOLK U. L. REV. 455, 456 (2005) ("Many of the elders that I have spoken with in Indian country tell me that they do not know any women in their community who have not experienced sexual violence").

33. *See* Deer, *Sovereignty of the Soul*, *supra* note 32 at 462.

34. Tribal Law & Order Act of 2010, 124 Stat 2258 (2010) provides for better communication among tribal law enforcement, federal authorities, and federal courts by deputizing special assistant US attorneys to prosecute reservation crimes in federal courts and gives tribes some greater authority to hold perpetrators accountable.

35. For documentation and discussion, *see, e.g.*, Beverly Balos, *A Man's Home Is His Castle: How the Law Shelters Domestic Violence and Sexual Harassment*, 23 ST. LOUIS U. PUB. L. REV. 77, 90–91 (2004).

36. Doe v. Karadzic, 866 F. Supp. 734 (S.D.N.Y. 1994).

37. *See* MACKINNON, SEX EQUALITY, *supra* note 16, at 835 (citing Judgment, Kadic v. Karadzic, (S.D.N.Y. No. 93 Civ. 1163 (Aug. 16, 2000)).

38. Prosecutor v. Karadzic, Case No. IT-95-5/18, Amended Indictment (May 31, 2000), *available at* http://www.icty.org/x/cases/karadzic/ind/en/kar-ai000428e.pdf.

39.   Lovelace v. Canada (Communication No. 24/1977), GAOR, 36th Sess., Supp. No. 40, at 166, U.N. Doc. A/36/40 (1981) (holding that Canada had abridged Lovelace's cultural rights).

40.   *See* R.L. et al. v. Canada, Communication No. 358/1989, U.N. Doc. CCPR/C/43/D/358/1989, at 16 (1991) ("By virtue of Bill C-31 women who, on account of their marriage to non-Indians prior to 17 April 1985, had lost their Indian status under the former Indian Act, together with any of their children who had lost status with them, could be reinstated and thus be re-considered band members"), *available at* http://www1.umn.edu/humanrts/undocs/html/ dec358.htm.

41.   *See* Valencia-Weber, *Three Stories in One, supra* note 9, at 484 (documenting this through 2010).

42.   Elder Noranjo takes this position. *See id.* at 482 n.104. For various views within the Pueblo on the question, including support for gender equality, *see id.* at 482–83.

43.   The U.N. Declaration on the Rights of Indigenous Peoples, GA Res. 61/295 (Sept. 13, 2007) is a major step in this direction. *See* DRIP, *supra* note 22.

CHAPTER 3

40 Years of the Indian Civil Rights Act: Indigenous Women's Reflections

═══

GLORIA VALENCIA-WEBER, RINA SWENTZELL,
AND EVA PETOSKEY

Gloria Valencia-Weber

First, I want to thank the people at Michigan State University Law School for planning this conference. The Indian Civil Rights Act (ICRA)[1] as the core statute and then *Santa Clara Pueblo v. Martinez*[2] as the foundational case that continues with power in Indian life on the ground are very important. And I want to thank everyone. I know Matthew Fletcher and Wenona Singel led, but you had some great staff people and I thank you all. I especially want to thank the panelists for their perspectives. I come from Mexican indigenous people, Yaquis who crossed over into territorial Arizona, and Indianness does not end with formal borders. We always speak about all our relations, and I am especially pleased to be here with my relations and particularly my sisters that include not only Rina Swentzell, but it is always gratifying for a law professor to see several of her former students on the program. I also want to acknowledge my appreciation for Professor MacKinnon.[3] One of the highlights of my career as a law student was to hear her speak at the Harvard Law School. I think all women who have faced less than friendly work environments owe a great deal to the development of the doctrine of the hostile work environment and what complications arise for all women in the workplace, and they have not all gone away, as we know.

I approach this discussion by noting that *Martinez* raises two critical oppositional principles: the collective political right versus the individual rights norm. Individual rights are the keystone in the Constitution of the United States. However, tribal rights for collective political entities are also affirmed in the Constitution in the provisions that establish relationships with the tribal nations. This political, nation-to-nation relationship was explicitly acknowledged and reaffirmed in *Morton vs. Mancari*.[4] The most important right that tribal people claim for themselves is that as sovereigns. We have to remember that tribes were first sovereigns within the United States. And, as the noted scholar Charles Wilkinson reminds us, the tribal sovereigns

– 39 –

were pre-constitutional, post-constitutional, and, in the international law context of indigenous law, extra-constitutional.[5]

As an Indian law teacher who also teaches constitutional law, I'm quite aware of the different pushes and pulls of those two doctrines. It's very hard for some students to understand why this political sovereignty right exists and how it functions as the guiding principle of *Martinez*. Many a student comes into law seeing that Indians are just another minority group, an aggregate collection of individuals. Why not apply the universal norms of equal protection and due process, and transfer them from the constitutional law doctrines over into the Indian law area? Yet they ignore or are unaware throughout their law education that Indian law is, as we call it in law, *sui generis*, a unique form of historical and legal relationship-based law. The fact remains that within the borders of the United States, the tribes are unique, culturally based governments—the only legal theocracies—and that has always guided my own perspective of what every question starts with: the sovereignty foundation.

From the law professor perspective, I'm working on the *Martinez* case for a book and some other writings. I enjoy looking at the Library of Congress archives of our justices to see how they reasoned, not only in *Martinez* but in other cases. You have to recognize that *Martinez* is one of the most cited cases. It has endless numbers of articles written about it. If you look just in the federal courts from the Supreme Court down to bankruptcy court, almost 350 citations to *Martinez* and to ICRA appear, and the number is growing.[6]

On the ground, life is different from legal study. I'm very aware of this as I engage in this long-term study with Santa Clara Pueblo tribal member and scholar Rina Swentzell on this matter. I am writing a law chapter using the Library of Congress, the justices' archives, but am very aware all the time that life on the ground in Indian country where I live and have lived most of my life is quite different. The ICRA is one of a number of Indian statutes, but one that nonetheless has complete and pervasive impact, much the way Lawrence Baca described it when it is invoked for a variety of reasons, some not so honorable.[7]

The underlying question very much is as my former student Casey Douma states it in the federal bar article in the conference materials.[8] He raises the question: "Can tribal law and can tribal courts provide justice to the persons who are within the authority exercised by that tribe?" Let us remember that the act is about "persons" within the authority of that tribe. In the legislative history, as described in Donald Burnett's great article in the *Harvard Journal on Legislation*, there was much active discussion on this point.[9] As truncated and spread-out as those hearings were, there was one continuing discussion: Should the ICRA protect the rights of "Indians," "members," or "persons?" The final statutory term "persons" is significant in how life on the ground is lived among Indians and non-Indians and how government authority is exercised under the ICRA.[10] Issues of equality, equal protection, and due process raise the question in *Martinez* as well as now: Who defines these terms and how do we go about determining that equality exists?

Of the 565 tribes that are federally recognized, each has a unique culture and perspective, but there are some commonalities. The story on the ground in Santa Clara Pueblo is that before and after the case there had always been a core of people who, by their own designation, called themselves progressives, who felt that true equality and treatment of female members should exist. They are the same people who presented a proposal in the last two years to the Pueblo council to change that ordinance. I will leave it to Rina to address this.

What's important is that *Martinez* left to the tribe, in the exercise of its authority, community dialogues and process, to resolve how—in the sense of all my relations—we are going to live with each other. The fact that *Martinez* preserves a collective communal right does not mean that equality of individuals will be overlooked. In mainstream scholarship, Martha Minow, who writes about relations and community, has suggested that when our role in the community is based on relationships, these relationships are the core from which our individual rights, entitlements, and duties arise.[11] What we are entitled to—how we are going to be protected in enjoying the entitlements that arise from those relationships, families, clans, and orders—depends on a Pueblo perspective. In *Martinez,* specifically, what the western lens looks at is ideas of male dominance and patriarchy. These ideas are the very reasons why Alfonso Ortiz, a professor at the University of Chicago, returned to New Mexico: to write about the Pueblo perspective. In his book, *The Tewa World*, Ortiz tells us that perspective is not about matriarchy or patriarchy, the narrowing paradigms that western intellectual academic study uses to analyze the Pueblo world.[12] That world is about loyalties, moieties or societies, whether you are part of the winter people who govern and carry out the order of the pueblo in the winter and then hand it to the summer people. It is in those core societies that our relationships, our status, our responsibilities, our protections arise.

And so you have this set of clearly different views. Life on the ground was different even at the time of the case. Through detective work, I got the transcript of the trial and you can now, if you go on our law school Web space, get it through our law library.[13] One would think, reading the law-review articles, that the day after the Supreme Court issued its decision upholding the sovereignty and the sovereign immunity of the tribe, that the moving vans showed up and ejected the Martinezes from the community, threw the kids out of the school, cut off the water, cut off the firewood, and cut off all those amenities. That is not what happened.

We have to step back and ask, "Is this the lens, are these the principles by which we try to understand what was going on internally at Santa Clara Pueblo?" We find that during that time the Martinez family continued to function as community members; they do to this very day. Two weeks ago, we were doing interviews in Santa Clara Pueblo and passed by the Martinez house still used, inhabited by members. Outsiders bring a western cultural perspective that is not invaluable, but it is different. And life on the ground continues that way. On the ground today in tribes across the US, the power of *Martinez* in the affirmation of sovereignty and sovereign immunity is critical for daily life.

When I teach *Martinez,* I have the students read the Swentzell essay[14] and I also show them the excerpt from a PBS documentary called *Winds of Change,* showing that the Onondaga Nation uses its sovereignty differently.[15] At Onondaga, it is a female clan system and the woman that heads the clan selects the Faith Keeper, a male. If he fails in his duty on the Faith Keeper council that governs the Onondaga, she alone has the power to remove him. Note that in a George W. Bush era, there is no democracy here. No one elects the clan mother. No one elects or votes for the Faith Keeper. And I show a special excerpt from *Winds of Change* with this grainy footage of the all-male Faith Keeper council seeing that their cultural foundation based on clan mothers and clan systems is falling apart. Why? Because when the high school on the reservation closed and was merged with the in-town high school, high school hormones and hot love resulted in all kinds of marriages. So the question comes when you have a finite amount of land, space, and resources: Who is going to have a piece of Onondaga land? You see the newsreel footage of the all-male council voting to preserve their clan mother system. For the males who out-marry, it is they and their children who will be disadvantaged. This is how the Onondaga used the tribal culturally based governance to preserve themselves.

This past May, in New York I had an opportunity to talk to Oren Lyons, the head Faith Keeper. Chief Lyons said that there has been no change in the rule at Onondaga. It remains the same. Males who out-marry, who marry non-Onondaga women, the price is that their children will suffer some membership losses. But again, on the ground if you go to Onondaga, as soon as you get off the tribal land, at the boundaries surrounding Onondaga are homes where these males who out-married live with their wives and children. They partake of what goes on in that society. And no one who sees that film and sees the clan mothers that are featured there would think that these are women without power. So this is just one example of how it plays out within other communities.

Now on the ground in Indian country where I live, *Martinez* matters beyond membership issues. Remember that the ICRA applies to "persons" and not just "Indians" or "members." As non-Indians come onto Pueblo lands for all kinds of commercial business, and economic-development ventures, we are seeing those issues arise. For example, outside of Santa Fe, right next to the ritzy Santa Fe Opera, is the Tesuque Flea Market. It is quite a large and enjoyable flea market, and it is commercially run by the Tesuque Pueblo. A non-Indian vendor who had a vendor's license and contract got into a physical dispute with other vendors, was ejected, and then had his vendor license canceled. He exhausted his remedies in tribal court, but was not satisfied, so then tried to get into federal court. Of course, he did have his liberty interest, his livelihood, and his income stopped. But then again he had violated the conditions. In a way, the vendor was trying to invoke *Oliphant*[16] wherein non-Indians cannot be prosecuted by the Indian tribe. There is a hint of that in some of his filings. After losing at the Pueblo's court of appeals, he tried to get into federal district court, which dismissed the case. Then he filed a cert petition and the Supreme Court denied review. But you see how he could invoke the rights he claimed and he was fairly treated. However, he had violated the terms of the contract and the tribe had every right to control the activities on tribal land and to deny him further presence on their land.[17] For Tesuque in that area, there are continuing struggles in which non-Indians challenge tribal authority even though there is cross-deputization with the state and county police authorities.

I will finish with tribal sovereignty as a recognized authority to enforce law. We have a lot of cross-jurisdictional agreements involving tribes and the state in New Mexico of necessity because of the way Indian land weaves in and out. And there again that busy highway that goes by the Santa Fe Opera and the Tesuque Flea Market is a place where cross-deputized Tesuque police officers frequently stop people who are speeding like crazy, or maybe driving under the influence, or engaging in other kinds of offenses that are dangerous to people on the road. Continuously, non-Indians challenge the Tesuque Pueblo officer. Even though the officer shows the cross-deputization document, the non-Indian says, "No, they can't stop me and they shouldn't be able to arrest me or anything else." It's what those of us living in New Mexico call "the non-Indian guys who hate getting tickets from Indian police officers." This goes on in other places. In some instances, cross-deputization occurs with the federal authorities. You cannot have some federal law enforcement activity occur in the hinterlands without the assistance of some tribes. When an offender flees, cooperation is essential. One incident involved violent killings on an interstate amid canyons and mountains; the only people who could help find the suspects were the tribal people and the tribal trackers! So life on the ground is different. Life on the ground involving the ICRA and *Martinez* is about real people living daily lives trying to be productive. This is a concern not only within their tribal community, but shared with the other communities with which they have mutual interests in safe and productive lives.

Rina Swentzell

I am a woman from Santa Clara Pueblo. I was forty years old when the US Supreme Court ruled in favor of the tribe during the *Santa Clara v. Martinez* case. The entire Santa Clara community was happy with the decision, as was I. The ruling in favor of tribal sovereignty meant we were a group of people who could make decisions for ourselves. We felt that the ordinance of our constitution, which treated women unfairly, was something the community had to deal with internally.

This remains a complicated issue through today because, as you know, Santa Clara has not dealt with this issue of injustice against its women. But the statement that Lawrence Baca left us with is that the world is complicated. If you decide one way, you have this set of problems; if you go that way, you have a different set of problems. Santa Clara is not unique in that sense. But Santa Clara, and other tribes, do have something that we Santa Clarans need to remember and the rest of the world really needs to hear—not just about the law or social institutions. It is about an old way of life. It is a philosophical stance.

It is related to the gender issue. In our old way of thinking, the acknowledgment of different energies, such as male and female, winter and summer, hot and cold, influences our daily lives because every person in our community is born with winter or summer, hot or cold, male or female energy. Our traditional social/political structuring emulates the seasons so our community is made up of Winter and Summer people. Every six months, from one equinox to the other, community leadership is transferred from one group to the other. Sometime, way back long time ago, our people knew there are basic tensions in the world, that there are opposite forces in the world, different energies in the world. Male and female are a pair of these forces. Alfonso Ortiz and other archaeologists have argued that there are matrilineal or patrilineal societies and one or the other is dominant. In traditional Santa Clara thinking it is not about one or the other. It is about both and each is needed for the other to exist, or to assure the health of the whole. If winter and summer are put together, we've got the whole year. It's not just about winter, it's not just about summer, it's about the whole cycle of the year. And without one or the other we'd be in sad shape. Our people somewhere back there realized that and began to define the world, the community, our daily lives, accordingly. They didn't conclude that one is better than the other. They accepted that these opposite forces bring tension but that the thing to do is to figure out how to bring them together to create a balance of the two within the whole. This meant that the whole is bigger than its parts. So with this thinking, we were in favor of the US Supreme Court ruling in favor of the whole, in favor of the community.

We have a word in our language that encapsulates this thinking. The word is *gia*, which in Tewa literally means "mother." It is a very important concept because mother is an idea, a place that contains everything. It represents the whole. All Native tribes assume that people dwell, exist, within nature. Everybody in the world acknowledges that earth and mother are synonymous. And so we go to that place, the earth. In our language we talk about being the children of the earth. We are the children of the mother. Males and females are the children of the mother. Femaleness becomes a mere gender classification. We do not accept the adversarial philosophy of the western world. We went someplace else. We went to seeing that tensions were an opportunity to create a relational whole. That is what Gloria was talking about. In our world, it is about relationships. Mother is about relationship. That sets up a whole different way of looking at the world and about how we treat each other, how we make decisions, what kind of rules we make for each other. Imagine, if laws were made by the mother, we would live in a different kind of world.

I grew up in Santa Clara, with my great-grandmother, right in the middle of the Pueblo plaza. Growing up during those years, I experienced a relational community. During those years, when big decisions like the *Martinez* case happened, these female mothers were consulted. The men were the caretakers of the outside world. They were the ones who were out in the mountains, out in the fields, farming, gathering, hunting. The women and the children were of the inside world. The traditional role of the males was to take care of that inside space, to keep things in balance, to keep it so it moves well for the children for whom they are responsible.

In that world, the men had a serious responsibility to take care of that inside space and the operative word here is care, nurture, in the best way possible. They dealt with the outside forces, like the Plains people coming early on. Then there were the Spanish and Anglos and it was the men meeting them. But, inside, every morning at her kitchen stove, my great-grandmother would wait for the men to come. There would be a parade of men coming to talk: "we've got this problem, let's talk about it. What do you think we should do about this? How does it work?" She was there, as one of the five women during the time I was growing up known as a *gia*. They were mothers of large extended families. They were all contacted about what could be done in major issues affecting the whole community.

But there was another interesting thing happening. The men who came to visit my great-grandmother were usually those who met in the kivas, or meeting places for men. They were people who did ceremonies and coordinated large public functions. If they acted appropriately as nurturing and caring people of the community, they were also called *gias*. They were also mothers! In the *Santa Clara v. Martinez* transcripts that Gloria talked about, there was the testimony of an elderly man, Alcario Tafoya.[18] When he was questioned about religious stuff, he said, "I can't talk about it. But, I am the *ogikay* of the winter people." He was a winter mother. He was not the winter leader or a winter man; he was the winter mother. That is what we have. We have winter mothers, we have summer mothers, and they are men.

These mothers, both female and male, agreed to the 1936 constitution written for us by people from Washington because that was the way to save our culture and place from the intruding outside world. The 1939 ordinance, which discriminates against women, was a way to fend off male intruders who were marrying into the community, claiming land and resources. The male outsiders were more of a threat than were female outsiders because men were, generally, more inclined to claim land and other resources for private use. Hence, the ruling against women who married outsiders. Intermarriage, however, for either males or females was not halted. It has increased and the traditional cohesiveness and definition of the community has changed. There are today more nonmembers than members in the Pueblo due to intermarriage.

This is the kind of complication that we have in our community, as outsiders say that Santa Clara has explicit gender discrimination. Of course, from a Western perspective, there is absolute gender discrimination. And how do we, as a tribe that still struggles to keep a very different philosophical way, deal with this? I did not live in the Santa Clara community for a long time because I married a non-Indian person. My children are not members. My brother, who married a non-Santa Clara, has children who are members. My male cousin, who married a non-Indian and does not live in the Pueblo, has children who are members. And so it goes. Two of my children live in the Pueblo. My grandchildren and great-grandchildren from these two children live in the Pueblo. They are in the community and that is where they belong. They live in houses that everyone acknowledges as theirs. We know they are not going to be thrown out. It is their home. That's just the way it is. How do we work through this confusion of living there but not being members, primarily not being able to vote or assume political roles, but mostly being treated as if one belongs? The only thing we can do is work it out within the community— to work within our own sensibilities. And it will happen. It will change in such a way that we can feel that we haven't given ourselves over completely to being the other, which represents foreign rules and regulations with pointed, linear actions. We can change this situation that was made static by a constitution written by outsiders for us—and the fear that gripped our mothers. Hopefully, we can remember to change in a relational way by using current tensions to create a healthy whole community.

Eva Petoskey

I want to say *miigwetch* for inviting me here today, to Matthew and Weriona and the rest of the staff here at the law school. It's a pleasure to be here at the Michigan State University campus. My daughter's a freshman here and I think she might be coming in here soon so she'll have a chance to hear her mom talk, which will be wonderful. Good for her, good for me, good for the family. Also, I want to say, *miigwetch* to the other women on the panel. I had the privilege of walking over from the hotel with Rina this morning and she kept a good pace. *I* had to keep up with *her*! We were both walking so fast we almost went past the law school! But also she inspired me to just be myself today. So in light of that inspiration let me introduce myself in our language, if you will: [*in Eva's language*].

I think it's really important for native people to feel liberated enough to use our language anywhere. But it's hard, it's hard to do that. It's hard to stand up and speak my truth. I wonder do any of you really care what my Anishnaabek name is? Or am I trying to put on some kind of show here for you to let you know that I actually have one? It is hard for me to know what is in your mind. But to me, it's important for me to introduce myself with my Anishnaabek name because my name reflects how I see the world. If I have to stand in front of a group of people it's more comfortable for me to say my name before I speak because it acknowledges my spiritual connection to who I am. If you're going to ask me to come and speak here, I have to ask for spiritual help in doing that. And the way I do that within the Anishnaabek worldview is to first speak my name and recognize my spiritual helpers. My name helps me feel grounded and unafraid. I'll be honest with you, that's hard. It's hard to speak my truth in this context.

But when I was asked to come here and speak, I read Catharine MacKinnon's article, and I don't know if she's here? Is she here? Hi Catharine. I read your article and I'll be honest again, I was kind of intimidated by it. I thought, I don't really understand this. And I'm an educated person, so to speak; I've gone to college and I have a couple different degrees and this and that, but I had a really hard time understanding it. I think because I've lived at home too long. I've lived on the reservation for twenty years, I served in tribal government, I raised our children, I'm married to another tribal member, so maybe I've forgotten. Sometimes I don't even go away from my home for weeks at a time other than to go to the grocery store! So I get really into this mind-set that's really pretty connected to where I live. I had a hard time with this presentation, because I thought, well Matthew, what are you asking me to talk about here? And at first I said, I'm not going to do it! I don't want to do it! I mean, what are you asking *me* for? [laughter] Then I realized that what I had to do is just tell myself I'll just speak from my own place. And we all speak from our own place. And Catharine, you speak from your own place, an honorable place, the place of your life experience and the view and the life of a woman. And that I can understand. I've certainly lived the life of a woman: a native woman.

I can speak as an Anishnaabek woman. I'm a member of the Grand Traverse Band of Ottawa and Chippewa Indians and I served on our tribal council for a number of years. When I think about feminism, if you will, from a native point of view, I really share Rina's view. Rina did such a wonderful job of describing the inner life of her community. I can only speak of the inner life of the Anishnaabek community as I know it today. We still have some speakers of our native language, unfortunately, not a lot. But I had the privilege to be born in a family where my mother was a fluent speaker of the language. So I was able to learn certain things that maybe some people my age, and I'm fifty-six, didn't have the opportunity to learn. When the *Martinez* case was decided [laughter], I was about twenty-some years old, twenty-five maybe, and I had just finished my undergraduate degree at the University of Wisconsin and I was in graduate school, but in the summer of 1978 I participated in the Longest Walk, a treaty walk, and I am sure some of you probably don't even know what I'm talking about. But people walked across the United States to protest legislation that had been introduced to abrogate treaty rights. I joined the walk in Pennsylvania and walked for maybe the last 150 miles or so. Not that this was a particularly successful political initiative but it was a formative experience, one of many at that time. This time period was about building empowerment for many people. After that summer I went to work in the basement of a place called Great Lakes Intertribal Council, which was in an old Catholic school on the Bad River Reservation. It was a great place to work fresh out of graduate school; I worked in the alcoholism program, of all things. I have always been concerned about where our people walk and where we live, and I decided to go there because of all of the issues associated with the destructive use of alcohol in our family and in the community.

But enough about me: Let me share a little bit from our language. There is a concept that expresses the egalitarian views of our culture. In our language we have a concept, *mino-bimaadziwin*, which essentially means to live a good life and to live in balance. But what you're really saying is much different, much larger than that; it's an articulation of a worldview. Simply said, if you were to be standing in your own center, then out from that, of course, are the circles of your immediate family. And then out from that your extended family, and out from that your clan. And then out from that other people within your tribe. And out from that people, other human beings within the world, other races of people, all of us here in the room. And out from that, the other living beings . . . the animals, the plants, the water, the stars, the moon and the sun, and out from that, the spirits, or the *manitous*, the various spiritual forces within the world. So when you say that, *mino-bimaadziwin,* you're saying that a person lives a life that has really dependently arisen within the web of life. If you're saying that a person is a good person, that means that they are holding that connection, that connectedness within their family, and within their extended family, within their community.

I just learned a new Anishnaabek word the other day. I'm a person that likes to ask for the deeper meaning in a word, so whenever I find someone who can speak our language, I go and ask questions. Well, one word I was wondering about in preparation for today is the word for *mother*.

In our language if you say *mother*, you say *ne'gasheh*; if you say *my mother*, that's *ne'gasheh*. *Gasheh* is a mother. So the other day I was thinking, well, before I come down here, maybe I should ask somebody, what are you really saying? In our language there's a lot more to a word than what appears on the surface. In our language, *ne'gasheh* actually means *my mother*—or *ne'dudu*, you could say also. And *ne'dudu* is an older word that people don't often use anymore. But *ne'dudu* actually refers to breast-feeding. Here is the mother, the woman who fed me. But *ne'gasheh* is even more earthy; *ne'gasheh* is actually, you're saying, here is the person's body from which I came. Say you introduced your mother with a literal translation to English, you would say, here's the person's body from where I came. But I think our people in our expression of our language are much more natural, and we speak of reality in a more natural way.

So why do I mention all that? Because I think in a way I kind of stand here as an anomaly maybe; you could look at me and say, well, who are you anyway? And I could look at myself and say that too. But I think that it is important to remember that throughout the whole country, it's very important to speak to lawyers this way—I'm married to a lawyer, and actually when I asked him about, well, what do you think I should talk about, he started talking for five minutes and I realized, NO WAY. [laughter] I am not, there's just no way I'm going to be able to talk about that! Maybe they should have invited you to be on the panel! Because I can't speak the way that you do! And that's when I started to realize I had to speak from my view as an Anishnaabek woman and mother.

I think it's important for us as women to feel liberated even in this context of a fairly intellectual discussion about federal Indian law. Which is extraordinarily important. Probably my husband and I are the best example of people who are very different: an intellectually oriented lawyer and someone who, like me, is mainly interested in watching the birds, but we can live happily together and love one another. Because both things are really needed. In a marriage, differing views can be respected in our home, but also in a forum like this, so that you can bring people who can come to speak from the internal perspective of the tribe and the culture, and what is still alive today. Because you might look around in Michigan and think, well gee, you folks should be fairly well acculturated. Well yeah we are, but yeah we aren't. Because you still have people like myself who, and many others, who are still affiliated with the language and the culture and the ceremonial life of the community.

Let me switch gears a little bit to talk about my experience as a member of our tribal council. I'll get lost in a story somewhere so you'll have to tell me to stop. But I was an elected official within our tribe; I was elected to our tribal council in 1990, so it's been a little while ago. Eighteen years ago . . . I had one child, and in fact I was pregnant at the time, so I was an old mother. But my daughter, if she ever comes in here, she is the one I was pregnant with in 1990 when I was elected as a tribal council member. In fact I was enormously pregnant—I think I was about seven months' pregnant when I was sworn into office—and I served for six years as a tribal council member. I actually had two children during that time, so I often brought my babies to the tribal council meetings. I even nursed my child occasionally at meetings. [laughter] I've always been just a little bit of my own person, and I actually come from a family like that. My mother was like that, my grandmother—so when people would sometimes view from the outside native women as somehow walking two steps behind the man, I could never understand that, because I never observed that other than maybe subtly so. But if someone was going to—exactly what you were speaking of Rina—if someone was going to really make a decision or get some advice . . . even my own husband, if you ask him anything about what's going on in the family, he'll just defer to me. You know, that's how our dynamic works. And I think that's still very much alive today.

But in our tribal government we have a constitution also that incorporates the Indian Civil Rights Act, and although I would venture to say that in the six years I served on the council and in the twenty-some years I've lived at home, I have seen very few situations in which people have actually used that in our tribal court. I am really a strong advocate for strengthening our tribal governments. I like the *Martinez* case, I can tell you that right now. Catharine, I think a comment in your article was that the only time the Supreme Court has really upheld sovereignty was at the expense of an Indian woman, and I say, I would pay that cost. I would pay that price! I would pay that price because I know a slightly different world. Oh, and here's my baby! What a good time for her to come in the door! Hi, Rosie.

So, I would pay that price. Because I don't really have a life without the sovereignty of the tribe. We don't have our land without the tribe's sovereignty. We don't have much hope of preserving our language. We don't have much hope of being able to live at home and raise our children where they can know about who they are.

We don't really have much hope of anything. And truly, I've lived in the outside world, I went to college, I did all these things. I actually have never worked there because I came home and I started working for the tribes, so I don't know, the only discrimination that I've experienced has been somewhat in interfacing with the outside world, but not so much as employment. I have seen what I would characterize as discrimination in employment within our tribal system. I've seen a lot of situations where I thought that people were not treated fairly, and sometimes didn't feel that they had adequate recourse, even within our tribal judicial system. And particularly I would say this is true for women. In fact, one of the bolder things that we did one time several years ago is a number of women felt mistreated in employment practices within our tribe. It seemed as though some of our tribal council members had developed the opinion that non-natives are smarter than us. Internally we treat each other rather poorly sometimes, because we think that if we employ a non-Indian within our government system they might be able to figure out something better than we can. I'm talking rather directly about our internalized oppression; some of you aren't familiar with this, so maybe I'm in the wrong audience to really get into that too much … but I'm just going to say that when you serve on a tribal council you have to deal with all of these issues as an elected official. One of the biggest challenges you have as an elected official is how to balance the rights of the individual against the collective rights of the tribe, and how to do that considering *mino-bimaadziwin*, how to do that from the interconnectedness of the people. Someone will say, "I'm going to get in there and do the right thing." Well, having served as a council member six years, the right thing is not always evident; you have to really work to find what the right thing is.

But I was starting to say, a group of women and I organized this campaign because we felt as though the non-native employees were treated better than the native employees. And so we made some buttons that said "stop the abuse of member employees (SAME)." But we didn't get anywhere; we were just trying to raise consciousness. We really didn't solve the problem. But even though this was more than eight years ago, when I visit people I often see this button still stuck to their bulletin board, a big bear with the letters SAME. I usually have a chat about the experience and we laugh. Change is gradual. If you live in a tribal community and you want change to happen quickly, it's not going to happen. But people do talk and people do change.

So I'm just going to close my session, I'm going do the bold thing. I told John, my husband, I might just go down there and read poetry. This speaks to the issue of feminism from the inside, from the tribal view. And actually this was a dream that I had and I wrote it down in a poem:

Our Place of Vision

There is a place where women gather, a place deep in the maple forest.
[And some of you haven't seen the maples, they
are changing now, and I know Rina was com-
menting how beautiful that is, it's an orange,
beautiful glow that comes in the fall.]
We bring our food, we clang our pots, we gather our voices and
speak our truth. We prepare a feast of birth and feast for death. We
nurture our spirits with the foods of life. From the fiber of our lives
we weave a basket, strong, soft, and pure. Deep in the eye of this basket, at the center of the spokes is where the past, present, and future
of our community resides. From the center, our lives unfold. From
this place of vision, we nourish our ancestors and our unborn children.

Miigwetch.

NOTES

1. Indian Civil Rights Act, Pub. L. 90-284, 82 Stat. 77-80 (1968) (codified at 25 U.S.C. §§ 1301–03, 1311–12, 1321–26, 1331, 1341).

2. Santa Clara Pueblo v. Martinez, 436 U.S. 49 (1978).

3. Catharine A. MacKinnon, Martinez *Revisited*, in THE INDIAN CIVIL RIGHTS ACT AT FORTY (2012).

4. Morton v. Mancari, 417 U.S. 535 (1974).

5. CHARLES F. WILKINSON, AMERICAN INDIANS, TIME, AND THE LAW: NATIVE SOCIETIES IN A MODERN CONSTITUTIONAL DEMOCRACY 112–113 (1987).

6. Before presenting this talk, this was the rough count from Westlaw and Lexis. It has now increased.

7. Lawrence R. Baca, *Reflections on the Role of the United States Department of Justice in Enforcing the Indian Civil Rights Act*, in THE INDIAN CIVIL RIGHTS ACT AT FORTY (2011).

8. Casey Douma, *40th Anniversary of the Indian Civil Rights Act: Finding a Way Back to Indigenous Justice*, 55 The Federal Lawyer 34 (March/April 2008).

9. Donald J. Burnett, Jr., *An Historical Analysis of the 1968 "Indian Civil Rights" Act*, 9 HARV. J. ON LEGIS. 557, 574–575 (1971–1972).

10. *Id.* at 602, n. 239.

11. MARTHA MINOW, MAKING ALL THE DIFFERENCE: INCLUSION, EXCLUSION, AND AMERICAN LAW 308–309 (1990).

12. ALFONSO ORTIZ, THE TEWA WORLD (1969).

13. See Gloria Valencia-Weber, *Santa Clara Pueblo v. Martinez*, in INDIAN LAW STORIES (2011). *Also see* transcript of the District Court Trial at the University of New Mexico School of Law: Transcripts of Federal District Court Trial, Santa Clara v. Martinez, No. 9717 Civil (D. N.M. Nov. 25, 1974), http://hdl.handle.net/1928/342.

14. Rina Swentzell, *Testimony of a Santa Clara Woman*, 97 (2004).

15. THE WINDS OF CHANGE: A MATTER OF PROMISES (PBS 1990).

16. Oliphant v. Suquamish Tribe, 435 U.S. 191 (1978).

17. Walton v. Tesuque Pueblo, 443 F. 3d 1274 (10th Cir. 2006).

18. Martinez v. Santa Clara Pueblo, 540 F.2d 1039, 1044 (10th Cir. 1976), Record on Appeal, U.S. Court of Appeals, 10th Cir., Transcript of Trial, November 25–26, 1971, Vol. II at 382, Testimony of Alcario Tafoya.

CHAPTER 4

Sex Discrimination under Tribal Law

ANN E. TWEEDY

BACKGROUND AND INTRODUCTION

T his chapter broadly identifies and then briefly examines tribal laws that prohibit sex discrimination and secondarily addresses laws that make sex-based
distinctions. Specifically, this chapter addresses tribal equal protection guarantees as well as all types of tribal statutory and constitutional laws that explicitly
prohibit sex discrimination. It also discusses tribal case law addressing such discrimination, including case law addressing equal protection guarantees, cases interpreting tribal codes or policies, and case law creating tribal common law.

The Indian Civil Rights Act

Any work that attempts to comprehensively explore tribal laws that protect against
discrimination based on a suspect classification has to address, in some measure, the
Indian Civil Rights Act (ICRA),[1] the 1968 law through which Congress imposed
many Bill of Rights obligations, including equal protection, on Indian tribes.[2] This
is particularly true of tribal sex discrimination laws[3] because the Supreme Court's
1978 decision in *Santa Clara Pueblo v. Martinez*[4] led to a widespread, monolithic
impression that tribes were not protective of the rights of women.

Although the final version of the ICRA reflects important compromises between
protection of the tribal right to self-government and individual rights,[5] the statute was
initially motivated by a perception that tribal courts were not adequately protecting the
rights of individual Indians.[6] Ten years after the act was passed, in *Santa Clara Pueblo v.
Martinez*,[7] the Supreme Court concluded that the civil rights obligations that the ICRA
imposed on tribes could not be enforced via a private right of action in federal court,
except through the limited remedy of habeas corpus. As explained further below, while
it was a strong victory for tribal sovereignty, the decision also arguably had the unin-

tended effect of fueling both prejudice against tribal courts and future judicial incursions on tribal sovereignty.[8]

The Supreme Court's Decision in *Santa Clara v. Martinez*. *Martinez* was a sex-based equal protection case brought under the ICRA. The plaintiff in *Martinez* was a mother whose daughters could not be enrolled in the tribe under current tribal enrollment provisions, which allowed enrollment of children whose fathers had married outside the tribe but not children whose mothers had married nonmembers.[9] The Supreme Court's decision meant that Ms. Martinez could only sue for this purported violation of the ICRA's equal protection guarantee in tribal court.[10]

Martinez was decided in 1978, just a few years after the US Supreme Court had begun to strike down sex-based classifications under the equal protection clause of the Fourteenth Amendment,[11] and only two years after the Court had adopted the intermediate scrutiny test for sex-based classifications alleged to violate the equal protection clause, which it still applies today.[12]

Although US federal policy prohibiting sex discrimination was still in its early stages when *Martinez* was decided, the outcry against the *Martinez* case by mainstream feminists and other advocates of individual rights was extensive and has been well documented.[13] In fact, feminist "discontent with the decision continues to fuel discourse about gender equality and whether tribal law should be force-fit into an external norm."[14] In contrast, proponents of the decision point to the important cultural values and traditions that the decision supports and protects.[15] Additionally, some Native scholars and commentators argue that sex-based oppression in tribal cultures derives from Western colonial influences,[16] specifically stemming from the hierarchical nature of Western society and its valuing of all opposites as good or bad.[17]

Rather than further exploring this dichotomy between those who bemoan the decision and those who applaud it, however, this chapter examines how tribal laws approach sex-based categorizations, particularly focusing on tribal prohibitions of sex discrimination. Scant scholarly attention has been devoted to analysis of tribal law,[18] and this lack of analysis undoubtedly contributes to federal courts' and other outsiders' misconceptions and prejudice with respect to tribal systems of governance and tribal laws.[19] Indeed, the outcry against *Martinez* can be understood as part of a widespread mistrust of tribal justice systems generally.[20]

Thus, this chapter attempts to begin to set the record straight about tribal laws in the specific area of sex discrimination. Tribal laws prohibiting sex discrimination (and those few tribal laws providing for sex-based distinctions) illuminate the diverse approaches that tribes take toward the concept of sex-based equal protection and sex discrimination.[21] Accordingly, this chapter undertakes a broad-based survey of tribal laws that pertain to sex-based classifications.

Organization of the Chapter

The most important part of this chapter, Tribal Sex Discrimination Laws, contains a survey of tribal sex discrimination laws, beginning with broader laws and proceeding to more specific laws. This section first examines equal protection guarantees and similar provisions,[22] as well as related case law.[23] Secondly, this part examines explicit steps that tribes have taken to protect those within their jurisdictions from sex discrimination. Tribal court case law that interprets specific code or policy provisions or establishes relevant common law is also examined.

Next, tribal laws that create sex-based distinctions are briefly analyzed as is the impact of tribal sovereign immunity laws on sex discrimination claims. Finally, the possibility that potential sex discrimination plaintiffs may be pursuing other avenues of relief in tribal courts and tribal agencies is briefly examined.

Methodology

Sources for this chapter include the tribal codes, constitutions, and cases available online from the National Tribal Justice Resource Center, cases included in the *Indian Law Reporter* from 1983 through early 2008,[24] the University of Washington's 1988 microfiche compilation of tribal codes and constitutions, the decisions of the Northwest Intertribal Courts, the limited tribal law resources available on Westlaw, and legal resources downloaded from the websites of individual tribes and obtained from other miscellaneous sources.

Researching tribal law is inherently difficult, and it is literally impossible without visiting each tribe's reservation to ensure that one has the most recent and comprehensive set of tribal laws available from each tribe.[25] Indeed, in most cases, the particular sources I relied on did not purport to be comprehensive even as to the tribes whose laws were included. For example, the *Indian Law Reporter*, which exists solely in hard copy format, is the "only national reporter of tribal court decisions."[26] However, it does not publish all of the tribal court decisions submitted to it, typically publishing about "one hundred decisions per year that come from about twenty-five tribes."[27] Moreover, some of the *Indian Law Reporter* volumes I used had missing pages, and the *Indian Law Reporter* also has irregular indexing over time, which made it difficult to ensure consistency.

Similarly, the 1988 microfiche compilation contains codes and constitutions from only fifty-six tribes and is not only now out-of-date, but is also incomplete even with respect to the tribes that are represented.[28] Additionally, visually searching microfiche tends to be an inexact science, and my search of the microfiche was primarily limited to provisions explicitly mentioning "sex" or "gender." Finally, the National Tribal Justice Resource Center does not guarantee that its sources are up-to-date or comprehensive with respect to the tribes that are included,[29] and I identified a couple of instances in which codes or constitutional provisions provided on the site were in fact not currently in place.[30] Thus, this chapter provides a snapshot of numerous tribal approaches to sex as a classification in the hope of facilitating greater understanding of the diverse ways that tribes approach the issue of sex discrimination and the significant protections that many tribes afford against it.

The most comprehensive portion of this survey consisted of searches of tribal codes and constitutions available online at the National Tribal Justice Resource Center site. On that site, I examined all of the hits for the following terms: "sex," "gender," "equal protection" (with quotes), "male," "female," "father," "mother," "sexual harassment" (with quotes), and "sexually harass" (without quotes). During the period of my searches, which took place in August 2008, the National Tribal Justice Resource Center webpage stated that it had archived on its site the codes and resolutions of sixty-nine tribes[31] and the constitutions and bylaws of 116 tribes.[32] Despite the incompleteness of this resource, I nonetheless provide some percentages of tribes that had particular types of sex discrimination laws in place, usually in the footnotes to the discussions of such laws.

In fall 2008, additional tribal law resources became available on Westlaw (although still of a very limited scope). Thus, in late January and in February 2009, I ran the following search in the Westlaw Tribal Cases and the Tribal Codes and Indexes databases: "sex gender 'equal protection' male female father mother 'sexual harassment' 'sexually harass.'" Under Westlaw's "Terms & Connectors" searching framework, this search resulted in each word not in quotation marks being searched for individually, while phrases in quotation marks, such as "equal protection," were searched for as phrases. During this period, Westlaw had cases from nine tribes online as well as a somewhat overlapping database of Oklahoma tribal decisions. Additionally, it had the tribal codes of two tribes, the Navajo Nation and the Mashantucket Pequot Tribe, in its tribal codes database. In many instances, materials found through Westlaw had already been identified through earlier searches of other resources. However, any newly discovered sex discrimination materials were added to the chapter at that point.

TRIBAL SEX DISCRIMINATION LAWS

At the outset, it should be noted that whether a tribal code or constitution protects against sex discrimination is not determinative of whether its tribal court would recognize such a claim. Even in the absence of a code provision or constitutional provision that prohibits sex discrimination, either explicitly or implicitly, a tribal court may hold such conduct to be actionable as a matter of common law.[33]

Equal Protection and Related Guarantees

Numerous tribal laws provide equal protection guarantees that, like the language in the Fourteenth Amendment of the United States Constitution, generally provide that the tribe "will not deny to any person within its jurisdiction the equal protection of its laws."[34] Many such laws are part of tribal constitutions,[35] while others have been enacted as part of the tribal code.[36] Still other tribes have enacted equal protection guarantees, or other guarantees of equality, that apply in specialized circumstances.[37] These context-specific protections may be in addition to general equal protection guarantees,[38] or they may stand alone.[39] Finally, some tribes have expressly adopted the provisions of the ICRA as a matter of tribal law, and, to the extent that any of them lack separate equal protection guarantees, these tribes should be viewed as having such guarantees in place, based on the terms of the ICRA.[40]

Without tribal court case law on point, however, it is difficult to know how a particular tribe would apply such equal protection guarantees in the context of a sex discrimination claim and whether, even if it followed the federal model of differing levels of scrutiny for different types of classifications, the tribal court would apply heightened scrutiny to a sex-based classification.[41] This uncertainty is due to the fact that tribal "needs, values, customs, and traditions" play an important role in tribal interpretation of civil rights guarantees,[42] regardless of whether a litigant is proceeding under tribal law or the ICRA.[43] Therefore, especially with regard to a facially sex-neutral guarantee like "equal protection," tribal court case law, where available, is an enormously important resource.[44]

For most of the tribal laws cited above, I was unable to locate tribal court case law construing the equal protection guarantee in the context of a sex discrimination case. However, the Northern Plains Intertribal Court of Appeals has considered the scope of the ICRA's equal protection guarantee in the context of a custody dispute, and it invalidated a family law provision of the Turtle Mountain Tribal Code that severely limited the rights of an unmarried father.[45] By contrast, the Winnebago Tribal Court upheld a sex-neutral tribal criminal prohibition on sexual intercourse with an unemancipated minor against an as-applied challenge that was based on the equal protection guarantee in the tribal constitution, and its decision was affirmed by the Winnebago Supreme Court.[46] The Tribal Court of the Grand Traverse Band of Ottawa and Chippewa Indians took something of a middle ground, rejecting a former employee's equal protection claim based on the court's conclusion that the female plaintiff was not similarly situated to a male who had not been discharged three years before.[47] Finally, the Mashantucket Pequot Tribal Court has suggested that sex discrimination is covered by its statutory equal protection clause, although it does not appear that a litigant has yet successfully brought a sex discrimination claim under the clause.[48]

The Northern Plains Intertribal Court of Appeals' decision regarding the application of ICRA's equal protection guarantee in the context of the Turtle Mountain Band of Chippewa Indians' law. In *Griffith v. Wilkie*, the Northern Plains Intertribal Court of Appeals examined a provision of the Turtle Mountain Tribal Code that granted the "custody, services, and earnings" of an illegitimate child to the mother.[49] The court had ordered, and considered supplemental briefing, on the issue of "the constitutionality" of the provision.[50] Without providing the details of its analysis on the issue, the court concluded that "in situations where paternity is established or acknowledged," the provision "denie[s the father] equal protection of the law," and therefore violates 25 U.S.C. § 1302(8).[51] It thus remanded the case to the trial court to determine the best interests of the child.[52]

While *Griffith* appears to be a strong affirmation of the concept of equal protection as construed in American culture, it is important to recognize the harshness of the law at issue, which accorded the mother of an illegitimate child custody as a matter of law. Given the severity of the law, the case does not necessarily shed light on how the court would respond to a less drastic incursion on the unmarried father's rights, such as a presumption in favor of maternal custody. Moreover, perhaps also due to the harshness of the law, the court is not explicit about its methodology for evaluating equal protection questions. Thus, these issues will most likely have to await a more difficult case for definitive resolution.

The Winnebago Courts' construal of the equal protection guarantee in the tribal constitution. This subsection examines the trial court's decision in *Bigfire* and the appellate decision of the Winnebago Supreme Court. The Winnebago courts' decisions do not entirely reject traditional federal analysis and do, in fact, incorporate some federal concepts, such as requiring a plaintiff to show that she was similarly situated to someone not in the protected class who was treated more favorably and applying the concept of differing levels of scrutiny. Nonetheless, the decisions reveal considerable discomfort with, and resistance to, the federal approach, at least in the context of a claim based on the tribal constitution.

(1) The tribal court's decision upholding the law. In *Bigfire*, the Winnebago Tribal Court upheld a facially neutral statutory rape law against the defendant's allegation that prosecuting only the male under such a law violated the equal protection provision of the tribe's constitution.[53] The trial court appeared dismissive of federal law as persuasive authority and skeptical both of whether the federal three-tiered approach to equal protection analysis based on the type of classification at issue would serve the interests of the Winnebago Tribal Court and of whether intermediate scrutiny would be an appropriate standard for sex-based classifications.[54] Additionally, because the parties had not provided any information on traditional tribal approaches to rape, the court solicited its own expert information on the matter and set forth in the opinion the substance of that information, which detailed violent disfigurement as a punishment for a wife's unfaithfulness and the punishment of death for a man's rape of a female aged thirteen or above.[55]

In rejecting the defendant's challenge to the law, the tribal trial court did not officially reject intermediate scrutiny or rely on the traditional punishments.[56] Rather, having determined that it was premature to make decisions on those issues, the trial court rejected the defendant's arguments because it determined, in essence, that he was not similarly situated to the female victim.[57] The court referred to the "ample evidence that force or coercion was present," the fact that the statute was facially neutral or "benign," the fact that the defendant had failed to provide evidence that the law was being applied in a discriminatory fashion, and finally, possibly based on the evidence of force or coercion, the fact that "consent was not an issue" in this case.[58] Thus, in rejecting the defendant's challenge, the trial court concluded that "there seems to be little gained and huge detriments both psychologically and in law enforcement in charging victims of violent sexual assault with criminal sanctions."[59] Most likely, the fact that the victim was twelve at the time of the attack while the perpetrator was seventeen-and-a-half also played a part in the court's decision.[60]

(2) The Winnebago Supreme Court's decision. The Winnebago Supreme Court later affirmed the opinion of the Winnebago Tribal Court. In that case, the court heard two consolidated appeals, that of Mr. Bigfire and that of C.L., a fifteen-year-old male who was charged with second-degree sexual assault (i.e., statutory rape) of a thirteen-year-old-girl; a third appeal had been dismissed on double jeopardy grounds.[61] The Winnebago Supreme Court adopted a strict scrutiny test for sex but determined that the compelling tribal interest requirement was satisfied in the case because traditional cultural differentiations based on sex always constitute a compelling tribal interest.[62] The court considered "whether the use of different roles based on gender, particularly in areas of sex and procreation, is of a similar discriminatory and patriarchal nature [as in Anglo culture] when employed within the Winnebago Tribe."[63] The court concluded that "[i]n Ho-Chunk [or Winnebago] culture . . . gender differences or disparities in treatment do not signal hierarchy, lack of respect or invidious discrimination," and therefore held that "it is not accurate to attribute archaic stereotypes of the Anglo-American culture to the Winnebago Tribe's culture."[64] This conclusion was supported in part by the statement of one of the judges deciding the case, a woman who was a member of a related tribe; she explained that she had "no . . . feeling of inequality" as a result of tribal differentiations in sex roles.[65]

Some scholars consider the Winnebago Supreme Court's decision troubling because of its indication that culture would always trump the guarantee of equal protection.[66] However, the court also emphasized the age differences between the perpetrators and the victims in the cases, and the fact that there were only three prosecutions, a number that was too small, in the court's view, to demonstrate a pattern of sex discrimination.[67] Furthermore, the court appeared to place importance on the fact that it was not construing the ICRA but rather the tribal constitution.[68] Additionally, the court recognized that the result in the case, namely the Winnebago Supreme Court's decision to uphold this sex-neutral statutory rape law against a selective enforcement challenge, is not at variance with federal law, given that the US Supreme Court has upheld a sex-based statutory rape law based on its conclusion that young women and men are not similarly situated with respect to pregnancy.[69] Also, the lower court opinion in *Bigfire* demonstrates the weakness of the defendant's equal protection challenge considering the circumstances of the case and the injustice that would evidently occur if the crime of forcible rape of a twelve-year-old girl were to go unpunished.[70] Finally, the Winnebago Supreme Court indicated that if the arguably sex-based prosecutions continued, it might begin to strike them down as violative of the sex-neutral statute; thus, it saw the statute as overriding, at least to some extent, traditional tribal customs.[71]

In both the Winnebago Supreme Court's discussion of the fact that it was construing the tribal constitution rather than the ICRA and its intimation that it might hold that future prosecutions, if shown to be sex-based, violate the sex-neutral statute, the court evidenced a desire to protect the uniqueness of Winnebago law, especially as embodied in the tribal constitution, from being subsumed by federal law.[72] For instance, in the discussion preceding its conclusion that the "Ho-Chunk tradition and customary law certainly was not rendered illegal by the tribe's own constitution,"[73] the court explained:

> Since the legal concept of equal protection . . . is an Anglo-American legal concept, this Court must look in part to the current American legal tradition. . . . But this analysis must stop short of simply applying another standard to a different cultural system with a unique legal tradition without adjustments for or taking any account of that which is unique in that system.[74]

The court also noted that the sex-neutral statutory rape statute showed that the "Tribal Council plainly adopted a current tribal policy of furthering gender neutrality in this area as much as possible,"[75] and distinguished this current tribal policy from the more permanent equal protection guarantee of the tribal constitution, which, in the court's view, did not mandate treating both sexes the same.[76] Thus, the Winnebago Supreme Court's decision in *Bigfire* should be read in part as an attempt to preserve the uniqueness of tribal custom and tradition against the threat of a wholesale incorporation of federal ideas. At the same time, however, the court showed a willingness to enforce federal legal constructs such as gender neutrality if it could be demonstrated both that the tribal council had adopted them as law and that they were being violated by the tribal prosecutor. Thus, it could be said that the Winnebago Supreme Court in *Bigfire* simply adopted a presumption against construing tribal constitutional provisions identically to the way similar provisions would be interpreted in a federal court, but that, outside of the context of the tribal constitution, for example, in construing the ICRA or a law adopted by the tribal council, the court may well be more open to federal analysis.

The decision of the tribal court in *Koon v. Grand Traverse Band of Ottawa and Chippewa Indians.* In *Koon*, a tribal conservation officer who had been dismissed from employment after she was convicted of drunk driving brought suit alleging violation of the tribal constitution's equal protection guarantee.[77] The basis of her claim was that a male employee had not been dismissed for a similar incident three years before.[78] The court, however, accepted the defendant's argument that the plaintiff was not similarly situated to this male employee because, although both the plaintiff's job and that of the male employee involved driving, insuring those convicted of drunk driving had become much more difficult in the intervening three years.[79] Thus the *Koon* Court applied the federal requirement that a plaintiff show that she is similarly situated to a male employee who was treated more favorably before she can win a sex-based equal protection case.[80]

Summary of tribal equal protection cases. The few available tribal cases on sex-based equal protection demonstrate that tribes take different approaches to construing equal protection guarantees in the context of a charge of sex discrimination. Some tribes, such as Turtle Mountain and Grand Traverse, appear to undertake an equal protection analysis that resembles the federal approach to the question, while other tribes, such as Winnebago, will be more likely to reject sex discrimination claims that implicitly challenge traditional tribal gender roles. Given the legacy of colonialism and the fact that tribes have had to strive to maintain their separate existence against numerous federal policies that were designed to assimilate them,[81] it is not surprising to see at least some tribes forging definitions of equal protection that differ from federal definitions. It is perhaps more surprising that some tribes appear to accept the federal framework as is.[82] Regardless of whether one sees it as advantageous for tribes to adopt discrimination laws that are similar to federal laws or hopes that tribes will adopt unique frameworks of discrimination law, even this small number of cases clearly demonstrates that tribes take diverse approaches to the issue of sex discrimination and that the tribes whose laws were examined here view equal protection guarantees as protecting individuals from sex discrimination.

Tribal Constitutions Explicitly Incorporating US Constitutional Rights

In addition to the tribal statutes and constitutions providing general guarantees of equal protection, several tribal constitutions were identified that explicitly incorporate federal constitutional rights.[83] For example, the Minnesota Chippewa Tribe's Constitution provides that "no member shall be denied any of the constitutional rights or guarantees enjoyed by other citizens of the United States."[84] In contrast to a general equal protection guarantee under the applicable tribal constitution or under the ICRA, which may, as discussed above, be subject to diverse interpretations in the context of a sex-based classification, tribal courts construing tribal constitutional provisions that explicitly incorporate federal constitutional rights appear to be likely to treat sex-based classifications similarly to federal courts construing the US Constitution and therefore will most likely view such classifications as inherently suspect and subject to intermediate scrutiny.[85] It is possible that these provisions are common, and they should be taken into account in any attempt to determine whether a given tribe prohibits sex discrimination.[86]

The Navajo Nation's Broad-Based, Explicit Prohibition on Sex Discrimination. The Navajo Nation was the only tribe identified that had a broad-based provision of law in place that prohibits governmental sex discrimination in all facets of tribal life.[87] The Navajo Nation Bill of Rights provision, enacted in 1980, provides that "[e]quality of rights under the law shall not be denied or abridged by the Navajo Nation on account of sex."[88] Moreover, Navajo's broad-based statutory provision functions similarly to a constitutional provision in that it empowers the tribal court to strike down conflicting statutory enactments.[89]

No tribal constitution containing a similarly broad prohibition on sex discrimination[90] was identified, although several tribes constitutionally prohibit sex discrimination in voting,[91] and it appears that at least two tribes have seriously considered adopting broad-based constitutional proscriptions against sex discrimination.[92]

To the extent that a culture's responsiveness to sex discrimination can be seen as a measure of its progressiveness, Navajo appears to be more progressive than the United States, given the United States' failure to ratify a proposed amendment to the constitution that would have definitively outlawed sex discrimination.[93] The Navajo law is written to capture a broad spectrum of discriminatory conduct. The Nation's Bill of Rights prohibits the Navajo Nation from "den[ying] or abridg[ing]" "[e]quality of rights under the law . . . on account of sex."[94] Although it is not clear whether the concept of "equality of rights" differs from that of "equal protection," the Nation's prohibition on abridging equality increases the breadth of the provision because, as the Navajo Supreme Court has suggested, the provision allows for challenges to practices that burden some groups more than others (rather than requiring a stronger showing of explicit or intentional discrimination).[95] In consonance with the provision's language, the Court of Appeals of the Navajo Nation has interpreted the provision regarding sex discrimination very broadly, in a manner that would appear to invalidate any sex-based distinction that causes either sex disproportionate harm:

> The proper analysis of the Navajo Equal Rights guarantee is that there
> can be no legal result on account of a persons [sic] sex, no presump-
> tion in giving benefits or disabilities gaged by a person's sex and no
> legal policy which has the effect of favoring one sex or the other.[96]

Although based on this opinion and other case law, any sex-based distinction that favors one sex over the other in any measure would seem to be unlikely to survive a Navajo Nation Bill of Rights challenge,[97] one Navajo Supreme Court case allowed sex, based on traditional Navajo cultural norms that highly valued grazing rights generally are to descend to female relatives, to factor into the issue of the descent of such rights.[98] From the main opinion, the Bill of Rights issue does not appear to have been raised by the parties, but Justice Benally argued in a concurring opinion that the court's holding violated the Bill of Rights's prohibition of sex discrimination.[99] The majority responded to this argument in a footnote, stating that

[c]ontrary to the characterization in the dissenting[100] [*sic*] opinion, this opinion does not mean that the gender of the claimant is dispositive. . . . In fact, the rule set out in this opinion is that the *Keedah* factors[101] and traditional law on women's role in Navajo society should be considered together to decide the most logical trustee, not that if a female and a male both claim the permit, regardless of their connections to the land, the permit automatically must go to the female.[102]

Thus, in the above footnote, the court functionally characterizes the language set forth below, which occurs slightly earlier in the opinion, as allowing sex to be factored into the grazing permit descent decision:

Traditionally, women are central to the home and land base. They are the vein of the clan line. The clan line typically maintains a land base upon which the clan lives, uses the land for grazing and agricultural purposes and maintains the land for medicinal and ceremonial purposes. . . . This is why women are attached to both the land base and the grazing permits. For the most part, Navajos maintain and carry on the custom that the maternal clan maintains traditional grazing and farming areas.[103]

The majority's characterization of woman's traditional role is, as the concurring opinion acknowledges, consistent with the matrilineal and matrilocal character of Navajo society.[104]

Thus, despite very strong language prohibiting sex discrimination in Navajo's Bill of Rights and the absolute terms of one Navajo Appellate opinion, the Navajo Supreme Court appears willing to allow sex to be a factor when consistent with traditional Navajo culture, at least in the context of grazing rights inheritance. Nonetheless, depending on how broadly or narrowly the Navajo Supreme Court is willing to make such distinctions, Navajo law concerning sex discrimination may well be considerably more stringent than US law in terms of the types of distinctions the Navajo courts will uphold.[105] In fact, such distinctions may quite possibly be limited to highly traditional aspects of Navajo culture. Moreover, given the Navajo Supreme Court's statement that disparate impact falls within the purview of the Bill of Rights provision,[106] the Navajo Bill of Rights provision appears to be considerably broader than the US concept of equal protection in the very significant area of disparate impact.[107]

Context-Specific Protections

In addition to Navajo's explicit, broad-based provision and the more general equal protection provisions discussed above, twenty-five tribes were identified that have at least one context-specific law explicitly prohibiting sex discrimination.[108] Although most of the provisions identified were part of tribal codes, some were constitutional provisions, and a few were either created by common law or contained in administrative materials.[109] In terms of code-based laws alone, this finding means that roughly 22 percent of tribes whose codes were available online from the National Tribal Justice Resource Center had some statutory protection from sex discrimination in place.[110] All of the sex discrimination laws cited above generally demonstrate that each of these twenty-five tribes has a policy against sex discrimination, although in the case of tribes that both legally prohibit sex discrimination in some circumstances and make sex-based distinctions in others, the policy is necessarily a complicated one.[111] Some tribes, such as the Eastern Band of Cherokee Indians, have several anti-discrimination laws that cover sex discrimination in different, rather broad contexts, whereas other tribes, such as Chitimacha Tribe, appear to have only one or two very narrow laws in place.[112] Below is a brief summary of the sex-discrimination laws by category, beginning with broader laws and proceeding to narrower ones.

Employment: Sex discrimination explicitly prohibited in employment generally. Four tribes have broadly worded, explicit prohibitions on sex discrimination in employment in their tribal codes,[113] and two other tribes appear to have such laws in place based on discussions in tribal court opinions.[114] One of the four tribes, the Little River Band of Ottawa Indians, carves out an exception to the prohibition where sex is a bona fide occupational qualification (BFOQ).[115] This BFOQ exception also applies to age and disability; however, it does not apply to race, marital status, national origin, or other specified suspect classes.[116] This differentiation may indicate that the Little River Band of Ottawa Indians considers sex to be less inherently suspect than categories such as race, which are not subject to the exception.[117] Federal law similarly provides that a bona fide occupational qualification may be a defense to allegations of sex discrimination but not of race discrimination.[118] It may be the case that the three tribes whose codes do not provide for a BFOQ defense would not allow for such a defense under common law if the issue were raised in a case or administrative proceeding. Thus, these three tribes may take a harder line on sex discrimination than would a federal court.[119] However, it is difficult to make predictions about such issues.

(1) Specialized categories of employment: employment by contractors and subcontractors. The Oglala Sioux, one of the six tribes that has in place a general prohibition on sex discrimination in employment, also has a law providing that "[c]ontractors or subcontractors extending such preference [to Indians] shall not, however, discriminate among Indians on the basis of religion, sex, or tribal affiliation, and the use of such a preference [for Indian employees] shall not excuse a contractor or subcontractor from complying with the other requirements contained in this chapter."[120]

(2) Specialized categories of employment: gaming. A total of six tribes, including two of the six that have prohibitions on sex discrimination in employment and one, the Navajo, which has a broad-based general prohibition on sex discrimination generally, prohibit sex discrimination in the operation of their gaming enterprises.[121] Given that these gaming enterprises may well be the largest employer among the tribal government and its enterprises—or even in the geographical area for some of the more rural tribes—these laws are a significant source of protection.

(3) Sexual harassment. Evaluating tribal protections against sexual harassment is complicated somewhat by the fact that some tribes, contrary to the traditional federal view, consider sexual harassment to be an act perpetrated by one individual against another, rather than an employment rights issue.[122] Such tribes may treat harassment, implicitly or explicitly including sexual harassment, as a civil infraction, a misdemeanor, or even a tort.[123] Other tribes consider sexual harassment to be an employment issue but define it as a potential basis for discipline of the harassing employee rather than explicitly defining it as the basis for a cause of action by the injured employee.[124]

Because this subpart is limited to laws that explicitly apply to sex discrimination, this section on sexual harassment does not include the laws that simply provide protection against harassment without discussion of sexual harassment. The Ysleta Pueblo del Sur law that defines "sexual harassment" as a prohibited type of harassment is included, although the application of that law is personal to the perpetrator and applies more broadly than just to the employment context.[125] Although some ambiguities remain, in all, nine tribes appear to have policies or laws in place that prohibit sexual harassment in the workplace,[126] and one tribe has directed its general manager to create such a policy,[127] so it may now in fact have a policy in place. Two of these tribes also prohibit employment discrimination based on sex generally, and two of them prohibit it in the gaming context.[128] Finally, Navajo, one of the two tribes that has both a prohibition on sexual harassment and a prohibition on sex discrimination in its gaming operation, also has a broad-based, tribal prohibition on sex discrimination, as discussed above. Thus, it appears that some tribes that recognize sexual harassment do not explicitly recognize other forms of sex discrimination.

(4) Maternity and paternity leave and related laws. Though not a sex discrimination law per se, at least one tribe, the Little River Band of Ottawa Indians, has enacted a law allowing its employees to take maternity or paternity leave.[129] Such laws are relevant to sex discrimination because of the disproportionate impacts that women suffer in employment because of pregnancy.[130] Similarly, the Ho-Chunk Nation currently has a law in place that prohibits pregnancy-based discrimination[131] and the Navajo Nation progressively requires all on-reservation employers to provide breastfeeding accommodations for employees who are working mothers.[132]

One interesting aspect of the Little River Band of Ottawa Indians's law is that its express purpose is to protect the children that would be affected by a failure to grant maternity (or paternity) leave to full-time employees: "The Little River Band recognizes that its children are its most precious asset and that the promotion of strong families is critical. With this recognition, the Tribe has adopted the following policies regarding maternity leave."[133] Thus, although it clearly protects women's ability to maintain employment while pregnant (and therefore protects women from discrimination), this particular tribal law does not have as its primary purpose protection against employment discrimination.

(5) Summary of employment-related tribal sex discrimination laws. A significant percentage of tribes appear to have in place some statutory protection against sex discrimination that applies to employment.[134] The most common types of anti-discrimination laws appear to apply to employment generally, gaming, and sexual harassment. There are likely to be many additional protections in tribal personnel policies, but, because they are not widely available, such policies are not addressed here except to the extent that discussion of them was included in tribal case law or the policies were codified in tribal ordinances.

Voting and other political rights.   The constitutions of three tribes, namely the Fort Belknap Indian Community, the Muscogee (Creek) Nation, and the Confederated Tribes of the Warm Spring Reservation, outlaw sex discrimination in voting.[135] These provisions are roughly analogous to the Nineteenth Amendment to the United States Constitution.[136] The constitution of the Sac and Fox Tribe of the Mississippi in Iowa proscribes sex-based disqualification from holding public office.[137]

Application of the laws and rules of procedure.   Three tribes have code provisions that either prohibit or set a policy against sex discrimination in the application of laws or the rules of procedure.[138] For instance, the Rules of Criminal Procedure for the White Earth Band of Chippewa set out an intent not to discriminate in purpose or effect: "These rules are intended to provide for the just and speedy determination of criminal proceedings without the purpose or effect of discrimination based upon race, color, creed, religion, national origin, sex, marital status, status with regard to public assistance, disability, handicap in communication, sexual orientation, or age."[139] Protection against discrimination in both "purpose" and "effect" appears to evince a legislative intent that the operation of the rules be free from discriminatory intent as well as from disparate impact on suspect classes such as sex. Although, given the use of the word "intent," the section may be merely precatory rather than creating an enforceable obligation, it is interesting that it encompasses such a broad conception of fairness, which can be contrasted to the "fear of too much justice" that often characterizes the American judicial system.[140]

Because the Blackfeet provision is part of the Family Court's "Code of Ethics," like the White Earth Chippewa provision, it may not be directly enforceable, although, alternatively, its strong language could be interpreted to dictate enforceability: "The Blackfeet Family Court Members will serve and respond to requests without bias because of race, religion, sex, age, national origin or handicap."[141]

Finally, the Eastern Band of Cherokee provision utilizes even stronger wording and therefore probably creates enforceable obligations.[142] Additionally, the Cherokee provision may be the most remarkable in that it appears to put a complementary onus on the individual not to seek exemptions or more favorable treatment based on membership in a particular class:

> (a) All persons, regardless of race, age, or sex will comply and be subject to the laws of the Eastern Band of Cherokee Indians whenever they are within the boundaries of Qualla Boundary and its territories.

> (b) All persons, regardless of race, age, or sex will be subject to all of the same charges, convictions, and fines that enrolled members of the Eastern Band are subject to.

> . . .

> (e) Tribal jurisdiction on all persons shall be equal and nondiscriminatory towards anyone, regardless of race, age, or sex as long as they are visiting or living or doing business on the lands of the Eastern Band of Cherokee Indians. [143]

Prohibition on the use of sex-based presumptions in child custody matters. Somewhat similar to above-described laws prohibiting discrimination in the application of rules and laws, the code provisions of three tribes prohibit the use of sex-based presumptions for one parent or another in custody matters.[144] A fourth tribe has, in case law, rejected as "sexist" the American rule that the domicile of a nonmarital child follows that of his or her mother.[145]

Miscellaneous prohibitions on sex discrimination. Finally, a few tribes have prohibitions on sex discrimination that apply in other diverse contexts, such as applications for financial credit, housing, provision of health services, treatment of prisoners, and education.

(1) Credit applications. The Blackfeet Tribe disallows creditors from discriminating based on sex or other listed grounds "in any aspect of a credit transaction."[146] This provision contains much of the same language as the Federal Equal Credit Opportunity Act and was most likely modeled on that act.[147]

(2) Health services. The bylaws of Susanville Indian Rancheria's health clinic require the board of directors "[t]o ensure operation of the clinic without limitation by reason of race, creed, sex or national origin except as provided by Congress and federal rules and regulations."[148]

(3) Education. The Oglala Sioux Education Code requires the local school board "to develop and implement a student activity program" and necessitates that the development and implementation be conducted in an "equitable manner with respect to . . . gender. "[149] Whereas the United States has a statute generally pro-

hibiting discrimination in education based on sex or other enumerated grounds,[150] the Oglala Sioux provision applies in a much narrower context.

(4) Treatment of prisoners. Probably the most unique provision at least among these miscellaneous provisions is the Sisseton–Wahpeton Sioux Tribe's anti-discrimination provision for prisoners: "(1) There shall be no discrimination on grounds of race, color, sex, language, religion, political or other opinion, national or social origin, property, birth or other status. (2) On the other hand, it is necessary to respect the religious beliefs and moral precepts of the group to which a prisoner belongs."[151]

While it is difficult to know how it operates in practice, the law is clearly at odds with the federal trend of limiting prisoners' rights and their ability to seek relief.[152] Moreover, there appears to be no federal statutory counterpart to the law; rather, state and federal prisoners typically seek relief for sex discrimination by alleging a constitutional violation of their right to equal protection under the Fourteenth Amendment's Equal Protection Clause or the Fifth Amendment's due process clause.[153] Additionally, whereas federal courts do, at least formally, apply intermediate scrutiny in such cases, deference to the prison administration plays a large role.[154] By contrast, this law, on its face, unqualifiedly prohibits sex discrimination.

Thus, like the White Earth Chippewa provision requiring equal treatment under the tribe's rules of criminal procedure and like the broad-based Navajo proscription on sex discrimination, this Sisseton–Wahpeton Sioux provision evidences a strong concern for substantive fairness. Moreover, the Sisseton–Wahpeton Sioux provision extends the concern to one class of persons whose right to fairness under federal law has been considerably diminished.

Allowing tenants to defend against eviction based on a landlord's sex-based discrimination. Two tribes have adopted laws that allow a tenant to defend against an eviction on the basis that the eviction is occurring because of the tenant's sex or for other specified discriminatory reasons.[155] These laws are similar to a federal Fair Housing Act regulation that prohibits landlords from evicting tenants based on sex or other prohibited grounds.[156] Thus, as with the Oglala Sioux education provision, these two provisions accord with a corresponding federal policy against housing discrimination, but they apply more narrowly.[157]

Prohibition on sex discrimination by telecommunications service providers. The Navajo Nation has a law in place that provides that "[n]o telecommunications service provider shall, as to rates or service, make or grant any unreasonable preference or advantage to any person, or subject any person to unreasonable prejudice or disadvantage based upon . . . sex."[158] It is not clear how the qualifier "unreasonable" would be interpreted here, but it appears to allow the companies to make some types of sex-based distinctions. At least one state, Texas, has a similar administrative rule prohibiting telecommunications service providers from discriminating based on sex.[159]

Workers' compensation for sex organ losses. Mashantucket Pequot's inclusion, as of 2000, of loss of female genitalia on its table of compensable injuries is another apparent move toward gender equity, given that the loss of male genitalia had already been included in the table.[160] The amendment was apparently based upon a similar amendment enacted by the State of Connecticut.[161]

SUMMARY OF CONTEXT-SPECIFIC SEX DISCRIMINATION LAWS

Tribes have adopted a broad range of policies and laws that protect against sex discrimination in myriad contexts. Whereas many of them apply in narrow circumstances, such as eviction, others are quite broad, applying, for example, to all sex-based employment discrimination. Often these laws appear to reflect a deeper level of concern for substantive fairness than do federal laws, and the laws sometimes apply in contexts, such as prisoner rights, that are unusual by US standards. In a few cases, the laws appear to be modeled after similar federal laws. The diversity of these laws suggests that tribes are indeed "'laboratories for democracy,'" as Raymond Etcitty, legislative counsel for the Navajo Nation, has argued.[162]

SEX-BASED DISTINCTIONS UNDER TRIBAL LAW

As might be expected given the vast diversity of tribal cultures, although a significant portion of tribes have prohibitions on sex discrimination in place, some tribes continue to make sex-based distinctions in their laws. Indeed, some of the tribes that have enacted context-specific prohibitions on sex discrimination make sex-based distinctions in other contexts.[163]

One of the most well known of tribal laws that makes sex-based distinctions is the membership rule for Santa Clara Pueblo, which is reportedly still in place.[164] Although most membership provisions appear to be sex-neutral, I identified one additional sex-based enrollment law that favors women[165] and one that appears to limit the rights of unmarried fathers with respect to their children's eligibility for membership.[166] With a few exceptions,[167] most other sex-based laws that were identified pertained to the family law context,[168] an area where sex-based distinctions have been, and to some extent continue to be, common in American law.[169]

Two of the most interesting sex-based laws relate to traditional tribal governmental functions. The Constitution of the Iroquois Nations—The Great Binding Law, *Gayanashagowa*—sets out male and female roles in the traditional government.[170] One section provides that a Lord who oversteps his rightful authority will be dismissed after repeated warnings, and "[h]is nation shall then install the candidate nominated by the female name holders of his family."[171]

Another law that appears to codify tribal tradition is an alternative dispute resolution provision of the Little River Band of Ottawa Indians, which utilizes a "Peacemaking System"'"to provide a traditional conflict resolution process to children, youth and families."[172] This law provides that "[p]eacemaking sessions are conducted by two Peacemakers: one male and one female to create balance."[173]

Both the Little River Band of Ottawa Indians' law and the Constitution of the Iroquois Nations appear to be integral to preserving those tribes' unique traditions. Whereas some tribal laws make sex-based distinctions that may be troubling to other Americans, it is hard to fathom the degree to which tribal cultures would be compromised if all such distinctions were outlawed.[174]

TRIBAL SOVEREIGN IMMUNITY

It is very possible that tribal sovereign immunity could impede a plaintiff's ability to enforce equal protection guarantees or tribal prohibitions on sex discrimination or to challenge a law creating a sex-based distinction. Therefore, a brief discussion of the doctrine is warranted here. Under the doctrine of tribal sovereign immunity, tribes, like other sovereigns,[175] are immune from suit in state, federal, and tribal courts, although either the tribe or the federal government may expressly waive this immunity.[176]

However, most tribes will permit ICRA suits in which the plaintiff is only seeking equitable relief to be brought against them in tribal court.[177] Other civil rights claims based on the tribal constitution or a statutory bill of rights also appear to be permitted fairly commonly when only equitable relief is sought.[178] However, more difficult issues tend to arise when a plaintiff seeks to sue under an ordinary tribal code provision. Many tribes appear to have enacted narrow waivers for specific types of such claims, and thus tight filing deadlines and sharp limitations on the claims that may be pursued and the remedies available should be expected.[179] In some cases, a waiver may not be available at all,[180] although, in rare cases, plaintiffs have convinced tribal councils to create waivers especially for them.[181] Even if no waiver is available, however, the policy inherent in law can still serve important functions and can influence community standards of right and wrong.

OTHER AVENUES OF RELIEF

Despite the fairly widespread existence of tribal sex discrimination laws, case law construing such laws appeared to be largely lacking. Given the numerous cases regarding employment-related due process claims, it is possible that plaintiffs who could bring sex discrimination claims are focusing on due process instead.[182] Another possibility is that some tribes take a broader view of discrimination, not conceptualizing it as limited to suspect classes; therefore, plaintiffs may be bringing generic discrimination claims, rather than sex discrimination claims.[183] Undoubtedly, however, a proportion of potential sex discrimination claims are not heard on the merits due to plaintiffs' failure to meet the strict filing deadlines that many tribes apply to employment discrimination claims or claims against the tribe generally.[184]

CONCLUSION

Numerous tribal protections against sex discrimination are in force, ranging from equal protection guarantees and explicit broad-based constitutional or statutory protections, to context-specific proscriptions against discrimination that apply in anywhere from fairly broad to quite narrow contexts. Although it is difficult to generalize, the wording of several statutory laws and some case law suggests a greater concern for disparate impact than inheres in federal anti-discrimination law. Moreover, all of these protections evidence tribal policies against sex discrimination. However, it is important to be realistic about the fact that all tribes do not have such protections in place, and, like the United States, some tribes continue to make sex-based distinctions (including a few of the tribes that prohibit sex discrimination in some contexts). Nonetheless, the diversity of tribal approaches to the issue of sex discrimination and the breadth of existing legal protections are impressive.

More research is needed to better understand the scope, application, and frequency of these laws. As more tribes begin to make their laws available outside of their judicial systems, this research will become more feasible. In the meantime, it is possible to focus in significant depth on individual tribes that have codes and case law that either are available on their own websites or by visiting the tribal courts in person. Though obtaining materials in either of these two ways is less likely to allow for electronic searching or to facilitate large-scale comparisons among tribes, research focused on one specific tribe would add significantly to the growing base of scholarship on tribal law.

What should be clear from the existing information is that tribes collectively do not take a monolithic approach to sex discrimination and that many tribes have made a significant commitment to eradicating it. Moreover, it should also be apparent that individual tribes' laws can, in many circumstances, be located, albeit with some work.

NOTES

1. 25 U.S.C. §§ 1301–1303 (2006). Federal courts have held, in addition to the protections imposed under the ICRA, that some federal anti-discrimination statutes of general applicability apply to tribes, whereas others do not. See, e.g., Arostook Band of Micmacs v. Ryan, 484 F.3d 41, 56 (1st Cir. 2007) (reciting the fact that tribes are specifically excluded from the definition of "employer" under Title VII of the Civil Rights Act, but holding that particular tribe to be subject to state employment laws); San Manuel Band of Mission Indians v. Nat'l Labor Relations Bd., 475 F.3d 1306, 1315 (D.C. Cir. 2007) (citing cases addressing the applicability of the Age Discrimination in Employment Act and the Americans with Disabilities Act to tribes). Aside from tribal enforcement of the ICRA, tribal enforcement of federal statutes pursuant to federal law is beyond the reach of this chapter.

2. See 25 U.S.C. §§ 1301–1303 (2006).

3. I generally use the term sex rather than gender throughout this chapter because it refers more precisely to distinctions and discrimination based on biological sex, in other words to being male or female. See, e.g., Lara Stemple, Male Rape & Human Rights, 60 HASTINGS L. J. 605, 619 nn.138–39 (2009).

4. 436 U.S. 49 (1978).

5. *See, e.g., id.* at 62.

6. Robert J. McCarthy, *Civil Rights in Tribal Courts: The Indian Bill of Rights at Thirty Years*, 34 IDAHO L. REV. 465, 469–70 (1998).

7. 436 U.S. 49 (1978).

8. *See, e.g.,* Sarah Krakoff, *A Narrative of Sovereignty: Illuminating the Paradox of the Domestic Dependent Nation*, 83 OR. L. REV. 1109, 1133 (2004).

9. *Martinez*, 436 U.S. at 59.

10. *See id.* The ICRA's equal protection guarantee can be found at 25 U.S.C. § 1302(8) (2006).

11. U.S. CONST. amend. XIV, § 1 ("No State shall . . . deny to any person within its jurisdiction the equal protection of the laws"); *see, e.g.,* Reed v. Reed, 404 U.S. 71 (1971) (holding that an Idaho state law preferring males to administer estates violated the Fourteenth Amendment).

12. Craig v. Boren, 429 U.S. 190 (1976), represents the Court's first application of the intermediate scrutiny standard for sex-based classifications. The standard was applied most recently by the Supreme Court in Nguyen v. I.N.S., 533 U.S. 53 (2001).

13. *See, e.g.,* Gloria Valencia-Weber, Santa Clara Pueblo v. Martinez: *Twenty-Five Years of Disparate Cultural Visions: An Essay Introducing the Case for Reargument Before the American Indian Nations Supreme Court*, 14 KAN. J.L. & PUB. POL'Y 49, 50, 53–54 (2004); *see generally* Catharine A. MacKinnon, *Whose Culture? A Case Note on* Martinez v. Santa Clara Pueblo (1983), *in* FEMINISM UNMODIFIED: DISCOURSES ON LIFE & LAW 63–69 (1987).

14. Valencia-Weber, *supra* note 13, at 53.

15. *Id.* at 54–57; *see generally* Rina Swentzell, *Testimony of a Santa Clara Woman*, 14 KAN. J.L. & PUB. POLY'Y 97 (2004).

16. ANDREA SMITH, CONQUEST: SEXUAL VIOLENCE AND AMERICAN INDIAN GENOCIDE 18, 139 (2005); Swentzell, *supra* note 15, at 99, 101.

17. Swentzell, *supra* note 15, at 98, 101; *see also* SMITH, *supra* note 16, at 18 (stating that, in Indian societies prior to colonization, "[a]lthough there existed a division of labor between women and men, women's labor and men's labor was accorded similar status").

18. Robert D. Cooter & Wolfgang Fikentscher, *American Indian Law Codes: Pragmatic Law & Tribal Identity*, 56 AM. J. COMP. L. 29, 30 (2008).

19. *See, e.g.,* McCarthy, *supra* note 6, at 468, 485–89.

20. *See, e.g.,* Nell Jessup Newton, *Tribal Court Praxis: One Year in the Life of Twenty Indian Tribal Courts*, 22 AM. INDIAN L. REV. 285, 285–87 (1998).

21. Tribes take diverse approaches to their ICRA obligations based on tribal needs, values, customs, and traditions; accordingly, ICRA-based rights under tribal law do not necessarily mirror the corresponding protections under federal law. Mark D. Rosen, *Multiple Authoritative Interpreters of Quasi-Constitutional Federal Law: Tribal Courts & the Indian Civil Rights Act*, 69 FORDHAM L. REV. 479, 487 (2000). Additionally, of course, tribal guarantees of equality and tribal prohibitions on sex discrimination that are not related to the ICRA may well be interpreted differently than would similar provisions under federal law. *See id.* at 487–89.

22. Many tribes include an equal protection guarantee in their constitutions. *See, e.g.,* CONST. OF THE COQUILLE INDIAN TRIBE, art. VI, § 3(b)(11), *available at* http://www.narf.org/nill/Constitutions/coquilleconst/coqconsttoc.htm (last visited Feb. 23, 2011); CONST. OF THE SAC & FOX NATION, art. X, § 8, *available at* http://www.sacandfoxnation-nsn.gov/departments/government/constitution/ (last visited Feb. 23, 2011); CONST. & BYLAWS OF THE SAULT STE. MARIE TRIBE OF CHIPPEWA INDIANS, art. VIII, *available at* http://www.narf.org/nill/Constitutions/saultconst/saultconsttoc.htm (last visited Feb. 23, 2011). Such constitutional guarantees may pre-date the ICRA and thus may be unrelated to it. *See* Cooter & Fikentscher, *supra* note 18, at 31. Additionally, even equal protection guarantees that came into effect after the ICRA may not be related to the ICRA, and a lack of detailed legislative history often makes it impossible to tell.

23. While the published tribal court cases construing the ICRA are by no means numerous—for example, *see* McCarthy, *supra* note 6, at 491—a few such cases are available that address sex discrimination claims. *See, e.g.,* Winnebago Tribe of Nebraska v. Bigfire, 24 Indian L. Rptr. 6232 (Winnebago Tribal Ct. 1997), *aff'd* 25 Indian L. Rptr. 6229 (Winnebago Sup. Ct. 1998); Griffith v. Wilkie, 18 Indian L. Rptr. 6058 (Northern Plains Intertribal Ct. App. 1991); *see also* Rosen, *supra* note 21, at 541 (discussing the Winnebago Supreme Court's opinion in *Bigfire* as well as two earlier Winnebago equal protection cases relating to sex discrimination).

24.   The *Indian Law Reporter* first began including tribal court decisions in 1983. David A. Castleman, *Personal Jurisdiction in Tribal Courts*, 154 U. PA. L. REV. 1253, 1254 (2006).

25.   *See* Cooter & Fikentscher, *supra* note 18, at 32–34 (explaining the difficulty of researching tribal law).

26.   Frank Pommersheim, *Looking Forward and Looking Back: The Promise and Potential of a Sioux Nation Judicial Support Center and Sioux Nation Supreme Court*, 34 ARIZ. ST. L.J. 269, 275 (2002).

27.   Rosen, *supra* note 21, at 510; *accord* Cooter & Fikentscher, *supra* note 18, at 35 (describing the *Indian Law Reporter* as "collect[ing] a small number of cases from reservations throughout the United States").

28.   Cooter & Fikentscher, *supra* note 18, at 33.

29.   *See id.* at 33 (noting that online collections, such as that of the National Tribal Justice Resource Center, are not yet "close to complete" and that "[t]o gain access to a complete set of codes for a tribe, one must go to reservations and speak to officials").

30.   *See infra* notes 35 and 92.

31.   Unfortunately, this website is no longer operational.

32.   *See supra* note 31.

33.   *See, e.g.*, Michael Taylor, *Modern Practice in Indian Courts*, 10 U. PUGET SOUND L. REV. 231, 239 (1986–87); *see also* Bank of Hoven v. Long Family Land & Cattle Co., No. 03-002-A/R-120-99, slip op. at 6–9 (Cheyenne River Sioux Tribal App. Ct., Nov. 24, 2004), *available at* http://turtletalk.files.wordpress.com/2007/12/tribal-coa-opinion-bank-of-hoven.pdf (recognizing a race discrimination claim under tribal common law), *aff'd*, Plains Commerce Bank v. Long Family Land & Cattle Co., 440 F. Supp. 2d 1070 (D.S.D. 2006), *aff'd*, 491 F.3d 878 (8th Cir. 2007), *rev'd on other grounds*, 128 S. Ct. 2709 (2008).

34.   CONST. OF THE STANDING ROCK SIOUX TRIBE, art. XI, § 8. *microformed on* Indian Tribal Codes: A Microfiche Collection of Indian Law Codes (Ralph Johnson ed. 1988).

35.   CONST. OF THE CITIZEN POTAWATOMI NATION, art. 16, §1(h), *available at* http://www.potawatomi.org/index.php?option=com_content&view=category&id=98:constitution&Itemid=29&layout=default; CONST. & BYLAWS OF THE COLORADO RIVER INDIAN TRIBES OF THE COLORADO RIVER INDIAN RESERVATION ARIZONA AND CALIFORNIA, art. III, § 3 *microformed on* Indian Tribal Codes: A Microfiche Collection of Indian Law Codes (Ralph Johnson ed. 1988); CONST. OF THE COQUILLE INDIAN TRIBE, art. VI, § 3(b)(11), *available at* http://www.narf.org/nill/Constitutions/coquilleconst/coqconsttoc.htm; CROW TRIBAL CONST., art. XI, §4(h), *available at* http://www.indianlaw.mt.gov/crow/constitution/ default.mcpx; CONST. OF THE DUCKWATER SHOSHONE TRIBE OF THE DUCKWATER RESERVATION, NEVADA, art. IV, § 2(h), *available at* http://thorpe.ou.edu/IRA/shoshcons.html; CONST. & BYLAWS OF THE ELY SHOSHONE TRIBE, art. VIII, §§ 1, 2(h), *available at* http://www.narf.org/nill/Constitutions/elyconst/elyconsttoc.htm; CONST. & BY-LAWS OF THE CONFEDERATED TRIBES OF THE GRAND RONDE COMMUNITY OF OREGON, art. III, § 3(k), *available at* http://www.narf.org/nill/Constitutions/Grand%20Ronde%20Constitution/grandrondeconsttoc.htm; CONST. OF THE GRAND TRAVERSE BAND OF OTTAWA AND CHIPPEWA INDIANS, art. X, § 1(h), *available at* http://www.narf.org/nill/Constitutions/grandtraverseconst/index.htm; CONST. OF THE HO-CHUNK NATION, art. X, § 1(a)(8), *available at* http://www.narf.org/nill/ Constitutions/hochunkconst/hochunkconsttoc.htm; CONST. OF THE NATIVE TRIBE OF HUSLIA, ALASKA, art. 12, § 3(8), *available at* http://thorpe.ou.edu/constitution/huslia/index.html; CONST. OF THE KICKAPOO TRADITIONAL TRIBE OF TEXAS, art. X, § 2(h), *available at* http://thorpe.ou.edu/constitution/kickapoo/; CONST. OF THE NATIVE TRIBE OF KOYUKUK, ALASKA, art. 11, § 3(8), *available at* http://thorpe.ou.edu/constitution/ koyukuk/index.html; LITTLE RIVER BAND OF OTTAWA INDIANS CONST., art. III, § 1(h), *available at* http://thorpe.ou.edu/constitution/ottawa2.html; REVISED CONST. & BYLAWS OF THE MINNESOTA CHIPPEWA TRIBE, art. XIII, *available at* http://www.narf.org/nill/Constitutions/mnchippconst/mnconsttoc.htm; CONST. & BYLAWS OF THE MISSISSIPPI BAND OF CHOCTAW INDIANS, art. X, § 1(h), *available at* http://www.choctaw.org/Government/Document%20of%20Governance/Tribal%20Constitution% 20&%20Bylaws.html; CONST. OF THE SIPAYIK MEMBERS OF THE PASAMAQUODDY TRIBE, art. IV, § 1(h), *available at* http://www.narf.org/nill/Constitutions/passconst/passconsttoc.htm; CONST. & BYLAWS OF THE ROSEBUD SIOUX TRIBE OF SOUTH DAKOTA, art. X, § 3, *available at* http://www.narf.org/nill/Constitutions/ rosebudconst/rstconsttoc.htm; CONST. OF THE SAC & FOX NATION, art. X, § 8, *available at* http://meskwaki.org/trcode.html; SALISH & KOOTENAI CONST. & BYLAWS CODIFIED, app., *available at* http://www.narf.org/nill/Constitutions/salishconst/skconsttoc.htm (explicitly incorporating and setting forth the text of the ICRA, including its equal protection guarantee); CONST. & BYLAWS OF

THE SAULT STE. MARIE TRIBE OF CHIPPEWA INDIANS, art.VIII, *available at* http://www.narf.org/nill/Constitutions/saultconst/saultconsttoc.htm; CONST. OF THE SKOKOMISH INDIAN TRIBE [AND RELATED DOCUMENTS], art. IX, *available at* http://www.narf.org/nill/Constitutions/skoconst/skokomishconsttoc.htm; SAINT REGIS MOHAWK TRIBE CONST., art. IV, § 1(h), *available at* http://www.narf.org/nill/Constitutions/ StRegis-Const/constitutiontoc.htm; CONST. OF THE STANDING ROCK SIOUX TRIBE, art. XI, § 8 *microformed on* Indian Tribal Codes: A Microfiche Collection of Indian Law Codes (Ralph Johnson ed. 1988); CONST. OF THE TORRES MARTINEZ DESERT CAHUILLA INDIANS TORRES MARTINEZ RESERVATION, CALIFORNIA, art. V, § 1(H), *available at* http://www.narf.org/nill/Constitutions/ tmarconst/index.htm; CONST. & BYLAWS OF THE TURTLE MOUNTAIN BAND OF CHIPPEWA INDIANS, art. XIV, § 3, *available at* http://www.tmbci.net/PDF/Constitution.pdf (judiciary to ensure "equal protection"); CONST. OF THE WAMPANOAG TRIBE OF GAY HEAD (AQUINNAH), art. III, § 1(d), *available at* http://thorpe.ou.edu/constitution/wampanoag/index.html; CONST. OF THE YAVAPAI- APACHE NATION, art. IX, § (h), *available at* http://www.narf.org/nill/Constitutions/ YavapaiApache/yavtoc.htm; CONST. OF THE FORT MCDOWELL YAVAPAI NATION, art.VIII, § 1(H), *available at* http://www.narf.org/nill/Constitutions/FtMcDowellConst/ftmcdowellconsttoc.htm.

Roughly 20 percent of the tribal constitutions that were available on the National Tribal Justice Resource Center site during the period of my search had equal protection clauses. *See* Methodogy section, *supra* (explaining that 116 tribal constitutions and bylaws were archived on the National Tribal Justice Resource Center site during the relevant period). Note that the Turtle Mountain Band of Chippewa Indians' constitution was available online on the National Tribal Justice Resource Center website but that another of that tribe's documents downloaded from the National Tribal Justice Resource Center appeared to be out-of-date, so I downloaded the constitution from the tribe's own website to ensure I had the most current version. *See infra* note 92. Because the Turtle Mountain Band of Chippewa Indians' Constitution was available on the National Tribal Justice Resource Center website, I included it in the count of tribal constitutions available from that website and also included its equal protection clause in the calculation of the number of tribes having such clauses. Similarly, the Pasamaquoddy Constitution was designated a draft on the National Tribal Justice Resource Center site, so I downloaded the version from that tribe's own website. Likewise, the Hopi Constitution on the National Tribal Justice Resource Center site had both an equal protection clause and an explicit, broad-based prohibition on sex-discrimination, CONST. OF THE HOPI TRIBE, art. IX, § 1(i), but it appears to have been an unapproved draft, based on information communicated by the Hopi Tribal Secretary's Office. Personal communication with Hopi Tribal Secretary's Office (Oct. 1, 2008); *see also* CONST. & BY-LAWS OF THE HOPI TRIBE, art. IX, § 1 (1993), *available at* http://hopicourts.com/ index.php?option=com_docman&Itemid=50&group=13. Therefore, the Hopi provision from the Tribal Justice Resource Center was not counted, although the Pasamaquoddy Tribe's Constitution was counted.

36. *See* Colville Tribal Civil Rights Act, ch.1–5, § 1-5-2(h), *available at* http://www.narf.org/nill/Codes/colvillecode/cc1.htm; CONFEDERATED TRIBES OF THE COOS, LOWER UMPQUA AND SIUSLAW INDIANS TRIBAL CODE, tit. I, ch. 1–5, § 1-5-1(g), *available at* http://www.narf.org/nill/Codes/cooscode/index.htm; MASHANTUCKET PEQUOT TRIBAL LAWS, tit. XX, ch. 1, § 1(a)(8), *available at* http://www.narf.org/nill/Codes/mpcode/index.htm; STATUTES OF THE NON-REMOVABLE MILLE LACS BAND OF CHIPPEWA INDIANS, BAND STATUTE 1011-MCL-5, § 8; SISSETON, S.D., ORDINANCE No.79-02 (1979) (stating that judiciary of the tribe is to provide "equal protection and justice" pursuant to the Indian Civil Rights Act), *available at* http://www.narf.org/nill/Codes/mlcode/mltitle1civrights.htm.

37. *See, e.g.,* CONST. & BYLAWS OF THE COLORADO RIVER INDIAN TRIBES OF THE COLORADO RIVER INDIAN RESERVATION ARIZONA AND CALIFORNIA, art. III, § 3, *microformed on* Indian Tribal Codes: A Microfiche Collection of Indian Law Codes (Ralph Johnson ed. 1988) (providing for "equal political rights and equal opportunity to participate in the economic resources and activities of the tribes" in addition to equal protection); NISQUALLY TRIBAL CODE, tit. 38, § 38-01-03 ("no person shall be denied the equal protection of the terms of" the sub-chapter pertaining to tobacco revenue taxation), *available at* http://www.narf.org/nill/Codes/ nisqcode/nisqcode38.htm; CONFEDERATED TRIBES OF THE SILETZ INDIANS, OR., STANDING COMMITTEE ORDINANCE 84-06, § 4 (1999) ("Committee Members may also be removed for cause following a hearing before the Tribal Council, which provides applicable standards of due process and equal protection"), *available at* http://www.narf.org/nill/Codes/siletzcode/silcodetoc.htm; *id.* § 12 ("The Tribal Chairman shall attempt to ensure that all members of the Siletz Tribe have an equal oppor-

tunity to serve on committees . . . ."); CONST. OF THE WAMPANOAG TRIBE OF GAY HEAD (AQUINNAH), art. III, § 3(b), *available at* http://thorpe.ou.edu/constitution/ wampanoag/index.html (requiring the Tribal Council to "[e]nsure that tribal members have free access to the clay in the cliffs on an equal basis provided that such access is subject to reasonable regulation in order to protect and preserve the resource").

38.   *See, e.g.*, STANDING ROCK SIOUX CODE OF JUSTICE, tit. XVIII, ch. 1, § 18–102(c) ("compensation for work will be based on the principles of equal pay for equal work"), *microformed on* Indian Tribal Codes: A Microfiche Collection of Indian Law Codes (Ralph Johnson ed. 1988); *see also* CONST. OF THE STANDING ROCK SIOUX TRIBE, art. XI, § 8, *microformed on* Indian Tribal Codes: A Microfiche Collection of Indian Law Codes (Ralph Johnson ed. 1988) (providing general equal protection guarantee).

39.   For example, nothing in the Nisqually Tribe's constitution or code, assuming the complete version is available on the National Tribal Justice Resource Center website, appears to provide for "equal protection" except for the provision relating to tobacco revenue taxation. NISQUALLY TRIBAL CODE, tit. 38, § 38-01-03, *available at* http://www.narf.org/nill/Codes/nisqcode/nisqcode38.htm ("no person shall be denied the equal protection of the terms of" the sub-chapter pertaining to tobacco revenue taxation). However, the tribe's constitution does provide for "[a]ll members of the Tribe . . . [to] be accorded equal opportunities to participate in the economic resources and activities of the Tribe." CONST. & BYLAWS OF THE NISQUALLY TRIBE OF THE NISQUALLY INDIAN RESERVATION, art. VII, § 2, *available at* http://www.ntjrc.org/ccfolder/nisqconst.htm.

40.   *See, e.g.*, CONST. OF THE COQUILLE INDIAN TRIBE, art. VI, § 3(b)(11), *available at* http://www.narf.org/nill/Constitutions/coquilleconst/coqconsttoc.htm; CONST. & BY-LAWS OF THE CONFEDERATED TRIBES OF THE GRAND RONDE COMMUNITY OF OREGON, art. III, §3(k), *available at* http://www.narf.org/nill/Constitutions/Grand%20Ronde%20Constitution/ grandrondeconsttoc.htm; SAN ILDEFONSO PUEBLO CODE, tit. XVIII, ch. 57, § 57-3, *available at* http://www.narf.org/nill/Codes/sicode/sanildcodet18consumer.htm#chapter57; CONST. OF THE SKOKOMISH INDIAN TRIBE [AND RELATED DOCUMENTS], art. IX, *available at* http://www.narf.org/nill/Constitutions/skoconst/skokomishconsttoc.htm; SALISH & KOOTENAI CONST. & BYLAWS CODIFIED, APPENDIX, *available at* http://www.narf.org/nill/Constitutions/salishconst/skconsttoc.htm (explicitly incorporating and setting forth the text of the ICRA, including its equal protection guarantee); CONST. & BYLAWS OF THE TURTLE MOUNTAIN BAND OF CHIPPEWA INDIANS, art. XIV, § 3, *available at* http://www.tmbci.net/PDF/Constitution.pdf.

41.   *See, e.g.*, Rosen, *supra* note 21, at 487–88, 511; Taylor, *supra* note 33, at 255–57; Matthew L.M. Fletcher, *Tribal Employment Separation: Tribal Law Enigma, Tribal Governance Paradox, and Tribal Court Conundrum*, 38 MICH. J.L. REFORM 273, 273–74 (2005).

42.   Rosen, *supra* note 21, at 487; *see also* Colville Confederated Tribes v. Bearcub, 35 Indian L. Rptr. 6011, 6012 (Confederated Tribes of the Colville Tribal Ct. 2005) (explaining tribe's right to interpret free speech rights differently under the ICRA than a federal court would under the U.S. Constitution).

43.   Rosen, *supra* note 21, at 511; Taylor, *supra* note 33, at 239, 255–56; *see also* Winnebego Tribe of Nebraska v. Bigfire, 25 Indian L. Rptr. 6229, 6230 (Winnebago Sup. Ct. 1998); *accord* Winnebago Tribe of Nebraska v. Bigfire, 24 Indian L. Rptr. 6232, 6235–36 (Winnebago Tribal Ct.1997), *aff'd* 25 Indian L. Rptr. 6229 (Winnebago Sup. Ct. 1998); Fletcher, *supra* note 41, at 273–74. However, the Winnebago Supreme Court in *Bigfire* suggested that its analysis of equal protection might be somewhat different under the ICRA than under the tribal constitution. *Bigfire*, 25 Indian L. Rptr. at 6230, 6233.

44.   While some scholars have suggested that tribal courts are much less likely to follow precedent than American courts, Cooter & Fikentscher, *supra* note 18, at 59, my limited experience practicing before tribal courts in the Northwestern United States suggests that precedent from the particular tribal court deciding a case, where available, is immensely important and that tribal courts often look to opinions from other tribes as persuasive authority. *See also* Taylor, *supra* note 33, at 240 ("Tribal courts will generally follow their own precedents and give considerable weight to the decisions of other Indian courts"); *accord* Nevayaktewa v. Hopi Tribe, 1998.NAHT.00000019, No. 97AC000004 ¶¶ 29–30 (App. Ct. of the Hopi Tribe, Mar. 20, 1998) (considering whether defendants' allegations meet the requirements of an equal protection test created by Burns Pauite Court of Appeals), *available at* http://www.tribal-institute.org/opinions/1998.NAHT.0000019.htm.

45.   Griffith v. Wilkie, 18 Indian L. Rptr. 6058, 6059 (Northern Plains Intertribal Ct. App. 1991).

46. *Bigfire*, 24 Indian L. Rptr. 6232 (Winnebago Tribal Ct. 1997), *aff'd* 25 Indian L. Rptr. 6229 (Winnebago Sup. Ct. 1998). The Winnebago Tribal Court also decided three other cases dealing with similar issues, two of which were ultimately consolidated on appeal with *Bigfire*. Winnebago Tribe of Neb. v. Frazier, 25 Indian L. Rptr. 6021 (Winnebago Tribal Ct. 1997); Winnebago Tribe of Neb. v. Levering, 25 Indian L. Rptr. 6022 (Winnebago Tribal Ct. 1997); Winnebago Tribe of Neb. v. Whitewater, 25 Indian L. Rptr. 6022 (Winnebago Tribal Ct. 1997); *see also Bigfire*, 25 Indian L. Rptr. at 6229; Rosen, *supra* note 21, at 541.

47. Koon v. Grand Traverse Band of Ottawa & Chippewa Indians, Case No. 95-067-048-CV (Tribal Ct. of the Grand Traverse Band of Ottawa & Chippewa Indians, July 20, 2001), slip op. at 3–4.

48. *See, e.g.*, Barnes v. Mashantucket Pequot Tribal Nation, 4 Mashantucket Rptr. 477, 485, 2007 WL 2728330 (Mashantucket Pequot Tribal Ct. 2007); *see also* Sawyer v. Mashantucket Pequot Tribal Nation, 3 Mashantucket Rptr. 413, 2001 WL 36037904 (Mashantucket Pequot Tribal Ct., Nov. 27, 2001).

49. *Griffith*, 18 Indian L. Rptr. at 6059.

50. *Id.*

51. *Id.*

52. *Id.* at 6059–60.

53. Winnebago Tribe of Nebraska. v. Bigfire, 24 Indian L. Rptr. 6232, 6236, 6239 (Winnebago Tribal Ct. 1997), *aff'd* 25 Indian L. Rptr. 6229 (Winnebago Sup. Ct. 1998). Other tribal court decisions had gone the other way but were either overruled or reversed by the tribal supreme court. *See* Winnebago Tribe of Nebraska v. Frazier, 25 Indian L. Rptr. 6021 (Winnebago Tribal Ct. 1997); Winnebago Tribe of Nebraska v. Levering, 25 Indian L. Rptr. 6022 (Winnebago Tribal Ct. 1997); Winnebago Tribe of Nebraska v. Whitewater, 25 Indian L. Rptr. 6022 (Winnebago Tribal Ct. 1997); *see also Bigfire*, 25 Indian L. Rptr. at 6229; Rosen, *supra* note 21, at 541.

54. *Bigfire*, 24 Indian L. Rptr. at 6238–39.

55. *Bigfire*, 24 Indian L. Rptr. at 6239.

56. *Bigfire*, 24 Indian L. Rptr. at 6238–39.

57. *Id.* at 6239.

58. *Id.*

59. *Id.*

60. *Id.* at 6233.

61. Winnebago Tribe of Nebraska v. Bigfire, 25 Indian L. Rptr. 6229, 6229 (Winnebago Sup. Ct. 1998).

62. *Id.* at 6231; Rosen, *supra* note 21, at 541–44 (citing *Bigfire,* 25 Indian L. Rptr. at 6229). This was not a traditional federal-style strict scrutiny analysis because the court did not look at whether the governmental action was narrowly tailored to the compelling tribal interest. *See, e.g.*, Fed. Election Comm'n v. Wisconsin Right to Life, 551 U.S. 449, 464–65 (2007).

63. *Bigfire*, 25 Indian L. Rptr. at 6232.

64. *Id.*

65. *Id.* at 6233.

66. Rosen, *supra* note 21, at 543–44.

67. *Bigfire*, 25 Indian L. Rptr. at 6231.

68. *Id.* at 6230, 6233.

69. Michael M. v. Super. Ct. of Sonoma County, 450 U.S. 464, 467 (1981); *Bigfire*, 25 Indian L. Rptr. at 6233.

70. *See generally Bigfire*, 24 Indian L. Rptr. at 6236, 6239, *aff'd* 25 Indian L. Rptr. 6229 (Winnebago Sup. Ct. 1998). Although the defendant objected on appeal to the trial court's conclusion that force or coercion had been at play, the evidence of force to which the lower court alluded may still have had an emotional effect on the appellate judges. *Bigfire*, 25 Indian L. Rptr. at 6229.

71. *Bigfire*, 25 Indian L. Rptr. at 6233–34.

72. *Id.* at 6233–34.

73. *Id.* at 6233.

74. *Id.*

75. *Id.*

76. *Id.* at 6234.

77. *See generally* Koon v. Grand Traverse Band of Ottawa & Chippewa Indians, Case No. 95-067-048-CV (Tribal Ct. of the Grand Traverse Band of Ottawa & Chippewa Indians, July 20, 2001); *see also* Koon v. Grand Traverse of Ottawa & Chippewa Indians, Case No. 95-067-048-CV (Tribal Ct. of the Grand Traverse Band of Ottawa & Chippewa Indians, Aug. 31, 1996).

78. Koon v. Grand Traverse Band of Ottawa & Chippewa Indians, No. 95-067-048-CV, slip op. at 3–4 (Tribal Ct. of the Grand Traverse Band of Ottawa & Chippewa Indians, July 20, 2001).

79. *Id.* slip op. at 4.

80. *Id.; see also* Matthew L.M. Fletcher & Zeke Fletcher, *A Restatement of the Common Law of the Grand Traverse Band of Ottawa & Chippewa Indians*, 7 TRIBAL L. J. § 6.02 & n.117 (2006–07), *available at* http://tlj.unm.edu/tribal-law-journal/articles/volume_7/a_restatement_of_the_common_law_of_the_grand_traverse_band_of_ottawa_and_chippewa_indians/index.php.

81. *See, e.g.*, ANDERSON ET AL., AMERICAN INDIAN LAW: CASES & COMMENTARY 103–04, 139–42 (2008) (describing federal assimilationist policies such as allotment and termination).

82. *See, e.g.*, Fletcher, *supra* note 41, at 273, 279.

83. *See, e.g.*, CONST. & BYLAWS OF THE COLORADO RIVER INDIAN TRIBES OF THE COLORADO RIVER INDIAN RESERVATION ARIZONA AND CALIFORNIA art. III, § 3, *microformed on* Indian Tribal Codes: A Microfiche Collection of Indian Law Codes (Ralph Johnson ed. 1988); Hudson v. Hoh Tribal Bus. Comm., No. HOH-CIV-4/91-015, 2 Tribal Appellate Court Opinions of the Northwest Intertribal Ct. Sys. 160, 161 (Hoh Tribal Ct. of App., May 28, 1992); CONST. & BYLAWS OF THE LUMMI TRIBE OF THE LUMMI RESERVATION, WASHINGTON AS AMENDED art. VIII, *microformed on* Indian Tribal Codes: A Microfiche Collection of Indian Law Codes (Ralph Johnson ed. 1988); REVISED CONST. & BYLAWS OF THE MINNESOTA CHIPPEWA TRIBE art. III, *available at* http://www.narf.org/nill/Constitutions/mnchippconst/mnconsttoc.htm.

84. REVISED CONST. & BYLAWS OF THE MINNESOTA CHIPPEWA TRIBE art. III, *available at* http://www.narf.org/nill/Constitutions/mnchippconst/mnconsttoc.htm.

85. *See, e.g.*, *Hudson*, 2 Tribal Appellate Court Opinions of the Northwest Intertribal Ct. Sys. at 163–64 (construing right to petition for redress of grievances provided for in the Hoh tribal constitution according to federal constitutional principles because the tribal constitution explicitly incorporated federal constitutional rights).

86. Because my electronic searches were for explicitly sex-based terms, the prevalence of such provisions is probably significantly underrepresented here. *See* methodology section, *supra* (explaining searching methodology).

87. 1 NAVAJO NATION CODE § 3, *available at* http://www.navajocourts.org/Harmonization/NavBill-Rights.htm.

88. *Id.*; Bennett v. Navajo Bd. of Election Supervisors, No. A-CV-26-90, 1990.NANN.0000016, ¶ 63 (Navajo Sup. Ct., Dec. 12, 1990), *available at* http://www.tribal-institute.org/opinions/1990.NANN.0000016.htm.

89. *Bennett*, No A-CV-26-90, 1990.NANN.0000016, ¶¶ 39–40.

90. Additionally, Elmer Rusco undertook a survey of the civil liberties protections provided for in 220 tribal constitutions that were in place as of September 1981, and he identified no broad-based prohibitions on sex discrimination. Elmer R. Rusco, *Civil Liberties Guarantees Under Tribal Law: A Survey of Civil Rights Provisions in Tribal Constitutions*, 14 AM. INDIAN L. REV. 269, 270, 284, 290 (1990). However, as his survey is now out-of-date, it is possible that some tribal constitutions explicitly prohibit sex discrimination generally, although I was not able to locate them in my searches.

91. CONST. OF THE FORT BELKNAP INDIAN COMMUNITY OF THE FORT BELKNAP RESERVATION MONTANA art. VII, § 1, *available at* http://www.indianlaw.mt.gov/content/fortbelknap/constitution/1935_constitution.pdf; CONST. OF THE MUSCOGEE (CREEK) NATION art. IV, § 2, *available at* http://thorpe.ou.edu/constitution/muscogee/index.html; CONST. & BY-LAWS OF THE CONFEDERATED TRIBES OF WARM SPRINGS RESERVATION OREGON AS AMENDED art. IV, § 5, *available at* http://www.warmsprings.com/Warmsprings/Tribal_Community/History__Culture/Treaty__Documents/Tribal_Constitution_and_By-Laws.html; *see also* CONST. & BY-LAWS OF THE SAC & FOX TRIBE OF THE MISSISSIPPI IN IOWA art. IV, § 4 *available at* http://thorpe.ou.edu/IRA/ias&fcons.html (prohibiting sex-based disqualification from holding tribal office).

92. Initially, it appeared that the Turtle Mountain Band of Chippewa Indians had in place such a broad-

based provision, based on a document downloaded from the National Tribal Justice Resource Center. *See* TURTLE MOUNTAIN BAND OF CHIPPEWA BILL OF RIGHTS (2001). However, the document appeared to be a draft and was not included in the tribe's constitution, which was also available from the National Tribal Justice Resource Center. CONST. & BY-LAWS OF THE TURTLE MOUNTAIN BAND OF CHIPPEWA INDIANS BELCOURT, NORTH DAKOTA. To resolve the question, I contacted the tribal government; the records manager reported that she had no knowledge of the Bill of Rights and did not believe it was current law. E-mail from Jolean Peltier, Records Manager, Turtle Mountain Band of Chippewa Indian Belcourt, North Dakota, to Ann Tweedy, Teaching Fellow, California Western School of Law (Aug. 8, 2008, 4:37 pm Pacific Time) (on file with author). Similarly, the Hopi Tribe initially appeared to have such a constitutional provision in place, CONST. OF THE HOPI TRIBE art. IX, § 1(i), but, based on my communication with the Hopi Tribe Secretary's Office, it appears that only a 2003 unapproved Draft Constitution contains this provision. Interview with Hopi Tribal Secretary's Office (Oct. 1, 2008); *see also* CONST. & BY-LAWS OF THE HOPI TRIBE art. IX, § 1 (1993), *available at* http://hopicourts.com/index.php?option=com_docman&Itemid=50&group=13.

93. *See, e.g.*, Joseph Blocher, *Amending the Exceptions Clause*, 92 MINN. L. REV. 971, 971 n.2 (2008); Krakoff, *supra* note 8, at 1138 & n.160.

94. 1 NAVAJO NATION CODE § 3, *available at* http://www.navajocourts.org/Harmonization/NavBillRights.htm.

95. Bennett v. Navajo Bd. of Elections Supervisors, No. A-CV-26-90, 1990.NANN.0000016, ¶ 64 (Navajo Sup. Ct., Dec. 12, 1990), *available at* http://www.tribal-institute.org/opinions/1990.NANN.0000016.htm (suggesting that a law that caused disparate impact based on sex would violate the Navajo Bill of Rights). The language regarding denial or abridgment is derived from the proposed Equal Rights Amendment to the United States Constitution. *Bennett*, No. A-CV-26-90, 1990.NANN.0000016 at ¶ 63. Similar language is contained in the voting rights amendments to the United States Constitution. U.S. CONST. amend. XV, § 1; U.S. CONST. amend. XIX. But these amendments, by their terms, are limited to voting issues. Outside of the voting context, the United States has been less protective of potential victims of discrimination than the Navajo Nation appears to be, and the United States has upheld sex-based classifications in some circumstances and has sharply limited disparate impact claims, particularly in the equal protection context. *See, e.g.*, Nguyen v. I.N.S., 533 U.S. 53 (2001) (upholding the validity of federal distinctions between unmarried mothers and unmarried fathers that affect a child's ability to benefit from the parent's immigration status in order to gain admittance to the United States); McCleskey v. Kemp, 481 U.S. 279 (1987) (holding that statistical evidence that black defendants were more likely to get the death penalty for killing white victims was not problematic under the equal protection clause of the Fourteenth Amendment because of the lack of evidence of discriminatory intent); *cf.* 42 U.S.C. § 2000e-2(k) (2006) (providing for employment discrimination claims based on disparate impact under Title VII of the Civil Rights Act of 1964 but only where the employer cannot show that the challenged practice is "job related for the position in question and consistent with business necessity"). Furthermore, the Supreme Court recently made clear that it views disparate impact as merely a secondary part of Title VII, which it sees as more directly concerned with disparate treatment, and that an employer who wishes to voluntarily eliminate disparate impacts will face a high burden to justify its behavior when affected employees can plausibly claim disparate treatment as a result of the employers' efforts. *See generally* Ricci v. DeStefano, 129 S.Ct. 2658 (2009).

96. Help v. Silvers, No. A-CV-01-82, 1983.NANN.0000001, ¶ 32 (Navajo May 6, 1983), *available at* http://www.tribal-institute.org/opinions/1983.NANN.0000001.htm.

97. Bennett v. Navajo Bd. of Elections Supervisors, No. A-CV-26-90, 1990.NANN.0000016, ¶¶ 63–65 (Navajo Dec. 12, 1990), *available at* http://www.tribal-institute.org/opinions/1990.NANN.0000016.htm (rejecting the plaintiff's unelaborated claim that a requirement of prior tribal employment for holding elected office constituted impermissible sex discrimination under the Navajo Bill of Rights and stating that "Bennett did not show how or why it caused a discriminatory or disparate impact on those of her gender, excluding or inhibiting them from public elective office" and that "[w]hile it may be true that in the past women have been excluded or discouraged from the ranks of the Navajo Nation Council . . . Bennett was denied a place on the ballot because she had not been employed by the Navajo tribal organization. The Court is sensitive to the possibility of a past pattern and practice of excluding women from public office, but there are sufficient numbers of women employed by the Navajo Nation to make it possible for many to run for public office under the statute").

98. Riggs v. Estate of Attakai, No. SC–CV–39–04, slip op. at 3–4 & 4 n.5 (Navajo June 13, 2007), *available at* http://www.navajocourts.org/NNCourtOpinions2007/09Sista%20Riggs%20v%20Estate%20of%20Tom%20Attakai.pdf.

99. *Id.* at 7 (Benally, J., concurring).

100. The majority appears to be mistakenly characterizing the concurrence as a dissent. *See id.*

101. Begay v. Keedah, No. A–CV–09–91, 1991.NANN.0000007 (Navajo Nov 26, 1991) *available at* http://www.tribal-institute.org/opinions/1991.NANN.0000007.htm.

102. *Riggs*, No. SC–CV–39–04, slip op. at 4 n.5.

103. *Id.*, at 3.

104. *Id.*, at 7 (Benally, J., concurring).

105. *See, e.g., supra* notes 69, 95 (citing US law).

106. *Bennett*, No. A–CV–26–90, 1990.NANN.0000016, at ¶ 64.

107. *See supra* note 95 and accompanying text.

108. CONST. OF THE FORT BELKNAP INDIAN COMMUNITY OF THE FORT BELKNAP RESERVATION MONTANA art. VII, § 1 (providing for voting rights regardless of sex), *available at* http://www.indianlaw.mt.gov/content/fortbelknap/constitution/1935_constitution.pdf; CONST. OF THE MUSCOGEE (CREEK) NATION art. IV, § 2 (providing for voting rights regardless of sex), *available at* http://thorpe.ou.edu/constitution/muscogee/index.html; CONST. & BY-LAWS OF THE SAC & FOX TRIBE OF THE MISSISSIPPI IN IOWA art. IV, § 4 (prohibiting sex-based disqualification from holding tribal office), *available at* http://thorpe.ou.edu/IRA/ias&fcons.html; CONST. & BY-LAWS OF THE CONFEDERATED TRIBES OF WARM SPRINGS RESERVATION OREGON AS AMENDED art. IV, § 5 (providing for voting rights regardless of sex), *available at* http://www.warmsprings.com/Warmsprings/Tribal_Community/History__Culture/Treaty__Documents/Tribal_Constitution_and_By-Laws.html; BAY MILLS INDIAN COMMUNITY LAW & CODES, ORD. TO REGULATE THE OPERATION OF GAMING BY THE BAY MILLS INDIAN COMMUNITY § 7.27 (prohibiting sex discrimination in operation of gaming enterprise), *available* at http://www.narf.org/nill/Codes/baymillscode/baymillscodetoc.htm; BLACKFEET TRIBAL LAW & ORDER CODE ch. 3, § 4(A)(1) (prohibiting creditors from engaging in sex discrimination), *available at* http://www.narf.org/nill/Codes/blackfeetcode/blftcodetoc.htm; THE CHEROKEE CODE: PUBLISHED BY ORDER OF THE EASTERN BAND OF CHEROKEE INDIANS ch. 95, art. II, § 95-13(c) (prohibiting sex discrimination in employment), *available at* http://www.narf.org/nill/Codes/ebcicode/index.htm; CHITIMACHA COMPREHENSIVE CODES OF JUSTICE & CHITIMACHA COMPREHENSIVE "RULES OF THE COURT" tit. VI, ch. 3, § 304(e) (providing that there should be no sex-based presumption in child custody cases), *available at* http://www.narf.org/nill/Codes/chitimachacode/chitimcodetoc.htm; THE CONFEDERATED TRIBES OF THE GRAND RONDE COMMUNITY OF OREGON [ORDINANCES], § 480(P)(5)(F) (providing that the landlord's sex discrimination against the tenant can be used as a defense to eviction), *available at* http://www.narf.org/nill/Codes/grcode/grtoc.htm; GRAND TRAVERSE BAND CODE: STATUTES OF THE GRAND TRAVERSE BAND OF OTTAWA & CHIPPEWA INDIANS, tit. 18, ch. 8, § 825 (prohibiting gaming operators from discriminating based on sex), *available at* http://www.narf.org/nill/Codes/gtcode/index.htm; FORT PECK COMPREHENSIVE CODE OF JUSTICE 2000, tit. X, ch. 3, § 304(b) (providing that "there shall be no presumption that a parent is better suited to be custodial parent based on that parent's gender"), *available at* http://www.fptc.org/code.html; LITTLE RIVER BAND OF OTTAWA INDIANS ORDINANCES & REGULATIONS ch. 600, § 2.2 (prohibiting sex discrimination in employment except where sex is a bona fide occupational qualification), *available at* http://www.narf.org/nill/Codes/lrcode/lrcodetoc.htm; OGLALA SIOUX LAW & ORDER CODE ch. 17, pt. II.B., § I (declaring it to be the policy of the tribe not to discriminate in employment based on sex or other grounds), *available at* http://www.narf.org/nill/Codes/oglalacode/oglalatoc.htm; SAULT STE. MARIE TRIBE OF CHIPPEWA INDIANS TRIBAL CODE ch. 83, subch. VII, § 83.702(6) (providing that the landlord's sex discrimination against the tenant can be used as a defense to eviction), *available at* http://www.narf.org/nill/Codes/saultcode/ssmcodetoc.htm; SISSETON-WAHPETON SIOUX TRIBE ch. 59, § 59-07-03 (setting out an administrative complaint procedure for a worker who believes she has been discriminated against based on sex or other grounds), *available at* http://www.narf.org/nill/Codes/sissetonwahpeton%20code/tableofcontents.htm; SKOKOMISH TRIBAL CODE tit. 4, § 4.02.150(ee) (prohibiting gaming operators from discriminating based on sex and other grounds), *available at* http://www.narf.org/nill/Codes/skocode/index.htm; SUSANVILLE RANCHERIA [TRIBAL ORDINANCES] tit. I, § 7.6.2 (prohibiting

gaming operation from discriminating based on sex), *available at* http://sir-nsn.gov/onlinedocuments.html; WHITE EARTH BAND OF CHIPPEWA RULES OF CRIM. P. 1.02 (prohibiting discrimination based on sex and other grounds in application of rules of criminal procedure), *available at* http://www.whiteearth.com/gaming.html; YSLETA DEL SUR PUEBLO CODE OF LAWS, art. 4, pt. 6, § 4.6.20(F) (defining intentional sexual harassment as a civil infraction), *available at* http://www.narf.org/nill/Codes/ysletacode/ysletatoc.htm; Brooks v. Cherokee Nation, 5 Okla. Trib. 178, 1996 WL 1132752 (Cherokee Nov. 6, 1996) (discussing the sexual harassment law of the Cherokee Nation of Oklahoma); White v. Day, 7 AM. TRIBAL L. REP. 246, 2008 WL 2690792, at *2 (Ho-Chunk Trial Ct., 2008) (quoting the Employment Relations Act of 2004, which prohibits "discriminat[ion] based on individual's sex"); Hoopa Forest Industries v. Jordan, 25 Indian L. Rptr. 6159 (Hoopa Valley Tribal Ct., 1998) (reviewing and reversing, apparently under tribal common law while look-ing to federal law in an advisory capacity, an agency determination of hostile work environment sexual harass-ment because the conduct alleged failed to rise to the required level of severity and because of other evidentiary problems and also quoting the tribal personnel policy's narrower proscription against sexual harass-ment); Fargo v. Mashantucket Pequot Gaming Enterprise, 2 Mash. Rep. 145, 147, 153 (Mash. Pequot Tr. Ct. Oct. 6, 1997) (upholding plaintiff's termination due to sexual harassment), *available at* http://www.tribal-institute.org/opinions/1997.NAMP.0000030.htm; LaVigne v. Mohegan Tribe of Indians, 32 Indian L. Rptr. 6044 (Mohe-gan Tribal Ct. 2005) (upholding the plaintiff's termination from employment due to "sexual harassment"); *cf.* Renecker v. Tulalip Casino, No. TUL-EMP-11/96-667, 5 Northwest Intertribal Court App. 1, 1–2 (May 29, 1997) (reversing appellant's termination because of procedural errors in the administrative process but not-ing that "any one of the four allegations [of racial and gender slurs] involves 'major offenses'" as defined in the tribe's Human Rights Ordinance).

109. *See supra* note 108 and accompanying text.

110. *See supra* note 108. Fifteen of the laws cited in note 108 are code provisions downloaded from the National Tribal Justice Resource Center. *See also supra* methodology section. The methodology section explains that the codes of sixty-nine tribes were available on the site during the period of my research.

111. The Oglala Sioux and the Blackfeet are two of the tribes that have both multiple laws prohibiting sex dis-crimination as well as laws that explicitly make sex-based distinctions. *See, e.g.,* BLACKFEET TRIBAL LAW & ORDER CODE ch. 3, § 4(A)(1) (prohibiting creditors from engaging in sex discrimination), *available at* http://www.narf.org/nill/Codes/blackfeetcode/blkftcode3domestic.htm; THE FAMILY COURT OF THE BLACK-FEET TRIBE OF THE BLACKFEET INDIAN RESERVATION FAMILY CODE, CODE OF ETHICS FOR BLACKFEET FAMILY COURT MEMBERS R. 6 (providing that "[t]he Blackfeet Family Court Members will serve and respond to requests without bias because of race, religion, sex, age, national origin or handicap."), *available at* http://www.narf.org/nill/Codes/blackfeetcode/ blkft1to22familyct.htm; BLACKFEET TRIBAL LAW & ORDER CODE ch. 2, § 7 (allowing for imprisonment of only male debtors in cases of fraud, potential abscondment, or removal or concealment of property), *available at* http://www.narf.org/nill/Codes/blackfeetcode/blkftcode2civil.htm; OGLALA SIOUX LAW & ORDER CODE ch. 17, pt. II.B., § I (declaring it to be the policy of the tribe not to discriminate in employment based on sex or other grounds), *available at* http://www.narf.org/nill/Codes/ oglalacode/chapter17-personnel1.htm; OGLALA SIOUX LAW & ORDER CODE ch. 18, ch. 1, ¶ 8 (stating, in "Declaration of Policy" that Contractors and Sub-Contractors shall not, in exercising the Tribe's employment preference for Indians, discriminate among Indians on the basis of sex or on other grounds), *available at* http://www.narf.org/nill/Codes/ oglalacode/chapter18-tero.htm; OGLALA SIOUX LAW & ORDER CODE ch. 9, § 104 (creating the crime of having carnal knowledge of a female under the age of sixteen), *available at* http://www.narf.org/nill/Codes/oglalacode/chapter09-penal.htm.

112. *Compare* THE CHEROKEE CODE: PUBLISHED BY ORDER OF THE EASTERN BAND OF CHEROKEE INDI-ANS, ch. 95, art. II, § 95-13(c) (prohibiting sex discrimination in employment), *available at* http://www.narf.org/nill/Codes/ebcicode/95wages.pdf, *and* THE CHEROKEE CODE: PUBLISHED BY ORDER OF THE EASTERN BAND OF CHEROKEE INDIANS ch. 16, art. IV, § 16-4.09(a)(4) (providing that "[t]here shall be no discrimination in any gaming operations by reason of race, color, sex or creed"), *available at* http://www.narf.org/nill/Codes/ebcicode/16gaming.pdf, *and* THE CHEROKEE CODE: PUBLISHED BY ORDER OF THE EASTERN BAND OF CHEROKEE INDIANS, ch. 14, art. I, § 14-1.5 (providing for compliance with, sub-jection to, charging under, and jurisdiction pursuant to criminal laws to be without regard to sex or other pro-hibited grounds), *available at* http://www.narf.org/nill/Codes/ebcicode/index.htm, *with* CHITIMACHA

COMPREHENSIVE CODES OF JUSTICE & CHITIMACHA COMPREHENSIVE "RULES OF THE COURT" tit. VI, ch. 3, § 304(c) (no sex-based presumption in custody cases), *available at* http://www.narf.org/nill/Codes/chitimachacode/chitimcodet6family.htm.

113. THE CHEROKEE CODE: PUBLISHED BY ORDER OF THE EASTERN BAND OF CHEROKEE INDIANS ch. 95, art. II, § 95-13(c), *available at* http://www.narf.org/nill/Codes/ ebcicode/95wages.pdf; LITTLE RIVER BAND OF OTTAWA INDIANS ORDINANCES & REGULATIONS ch. 600, § 2.2, *available at* http://www.narf.org/nill/Codes/lrcode/lrcodetoc.htm; OGLALA SIOUX LAW & ORDER CODE ch. 17, pt. II.B, § I, *available at* http://www.narf.org/nill/Codes/oglalacode/chapter17-personnel1.htm; SISSETON-WAHPETON SIOUX TRIBE ch. 59, § 59-07-03, *available at* http://www.narf.org/nill/Codes/sisseton_NTJRC/sisseton_wahpeton_codeoflaw59.htm.

114. White v. Day, 7 AM. TRIBAL L. REP. 246, 2008 WL 2690792, at *2 (Ho-Chunk Trial Ct. Jan. 14, 2008); Renecker v. Tulalip Casino, No. TUL-EMP-11/96-667, 5 Northwest Intertribal Court App. 1, 1–2 (May 29, 1997).

115. LITTLE RIVER BAND OF OTTAWA INDIANS ORDINANCES & REGULATIONS ch. 100, § 2.2, *available at* http://www.narf.org/nill/Codes/lrcode/lrcodetoc.htm; *see also* ANNA KIRKLAND, FAT RIGHTS 90–93 (2008) (explaining the concept of a BFOQ exception and its meaning under federal law, particularly its indication that sex differentiations need not be eliminated in all cases, in contrast to race differentiations).

116. LITTLE RIVER BAND OF OTTAWA INDIANS ORDINANCES & REGULATIONS, ch. 100, § 2.2, *available at* http://www.narf.org/nill/Codes/lrcode/lrcodetoc.htm.

117. *See e.g.*, KIRKLAND, *supra* note 115, at 90–93.

118. 42 U.S.C. § 2000e-2(e) (2006); *see also* KIRKLAND, *supra* note 115, at 90–93 (explaining the concept of a BFOQ and its meaning under federal law).

119. *See* Cooter & Fikentscher, *supra* note 18, at 35 (explaining that tribal "codes usually aspire to cover all eventualities").

120. OGLALA SIOUX LAW & ORDER CODE, ch. 18, ch. 1, ¶ 8, *available at* http://www.narf.org/nill/Codes/oglalacode/chapter18-tero.htm.

121. BAY MILLS INDIAN COMMUNITY LAW & CODES, ORDINANCE TO REGULATE THE OPERATION OF GAMING BY THE BAY MILLS INDIAN COMMUNITY, § 7.27, *available at* http://www.narf.org/nill/Codes/baymillscode/baymillscodetoc.htm; THE CHEROKEE CODE: PUBLISHED BY ORDER OF THE EASTERN BAND OF CHEROKEE INDIANS, ch. 16, art. IV, § 16-4.09(a)(4), *available at* http://www.narf.org/nill/Codes/ebcicode/16gaming.pdf; GRAND TRAVERSE BAND CODE: STATUTES OF THE GRAND TRAVERSE BAND OF OTTAWA & CHIPPEWA INDIANS, tit. 18, ch. 8, § 825, *available at* http://www.narf.org/nill/Codes/gtcode/18.pdf; NAVAJO NATION CODE tit. 5, § 2039(B)(3) (2008); SKOKOMISH TRIBAL CODE, tit. 4, § 4.02.150(ee), *available at* http://www.narf.org/nill/Codes/skocode/4-02.pdf; SUSANVILLE INDIAN RANCHERIA [ORDINANCES], tit. I, § 7.6.2, *available at* http://sir-nsn.gov/onlinedocuments.html.

122. *See, e.g.*, YSLETA DEL SUR PUEBLO CODE OF LAWS, art. 4, pt. 6, § 4.6.20(F) (defining intentional sexual harassment as a civil infraction), *available at* http://www.narf.org/nill/Codes/ysletacode/ysletaarticle4.htm#4.

123. *See, e.g.*, POARCH BAND OF CREEK INDIANS CODE, ch. 8, § 8-2-2 (defining the crime of harassment, without explicit mention of sexual harassment, as a misdemeanor that involves "strik[ing], shov[ing], kick[ing], or otherwise touch[ing] a person or subject[ing] him to physical contact; or . . . direct[ing] abusive or obscene language or mak[ing] an obscene gesture toward another person"); YSIETA DEL SUR PUEBLO CODE OF LAWS, art. 4, pt. 6, § 4.6.20(F) (defining intentional sexual harassment explicitly as a type of harassment that is punishable as a civil infraction), *available at* http://www.narf.org/nill/Codes/ysletacode/ysletaarticle4.htm#4; Hoopa Forest Industries v. Jordan, 25 Indian L. Rptr. 6159, 6160 (Hoopa Valley Tribal Ct. 1998) (quoting the tribe's personnel policy as providing that "[e]mployees shall be provided a safe work environment, free from harassment of any sort, i.e., verbal, physical, visual. The Tribal Council accepts no liability for harassment of one employee by another. The individual who makes unwelcome advances, threatens or in any way harasses another employee is personally liable for such actions and their consequences").

124. *See, e.g.*, Brooks v. Cherokee Nation, 5 Okla. Trib. 178, 1996 WL 1132752 (Nov. 6, 1996); Fargo v. Mashantucket Pequot Gaming Enterprise, 2 Mashantucket Rptr. 145, 147, 153, 1997 WL 34639655 (Mashantucket

Pequot Tribal Ct. Oct. 6, 1997); LaVigne v. Mohegan Tribe of Indians, 32 Indian L. Rptr. 6044 (Mohegan Tribal Ct. 2005); *see also* Yazzie v. Sanitation, 7 AM. TRIBAL L. REP. 543, 2007 WL 5884947, *3–4 (Navajo July 11, 2007); *cf.* Schock v. Mashantucket Pequot Gaming Enterprise, 3 Mashantucket Rptr. 129, 1999 WL 34828705 (Mashantucket Pequot Tribal Ct. Sept. 20, 1999).

125. *See, e.g.*, YSLETA DEL SUR PUEBLO CODE OF LAWS, art. 4, pt. 6, § 4.6.20(F) (defining intentional sexual harassment as a civil infraction), *available at* http://www.narf.org/nill/Codes/ysletacode/ysletaarticle4.htm#4. Similarly, the Hoopa Valley Tribe is included based on case law that suggests that that tribe may allow both claims against the employer and claims against the individual perpetrator in the employment context. *Jordan*, 25 Indian L. Rptr. at 6160 & n.1.

126. OGLALA SIOUX LAW & ORDER CODE, ch.17, pt. III (under section heading entitled "Interviewing, Screening, and Testing," requiring comprehensive background check on all applicants for employment, including determination of whether the applicant has been subject to "dismissal[s] from previous jobs due to sexual harassment"); SUSANVILLE INDIAN RANCHERIA CONST. & BYLAWS, BYLAWS, art. III, § 4(6) (requiring the tribal council to "[c]ommit to providing an environment that is free of discrimination, harassment, violence, and intimidation and that is drug free, as required by law. The Tribal Business Council shall not tolerate any form of threatening or abusive behavior, nor tolerated [*sic*] sexual harassment or other forms of harassment or discrimination"), *available at* http://sir-nsn.gov/onlinedocuments.html; YSLETA DEL SUR PUEBLO CODE OF LAWS, art. 4, pt. 6, § 4.6.20(F) (defining intentional sexual harassment as a civil infraction), *available at* http://www.narf.org/nill/Codes/ysletacode/ysletaarticle4.htm#4; Brooks v. Cherokee Nation, 5 Okla. Trib. 178, 1996 WL 1132752 (Nov. 6, 1996) (upholding dismissal of tribal employee for sexual harassment); Lonetree v. Garvin, 34 Indian L. Rptr. 6126 (Ho-Chunk Nation Sup. Ct. Oct. 8, 2007) (Plaintiff, who had been dismissed from tribal employment for sexual harassment, challenged the administrative proceedings based on due process, and, "[b]ecause the [plaintiff did] . . . not deny that he committed sexual harassment," the Ho-Chunk Nation Supreme Court "affirm[ed] the trial court's decision to remand to the GRB [Grievance Review Board] to resolve the sole issue of whether the [defendant] . . . would have terminated the [plaintiff's] . . . employment even if the pre-deprivation hearing had occurred"); *Jordan*, 25 Indian L. Rptr. at 6160 & n.1 (reversing a tribal agency's determination that the employer was liable for sexual harassment based upon the facts that the agency had not entered findings of fact and conclusions of law, that the agency had relied on an exhibit that was not in the record, and that the conduct at issue did not rise to the level of severity required under federal standards, which the court appeared to be using in an advisory capacity despite the statement in tribal personnel policies that only an individual harasser could be held liable for sexual harassment); Fargo v. Mashantucket Pequot Gaming Enterprise, 2 Mash. Rep.145, 147, 153, 1997 WL 34639655 (Mashantucket Pequot Tribal Ct. Oct. 6, 1997) (upholding tribal employee's termination for sexual harassment and citing employee handbook's provision on sexual harassment); LaVigne v. Mohegan Tribe of Indians, 32 Indian L. Rptr. 6044, 6045 (Mohegan Tribal Ct. March 3, 2003) (finding as fact that "Mohegan Tribe Policy #51 strictly forbids sexual harassment in the workplace"); *Yazzie*, 7 AM. TRIBAL L. REP. 543, 2007 WL 5884947, at *3 (reciting the fact that Navajo Nation has a sexual harassment policy for tribal employees).

127. THE CONFEDERATED TRIBES OF THE GRAND RONDE COMMUNITY OREGON [ORDINANCES], § 370(d)(3), *available at* http://www.narf.org/nill/Codes/grcode/gr370personnel.htm.

128. NAVAJO NATION CODE tit. 5, § 2039(B)(3) (prohibiting sex discrimination by gaming operation); OGLALA SIOUX LAW & ORDER CODE, ch. 17, pt. II.B., § I (declaring it to be the policy of the tribe not to discriminate in employment based on sex or other grounds), *available at* http://www.narf.org/nill/Codes/oglalacode/chapter17-personnel1.htm; SUSANVILLE INDIAN RANCHERIA [ORDINANCES], tit. I, § 7.6.2 (prohibiting gaming operation from discriminating based on sex or other grounds), *available at* http://sir-nsn.gov/onlinedocuments.html; Funmaker v. Doornbos, 24 Indian L. Rptr. 6095, 6095 (Ho-Chunk Nation Tribal Ct. August 22, 1996) (quoting prohibition on sex discrimination in employment in the tribe's Personnel Policies & Procedures Manual).

129. LITTLE RIVER BAND OF OTTAWA INDIANS ORDINANCES AND REGULATIONS, ch. 600, § 6.10, *available at* http://www.narf.org/nill/Codes/lrcode/lrcode6.htm.

130. *See, e.g.*, 42 U.S.C. § 2000e(k) (2006) (codifying federal Pregnancy Discrimination Act); *see generally* Daniela M. de la Piedra, *Flirting with the PDA: Congress Must Give Birth to Accommodation Rights that Protect Working Women*, 17 COLUM. J. GENDER & L. 275 (2008).

131. White v. Day, 7 AM. TRIBAL L. REP. 246, 246, 2008 WL 269072, at *2 (Ho-Chunk Trial Ct. 2008).

132. NAVAJO NATION CODE tit. 15, § 704 (2008). Because my electronic searches of tribal codes and constitutions did not target the words "pregnancy," "breastfeeding," "maternity," or "paternity," there may be many other similar tribal laws in existence that I did not discover.

133. LITTLE RIVER BAND OF OTTAWA INDIANS ORDINANCES AND REGULATIONS, ch. 600, § 6.10 (2001), *available at* http://www.narf.org/nill/Codes/lrcode/lrcode6.htm.; *see also* NAVAJO NATION CODE tit. 15, § 702 (2008) ("The purpose of this Act is to provide for opportunities for working mothers to obtain the health benefits of breast-feeding").

134. As explained above, roughly 22 percent of tribes whose codes were available online from the National Tribal Justice Resource Center had some statutory protection from sex discrimination in place. This figure is based on the fact that fifteen of the laws cited in *supra* note 108 are code provisions downloaded from the National Tribal Justice Resource Center. The methodology section explains that the codes of sixty-nine tribes were available on the site during the period of my research. Eight, or about twelve percent, of tribal codes available on the National Tribal Justice Resource Center site contained some proscription against discrimination that applied to employment.

135. CONST. OF THE FORT BELKNAP INDIAN COMMUNITY OF THE FORT BELKNAP RESERVATION MONTANA art.VII, § 1, *available at* http://www.indianlaw.mt.gov/content/fortbelknap/constitution/1935_constitution.pdf; CONST. OF THE MUSCOGEE (CREEK) NATION art. IV, § 2, *available at* http://thorpe.ou.edu/constitution/muscogee/index.html; CONST.& BY-LAWS OF THE CONFEDERATED TRIBES OF WARM SPRINGS RESERVATION OREGON AS AMENDED art. IV, § 5, *available at* http://www.warmsprings.com/Warmsprings/Tribal_Community/History__Culture/Treaty__Documents/Tribal_Constitution_and_By-Laws.html.

136. U.S. CONST. amend. XIX.

137. CONST. & BY-LAWS OF THE SAC AND FOX TRIBE OF THE MISSISSIPPI IN IOWA art. IV, § 4, *available at* http://thorpe.ou.edu/IRA/ias&fcons.html.

138. THE FAMILY COURT OF THE BLACKFEET TRIBE OF THE BLACKFEET INDIAN RESERVATION FAMILY CODE, CODE OF ETHICS FOR BLACKFEET FAMILY COURT MEMBERS R. 6 (1999), *available at* http://www.narf.org/nill/Codes/blackfeetcode/blkft1to22familyct.htm; THE CHEROKEE CODE: PUBLISHED BY ORDER OF THE TRIBAL COUNCIL OF THE EASTERN BAND OF CHEROKEE INDIANS ch. 14, art. I, § 14-1.5 (2005), *available at* http://www.narf.org/nill/Codes/ebcicode/index.htm; WHITE EARTH BAND OF CHIPPEWA RULES OF CRIMINAL PROCEDURE R. 1.02 (2000), *available at* http://www.narf.org/nill/Codes/wearthcode/wecode10criminal.htm.

139. WHITE EARTH BAND OF CHIPPEWA RULES OF CRIMINAL PROCEDURE R. 1.02, *available at* http://www.narf.org/nill/Codes/wearthcode/wecode10criminal.htm.

140. McCleskey v. Kemp, 481 U.S. 279, 339 (1987) (Brennan, J., dissenting).

141. THE FAMILY COURT OF THE BLACKFEET TRIBE OF THE BLACKFEET INDIAN RESERVATION FAMILY CODE, CODE OF ETHICS FOR BLACKFEET FAMILY COURT MEMBERS R. 6 (1999), *available at* http://www.narf.org/nill/Codes/blackfeetcode/blkft1to22familyct.htm.

142. THE CHEROKEE CODE: PUBLISHED BY ORDER OF THE TRIBAL COUNCIL OF THE EASTERN BAND OF CHEROKEE INDIANS ch. 14, art. I, § 14-1.5 (2005), *available at* http://www.narf.org/nill/Codes/ebcicode/index.htm.

143. *Id.*

144. CHITIMACHA COMPREHENSIVE CODES OF JUSTICE & CHITIMACHA INDIAN TRIBAL COURT "RULES OF COURT" tit. VI, ch. 3, § 304(c) (2003), *available at* http://www.narf.org/nill/Codes/chitimachacode/chitimcodet6family.htm; FT. PECK COMPREHENSIVE CODE OF JUSTICE tit. X, ch. 3, § 304(b) (2000), *available at* http://www.fptc.org/title_x/title_x.html; GRAND TRAVERSE BAND CODE: STATUTES OF THE GRAND TRAVERSE BAND OF OTTAWA & CHIPPEWA INDIANS, tit. 10, ch.5, § 514(b) (2003), *available at* http://www.narf.org/nill/Codes/gtcode/10.pdf ; *see also In re* Custody of C.A.G., 5 AM. TRIBAL L. REP. 148, 2004 WL 5599397, at *2 (Fort Peck Ct. App. 2004) (applying the tribal code's prohibition on gender-based presumptions).

145. Father v. Mother, 3 Mashantucket 204, slip op. ¶ 28 (Mashantucket Pequot Tribal Ct. Mar. 9, 1999) (following a Cheyenne River Sioux Tribal Court opinion and rejecting in a child custody case "'the historically gendered and sexist rules of Western common law'" regarding a child's domicile), *available at*

http://www.tribal-institute.org/opinions/1999.NAMP.0000010.htm; *see also* Matthew L. M. Fletcher, *Tribal Courts, the Indian Civil Rights Act, and Customary Law: Preliminary Data* 18–20 (MSU Legal Studies Research Paper, No. 06-05, 2008), *available at* http://ssrn.com/abstract=1103474 (discussing *Father v. Mother*).

146. BLACKFEET TRIBAL LAW & ORDER CODE ch. 3, § 4(A)(1)(1999), *available at* http://www.narf.org/nill/Codes/blackfeetcode/blkftcode3domestic.htm.

147. 15 U.S.C. § 1691(a)(1) (2006).

148. SUSANVILLE INDIAN RANCHERIA [ORDINANCES], BYLAWS LASSEN INDIAN HEALTH CTR. art. II, § 2(15) (2003), *available at* http://sir-nsn.gov/onlinedocuments.html.

149. OGLALA SIOUX LAW & ORDER CODE, ch. 26, § VI, 600.10 STANDARD (1996), *available at* http://www.narf.org/nill/Codes/oglalacode/chapter26-education.htm.

150. 20 U.S.C. § 1681(a) (2006).

151. SISSETON-WAHPETON SIOUX TRIBE, ch. 31, § 31-01-01 (1998), *available at* http://www.narf.org/nill/Codes/sisseton_NTJRC/sisseton_wahpeton_codeoflaw31.htm.

152. *See, e.g.*, Risa E. Kaufman, *Access to the Courts as a Privilege or Immunity of National Citizenship*, 40 CONN. L. REV. 1477, 1509–10, 1509 n.159 (2008) (describing the Prison Litigation Reform Act and other recent developments in federal law).

153. *See, e.g.*, Jackson v. Thornburgh, 907 F.2d 194 (D.C. Cir. 1990); Ashann-Ra v. Commonwealth of Virginia, 112 F. Supp.2d 559 (W.D.Va. 2000).

154. *See Ashann-Ra*, 112 F. Supp. 2d at 570–71.

155. THE CONFEDERATED TRIBES OF THE GRAND RONDE COMMUNITY OF OREGON [ORDINANCES], § 480(p)(5)(F) (2003), *available at* http://www.narf.org/nill/Codes/grcode/grtoc.htm; SAULT STE. MARIE TRIBE OF CHIPPEWA INDIANS TRIBAL CODE, ch. 83, sub.-ch. VII, § 83.702(6) (2001), *available at* http://www.narf.org/nill/Codes/saultcode/ssmcode83evict.htm.

156. 24 C.F.R. § 100.60(b)(5) (2009).

157. *See, e.g.*, 42 U.S.C. § 3604 (2006).

158. NAVAJO NATION CODE, tit. 21, § 509(B) (2008).

159. Public Utilities Commission of Texas, Substantive Rules, ch.26, § 26.21 (1999), *available at* http://www.puc.state.tx.us/rules/subrules/telecom/26toc-I/26toc-I.pdf.

160. *See* MASHANTUCKET PEQUOT TRIBAL LAWS ANN., tit. 13, ch. 4, § 12(b) (2008), *available at* http://www.narf.org/nill/Codes/mpcode/13workerscomp.pdf; *see also id.* at tit. 13, ch. 4, § 12(b) cmt. B(6).

161. *Id.* at tit. 13, ch. 4, § 12(b) cmt B(6).

162. *See* Krakoff, *supra* note 8, at 1153 (quoting Navajo Nation Legislative Counsel Raymond Etcitty).

163. *See supra* note 111 and accompanying text.

164. Valencia-Weber, *supra* note 13, at 50.

165. CONST. & BYLAWS OF THE KIALEGEE TRIBAL TOWN OKLAHOMA, art. III, §§ 3-5 (allowing children of female members to automatically become members but requiring case-by-case approval for children of male members whose mothers are from other tribes), *available at* http://thorpe.ou.edu/IRA/kiacons.html.

166. FORT PECK COMPREHENSIVE CODE OF JUSTICE 2000, tit. IV, § 202, Group 4, *available at* http://www.fptc.org/title_iv/title_iv.html. A somewhat similar provision of federal immigration law was upheld in *Nguyen v. I.N.S.*, 533 U.S. 53 (2001). Additionally, I identified one sex-based voting provision but have serious doubts about whether it remains in force. CONST. FOR THE ISLETA PUEBLO, art. II, ¶ 2, *available at* http://thorpe.ou.edu/IRA/isnmcons.html. This constitution is dated 1947, *id.*, although other information indicates this tribe's constitution was revised in 1991. *See, e.g.*, Center for Legal Education, State Bar of New Mexico Indian Law Section, Tribal Justice & Court Systems, "Pueblo of Isleta Appellate Court & Tribal Court" 3 (2006), *available at* http://tlj.unm.edu/handbook/pdfs/isleta2006.pdf. Indeed, Rusco discusses the Isleta Pueblo Constitution in parts of his article but does not mention the tribe in his discussion of tribal sex discrimination. Rusco, *supra* note 90, at 273, 284.

167. BLACKFEET TRIBAL LAW & ORDER CODE, ch. 6, § 14(1), *available at* http://www.narf.org/nill/Codes/blackfeetcode/blkftcode6enforce.htm; BLACKFEET TRIBAL LAW & ORDER CODE, ch. 2, § 7, *available at* http://www.narf.org/nill/Codes/blackfeetcode/blkftcode2civil.htm ; MASHANTUCKET PEQUOT TRIBAL LAWS ANN., 24 M.P.T.L. ch. 8, § 7(d) (2008); OGLALA SIOUX LAW & ORDER CODE, ch. 9, §§ 64, 103–04, *available at* http://www.narf.org/nill/Codes/oglalacode/chapter09-penal.htm; SAN ILDEFONSO PUEBLO TRIBAL

CODE, ch. 31, § 31.2(10), *available at* http://www.narf.org/nill/Codes/sicode/sanildcodet11probate.htm#chapter31; WHITE MOUNTAIN APACHE PROBATE CODE, ch. 4, § 4.11(A), *available at* http://www.narf.org/nill/Codes/whitemountainapache/chapter_four.htm; *see also* Riggs v. Estate of Attakai, No. SC-CV-39-04 (Navajo June 13, 2007), slip op. at 3–4 & 4 n.5 (explaining that the tradition of prized grazing rights descending to female relatives should be part of the analysis in determining who should be awarded such rights in individual cases), *available at* http://www.navajocourts.org/NNCourtOpinions2007/09Sista%20Riggs%20v%20Estate%20of%20Tom%20Attakai.pdf.

168. *See, e.g.,* LAW & ORDER CODE OF THE FORT MCDOWELL YAVAPAI COMMUNITY, ARIZONA, art. III, § 10-34(a)(1)(d), *available at* http://www.narf.org/nill/Codes/ftmcode/ftmcodetoc.htm; OGLALA SIOUX LAW & ORDER CODE, ch. 3, § 30, ¶¶ 2–3, *available at* http://www.narf.org/nill/Codes/oglalacode/chapter03-domestic.htm; THE LAW & ORDER CODE OF THE UTE INDIAN TRIBE OF THE UINTAH & OURAY RESERVATION UTAH, tit. V, ch. III, § 5-3-9, *available at* http://www.narf.org/nill/Codes/uteuocode/utebodyt5.htm.

169. *See, e.g., Ex parte* Devine, 398 So.2d 686 (Ala. 1981) (striking down presumption in favor of mother's custody under equal protection clause); Gordon v. Gordon, 577 P.2d 1271 (Okla. 1978) (upholding presumption in favor of mother's custody against equal protection challenge). Note also that the US Supreme Court continues to uphold laws treating unmarried fathers less favorably than unmarried mothers. Nguyen v. I.N.S., 533 U.S. 53 (2001).

170. CONST. OF THE IROQUOIS NATIONS: THE GREAT BINDING LAW, GAYANASHAGOWA, *available at* http://www.fordham.edu/halsall/mod/iroquois.html.

171. CONST. OF THE IROQUOIS NATIONS: THE GREAT BINDING LAW, GAYANASHAGOWA § 25, *available at* http://www.fordham.edu/halsall/mod/iroquois.html.

172. LITTLE RIVER BAND OF OTTAWA INDIANS ORDINANCES AND REGULATIONS, GDA DWENDAAGNANANIK: PEACEMAKING GUIDELINES, §§ 1–2, *available at* https://www.lrboi-nsn.gov/council/docs/regulations/chapter-r300/chapter%20R300.pdf

173. *Id.* at § 3.

174. *See, e.g.,* Valencia-Weber, *supra* note 13, at 53–56.

175. *See, e.g.,* Alden v. Maine, 527 U.S. 706 (1999) (addressing state sovereign immunity).

176. *See, e.g.,* COHEN'S HANDBOOK OF FEDERAL INDIAN LAW § 7.05 (2007).

177. Taylor, *supra* note 33, at 253–55; *see also* Dupree v. Cheyenne River Sioux Housing Authority, 16 Indian L. Rptr. 6106, 6108 (Cheyenne River Sioux Ct. App. 1988); McCallister v. Spirit Mountain Gaming, 33 Indian L. Rptr. 6057, 6061 (Confederated Tribes of the Grand Ronde Community Tribal Ct. 2007); Healy v. Mashantucket Pequot Gaming Enterprise, 26 Indian L. Rptr. 6189, 6191 (Mashantucket Ct. of App. 1999); Jackson v. Kahgegab, 33 Indian L. Rptr. 6105, 6108 (Saginaw Chippewa Indian Tribe App. Ct. 2003); *see also* DeCoteau v. Ft. Peck Tribes, 4 AM. TRIBAL L. REP. 277, 2002 WL 34432659, *5, *7 (Ft. Peck. Ct. of App., Dec. 5, 2002) (holding that ICRA claims for equitable and injunctive relief may be brought against tribal officials and tribal employees but imposing heightened pleading requirements); *accord* Rosen, *supra* note 21, at 509 (explaining that ICRA suits for prospective injunctive relief are usually allowed but that allowance of such suits does not technically constitute a waiver of tribal sovereign immunity); *cf.* Thomas v. Coquille Indian Tribe, No. C03-001, 2004.NACQ.0000001, ¶¶ 77–78 (Coquille Indian Tribal Court, March 9, 2004) (noting that neither the ICRA nor the tribal constitution "create[s] remedies in this tribal court for denial of due process or equal protection . . ." but that, because the plaintiff failed to state a claim on which relief could be granted, "[w]hether such remedies exist . . . is an issue to be resolved, if at all, on another day"), *available at* http://www.tribal-institute.org/opinions/2004.NACQ.0000001.htm.

178. *McCallister,* 33 Indian L. Rptr. at 6061; Johnson v. Navajo Nation, 14 Indian L. Rptr. 6037, 6040 (Navajo 1987); *cf.* Thomas, No. C03-001, 2004.NACQ.0000001 at ¶¶ 77–78 (noting that neither the ICRA nor the tribal constitution "create[s] remedies in this tribal court for denial of due process or equal protection . . ." but that, because the plaintiff failed to state a claim on which relief could be granted, "[w]hether such remedies exist . . . is an issue to be resolved, if at all, on another day"), *available at* http://www.tribal-institute.org/opinions/1987.NANN.0000011.htm.

179. *McCallister,* 33 Indian L. Rptr. at 6058–59; Chatterson v. Confederated Tribes of the Siletz Nation of Indians of Oregon, 24 Indian L. Rptr. 6231, 6231–32 (Siletz Ct. App., Oct. 9, 1997); Beebe v. Ho-Chunk

Nation, 32 Indian L. Rptr. 6155, 6156 (Ho-Chunk Nation Sup. Ct., July 18, 2005); Schock v. Mashantucket Pequot Gaming Enterprise, 3 Mashantucket Rptr. 129, 1999 WL 34828705 (Mashantucket Pequot Tribal Ct., Sept. 20, 1999); Bethel v. Mohegan Tribal Gaming Authority et al., No. GDTC-T-98-105, 1998.NAMG.0000005 ¶¶ 34–35, 42–43 (Mohegan Gaming Disputes Ct. of App., Dec. 14, 1998), *available at* http://www.tribal-institute.org/opinions/ 1998.NAMG.0000005.htm; Long v. Mohegan Tribal Gaming Authority, 25 Indian L. Rptr. 6111, 6112–13 (Mohegan Gaming Disputes Tribal Ct., Dec. 5, 1997); Renecker v. Tulalip Tribes, No. TUL-EMP-11/96-667, 5 Northwest Intertribal Court System App. 1, 4–5 (May 29, 1997).

180. *See, e.g.*, Pawnee Tribe of Oklahoma v. Fransen, 19 Indian L. Rptr. 6006 (Ct. Indian App. 1991).

181. *See, e.g.*, Shippentower v. Confederated Tribes of the Umatilla Indian Reservation of Oregon, 20 Indian L. Rptr. 6026, 6026–27 (Umatilla Tribal Ct. 1993).

182. *See, e.g.*, Fletcher, *supra* note 41, at 293 (noting that "Tribal Courts are inundated with personnel cases" based on due process claims).

183. *See, e.g.*, LITTLE RIVER BAND OF OTTAWA INDIANS ORDINANCES & REGULATIONS, CH. 600, § 2.2 (prohibiting discrimination based on suspect class membership or "other non-merit factors"), *available at* http://www.narf.org/nill/Codes/lrcode/lrcodetoc.htm; SUSANVILLE INDIAN RANCHERIA CONST. & BYLAWS, BYLAWS, art. III, § 4(6) (requiring the tribal council to "[c]ommit to providing an environment that is free from discrimination . . . ."), *available at* http://sir-nsn.gov/onlinedocuments.html; *see generally* Warner v. Ho-Chunk Nation, 34 Indian L. Rptr. 6084 (Ho-Chunk Nation Sup. Ct. 2007) (addressing the possibility that the plaintiff's demotion was a pretext as defined under tribal law without appearing to view the concept of pretext to necessarily be tied to discrimination based on membership in a suspect class); *see also* DiPietro v. Mashantucket Pequot, 34 Indian L. Rptr. 6092 (Mashantucket Pequot Tribal Ct. 2007) (referring to plaintiff's disparate treatment claim without mention of the claim's being based on membership in a suspect class).

184. *See, e.g.*, Bethel v. Mohegan Tribal Gaming Authority et al., No. GDTC-T-98-105, 1998. NAMG.0000005 ¶¶ 34–35, 42–43 (Mohegan Gaming Disputes Ct. of App., Dec. 14, 1998), *available at* http://www.tribal-institute.org/opinions/1998.NAMG.0000005.htm; McCallister v. Spirit Mountain Gaming, Inc., 33 Indian L. Rptr. 6057, 6058–59; Chatterson v. Confederated Tribes of the Siletz Nation of Indians of Oregon, 24 Indian L. Rptr. 6231, 6231–32 (Siletz Ct. App. 1997).

CHAPTER 5

Redwashing History:
Tribal Anachronisms in the
Seminole Nation Cases

KEVIN NOBLE MAILLARD

I n Oklahoma, the Seminole Freedmen and their descendants have struggled for equal recognition and membership rights as Afro-Indian members for more than a century. Freedmen have been marginalized, disenfranchised, expelled, and somewhat restored to and excluded from membership in the Seminole Nation, generating cries of unbridled racism on behalf of "black" members and cries of political sovereignty by "Indian" members. These demands for inclusion raise important questions about interracial memory and selective remembrance.

Both Freedmen and Seminoles view their intertwined history differently, and these understandings emerge in a heated contemporary conflict. This clash stems from the Nation's effort to "redwash" history, that is, to paint a tribal past rooted in indigenous autonomy—one imagined to be completely unblemished by nontribal influences. "There is no Black Seminole," exhorted past Chief Kenneth Chambers.[1] A majority of tribal members concurred with Chambers in the belief that people of African descent had no place in the Seminole Nation. In addition, recent changes in tribal law severed an historic tie between blacks and Indians that had existed since the seventeenth century. In fervent objection to these changes in membership policy, affected bicultural members filed a lawsuit in federal court in an appeal to have their tribal status restored. Roosevelt Davis, "a man as dark as any of African descent,"[2] exemplifies the indefatigable resolve of the Freedmen who balk at such efforts to redefine their identity. "My folks is Indian," he declares; "I'm Seminole."[3]

The yes/no dialectic of tribal membership is now familiar: On one side sits a group of racially mixed people who have been denied inclusion in a group of which they had previously and historically been members. Narrative accounts and subjective beliefs comprise their evidence of membership in addition to treaties and court cases that declare tribal parity between Black and Blood Seminoles. On the opposing side, tribal members and government agents argue that personal stories and historical interpretation fail to qualify the Freedmen as Indians for tribal and federal purposes. This latter group has erected a standard for proving Indian identity that they argue cannot be met by mere desire and belief. Ironically, they require "hard evidence" as proof of membership.

Yet disagreement abounds over what defines "hard evidence." Federal court cases and treaties declare Freedmen as equal members within the Seminole Nation.[4] At the same time, other federal documents portray Freedmen as lacking "Indian blood."[5] This absence of blood precluded them from participating in tribal programs and invoked an atmosphere of differential treatment.[6] Despite compelling claims on both sides for exclusion and inclusion, the Nation relied upon sovereignty to define membership as it chose, without accountability. In response to this assertion of Indian political freedom, the federal government refused to acknowledge the Nation's existence during the policy of exclusion, which included curtailing federal funding and tribal programs.[7] As of October 26, 2003, the Nation restored the Freedmen as members in order to regain federal funding and governmental recognition.[8]

The status of people of African descent in indigenous nations generates important questions about what it means to be Indian. A fair understanding of the Freedmen controversy necessitates an explanation of the historical sites of contention that affect the Freedmen's inclusion in the Nation. This essay critically examines the plasticity of memory—how both parties remember and forget the past in order to justify the present. It directly addresses the radically disparate interpretations of government documents by "Indians" and " Blacks" and how these readings of federal texts are constitutive of Seminole membership. The rigid adhesion to "Indian blood" by tribal governments marks a curious manifestation of sovereignty and self-determination. This dogged claim to autonomy and authenticity exemplifies a misapplied and dangerous discrimination hiding behind the mask of political ideology.

MEMORY IN THE COURTS

Case #1: *U.S. v. Davis*

In 1996, Donnell Davis, a twelve-year-old registered member of the Seminole Nation of Oklahoma, applied to his tribe for a $150 school clothing allowance. As a federally recognized Indian ·tribe, the Seminole Nation provides financial assistance to its members for education, clothing, health care, food, and other family expenses from a federal land claims settlement.[9] Enrolled members may apply to the tribe for such assistance, and the fund distributes aid regardless of one's financial background—membership stands as one of the necessary requirements. The tribe rejected Davis's application because he failed to provide a copy of a Certificate of Degree of Indian Blood (CDIB). Davis and his mother, Sylvia, brought a discrimination suit in federal court against the Bureau of Indian Affairs (BIA).[10] The plaintiffs sought declaratory and injunctive relief on two grounds: that federal officials wrongfully allowed the Seminole Nation to exclude them from participation in its assistance programs and that the BIA improperly refused to issue CDIBs to members of the Freedmen bands.[11]

At trial, Judge Vicki Miles-LaGrange dismissed the case on grounds that the Seminole Nation was an indispensable party and not named as a defendant. This left the plaintiffs in a legal bind—they could not sue the tribe because of the doctrine of sovereign immunity,[12] yet the court ruled that the Nation was an indispensable party. The Davises appealed in 1999, and the Tenth Circuit remanded the case back to the district court to "determine whether, in equity and good conscience, Plaintiffs' Judgment Fund Award claim can proceed in the absence of the Tribe."[13] On remand, the district court dismissed the plaintiff's case once again,[14] which led to a final appeal in 2003, with the Tenth Circuit affirming the lower court's decision. After two appeals and two remands, the Freedmen lost their fight to gain equality within the Seminole Nation.

The Davises' legal problem stems from federal documentation that prioritizes their black ancestry over their tribal identification. As members of the Dosar-Barkus band of the Seminole Nation, they were not eligible for CDIB cards, thus precluding their full membership. Tribal membership rolls define these registered members as black Freedmen: part of the Seminole Nation, but without Indian blood—a necessary standard for full tribal membership.[15]

The plaintiffs object to this racial delineation, which taints the Freedmen's legacy in the tribe. Sylvia Davis argues, "My ancestors came to Indian Territory on the Trail of Tears with these people. This is something that I'm not going to be denied."[16] In the collective memory of Seminole Freedmen, the past prevails as a definitive element in their contemporary identity. This retreat to history reveals an avoidance of discussion about a modern day-to-day connection with tribal affairs or strong identification with Blood Seminoles, who view Freedmens' attenuated connection to the Nation as persuasive justification for their exclusion.

Aside from the Freedmen and Seminoles by blood, money is the third major component of the dispute. To support the contested assistance programs, the Nation draws upon the Judgment Fund, a $56-million-dollar settlement awarded to the Seminoles as payment for aboriginal lands ceded in Florida in 1823.[17] Most Seminole Freedmen did not have CDIB cards and were thus excluded because the BIA required proof of Indian blood to participate in the federal programs. Blood Seminoles capitalized upon this restriction as justification for excluding the Freedmen.[18] In addition to the principal from the Judgment Fund, the Nation has lobbied Congress for additional settlements for mineral rights from oil and gas leases that were taken by the federal government in 1908. The tribe has valued these leases at $95 million, almost twice the amount of the Judgment Fund.[19] Simple mathematics shows that fewer members means larger payouts.[20]

Case #2: *Seminole Nation v. Norton*

While *U.S. v. Davis* generated interest from Freedmen who wanted to reassert their right as tribal members, *Seminole Nation v. Norton* generated greater political and racial strife, which literally threatened the unity of the Seminole Nation. *Norton* concerns the political prerogative of a sovereign Indian nation to determine membership as it chooses. In July 2000, "Blood" tribal members passed a general-vote resolution to dissolve the Freedmen bands, along with a constitutional amendment to restrict membership to those Seminoles who could prove one-eighth degree of Indian blood.[21] One year later, in July 2001, the Nation held an election for chief, and voting officials did not allow Freedmen to participate.[22] Before the onset of a possible multimillion-dollar settlement, Freedmen status and blood dilution did not obscure one's right to vote as a member of the Seminole Nation. With the subject of the vote excluded from the electoral pool, a majority of Blood Seminoles succeeded in excluding the Freedmen from membership.[23] The Nation also held an election for principal and assistant chief, with Ken Chambers and Mary Ann Emarthle defeating Jerry Haney and James Factor in a runoff.[24] Freedmen did vote in this election, but their votes were not counted.[25]

With a majority vote supporting the blood minimum, band dissolution, and chiefs' selection, Seminoles of African descent became pariahs within the Nation.[26] The common link between Africans and Seminoles came to an abrupt halt. Freedmen were no longer considered a part of the Seminole Nation, and tribal privileges that had previously existed disappeared quickly. Freedmen could not vote in elections, hold tribal office, or participate in health, educational, and food benefits.[27] The new government aimed to streamline the tribe into a group of "real" Seminoles, based on a platform of indigenous sovereignty that boasted self-determination and governmental autonomy. Chambers spokesperson Jackie Warledo asked, "The issue is, does our tribal government have the right to govern itself and amend its constitution? The issue still remains one of sovereignty."[28] Her statement invites the question: At what point does sovereignty become a political veil for irreproachable autocracy and questionable ethics?

Accusations of racial injustice and threats of social opprobrium failed to deter the ambition of the new administration, as the protective cloak of sovereignty stood as their argumentative vehicle for discrimination. As a result, the Bureau of Indian Affairs, in a bold move, refused to recognize these elections or the new government without the electoral participation of the Freedmen.[29] The Seminole Nation filed suit in federal court, challenging the BIA's action.[30] In response, the court upheld both the Bureau's dismissal of the tribe's leadership and their repudiation of the constitutional amendment.

SHARED HISTORY, SEVERED TIES

*Historically we have exhaustive historical and anthropological research prov-
ing that African Seminoles not only owned land, but were also essential
chiefs, military and diplomatic leaders, and gave up their lives defending the
Seminole Nation for almost two hundred years. . . . I believe you will find
there can be no doubt that Estelusti (Freedmen) held an equal interest in the
Florida lands they were forced to exchange for their "Trail of Tears" to Indian
Territory.*

—Memorandum of the Dosar-Barkus Band, Feb. 23, 1995[31]

The cases above discuss the roots of the Seminole Nation of Oklahoma, a racially
mixed Indian tribe distinguished by its historic connection to freed blacks and
escaped slaves. Historically, escaped slaves and freed blacks found refuge and freedom
among Indian tribes in Florida, and the Seminoles adopted these emigrants into
their ranks.[32] Freedmen adopted the customs, language, and manners of the Seminoles, and developed extensive agricultural skills, which led the Seminoles to
dependency on the blacks, as argued by Joseph Opala:

> They were the chief agriculturalists of the Seminole Tribe, but they
> were required to turn over only a token share of the harvest as a
> tribute to their Indian masters . . . They owned their homes, carried
> guns, and dressed in the same fashion as the Seminoles. Several
> observers noted that the blacks were better off materially than the
> Indians.[33]

The freedmen lived in harmony with the Seminoles in Florida and accompanied
them during the 1838 removal to Indian Territory (now Oklahoma) after the tribe's
defeat by the United States.[34] This close community of red and black led to extensive intermixing, which created a hybrid group of Seminoles of African and Native
descent. The extent of racial blurring led colonial whites to express disdain at the
inability to classify the Seminoles as simply black or Indian.[35] United States Senator Joshua Giddings described the black Indians as "mostly half breeds, and are rapidly becoming amalgamated with the Indian race."[36]

Contemporary Freedmen's arguments for inclusion rely heavily on the memory of their distant ancestors' indispensability to the tribe. In recounting this past,
Freedmen demonstrate the historic existence of interracial cooperation to counter
the Nation's racially based restrictions. Accounts of military allegiance recur as standard arguments. Prior to Indian Removal, which occurred after 1838 and before
1866, blacks and Indians fought together against American forces that sought possession of Native ancestral lands in south Florida.[37] Seminoles of African descent
played a strong role in helping their comrades resist the encroachment of the gov-

ernment, to such an extent that Thomas Sidney Jesup, an American military commander attested, "This you can be assured is a Negro, not an Indian war."[38] In 1836, General Jesup also wrote, "Throughout my operations I found the negroes the most active and determined warriors; and during the conference with the Indian chiefs I ascertained that they exercised an almost controlling influence over them."[39] Dosar Barkus Band Chief Rosetta Noble Finney champions this history: "After we fought, bled and died right here to help them with their freedom, they want to delete us. We're warriors, we're fighters, we're not going to give up."[40] A similar narrative account of military memory emboldens Sylvia Davis, who claims that her fifth great-grandparents died in the Second Seminole War and that another great-grandparent walked on the Trail of Tears.[41]

Rejected by their tribal cousins as non-Indians, many Freedmen remain dedicated to the steadfast belief that the conjoined past of the Seminoles entitles them to equal membership with Blood Indians. Because their ancestors lived with, intermarried with, and fought with the Seminoles, they consider themselves "real Indians." One Freedman describes the history in the same rhetoric as naturalization: "We were Indian. It's like a white man who grows up in Mexico. He speaks their language, eats their food and thinks the way they do. He's Mexican; we're Indian."[42] Recognition of the shared history would validate the Freedmen's subjective conception of themselves as legitimate members of the Seminole Nation.

Categorical denial by Blood Seminoles of this shared heritage invokes a notable dilemma: Black and Blood Seminole inherit legacies from their ancestors, but only the latter inherit a tribal legacy. An alternative argument may be made that full membership is unnecessary to verify the Freedmen's origins. Tribal ratification of this ancestry would not change what Black Seminoles think about themselves. This may be true, but Freedmen persist in seeking external validation and equal treatment. "We consider ourselves a part of the Seminole Nation. We want no more than what they get. We want to be included as members of the tribe," says Lawrence Cudjoe, a Freedman and former tribal council member.[43] Like other Freedmen, he asserts a personal belief that he deserves membership in the tribe because his parents, grandparents, and great-grandparents viewed themselves as Seminoles. Cudjoe's argument for inclusion finds root in ancestral allegiances to the Nation. In this appeal to the past, he, like other Freedmen, eclipses the doctrine of hypodescent to assert a tribal connection. Another Freedman, Polly Gentry, of Seminole County, Oklahoma, does not allow her African American appearance to sway her from her subjective conception of identity. When interviewed by the *New York Times* in January of 2001, she described herself as "an Indian. A black Indian."[44]

Freedmen's accessions to the past sharply contrast with Blood Seminoles' conception of a rightful claim to membership. Despite historical links between blacks and Indians, Blood Seminoles insist on streamlining the tribe to "real Indians." Former Chief Jerry Haney justified the opposition by arguing that current Freedmen have drifted away from cultural identification as Indians.[45] Blood Indians, comfortably situated within the irreproachable ranks of secure membership, question the authenticity of a faction that rests upon a historical and past, rather than a cultural and current, claim to membership. In the effort to streamline the Nation, a majority of Blood Indians have divested themselves of the burden of history to forge a new, singular identity divorced from the influences of Freedmen. In this rupture with the past, the Seminole Nation redwashes history by turning a blind eye to a substantial portion of its Afro-Indian population.

The Nation's policy of exclusion in part conforms to other patters of interracial denial, yet still differs from previous examples because of the issue of Indian sovereignty. While amnesia towards mixed race may take the form of Chesnutt's familial avoidance, Mrs. Hubbell's testamentary interests, or the Jeffersons' categorical exclusion, the Seminoles, under the umbrella of sovereign immunity, may safely invoke racially restrictive policies. Even though the Nation's policy openly promotes race-based exclusion, the Nation, as a sovereign entity, nevertheless may determine membership as it chooses. Courts refrain from questioning tribes' political policies, particularly regarding membership issues where race and gender would otherwise receive a form of heightened scrutiny. As Justice Marshall opined in *Santa Clara Pueblo v. Martinez*, a tribe should "maintain itself as a culturally and politically distinct entity," a necessity which he saw as incompatible with judicial review.[46] Thus, courts shy away from alarming examples of discrimination in the interest of sensitivity to the autonomy of Indian nations.

Examples of isolated sound bites from Blood Seminoles generate additional sympathy for the Black Seminoles' plight while revealing racially charged sentiments from the other side. Chambers supporter Yogi Harjo curtly revealed, "We're not black—we're Indians . . . We're trying to keep the black people out."[47] A local official in Seminole Indian Country chided Sylvia Davis with outspoken hostility, telling her that the Freedmen needed to "go back to Africa."[48] Davis, a former Freedman representative on the tribal council, attests that at meetings, other members were "calling them animal names, cows, stomping feet, roaring at 'em, telling them to get out."[49] At a curiously titled "Walk for Unity" march organized by Chambers supporters, participants sported T-shirts emblazoned with the slogan, "Seminole by Blood."[50] These examples speak clearly of the racial tension that characterizes this historically Afro-Indian tribe.

This sympathy has its limits, however. Although I stand partial to the merits of Freedmen claims to interracial heritage, I question the singular reliance on the past as a method of establishing a contemporary identity. As a method of legitimating a claim to membership, Freedmen and their representatives recall unified glory days of the past as irreproachable arguments for inclusion. The oral and legal history that they employ undoubtedly prove the existence of an intertwined history, yet these demonstrations fail to trump the Nation's reliance on federal determinations of blood as definitive proof of tribal membership. This bureaucratic hurdle stands as a somewhat necessary evil, yet in this case, the established standard is tautologically

exclusionary. Because Freedmen records remain silent on the subject of actual ancestry, their contemporaries cannot calculate a degree of ancestry that would make
them eligible for membership.

The Blood Seminoles' motivation for denial runs less on suppressing misce-
genistic shame than on capitalizing upon opportunities for economic gain. This
alternative approach considers the subjective eye of memory as the basis for an
authoritative belief in one's Seminole identity. This way, we may witness the formulation of one history, but with two attendant interpretations of its facts. These
opposing versions harbor respectively forgotten and suppressed facts that do not
comport with a unified picture of the past. By expunging the unfavorable and ven-
erating the flattering, narrators conflate fact and fiction to present a contrasting version of the past—an engaging model on which to base the present.

ONE TREATY, TWO VERSIONS

In 1866, the federal government entered into a treaty with the Seminole Nation.
The clause in Article 2 of the 1866 Treaty stands as the Freedmen's crucial argument
for legal and political inclusion:

> [I]nasmuch as there are among the Seminoles many persons of
> African descent and blood, who have no interest or property in the
> soil, and no recognized civil rights, it is stipulated that hereafter these
> persons and their descendants . . . shall have and enjoy all the rights
> of native citizens, and the laws of said nation shall be equally bind-
> ing upon all person of whatever race or color, who may be adopted
> as citizens or members of said tribe.[51]

The treaty flows from an inability to separate black from red and also from the government's acknowledgment of a multiracial tribal population. The federal establishment of interracial citizenship marks the basis for the Black Seminoles' claim to
equal membership in the Nation. From this juridical framework, Freedmen circu-
late an oral history of equality, which stipulates that "as long as grass grows and
water flows . . . if the Indian gets a dollar, the Freedman gets a dollar."[52] According
to these oral, legal, and historical narratives, Freedmen and Blood Seminoles shared
a common history as conjoined citizens of an Indian nation.

For Freedmen, 1866 marks the legal culmination of their long history with the
Seminoles. It also solidifies the alliance of escaped slaves and free blacks with the
accepting Natives. Thus 1866 does not represent a beginning for the Freedmen, but
memorializes a past that until then had not been formalized. From this variegated
background, Freedmen have passed down an oral history securely established in
legal and historical documentation. This notion of equality and partnership establishes a collective consciousness of Freedmen entitlement to inclusion. Seeing them-

selves as kin of the Seminoles, modern-day Freedmen pledge to retain and celebrate this cultural inheritance.

Blood Seminoles maintain that Freedmen overstate the extent of their historical integration into the tribe. Under this interpretation, the 1866 Treaty represents a federal imposition of equal citizenship. The Seminoles recall the past from a paradigm of slavery, precluding consideration of the relationship as one of equality. This interpretation imagines the Nation's past as an agricultural state characterized by black enslavement. Similar to the Indian–black relations of the other Five Civilized Tribes, the Seminoles view themselves as southern slave owners: distinct, separate, and over the Freedmen.[53]

This interpretation insists on the fundamental difference between Black and Blood Seminoles. Former Chief Haney maintains that "they were always looked at as non-Indian. They were always a separate people."[54] Freedmen's slave status, they argue, precluded them from ownership of Seminole lands in Florida. Citing the same treaty that energizes the Freedmen's cause for inclusion, Blood Seminoles insist that Freedmen had "no interest or property in the soil."[55] Because Freedmen did not have citizenship or property before the treaty, they cannot receive contemporary money judgments, which concern compensation for the removal from Florida in 1838.

Freedmen perceive their interest in the soil less literally. Their conception of the past downplays their historical status within the Nation as slaves of the Seminoles. While Freedmen do not deny this fact, they distinguish this form of servitude as "nominal slavery." Lena Shaw, a Freedmen band chief, insists, "In order to keep the American people from taking the people of African descent from them, they decided to say, 'We're your slaves.'"[56] Joseph Opala succinctly explains: "Technically, a Seminole black was owned or controlled by an Indian master who could either free him or bequeath him to a relative at his death. Seminole blacks or 'Indian Negroes,' as the Americans called them at that time, were, however, free in almost every other way."[57] Opala explains further that the Afro-Indians served the tribe as "warriors, war leaders, interpreters, negotiators and spies."[58] Contemporary Freedmen gather this information proudly, insisting that they were not "true" slaves, but "Brothers in Arms" who played a significant historical role in tribal culture and warfare. As argued by Freedmen attorneys and supported by historical treaties,[59] Black Seminoles were a part of the Seminole Nation at the time of removal from Florida, and these "Indian" citizens too experienced the appropriation of lands on the part of the federal government.

The citizenship clause of the treaty does not influence the Nation's arguments for exclusion. Language exists that argues for the inclusion of the Black Seminoles, but the scope of this inclusion remains unsettled. Does the phrase "enjoy all rights" extend to tribal benefits based upon events before 1866? Blood Seminoles, as arbiters of their own membership, emphatically say no. However, it seems counterintuitive that the Freedmen's evidence of legal precedent from the 1866 Treaty fails to convince courts that their claims to inclusion are valid. The treaty provides an external declaration of equality within the tribe that attests to a variegated group whose members may enjoy the benefits and protections of tribal membership. Yet the plain language of the citizenship clause fails to influence the Seminole's interpretation of their tribal history. As law may establish a posterity of knowledge that declares some facts as true and others as false, the language of the treaty stands as a problematic site for the interpretation of past events and their intentions. According to language in the 1866 Treaty, it appears that the Freedmen were unequivocally intended to be absorbed into the body politic. At the same time, however, the membership standards of the Seminole Nation incite racial distinctions that stultify the egalitarian rhetoric of the 1866 Treaty.

If the Seminole Nation is to foment a contemporary tribal identity that balks at its African ties, is it feasible for courts to accept this revised version of history as legitimate? It appears counterintuitive to assert claims of indigenous ancestry as necessary elements of reparations while selectively ignoring the qualifying circumstances. In this partial remembrance of the past, the Nation runs the risk of declaring the 1866 Treaty as coerced, misrepresentative, and therefore illegitimate. Their belief that the treaty was not meant to genuinely extend full tribal citizenship to Freedmen jeopardizes the legal authority of all treaties between Indian nations and the federal government. To reject clear and convincing legal language that records a binding promise between governments can only endanger the historical foundation of federal recognition of the Seminole Nation. The treaty marks a basis for the government's payment for lands ceded in Florida, which provides the monetary foundation of the Judgment Fund. Its legitimacy is only as good as the Seminole's loyalty and faith to abide by it. Selective attention to treaty language not only defies the treaty's purpose, but also compartmentalizes its effectiveness.

DAWES COMMISSION, FREEDMEN OMISSION

In the late nineteenth century, agents of the Unites States government, liberal intellectuals, and Christian missionaries convened annually at Lake Mohonk in upstate New York to propose speeches and papers addressing solutions to the "Indian problem." Overwhelmingly, the majority of participants (collectively known as "Friends of the Indian") believed that the practice of communal living on Indian reservations entrenched indigenous people in pitifully savage ways of living. They perceived this problem as stemming from the absence of the stabilizing providence of property ownership. Their perceived solution, then, was the allotment of land in severalty, known as the General Allotment Act. Each adult citizen of the various Indian nations would receive plots of land—a physical testament to the Indians' "entry wedge" into the mainstream of American culture. Senator Henry Dawes, the primary author of the Act, said at the Fifth Lake Mohonk Conference,

> We had better be employed taking, one by one, all these Indians, and making citizens of them, and planting them on their 160 acres

of land, telling them how to go forth among the white men of this country and learn the ways of the white man, and stand up and take their part in the great work of the governing of the Union.[60]

Reformers hoped that property would eradicate the "savage" ways of Indians and replace them with tenets of civilization. Moreover, property conveyed Lockean values of use and Jeffersonian principles of entitlement through the political and theoretical enchantment of the tilling of land. Through ownership, the reformers sought to replace Indian cultural traditions with American cultural values, in addition to opening up ceded land for white settlement. The reformer Carl Schurtz argued, "They will have advances in immense step in the direction of the 'white man's' way."[61]

The policy of instituting ownership strangely figures as the basis for membership in the Seminole Nation. From the reformers' intentions to supplant Native pathologies with American pragmatism emerges a contemporary paradox that challenges the authority of tribal sovereignty. The Dawes Commission imposed "the ways of the white man" to eradicate Native culture, but this scheme underscored the notion of membership in a particular tribe. Thus, in order to receive the spoils of assimilation, federal officials had to answer the question, "Who is Indian?" Today, their determination of membership stands as the irreproachable basis for tribal sovereignty. From the Seminole Nation's perspective, the proposals from Lake Mohonk do not taint the integrity of tribal history. Exposing this foundation facilitates an analysis of the persistent and divisive anathema of Indian blood.

Formalizing the concept of "Indian blood" underscored bureaucratic and political peculiarities of racial intermixture. Federal bureaucrats, in the task of determining membership, separated the tribe into two groups: Seminoles by Blood and Seminole Freedmen. Generally, applicants of mixed Afro-Indian ancestry became Freedmen, while full-bloods and mixed-blood white Indians claimed membership as Seminoles by Blood. In certain cases, bureaucratic officials placed Black Indians on the Blood rolls, but only after meeting certain requirements. Paradoxically, white European ancestry did not categorically threaten membership as a Blood Seminole.[62] Thus, the Dawes Rolls, as they became known, could declare a person who was one-fourth Indian and three-fourths white as "Indian," while a person three-fourths Indian and one-fourth black received "Freedman" status. Consequently, those declared Freedmen at the time of the Dawes Rolls, even with incontrovertible proof of Seminole blood, were stripped of a juridical nod to their dual heritage, as their record as Freedmen lists no evidence of Indian blood. Under this system, racial identity was not determined by each individual, but rather withstood review by a government agent. At the time of allotment, Seminoles numbered approximately three thousand, one-third being Freedmen. This membership roll, drawn more than one hundred years ago, remains the authoritative source for determining Seminole ancestry.

Although the institutionalization of Indian blood aimed to create order from chaos, this basis of identification gave birth to problematic ambiguities. At present, the membership rolls preclude contemporary Freedmen from obtaining CDIB cards as a result of the failure of the Dawes Commission to recognize the "Indian blood" of their predecessors. This weight of the past on the present forces inheritance of the cultural constraints of previous generations in order to affirm the impossibility of the obvious. While an individual Freedman may claim Seminole ancestry, the authoritative source for determining membership declares otherwise. Even though Freedmen may rally to declare "we know who we are," their foes point to the rolls to protest, "we know who you are not." This purgatory of identity, where subjective beliefs clash with purportedly objective proof, reduces one's conception of personhood to an historic aberration.

The lasting influence of the Dawes Rolls does not appear to dissipate, yet these seemingly overwhelming forces belie a fragile foundation that finds little basis in irreproachable fact. To assume the authority of nineteenth-century racial categorizations without a critical eye to their historic influences presents a case of fatuous objectivism. Accepting without question the racial constructions of Indianness as represented by the Dawes Commission necessarily privileges those who benefit fully from its provisions, while subordinating those who do not. Expectably, those Seminoles whose full access to the tribe is protected and secured by membership rolls pose few questions about the derivation of their inclusion. Those on the margins, however, find themselves at the mercy of antiquated standards that persist in exercising total authority over contemporary manifestations of identity.

A BAD CASE FOR SOVEREIGNTY

The historic delineation of black and red standardizes racial segregation and, to a larger extent, racial supremacy within the Seminole Nation. At the same time, it propels the past into the present by serving as a point of mutual contention. Blood Seminoles wish to uphold the separation of the rolls because they testify to the initial intention of the government to disenfranchise those of African descent. In their view, the rolls clarify the misintentions of the Freedmen in their struggle for inclusion. Conversely, Freedmen point to the racial bias they view as inherent in the rolls and argue for dissolution of the restrictive standards that preclude access to their birthright.

The Nation argues that the determination of membership marks a fundamental right of tribal sovereignty. This assertion of autonomy revels in the fact of exerting power within a political sphere unadulterated by non-Indian influences. Regarding racial exclusion in the tribe, tribal spokesperson Jackie Warledo states, "It should be our decision to make."[63] This image and ideal of sovereignty raises the controversy to a fevered pitch—as accusations of racism and discrimination increase, Blood members turn to this bedrock concept as political refuge. In resisting the encroachment of traditional American jurisprudence, the Seminoles ask outsiders to respect their assertion of self-determination. Their survival and authority, they argue, depends heavily on the ability to maintain a distinct tribal identity at whatever cost. This premium on autonomy receives support from scholars who sharply describe federal intrusion as a "smothering paternalism that could ruin traditional Indian modes of social, political and religious life."[64]

But the question remains of separating oneself from the chain of earlier generations. Tribal leadership cannot persuasively spin the Dawes Rolls as internal articulations of Seminole nationhood. This method of maintaining a past of tribal independence reveals a crucial element of recollection. In order for Seminoles to assess the truth of their history, they must regulate the numerous details of their past. Forgetting and remembering exist as essential functions in the management of memory. As Richard Terdiman argues, "loss is what makes our memory of the past possible at all."[65]

The Nation downplays the impact of the Dawes Rolls on membership and sovereignty. Reformers aggressively advocated their support of assimilation through property. Carl Schurtz, a self-professed "Friend of the Indian," predicted that "[w]hen the Indians are individual owners of property, and as individuals enjoy the protection of the laws, their tribal cohesion will necessarily relax, and gradually disappear."[66] Surely, the goal of solving the "Indian problem" actually weakened the authority of cohesive Indian nations. The historical distinction of the Dawes Act is its paradoxical benevolence of claiming to aid Natives by eroding their societies. Without question, tribal members know its original intentions, and with fewer questions, tribal officials derive authority from it. Thus, the federal plan of eventual dissolution strangely reigns as the primary rubric for inclusion on the membership rolls.

The hyperbolic reaction to what the Seminoles see as encroachment on sovereignty matches the level of irony that makes their self-determination appear completely nonindigenous. The current tribal rubric for membership is fundamentally based on the draftings of the Dawes Commission. Even though the tribe retains the prerogative to determine membership as it chooses, it accepts the external and inorganic racial articulations of the all-white commission. This internalization of extratribal standards marks a peculiar flaw in the Seminoles' logic. The imposed and arbitrary concept of blood quantum as a current variable in the all-important area of membership haunts the idea of an unfettered and sovereign development of nation. The impossibility of avoiding and circumventing the past may be conceded, but this indefatigable specter of government incursion sets up a conundrum of memory.

The journey of the Dawes Act from a destructive policy conceived by whites to an irreproachable doctrine fortified by Indians is nothing short of a remarkable transformation. The Seminoles have overturned the negative aspects of the Dawes Act into an unavoidable tenet of indigenous authenticity. Indian blood remarkably retains its Victorian legitimacy; defined by whites and essentialized by Natives, it persists unchecked. Tribal spokesperson Jackie Warledo declares, "If you are not Seminole by blood, you are not a tribal member. If we can't pass that inheritance to our future, we will cease to be Seminole tribal members."[67] This dogged loyalty to the Dawes Rolls confounds a traditional understanding of self-determination and self-identification. In appropriating the external articulation of membership as a prerogative of sovereignty and a symbol of independence, the Seminoles fail to escape the state power they claim to be sovereign from. Notably, the Nation's redwash of the Dawes Rolls concedes nothing to the influence of "Friends of the Indian." Even though the tribe retains the prerogative to determine membership as it chooses, a twenty-first-century Indian tribe accepts the external and inorganic racial articulations of dead white Victorians in upstate New York.

Notes

1. Andrew Metz, *A Nation Divided*, Newsday, Dec. 22, 2003, at A7.

2. *Id.*

3. *Id.*

4. Treaty with the Seminole, July 19, 1866, U.S.-Seminole Nation, 14 Stats. 755, *available at* http://digital.library.okstate.edu/kappler/Vol2/treaties/sem0910.htm [hereinafter "Treaty"]. *See also* Seminole Nation v. US, 78 Ct.Cl. 455 (1933) (ruling that Seminole Nation cannot exclude Freedmen from receiving benefits).

5. Letter from Patricia Buckley, coordinator of the Seminole Nation Judgment Fund Program, to Sylvia Davis, Jan. 12, 1995 (claiming that Donnell Davis did not have Seminole blood to participate in the Clothing Assistance Program).

6. William Glaberson, *Who is a Seminole, and Who Gets to Decide?* N.Y. Times, Jan. 29, 2001, at A1 (A legal brief written by government attorneys reads: "Presuming the plaintiffs have no Seminole Indian blood, they cannot legitimately claim harm from exclusion of funds to which they are not entitled").

7. For a period, the BIA ceased federal monies to the tribe, and federal courts ordered their accounts frozen. This included a threat to close the Nation's Head Start program. Momentarily, the tribe remains at a standstill, and its government stands reluctant to accept Freedmen as equal members. Yet, as of September 2003, the BIA, circumventing the Seminole Nation, announced its recognition of enrolled Freedmen. *See* Carol Cole, *Haney Recognized as Seminole Chief*, Shawnee News-Star (Okla.), Dec. 6, 2002; *Government Recognizes Seminole Freedmen*, Shawnee News-Star (Okla.), October 26, 2003.

8. *See Government Recognizes Seminole Freedmen, supra* note 7.

9. Aaron Brown, *Judgments: "Brothers" Fighting Over Indian Money: The Right of Seminole Freedmen to a Portion of the Indian Claims Commission Judgment Fund*, 11 Am. Indian. L. Rev. 111, 112 (1983).

10. Davis v. United States, 199 F. Supp. 2d 1164, 1167 (W.D. Okla. 2002).

11. Filed complaint, Davis v. US (on file with author), 16–21.

12. *See* Turner v. United States, 248 U.S. 354, 358 (1919) (*quoted in* Santa Clara Pueblo v Martinez, 436 U.S. 49, 74 (1978) (Indian tribes have long been recognized as possessing the same common-law immunity from suit traditionally enjoyed by sovereign powers)).

13. Davis v. United States, 192 F.3d 951, 961 (10th Cir. 1999).

14. Davis, 199 F. Supp. 1164.

15. Eligibility to receive tribal benefits rests upon whether a person has descended from a member of the Seminole Nation as it existed in Florida in the 1800s. *See* Daniel E. Dawes, *Unveiling the Mask of Interracial Injustice: How the Seminole Nation Implicitly Endorses Dred Scott and Plessy*, 50 How. L.J. 319, 320 (2007).

16. Michael Dodson, *Sylvia Davis*, Shawnee News-Star (Okla.), July 10, 2002.

17. *See* Dawes, *supra* note 15 at 320.

18. Carla Pratt has characterized the exclusion as "not only dignitary or psychological, [but] also economic and educational." *See* Carla Pratt, *Tribes and Tribulations: Beyond Sovereign Immunity and Toward Reparation and Reconciliation for the Estelusti*, 11 Wash. & Lee Race & Ethnic Anc. L.J. 61, 104 (2005).

19. *Mineral Rights Money and Political Realities*, N.Y. Times, Jan. 29, 2001, at A1.

20. *See* John Rockwell Snowden, Wayne Tyndall, David Smith, *American Indian Sovereignty and Naturalization: It's a Race Thing*, 80 NEB. L. REV. 171 (2001) (Full-blood council member Dwayne Miller believes that Freedmen should receive compensation, but from an alternative, nontribal source. In an interview, he conceded, "I don't think they should take it out of *our* money." Glaberson, *supra* note 6 (emphasis added). Other scholars have argued that increased economic potentials of tribes, such as government settlements and Indian gaming, have created an atmosphere of greed. This monetary interest leads tribes to disenroll people to increase benefits for remaining members).

21. Terrioni Williamson, *The Plight Of "Nappy-Headed" Indians: The Role of Tribal Sovereignty in the Systematic Discrimination Against Black Freedmen by the Federal Government and Native American Tribes*, 10 MICH. J. RACE & L. 233, 236 (2004).

22. *Id.*

23. Metz, *supra* note 1 at A7.

24. Lydia Edwards, Protecting Black Tribal Members 26 (2005) (unpublished manuscript, on file with The Berkeley Electronic Press), at http://law.bepress.com/cgi/viewcontent.cgi?article=3098&context=expresso (last visited May 19, 2011).

25. *Id.*

26. *See* Pratt, *Tribes and Tributlations*, *supra* note 18. *See also*, Lydia Edwards, *Protecting Black Tribal Members: Is The Thirteenth Amendment The Linchpin To Securing Equal Rights Within Indian Country?* 8 BERKELEY J. AFR.-AM. L. & POL'Y 122, 131 (2006).

27. *Id.*

28. Ben Fenwick, *Racial Strife Splits American Indian Tribe*, Reuter News, July 5, 2002.

29. *See* Letter from Assistant Secretary of Indian Affairs to Hon. Jerry Haney, Seminole Nation of Oklahoma, Nov. 29, 2002 (on file with author) (The Department of the Interior, refusing to give credence to the restrictive platforms and policies of the Chambers administration, publicly recognized Jerry Haney, chief for twelve years prior to the election dispute, as Principal Chief); Michael Dodson, *Tribe's Old Leadership Won't Back Down*, Shawnee News-Star (Okla.), May 9, 2002 (Still, neither contender conceded defeat, with Chambers recognized by the people and Haney recognized by the government. The conflict escalated to a tense standoff in May 2002, with Chambers refusing to vacate tribal offices after an express order by the tribal court. Judge Phil Lujan froze all tribal assets, giving control to Haney).

30. Seminole Nation v. Norton, 206 F.R.D. 1 (D.D.C. 2001).

31. On file with author.

32. Natsu Saito, *From Slavery and Seminoles to Aids in South Africa: An Essay on Race and Property in International Law*, 45 VILL. L. REV. 1135, 1144 (2000) (Describing that "some of the members of the Seminole nation who were of African descent had never been enslaved, some had escaped from slavery, and others were the descendants of fugitive slaves"). *See also*, DANIEL F. LITTLEFIELD, JR., AFRICANS AND SEMINOLES 5 (1997); KENNETH PORTER, THE BLACK SEMINOLES 4–6 (1996).

33. JOSEPH OPALA, A BRIEF HISTORY OF THE SEMINOLE FREEDMEN 4–5 (1980).

34. Aaron Brown, *supra* note 9 at 122; ANGIE DEBO, AND STILL THE WATERS RUN (1968); GRANT FOREMAN, THE FIVE CIVILIZED TRIBES 255–57 (1934).

35. KEVIN MULROY, FREEDOM ON THE BORDER: THE SEMINOLE MAROONS IN FLORIDA, THE INDIAN TERRITORY, COAHUILA, AND TEXAS 2 (1993).

36. Isa Hamm Bryant, *We Florida*, Palm Beach Post, 1996.

37. Carla D. Pratt, *Contemporary Racial Realities: Tribal Kulturkampf: The Role of Race Ideology in Constructing Native American Identity*, 35 SETON HALL L. REV. 1241, 1246 (2005).

38. Porter, *supra* note 32 at 67.

39. Opala, *supra* note 33 at 10.

40. Kevin Hemstock, *Black Seminoles Detail Struggles of Their Nation*, Jupiter Courier (Fla.), December 3, 1997, at A1.

41. Davis states. "Not a day doesn't go by that I don't think about my ancestors. Sometimes I place myself back in history and think about the hard times they had to suffer through. A lot of them died at an early age. A lot of them died on the Trail of Tears." *Fighting To Be Heard Black Seminoles Sue For A Place In History*, The Sunday Oklahoman, November 7, 1999, at City Edition.

42. Scott Thybony, *Against All Odds*, SMITHSONIAN, August 1991 at 90, 90.

43. Lisa Beckloff, *Tribe's Freedmen Seek Share*, The Daily Oklahoman, Feb. 21, 1992, at 27.

44. Glaberson, *supra* note 6, at A1.

45. *Id.*

46. *Santa Clara Pueblo v. Martinez*, 436 U.S. 49, 72 (1978).

47. Megan Stack, *Tribal Matter is a Rift of Blood*, L.A. Times, May 16, 2002, *at* http://articles.latimes.com/2002/may/16/nation/na-chiefs16/3 (last visited May 19, 2011).

48. Brent Staples, *The Seminole Tribe, Running From History*, N.Y. Times, Apr. 21, 2002, *at* http://www.nytimes.com/2002/04/21/opinion/editorial-observer-the-seminole-tribe-running-from-history.html (last visited May 19, 2011).

49. CBSNews.com, *A Nation Divided*, *at* http://www.cbsnews.com/stories/2002/07/01/60II/main513944.shtml (last visited August 2, 2004).

50. Michael Dodson, *Seminole Tribe Walked for Unity*, Shawnee News-Star (Okla.), Apr. 23, 2002.

51. Treaty, *supra* note 4.

52. Josephine Johnston, *Resisting a Genetic Identity: The Black Seminoles and Genetic Tests of Ancestry*, J. L. MED & ETHICS, 31.2, 264 (Summer 2003) (*quoting* Rebecca Bateman, "We're Still Here": History, Kinship, and Group Identity Among the Seminole Freedmen of Oklahoma (1991) (unpublished Ph.D. dissertation, Johns Hopkins University) (on file with the Schomburg Center for Research in Black Culture, N.Y., N.Y.)).

53. The Five Tribes are: Seminole, Creek, Cherokee, Choctaw, and Chickasaw. Primarily based in Oklahoma, these Indian nations each have Freedmen branches in their membership. Or, considered from another angle, these tribes each practiced various forms of black slavery. As Grant Foreman describes, "through their contact with the white settles and missionaries, ...[they] had acquired the rudiments of the white man's culture and were making amazing progress in civilized ways[.]" Foreman, *supra* note 34 at 17. The Five Tribes were also distinguished by their acceptance of Christianity, the reliance on constitutional government, and frequent intermarriage with whites. *See* Debo, *supra* note 34 at 3–13.

54. Metz, *supra* note 1.

55. Treaty, *supra* note 4 at Article 2.

56. Mary Pierpont, *Jim Crow Legacy Still Disrupts Oklahoma Seminoles*, Indian Country Today, Mar. 5, 2002.

57. Opala, *supra* note 33 at 4–5.

58. Opala, *supra* note 33 at 8.

59. Treaty, *supra* note 51 at Article 2.

60. Henry Dawes, *Defense of the Dawes Act* (1887), *in* FRANCIS PAUL PRUCHA, AMERICANIZING THE AMERICAN INDIANS 101 (1973) [hereinafter "PRUCHA"].

61. *Id.*

62. Pratt, *Kulturkampf*, *supra* note 37 at 1250.

63. *Seminole Nation Postpones Election Until March 23*, Shawnee News-Star (Okla.), Jan. 17, 2002.

64. *See C.L. Stetson, Tribal Sovereignty: Santa Clara Pueblo v. Martinez: Tribal Sovereignty 146 Years Later*, 8 AM. INDIAN L. REV. 139, *152 (1980), available at* http://www.jstor.org/pss/ (last visited May 19, 2011).

65. RICHARD TERDIMAN, PRESENT PAST: MODERNITY AND THE MEMORY CRISIS 22 (1993).

66. Carl Schurz, *Present Aspects of the Indian Problem* (July 1881), in PRUCHA, *supra* note 60.

67. *One Arrest Made, Group Armed*, Shawnee News-Star (Okla.), May 10, 2002.

PART II
TRIBAL COURTS AND
DUE PROCESS

CHAPTER 6

Due Process and the Legitimacy
of Tribal Courts

FRANK POMMERSHEIM

T he essential legitimacy of tribal courts rests in many instances on their ability to provide basic civil rights such as due process within both a legal and cultural context grounded in affirmation and consent. General criticism of this effort arises from two different points of view. One view is that tribal courts do not implement such rights with sufficient vigor; the other view often suggests that the Indian Civil Rights Act of 1968 is yet another federal incursion into tribal sovereignty and thus exacerbates tension created by the due process rights of individuals in the tribal context, where notions of the group are predominant and ascendant. These concerns might be roughly thought of as tribes doing "too little" or being required to do "too much." Though such claims often have a formal and abstract appeal, my experience as a scholar and tribal appellate judge has been that these assessments are decidedly less manifest in the real daily legal and cultural world of tribal life on most reservations.

These criticisms are further minimized when there is a concrete tribal judicial ethos that is sensitive to cultural concerns and that eschews the dangers of either/or dichotomies that posit a false and rigid distinction between the indigenous and dominant, the inside and the outside. The best way to illustrate these points is to review a significant variety of tribal appellate cases that have been disposed of on due process grounds.[1] A good cross-section of issues may be drawn from an examination of cases involving the individual tribal member's relationship to the tribal political process, tribal criminal cases, and civil cases involving non-Indians.

TRIBAL MEMBERS AND TRIBAL POLITICAL AND
ELECTORAL PROCESSES

Many tribal constitutions include specific provisions that recognize certain collective political rights in the tribal polity. The most common of these include the right to recall electoral tribal officials and the right to challenge tribal legislation through the power of referendum.[2] With the growing participation of tribal members in the tribal political process, these provisions have increasingly generated tribal court litigation in which tribal members sue the tribe and tribal officials for failing to implement the right at all or for implementing the right in such a way as to deny them due process under the Indian Civil Rights Act of 1968.[3]

Several cases are illustrative. For example, the Saginaw Chippewa Tribal Court of Appeals confronted the issue of due process in the 2005 case of *Peters v. Saginaw Chippewa Indian Tribe of Michigan*,[4] which involved an attempt by members of the tribe to exercise the tribal constitutional right to remove four members of the tribal council because of their alleged neglect of duty, misconduct in office, and offenses involving dishonesty. The court decided that although it has the authority to pass an ordinance to establish procedural guidelines for implementing the tribal constitutional right of removal, the tribe may not establish rules that impair the substantive contours of the tribal constitutional right of removal. Specifically, the court held that Tribal Ordinance 4 properly allowed the tribal council and the tribal clerk to review the number of signatures on the petitions for removal and their authenticity without violating either the plaintiff's due process guarantees or the tribal constitutional right of removal. However, the court held that Tribal Ordinance 4 could not and did not authorize the tribal council to review the merits of the alleged grounds for removal.[5] The court noted that to permit such review would go too far and would fatally impair the substance of the plaintiff's constitutional right of removal. In this case, due process procedural guidelines were permitted up to the point that the guidelines *impaired* the substantive (constitutional) right of removal.

The Saginaw Chippewa Court of Appeals in this instance achieved a constitutional and due process balance between substance and procedure. Tribal constitutional rights that are substantive in nature, such as the right of removal, require implementation through procedures enacted by the tribal council. Such procedures must be designed to guarantee timeliness and orderly efficiency, but not to interfere with the substantive right itself. Individual and collective political rights that are accorded constitutional status cannot be meaningfully implemented without procedural guidance. Due process permits this regulation up to the point that the procedures impair the substantive (constitutional) right at issue, at which point they must fail.

Similar due process principles of balancing substance and procedure have been implemented in several other tribal court appellate cases involving the tribal constitutional right of referendum. Cases from the Lower Sioux Community of Minnesota Court of Appeals and the Cheyenne River Sioux Tribal Court of Appeals are representative. In the case of *Hernandez v. Lower Sioux Indian Community*,[6] several tribal members sued the tribal council for injunctive relief for its alleged failure to act on several referendum petitions submitted to it in accordance with the tribal constitutional right of referendum. Specifically, Article VII of the Lower Sioux Indian Community Constitution provides that:

> Any exercise of any enumerated powers lodged in the Community
> Council shall be subject to a referendum vote of the people upon a
> written petition signed by not less than 25 percent of the total num-
> ber of voters in the last regular election, provided that not less than 30
> percent of the eligible voters shall vote in any such referendum.

The tribal appellate court held *inter alia* that although the tribal council could (and
did) pass legislation implementing the (tribal) constitutional right of referendum,
such legislation could not infringe the substantive content of the constitutional
right of referendum; to do so would violate both the tribal constitutional right of
referendum itself, as well as the federal statutory right of due process.[7] For example, the tribal ordinance could permissibly allow the tribal council to review the
number of signatures or their authenticity, but not the merits of the referendum
claim itself.[8]

The Cheyenne River Sioux Tribal Court of Appeals dealt with the very same
issue in considerably more detail in the 2005 case of *In the Matter of Tribal Council
Ordinance 14*.[9] In this proceeding, the tribal council had enacted Tribal Council
Ordinance 14 with specific focus on implementing the tribal constitutional right
of referendum found in Article VII of the tribal constitution. Notably, the Cheyenne
River Sioux Tribe Rules of Civil Procedure contain a very innovative provision at
Rule 76(b), which provides the tribal court of appeals with "original jurisdiction
over actions initiated by the Tribal Council to validate any ordinance or resolution
adopted by Tribal Council."[10]

This case was thus in the form of an original proceeding brought in the tribal
court of appeals seeking a ruling on the validity of Ordinance 14. Enacted in 2004,
Ordinance 14 was the first piece of legislation enacted by the tribe to implement
the constitutional right of referendum, which is part of the original constitution
adopted in 1935. Rule 76 requires publication and public notice of the proposed
legislation and permits interested tribal members to file written "answers" that support or oppose the proposed ordinance. The Rule 76 proceeding culminates in a
hearing before the tribal court of appeals to receive "evidence and argument" as to
the validity of the proposed ordinance.

In this case,[11] the tribal court of appeals struck down proposed Ordinance 14
because it denied tribal members due process as required by the Indian Civil Rights
Act of 1968.[12] The specific focus of the court's due process analysis was the element of adequate notice of enacted tribal legislation that would be potentially subject to referendum action under the tribal constitution. Ordinance 14 created a
forty-five-day timeframe within which to challenge proposed tribal legislation
through the power of referendum; it contained no notice element whatsoever.

The tribal court of appeals found that this complete absence of notice violated
the principle of due process embedded in the Indian Civil Rights Act of 1968 and
also (substantively) impaired the constitutional right of referendum. The court—at

the request of all parties including the tribe itself—suggested that an approved due process notice timeframe should run for 180 days and include such express notice requirements as publication in the weekly *Eagle Butte News*, posting the proposed ordinance at the tribal council chambers and at the tribal courthouse, posting the proposed ordinance on the tribe's website, and posting the proposed ordinance in each of the fifteen districts or "precincts" recognized in the tribal constitution.[13]

In addition to such collective political and (tribal) constitutional rights as removal and referendum, there are basic individual rights such as voting and running for office. Accompanying this increase in the civic participation of members within the tribal electoral processes, basic voting issues often arise. For example, in *In re Constitutional Question re: Voting*,[14] a case from the St. Regis Mohawk Tribal Court, a basic question arose about the tribe's preparation of a "voters list" to determine the eligibility of voters in a 1998 tribal election. The tribal constitution specified the conditions for membership, as well as indicated that one of the "rights" of members was "voting in all tribal elections."[15]

Pursuant to a tribal ordinance, the tribal election board was charged with the responsibility of preparing a voters list within ninety days of any regularly scheduled election. Any tribal member whose name did not appear on the list had the right to file a written request for a "personal interview" to review his or her eligibility to vote. A final voters list was to be prepared seventy-two hours prior to the election.

In reviewing a challenge to this process, the court noted that "[t]he Indian Civil Rights Act safeguards those rights restated in entirety in the Constitution of the Saint Regis Mohawk Tribe. Under the Indian Civil Rights Act tribes are prohibited from depriving persons of rights without due process."[16] The court indicated that in the context of the eligibility to vote, due process "requires notice, [and] the right to be heard before an impartial decision maker."[17] The court specifically held that the process of registering to vote and the timeframes for review and challenge were wholly necessary, reasonable, and did not impermissibly burden the tribal constitutional right to vote in a tribal election.

Again we see, as in the previous cases, a rule of reasonableness and context guiding the determination of electoral due process. In so doing, the usual caveat that federal due process standards are not the norm is articulated, but then—presumably because of the absence of tribal precedent—the United States Supreme Court cases are cited as a persuasive, rather than controlling, authority.[18]

TRIBAL CRIMINAL CASES

Though no constitutional principle or federal statute limits tribal criminal jurisdiction over non-Indians, the Supreme Court nevertheless held in the 1978 case of *Oliphant v. Suquamish Indian Tribe*[19] that tribes do not have criminal jurisdiction over non-Indians. This decision appears rooted in the Court's policy preference rather than in any constitutional or statutory mandate.

This case is also significant for its express turn away from a presumption in favor of tribal jurisdiction absent any statute or treaty to the contrary toward a presumption against tribal (criminal) jurisdiction over non-Indians unless there is an express statute (or treaty) to the contrary. The Court posited that the exercise of such nonauthorized criminal jurisdiction over non-Indians was "inconsistent with their [dependent] status."[20]

In the case of *Seymour v. Colville Confederated Tribes*,[21] the defendant raised the issue of due process by claiming that the trial court's failure to grant his motion for a continuance and to order a competency hearing violated the guarantees of due process under both the Colville Tribal Civil Rights Act, § 50.02(h) and the federal Indian Civil Rights Act of 1968, 25 U.S.C. § 1302(8). The Colville Tribal Court of Appeals denied the claim.

The Court expressly held that due process under both the tribal statute and the Indian Civil Rights Act of 1968 is not "coextensive with the notion of constitutional due process."[22] This lower standard was coupled with "deference to the first hand observations of a sitting judge in the Tribal Court."[23] Having (apparently) rejected the applicability of due process, the Court looked to the Colville Confederated Tribes' choice of law provision. The Court chose "state common law" as the proper enumerated "priority'" under the provision and applied a Washington Supreme Court case employing an abuse of discretion standard in competency matters. The Court found no such abuse of discretion and affirmed the defendant's conviction.

The Court eschewed due process analysis altogether because it was apparently persuaded that it did not apply. This finding seems quite circular given that due process existed as a matter of both tribal statutory law and federal statutory law. Due process appears—especially given the ultimate liberty interest of potential incarceration—to have been wrongly removed from the analysis. Although the opinion doesn't say so, this case may represent an attempt by the Colville Tribe Court of Appeals to provide greater deference to the decision of the trial judge as the voice of the "community" rather than to extend the "individual" right of due process.

In another Colville case, *Hall v. Confederated Colville Tribes*,[24] the court of appeals in a short opinion held that there were no due process violations in a criminal case in which the trial court permitted one of the tribe's witnesses to testify telephonically, but did not allow one of the defendant's witnesses to do so. The court rested its decision on a finding that the defendant had failed to subpoena the witness for trial in a timely manner, especially when the defendant had had at least seventeen days' notice prior to trial that said individual was a potential witness.

As in the previous case, the court employed an abuse of discretion standard of review. It found no abuse of discretion, noting that the trial judge's decision was well within the parameters of trial management and that the decision was not manifestly unreasonable.[25] In addition, the court noted that tribe's telephonic witness had been properly subpoenaed.[26] With its focus on reasonableness, the analysis is on surer due process grounds than the *Seymour* case.

The Hopi Court of Appeals decision in the case of *Nevayaktewa v..The Hopi Tribe*[27] provides a very thoughtful analysis of due process in the context of both the Indian Civil Rights Act of 1968 and Hopi tradition and custom. In this case, the defendants were convicted at a bench trial of the illegal possession of marijuana, a violation of provisions in the Hopi Criminal Code.

The defendants raised a number of issues on appeal including a vague equal protection claim and a search and seizure issue. The essence of the due process claim was that the bench trial in the case lacked "fundamental fairness" in that the court admitted into evidence material that was "willfully altered" by the arresting officer. The court of appeals rather easily rejected this assertion because no such argument pertaining to tainted evidence was proffered, much less rejected, by the trial court.

The court did, however, further extend and explicate its interpretation of due process. The court stated that basic (civil) due process requires notice and the opportunity to be heard, but, perhaps more importantly, "[b]ecause of its basis in Hopi custom and tradition, fundamental fairness must always be determined within the context of Hopi values."[28]

The court went on to note that in the context of criminal cases, there can be certain "trial defects" that do not meet the test of fundamental fairness. Here the court cited with approval such well-known Supreme Court cases as *Cooper v. Oklahoma*,[29] *Mooney v. Holohan*,[30] *Wainwright v. Greenfield*,[31] and *Chambers v. Mississippi*.[32] The court's citation of those cases reveals a laudable convergence of fundamental fairness and due process within federal and tribal, national and local, and new and old realms of jurisprudence and decision-making.

In the case of *Means v. District Court of the Chinle Judicial District*,[33] the Navajo Supreme Court held that Russell Means, the well-known Oglala Sioux activist, was subject to the criminal jurisdiction of the Navajo Nation despite the fact that Mr. Means was not an enrolled member of the Navajo Nation.[34] The Navajo Supreme Court decided that Mr. Means was subject to the Navajo criminal law because of pertinent language in the Treaty of 1868 and his status as a *hadane* or in-law under Navajo common law.

Though the court's decision focuses largely on Mr. Means's equal protection claim under the Indian Civil Rights Act of 1968, 25 U.S.C. § 1302(8), the court does observe in passing that Mr. Means would not be denied any fundamental right under the Indian Civil Rights Act or the United States Constitution. For example, if Mr. Means were indigent, counsel would be appointed for him, and he would be "entitled to a jury composed of a fair cross section of Navajo Nation population, including non-Indians and non-member Indians."[35] This latter issue, relevant to jury composition, is a classic situation involving due process.[36]

Due process is likely the most flexible of the guarantees in the Indian Civil Rights Act, as well as in the United States Constitution. A good example of such flexibility is found in the case of *Fort Peck Tribes v. Azure*,[37] a 1989 case from the Fort Peck Court of Appeals. In this case, the tribes as appellant challenged an *ex parte* order issued by Chief Judge William McClammy to disqualify Judge Violet Hamilton, who was assigned as the trial judge in this matter.

The tribe apparently had not been served with the motion for disqualification and was not aware of the proceeding until it was served with the *ex parte* order. Upon service of the order, the tribe filed an interlocutory motion for a hearing on the disqualification order. The core of the *Tribes* claim was that such an *ex parte* order violated due process under the Indian Civil Rights Act of 1968.[38] The court easily found that the lack of notice and opportunity to be heard constituted a basic violation of due process. Although the court's reasoning is more conclusory than analytical, quibbling with the result is difficult.

The most interesting part of this case is that the Indian Civil Rights Act is expressly made part of the tribal code of ethics for judges and justices of the Fort Peck Tribal Court, specifically at Canon 3(A)(4):

> A judge should accord to every person who is legally interested in
> a proceeding, or his lawyer or advocate, the full right to be heard
> under the Code, the Indian Civil Rights Act, and any other related
> source of law.[39]

The question of whether the tribe itself is entitled to due process under the Indian Civil Rights Act appears dubious. Yet when that right is incorporated into a tribal code of ethics to provide "every person who is legally interested in a proceeding, or his lawyer or advocate the full right to be heard," the ethics code likely intends that exact result. Without such an interpretation, the tribe and its concern for community security might be unduly disadvantaged.

DUE PROCESS AND NON-INDIANS
IN TRIBAL COURT

Although by its title, the Indian Civil Rights Act of 1968 would appear to apply only to Indians, that is not the case. The actual text of the statute states that "no tribal government shall deny to *any person*" (emphasis added) the enumerated rights set out in the law. As a result, non-Indians may assert the protections—including due process—contained in the statute. The universal and inclusive reach of the statute is significant in ensuring that the guarantees are not limited to some individuals and groups and not others.

A particularly poignant decision in this regard is the case of *Bloomberg v. Dreamer*.[40] In this case, the Tribal Council of the Oglala Sioux Tribe voted to exclude Mr. Bloomberg, a non-Indian, from the Pine Ridge Reservation. No notice or opportunity to be heard was provided to Mr. Bloomberg. As a result, Mr. Bloomberg sued the tribal council in tribal court, asserting that failure to provide notice or an opportunity to be heard violated his due process rights under the Indian Civil Rights Act of 1968.[41]

The Oglala Sioux Supreme Court decided in favor of Mr. Bloomberg, holding that due process requires notice and a hearing before attempting to remove anyone from the Pine Ridge Reservation. Though it largely parallels the mainstream jurisprudence of due process, this decision insightfully notes that due process is an essential element of tribal tradition and custom as well:

> [i]t should not be for the Congress of the United States or the federal court of appeals to tell us when to give due process. Due process is a concept that has always been with us. Although it is a legal phrase and has a legal meaning, due process means nothing more than being fair and honest in our dealings with each other. We are allowed to disagree. . . . What must be remembered is that we must allow the other side the opportunity to be heard.[42]

In *Bank of Hoven v. Long Family Land and Cattle Co.*,[43] a non-Indian bank made a number of specific due process–like challenges to events that transpired in the tribal court's handling of a civil matter involving the bank and the Long Family Land and Cattle Co. Specifically, in this somewhat complicated case, the Long Family and its Indian-controlled corporation brought suit against the Bank of Hoven in the Cheyenne River Sioux Tribal Court, seeking a restraining order to prevent the bank from selling reservation land once owned by the Long Family and currently leased to the Longs with an option to purchase. Though the restraining order was denied, the Longs amended their complaint to include several causes of action against the bank, including seeking damages and other relief. The bank counterclaimed, seeking eviction of the Longs and other relief. After a two-day jury trial, the jury returned a verdict of $750,000 in favor of the plaintiffs.[44]

Both sides appealed, which brought the bank's due process–like claims into view. The bank neither used the phrase "due process" nor cited the Indian Civil Rights Act of 1968. The first due process–like claim involved an assertion that one of the Long family's causes of action, which alleged discrimination by the bank, did not exist as a matter of tribal law and was impermissibly premised on federal law. The second due process–like claim was that the all-Indian jury was "completely enflamed" by the discrimination claim against the non-Indian bank.[45]

The Cheyenne River Sioux Tribal Court of Appeals ruled against the bank by using the following rationale: Though it agreed that there was no tribal law discrimination cause of action based on federal law, the court stated that there was such a tribal cause of action grounded in tribal tradition and custom—that is, tribal common law. The court further indicated that there was no evidence introduced at the trial to suggest that the all-Indian jury was, in fact, "completely enflamed." Indeed, the bank admitted at oral argument that "it did not challenge any juror for cause, did not challenge the jury panel as a whole because it did not contain any non-tribal members and perhaps most importantly, did not request that the trial court use its discretionary power under Sec. 1-6-1(2) of the Tribal Code to 'adopt procedures whereby non-enrolled Indians and non-Indians may be summoned for jury duty in cases in which one or more non-Indian parties are involved.'"[46]

After this appeal, which fulfilled the exhaustion of tribal court remedies requirement of *National Farmers Union Ins. Cos. v. Crow Tribe of Indians*,[47] the bank appealed to federal court, asserting that tribal court did not have subject matter jurisdiction over the discrimination claim against the bank and, even if it did, the bank was denied due process pursuant to the Indian Civil Rights Act of 1968, 25 U.S.C. § 1302(8).

The district court granted summary judgment in favor of the Long family and the bank appealed to the Eighth Circuit. The Eighth Circuit ruled "that the tribal court of appeals appropriately upheld jurisdiction on the basis of tribal rather than federal law."[48] More importantly, for this chapter's purposes, the court expressly held that there was no denial of due process to the bank. "In this case," the court opined, "there was no deficiency in notice or opportunity to defend sufficient to make out a due process violation."[49] In addition the court affirmed the tribe's use of its common law to recognize a cause of action and stated that there was "no evidence" to support the bank's assertion that it was treated unfairly by an all-Indian jury.[50]

The bank abandoned its due process claim in its appeal to the United States Supreme Court, presumably doing so because it realized the unlikelihood of success. Nevertheless, the bank did prevail in the Supreme Court on its jurisdictional claim that the tribal court lacked jurisdiction over matters involving the sale of fee land by a non-Indian bank to tribal members.[51]

Two final cases illustrate the reach of due process—albeit unsuccessfully—in civil matters involving non-Indians. One is a basic case involving the alleged failure of a tenant to pay rent and the other is the more controversial decision to exclude a non-Indian from the Hopi Reservation.

In the 2005 case of *Monette v. Schlenvogt*,[52] the Turtle Mountain Court of Appeals held it a violation of due process under the Indian Civil Rights Act of 1968 for the trial court to permit entry of a default judgment in favor of a non-Indian landlord plaintiff against a tribal member defendant for the alleged failure to pay rent due and owing. Due process was not provided when the record failed to indicate that service of process was made against the defendant tribal member.

It is significant to note that in this case the court of appeals pointed out that the Indian Civil Rights Act had been expressly incorporated into the Turtle Mountain Constitution. Specifically, Article 14, Section 3a states:

> the judicial branch of government of the Turtle Mountain Band of Chippewa Indians shall have jurisdiction . . . to ensure due process, equal protection of rights arising under the Indian Civil Rights Act, as amended, for all persons and entities subject to the criminal and civil jurisdiction of the Turtle Mountain Tribe.[53]

Thus, due process was not only a federal statutory right, but also a tribal constitutional right. Such a situation offers striking evidence of mutual commitment to a premier legal value.

In the 2002 case of *Monestersky v. The Hopi Tribe*,[54] the Hopi Court of Appeals ruled that an order of exclusion issue by the chairman of the Hopi Tribe against a non-Indian did not violate due process standards as guaranteed by the Indian Civil Rights Act of 1968. The analysis in this case is particularly thoughtful, especially in light of growing concerns about the general trend of many tribes to use the remedy of exclusion in a variety of circumstances.[55]

To begin its opinion, the court established the foundation that the Hopi Tribe (and all Indian tribes) possessed "inherent power to exclude non-members as an exercise of their sovereign power in order to protect the health and safety of tribal members."[56] The court then went on to discuss Ordinance 46, which implemented this inherent power. Ordinance 46 was specifically designed to protect "tribal members, lands, resources."[57]

Ordinance 46 further states the Hopi Reservation is "closed and shall be for the exclusive use and benefit of members of the Hopi Indian Tribe."[58] Grounds for the exclusion of nonmembers include the violation of any tribal or federal law, as well as the much broader ground of entering and remaining upon a closed portion of the reservation.

Ordinance 46 also establishes a procedure with which to effectuate exclusion. Though an action of exclusion may be initiated by the tribal chairman, the targeted individual is entitled to notice and administrative hearing, including the right to be present and to cross-examine witnesses. All of these requirements were satisfied in the instant case. The court made it clear in this regard that admissibility of hearsay evidence was not prohibited as long as there was "other sufficient evidence to support the findings"[59] and the trial court had not committed any abuse of discretion.

Interestingly, the court made it clear that its review of procedural adequacy was not really necessary in that the non-Indian appellant in this case had not suffered any liberty or property deprivation, which is the necessary predicate to invoke a due process violation of the Indian Civil Rights Act in the first instance. Because the non-Indian individual was not a resident of the Hopi Reservation and no property was taken from her, she suffered no loss of liberty or property and, therefore, no substantive deprivation had even triggered the Indian Civil Rights Act concerns.[60] The analytical rigor and sophistication of the opinion as a whole is of the highest order.

CONCLUSION

As these diverse cases illustrate, the due process requirement of the Indian Civil Rights Act of 1968 has met with significant approval in a wide range of tribal court jurisprudence. This is so for two different, but overlapping reasons: First, the legal concept of due process readily translates into the basic notion of essential fairness.

Such a ubiquitous value easily migrates between cultures in both directions. Second, just as it has proved flexible and evolving within a national (and state) jurisprudence, due process has demonstrated a similar flexibility and arc of development within tribal court jurisprudence. This convergence is rooted in mutual respect and commitment to essential values.

NOTES

1. It is important to note in this regard that many tribes enacted due process guarantees within their tribal constitutions both before and after the passage of the Indian Civil Rights Act of 1968. Thus it is often true that the guarantee of due process is a tribal constitutional right in addition to being a federal statutory right. *See, e.g.*, ROSEBUD SIOUX CONST. art. X, § 3 (Bill of Rights); MISSISSIPPI BAND OF CHOCTAW CONST. art. X, §.1(h).

2. *See, e.g.* CHEYENNE RIVER SIOUX TRIBE CONST. art.VII, § 1; CROW TRIBAL CONST. art. IX, § 1.

3. 25 U.S.C. § 1302(8).

4. Peters v. Saginaw Chippewa Indian Tribe of Michigan, No. 04-CA-1019, slip op. (Saginaw Chippewa Indian Tribe of Michigan Mar. 8, 2008).

5. The trial court had interpreted Tribal Ordinance 14 as authorizing the tribal council to review the *merits* of the submitted removal petitions. *Id.* at 4–5.

6. Hernandez v. Lower Sioux Indian Community, No. 06-01, slip op. (Lower Sioux Indian Community in Minnesota 2006).

7. 25 U.S.C. § 1302(8).

8. *Id.* at 9–10.

9. In the Matter of Tribal Council Ordinance 14, No. 04-001-A, slip op. (Cheyenne River Sioux Tribal App. Ct. Sept. 24, 2004).

10. *Id.* at 1 n.1.

11. *Id.* at 3–4.

12. 25 U.S.C. 1302(8).

13. *Id.* at 4.

14. *In re* Constitutional Question re:Voting, 1998 NASR 0000001 (Saint Regis Mohawk Sept 10, 1998), http://www.tribal-institute.org/opinions/1998.NASR.0000001.htm.

15. The specific criteria for voting included the necessity to be eighteen years of age, reside on the United States side of the Canada/United States border, and be an enrolled member of the Saint Regis Mohawk Tribe. The residency requirement was struck down in earlier tribal court litigation. Thomas v. Saint Regis Mohawk Tribal Council, No. 96CI0080, 1996.NASR.0000004 (Saint Regis Mohawk June 06, 1996) (VersusLaw).

16. *Constitutional Question*, 1998.NASR.0000001, at para. 40.

17. *Id.*

18. *See id.* at para. 40 (citing Grannis v. Ordean, 234 U.S. 385 (1914) and Armstrong v. Manzo, 380 U.S. 545 (1962)).

19. Oliphant v. Suquamish Indian Tribe, 435 U.S. 191 (1978).

20. *Id.* at 208.

21. Seymour v. Colville Confederated Tribes, 3 CCAR 11, 23 ILR 6008, 1995.NACC.0000001 (Colville Confederated Nov.17, 1995) (VersusLaw).

22. *Id.* at n.5.

23. *Id.*

24. Hall v. Colville Confederated Tribes, 4 CTCR 107, 2003.NACC.0000009 (Colville Confederated Sept. 03, 2003) (VersusLaw).

25. *Id.* at para. 20.

26. *Id.* at para. 23.

27. Nevayaktewa v. Hopi Tribe, No. 97AC000004, 1998.NAHT.0000019 (Hopi 03/20/1998), http://www.tribal-institute.org/opinions/1998.NAHT.0000019.htm.

28. *Id.* at para. 47.

29. Cooper v. Oklahoma, 517 U.S. 348 (1996) (holding that Oklahoma law establishing presumption that a defendant is competent to stand trial unless he proves incompetence by clear and convincing evidence violates due process).

30. Mooney v. Holohan, 294 U.S. 103 (1935) (holding that due process "[is not] satisfied by mere notice and hearing if a state has contrived a conviction through the pretense of a trial which in truth is but used as a means of depriving a defendant of liberty through a deliberate deception of court and jury by the presentation of testimony known to be perjured").

31. Wainwright v. Greenfield, 474 U.S. 284 (1986) (holding that the use of petitioner's silence after being arrested and read Miranda warnings as evidence of his sanity violated due process).

32. Chambers v. Mississippi, 410 U.S. 284 (1973) (holding that preventing a defendant from cross-examining a witness whom the defendant called to the stand and who had orally confessed on three occasions to committing the crime for which the defendant was being prosecuted violated due process).

33. Means v. District Court of the Chinle Judicial District, No. SC-CV-61-98, 26 ILR 6083 (Navajo 05/11/1999), http://www.tribal-institute.org/opinions/1999.NANN.0000013.htm.

34. Note that this was a 1999 decision, arguably governed by *Duro v. Reina*, 495 U.S. 676 (1990) (holding that tribes do not have criminal jurisdiction over nonmember Indians). *Duro* was subsequently overturned by an amendment to the Indian Civil Rights Act of 1968, 25 U.S.C. § 1301, and upheld in *Lara v. United States*, 541 U.S. 193 (2004). *See also* Means v. Navajo Nation, 432 F.3d 924 (9th Cir. 2005) (rejecting the defendant's claim that the prosecution in the tribal court violated his due process rights under ICRA and his due process and equal protection rights under the US Constitution).

35. *Means*, 26 ILR 6083 at n.11.

36. *See, e.g.* Peters v. Kiff, 407 U.S. 493 (1972); Taylor v. Louisiana, 419 U.S. 522 (1975).

37. Fort Peck Tribes v. Azure, No. 081, 1989.NAFP.0000016 (Fort Peck 10/03/1989), http://www.tribal-institute.org/opinions/1989.NAFP.0000016.htm.

38. The court did not address the issue of whether the tribe itself, as opposed to individual persons, could be denied due process. It seems unlikely that the tribe could deny itself due process. *Id.*

39. *Id.* at para. 43.

40. Bloomberg v. Dreamer, Oglala Sioux Civ. Ap. 90-348 (1991).

41. 25 U.S.C. § 1302(8).

42. *Id.* at 5–6.

43. Bank of Hoven v. Long Family Land and Cattle Co., Slip Opinion, No. 03-002-A-4, R-120-99 (Cheyenne River App. Ct. Nov. 22, 2004), http://www.narf.org/sct/plainsvlong/crst_tcoa/crst_court_of_appeal_opinion.pdf.

44. *Id.* at 4.

45. *Id.* at 14.

46. *Id.*

47. National Farmers Union Ins. Cos. v. Crow Tribe of Indians, 468 U.S. 1315 (1985).

48. Plains Commerce Bank v. Long Family Land and Cattle, 491 F.3d 878, 888 (8th Cir. 2007).

49. *Id.*

50. *Id.*

51. Plains Commerce Bank v. Long Family Land and Cattle Co., 128 S.Ct. 2709 (2008).

52. Monette v. Schlenvogt, No. TMAC 04-2021, 2005.NATM.0000003 (Turtle Mountain 03/31/2005), http://www.tribal-institute.org/opinions/2005.NATM.0000003.htm.

53. *Id.* at para. 24.

54. Monestersky v. Hopi Tribe, No. 01AP000015, 2002.NAHT.0000003 (Hopi 06/27/2002), http://www.tribal-institute.org/opinions/2002.NAHT.0000003.htm.

55. *See, e.g.*, Patrice Kunesh, *Banishment as Cultural Justice in Contemporary Legal Systems*, 37 N.M. L. REV. 85 (2007).

56. *Monestersky*, 2002.NAHT.0000003, at para. 18 (citing *Merrion v. Jicarilla Apache Tribe*, 102 U.S. 894 (1982), *Babbitt Ford, Inc. v. Navajo Indian Tribe*, 710 F.2d 894 (9th Cir. 1983), and *Hardin v. White Mountain Apache*, 779 F.2d 476 (9th Cir. 1985)).

57. *Id*. at para. 19.
58. *Id*.
59. *Id*. at para. 50.
60. The court, however, did make it quite clear *in dicta* that the exclusion of a tribal member and the attendant loss of the right to even be on the reservation would likely constitute an adequate "liberty" deprivation with which to invoke substantive due process concerns under the Indian Civil Rights Act. *id*. at para. 32 (citing Poodry v. Tonawanda Band of Seneca Indians, 85 F.3d 874 (2nd Cir. 1996)).

CHAPTER 7

The Meaning of Due Process
in the Navajo Nation

PAUL SPRUHAN

H ow should a tribal court apply the concept of *due process*? Whether required by the Indian Civil Rights Act or by a tribal bill of rights, or applied as a matter of tribal common law, the term *due process* itself has no self-evident meaning. Whether a person has an interest that requires the protection of due process, and what process is due for that interest, depends upon the norms and values of the particular jurisdiction. How should tribal courts determine what interests require due process and, once identified, decide what process is appropriate? Should a tribal court simply adopt federal interpretations of due process, applying US Supreme Court precedent and tests, and merely predict what the outcome would be were a federal court to rule on the issue? Or should a tribal court attempt to find unique tribal ways of thinking about due process, developing its own jurisprudence based on the customs, traditions, and public policy of the tribe regardless of federal rulings?

These questions have driven the evolution of the concept of due process in the Navajo Nation, as its courts have been consistent with Navajo principles in giving meaning to the vague term, while considering and even sometimes incorporating federal approaches. Embedded in the Indian Civil Rights Act (ICRA) and the Navajo Nation's own Bill of Rights (separately adopted by the Navajo Nation Council), due process has been the subject of important cases over the life of the Navajo Nation court system. From the creation of the Navajo Court of Appeals, to the modern Navajo Supreme Court, the Navajo Nation has moved from a blanket adoption of federal concepts of due process, to a sophisticated and unique synthesis of federal concepts with Navajo principles. This unique approach ultimately transcends federal definitions of due process, in most cases recognizing a broader right than allowed by the federal courts. In this short essay, I discuss the Navajo approach to due process as a potential model for other tribal courts seeking to reconcile the rights conferred by the Indian Civil Rights Act with the fundamental values and principles embedded in tribal law.

The evolution of due process within the Navajo Nation is best understood in the context of the evolution of the Navajo court system itself. Until 1958,[1] the federal government operated a Court of Indian Offenses within the Navajo Nation. As a federal court, the Court of Indian Offenses was directly subject to the US Constitution and had to honor an individual's constitutional right to due process. The Nation took over the courts in 1958 by creating the Navajo Nation Judicial Branch, whose power derived from tribal law, not federal law.[2] Interestingly, according to the resolution that created the judicial branch, the council created tribal courts in part because elected federal judges were allegedly failing to uphold the people's rights, provoking the assertion of state court jurisdiction.[3]

Though the courts became Navajo tribal courts, the Navajo Nation Council retained the trappings of the prior federal court system, essentially adopting the Court of Indian Offenses' structure and procedures wholesale.[4] The courts operated, and continue to operate, on a plaintiff-versus-defendant adversarial model with Anglo-American pleading and procedure.[5] The council also established a court of appeals made up of a chief justice and two district court judges appointed by the chief to sit on a case.[6] Appeals were heard *de novo*.[7] As with the trial court, the court of appeals adopted the structure of an American appellate court, including a *stare decisis* system of precedent.[8]

What the Navajo courts were doing before the passage of the Indian Civil Rights Act in 1968 remains unknown, as opinions only began to be published in the following year. However, a prominent federal pre-ICRA case offers insight into at least one Navajo judge's view of due process. In *Native American Church v. Navajo Tribal Council* (1959), members of the Native American Church sued the Navajo Nation in federal district court alleging several violations of their civil rights after a crackdown on the church by the Nation's government.[9] The church members claimed that the Nation violated their freedom of religion, and, importantly, their right to due process when a Navajo judge refused to grant a jury trial or attorney in a tribal criminal proceeding.[10] The federal district court dismissed the case on the freedom of religion issue, but it is unclear from the appellate opinion what ruling, if any, the district court made on the due process issue.[11] The Tenth Circuit, following the US Supreme Court's ruling in *Talton v. Mayes*,[12] held that the Navajo Nation courts were not subject to constitutional restrictions, and that therefore the plaintiffs could not bring an action alleging a violation of federal civil rights.[13] The holding, and the US Supreme Court's later holding barring similar federal claims under the Indian Civil Rights Act in *Santa Clara Pueblo v. Martinez*,[14] shielded the Navajo courts from direct federal scrutiny and facilitated the development of unique Navajo jurisprudence on the meaning of due process. With the freedom to develop unique Navajo law on individual rights, the concept of due process has evolved significantly.

There were no explicit internal limits to Navajo government power over individuals until 1967, when the council passed the Navajo Bill of Rights one year before the Indian Civil Rights Act.[15] Interestingly, the council did not call its resolution "the Bill of Rights," but instead "A Declaration of Human Rights."[16] The term "Navajo Bill of Rights" is now used to describe the codified law.[17] The original Navajo Bill of Rights did not recognize a separate right to due process.[18] It did include an establishment clause, something Congress did not mandate in the Indian Civil Rights Act.[19] It also included rights to freedom of speech and freedom of the press, double jeopardy, and other rights clearly modeled after US constitutional rights.[20] Why the council omitted a due process right is unclear from the available record. The minutes of the council discussion of the resolution suggest that the sponsors were primarily concerned with freedom of religion and the rights of defendants in criminal proceedings.[21] Given that focus, the council may have considered due process rights to be already embedded in other stated rights, thus obviating the need to articulate a separate right.

Absent a direct Navajo legislative recognition of a due process right, early decisions by the Navajo Court of Appeals adopted and applied due process in line with ICRA[22] following federal interpretations of the scope of the right.[23] There was no indication that the concept of due process had any unique Navajo meaning; however, during this time, the Navajo courts, particularly the Window Rock District Court under Judge Tom Tso, did begin to recognize a role for Navajo custom and tradition, applying Navajo values and beliefs to declare a unique "Navajo common law."[24]

Two legislative events in the 1980s changed the landscape of the Navajo legal system. In 1985 the Navajo Nation Council reformed the judicial branch by abolishing the Navajo Court of Appeals and establishing a Navajo Supreme Court with three permanent justices.[25] In 1986 the council amended the Navajo Bill of Rights and for the first time recognized a right to due process.[26] Significantly, on the same day, the council explicitly waived the Nation's sovereign immunity for violations of the Navajo Bill of Rights.[27]

The new Navajo Nation Supreme Court infused its discussion of due process and other rights with unique Navajo principles derived from Navajo common law. The court articulated a distinct jurisprudence of "Navajo due process," which originates, according to the court, not from any congressional mandate in ICRA or even from a council mandate from the Navajo Bill of Rights.[28] According to the court, Navajo justice had always recognized and protected the right of people to be heard on matters affecting them:

> The concept of due process was not brought to the Navajo Nation by the Indian Civil Rights Act, 25 U.S.C. § 1302(8), or the Navajo Nation Bill of Rights, 1 N.T.C. § 3. The Navajo people have an established custom of notifying all involved parties in a controversy and allowing them, and even other interested parties, an opportu-

nity to present and defend their positions. This custom is still followed today by the Navajo people in the resolution of disputes.
When conflicts arise, involved parties will go to an elder statesman,
a medicineman, or a well-respected member of the community for
advice on the problem and to ask that person to speak with the one
they see as the cause of the conflict. The advisor will warn the
accused of the action being contemplated and give notice of the
upcoming group gathering. At the gathering, all parties directly or
indirectly involved will be allowed to speak, after which a collective
decision will be made. This is Navajo customary due process and it
is carried out with fairness and respect. The heart of Navajo due
process, thus, is notice and an opportunity to present and defend a
position.[29]

Though articulating a concept of due process similar to that recognized by the US
Constitution—focused, centrally, on a litigant's right to notice and opportunity to
be heard—the court identified the source of the right as transcending statutory
mandates. Instead, the notion of due process articulated by the court reflects the
preexisting values of the Navajo people applied to the problems of the modern day.

With this recognition of "Navajo due process," the Navajo Supreme Court
synthesized federal notions of due process with a Navajo sense of fundamental fairness, deviating from federal approaches when considered appropriate. Application
of the Indian Civil Rights Act practically disappeared, as the court focused on internal Navajo law to define individual rights. In subsequent cases, the court described
due process as "fundamental fairness in a Navajo cultural context,"[30] and stated that
it would define due process "in light of the enjoyment and protection of rights by
all Navajos."[31] The court also stated that claims to due process "are subject to considerations of the community good and Navajo perceptions of moral right."[32] The
court distilled the basic right of due process to mean "each litigant shall have the
opportunity to be heard at a meaningful time in a meaningful way."[33]

As defined through these principles, the court carved out its own conception
of due process by explicitly transcending federal law. For instance, in *Atcitty v. District Court for the Judicial District of Window Rock* (1996), the court recognized a right
to due process for recipients of public housing benefits and explicitly declined to
apply federal rulings to the contrary.[34] Rejecting an argument based on US Supreme
Court case law that applicants for government benefits have no property interest that
required due process protections, the court stated that there was a sufficient property interest based on Navajo concepts of fairness and egalitarianism because
"[d]istributive justice requires sharing of Navajo Nation resources among eligible
applicants."[35] The court also moved away from merely applying federal notions of
due process in deciding whether the Navajo courts had personal jurisdiction over
nonresident litigants. In *Billie v. Abbott* (1988), the court expanded the scope of the

"minimum contacts" analysis applied by the United States Supreme Court in similar cases under the Fourteenth Amendment's due process clause.[36] Based on distinctly Navajo notions of due process, the court concluded that the Navajo courts had personal jurisdiction over a Utah state official who had intercepted the federal tax refunds of Navajos receiving welfare benefits:

> When Navajo sovereignty and cultural autonomy are at stake, the Navajo courts must have broad-based discretion in interpreting the due process clauses of the ICRA [Indian Civil Rights Act] and NBR [Navajo Bill of Rights], and the courts may apply Navajo due process in a way that protects civil liberties while preserving Navajo culture and self-government. Abbott [the Utah official] has interfered with the domestic relations of Navajos, a subject with strong cultural ties. This has caused personal injury unique to Navajos residing on the reservation. We have just held that this personal injury occurred on the Navajo Reservation, thus, Abbott has made "minimum contact" with the Navajo Nation to satisfy the requirement of Navajo due process under the ICRA and under the NBR.[37]

As it became more confident in its ability to define legal concepts through Navajo customs and traditions, the Navajo Supreme Court moved away from relying on federal cases on due process, finding its meaning in the Navajo principle of *k'é*, as stated in *Atcitty*:

> The Navajo principle of k'é is important to understanding Navajo due process. K'é frames the Navajo perception of moral right, and therefore this Court's interpretation of due process rights. K'é contemplates one's unique, reciprocal relationships to the community and the universe. It promotes respect, solidarity, compassion and cooperation so that people may live in hozho, or harmony. K'é stresses the duties and obligations of individuals relative to their community. The importance of k'é to maintaining social order cannot be overstated. In light of k'é, due process can be understood as a means to ensure that individuals who are living in a state of disorder or disharmony are brought back into the community so that order for the entire community can be reestablished.[38]

The next step of legal evolution in the Navajo courts occurred after the council passed a statute in 2002 recognizing what it called "the Fundamental Laws of the Dine," or in the Navajo language as *Dine bi beenahaaz'áanii*.[39] In that statute, the council recognized four types of "fundamental laws": traditional law, customary law, natural law, and common law.[40] Though it explicitly declined to define fully the scope of such laws, the council mandated that the courts apply such laws when interpreting and applying all statutes.[41]

Applying the council's mandate, the court declared that past opinions interpreting ICRA or the Navajo Bill of Rights that only considered federal interpretations were not binding on the court.[42] Instead, the court could consider federal interpretations of equivalent rights in the United States Constitution as part of a comprehensive analysis consistent with Navajo ways of thinking about a problem.[43] Based on its definition of Diné Fundamental Law, the court has subsequently incorporated unique Navajo values into its interpretation of individual rights.[44] This approach emphasizes the protections of Navajo citizens from harsh results of procedural and statutory law, especially if results involve imprisonment.[45] Though it examines the meaning of due process or other individual rights as defined by federal law, the court ultimately defines the meaning of such terms in a distinctly Navajo context.

Several examples illustrate the current approach. In *Fort Defiance Housing Corp. v. Lowe* (2004), the court was faced with the question of whether residents of public housing had adequate notice and opportunity to be heard when appealing eviction cases under the Forcible Entry and Detainer statute.[46] The statute, clearly adopted from the Arizona eviction statute, allowed five days to appeal an eviction from the district court to the Supreme Court.[47] The question presented was whether five days provided adequate opportunity for such litigants to appeal.[48] The court answered the question in the context of the "absolute" right to due process when someone's home is being taken away, even where residents had no ownership interest in tribal public housing.[49] The court emphasized the importance of home in Navajo thought as a central place to the spiritual life of a Navajo family and the principle of *k'é*, which it described as ensuring "that individuals living in disharmony are brought back into right relationships."[50] Based on *k'é* and the unique Navajo values concerning homes, the court interpreted the appellate time period as five business days, and required the trial court to inform the evicted defendants of that period and of any other requirements necessary to perfect their appeal.[51]

In *Navajo Nation v. Rodriguez* (2004), the court explained its approach to the Indian Civil Rights Act and the Navajo Bill of Rights more generally, stating that both would be applied with Navajo values in mind.[52] In that case, the court adopted the requirement that the *Miranda* warning be given before a confession by the criminal defendant could be admissible.[53] However, the court expanded the requirements for law enforcement when administering the warning in light of the Navajo principle of *hazhó'ógo*, which requires patience and respect in interactions among Navajos.[54] Consistent with this principle, the court threw out the conviction because the *Miranda* warning had not been explained in a respectful way to the defendant before seeking a confession.[55] In so interpreting the right against self-incrimination, the court laid out its approach to individual rights, seemingly mandated by federal and Navajo statute:

[T]his Court does not have to directly apply federal interpretations of the Bill of Rights. In interpreting the Navajo Bill of Rights and the Indian Civil Rights Act, as with other statutes that contain ambiguous language, we first and foremost make sure that such interpretation is consistent with the Fundamental Laws of the Diné. That the Navajo Nation Council explicitly adopts language from outside sources, or that a statute contains similar language, does not, without more, mean the Council intended us to ignore fundamental Diné principles in giving meaning to such provisions. Indeed, Navajo understanding of the English words adopted in statutes may differ from the accepted Anglo understanding. Further, the Indian Civil Rights Act does not require our application of federal interpretations, but only mandates the application of similar language. . . . While we are not required to apply federal interpretations, we nonetheless consider them in our analysis. We consider all ways of thinking and possible approaches to a problem, including federal law approaches, and we weigh their underlying values and effects to decide what is best for our people. We have applied federal interpretations, but have augmented them with Navajo values, often providing broader rights than that provided in the equivalent federal provision. Our consideration of outside interpretations is especially important for issues involving our modern Navajo government, which includes institutions such as police, jails, and courts that track state and federal government structures not present in traditional Navajo society.[56]

In a quite recent case, *Office of the Navajo Nation President v. Navajo Nation Council* (2010), the Supreme Court applied this approach to due process to reject the attempted removal of the Navajo Nation president by the Navajo Nation Council.[57] In one of two high-profile, politically charged cases issued the same day, the court in effect struck down a statutory provision that allowed the Navajo Nation Council to place the Navajo Nation president on leave without a hearing.[58] The council had put President Joe Shirley, Jr. on leave for alleged improprieties, but did not allow him an opportunity to defend himself before voting to approve the leave.[59] The statute upon which the council relied did not allow a president to contest the allegations before a vote.[60] The court, again in the context of *k'é* as the "primary principle" informing Navajo due process, stated that the statute lacked due process protections for the president and therefore "should no longer be used."[61]

This new approach, however, does not always result in the process desired by individual litigants. In *Nelson v. Initiative Committee to Reduce the Navajo Nation Council*, the other high-profile case recently issued by the court, Navajo member Timothy Nelson challenged an initiative passed by the Navajo people to reduce the size of the Navajo Nation Council from eighty-eight to twenty-four members.[62] Nelson filed a petition under the process provided in the Navajo Election Code, alleging several defects in the initiative language and the election procedure.[63] His petition was first heard by the Office of Hearings and Appeals, a quasi-judicial administrative agency, which dismissed his petition without a hearing based on a motion to dismiss filed by the initiative committee.[64] The Election Code authorizes OHA to dismiss a petition summarily without a hearing if on the face of the petition it is "insufficient under the Election Code."[65] OHA dismissed the petition before Nelson even responded to the motion to dismiss.[66] Nelson appealed the dismissal, alleging that OHA had violated his right to due process.[67] Somewhat surprisingly, the court affirmed OHA, stating that the statutory procedure was proper in the context of the need for expediting election grievances, and that Nelson's due process right had not been violated by the summary dismissal.[68] At least in the context of election challenges, the court does not require an absolute opportunity to be heard before a claim is dismissed.

One area in which the court's current approach may provide less of a right to litigants than provided under federal law is personal jurisdiction. In *Navajo Transport Services v. Schroeder* (2007), the court expanded upon its approach in *Atcitty* (discussed above) to define when a Navajo court may exert jurisdiction over a person not physically present on the Navajo Nation:

> If the long arm statute allows jurisdiction over Appellees, the District Court must further analyze whether the long arm statute is consistent with Navajo concepts of fairness embedded in the Due Process Clause of the Navajo Bill of Rights. As stated previously by this Court, the Navajo concept of due process is unique, in that it applies concepts of fairness consistent with Navajo values. More generally, this Court has emphasized that federal concepts of civil rights may be considered, but that ultimately the rights set out in the Navajo Bill of Rights are to be interpreted in light of Navajo Fundamental Law. Under these principles, the District Court may consider the federal "minimum contacts" standard, and incorporate it into its analysis. However, such analysis cannot be used exclusively to decide the issue, as, regardless of federal concepts of due process, the District Court must decide whether, taking into account all the circumstances of the case, the assertion of personal jurisdiction over these Appellees is fair under Navajo values.[69]

The case concerned an action against a liquor store located off the Navajo Nation in Cortez, Colorado. The plaintiffs alleged that the liquor store was responsible for a car accident occurring within the Nation because it had provided alcohol to the driver of one of the vehicles.[70] The question was whether the Nation's courts had personal jurisdiction over the liquor store.[71] The store did no advertising within the Nation, and the only connection was that the driver who allegedly caused the accident had consumed liquor purchased at the store.[72] The Navajo Supreme Court did not answer whether there was personal jurisdiction; it remanded the case back to the trial court.[73] However, the court articulated a unique Navajo test for personal jurisdiction that emphasizes notions of "fairness" under Navajo values, which, in some circumstances, may allow for personal jurisdiction when such jurisdiction would be lacking under a straight application of federal law.

With these recent cases, the Navajo Nation Supreme Court has moved further away from reliance on federal concepts of due process. Though the term remains *due process*, its essence is uniquely Navajo. As the Navajo Nation faces more litigation that tests the limits of Navajo due process, particularly in the context of ongoing government reform, the Supreme Court will be called upon to further synthesize external and indigenous notions of fairness to resolve increasingly complex disputes.

CONCLUSION

Under its new approach, the Navajo Supreme Court has transcended federal interpretations of individual rights, including due process. The court will apply Navajo concepts of fairness to define when someone requires notice and opportunity to be heard. As interpreted within the context of the Navajo principle of *k'é*, the Nation's courts look to the good of the community as well as to the litigants to define when an interest requires due process, and whether the process provided is adequate. However, this approach does not mean that federal interpretations are to be ignored or disparaged; indeed, the Navajo method of incorporating all ways of thinking about an issue invites consideration of how federal courts conceive of due process.

This evolution of a distinctly Navajo notion of due process can be a model for other tribes. As a positive assertion of unique cultural values, the Navajo Nation Supreme Court's current approach bolsters the Nation's jurisprudential sovereignty by transcending a mere literal application of outside interpretations of individual rights. By applying Navajo language and Navajo thinking to interpretations of amorphous concepts like due process, the Navajo court system legitimizes Native ways of thinking about the world, and infuses the justice system of the Navajo Nation with values that are recognized and respected by its primary constituents, the Navajo people.

What of federal judicial reluctance to acknowledge and respect distinct tribal law? Recent US Supreme Court opinions actually cite the inclusion of tribal values in tribal courts as a basis for denying tribal jurisdiction over nonmembers.[74] Does a tribal justice system like the Navajo Nation's court risk sacrificing jurisdiction over nonmembers by overtly invoking Navajo language and culture to define its jurisprudence? Should such concerns drive or alter a tribe's approach to its own law in a way it otherwise would not if it were free to construct its own system outside the scrutiny of federal courts? The Navajo Nation Supreme Court is clearly aware of federal approaches to tribal jurisdiction, as it faces numerous challenges to the jurisdiction of the Navajo Nation by litigants claiming that federal law prohibits Navajo courts from hearing their cases.[75] However, as it does with individual rights, the court consciously deviates from a strict application of federal approaches, defining its own view of jurisdiction through the recognition of US Supreme Court opinions, but based on the construction of a unique Navajo vision of jurisdiction derived from the Treaty of 1868.[76]

From the perspective of tribes and tribal attorneys who believe deviation from federal law risks further diminution of tribal sovereignty, the Navajo Nation Supreme Court's approach to individual rights might seem unnecessarily provocative. However, the Navajo Nation Supreme Court is unlikely to alter its course to adhere to a narrow vision of tribal jurisprudence restricted by conformance to federal norms. Indeed, based on the case law, the Navajo judiciary consciously asserts a jurisprudential independence that it believes ensures the survival of a distinct Navajo view of law and society. If such survival is at least one goal of tribal judiciaries, then Navajo jurisprudence provides a worthy model for other tribes in applying their own unique values and norms in tribal court decisions. Navajo due process is but one manifestation of a larger approach to law and society that maintains the sovereignty of distinct tribal nations in the face of adversity.

NOTES

1. DAVID WILKINS, THE NAVAJO POLITICAL EXPERIENCE 138 (2003).

2. Navajo Nation Council Resolution No. CO-69-58 (October 16, 1958) (codified as amended at 7 N.N.C. § 101, et seq.).

3. *Id.*, whereas Clause 2.

4. *See* Resolution No. CO-69-58.

5. *See id.; see also, e.g.*, Navajo Rules of Civil Procedure; Navajo Rules of Civil Appellate Procedure; Navajo Rules of Criminal Procedure. There is a separate dispute resolution forum, the Navajo Peacemaking Program, where traditional methods are used to have parties in dispute "talk things out" to a mutually agreed-upon solution. The Peacemaking Program does not use formal Anglo-American derived procedures, but has guidelines derived from Navajo principles to facilitate discussion and resolution. *See* PEACEMAKING (A GUIDE TO THE PEACEMAKING PROGRAM OF THE NAVAJO NATION) (2004).

6. Resolution No. CO-69-58, § 3.

7. *Id.*

8. *See generally*, NAVAJO REPORTER, volumes 1–8 (official reporter of opinions from the Navajo Court of Appeals and Navajo Supreme Court). Opinions are also available from Westlaw or VersusLaw.

9. 272 F.2d 131, 132 (10th Cir.).

10. *Id.*

11. *See id.* On the due process claim, the Tenth Circuit states only that it was not at issue in the appeal. *Id.*

12. 163 U.S. 376 (1896).

13. Native American Church, 272 F.2d at 134–35.

14. 436 U.S. 49 (1978). In that case, the US Supreme Court held there was no federal cause of action under the Indian Civil Rights Act except for habeas corpus. *Id.* at 65.

15. Navajo Nation Council Resolution No. CO-63-67 (codified as amended at 1 N.N.C. § 1, et seq. (2005)).

16. *Id.*
17. *See* 1 N.N.C. § 1 (2010).
18. *See* Navajo Nation Council Resolution No. CO-63-67.
19. *Id.*, § 1.
20. *See id.*, §§ 2–7. Interestingly, the Council included the right to bear arms as one enumerated right. *Id.*, § 2. The Indian Civil Rights Act includes no such right.
21. *See* Minutes of the Navajo Nation Council, October 9, 1967, at 9–27.
22. *See, e.g.,* Holona v. McDonald, 1 NAV. REP. 189, 205–6 (1978); Navajo Nation v. Browneyes, 1 NAV. REP. 300, 302 (1978); *In re* Guardianship of Chewiwi, 1 NAV. REP. 120, 122–23 (1977).
23. *See, e.g.,* George v. Navajo Indian Tribe, 2 NAV. REP. 1, 5 (1979); Keeswood v. Navajo Tribe, 1 NAV. REP. 362, 375 (1978); Deswood v. Navajo Bd. of Election Supervisors, 1 NAV. REP. 306, 309–10 (1978).
24. *See, e.g.,* Johnson v. Dixon, 4 NAV. REP. 108, 110–12 (Ct. App. 1983); *In re* Estate of Apachee, 4 NAV. REP. 178, 179–81 (W.R. Dist. Ct. 1983); Apache v. Republic Nat'l Life Ins. Co., 3 NAV. REP. 250, 251–53 (W.R. Dist. Ct. 1982).
25. *See* Navajo Nation Council Resolution No. CD-94-85, § 301 (codified at 7 N.N.C. § 301 (2005)).
26. Navajo Nation Council Resolution No. CD-59-86, § 3 (December 11, 1986) (codified at 1 N.N.C. § 3 (2005)).
27. Navajo Nation Council Resolution No. CD-60-86, § 1 (codified at 1 N.N.C. § 554(F)(5) (2005)).
28. *See, e.g.,* Begay v. Navajo Nation, 6 NAV. REP. 20, 24 (1988).
29. *Id.*
30. Navajo Nation v. Platero, 6 NAV. REP. 422, 424 (1991).
31. *In re* Estate of Plummer, Sr., 6 NAV. REP. 271, 275 (1990).
32. *Id.* at 276.
33. *Id.* at 275.
34. 7 NAV. REP. 227, 230–31.
35. *Id.* at 231.
36. 6 NAV. REP. 66, 74.
37. *Id.*
38. *Atcitty*, 7 NAV. REP. at 230. For a detailed and accessible discussion of the meaning of *k'é* and other foundational Navajo principles, see RAYMOND D. AUSTIN, NAVAJO COURTS AND NAVAJO COMMON LAW: A TRADITION OF TRIBAL SELF-GOVERNANCE (2009).
39. Navajo Nation Council Resolution No. CN-69-02 (November 1, 2002) (codified at 1 N.N.C. § 201, et seq. (2005)). For discussions of the statute, see Kenneth Bobroff, *Dine Bi Beenahaz'áanii: Codifying Consuetudinary Law in the 21st Century*, 5 TRIBAL L.J. 4 (2004–05); Ezra Rosser, *Customary Law: The Way Things Were, Codified*, 8 TRIBAL L.J. 18 (2007–08); Paul Spruhan, *The Origins, Current Status, and Future Prospects of Blood Quantum as the Definition of Membership in the Navajo Nation*, 8 TRIBAL L.J. 1, 12–14 (2007–08).
40. 1 N.N.C. §§ 203–206.
41. 1 N.N.C. § 203(E).
42. Eriacho v. Ramah Dist. Ct., 8 NAV. REP. 617, 629, n. 1 (2005).
43. *Id.*
44. *See, e.g., Eriacho* (waiver of jury trial); Navajo Nation v. Kelly, No. SC-CR-04-05 (July 29, 2006), *available at* http://www.navajocourts.org/NNCourtOpinions2006/13Navajo%20Nation%20v%20James%20Kelly.pdf (double jeopardy); Navajo Nation v. Morgan, 8 NAV. REP. 732 (2005) (waiver of trial through guilty plea).
45. *See id.*
46. 8 NAV. REP. 463, 473.
47. *Id.* at 474; *see* 16 N.N.C. § 1807 (2005).
48. *Lowe*, 8 NAV. REP. at 474–75.
49. *Id.* at 474.
50. *Id.* at 473–75.
51. *Id.* at 475.

52. 8 Nav. Rep. 604, 613–14. For a detailed discussion of this case, see Philip Morin, *Navajo Nation v. Rodriguez and the Traditional Navajo Principle of Hazhó'ógo*, 7 Tribal L. J. (2006–07).

53. *Id.* at 614–15.

54. *Id.*

55. *Id.* at 615–16.

56. *Id.* at 613–14 (internal citations omitted).

57. No. SC-CV-02-10, slip op. at 44 (June 2, 2010) (amended opinion), *available at* http://www.navajocourts.org/NNCourtOpinions2010/06MorganvShirleyCorrected.pdf.

58. *See id.*

59. *Id.* at 42.

60. *See id.* at 44; 11 N.N.C. § 240(C) (2005).

61. *Navajo Nation President*, No. SC-CV-02-10, slip op. at 4, 44.

62. No. SC-CV-03-10, slip op. at 1 (June 2, 2010) (amended opinion), *available at* http://www.navajo-courts.org/NNCourtOpinions2010/07NelsonvIPCCorrected.pdf.

63. *Id.* at 4–5.

64. *Id.* at 5.

65. 11 N.N.C. § 341(A)(1) (2005).

66. *Nelson*, No. SC-CV-30-10, slip op. at 5.

67. *Id.* at 18.

68. *Id.* at 9, 12.

69. No. SC-CV-44-06, slip op. at 7–8 (April 30, 2007) (internal citations omitted), *available at* http://www.navajocourts.org/NNCourtOpinions2007/05Navajo%2520Transport%2520Services%2520v%2520Charles%2520Schroeder,%2520et%2520al..pdf.

70. *Id.* at 1.

71. *Id.* at 2.

72. *Id.* at 4.

73. *Id.* at 6.

74. *See, e.g.,* Plains Commerce Bank v. Long Family Land and Cattle Co., 128 S. Ct. 2709, 2724–25 (2008); Nevada v. Hicks, 533 U.S. 353, 382–84 (2001) (Souter, J., concurring); Duro v. Reina, 495 U.S. 676, 693 (1990). In his concurring opinion in *Hicks,* Justice Souter cites the claimed ability of tribal courts to interpret due process differently from federal courts as one reason tribal court jurisdiction over nonmembers is problematic. *See Hicks,* 533 U.S. at 382–84.

75. *See, e.g.,* Ford Motor Co. v. Kayenta Dist. Ct., No. SC-CV-33-07 (December 18, 2008), *available at* http://www.navajocourts.org/NNCourtOpinions2008/Ford%20v.%20Kayenta.pdf; Cedar Unified Sch. Dist. v. Navajo Nation Labor Comm'n, No. SC-CV-53-06 (Nov. 21, 2007), *available at* http://www.navajocourts.org/NNCourtOpinions2007/ar%20Unified%20School%20District%20v%20NNLC,%20and%20concerning%20Hasgood,%20et%20al.,;%20Red%20Mesa%20School%20District%20v.%20NNLC%20concerning%20Yellowhair.pdf; Nelson v. Pfizer, 8 Nav. Rep. 369 (2003).

76. *See, e.g., Ford Motor Co.*, No. SC-CV-33-07, slip op. at 6–8 (holding *Montana v. United States* test for jurisdiction not applicable on Navajo trust land due to Treaty if 1868); Dale Nicholson Trust v. Chavez, 8 Nav. Rep. 417, 424 (2004) (same).

PART III
SPEECH AND RELIGION

CHAPTER 8

Resisting Congress:
Free Speech and Tribal Law

≡

MATTHEW L. M. FLETCHER

C ongress codified the unsettled tension between American civil rights law and American Indian tribal law, customs, and traditions in American Indian communities by enacting the Indian Civil Rights Act (ICRA) in 1968.[1] Concerned that individual rights were receiving short shrift in tribal courts and by tribal governments, Congress chose to apply a modified form of the Bill of Rights on tribal governments.[2] In other words, Congress chose to *impose* American legal norms on Indian governments in order to *protect* those under tribal jurisdiction. As it had done previously in statutes such as the Indian Reorganization Act,[3] Congress affirmatively sought to displace tribal law—and all the attendant customs and traditions, as well as Indian values—with American law.[4] Ironically, after the Supreme Court interpreted ICRA in 1978, this law could only be interpreted and enforced by tribal courts.[5] Tribal law and American civil rights law have been at odds in many tribal communities ever since, as tribal voters, legislatures, and courts have struggled with how (and whether) to apply American civil rights law in Indian country.

In this chapter, I explore several questions relating to tribal courts, tribal governments, and the Indian Civil Rights Act. For example, do tribal decision makers (i.e., voters, legislatures, and especially courts) deviate from the state and federal government and court interpretations of the Bill of Rights in applying ICRA; and if so, how much and in what way? Do tribal decision makers apply or incorporate tribal law, customs, and traditions into their decisions relating to civil rights under ICRA (and tribal laws that incorporate ICRA's provisions); and if so, how? Are tribal decision makers truly bound by the provisions of the ICRA? The last question begs a final question: Does Congress have authority to force tribal decision makers how to decide civil rights disputes?

Since ICRA's enactment, literally thousands of tribal court decisions have invoked ICRA in some manner. I will discuss tribal court decisions in only one key context: freedom of speech. The very first ICRA case, *Dodge v. Nakai*,[6] involved free speech—

and that was no accident. Free speech protections under the First Amendment guarantee certain activities of American citizens from government restriction in a manner that may or may not comport in fundamental ways with tribal values.

The intent of this chapter is to give meaning, from a lawyer's perspective, to Frank Ettawageshik's important dictum that outsider court pronouncements of tribal authority should not—and do not—operate to limit tribal sovereignty effectively.[7]

TRIBAL "CIVIL RIGHTS" BEFORE THE INDIAN BILL OF RIGHTS

Tribal decision makers prior to 1968 dealt with issues of government activity and fundamental fairness toward and among individuals in manners that tended to differ fundamentally from American decision makers. The differences can be boiled down, in general terms, to two themes. First, the forum by which Indian governments dealt with fundamental fairness frequently had no relation to an adversarial-style court structure, although dozens of Indian tribes did utilize tribal court systems. Second, tribal decision makers tended to weigh individual claims to fundamental fairness against the interests of the entire tribal community in a manner likely unfamiliar to American decision makers.

Tribal Decision-Making Forums

One of the key features of traditional American Indian government was its focus on resolving disputes as they arose, rather than on legislating and enforcing. According to Vine Deloria and Clifford Lytle, "[T]he primary thrust of traditional government was more judicial than legislative in nature."[8] For example, the Zuni dispute-resolution system consisted of both secular and religious leaders of the community who would convene as a "court":

> When the Council sits as a court it acts in the capacity of both judge and jury. Since there are no verbalized limits to its judicial authority, its powers in this field have been built up by accretion and precedent to the point where it may consider and determine almost any controversy of daily life among the people.[9]

Tribal traditional government that is focused on the reactionary business of resolving disputes as they arise slowly, over time, could become more of a policymaking body, preventing future disputes by establishing the ground rules before arguments arise. Deloria and Lytle described traditional tribal governments as "more judicial than legislative in nature."[10]

Scholars took to examining the "cases" decided by American Indian councils as if they were case law analogous to Anglo-American common law. Most famously, Karl N. Llewellyn and E. Adamson Hoebel published *The Cheyenne Way: Conflict and Case Law in Primitive Jurisprudence* in 1941, a deeply influential work of legal anthropology involving the reduction of Cheyenne dispute-resolution outcomes to writing.[11] Other legal anthropologists followed this methodology of reporting "case law."[12] Better scholarship has focused on the overall legal structures developed by Indian communities, the best such work being Rennard Strickland's *Fire and the Spirits: Cherokee Law from Clan to Court.*[13]

Many Indian communities recognized governmental and decision-making authority in a particular leader. The Michigan Anishinaabe (Odawa, Ojibwe, and Bodewadmi) structure is illustrative. The authority and responsibility of the family *ogema* (headman) is captured in the story of how one Grand Traverse Bay region family's traps intruded on the trapping territories of another family:

> Some years ago, a Chippewa hunter of Grand Traverse Bay, Lake Michigan, found that an Indian of a separate band had been found trespassing on his hunting grounds by trapping furred animals. He determined to visit him, but found on reaching his lodge the family absent, and the lodge door carefully closed and tied. In one corner of the lodge he found two small packs of furs, these he seized. He then took his hatchet and blazed a large tree. With a pencil made of a burned end of a stick, he then drew on this surface the figure of a man holding a gun, pointing at another man having traps in his hands. The two packs of furs were placed between them. By these figures he told the tale of the trespass, the seizure of the furs, and the threat of shooting him if he persevered in his trespass.[14]

This demonstration ended the dispute.

Anishinaabe *ogemaag* (headmen) had a variety of tools at their disposal to enforce territorial rights and obligations. Penalties could range from confiscation to violence. For example, Peter Dougherty, a Presbyterian missionary living at Grand Traverse Bay in the 1840s and 1850s, stated that the penalty for trespassing on another band's hunting territories could be severe:

> Each family has a certain hunting ground and trespass was in former times considered to be a sufficient cause for retaliation on the life of the trespasser. Now the one against whom the trespass is committed has the right to go to the lodge of the offender and take from him property to satisfy himself. In case of trespass by one tribe on the hunting ground of another tribe, the injured party sends a message to the other, and if satisfaction is not rendered it becomes a just cause of war.[15]

Ogemaag even enforced Anishinaabe community rights against non-Indians: "When the American, Samual Ashman, started fishing commercially in Goulais Bay, Shingwaukonse, a Sault Ste. Marie *ogema*, had Ashman's property seized and the fish distributed to the Indians to whom they of right belonged."[16]

Even in the mid-nineteenth century, Michigan Indians spoke about the sovereignty of their communities and leaders. Francis Assikinack, an Odawa Indian from Drummond Island who lived at L'Arbre Croche at a young age, asserted that tribal sovereignty originates in these territorial boundary questions:

> Each of these tribes had to maintain a small sovereignty of its own and for its own use. The members of the neighboring tribes had no right to go beyond the limits of their respective districts on their hunting excursions, and encroach upon that belonging to others. Any hunter that was caught trespassing upon the rights of other tribes, or taking beaver in the rivers running through their lands, was in danger of forfeiting his life on the spot for his rashness.[17]

Tribal communities nationally followed a complex series of steps in moving from traditional justice systems to the adversarial Anglo-American constitutional structures now in place in more than three hundred Indian communities. The United States bureaucracy had imposed, *without* express Congressional authorization but *with* federal court acquiescence, piecemeal and roughshod justice systems in many parts of Indian country in the nineteenth century, structures that survived well into the twentieth century.[18] These court structures operated with few of the protections afforded criminal defendants in the modern era, with judges, police, and laws imposed on tribal communities largely by federal bureaucrats.[19] Beginning slowly in the mid-twentieth century, Indian nations began to take over these court systems and retask them according to their own values and vision, the most impressive example of this being the Navajo Nation.[20]

INDIVIDUAL VERSUS GROUP RIGHTS

Tribal law prior to the Indian Civil Rights Act, generally speaking, was much more oriented toward the rights of the group over the rights of the individual. Angela Riley has succinctly described this legal paradigm of American Indian people:

> Native peoples . . . understand their place in the world as that of a people born into a network of group relations, and whose rights and duties in the community arise from, and exist entirely within, the context of the group. For these groups, one's clan, kinship, and family identities make up personal identity. The individual sees his/her rights and responsibilities as arising exclusively within the framework of such familial, social, and tribal networks. Rights are part of group membership; individual rights exist in contemplation of how they may be suited to the larger political group.[21]

The kind of coercive, arbitrary, and violent government actions generated by Euro-American governments—imprisonment, execution, police brutality, denial of governmental benefits and services, eminent domain, interrogation, entrapment, surveillance, quartering of soldiers, and so on—were rarely, if ever, perpetuated by Indian communities. A classic Supreme Court case analyzing the dark side of Anglo-American law is *Miranda v. Arizona*,[22] in which the Court concluded that the long history and custom of police abuse of suspected criminals required a constitution-based prophylactic rule prohibiting the interrogation of suspects unless they were aware of their rights to silence and to counsel.[23] As the Navajo Nation Supreme Court recently noted, no such tradition of law enforcement exists at Navajo,[24] and likely no such tradition exists in the vast majority of American Indian communities.[25]

Consider, for example, the political murder of Spotted Tail by Crow Dog—two Lakota leaders—in the 1880s, resulting in the United States Supreme Court's decision in *Ex parte Crow Dog*.[26] The families settled the dispute "for $600 in cash, eight horses, and one blanket."[27] Federal officers dissatisfied with the tribe's version of justice—which took into account much broader concerns of the community than recognized by federal officials, such as leadership, family, and economic considerations—brought a federal prosecution. The Dakota territorial court sentenced Crow Dog to hang, but the Supreme Court reversed. Congress would enact the Major Crimes Act in 1885 in a successful effort to overturn the Court's decision.[28]

Like criminal law and procedure, free speech and religion are areas of American Indian law and policy that may differ dramatically from American versions, perhaps causing tribal interpretations of those civil rights to vary from those of federal and state courts and legislatures.

HOW DECISION MAKERS APPLY ICRA'S FREE SPEECH PROTECTIONS

The Indian Bill of Rights incorporates aspects of the First Amendment critical to this chapter. The statute prohibits "Indian tribe[s] in exercising powers of self-government [from] ... mak[ing] or enforc[ing] any law prohibiting the free exercise of religion, or abridging the freedom of speech, or the press, or the right of the people peaceably to assemble and to petition for a redress of grievances."[29] This chapter discusses some aspects of freedom of religion, but is focused more on freedom of speech and of the press, and the political implications of those civil rights.

The freedom of speech (and of the press) is uniquely linked to the participation of individuals in government and politics. In the American constitutional structure, these political rights help to form the core of American governance and liberty. In American politics, individual free speech honors the right of individuals to speak and express an opinion, nonetheless doing so within certain nondiscriminatory limitations that help to avoid an anarchic free-for-all.[30] Though freedom of speech is not absolute, the federal common law defining free speech grants enormous deference to the speaker.[31]

In American Indian politics, the right to speak is also a core aspect of government, but in ways that sometimes differ from American politics. In general, tribal communities have always presumed the right to speech, whereas free speech in American politics is a new creature, subject to continued and varied restrictions in spite of the First Amendment. Russel Barsh writes, "Leaders are inherently powerless to deprive any family of its means of subsistence. As long as each family stays within its ancestral lands and retains its economic autonomy, the right to dissent is a practical reality."[32]

Nevertheless, with the imposition of hierarchical tribal governments through the creation of leadership roles for the purpose of executing treaties and through the creation of tribal governments as we know them today under the Indian Reorganization Act, governmental restrictions on speech inherent in such governments began to manifest themselves in tribal governments, for better or worse. The legislative history provides somewhat of a snapshot of the rise of speech restrictions in Indian country, focusing attention on the "protection of the 'outside agitator'" in order to preserve pan-tribal "militant Indian movements."[33] Legal commentators argued against tribes that imposed criminal penalties on individuals for charges such as "spreading malicious gossip" and "witchcraft."[34] One critical argument was that individual Indians should be allowed greater leeway to criticize their government.[35]

And yet, some deferred to tribal decision making on the issue of whether speech should be protected and which speech should be limited: "The wisdom of affording [freedom of speech] protection to dissident members of closely knit tribes is questionable. Indian tribes being more like families than governmental units, the risk exists that barriers raised against 'intra-family' discipline could well lead to a further breakdown of tribal society."[36] As one commentator put it, "Tribal politics is a closed circle; it is intense and deeply personal."[37]

And so ICRA allows Indian tribes to decide for themselves what individual speech rights mean in each tribal community. The "legislative history makes clear that Congress found it necessary to impose a specially designed set of restraints upon tribal government ... operating within the structure of tribal government."[38] One influential commentary on the legislative history of ICRA written by Harvard law students contended that "[i]n construing the statute, courts should remember that Congress has strongly supported the policy of allowing Indian tribes to maintain their governmental and cultural identity."[39]

Early Federal Court Decisions

The first ICRA cases arose in federal courts (raised before the Supreme Court recognized a bar on such claims in 1978), and exemplify key differences between American and tribal politics. In *Dodge v. Nakai*,[40] a federal court took jurisdiction over the ICRA claim[41] and ruled that the Navajo Nation's expulsion of an attorney in charge of Dinebeiina Nahiilna Be Agaditahe, Inc. (DNA), the reservation's legal aid office, violated the attorney's freedom of speech and constituted an unlawful bill of attainder.[42] Though the court acknowledged that the attorney had actually laughed at tribal leaders and tribal elders during a critical tribal leadership meeting—behavior the defendants argued was full of "ridicule and scorn" and "so obnoxious as to provoke an assault" by a tribal elder[43]—the court ruled that the attorney's rights under ICRA had been violated and vacated the tribe's decision. Alvin Ziontz argued:

> Unfortunately, the court gave no consideration to the significance such an act may have had to Indians. For a white man who had previously placed himself in defiance of tribal government to enter into the seat of government of that tribe, on their reservation and to laugh scornfully in the face of tribal government, may, within the culture of the Navajo tribe, constitute a grave transgression.[44]

Ziontz concluded that "[t]he actions of the federal court in deciding that banishment was 'unreasonable' may reflect either mere ignorance of tribal values or a decision to reject those values in favor of Anglo-Saxon standards of acceptable conduct."[45]

In another federal case, *Big Eagle v. Andera*,[46] the federal courts took jurisdiction under the habeas provision of ICRA[47] of a claim that a tribal law prohibiting disorderly conduct had been used to violate the free speech rights of tribal members. The Eighth Circuit first opined that the disorderly conduct statute appeared—"if tested by standards applied to communities outside an Indian reservation"—to satisfy free speech protections,[48] but remanded the case back to the district court. The district court then applied to the tribal ordinance standards that would normally be applied off the reservation, noting that "[t]he tribal court is not a court of record."[49] Judge Bogue's district court found that the tribal court had allowed the disorderly conduct statute to be applied to individuals who merely swore at police officers or merely demanded their rights.[50] The court held that since the ordinance was used as a "catch-all" where "a confusing variety of words, acts, and human conditions have been found to be within its prohibitions," the ordinance was void for vagueness.[51] Another example of federal courts applying American conceptions of justice to tribal communities is *Janis v. Wilson*.[52] In *Janis*, several tribal employees who had been caught protesting against the tribal government while on the clock argued that the tribal ordinance prohibiting such conduct violated ICRA's free speech guarantees.[53] Judge Bogue first wrote: "[T]his Court is of the opinion that the meaning and application of 25 U.S.C. § 1302 to Indian tribes must necessarily be somewhat different than the established Anglo-American legal meaning and application of the Bill of Rights on federal and state governments."[54] But then he relied exclusively on First Amendment jurisprudence in deciding that the ordinance did not violate the free speech guarantees of ICRA.[55]

Tribal Law

Tribal law develops daily and, since the federal courts will generally no longer hear civil rights claims brought under ICRA, focusing on modern tribal law relating to free speech is appropriate.

Tribal constitutions. Many tribal constitutions guarantee free speech rights in varying forms. Some tribes guarantee free speech even without the "state action" requirement imposed by the First Amendment's language, "Congress shall make no law . . ."[56] The Confederated Tribes of Warm Springs Reservation of Oregon provides that "[a]ll members of the Confederated Tribes may enjoy without hindrance, freedom of worship, speech, press and assembly."[57] The Comanche Indian Tribe's constitution has nearly identical language: "All members of the Comanche Indian Tribe shall enjoy without hindrance freedom of worship, conscience, speech, press, assembly and association."[58] The Sisseton-Wahpeton Oyate Tribe's constitution similarly states that "no person shall be denied freedom of conscience, speech, association, or assembly."[59] Some tribes limit this protection to tribal members. The Blackfeet Constitution states, "All members of the tribe may enjoy without hindrance freedom of worship, conscience, speech, press, assembly, and association."[60]

Some tribal constitutions regulate only governmental conduct that would otherwise restrict speech. The Chickasaw Constitution provides that "[e]very citizen shall be at liberty to speak, write, or publish his opinions on any subject, being responsible for the abuse of that privilege, and no law shall ever be passed curtailing the liberty of speech, or of the press."[61] Others constitutions substantially mirror the provisions contained in the Indian Civil Rights Act,[62] whereas other tribes adopt ICRA's provisions.[63] Many tribal constitutions do not have constitutional protections relating to freedom of speech at all.[64]

Tribal court jurisprudence and constitutional law. Tribal courts have generally interpreted the provisions of the Indian Civil Rights Act in accordance with the principle that, where no tribal "custom or tradition has been argued to be implicated . . . [tribal courts] will look to general U.S. constitutional principles, as articulated by federal and [state] courts, for guidance."[65] One critical element that tends to guide tribal court analysis of fundamental individual rights is whether the activity at issue is a distinctly Anglo-American construct versus a traditional or cultural construct. In other words, federal and state constitutional law is less likely to be persuasive to tribal courts deciding uniquely tribal questions of law.

Applying federal law. Since many free speech claims heard in tribal courts arise during the course of employment or in the exercise of political rights, tribal courts most often apply federal law as persuasive authority to decide these cases. In *LaPorte v. Fletcher*,[66] the tribal court rejected a freedom of speech challenge to an employee's demotion from chief of police and his challenge to a tribal statute that prohibited employees from making statements to the media regarding issues under negotiation.[67]

The employee as chief of police had allegedly stated to a local newspaper that the tribe had entered into an agreement with a local sheriff's department when, in fact, the tribe had not.[68] Relying on several federal cases,[69] the court upheld the tribal statute and the demotion. On appeal, the tribal court of appeals affirmed the trial court's decision without citation to any cases (although seemingly agreeing with the trial court's description of the law), instead asserting a pragmatic approach to the question of whether a tribal employee in the course of duty has free speech rights:

> It is clear that tribal government must be able to control its com-
> munications to the general public. This recently-reaffirmed Tribe is
> in its early formative years. Its governmental institutions are in their
> infancy. Governmental systems and relationships are very fragile.
> These relationships are both internal and external. The eye of the
> surrounding community is on the Tribe. It is a time of uncertainty
> and the chaos that is attendant to an emerging contemporary Indian
> tribal government. This is the context of the matter now before this
> Court. It is clear beyond a doubt that in this context tribal govern-
> ments must be able control their communications. Government's
> duty and responsibility in this regard are never more critical than
> they are right now for this tribal community.
> [LaPorte] was the Director of Public Safety. As such, he was more
> than an ordinary tribal employee. [He] was an official of tribal gov-
> ernment. [His] communication, which is at the root of this matter,
> was a government communication any way you look at it, although
> he would have this Court understand that it was as an ordinary
> tribal member he communicated with the media. This self-serving
> characterization defies reality and common sense.[70]

In instances where an individual's speech rights as a candidate for tribal election are implicated, at least one court applied a sliding scale standard of review, choosing to apply intermediate scrutiny where the tribe imposed nondiscriminatory restrictions on candidate eligibility imposed to avoid a chaotic tribal caucus process. In *Rave v. Reynolds*,[71] both the trial court and the appellate court relied exclusively on federal constitutional law to determine the constitutionality of a tribal statute that restricted the right of tribal members to attend more than one electoral caucus, where even an unknowing violation of this rule by an individual other than an electoral candidate resulted in the removal of the candidate from the ballot.[72] Relying on two United States Supreme Court cases that generally discussed the right to freedom of association in the national electoral context, the tribal court struck down the tribal statute.[73] On appeal, the court at least raised the possibility that tribal law—or "special facts in the Winnebago tribal community"—might counsel in favor of rejecting the application of Federal Constitutional law, but no party chose to assert alternative authority.[74] The court then compared the tribal constitutional provision to the Indian Civil Rights Act provision dealing with free speech and concluded that "the language of these rights is virtually identical to the rights protected against federal governmental action under the first amendment to the United States Constitution."[75] The appellate court adopted the federal "sliding scale of scrutiny in election rights cases involving the right of political association depending on whether the election regulations in question severely burden political association rights or merely constitute 'reasonable nondiscriminatory restrictions.'"[76] As such, the appellate court applied "intermediate scrutiny," which required the government to prove an important governmental interest to justify the tribal statute, and upheld the rule.[77] The court noted that the purpose of the rule was to prevent "the then common practice of tribal members going from caucus to caucus, thereby creating a disorderly election process."[78] Because voters could still write in the candidate removed from the ballot, the court held that the restriction was not severe enough to render the statute unconstitutional.

Similarly, the Mohegan courts twice have relied exclusively upon federal constitutional law to decide challenges to elector qualifications and tribal "good standing" requirements. In *Bauer v. Mohegan Council of Elders*,[79] the court rejected an effort to enjoin the initiation of "good standing" proceedings that would have adjudicated the petitioner's continuing standing as a tribal member. Relying upon federal law, the court concluded that no injunction was necessary, as no adjudication had yet taken place and the petitioner had had adequate notice of the proceedings.[80] In *Davison v. Mohegan Tribe Election Committee*,[81] the court rejected a constitutional challenge to a tribal voting statute requiring each voter to vote for each elective position available.[82] The court applied federal constitutional law once again and adopted a standard of review requiring the petitioner to prove that the government's restriction on speech in the context of the vote was "severe" before it would apply strict scrutiny.[83]

Some tribal courts, confronted with the claim that a tribal criminal statute had been used to restrict the speech activities of individuals, apply the federal void-for-vagueness doctrine. In *Hopi Tribe v. Lonewolf Scott*,[84] the Hopi Tribal Court upheld a tribal ordinance prohibiting "injury to public property."[85] In that case, the defendants argued, as the *Big Eagle v. Andera* defendants argued,[86] that the tribal law enforcement officials used the statute as a catch-all that operated to "include their alleged criminal activity within the penumbra of constitutionally protected speech and conduct."[87] However, unlike the *Big Eagle* defendants, the defendants in *Lonewolf Scott* had engaged in actions that "constituted civil disobedience that resulted in physical damage and was not conduct that may be construed as protected or within constitutional protection."[88] The tribal court relied exclusively on *Big Eagle*.

Applying state law. Occasionally, tribal courts apply the law of the state where the tribe is located as persuasive authority. In *Chase v. Mashantucket Pequot Gaming Enterprise*,[89] the court warned the tribal gaming enterprise that it should be "extremely careful when seeking to regulate their employees' off-duty conduct so as to not infringe upon the employee's right to free speech." The court cited a Connecticut statute as an example of a law that would support an employee's right to off-duty free speech as long as that exercise "does not substantially or materially interfere with the employee's bona fide job performance."[90] Another case, *Gwin v. Bolman*,[91] exemplified a circumstance where a tribe chose to import state law into its election laws, and the tribal court applied state and federal free speech jurisprudence in construing the statute.[92]

Influenced by tribal customary or traditional law. Other cases exemplify a tribal court's nod to federal law, but where the results change depending on the sometimes unspoken influence of tribal customary or traditional law. The standard of review changes depending on the tribe's collective interest, as opposed to the tribe's governmental interest. Federal courts, in contrast, are unable and unqualified to determine the collective interest of the American public, whereas many (but not all) tribal courts are in the unique position not only to have authority to invoke collective rights, but also the capability to do so.

Tribal courts apply a reduced standard of review on restrictions on the behavior of elected tribal leaders. *Brandon v. Tribal Council*,[93] is an example where a tribal court relies almost exclusively on federal law but issued an opinion contrary to what federal constitutional law scholars would have expected in an analogous federal case.[94] In *Brandon*, the tribal council suspended one tribal council member who had made a "vulgar" statement during a public meeting for three months in accordance with a tribal statute that prohibited tribal council members from behaving in a manner that would bring discredit or disrespect to the tribe. The tribal court noted that tribal leaders had a restricted right of expression, stating, "Being a tribal councilmember [*sic*] is a privilege, not a right, and council members should be expected to conduct themselves at a higher level of restraint than other tribal members."[95] The court adopted a form of the strict scrutiny standard of review, finding that "[w]hen there is a valid and compelling reason, a governmental body is free to ban certain expressions or conduct on the part of its citizens. These reasons may include prohibiting obscenity or 'fighting words' or phrases likely to result in a violent reaction by the person addressed."[96] The court then found a "compelling" reason for the statute, based in part on tribal traditions:

> The Grand Ronde Tribe has compelling reasons to have interpreted the ordinance so as to limit the vulgar language that may be uttered by councilmembers [*sic*] in public. . . . [T]he Tribe has the right to expect its councilmembers to conduct themselves in public with dignity and respect, and refrain from using words or phrases that a normal tribal member is privileged to use. Secondly, the type of language used by Mr. Brandon was arguably 'fighting words' that were likely to create a violent or hostile situation, as indeed was created here. The tribe has a right to expect its tribal councilmembers to refrain from using such language so as to avoid fights or other altercations. Finally, the Grand Ronde Tribe has a vested interest in protecting its reputation throughout the community.[97]

The *Brandon* court created a doctrine of free speech that applied only to the tribe's elected officials. Finding that preserving the reputation of the tribe through the regulation of the expression of the tribe's leaders was a compelling governmental interest, the court saw no need to engage in discussing whether the statute was narrowly tailored to accomplish that goal while preserving free speech rights as much as possible, unlike the *Rave II* court. A tribe's reputation in business and intergovernmental negotiation is directly related to the quality and behavior of its elected leaders. As Professor Mark Rosen has noted, the court appeared to be adopting an analog of the federal doctrine that validly restricts the expression of federal employees.[98] But the tribal court went further in issuing a decision that appeared to recognize the critical role that tribal leaders play in representing the tribe in tribal meetings, in government-to-government negotiations, and in business relationships.

The factual converse of the *Brandon* decision is likely *Flute v. Labelle*.[99] There, an elected tribal leader who was the subject of an unflattering letter to the editor of the local newspaper sued the author of the letter for defamation. The tribal court applied federal and South Dakota constitutional law in analog and found that the plaintiff's petition met the requirements of libel *per quod*. Because the plaintiff could not show actual damages, the court awarded only nominal damages and ordered the defendant to "write a retraction letter to the Tribal newspaper correcting the false impression she left with readers."[100] The court noted the political history of the defendant in particular, stating that she had been "one of many persons who several years ago engaged in a protest of tribal council action by occupying the Tribal Council chambers after a Council meeting ended."[101] In short, the court applied federal and state common law that established the defendant's culpability, but applied that law to fashion a tribe-specific remedy that severely limited the defendant's liability.

In a case with many of the same circumstances, *Chavez v. Tome*,[102] the Navajo Nation Supreme Court affirmed a trial court's decision finding liability in libel for the publication of false statements about an attorney employed by the Navajo Nation. Unlike the Sisseton-Wahpeton Oyate Court in *Flute*, the Navajo Nation applied federal free speech jurisprudence to prohibit the lower court from ordering the publisher from printing a retraction.[103]

Applying tribal traditional or customary law. Other tribal courts often express no hesitation in examining a free speech claim using traditional or customary law, even in an employment context. The Navajo Nation Supreme Court in *Navajo Nation v. Crockett* held that Navajo courts apply "Navajo common law to determine whether an individual's right to free speech has been violated."[104] The general rule is:

> [Navajo common law provides] that an individual has a fundamental right to express his or her mind by way of spoken word and/or actions. As a matter of Navajo custom and tradition, people speak with caution and respect, choosing their words carefully to avoid harm to others. This is nothing more than freedom with responsibility, a fundamental Navajo traditional principle.[105]

The Navajo court discussed how Navajo customary law includes certain restrictions on free speech, such as, "For example, on some occasions, a person is prohibited from making certain statements, and some statements of reciting oral traditions are prohibited during certain times of the year."[106] Additional restrictions include how speech should be delivered and, in conflict situations, to whom:

> Furthermore, speech should be delivered with respect and honesty. This requirement arises from the concept of *k'e*, which is the "glue" that creates and binds relationships between people. To avoid disruptions of relationships, Navajo common law mandates that controversies and arguments be resolved by "talking things out." This process of "talking things out," called *hoozhoojigo*, allows each member of the group to cooperate and talk about how to resolve a problem. This requirement places another limitation on speech, which is that a disgruntled person must speak directly with the person's relative about his or her concerns before seeking other avenues of redress with strangers.[107]

Applying these rules to a circumstance where a Navajo government employee has a complaint with a supervisor, the Navajo court invoked "the Navajo common law of *nalyeeh*" and advised employees to "not seek to correct the person by summoning the coercive powers of a powerful person or entity, but should seek to correct the wrongful action by 'talking things out.'"[108] The court concluded that if this process failed, the employee could then resort to speaking to strangers, that is, by accessing "an internal employment grievance process."[109] The court noted that, even within the employment grievance process, "the traditional rules of respect, honesty, and kinship apply."[110]

In *Crockett*, the Navajo Nation fired an employee for, as alleged by the employee, speaking at a government meeting about alleged government misconduct and distributing documents that supported the allegations of government misconduct.[111] The court held that this speech was protected by Navajo law by apparently carving a kind of "public concern" exception to the law of *hoozhoojigo* and *nalyeeh*.[112] Though not explicitly noting an exception, the court did note that "an initial inquiry with management to 'talk things out' is [merely] encouraged,"[113] not mandated. The court also stated, "When an employee gives a statement before an official government committee, he or she speaks in a context that is inherently public in nature. This includes any documents which the employee may distribute."[114] As such, though it appeared that the employees had not specifically attempted to "talk things out" prior to surprising the governmental body in a public meeting with the allegations, the court still found the speech protected, in large part, because of the importance of the information to the public:

> This Court finds the speech in question was "a matter of public concern." At the meeting, the employees expressed safety and envi-

ronmental concerns, undue interference by the Bureau of Indian Affairs in P.L. 96-638 contracts, and allegations and misconduct on the part of . . . management. The disclosure of misconduct or malfeasance by a government entity is a matter of public concern, as are questions of effectiveness and composition of the . . . management board. Likewise, safety and environmental concerns have the potential to directly impact the general public, and therefore, are a matter of public interest.[115]

In this case, the Navajo court came to the same conclusion that an Anglo-American court likely would have, but took a far different route. Former Navajo Nation Supreme Court Justice Raymond Austin noted:

Traditional Navajos believe that knowledge is power—this means that knowledge formed as thought, which is expressed through language (i.e., everyday spoken Navajo, or words or symbols, can be used to coerce, control, destroy, manipulate, or persuade. The process through which the goal is achieved follows this pattern: knowledge precedes thought; thought precedes language; and language precedes words; thus, a word, as the ultimate manifestation of knowledge, is sacred and powerful.[116]

Later, in *Judy v. White*,[117] the Navajo Nation Supreme Court "introduced the traditional Navajo concept of 'community free speech'":[118]

It is without question that in recognizing and giving formality to the Navajo People's fundamental principles and tenets of the *Diné bi'ó'ool'ii ł*, or the Diné Life Way, the Council conceded that despite its statutory pronouncements there exists a deeper, more profound system of governance. It is abhorrent to the Diné Life Way to violate the right of a community member to speak or to express his or her views or to challenge an injury, whether tangible or intangible. This right is protected to such an extent that the right to speak to an issue is not limited to the "real party in interest." Rather, the right belongs to the community as a whole, and any member of that community may speak. The non-Navajo concept of governance protects one's right to speak because that right has historically been oppressed. The Diné Life Way has always accepted that right unconditionally. Therefore, we do not focus on the existence of a right to speak or express our opinions; instead, we seek to protect the exercise of what we inherently know to exist.[119]

Some tribal courts provide additional tribe-specific reasons for restricting or otherwise rewarding speech. In *Garcia v. Greendeer-Lee*,[120] the Ho-Chunk Supreme

Court rejected a claim by a nonmember employee of the Ho-Chunk Nation that the tribe's personnel policies violated her right to choose her own religion. The employee, a Jehovah's Witness, sought paid leave for the time she had taken to attend a religious event. The tribe's Waksig Wogsa Leave Policy allowed paid leave for attendance of certain tribe-specific religious events, but only unpaid leave for other events. The court majority found that the employee was not prohibited from participating in her religion and rejected the claim. The interesting portion of the opinion came in a concurring opinion of the court's chief justice, who interpreted the phrase "Waksig Wagsa" to mean "Indian Ways," and noted that the purpose of the leave policy was to "provide a means in which enrolled Tribal member employees can practice religion, culture and tradition . . . without the threat of losing a job or losing pay."[121] Finding that the practice of these "Indian Ways" is both "the essence of tribal sovereignty" and "the backbone of cultural support that makes us distinctly Ho-Chunk,"[122] the chief justice had no problem rejecting the constitutional challenge. Here, the chief judge viewed tribal member religious activities as fundamental to the survival of the tribe and its sovereignty, surely a compelling governmental interest.

In short, tribal courts have no obligation to apply federal and state constitutional law as it relates to free speech. Some tribal courts apply strict, intermediate, or rational basis scrutiny to analyze government restrictions on speech in relevant contexts, whereas others do not. Some courts rely heavily on tribal customary or traditional law whereas others rely less. However, depending on the strength or intensity of the customary or traditional interest in the free speech restriction, tribal courts are more likely to invoke tribal customary or traditional law. If a legal dispute involving a uniquely tribal practice, tradition, art, or custom arises, it is far more likely (and reasonable, if not desirable) for a tribal court to apply traditional or customary law.

RESISTING CONGRESS

A key unanswered question is whether tribal decision makers *must* comply with the Indian Civil Rights Act at all. As a normative matter, perhaps Indian nations should comply with the congressional mandate—and most tribes have agreed to do so. However, some tribal courts have explicitly kept the question open. Indeed, this question is valid, given the American Constitution's ambiguous grant of authority to Congress over Indian affairs.[123]

What if a tribal court or tribal legislature actively resists applying, interpreting, or enforcing ICRA? What if a tribal court holds that Congress had no real authority to enact ICRA?

Currently, these questions often are more or less irrelevant for two reasons. First, few, if any, tribes overtly resist the substantive rules that the ICRA requires. Additionally, ICRA largely is redundant in many tribal communities. Tribal constitutional and statutory law, not to forget tribal common law, already mirror and even expand upon ICRA's due process and equal protection rules, generating rules equivalent to the protections offered in federal and state courts. Many tribal courts invoke "fundamental fairness" in deciding claims.[124] And, just as in federal and state courts, the rules may be the same but the protections offered individuals case-by-case may differ.

Second, because tribal decision makers can interpret the rules required by the ICRA in accordance with tribal law, customs, and traditions, ICRA itself borders on irrelevance as a substantive matter, while still retaining important symbolic meaning. As the preceding part on free speech cases demonstrates, tribal decision makers are free to directly apply federal and state law, apply modified versions of federal and state law, or even disregard federal and state law in favor of tribal common law.

That said, there are certain flashpoints where tribal law and ICRA may collide. In a few narrow and exceptional cases, federal courts have taken jurisdiction under ICRA's criminal habeas provision over claims made by persons under tribal authority that are most certainly civil claims. One example is where an independent and impartial tribal forum is unavailable to adjudicate what appears to be a straight-up example of a tribal government violating the civil rights of an individual, as in the case of *Dry Creek Lodge, Inc. v. Arapahoe and Shoshone Tribes.*[125] Nothing in ICRA mandates an independent and impartial forum, except the due process clause perhaps (but not likely), and some tribal communities continue to decide hard cases by relying upon a monolithic government decision maker that likely created the mess in the first place. These kinds of cases are exceptionally rare in reality, although outsiders to tribal law apparently perceive that such occurrences are commonplace. Additional kinds of cases meeting these criteria are some tribal member disenrollment or banishment actions, as in *Poodry v. Tonawanda Band of Seneca Indians.*[126] All too frequently, no credible tribal forum exists to adjudicate challenges to tribal disenrollment or banishment. And even where one exists, the forum may be inadequate as a practical matter to stop civil rights violations or may be forced under tribal law to affirm the government action.

Assuming that ICRA protections could not be massaged by a tribal court to avoid serious conflict in cases like these, a tribal decision maker (likely a tribal court) may simply assert that Congress had no authority to impose federal constitutional rules on internal tribal matters and utterly reject ICRA. There are claims perhaps not yet considered that may pit tribal law even more directly against ICRA and federal and state civil rights norms, potentially placing a tribal court in this position.

A Case Study in Free Speech: Indigenous Biological Knowledge

Some Indian nations have begun the process of developing statutory prohibitions on the exportation of "Indigenous biological knowledge." The most sophisticated proposal to govern the export of Indigenous biological knowledge is entitled Model Tribal Research Code, developed by the American Indian Law Center, Inc.[127] Section 006 of the Code would criminally prohibit research "with respect to materials wherever located as to which the _____ Tribe has a legal or equitable claim of intellectual or cultural ownership."[128] This Code provision raises the question of whether such a prohibition would violate a person's freedom of speech under tribal law. Tribal legislatures could also enact much stricter prohibitions against the disclosure, dissemination, or the export of Indigenous biological knowledge from Indian communities by both tribal members and nonmembers. Tribal legislatures and executives might also take other action as incidents or facts arise—their powers are not limited to legislation. They could also enact statutes calling for the removal of nonmembers from the reservation for violations of tribal law. In fact, as Alvin Ziontz has noted, "[T]he exclusion power may well be the only way a tribe can deal with a non-Indian whose conduct is offensive, particularly if it has no jurisdiction over non-Indians in tribal courts."[129]

Some Indian nations have already asserted a tribal property interest in Indigenous biological knowledge. The governor of the A:shiwi (Zuni Indian Tribe) argued in 2002 that the "Zuni people rely on … the Zuni Tribal Council[] to guide, direct and mediate all facets of our Zuni Indian Nation. [T]he tribal council is entrusted with the protection and welfare of our people, resources, and lands."[130] The Zuni Pueblo, for example, asserts that "the tribe owns the data, results and manuscripts prior to publication or presentation."[131] Scientists have already begun to warn Indian tribes and their institutional review boards against "censor[ing]" research studies.[132] One commentator added that tribal restrictions on the disclosure and publication of Indigenous biological knowledge amount to an "effort to censor the data and the commentary that flow out of scientific research [and are] generally misbegotten."[133] Censorship rightfully brings up the question of whether scientists and other researchers have a free speech right to publish and disclose their findings under ICRA, and whether an Indian tribe can lawfully prohibit or restrict the flow of Indigenous biological information—a restraint on free speech.

This issue is not merely hypothetical. In an ongoing case, the Havasupai Tribe and many of its members sued the Arizona Board of Regents for using deception and other tactics to induce consent to the use of genetic material in scientific research.[134] Moreover, the Office of Legal Counsel in the Department of Justice under the Clinton Administration offered a legal opinion on the question, perhaps concerned that an Indian tribe's enforcement of its laws might somehow interfere with free trade under the North American Free Trade Agreement.[135] According to the memorandum, the answer to whether tribal restrictions on the disclosure of Indigenous biological knowledge are unconstitutional depends on several factors:

> In particular, the analysis could turn on who holds the information that the tribe seeks to protect; whether those who hold the information have a particular relationship of trust with the tribe; the magnitude of the tribal interest underlying the tribe's effort not to disclose the information; and whether the information in question can be viewed as tribal property under an intellectual property rights regime that is otherwise consistent with applicable law.[136]

This legal opinion presumes too many facts to be persuasive, including an assumption that Indian tribes are analogous to municipal governments or corporations.[137] But the opinion correctly concludes that only each individual tribe can make a determination as to the constitutionality of its statutes restricting the export of Indigenous biological knowledge.

The question, then, is do tribal governments have a compelling, important, or rational governmental interest in restricting the speech rights of tribal members and nonmembers?

Collective identity as a compelling interest. Indian tribal governments can make a very strong case that the preservation of Indigenous biological knowledge is an extremely compelling governmental interest. As Professor Riley established, "tribal people ... define their individual identity largely based on their identification with the group. . . . For individuals within these distinct groups, flourishing in the world as a person is intimately related to cultural identity."[138] Relinquishing the group rights over Indigenous biological knowledge in favor of the individual right to export (and exploit) such knowledge would portend the end of a tribe's identity and even existence. Professor Riley continues:

> But identity for tribal peoples reaches further, to form a forceful nexus between the group and its cultural property. For a tribe, the authority to control that property is essential for group survival, as it links its very existence to group creations. Cultural property situates indigenous people[s] in a historical context, tying them to a place from which they came and the point of their creation. Tribal members become linked to the goods of the tribe—turtle rattles, trickster narratives, religious bundles—often resulting in a commitment to the objects outside of themselves; this commitment is the Native peoples' definition of what life is about.[139]

Professor Riley's argument applies to Indigenous biological knowledge as well as to cultural property, establishing the key relationship between community identity and group rights and how individual rights often have lesser importance.

Professor Riley's view is consistent with the point of view of Indians and tribes.. Indian tribes are much more than merely governments. Tribes are, without limitation, social organizations, family structures, community social control mechanisms, and protectors of tribal culture, tribal law, tribal sovereignty, both individual and collective fundamental rights, and both individual and collective property rights. And because tribal members have greater and greater confidence in and expectations of their tribal governments, these additional responsibilities acquire a greater importance. Of importance also is the fact that tribal cultures are usually oral cultures. Restrictions on free speech take on a different meaning in this mixture of group rights over individual rights in predominantly oral cultures. Professor Barsh has noted the critical relationship between speech and tribal culture and identity:

> The role of language in caring for country cannot be over-stated. Ecological knowledge, the stories embedded in places, place-names, and their meanings, and the key logical relationships between place-names, family names, family chronicles, ceremonies, and ecological processes—are documented in indigenous peoples' languages.[140]

On the surface the restriction of speech in an oral culture would seem to be anathema, but the link between the group right to Indigenous biological knowledge to preserve the identity of the community and the method of communication is an unusually strong argument for limiting the export of such speech, communication, knowledge, and so on. Certain tribal ceremonies are linked to very specific landmarks—landmarks often open to the public—so much so that the tribe has a very strong interest in keeping the ceremonies practically secret. Restrictions on the exportation of this knowledge are essential to its preservation. Tribal restrictions on the exportation of this type of knowledge are essential to tribal governments, especially because federal and state laws simply do not cover the contingencies of non-Indian tourism and scholarly research. Simple curiosity about Indigenous knowledge may be the tool that ultimately destroys that knowledge.

This interest is consistent with other speech restrictions imposed by tribal governments. The charge of "spreading malicious gossip," for instance, is to prevent "the ever present possibility of divisive factionalism breaking out between members of a close homogeneous group."[141] "Social harmony," then, is a compelling government interest for Indian tribes. One commentator in favor of advancing a free speech agenda in tribal law grudgingly acknowledged, "The amount of social disorganization among Indian groups appears to rise in proportion to the breakdown of social order within the tribe."[142] More fundamental than simply preserving civility is the fact that Indian tribes are far more than mere governments.

Intergenerational justice as a compelling interest. Preserving Indigenous biological knowledge supports a second compelling or important tribal governmental interest—"intergenerational justice."[143] In a way, both past and future generations have standing to assert rights in tribal courts (through the spokespersons of the present) and "[p]reserving the divine nature of cultural works and sheltering them from the market demonstrates Indian respect for those who have walked on, and sets the work aside for use and honor by future generations."[144] There is compelling governmental interest in restricting the export of Indigenous biological knowledge. Though the paradigm of group rights over individual rights does not appear explicitly in tribal court decisions, in an area of the law so inherently related to the future of Indian tribes and to the identity of individual Indians, tribal court decisions upholding the constitutionality of these theoretical restrictions should not be a surprise.

The establishment of these compelling (or important) tribal governmental interests would "necessarily imply an extremely narrow application of the Indian Civil Rights Act where there is a showing of countervailing customary tribal values, beliefs or standards."[145] Alvin Ziontz reached a similar conclusion two decades ago concerning the power and right of tribes to exclude certain persons. He would impose a rational basis test: "Tribes should have the right to exclude outsiders under appropriate ordinances with standards bearing a reasonable relationship to the preservation of peace and harmony within the community."[146]

As a matter of history, "[a]n Indian reservation must be seen as an ethnic community banded together under the pressure of being surrounded by an alien society, given ownership of compact geographical areas, and allowed a great measure of self-government. Separation has been fostered by the desire to retain—and has in turn fostered the retention of—a traditional culture."[147] Given the enormous and quantifiable destruction visited upon Indian tribes that, as a result, suffer the loss of their culture, often the only acceptable course is for a tribe to take action to prevent this loss—and tribal courts are obliged to uphold that choice.

Considering these factors and interests, a tribal court interpreting tribal law may well conclude that the ICRA cannot be a bar to tribal suppressions of the exportation of Indigenous biological knowledge. In fact, as some tribal courts have suggested, Congress might have had no authority to export American civil rights law to Indian country at all, or at the very least, not free speech protections.

ICRA as a Dead Letter in Tribal Forums?

Even absent a free speech question involving a subject such as Indigenous biological knowledge, tribal courts may conclude that Congress never had authority to impose American constitutional limitations on Indian tribes. Congressional authority to regulate Indian affairs is plenary and exclusive (as to states), but that plenary power generally does not involve authority over the internal affairs of Indian tribes.

The evolution of ICRA through judicial interpretation and legislative amendment strongly suggests that Congress's legal and actual authority over internal tribal affairs is tenuous. At ICRA's enactment, Congress appeared to assume that Indian tribes retained substantial authority over tribal members and nonmembers, including non-Indians, by not defining which persons could be under tribal jurisdiction. It wasn't until 1978 that the Supreme Court interpreted ICRA's silence as being relevant to the race or political status of the individuals under tribal jurisdiction, when it held that Indian tribes had no criminal jurisdiction over non-Indians.[148] It also held in 1978 that no federal court forum exists to adjudicate civil suits under ICRA.[149] Moreover, three years later, the Court adopted a general rule that tribes do not have jurisdiction over nonmembers absent two narrow exceptions.[150] Until 1991, in the so-called "*Duro* fix," ICRA did not distinguish between members and nonmembers.[151] Put differently, Congress seemed originally to intend to apply ICRA to members and nonmembers, but the Supreme Court's (and Congress's) actions have effectively cut off application to non-Indians except in unusual circumstances. Moreover, that the Supreme Court's continuing skepticism about fairness in tribal courts seems to revolve around the inapplicability of the federal constitution to the tribes[152] suggests that, at least to the Court, ICRA is of little import. All that remains of ICRA is its application to tribal members and non-member Indians in criminal cases. These are almost entirely, as a general matter, internal tribal affairs.

It is very conceivable that one or more tribal courts will reject ICRA, and that tribal legislatures may do the same. Though ICRA has significant symbolic value, as suggested by the importation of its language into tribal constitutions and federal jurisprudence into tribal court decisions, its specific import in many cases is truly narrow.[153] ICRA now looks like nothing more than Congressional interference with internal tribal affairs.

ICRA may be dying a slow death, but that does not mean that civil rights norms applicable in the United States generally are inapplicable in Indian country. In fact, tribal courts tend to hold tribal governments to a higher standard than federal and state courts due to their own government defendants. The real test in the coming years for tribes facing difficult internal political questions about budgetary and economic crises, criminal jurisdiction, and outsider intrusions in tribal affairs is whether tribes will maintain their good governance.[154]

NOTES

1. 25 U.S.C. §§ 1301-1303 (1968).
2. VINE DELORIA, JR., & CLIFFORD M. LYTLE, AMERICAN INDIANS, AMERICAN JUSTICE 126–30 (1983).
3. *See* 25 U.S.C. § 476 (1934) (authorizing tribes to reorganize as American-style constitutional governments).
4. *See* Lawrence Baca, "Reflections on the Role of the United States Department of Justice in Enforcing the Indian Civil Rights Act," in THE INDIAN CIVIL RIGHTS ACT AT FORTY (2012) (describing efforts by the United States Department of Justice to enforce ICRA in federal courts).
5. *See* Santa Clara Pueblo v. Martinez, 436 U.S. 49 (1978).
6. 298 F. Supp. 17 (D. Ariz. 1968) [hereinafter *Dodge* I]; 298 F. Supp. 26 (D. Ariz. 1969) [hereinafter *Dodge* II].
7. Frank Ettawageshik, Former Tribal Chairman, Little Traverse Bay Bands of Odawa Indians, "Looking Inward: Tribal Governance," address at the University of Michigan Native American Law Students Association 2010 Indian Law Day (April 2, 2010).
8. DELORIA & LYTLE, *supra* note 2.
9. WATSON SMITH AND JOHN M. ROBERTS, ZUNI LAW: A FIELD OF VALUES 36 (1954). Smith and Watson further reported:

> [M]eetings of the Great Council were formerly held for the purpose of providing a public hearing of cases of extraordinary interest... [S]uch meetings could be convened by the Tribal Council on its own authority or at the request of an individual. They were announced by the crier four days in advance and were held in the plaza. As many as 400 to 500 people might attend.

Id. at 114. But these public hearings ceased some time in the 1930s.
10. DELORIA & LYTLE, *supra* note 2, at 89. *See also* MATTHEW L.M. FLETCHER, AMERICAN INDIAN TRIBAL LAW 5–10 (2011) (collecting cases in this vein).
11. KARL N. LLEWELLYN AND E. ADAMSON HOEBEL, THE CHEYENNE WAY: CONFLICT AND CASE LAW IN PRIMITIVE JURISPRUDENCE (1941).
12. *See* JOHN A. NOON, LAW AND GOVERNMENT OF THE GRAND RIVER IROQUOIS (1949); JANE RICHARDSON, LAW AND STATUS AMONG THE KIOWA INDIANS (1940); SMITH & ROBERTS, *supra* note 8.
13. RENNARD STRICKLAND, FIRE AND THE SPIRITS: CHEROKEE LAW FROM CLAN TO COURT (1975).

14. Gregory E. Dowd, Expert Report, *The Meaning of Article 13 of the Treaty of Washington, March 28, 1836*, at 92, Expert Report prepared for the Chippewa Ottawa Resource Authority, United States v. Michigan, No. 2:73 CV 26 (W.D. Mich., Oct. 11, 2004) (quoting HENRY ROWE SCHOOLCRAFT, PERSONAL MEMOIRS OF A RESIDENCE OF THIRTY YEARS WITH THE INDIAN TRIBES OF THE AMERICAN FRONTIERS 695 (AMS Press 1978) (1851)).

15. Dowd, *supra* note 12, at 90 (quoting letter from Peter Dougherty to War Department, Office of Indian Affairs, Grand Traverse Bay (Jan. 21, 1848)).

16. Robert Doherty, *Old-Time Origins of Modern Sovereignty: State-Building among the Keweenaw Bay Ojibway, 1832–1854*, 31 AM. INDIAN Q. 165, 170 (2007) (quotation and citation omitted).

17. Francis Assikinack, *Legends and Traditions of the Odawah Indians*, 3 CAN. J. OF INDUSTRY, SCI., & ARTS 115, 117 (1858).

18. See DAVID H. GETCHES & NATIONAL AMERICAN INDIAN COURT JUDGES ASSOCIATION, INDIAN COURTS AND THE FUTURE 7–13 (1978).

19. See JUSTIN B. RICHLAND & SARAH DEER, INTRODUCTION TO TRIBAL LEGAL SYSTEMS 92–100 (2d ed. 2010).

20. See RAYMOND D. AUSTIN, NAVAJO COURTS & NAVAJO COMMON LAW: A TRADITION OF TRIBAL SELF-GOVERNANCE 18-29 (2009).

21. Angela R. Riley, *Recovering Collectivity: Group Rights to Intellectual Property in Indigenous Communities*, 18 CARDOZO ARTS & ENT. L. J. 175, 203 (2000).

22. 384 U.S. 436 (1966).

23. *E.g., id.* at 442–43 (describing the coercive character of Anglo-American criminal procedure).

24. See Navajo Nation v. Rodriguez, 8 NAV. REP. 604, 615–16; 5 AM. TRIBAL L. 473 (Navajo Nation Supreme Court 2004).

25. *But cf.* Bob L. Blackburn, *From Blood Revenge to the Lighthorsemen: Evolution of Law Enforcement Institutions among the Five Civilized Tribes to 1861*, 8 AM. INDIAN L. REV. 49, 53–54 (1988) (detailing the rather rough treatment—by today's standards—of suspected criminals by the lighthorsemen).

26. 109 U.S. 556 (1883).

27. SIDNEY L. HARRING, CROW DOG'S CASE: AMERICAN INDIAN SOVEREIGNTY, TRIBAL LAW, AND UNITED STATES LAW IN THE NINETEENTH CENTURY 1 (1994).

28. See United States v. Kagama, 118 U.S. 375 (1886).

29. 25 U.S.C. § 1302(1) (1968).

30. *Political Freedom, in* THE FIRST AMENDMENT: A READER 101, 101–03 (John H. Garvey & Frederick Schauer, eds., 2d ed. 1996).

31. See generally LEE C. BOLLINGER, THE TOLERANT SOCIETY: FREEDOM OF SPEECH AND EXTREMIST SPEECH IN AMERICA (1986).

32. Russel Lawrence Barsh, *The Nature and Spirit of North American Political Systems*, 10 AM. INDIAN Q. 181, 186 (1986).

33. Joseph de Raismes, *The Indian Civil Rights Act of 1968 and the Pursuit of Responsible Tribal Self-Government*, 20 S.D. L. REV. 59, 72–74 (1975).

34. Burton D. Fretz, *The Bill of Rights and American Indian Tribal Governments*, 6 NAT. RESOURCES J. 581, 609 (1966).

35. See id. at 610.

36. G. Kenneth Reiblich, *Indian Rights under the Civil Rights Act of 1968*, 10 ARIZ. L. REV. 617, 623–24 (1968).

37. Donald L. Burnett, Jr., *An Historical Analysis of the 1968 'Indian Civil Rights' Act*, 9 HARV. J. ON LEGIS., 557, 577 (1971).

38. Alvin J. Ziontz, *In Defense of Tribal Sovereignty: An Analysis of Judicial Error in Construction of the Indian Civil Rights Act*, 20 S.D. L. REV. 1, 6 (1975).

39. Note, *The Indian Bill of Rights and the Constitutional Status of Tribal Governments*, 82 HARV. L. REV. 1343, 1355 (1969).

40. 298 F. Supp. 17 (D. Ariz. 1968); 298 F. Supp. 26 (D. Ariz. 1969).

41. See Dodge I, 298 F. Supp. at 23–25.

42. *See Dodge* II, 298 F. Supp. at 32–34.

43. *Id.* at 30–31. *See also* ALVIN J. ZIONTZ, A LAWYER IN INDIAN COUNTRY: A MEMOIR 174–75 (2009).

44. Ziontz, *supra* note 41, at 50–51.

45. *Id.* at 51.

46. 508 F.2d 1293 (8th Cir. 1975) [hereinafter *Big Eagle* I]; 418 F. Supp. 126 (D. S.D. 1976) [hereinafter *Big Eagle* II].

47. 25 U.S.C. § 1303.

48. *Big Eagle* I, 508 F.2d at 1296.

49. *Big Eagle* II, 418 F. Supp. at 129.

50. *Id.* at 130.

51. *See id.* at 131.

52. 385 F. Supp. 1143 (D. S.D. 1974).

53. *See* Janis, 385 F. Supp. at 1146–48.

54. *Id.* at 1150.

55. *See id.* at 1152 ("[T]his Court is of the opinion that the First Amendment imposes no greater restraint on Indian tribes through 25 U.S.C. 1302(1) than it imposes on the federal government").

56. U.S. CONST. amend. I.; see Charles Black, *The Supreme Court 1966 Term—Foreword: "State Action," Equal Protection, and California's Proposition 14*, HARV. L. REV. 69, 95 (1967).

57. CONFEDERATED TRIBES OF WARM SPRINGS RESERVATION OF OREGON CONST. art. VII, § 2.

58. COMANCHE INDIAN TRIBE OF OKLAHOMA CONST. art. X, § 1.

59. SISSETON-WAHPETON SIOUX TRIBE, SOUTH DAKOTA CONST. AND BY-LAWS art. IX, § 1.

60. BLACKFEET TRIBE OF THE BLACKFEET INDIAN RESERVATION OF MONTANA CONST. AND BY-LAWS art. III, § 3.

61. CHICKASAW NATION CONST. art. IV, § 4.

62. *E.g.*, GRAND TRAVERSE BAND OF OTTAWA AND CHIPPEWA INDIANS CONST. art. X, § 1(a); HO-CHUNK NATION CONST. art. X, § 1(a)(1); LITTLE TRAVERSE BAY BANDS OF ODAWA INDIANS CONST. art. II, § 1; TURTLE MOUNTAIN BAND OF CHIPPEWA INDIANS CONST. art. III, §§ 1–2.

63. *E.g.*, CHEROKEE NATION OF OKLAHOMA CONST. art. II, § 1; CHEYENNE-ARAPAHO TRIBES OF OKLAHOMA CONST. AND BY-LAWS art. III, § 1; CONFEDERATED TRIBES OF THE COOS, LOWER UMPQUA AND SIUSLAW INDIANS CONST. art. IV, § 1.

64. *E.g.*, BAY MILLS INDIAN COMMUNITY CONST. AND BY-LAWS; CHEYENNE RIVER SIOUX TRIBE CONST. AND BY-LAWS.

65. Louchart v. Mashantucket Pequot Gaming Enter. 27 Indian L. Rep. 6176, 6179 (Mashantucket Pequot Tribal Ct., 1999). *See also* Note, *supra* note 37, at 1355 ("Unless the record shows a willingness to modify tribal life wherever necessary to impose ordinary constitutional standards, courts should take this legislation as a mandate to interpret statutory standards within the framework of tribal life").

66. LaPorte v. Fletcher, No. 04-0-023-GC, 2004 WL 5748553 (Little River Band of Ottawa Indians Tribal Court 2004) [hereinafter *LaPorte* I], *aff'd,* LaPorte v. Fletcher, No. 0442AP, 2005 WL 6344557 (Little River Band of Ottawa Indians App. Ct., 2005) [hereinafter *LaPorte* II].

67. *See LaPorte* I, 2004 WL 5748553 (2004), at *1.

68. *See id.*

69. *See id.* at *3 (citing Pickering v. Board of Education, 391 U.S. 563 (1968); Gonzales v. Chicago, 239 F.3d 939 (7th Cir. 2001); Youker v. Schoenenderger, 22 F.3d 163 (7th Cir. 1994); Koch v. Hutchinson, 847 F.2d 1436 (10th Cir. 1988)).

70. *LaPorte* II, 2005 WL 6344557 (2005), at *2.

71. Rave v. Reynolds, 23 Indian L. Rep. 6021 (Winnebago Tribal Court 1995) [hereinafter *Rave* I], *aff'd in part and rev'd in part*, Rave v. Reynolds, 23 Indian L. Rep. 6150 (Winnebago Supreme Court 1996) [hereinafter *Rave* II].

72. *See Rave* I, 23 Indian L. Rep. at 6024; *Rave* II, 23 Indian L. Rep. at 6165–68.

73. *See id.* (citing NAACP v. Alabama, 357 U.S. 449 (1958), and Buckley v. Valeo, 424 U.S. 1 (1976)).

74. *Rave* II, 23 Indian L. Rep. at 6165.

75. *Id.* (citing Winnebago Tribe of Nebraska Const. art. IV, § 3(a), and 25 U.S.C. § 1302(1)).

76. *Id*. at 6166–67 (quoting Burdick v. Takushi, 504 U.S. 428, 434 [1992]).

77. *Id*.

78. *Id*. at 6166.

79. Bauer v. Mohegan Council of Elders, 8 AM. TRIBAL L. REP. 99 (Mohegan Tr. Ct. 2009).

80. *See id*. at 103 (citing Laird v. Tatum, 408 U.S. 1 (1972)).

81. Davison v. Mohegan Tribe Election Committee, 8 AM. TRIBAL L. REP. 121 (Mohegan Tr. Ct. 2009).

82. *See id*. at 123 (quoting Mohegan Tribal Code § 1-205(a)).

83. *See id*. at 127 (quoting Timmons v. Twin Cities Area New Party, 520 U.S. 351 (1997), and Burdick v. Takushi, 504 U.S. 428 (1992)).

84. Hopi Tribe v. Lonewolf Scott, 14 Indian L. Rep. 6001 (Hopi Tribal Court 1986).

85. *Id*. at 6005.

86. *See* Big Eagle v. Andera, 418 F. Supp. 126, 131–33 (D.S.D., 1976).

87. *Lonewolf Scott*, 14 Indian L. Rep. at 6005.

88. *Id*.

89. Chase v. Mashantucket Pequot Gaming Enterprise, 2 Mash. Rep. 387, 397 at n. 1, 1998 WL 35234940 (Mashantucket Pequot Tribal Court, 1998).

90. *Id*.

91. Gwin v. Bolman, 25 Indian L. Rep. 6121 (Three Affiliated Tribes of the Fort Berthold Reservation D. Ct. 1998).

92. *See id*. at 6122 ("This harms plaintiff's First Amendment rights and equal protection rights under the ICRA, 25 U.S.C. ¶ 1302(1) [&] (8); and alternatively under the U.S. Constitution as state law is being utilized").

93. Brandon v. Tribal Council for the Confederated Tribes of the Grand Ronde Community of Oregon, 18 Indian L. Rep. 6139 (Confederated Tribes of the Grand Ronde Community Tribal Court 1991).

94. See Mark D. Rosen, *Multiple Authoritative Interpreters of Quasi-Constitutional Federal Law: Of Tribal Courts and the Indian Civil Rights Act*, 69 FORDHAM L. REV. 479, 553 (2000) ("It is unlikely that a provision such as the tribe's [in *Brandon*] would be found to fall within the 'fighting words' exception under ordinary federal doctrine").

95. *Brandon*, 18 Indian L. Rep. at 6140.

96. *Id*. at 6141 (citing Cohen v. California, 403 U.S. 15, 20 (1971)).

97. *Id*.

98. *See* Rosen, *supra* note 87, at 554 (citing United States Civil Serv. Comm'n v. Nat'l Ass'n of Letter Carriers, 413 U.S. 548, 550, 564 (1973)).

99. Flute v. Labelle, case number not available (Sisseton-Wahpeton Oyate Court, May 14, 2004), excerpted in Fletcher, *supra* note 10, at 350.

100. *Id*.

101. *Id*.

102. Chavez v. Tome, 14 Indian L. Rep. 6029 (Navajo Nation Supreme Court 1987).

103. *See id*. at 6032 (citing Miami Herald Publishing Co. v. Tornillo, 418 U.S. 241 (1974)). The court did note, however, that "the printing of a retraction can serve as a method of mitigating damages." *Id*.

104. Navajo Nation v. Crockett, 7 NAV. REP. 237, 240 (Navajo Nation Supreme Court, 1996).

105. *Id*.

106. *Id*. at 240–41. *See also* AUSTIN, *supra* note 18, at 123–24 (describing subject areas where there are limitations on speech; most notably, "[a] prohibition on discussing the property of a deceased [person] during the four-day mourning period").

107. *Id*. at 241.

108. *Id*.

109. *Id*.

110. *Id*.

111. See *id*. at 237–38. See also AUSTIN, *supra* note 18, at 121 (describing the case).

112. *See Crockett*, 7 NAV. REP. at 242.

113. *Id*. at 241.

114. *Id*. at 242.

115. *Id.*

116. Austin, *supra* note 18, at 122.

117. Judy v. White, 8 Nav. Rep. 510; 5 Am. Tribal L. Rep. 418 (Navajo Nation Supreme Court, 2004).

118. Austin, *supra* note 18, at 120.

119. *Judy*, 8 Nav. Rep. at 531.

120. Garcia v. Greendeer-Lee, 30 Indian L. Rep. 6097 (Ho-Chunk Supreme Court 2003).

121. *Id.* at 6099 (Hunter, C.J., concurring).

122. *Id.* (Hunter, C.J., concurring).

123. *See, generally,* Robert N. Clinton, *There Is No Federal Supremacy Clause for Indian Tribes*, 37 Ariz. St. L. J. 113 (2002).

124. *E.g.*, Crampton v. Election Board, 8 Am. Tribal Law 295, 296 (Little River Band of Ottawa Indians Tribal Court, 2009); Johnny v. Greyeyes, 8 Am. Tribal Law 140, 143–44 (Navajo Nation Supreme Court, 2009); Bailey v. Grand Traverse Band Election Board, No. 2008-1031-CV-CV, 2008 WL 6196206, at ★9, ★11 (Grand Traverse Band Tribal Judiciary, Aug. 8, 2008) (en banc); Kaquotosh v. Oneida Bingo & Casino, Table Games Dept., No. 07-AC-027, 2008 WL 7438746, at ★2–3 (Oneida Tribal Judicial System Appellate Court, April 28, 2008).

125. Dry Creek Lodge, Inc. v. Arapahoe and Shoshone Tribes, 623 F.2d 682 (10th Cir. 1980), *cert. denied*, 449 U.S. 1118 (1981).

126. Poodry v. Tonawanda Band of Seneca Indians, 85 F.3d 874 (2d Cir.), *cert. denied*, 519 U.S. 1041 (1996).

127. American Indian Law Center, Inc., Model Tribal Research Code with Materials for Tribal Regulation for Research and Checklist for Indian Health Boards (3rd ed., Sept. 1999), *available at* http://www.ihs.gov/MedicalPrograms/Research/pdf_files/mdl-code.pdf.

128. *Id.* at 20.

129. Ziontz, *supra* note 36, at 53.

130. Malcom B. Bowekaty, *Perspectives on Research in American Indian Communities*, 42 Jurimetrics J. 145, 146 (2002).

131. *Id.* at 148.

132. *E.g.*, Andrew Askland, *A Caution to Native American Institutional Review Boards about Scientism and Censorship*, 42 Jurimetrics J. 159, 162 (2002).

133. *Id.* at 162.

134. See Havasupai Tribe v. Arizona Board of Regents, 204 P.3d 1063 (Ariz. App. 2008). *See generally* Kimberly TallBear, *Narratives of Race and Indigeneity in the Genographic Project*, 35 J. L. Med. & ethics 412 (2007).

135. See Randolph D. Moss, Acting Assistant Attorney General, Office of Legal Counsel, United States Dept. of Justice, *Tribal Restrictions on Sharing of Indigenous Knowledge on Uses of Biological Resources* (Oct. 12, 1999), available at 1999 WL 33229993.

136. *Id.* at ★1.

137. *See id.* at ★2 n. 2.

138. *See* Riley, *supra* note 19, at 203–04 (citing John S. Harbison, *The Broken Promise Land: An Essay on Native American Tribal Sovereignty Over Reservation Resources*, 14 Stan. Envtl. L. J. 347, 349 (1995)).

139. *Id.* at 204 (citing Peter Matthiessen, Indian Country 5 (1984); Lesley A. Jacobs, Rights and Deprivation 70 (1993)).

140. Russel L. Barsh, "*Grounded Visions: Native American Conceptions of Landscapes and Ceremony*, 13 St. thomas L. Rev. 127, 133 (2000). *See also* Austin, *supra* note 18, at 123–24 (discussing how "words are sacred" at Navajo, and form a part of Navajo common law).

141. Fretz, *supra* note 32, at 609.

142. *Id.* at 615.

143. *See* Riley, *supra* note 19, at 205 (citing John Moustakas, *Group Rights in Cultural Property: Justifying Strict Inalienability*, 74 Cornell L. Rev. 1179, 1208-09 (1990)).

144. *Id.*

145. Ziontz, *supra* note 36, at 47.

146. *Id.* at 53.

147. Note, *supra* note 37, at 1356.

148. *See* Oliphant v. Suquamish Indian Tribe, 435 U.S. 191 (1978).

149. *See* Santa Clara Pueblo v. Martinez, 436 U.S. 49 (1978).

150. *See* Montana v. United States, 450 U.S. 544 (1981). Of course, no one really knew how narrow the exceptions were for several years. *See* Strate v. A-1 Contractors, 520 U.S. 438 (1997).

151. Congress in 1991 added this phrase to 25 U.S.C. § 1301(2): "and means the inherent power of Indian tribes, hereby recognized and affirmed, to exercise criminal jurisdiction over *all Indians*" (emphasis added).

152. *See* Plains Commerce Bank v. Long Family Land and Cattle Co., 554 U.S. 316, 337 (2008) (citing Talton v. Mayes, 163 U.S. 376 (1896)).

153. *See, generally*, FLETCHER, *supra* note 10, at 319–82 (canvassing tribal court cases on civil rights).

154. *Cf.* Angela R. Riley, *Good (Native) Governance*, 107 COLUM. L. REV. 1049 (2007).

CHAPTER 9

Individual Religious Freedoms in American Indian Tribal Constitutional Law

≡≡≡

KRISTEN A. CARPENTER

Environment, culture, religion, and life are very much interrelated. Indeed, they are often one and the same. Water for example, is the lifeblood of the people. I recall taking a draft tribal water code for public input into the five villages. . . . Protection of the water spirits was a major concern throughout the reservation. And the water spirits were varied, depending whether the water source was a river, lake, or spring. I reported back to the attorneys and they laughed at my findings. However it was no laughing matter when an elderly Cheyenne with a rifle kept [a] drilling team from crossing his water spring. "Today is a good day to die," he said as he held his own hunting rifle before him. I defended him in tribal court the next morning and I cried with him when he told me how the water spirits sometimes came out and danced in the spring.[1]

Gail Small, Northern Cheyenne

A s American Indian nations revitalize their legal systems, there is renewed interest in "tribal law," that is the law of each of the 565 Indian nations within the geographic boundaries of the United States.[2] Tribal law refers to the internal laws of American Indian tribes, and includes each tribe's customary, constitutional, codified, common, decisional, and regulatory law. Several constituencies are closely focused on "individual rights" under tribal law.[3] In tribal communities, people are highly interested in the legal institutions and rules that govern their lives, especially as many tribes are experiencing a period of great political, social, and economic change.[4] In federal Indian law jurisprudence, the United States Supreme Court repeatedly expresses concern about whether individuals, especially non-Indians, will be treated fairly in tribal courts.[5] For scholars, the question of individual rights under tribal law raises a number of issues including potential tension between individual rights and the collective interests and cultures of Indian tribes,[6] the expectation of reservation residents that the law will protect their individual rights,[7] and the meaning of tribal sovereignty in the contemporary era.[8] For those outside the Indian law field, the American Indian context seems to inspire reflection on the broader question of individual rights under law.[9]

Much of the debate about individual Indian rights stems from the fact that the US Constitution, including its Bill of Rights, does not limit the powers of American Indian tribal governments.[10] As the US Supreme Court has held, Indian tribes predate the Constitution and the Bill of Rights does not extend to internal tribal governance.[11] Yet Congress has broad legislative powers over tribes and, in 1968, Congress responded to concerns about individual rights in tribal communities by enacting the Indian Civil Rights Act ("ICRA").[12] ICRA purports to extend a version of the Bill of Rights to Indian nations, attempting to accomplish by statute what the Constitution does not. Thus the ICRA plays a major role in a vibrant discussion now occurring among tribal citizens, judges, scholars, and others about the role of individual rights in tribal communities and beyond.[13] This chapter contributes to the discussion by examining the specific area of individual religious freedoms.

More specifically, I explore, in the religious freedoms context, a scholarly viewpoint that the presence of individual rights in tribal settings problematically perpetuates the "assimilation" of American Indian peoples.[14] In federal Indian law, "assimilation" refers to nineteenth and early twentieth century federal policy designed to eradicate tribal governments and cultures, replacing traditional community values through programs aimed to "civilize" and "Christianize" American Indians.[15] Propounded through various federal statutes, orders, and regulations, assimilation programs such as the "allotment" of tribal lands, criminalization of tribal religious practices, assignment of Christian missionaries to reservation communities, and Indian boarding schools have now been widely discredited and firmly rejected as a matter of federal law.[16] Yet vestiges of assimilation arguably remain. The federal government no longer tries to eradicate tribal governments, but continues to wield influence over tribal law through statutes including the Indian Reorganization Act of 1934, which provides for the adoption of federally approved tribal constitutions, and the ICRA, which encourages tribes to afford certain individual rights to persons under tribal jurisdiction.[17]

To supporters of tribal sovereignty, the imposition of individual rights on tribal government seems to further the assimilationist goals of past policy. Defining "individual rights" as "individual claims that preclude or limit collective pursuits—the type of rights enshrined in the United States Bill of Rights and central to liberal political theory," Professor Carole Goldberg notes that such individual rights "can trump the interests of others, the good of society, and the will of the majority because they are understood to derive from moral principles independent of any social conceptions of the good."[18] Goldberg and other scholars find the privileging of individual rights over group rights threatening for Indian tribes, which are insufficiently protected even by an associational or contextual theory that would link individual autonomy with the culture or community where individual rights are practiced. The problem, for Goldberg, is that "grounding what is essentially a group rights claim on the rights of individual group members commits one to an individual rights critique of the group itself, a result that may tear at tribal cultures which do not privilege individual rights in the same way United States law does."[19] With the modern movement in favor of tribal self-determination and self-government closely connected to the revitalization of tribal cultures, individual rights may undermine tribal sovereignty.[20]

The assimilation critique seems intuitively correct and applicable in the religion context. Whereas federal law provides for religious freedoms in terms of individual rights, tribes have traditionally practiced religions as a matter of collective responsibility to the natural world. Moreover, tribal leaders explicitly connect traditional tribal religions with contemporary tribal self-determination, as in the following testimony by a Lakota leader in federal litigation over a sacred site:

> [Certain religious ceremonies] are vital to the health of our nation and to our self-determination as a Tribe. Those who use the butte to pray become stronger. They gain sacred knowledge from the spirits that helps us to preserve our Lakota culture and way of life. They become leaders. Without their knowledge and leadership, we cannot continue to determine our destiny.[21]

Despite this emphasis on the collective aspect of tribal religious practice, however, many tribal constitutions now contain religious freedoms provisions that resemble the First Amendment or ICRA's free exercise clause, with their obvious emphasis on the individual aspect of religious freedoms.[22] As a matter of federal constitutional law, the free exercise clause has been interpreted to protect an individual's right to hold religious beliefs free from government compulsion.[23] Some commentators, perhaps most notably US Supreme Court Justice Brennan, have argued that, in this respect, the free exercise clause fits better with "Western" religions than it does with Native American religions:

> While traditional Western religions view creation as the work of a deity who institutes natural laws which then govern the operation of physical nature, tribal religions regard creation as an on-going process in which they are morally and religiously obligated to participate....
>
> In marked contrast to traditional Western religions, the belief systems of Native Americans do not rely on doctrines, creeds, or dogmas. Established or universal truths—the mainstay of Western religions—play no part in Indian faith. Ceremonies are communal efforts undertaken for specific purposes in accordance with instructions handed down from generation to generation....Where dogma

THE INDIAN CIVIL RIGHTS ACT AT FORTY

lies at the heart of Western religions, Native American faith is inextricably bound to the use of land. The site-specific nature of Indian religious practice derives from the Native American perception that land is itself a sacred, living being. [24]

Brennan's quote comes from his dissenting opinion in *Lyng v. Northwest Indian Cemetery Protective Association* in which the majority of the Supreme Court held that the free exercise clause does not prevent the federal government from destroying an Indian sacred site located on federal public lands. Under *Lyng*, the practice of traditional tribal religions, with their emphasis on collective, intergenerational obligations between humans and the natural world, seems beyond the purview of the First Amendment. [25]

The legal scholar and theologian Vine Deloria, Jr., once wrote: "[t]here is no salvation in tribal religions apart from the continuance of the tribe itself."[26] Under this view, an individual rights model of religious freedom seems poorly suited to the American Indian context. The definition of "free exercise" in terms of individual rights to believe—versus collective responsibilities to steward the natural world through ceremony—may subvert tribal values and experiences. In *Lyng*, because no individual could show the harm (denial of a government benefit or imposition of a sanction) necessary to maintain a First Amendment claim, the Forest Service was legally permitted to destroy the sacred site, even if it would "virtually destroy" the religion of three tribes.[27] Religious freedoms modeled on this standard would seem antithetical to the survival of Indian religion and culture.

To a significant extent, then, I accept the validity of the assimilation critique as applied to the religious freedoms context: adopting a federally modeled free exercise clause may present tribal governments with serious challenges of cultural revitalization and self-government based on traditional norms. However, I also suggest that individual rights do not *necessarily* equal assimilation in the context of traditional American Indian religions.[28] Tribes might have their own indigenous traditions of individual religious expression and/or contemporary expectations of individual religious rights. They may have adopted constitutional or other law containing individual religious freedoms rights for a variety of reasons, some of which could still be apt today. They may be engaged in an ongoing process of reconciling modern law with traditional values, through legal developments that respect individual and collective interests. For all of these and other reasons, this chapter explores the possibility that, notwithstanding the important cautions of the assimilation critique, some tribes maintain and implement individual religious freedoms provisions in ways that actually affirm tribal culture and advance tribal sovereignty today.[29]

Part I acknowledges that the topic of tribal religious freedoms is a sensitive one and describes the author's approach to these topics. Part II discusses the legal framework of American Indian religious freedoms in tribal settings, noting that precisely because the Constitution is not binding on Indian tribes, the Indian Civil Rights Act and tribal law are the key legal sources in such matters.[30] This section analyzes several examples of religious freedoms provisions found in tribal constitutions, describing the extent to which they reflect or depart from ICRA's free exercise language. Part III outlines scholarly concerns about individual rights under tribal law, especially the critique that individual rights threaten tribal norms and harm tribal sovereignty. It then evaluates the critique by reference to tribal constitutional provisions, case law, and other sources of information on tribal religious rights and responsibilities. As suggested above, this part argues that the assimilation critique is valid, if potentially overstated, in the tribal religious freedoms context. In Part IV, the article offers some thought about how tribes can, and do, effectuate religious freedoms in ways that protect both individual interests and tribal sovereignty. These include: (1) using tribal custom as a basis for interpreting positive law on individual religious rights, (2) maintaining separate institutions for the resolution of legal disputes about religion, and (3) engaging in constitutional reform to change religious rights provisions that are inconsistent with tribal values. In Part V, the chapter concludes with a detailed description of one tribal court's attempt to reconcile religious freedoms and tribal tradition in a dispute among Sun Dance practitioners, offering it as a poignant example of just how difficult and important these issues are.

PART I: WRITING ABOUT RELIGIOUS FREEDOM

Writing about religious freedom and American Indian religious practices presents a number of challenges for scholars.[31] First, the English word *religion* may not fully capture tribal peoples' spiritual practices. In its Western sense, *religion* means "the service and worship of God or the supernatural" or "a personal set or institutionalized system of religious attitudes, beliefs, and practices."[32] But across the many tribal cultures and languages, different understandings may be operative. For example, the Cherokee Nation offers the word *dinelvdodi* as a direct translation of the English word *religion*.[33] At the same time, the Cherokee word *eloh* or *elohi*, meaning "earth" or "world," has also been translated to mean "religion," and simultaneously means "history, culture, law, and land." [34]

In many Native cultures, religion is inseparable from relationships and rituals, from stories and place.[35] In a Navajo setting, for example, it may be more appropriate to conceptualize an entire way of living in harmony with one's surroundings, relatives, and circumstances—rather than a discrete "religion."[36] James Zion, former solicitor to the Courts of the Navajo Nation, explains: "One of the fundamental principles of Navajo life is the phrase *sa'ah naaghai bik'eh hozho* which has been translated as 'the conditions for health and well-being are harmony within and connection to the physical/spiritual world.'" [37] For many indigenous peoples, a spiritual relationship with the land is a fundamental aspect of their identity as human beings. According to the Cheyenne scholar Henrietta Mann, for example, the Cheyenne word *Xamaa-vo'-estaneo'o,* which translates as "indigenous, aboriginal, or ordinary people," also evokes the sacred relationship that the people have with the land.[38] Within tribal communities, then, religious and spiritual life merits deep reflection not easily captured in scholarly discourse.

American Indian religions have been poorly understood by outsiders.[39] Former Principal Chief of the Cherokee Nation Wilma Mankiller once argued that "stereotypes . . . particularly with regard to spirituality" persist "because of the dearth of accurate information about Native people."[40] The hundreds of tribal religions and cultures are often lumped into generalities about Indian relationships with the natural world. But, on the other hand, when scholars try to move past stereotype and examine religion in specific tribal settings, they risk misunderstanding practices grounded in cultural traditions with which they may have inadequate familiarity.[41] They also risk violating privacy norms that may dictate that religious and cultural traditions be kept confidential among members, clans, societies, or practitioners within the tribal community.[42] Violation of these privacy norms and, at the worst extreme, appropriation of tribal religious ceremonies by outsiders, can have devastating effects for everyone involved.[43]

In some tribal communities, contemporary privacy norms are a response to religious persecution. Historically, the United States and Christian organizations have undertaken practices designed to eradicate American Indian religious practices.[44] As the Tenth Circuit recognized recently:

> [P]ast federal policy was to assimilate American Indians into United States culture, in part by deliberately suppressing, and even destroying, traditional tribal religions and culture in the 19th and early 20th centuries. The government provided direct and indirect support to Christian missionaries who sought to convert and civilize the Indians, and from the 1890's to 1930's, the government moved beyond promoting voluntary abandonment of tribal religions to, in some instances, affirmatively prohibiting those religions. By the late 19th Century federal attempts to replace traditional Indian religions with Christianity grew violent. In 1890 for example, the United States Calvary shot and killed 300 unarmed Sioux men, women and children en route to an Indian religious ceremony called the Ghost Dance. . . . In 1892, Congress outlawed the practice of traditional Indian religious rituals on reservation land. Engaging in the Sun Dance, one of the ceremonies at issue in this case, was punishable by withholding 10 days' rations or 10 days' imprisonment. This and other laws disrupted and harmed Indian practices, but many, including the Sun Dance and others at issue in this case, survived.[45]

Attitudes and practices have evolved considerably since the late nineteenth century. The American Indian Religious Freedom Act of 1978 states that "it shall be the policy of the federal government . . . to protect and preserve for American Indians their inherent right of freedom to believe, express, and exercise the traditional religions . . . including but not limited to access to sites, use, and possession of sacred objects, and the freedom to worship through ceremonials and traditional rites."[46] Yet American Indian religious practitioners face contemporary challenges. As described above, the Supreme Court held in its 1988 *Lyng* decision that the federal government's decision to build a road through an American Indian sacred site did not violate the First Amendment even if it would "virtually destroy" the Indian religion.[47] In 2009, the Ninth Circuit held that the federal government could desecrate an Indian sacred site notwithstanding the Religious Freedom Restoration Act's protection against government actions that "substantially burden" religious exercise.[48] Thus the discussion of contemporary individual religious freedom occurs against a continuing history of Indian religious oppression. Scholars must acknowledge that many traditional tribal religions are still vulnerable, and the question of individual religious "freedom" may be highly charged in the context of communities that have been harmed by outside religions, governments, and citizens. In some communities, the struggle of tribal religions to survive against external threats may be more immediately pressing than questions of individual rights against tribal governments.[49]

Despite all of these challenges, the topic of religious freedom is important to tribal citizens concerned with their own rights[50] and to tribal governments as they develop and reform their law and governing institutions.[51] This chapter thus addresses the issue of religious freedoms, but with an awareness of the challenges described above.[52] Where possible, it comments on the legal experiences of specific tribes and tries not to over-extrapolate. Instead of discussing details of tribal rituals or practices,[53] this piece focuses on the law, relying primarily on the published constitutions, codes, and judicial decisions of tribal nations. It cites and describes the works of anthropologists with attention to the limitations of those works, offering them as sources to the extent that they may ultimately be helpful to tribal lawmakers.[54] With respect to the historical backdrop, the chapter makes observations about instances where individual claims might threaten tribal cultural and religious revitalization efforts, and ultimately leaves to tribal leaders and members the decisions about where and how to draw the lines. This chapter uses the word *religion* in its common sense, to refer to major world religions like Christianity, and also to refer to the ceremonial practices, spiritual beliefs, and cultural lifeways of American Indians.

PART II: LEGAL SOURCES ON INDIAN RELIGIOUS FREEDOMS

The First Amendment

The First Amendment of the US Constitution provides: "Congress shall make no law respecting an establishment of religion, or prohibiting the free exercise thereof."[55] As described above, however, the Constitution does not restrict the powers of tribal governments.[56] The Supreme Court explained in *Talton v. Mayes* that "the powers of local self-government enjoyed by [an Indian tribe] existed prior to the Constitution," and these powers are not subject to the limitations on the federal and state governments contained in the Constitution.[57] Two federal cases predating ICRA illustrate the development of this principle in the religious freedoms arena.

In *Native American Church v. Navajo Tribal Council*, plaintiffs challenged a Navajo Nation ordinance criminalizing peyote on the reservation.[58] The Native American Church is an intertribal indigenous religion whose practitioners ingest peyote as a sacrament. The legislation provided:

> Whereas ... use [of peyote] is not connected with any Navajo religious practices and is contradiction to the traditional ceremonies of the Navajo people: therefore be it resolved that as far as the Navajo people are concerned peyote is harmful and foreign to our traditional way of life: be it further resolved that the introduction into the Navajo country of the use of peyote by the Navajo people be stamped out and appropriate action be taken by the Tribal Courts to enforce this action.[59]

The ordinance levied punishment of nine months' labor or a fine of $100 against anyone convicted of sale, use, or possession of peyote.[60]

Members of the Native American Church sued to enjoin the anti-peyote ordinance on grounds that it violated freedom of religion under the First Amendment.[61] The Tenth Circuit held that the federal courts lacked jurisdiction in the case because "the First Amendment applies only to Congress," and whereas the Fourteenth Amendment made it applicable to states, the same was not true of tribes.[62] According to the court, tribes had a "higher status than that of states" and had surrendered to the United States only to the extent explicitly provided in a treaty or statute.[63] Although the Navajo plaintiffs could not sue in federal court, the Navajo tribal council ultimately decided to adopt a legislative provision in favor of the freedom of religion and specifically abolish the prohibition on peyote.[64]

A second pre-ICRA case on the inapplicability of the First Amendment to tribal governments is *Toledo v. Pueblo de Jemez*.[65] The plaintiff tribal members claimed that because of their Protestant faith, the Pueblo government had denied them the right to bury their dead in the community cemetery, the right to build a church on Pueblo land, the right to have missionaries, and the right to use a communal wheat threshing machine.[66] The plaintiffs further claimed that the Pueblo government had "threatened them with the loss of their birthrights, homes and personal property unless they accept the Catholic religion."[67] All of these transgressions had occurred, the Protestant members alleged, even though the Pueblo had legislative provisions ensuring the freedom of religion.[68]

In *Toledo*, the plaintiffs sued under the Civil Rights Act providing for liability where any person "acting under color of state or territorial law" deprives another of "rights, privileges, or immunities secured by the Constitution and laws."[69] The court found that the tribal government officials could not have acted under New Mexico law because the Pueblo was under the guardianship of the United States. Moreover, the court recognized: "[T]he Pueblos do not derive their governmental powers from the State of New Mexico .... Indeed ... the powers of an Indian tribe do not spring from the United States although they are subject to the paramount authority of Congress."[70]

Following *Native American Church* and *Toledo*, tribal plaintiffs appeared to have little, if any, basis for bringing religious freedoms lawsuits against tribal governments in the federal courts.[71] The only possibility alluded to by the courts was that Congress might enact some legislation authorizing such suits.[72] Congress seemed to take some steps in that direction when it enacted the Indian Civil Rights Act of 1968.[73]

The Indian Civil Rights Act

Often called the "Indian Bill of Rights," ICRA provides that tribal governments may not intrude on certain individual civil rights.[74] Among the rights enumerated in the statute is ICRA's equivalent of a free exercise clause: "No Indian tribe in exercising powers of self-government shall make or enforce any law prohibiting the free exercise of religion."[75] ICRA does not, however, contain any equivalent of the establishment clause.[76] Legislative history suggests that Congress omitted an establishment clause "out of respect for the religious-based governments of the Pueblos of the southwest."[77] For this reason, the rest of this chapter focuses largely on free exercise-type laws and claims.

For the most part, ICRA's substantive provisions are not enforceable in federal courts. As the Supreme Court explained in *Santa Clara Pueblo v. Martinez*, ICRA does not waive tribal sovereign immunity, nor does it provide a federal cause of action for civil rights claims against tribal governments.[78] In fact, the only federal remedy ICRA provides is a habeas corpus petition for individuals held in custody by a tribal government.[79] This exception for habeas jurisdiction will not typically be helpful to individuals making religious freedoms claims, unless perhaps a tribe detains or banishes an individual for religious reasons or imposes a penalty that impedes his or her religious practice.[80]

Moreover, the policy rationales articulated in *Martinez* are apt in the religion context. In *Martinez*, the Supreme Court described what it saw as ICRA's goals of promoting both individual rights and tribal government.[81] Because these goals are competing, Congress struck an appropriate balance between them by providing a federal remedy only where an individual's physical liberty was at issue. Moreover, the tribal interest is heightened and the federal interest diminished in cases involving internal matters like tribal citizenship.[82] As a practical matter, tribal legal institutions are more likely to have access to the kind of spiritual, cultural, and linguistic information that would allow them to decide religious freedoms cases.[83]

Indeed, ICRA is often enforceable in tribal courts, either because a particular tribal court has held that the ICRA waives sovereign immunity and creates a cause of action in tribal court or because tribal statutory or constitutional provisions have done the same.[84] Many tribes allow suits against tribal officials for declaratory and injunctive relief with respect to claims under civil rights laws or the tribal constitution.[85] The upshot is that if tribal citizens want to sue tribal governments for intrusions into their religious freedoms, the most likely forum is tribal court.

Tribal Constitutions

With this background in mind, we can now turn to the question of tribal law on religious freedoms and eventually to the question of whether the law advances assimilation, adaptation, or something else. In many cases, the tribal law is ICRA's free exercise provision, either adopted by the tribal constitution or applied as a federal statute. In other cases, tribes have statutory, decisional, regulatory, or customary law on religious freedom—or perhaps no law on religious freedom at all.

For purposes of narrowing the discussion somewhat, this section focuses on individual religious freedoms that are found in tribal *constitutions*, with some attention to the other sources of law. The chapter does not attempt to survey each of the several hundred tribes with written constitutions, but rather discusses several examples of tribal constitutional approaches to religious freedoms.[86] It groups these approaches into four categories: (1) constitutions with religious freedom language that references, incorporates, or tracks the ICRA; (2) constitutions that do not use ICRA but echo the principles of individual religious freedom found in the First Amendment; (3) constitutions with unique language on religion, clearly expressing distinct tribal values and norms (even if they also reference ICRA); and (4) constitutions that do not reference religion or related concepts at all.

The first group consists of tribal constitutions with religious freedom provisions that reference, incorporate, or track the language of the ICRA. Several of these constitutions expressly incorporate and set forth the ICRA. For example, the Crow Tribal Constitution provides: "In accordance with Title II of the Indian Civil Rights Act of 1968 (82 Stat. 77), the Crow Tribe of Indians in exercising its powers of self-government shall not: (a) make or enforce any law prohibiting the full exercise of religion."[87] Other tribal constitutions may have a section on the "Rights of Indians" or "Bill of Rights" that tracks the language of the Indian Civil Rights Act without referencing it explicitly. Tribal constitutions in this group, such as that of the Mississippi Choctaw Band of Indians, provide that the tribal government "shall not: (a) Make or enforce any law prohibiting the free exercise of religion."[88] Still other constitutions generally prohibit the tribal government from denying religious freedom and then expressly incorporate ICRA. For example the Constitution of the Skokomish Tribe provides: "The Skokomish Tribal Government shall not deny to any person within its jurisdiction freedom of . . . religion. . . . The tribe shall provide to all persons within its jurisdiction the rights guaranteed by the Indian Civil Rights Act of 1968."[89] Still other tribal constitutions expressly incorporate ICRA, without making separate mention of "religion" or "free exercise," as in the following example:

> The Miami Tribe, in exercising its powers of self-government, shall not take any action which is in violation of the laws of the United States as the same shall exist from time to time respecting civil rights and civil liberties of persons. This chapter shall not abridge the concept of self-government or the obligations of the members of the Miami Tribe to abide by this Constitution and the ordinances, res-

olutions, and other legally instituted actions of the Miami Tribe. The protections guaranteed by the Indian Civil Rights Act of 1968 (82 Stat. 78) shall apply to all members of the Miami Tribe.[90]

The second group consists of tribal constitutions with religious freedoms provisions that do not reference, track, or incorporate the ICRA, but echo the general principles of the First Amendment. For example, the Big Lagoon Rancheria Constitution provides that: "no member shall be denied freedom of . . . religion . . . or other rights guaranteed by applicable federal law."[91] The Ute Indian Tribe of the Uintah and Ouray Reservation provides: "All members of the . . . Tribe . . . may enjoy, without hindrance, freedom of . . . worship."[92] One provision recurring in a number of constitutions, such as the Choctaw Nation of Oklahoma's, is that "no religious test shall ever be required as a qualification to any office of public trust in this Nation."[93] Others, such as that of the Muscogee Creek Tribe of Oklahoma, have a similar statement declaring that all citizens have the right to vote in tribal elections "regardless of religion, creed, or sex."[94] Some of these latter provisions may involve establishment clause-type concerns.

The third group consists of tribal constitutions with unique language on religion, clearly expressing distinct tribal values and norms. Some of these speak in terms not only of individual, but also of collective rights and objectives. Some expressly reference not only religion but also Indian tradition and culture. Still others contain specific protections for their tribal ceremonies or rights associated with sacred places.[95] Of particular interest is the "Constitution of the Iroquois Nations or The Great Binding Law, Gayanashagowa."[96] This constitution is traditional, given to the Iroquois people by the Peacemaker Dekanawidah, rather than one of modern vintage.[97] The Iroquois Constitution is notable in that these constitutional protections seem to be for the religion itself, and the people have responsibilities. In a section called "Religious Ceremonies Protected," the Iroquois Constitution provides that:

> 99. The rites and festivals of each nation shall remain undisturbed and shall continue as before because they were given by the people of old times as useful and necessary for the good of men.

> 100. It shall be the duty of the Lords of each brotherhood to confer at the approach of the time of the Midwinter Thanksgiving and to notify their people of the approaching festival. They shall hold a council over the matter and arrange its details and begin the Thanksgiving five days after the moon of Dis-ko-nah is new. The people shall assemble at the appointed place and the nephews shall notify the people of the time and place. From the beginning to the end the Lords shall preside over the Thanksgiving and address the people from time to time.

101. It shall be the duty of the appointed managers of the Thanksgiving festivals to do all that is needed for carrying out the duties of the occasions.

The recognized festivals of Thanksgiving shall be the Midwinter Thanksgiving, the Maple or Sugar-making Thanksgiving, the Raspberry Thanksgiving, the Strawberry Thanksgiving, the Cornplanting Thanksgiving, the Corn Hoeing Thanksgiving, the Little Festival of Green Corn, the Great Festival of Ripe Corn and the complete Thanksgiving for the Harvest.

Each nation's festivals shall be held in their Long Houses.

102. When the Thanksgiving for the Green Corn comes the special managers, both the men and women, shall give it careful attention and do their duties properly.

103. When the Ripe Corn Thanksgiving is celebrated the Lords of the Nation must give it the same attention as they give to the Midwinter Thanksgiving.

104. Whenever any man proves himself by his good life and his knowledge of good things, naturally fitted as a teacher of good things, he shall be recognized by the Lords as a teacher of peace and religion and the people shall hear him.[98]

The Iroquois Constitution makes clear that the people must fulfill duties to ensure the perpetuation of the ceremonies. Indirectly, of course, the duty of the people to protect the ceremonies also means that individuals will be able to partake in the ceremonies. Viewed in this light, the constitution could be read as recognizing an individual right to religious practice, but the more obvious focus of the provisions on festivals and ceremonial events seems to be on responsibilities. And though various other sections of the constitution outline the rights of people in the community, including "lords," "war chiefs," and people from "foreign nations," these rights are similarly framed in terms of collective duties and welfare, and in the context of the Great Law. This constitution seems to express the interconnected nature of people's rights and duties.[99]

Tribal constitutions adopted more recently also explicate traditional religious and cultural values. The Land Policy and Constitution of the Yup'ik people of Bill Moore's Slough, for example, offers explicit statements on the collective nature of tribal rights and the relationship among land, tradition, and culture.[100]

We the Yup'ik people of Bill Moore's Slough being the original inhabitants of our land, having been placed here by our creator, to be the keepers of our land and having maintained this land as our creator intended us to keep it since the beginning, hereby declare our intent to continue managing it as we have always managed it in the past.

In the past as well as the present our land and the culture of our people have been intertwined to the point where it would not be possible to maintain our traditional values and lifestyle should our land be alienated, altered or otherwise changed from its traditional relationship with our people.

Therefore, it is our intent and the intent of this policy to maintain our land for all time forever for traditional uses.

Furthermore, while others may attempt to change or eliminate our culture by methods of separating our people from our land, let it be known that we will resist such attempts.

Let there be no misinterpretation nor ambiguities in this policy, it is a policy dedicated to the preservation of our traditional values, culture and lifestyle that we have maintained since the beginning.

As a further point of clarification it is the position of Bill Moore's Slough that our people would not have survived as a people without maintaining our traditional relationship with the land. Therefore let this written land policy be considered by all parties concerned to be not only an integral part of the constitution of the people of Bill Moore's Slough but to be the primary law of our people and the basis for our cultural survival.[101]

Having articulated the relationship between land, tradition, and survival, Bill Moore's Slough Constitution then sets forth specific limitations on government and rights of individuals:

ARTICLE I

A) The Bill Moores Slough Elders Council shall pass all resolutions and laws dealing with land issues in conformity with the Bill Moores Slough Land Policy.

B) The Bill Moores Slough Elders Council shall protect, preserve and defend the Bill Moores Slough land, land policy and its peoples' traditional relationship with the land to the best of its ability.

ARTICLE II

A) The Bill Moores Slough Elders Council shall pass no laws jeopardizing certain freedoms and rights deemed to be given our people by our peoples creator.
Amongst these freedoms and rights are:
The freedom to government by and for the people.
The right to speak ones Conscience.

The right to an education relevant to ones way of life.
Freedom from want, hunger, pain and fear.
The right to liberty.
The right to be Yupik.
All rights guaranteed by Federal law including but not limited to
Title II of the Indian Civil Rights Act of 1968.[102]

The Poarch Creek Constitution speaks in terms of *tribal* interest, connecting religion and community survival, explaining that the purpose of the tribal government is to:

(1) Continue forever, with the help of God our Creator, our unique identity as members of the Poarch Band of Creek Indians, and to Poarch identity from forces that threaten to diminish it;

(2) Protect our inherent rights as members of a sovereign American Indian tribe;

(3) Promote our cultural and religious beliefs and to pass them in our own way to our children, grandchildren, and grandchildren's children forever;

. . .

(8) Insure that our people shall live in peace and harmony among ourselves and with all other people.[103]

In such a context of intergenerational cultural and religious interests, kinship with others, and political sovereignty, the Poarch Creek Constitution affords its members "the right to exercise the tribal rights and privileges of members of the Poarch Band of Creek Indians."[104]

Finally, there are tribal constitutions with no express provision on religion. The White Mountain Apache Constitution, for example, does not expressly mention religion but provides for "freedom of conscience."[105] Of course, some of these tribes may deal with religion in their legislative codes. The White Mountain Apache code offers extensive protection for sacred sites within the reservation.[106] The Colville Constitution does not mention religion, but the Colville Tribal Civil Rights Act contains a free exercise provision.[107]

Still other tribes, like the Navajo Nation, do not have written constitutions. Tribes without written constitutions might have: (1) other written law, such as tribal codes or judicial decisions, on religion; (2) oral or customary law on religion; or, perhaps (3) no written or oral law on religion at all. In the Navajo Nation, for example, legal provisions on religion are found in the legislative code, the Fundamental Law of the Dine, and possibly in other sources as well.[108]

PART III: CONSIDERING THE "ASSIMILATION CRITIQUE"

The above examples suggest at least four tribal constitutional approaches to the freedom of religion: (1) constitutions that reference, track, or incorporate ICRA; (2) constitutions that do not use ICRA but echo US principles of individual religious freedom; (3) constitutions with unique language on religion, clearly expressing distinct tribal values and norms; and (4) constitutions that do not reference religion or related concepts at all.[109] This section considers possible ramifications of these approaches to individual religious freedom vis à vis scholarship critiquing individual rights in tribal law as a general matter.

In a recent article, Carole Goldberg points out that "[m]ost contemporary scholars concerned with what may be called tribal revitalization—the strengthening of political and cultural sovereignty for Native nations—treat individual rights as an impediment to achieving that objective, not a positive tool."[110] Surveying leading scholars, she cites Robert Porter, who describes "the introduction of individual rights into tribal litigation" as "fatal to tribalistic norms" and "therefore damaging to tribal sovereignty."[111] Similarly, Vine Deloria and Clifford Lytle argue "that individual rights requirements imposed on Indian nations transpose societies which understand themselves as a complex of responsibilities and duties into societies based on rights against the government and eliminate any sense of responsibility that the people might have felt for one another."[112] Finally, Kevin Washburn has argued that "the introduction of individual rights into tribal justice systems tended to standardize the cultures of Indian nations."[113]

Together these scholarly viewpoints represent what I call an "assimilation critique" of individual rights in tribal law. The assimilation critique suggests that individual rights are usually foreign and contrary to traditional tribal law and largely imposed on tribal communities by outside forces, especially the federal government. The imposition of US-styled rights is, in turn, harmful to Indian culture and sovereignty because it displaces or alters traditional tribal laws, values, and institutions. Taking the assimilation critique as a point of departure, this part of the chapter will first explore ways in which tribal constitutions with individual religious freedoms may indeed represent assimilation and be harmful to tribal sovereignty. It will then consider alternative explanations and ramifications for the presence of individual religious freedoms in tribal constitutions.

Individual Religious Freedoms as Representing and Effectuating Assimilation

The role of the federal government in drafting tribal constitutions. The above discussion reveals that some tribal constitutions repeat the principles, or even the very words, of the First Amendment or ICRA. On the one hand, tribes may have decided on their own to incorporate the substantive provisions of ICRA after it was passed. On the other hand, it is important to acknowledge that the federal government has long played a role in the development of tribal constitutions, a role set forth in the Indian Reorganization Act of 1934 (IRA).[114] After a long period of federal opposition to tribal governments through the reservation and assimilation eras, the IRA allowed tribes to reorganize as modern governmental entities, with eligibility for enhanced federal funding.[115] Tribes had the opportunity to accept or reject IRA constitutions by popular vote of the tribal citizenry. Those who voted in favor typically adopted a constitution or bylaws providing for governance by a tribal council that would manage tribal resources through a political or corporate entity.[116]

The IRA has been critiqued as imposing Anglo-American norms, institutions, and procedures on tribal communities.[117] Indeed, many tribes had traditional governments still functioning at the time of the IRA—whereas other tribes maintained traditional norms and values that had only gone underground during the nineteenth and early twentieth centuries. The IRA seemed to supplant those traditional governments with Anglo-American style governments by encouraging tribes to adopt constitutions and through other measures.

Among other things, the Interior Department provided tribes with various models of substantive constitutional law during the IRA period.[118] These included a "Basic Memorandum" of advice on adopting a constitution and, in some instances, a "Model Constitution" and/or "Outline of Tribal Constitution and Bylaws."[119] Yet recent scholarship on the papers of Felix Cohen, who served as associate solicitor of the Interior Department during the IRA era, also suggests that these documents may not have been widely distributed or intended to impose boilerplate language to the extent that scholars had previously argued.[120]

With respect to religious freedom specifically, neither the generic Model Constitution nor the Outline of Tribal Constitution and Bylaws provided by the government to some tribes during the IRA era appears to contain any free exercise clause provision.[121] Cohen's *Basic Memorandum on Drafting of Tribal Constitutions* to tribes stated:

> If it is thought desirable to include in the constitution a declaration of the rights of the people, the following provisions, taken from the constitution of the Choctaw Nation, adopted in 1890, may provide a helpful guide.
>
> . . .
>
> Section 3. That there shall be no establishment of religion by law. No preference shall ever be given to any religious sects, society, denomination, or mode of worship, and no religious test shall ever be allowed as a qualification to any public trust under his government.
>
> Section 4. That no human authority out in any case whatever control or interfere with rights of conscience in matters of religion.[122]

Thus, tribes would have had this guidance in favor of freedom of conscience and against the establishment of religion as they prepared IRA constitutions. And tribes would have also had the federal First Amendment as a model. By providing such models and encouraging tribes to adopt constitutions, the government may well have influenced tribes to adopt religious freedoms provisions based on norms and provisions of federal law. Yet the IRA period also marked federal attention to traditional tribal religions. As Charles Wilkinson has written, Commission of Indian Affairs John Collier took measures to protect the Sun Dance and other ceremonies, issuing the order that "no interference with Indian religious life or ceremonial expression will hereafter be tolerated."[123]

In addition to government's involvement in some substantive aspects of IRA constitutions, the IRA also provided a process for adopting and ratifying constitutions. The IRA contemplates that the secretary of the Interior shall "call and hold" the election, provide "technical assistance," and "review the final draft of the constitution and bylaws, or amendments thereto to determine if any provision therein is contrary to applicable laws."[124] The secretary shall then "notify the tribe, in writing, whether and in what manner the Secretary has found the proposed constitution and bylaws or amendments thereto to be contrary to applicable laws."[125] After the election, the secretary shall approve of the constitution chosen by the tribe, unless he or she finds it contrary to applicable laws.[126] To some extent, this process continues to influence tribes' constitutions today,[127] especially by requiring that the secretary of the Interior approve tribal constitutions.[128]

Unlike the recent works on the IRA described above, there is, to my knowledge, less scholarship studying the role of the federal government in tribal constitutional adoption and amendment following ICRA. I would agree with Professor Goldberg that "tribal protection for individual rights became considerably more prevalent after Congress passed the Indian Civil Rights Act in 1968,"[129] but I do not know if this growth was the result of independent tribal decision making, influence by the federal government, or some combination of these.

For a future project, it might be revealing to study the extent to which the secretary has employed this approval power to encourage tribes to insert ICRA language into their constitutions. At least one tribe has recently rejected this requirement of secretarial approval—adopting a new constitution that also strikes references to the ICRA that had been present in the tribe's earlier constitution.[130] Whether through secretarial approval or other mechanisms, the federal government seems to have had some influence on tribes' decisions to incorporate ICRA into their constitutions—a conjecture that would benefit from additional investigation. More generally, it is safe to say that the federal government has historically had a role in modeling and approving tribal constitutions, and this role may have led some tribes to adopt individual religious freedoms resembling federal law.[131]

Substantive law and assimilation. Whether as a result of independent tribal decision making, federal influence, or some combination thereof, many tribal constitutions now contain language from the First Amendment, ICRA, or other federal law on religion. From a substantive perspective, these provisions may express a view of religion that is too narrow—or just a bad fit—for tribal worldviews and cultures. As discussed earlier, in *Lyng*, the Court held that the First Amendment did not prevent the federal government from destroying a sacred site.[132] The Court explained that the First Amendment only prohibited government actions that "coerced belief."[133] It did not protect specific practices or limit the government's right to develop its land.[134] Then in *Employment Division v. Smith*, the US Supreme Court upheld a state statute denying unemployment benefits to an employee and member of the Native American Church who had been terminated for peyote use.[135] The Court found no violation of the federal free exercise clause because the law was facially neutral and generally applicable, even though the law effectively punished Smith for practicing his religion.[136]

Thus a tribal law modeled on the First Amendment—or on ICRA's language closely resembling the free exercise clause—might not protect religions that are place-based or require certain ritual activities.[137] The particular outcome in any given case would depend on the tribal court's interpretation and application of the religious freedom provision.[138] A tribal court may very well depart from the narrow conception of free exercise propounded by the Supreme Court in *Smith* and *Lyng*—and choose instead to interpret an ICRA-like provision consistent with tribal norms.[139] On the other hand, scholars have documented the tendency of some tribal courts to follow relevant federal and state law, even when it conflicts with tribal custom.[140] Examples of tribal court cases representing each of these modes of interpretation are discussed below.[141]

Additionally, with their focus on individual rights, tribal constitutions modeled on federal law may ignore the duties of tribal people and the collective nature of their religious experiences.[142] In fact, neither the ICRA nor the federal free exercise clause has any statement of individuals' religious or cultural duties to each other at all. In tribal contexts, this omission may be problematic. As Dean Suagee has written:

> Carrying on traditional tribal traditions is more than the freedom to choose, more than the right to "enjoy" one's culture. . . . The culture and religion must be passed down through the generations or the culture and religion cannot survive, and this means that some people in each generation are obligated to perform certain roles.[143]

The very survival of Indian cultures and religions is about the duty of some individuals more than it is about their liberties. Effectively linking collective responsibility to individual freedom, Suagee explains, "[i]f some people do not accept responsibility for carrying on the culture and religion, others will not have the freedom to choose the tribal religion because it will no longer exist."[144]

Many examples exist of tribal people's collective duties to maintain and practice religion for the benefit of the entire community. Some of these examples come from classic anthropological literature.[145] Ruth Underhill writes of Hopi religion:

No individual need seek a vision. His welfare was wrapped up with the welfare of the village and that was assured by the calendric round of cere-monies. Even the priest need not seek individual power. Power had been given to his clan or, perhaps, to the ruling family in his clan, long ago. What he had to do was to carry through the rites without error and to lead an upright life, free from quarreling or breach of taboo.[146]

Underhill explains that the hunting ceremonies of Plains Indians were undertaken to ensure food for the people and to maintain humans' relationship with the natural world. Individuals had duties not only to each other, but also to the animals and plants:

"Hunting is a holy occupation," said the Naskapi. So was the gather-ing of plants, the cutting of trees, even the digging of clay. For these Nature Persons had long ago offered their "flesh" for Indian use—but on certain conditions. Every step in obtaining the flesh must be taken with care and ceremony, or the gift would be withdrawn.[147]

Underhill also describes the Sun Dance of the Plains people as occurring "for the general welfare" of the people.[148]

Contemporary accounts of Indian religious practices also reflect their collec-tive and relational qualities. In the *Lyng* case, the district court described Yurok, Karuk, and Tolowa practices as follows:

The religious power these individuals acquire in the high country lends meaning to these tribal ceremonies, thereby enhancing the spiritual welfare of the entire tribal community. Medicine women in the tribes travel to the high country to pray, to obtain spiritual power, and to gather medicines. They then return to the tribe to administer to the sick the healing power gained in the high coun-try through ceremonies such as the Brush and Kick Dances.[149]

These ceremonies and dances provided the "World Renewal" essential to the tribes' religious belief system,[150] making the Supreme Court's ultimate decision not to protect them in *Lyng* particularly difficult to understand.[151]

Some contemporary indigenous leaders describe ceremonies that not only require cooperative behavior, but also have as their primary purpose and effect the renewal of relationships. The late Wilma Mankiller explained, "The Creator provided us with ceremonies to remind us of our place in the universe and our responsibil-ities as human beings."[152] With respect to Cherokee practices, she recounts:

Each year one Cherokee ceremony in a series was conducted in each settlement for the explicit purpose of rekindling relationships, requesting forgiveness for inappropriate conduct during the previ-

ous year, and cleansing the minds of Cherokee people of any negative thoughts towards each other. . . . The primary goal of prayer is
to promote a sense of oneness and unity.[153]

A number of tribes emphasize the collective, relational nature of religion in
their laws. The Iroquois Constitution described above offers a detailed example. In
other tribes, legislation fills the same purpose; for example, a Navajo Nation Resolution provides:

> This religion, Beauty Way of Life, holds this land sacred and that
> we, the Navajo People, must always care for it. Through this sacred
> covenant, this sacred ancestral homeland is the home and hogan of
> all Navajo people. Further, if the Navajo left their homelands, all
> prayers and religion would be ineffective and lost forever.[154]

In still other tribes, these principles may be enforced through unwritten customary
law, the expectations and teachings of families, clans, and societies. In any of these
settings, where a key purpose of the religion or spiritual practice is to achieve harmony for the community, the assertion of individual rights may threaten the fabric
of tribal life—or just seem beside the point.

Tribal constitutions modeled on ICRA or the free exercise clause may also fail
to reflect the history of suppression of Indian religions. As described above in Part
I, religious and governmental institutions collaborated to Christianize and civilize
Indians from contact through the better part of the twentieth century.[155] These programs, occurring alongside the broader project of colonization, threatened the very
existence of tribes.[156] This history means that today, the survival of tribes might
hinge more on the collective recovery and revitalization of Indian religions—
including the maintenance of a land base, the instruction of young people in ritual
duties and tribal language, and the repatriation of sacred items—than on the right
to maintain an individual belief system.[157]

Tribal procedures, institutions, and assimilation. Finally, to the extent that
tribes allow individuals to bring religious freedoms claims into tribal courts, this
decision may be inconsistent with tribal procedural and institutional norms and
practices. In some communities, religious issues may be handled by elders, clan leaders, or religious societies.[158] Providing a basis for a legal claim in tribal court might
undermine these traditional bases of authority and decision making, and vest power
in a body that is not experienced or able to handle spiritual matters. Several cases
discussed below, from the Cheyenne-Arapaho Tribal Court, reflect this problem.[159]
Even if tribal court jurisdiction is appropriate, one can imagine the challenge for
tribal judges who may not be fluent speakers of the tribal language, well-versed in
tribal custom, or enjoy access to the generations of community knowledge necessary to having full understanding of religious issues.[160]

This problem is particularly fraught given that many tribal courts originated through the federal government's installation of reservation courts staffed by federal agents to bring law and order to Indian country. According to one recent tribal court opinion, the Code of Federal Regulation courts were created in the 1880s "as tools of assimilation to bring non-Indian education and discipline to help 'civilize' reservation communities."[161] Some of these courts were charged with carrying out federal regulations sanctioning Indian religious practices. Indeed, CFR courts may have been "little more than social control mechanisms that resulted in the destruction of tribal religion and traditional culture."[162] In some communities, these courts or their descendants are the ones now called on to interpret ICRA and its religious freedoms provisions.

Of course, tribal courts have been completely transformed in the contemporary period and now act as institutions of self-government.[163] Questions of judicial qualification and cultural competency may be addressed through judicial selection processes or training programs. Yet tribal courts are usually still adversarial in nature—casting parties in oppositional roles, fomenting argument, and deciding a "winner" and "loser."[164] Moreover, in some communities, even the most traditional judge may not be authorized to make decisions about religious matters. Tribal life may be better served by respecting the traditional structures of dispute resolution and allowing religious or cultural leaders to resolve religious or cultural disputes in a way that maintains community norms.[165]

In all of these ways, wholesale adoption of ICRA or the First Amendment could reflect or facilitate an assimilationist agenda, ultimately reframing the struggle for sovereignty away from maintenance of a kinship-based way of life and toward the acquisition of Western-defined rights.[166]

Non-Assimilationist Explanations for Tribal Constitutional Provisions on Individual Religious Freedoms

In contrast to the discussion above, this section considers the possibility that tribal constitutions with individual religious freedoms provisions may be animated by principles and practices other than assimilation.[167] First, some tribes may have long-standing values in favor of individual rights generally. Among the Hopi and Zuni, for example, "there is a strong belief that adult individuals are ultimately free to act as they see fit and are not to be judged by other humans for their actions. . . . In Hopi, this respect for individual freedom is expressed by the phrase, '*Pi um pi*' or 'it's up to you.'"[168] This respect for individualism exists alongside the "obligations and duties toward one's kin . . . necessary for the proper order of Hopi or Zuni society."[169] The Navajo tribe holds a core value that "no one and no institution has the privilege to interfere with individual action unless it causes an injury to another or the group."[170]

The above examples have to do with individual freedoms generally. But it is also possible that tribes historically accommodated or even encouraged individuals' religious freedom. Whereas tribes should not be bound to the practices of any particular point in history,[171] "[t]radition plays a very important role" [in contemporary questions of Indian governance] since it lays out values and presents social and cultural justifications."[172] Therefore, it may helpful to situate contemporary individual religious freedoms against several examples from earlier anthropological and ethnographic studies.

Karl N. Llewellyn and E. Adamson Hoebel's *The Cheyenne Way* presents in the form of case studies certain data on Cheyenne lawmaking from 1821 to 1880.[173] In a case called *The Tribal Ostracism and Reinstatement of Sticks Everything Under His Belt*, Llewellyn and Hoebel recount the story of an individual who declared, "I am hunting for myself," ostensibly breaking tribal rules against individual hunting.[174] According to Llewellyn and Hoebel, the tribal chiefs met to decide how to handle Sticks Everything Under His Belt, ruling that "no one could help [him] in any way, no one could give him smoke, no one could talk to him."[175] Anyone who violated this ruling would have to give a Sun Dance.[176] After some years passed, a brother-in-law "took pity" on Sticks Everything Under His Belt and pledged a Sun Dance "to bring him back in."[177] The chiefs agreed and Sticks Everything Under His Belt promised to abide by tribal rules. Before the Sun Dance took place, a young man named Black Horse asked the chiefs if he could "sacrifice himself" alone up in the hills.[178] The chiefs sent Black Horse to the brother-in-law who pledged the Sun Dance, saying he should decide whether to grant Black Horse's request. The Sun Dance pledger initially denied the request saying, "you know my rule is that all must be there."[179] But Black Horse made his case for doing the ceremony his own way: "[B]rother-in-law, won't it be all right if I set up a pole on the hill and hang myself to it through my breasts? I shall hang there for the duration of the dance."[180] The pledger still demurred, saying the chiefs had agreed that everyone must act together. When Black Horse suggested that the pledger handle the situation by making "everyone . . . swing from the pole," the pledger finally said: "No, that was not mentioned in the meeting. If you want to swing from the pole, that is all right, but no one else has to unless he wishes to."[181]

On the one hand, this account may not perfectly represent traditional Cheyenne religious practices, especially given the challenges of linguistic and cultural interpretation that surely characterized Llewellyn and Hoebel's work. Yet the story might indicate room for individual expression (or even "individual rights") in instances where the individual abides by "tribal procedures." When Sticks Everything Under His Belt unilaterally declared his intent to hunt for himself, he became "a man out of the tribe." But, by contrast, Black Horse presented his individualized request first to the "head chiefs" and then to the Sun Dance pledger, ultimately securing permission in a way sanctioned by the tribe.[182] It appears that the tribe was able to accommodate Black Horse's individual interests in a way that preserved tribal order and harmony. Llewellyn and Hoebel conclude: "When they had the Sun Dance everyone had a good time. Black Horse was the only one on the pole, and there were so many in the lodge that there was not room enough for all to dance."[183]

Another example comes from the Dakota ethnographer Ella Cara Deloria, who wrote extensively about her Dakota people, emphasizing above all else the relational nature of tribal life: "One must obey kinship rules: one must be a good rela-tive. No Dakota who has participated in that life will dispute that. In the last analy-sis every other consideration was secondary—property, personal ambition, glory, good times, and life itself."[184] These rules are enforced by social norms and expec-tations, as well as by a group of "magistrates."[185] Spirituality infuses all aspects of the story. Deloria writes movingly of the Dakota Sun Dance that "might vary in minor details from band to band, but in essentials was all the same. . . . For there was brought together, into one great religious event, the fulfillment of all the vows that men in their distress had made in the preceding year; there were also the corporate prayer's for the tribe's well-being . . . offered, in tears."[186]

But even in this culture of relatives, kinship, and communal ceremony, Deloria describes individual interactions with the sacred. In her fictional though ethnograph-ically rich work *Waterlily,* she recounts the experience of Bluebird, whose daughter is dying. Bluebird engages in her own private ceremony to save the baby:

> She knew she must make some sacrificial offerings. Fumbling in her haste, she muttered to herself, "Is that right? Alas, what do I know about it? Those who know tell of the Something Holy— Taku Wakan—that has supreme power, but I never understood. It is so remote. What right have I?[187]

Despite this doubt about her "right" to make an offering, Bluebird does her best to follow what "everyone knew" about spiritual matters.[188] She goes off on her own, except for the sick baby, and makes a prayer, attempting to go to the correct place and make the correct offering. Finally she finishes the private ceremony and steps back: "Right or wrong, that was her prayer. Overwhelmed by her daring, she stood motionless, waiting—for what, she did not know. Presently someone said in her ear quite clearly, 'Hao!' It was the Dakota word of approval and consent."[189] Immedi-ately, the baby is healed, and Bluebird knows the Great Spirit has heard her. She prays to her relatives and takes the baby back to camp.[190]

This example suggests not that individual religious freedoms ever trumped col-lective duties and experiences in Dakota life, but that in Ella Deloria's view, indi-vidual religious experiences have, at times, been necessary (and perhaps tolerated), even if the individual was not sure he or she was following the rules.

From these examples, it appears that some tribes traditionally provided space for individual religious expressions and interests within the duty-bound, relational nature of the tribal community. The late Vine Deloria, Jr., the leading contempo-rary scholar writing at the intersection of Indian religion and law (and Ella Delo-ria's nephew), more explicitly addresses the complex nature of individual expression in the tribal community.[191] Deloria dismisses "the concept of an individual alone in the tribal religious sense" as "ridiculous," given the "interdependence of people" in tribal life.[192] But Deloria nonetheless accepts that "Indian tribal religions have an individual dimension."[193] He points to the individual experience in vision quests, dreams, and naming ceremonies, the designation of certain individuals to become keepers of medicine bundles or leaders in the tribal religion.[194]

For Indians, this individual experience has always been linked to the tribal community—in sharp contrast, Deloria argues, to Christianity, which has "the individual as the primary focal point and his or her relationship with the deity as her or her primary concern."[195] In Deloria's view, Indian religions traditionally "supported the individual in his or her community context, because they were community religions and not dependent on abstracting a hypothetical individual from his or her community context. One could say that the tribal religions created the tribal community, which in turn made a place for every tribal individual."[196]

Individuals' interests in religion may also arise when new religions appear in, or come to, tribal communities. Well-known examples include Handsome Lake bringing a new religion to the Seneca,[197] the arrival of the Ghost Dance on the Plains,[198] and the spread of the Native American Church.[199] When these religions reached tribal people, there were probably some conversations and struggles about whether it was acceptable for members to practice the new, as opposed to the old, religion. Perhaps more research into these historical events could serve as a basis for examining religious freedom in indigenous communities. The openness of some Indians towards Christian missionaries, and Indians' surprise about the missionaries' own closed-mindedness, suggests that some Indians tolerated people who practiced religions different from their own.[200]

The idea that Indians may have mechanisms for accepting various religions and individuals' choices about them seems to be reflected in contemporary experience. Similarly, former Principal Chief of the Cherokee Nation Wilma Mankiller writes about "traditionally minded" Indian women who practice both Christianity and tribal religions. The late Cherokee elder Florence Soap, for example, recounted how she experienced both types of religion:

> I started going to church when I was about thirteen years old. We went to church a lot. We used trails in the woods to walk to and from church. . . . As Christians we are taught to love everybody because God wants us to love each other. When I was well, I would go to the hospital and sit with people or cook for people. God taught me that. We also went to Cherokee Stomp Dances and we used traditional Cherokee medicine. My mother-in-law, Molly Soap, taught me a lot about medicine. I used to help her gather medicine in the woods. She was a good woman and a good healer who lived to be more than 110 years of age.[201]

LaDonna Harris tells about her Comanche family's experiences with religious freedom:

> My grandfather took me and my grandmother to church, and he would sit outside because he did not accept church teachings. He would sit outside and wait for us. That evening he would be singing

> peyote songs. He was a powerful man who could cure certain kinds
> of illnesses with his Indian medicine. . . . When I asked him if it
> bothered him that the church preached against the Native Ameri-
> can Church and peyote, he said no one should try to take away any-
> one else's religious beliefs. He said it would be harmful to everyone
> involved to try to take away the religious beliefs of others.[202]

These examples suggest that some individuals and families in tribal communities have the freedom to practice Christian and other religions, even as they continue to practice traditional tribal religions.[203] This tolerance for Christian practices
and beliefs exists even though several women interviewed in Mankiller's book
acknowledge the harmful, divisive, and assimilative history of Christianity in tribal
communities,[204] and some express a strong preference for tribal traditions.[205] For
some, it is the tribal religion itself that facilitates such tolerance. Linda Arandayo
describes: "I've had to wrestle with the concept of Christianity and what churches
and religions did to our people, but then Christ's messages are not violent. I finally
made peace with all that. When my family comes back to Oklahoma for the Green
Corn Ceremony at Hillubee Stomp Grounds, we take medicine together. . . . We let
go of all negative things, get well together, and get into a good relationship with the
world."[206]

From these and other descriptions, some tribal religious traditions would seem
to allow for individual freedom and expression,[207] while emphasizing communal
duties and experiences.[208] As LaDonna Harris explains, "One of the things I respect
about Comanche spirituality is there is no hierarchy or rigid structure. There are
common beliefs, including that of a Creator, but each individual finds his or her own
way to that place."[209]

Even the express incorporation of ICRA or the First Amendment may represent the always changing nature and dynamism—not just the assimilation—of tribes.
First of all, as suggested above, some tribes have long-standing value in favor of individual freedoms, limited when the exercise of individual rights would harm the
group.[210] But, even if individual legal freedom is a relatively new concept, it makes
sense for tribal people to evolve as all people do. In early America, religious freedom meant the right to be a Puritan, free from persecution by the Church of England; today it gives rise to our national tolerance for everything from Buddhism to
Santeria.[211] Tribal people have, over time, shown a similarly capacity to adopt new
ideas, whether religious as in the above examples or otherwise, and to incorporate
them into tribal culture.

Admittedly, in some tribes, however, the concept of individual religions freedoms, or even religion separate from other aspects of tribal life, may seem particularly alien.[212] But it is at least worth considering that even when American Indians
have borrowed individual freedom of religion from the ICRA or the free exercise
clause, they have managed to make it their own, in an act of dynamic sovereignty.[213]
Indeed, there are a number of reasons, not fully attributable to assimilation, why a

tribe might want an individual religious freedom provision in its constitution.[214] Tribal members may demand what they see as basic civil rights including religious freedoms.[215] The tribal government may decide that it is important for the tribal legal system to have readily observable indicia of democratic principles,[216] particularly in an era where the Supreme Court is restricting the jurisdiction of tribal courts over concerns about the treatment of non-Indian litigants.[217] In some cases, the modern rise to power of the tribal council may necessitate protections for members' religious and cultural interests that were not required when tribal government was less centralized.[218] In other cases, customary law and institutions may have been irretrievably lost, leaving tribes with the need for law to fill in the gaps. Perhaps a tribe needs to provide religious freedoms (or duties) in response to particularized events in the history of the tribe.[219]

Most important is that tribes' legal systems are functional and meaningful today. As tribal law scholars Justin Richland and Sarah Deer have argued:

> A tribal nation can choose to adopt a nontraditional legal principle as part of their tribal law (perhaps because it most closely matches the ways in which at least some members live their lives), and this does not necessarily violate their sovereign authority. In fact, it is the very essence of the sovereignty of any nation to choose what legal principles—traditional or nontraditional—they wish to incorporate into their law. [220]

In the next section, I offer some ideas about how tribes might approach individual religious freedoms in the context of tribal sovereignty—and then reviews recent tribal court decisions that have dealt with these issues.

Addressing the Assimilation Critique in Tribal Law Practice

Whatever form of religious freedom provision appears in a tribal constitution—and even if it was originally imposed by the federal government—tribes can take steps now to ensure that the application of such provisions reflects tribal norms and enhances tribal sovereignty. One mechanism is to use tribal custom, or the traditionally accepted law of the tribe, as an interpretive guide when tribal courts interpret modern constitutional provisions on religious freedoms. Though challenges are associated with the use of customary law, including "questions of authenticity, legitimacy, and essentialism,"[221] tribes can rely on a growing body of jurisprudence and scholarship discussing customary law.[222] Most notably, Matthew Fletcher has authored a series of articles on tribal customary law providing guidance on the challenges of identifying customary law, deciding when and how to apply it, and evaluating the ramifications of such decisions.[223]

Addressing the challenges associated with customary law is worthwhile, at least in some tribes' view. The Navajo Nation Supreme Court has articulated the act of relying on tribal law and custom as a sovereignty-enhancing measure: [224]

> As a sovereign Indian nation that is constantly developing, the Navajo Nation must be forever cautious about state or foreign law infringing on Navajo Nation sovereignty. The Navajo Nation must control and develop its own legal system because the concept of justice has its source in the fabric of each individual society. The concept of justice, what it means for any group of people, cannot be separated from the total beliefs, ideas, and customs of that group of people. [225]

Under similar reasoning, a tribal court could interpret a constitutional provision on religious freedoms consistent with the tribal custom—instead of under the US Supreme Court's restrictive approach in First Amendment cases. Compare two examples.

In *Townsend v. Port Gamble S'Klallam Housing Authority*, the tribal court of appeals rejected a tribal citizen's claim that the tribe had violated her religious freedom when it evicted her from tribal housing on the ground that her religious drumming constituted a nuisance. [226] In reviewing the tribal citizen's ICRA claim, the court explicitly "looked . . . for guidance" to the US Supreme Court's First Amendment jurisprudence (because, the court said, it could find no tribal court decisions on point). Thus the tribal court adopted from federal case law the principle that "freedom of religion does not provide anyone with the right to conduct a true nuisance." [227] Next, the court considered the tribal constitution's provision: "members of the Community shall enjoy without hindrance, freedom of worship, . . . speech, . . . assembly, and association." [228] Holding that this constitutional right was "not absolute," the court held that the individual's religious freedom must yield to the tribe's interest in regulations that "protect the health, safety, and welfare of the community and its members," particularly where the appellant had had an opportunity to comply with the regulation before she was evicted. [229]

Without more information about religion, culture, and community in the Port Gamble S'Klallam tribe, knowing whether the *Townsend* case is considered consistent with tribal values or not isn't possible. It is plain from the opinion, however, that the court used federal law to interpret the religious freedoms provisions of ICRA and the tribal constitution. For this reason, it is interesting to contrast *Townsend* with cases that appeal more obviously to tribal custom on religious matters. For example, in *Garcia v. Greendeer-Lee*, the Ho-Chunk Supreme Court rejected a tribal employee's religious freedom challenge to the tribe's "Waksig Wagsa Leave Policy." The policy gave paid leave for employees attending traditional tribal religious events but did not cover the plantiff's activities as a Jehovah's Witness. [230] As Matthew Fletcher writes about the *Garcia* case:

> The interesting portion of the opinion came in a concurring opinion of the court's chief justice . . . [i]nterpreting the phrase, Waksig Wagsa, to mean "Indian Ways," and noting that the purpose of the

leave policy was to "provide a means in which enrolled Tribal member employees can practice religion, culture and tradition . . . without the threat of losing a job or losing pay." Finding that the practice of these "Indian Ways" is both "the essence of tribal sovereignty" and "the backbone of cultural support that makes us distinctly Ho-Chunk," the chief justice had no problem rejecting the constitutional challenge. Here, the chief judge viewed tribal member religious activities as fundamental to the survival of the tribe and its sovereignty, surely a compelling governmental interest.[231]

The Ho-Chunk Constitution provides that the tribal government "shall not make or enforce any law prohibiting the free exercise of religion,"[232] thus tracking the First Amendment and ICRA. Yet the *Garcia* case demonstrates the Ho-Chunk Supreme Court's willingness to use tribal custom and language as an interpretive device, with express attention to the sovereignty-enhancing aspects of its decision.

Tribal court jurisprudence also reveals a growing body of cases wherein courts use tribal custom on religion and spirituality as a basis for deciding land use and other property disputes.[233] Admittedly, these are not cases where an individual tribal citizen has claimed a religious freedom right under ICRA or the First Amendment. Nevertheless, they are interesting examples of tribal court decisions relying on customary law with a substantive religious or spiritual component (versus customary law with a procedural or jurisdictional component as discussed in later cases).

In *Hoover v. Colville Confederated Tribes*,[234] for example, informed by tribal custom, the Colville Court of Appeals offered expansive protection of tribal citizens' religious interests in lands. This case arose under the tribal regulatory code, which the court interpreted to protect lands with ceremonial importance against development by a non-Indian that threatened to harm tribal religious interests. The case thus turned on the authority of the tribe to regulate non-Indian fee land.[235] The trial court had found that the proposed land development would have a direct effect on the "health and welfare of the tribe," by harming tribal religious and ceremonial practices:[236]

> Plants and animals preserved through comprehensive management in the reserve are not only a source of food, but also play a vital and irreplaceable role in the cultural and religious life of Colville people. Annual medicine dances, root feasts, and ceremonies of the Longhouse religion all incorporate natural foods such as deer and elk meat and the roots and berries found in the Hellsgate Reserve. The ceremonies play an integral role in the current well being and future survival of Colville people, both individually and as a tribal entity. . . .

> It is well known in Indian Country that spirituality is a constant presence within Indian tribes. Meetings and gatherings all begin with prayers of gratitude to the Creator. The culture, the religion,

the ceremonies—all contribute to the spiritual health of a tribe. To approve a planned development detrimental to any of these things is to diminish the spiritual health of the Tribes and its members. The spiritual health of the American Indian is bound with the earth. Their identity as a people becomes invisible in the city, away from nature. It is the land and the animals which renew and sustain their vigor and spiritual health.[237]

Moreover, the trial court had found "highly persuasive [evidence] that the encroachment of human habitation would have a detrimental effect on the animals, plants, and herbs used for sustenance, medicinal, and ceremonial purposes—the continued existence of which is vital to the spiritual health of the Tribes and their members."[238] Therefore, the appellate court upheld the injunction preventing the land development. [239]

The *Hoover* court explicitly recognized individual interests in religious practice, explaining that "the ceremonies play an integral role in the current well being and future survival of Colville people, both *individually* and as a tribal entity."[240] Proponents of the assimilation critique might argue that *Hoover* only proves their point: the fact that it (unlike *Townsend*) is *not* a case brought under an individual constitutional rights model allows the court to conceive broadly of the interests of the entire tribal community. The Colville Constitution, as described above, contains no express provision on religion, recognizing individual religious freedoms in the Tribal Civil Rights Act, a provision that is not cited in the *Hoover* opinion.[241] But, most importantly for this discussion, *Hoover* reveals a tribal court going beyond a *Lyng*-like approach and, instead, using tribal custom to recognize and protect the relationship among land, ceremonies, and living beings. This is not a tribal court confined to Anglo-American notions of justice in the application of religious principles to contemporary disputes.

A second mechanism for implementing individual religious freedoms in a way that resists assimilation is to maintain institutions apart from tribal courts, such as elders' councils and clan-based decision makers. The Ho-Chunk Tribe, for example, has a "traditional court," with decision makers selected by the clans and proceedings conducted primarily in Ho-Chunk, which hears matters implicating culture and serves as a resource on customary law.[242] In some tribes, deference to such dispute resolution entities may be required in matters involving cultural and religious questions. For example, Gloria Valencia-Weber has found that "disputes involving cultural beliefs and a failure to comply with custom are the subject matter for bodies such as the Peacemaker Court in the Navajo and Seneca Nations, the Court of Elders in the Sitka Community Association, and the Northwest Intertribal Court System."[243] To implement individual religious freedoms in a way that comports with tribal custom, tribes can work to ensure that traditional decision-making bodies retain decision-making authority over disputes involving religion and culture.

Consider, for example, *Elk Horn Society v. Red Hat,* in which four traditional societies asked the Cheyenne-Arapaho court to rule in a dispute over possession of the Sacred Arrows and other items used in rituals of the Cheyenne people.[244] At first, the trial court issued an order requiring the return of the items to the Arrow Keeper and directing the tribal police to offer peaceful assistance in the restoration of the items.[245] When fighting erupted between the disputants, a number of tribal members contacted the court about resolving the situation according to traditional procedures. Thus, after issuing a stay order to prevent any more conflict, the Cheyenne-Arapaho District Court issued a new ruling that "the Tribal Court cannot decide who the Arrow Keeper is."[246] Instead, it left this question "to the Headsmen, Chiefs, and the Cheyenne tribal members themselves . . . in accordance with traditional practice and procedure."[247] The record does not indicate what ultimately happened to the Sacred Arrows in this case.[248]

A third approach would be for tribal lawmakers and citizens to engage in constitutional reform with the specific and conscious goal of providing for religious freedom in a way that reflects tribal values.[249] As mentioned briefly above, the Cherokee Nation of Oklahoma, after an extensive process of constitutional reform beginning in 1999,[250] adopted a new constitution that omitted reference to ICRA. The 1975 constitution had a general "Bill of Rights," including the statement that: "The appropriate protections guaranteed by the Indian Civil Rights Act of 1968 shall apply to all members of the Cherokee Nation."[251] By contrast, the 1999 constitution specifically enumerates certain rights including due process, equal protection, rights to counsel, jury trial, and "the free exercise of religion."[252] On the one hand, religious freedoms do not seem to have been a primary concern in the 1999 constitutional reform process.[253] On the other hand, one participant in the Cherokee Constitutional Convention explained:

> I'd like to stress that enumerating our own Bill of Rights as opposed
> to just by implication taking the Indian Civil Rights Act, will allow
> us to develop our own notions of due process and protection, which
> I think is important for any sovereign people who are concerned
> with individual rights.[254]

Indeed, the Cherokee Nation's Constitutions of 1827 and 1839 had both provided a "free exercise" clause not completely unlike the one adopted in the 1999 constitution—suggesting an historical (and certainly pre-IRA or pre-ICRA) concept of religious freedom.[255] More broadly, other aspects of the Cherokees' 1999 constitution clearly reflect a move away from federal influence—most notably, the 1999 constitution no longer contains the requirement of approval by the secretary of the Interior found in the 1975 constitution.[256]

Though constitutional reform must be specific to the tribe, some of the constitutions discussed above provide models that could be adapted to the particular culture, religion, and other community norms. A tribe could follow the Bill Moore's Slough Yupik constitution and supplement boilerplate ICRA or free exercise language with a statement of its own tribal-specific religious duties and broader context for the realization of such rights. A tribal constitution could specifically reference certain religious practices. The Fort Mojave Constitution provides, for example that "Members shall continue undisturbed in their customs, culture, and their religious beliefs, including, but not limited to, the customs, ceremonial dancing and singing, and no one shall interfere with these practices, recognizing that we have been a people and shall continue to be a people whose way of life has been different."[257] If external or internal challenges to the tribal religion persist, a tribal constitution could be reformed to include specific language addressing specific threats to the tribal religion. The Salt River Pima-Maricopa Constitution, for example, has special provisions about missionaries, requiring them to be either tribal members or to present "proof satisfactory to the community council that they are of good moral character and that their presence within the reservation will not disturb peace and good order."[258]

As part of the reform process, any constitutional provisions for substantive religious rights and duties could be enhanced by procedural reforms that ensure that jurisdiction over religious matters rests in the appropriate forum.[259] In other communities, it may be perfectly consistent with tribal norms to keep ICRA or ICRA-like religious freedoms provisions and to lodge jurisdiction in the tribal court.

This section has described just three ways—using tribal custom as an interpretive force, maintaining traditional dispute resolution mechanisms, and engaging in constitutional reform—for tribes to implement individual religious freedoms in ways that resist assimilation and enhance tribal sovereignty. In the final analysis, tribes will decide for themselves whether these or other approaches work for them.[260]

REALITY CHECK

On September 11, 2003, a group of Northern Arapaho ceremonial elders from Wyoming sued several traditional Southern Arapaho chiefs in the Cheyenne-Arapaho tribal court of Oklahoma to prevent the Southern Arapahos from conducting a Sun Dance in Oklahoma. The case came to be known as *Redman v. Birdshead.*[261] The Northern Arapaho plaintiffs claimed that the Southern Arapaho defendants had announced their intent to conduct the Sun Dance without complying with "the proper traditional way to seek permission and properly hold an Arapaho ceremony."[262] The Northern Arapahos from Wyoming filed their case in the Cheyenne-Arapaho tribal court located in Oklahoma, where four years of litigation ensued.

The case pitting certain Northern Arapahos against certain Southern Arapahos reflects, in some respects, historical events involving the tribe. Traditionally, the Arapaho people lived on the plains of present-day Colorado and Wyoming, with a distinction between the Northern and Southern bands tracing back to the mid-nineteenth century. After experiencing hostilities from the United States and its citizens, including violations of the Treaty of Fort Laramie of 1851 and the Sand Creek Massacre of 1864, the Arapaho people were largely removed from Colorado and other traditional lands.[263] Since approximately 1867 the Southern Arapaho have resided in Oklahoma, alongside the Southern Cheyenne, with whom they formed the joint federally recognized Cheyenne-Arapahoe Tribe of Oklahoma in 1937.[264] Since 1878, the Northern Arapaho have resided alongside the separately recognized Shoshone Tribe on the Wind River Reservation in Wyoming.[265]

The Arapaho people have long been practitioners of the Sun Dance, a multiday ritual involving prayer and sacrifice for the community.[266] In the years leading up to the *Redman v. Birdshead* case, the Arapaho Sun Dance had occurred regularly on the Northern Arapaho reservation, under the direction of the plaintiffs, with Southern Arapahos often attending. In 2003, Southern Arapaho Saul Birdshead announced his intent to conduct a Sun Dance in Oklahoma by sending a letter to the chairman of the Cheyenne-Arapaho Tribes, informing him and the tribal council of his vow and asking for their help. His letter indicated he thought this was the proper way to ask for support.[267] But the Northern Arapaho ceremonial elders said that the defendants had to seek *their* permission. The Northern Arapaho plaintiffs further charged that the Southern Arapahos had "lost" their Sun Dance in the 1930s after sharing their tradition with the white anthropologist George Dorsey. According to the plaintiffs, "the people with the authority to conduct the ceremonies died out from violating the secrecy of the ceremonies."[268] To make matters worse, the Southern Arapahos were now relying on the same anthropologist's books as a source of "proper Arapaho ways," at least according to a letter that one individual had submitted to the tribal newspaper.[269]

After the allegations came to light, the Northern Arapaho and Cheyenne-Arapaho business committees each passed (slightly different) resolutions barring the Sun Dance proposed by the Southern Arapaho individuals until they complied with "the traditional ways" of seeking permission and holding the ceremony.[270] But when it looked like Southern Arapaho individuals were going ahead with their plans anyway, the Cheyenne-Arapaho tribal court granted a temporary restraining order to prohibit the Sun Dance.[271] The Southern Arapaho defendants challenged the temporary restraining order on grounds that the tribal court lacked jurisdiction to decide "these traditional type matters."[272] Finding that the dispute "related to the centuries old spiritual matters of the Arapaho," the court agreed, holding:

> [T]he case at hand ... deals with a matter not addressed in any written way, at least as to the tribal codes and laws. Thus, this Court lacks jurisdiction to decide this case.... The Court notes that there is a proper procedure to spiritual matters, and the parties are directed to submit this matter for the property traditional way of resolving these types of disputes.[273]

Urging the parties to "comply with the proper traditional ways," the court said it would "give recognition and 'full faith and credit' to the decisions of the traditional leaders in this dispute."[274] But despite the court's clear rejection of jurisdiction and many admonitions to take the matter to the traditional leaders, the case of *Redman v. Birdshead* did not end with the 2003 decision.

In 2005, the Northern Arapaho plaintiffs again sued in the Cheyenne-Arapaho tribal court to prevent the defendants from running "Arapaho ceremonials" in Oklahoma, arguing that the individuals had not sought authorization in the traditional manner and that the only proper location for Arapaho ceremonies was Wyoming.[275] Whereas the substantive issue was the same, the emphasis of the court's legal analysis had changed from the previous cases. This time, the court separated the case into its "spiritual aspects" and its "legal aspects."[276] On the former point, the court reiterated its earlier view that "the Court is no place for determining traditional aspects of ceremonies."[277] Indeed, the Arapaho had unwritten law on spiritual matters, along with "police, prosecutors, and judges of the unwritten law."[278] These were the entities with jurisdiction over the spiritual matter. On the legal issue, however, the court found the tribal court "may, consistent with the 1975 Constitution and the Indian Civil Rights Act, enforce a Resolution of the Cheyenne-Arapaho Business Committee."[279] The court therefore upheld as "good law" the tribal resolution prohibiting the defendants "from proceedings with, holding, condoning . . . Arapaho ceremonies until they proceeded with such in a traditional manner," and issued a permanent injunction to enforce it. The court further held that the Southern Arapaho defendants would have to sue the tribe directly on their Indian Civil Rights Act and freedom of religion claims.

Despite issuing the permanent injunction, the court voiced a "word of concern," as follows:

> Traditions of tribes vary. With some tribes I am familiar with, if a ceremony is "lost" then some tribes see it as gone forever and not to be restored or bad things will occur to the people. Other tribes say that only those with proper authority may revive the ceremony, and that it must be done in a certain way. I do not know the situation with the Arapaho (Southern and Northern) people, but please do not take this lightly.
>
> Also, it is certain that the Arapaho have been separated in the neighborhood of 140 years. It is also certain that being separated can create the need for change or cause differences to occur between those separated. But the change was not created by the tribes, but rather by the United States government. That is to say, there is only a Southern and a Northern Arapaho because the United States put one group on a reservation in the South and the other on a reservation in the North. This means they are separate in terms of how the United States deals with them; thus there are governmentally distinct. This is a different idea than whether they are culturally, traditionally distinct. I would believe that at one point they were all the same people.[280]

Redman v. Birdshead did not end with the court's permanent injunction order in 2005. In 2006, the Southern Arapaho defendants "began to erect an offerings lodge in preparation for an Arapaho Sun Dance in Oklahoma" and the Northern Arapaho plaintiffs sued for "contempt relief," claiming the defendants were violating the court's earlier injunction.[281] By this point, the tribal law landscape had changed in some important respects. The recently renamed "Cheyenne and Arapaho Tribes" of Oklahoma had adopted a new constitution that year. It contained a free exercise clause, prohibiting the tribe from making or enforcing "any law which infringes upon the religious or cultural beliefs or prohibits the free exercise clause thereof."[282] But, at the same time, the new constitution expressly prohibited the tribal courts from exercising "jurisdiction over traditional matters such as the conduct of ceremonies."[283]

Analyzing the case under the new constitution, the trial court of the Cheyenne-Arapaho Tribes vacated the 2005 permanent injunction, which had been based on the Resolution of Business Committee of the Cheyenne-Arapaho Tribes prohibiting the defendants from conducting any ceremony "purporting" to be a traditional Arapaho Sun Dance.[284] In the court's view, the resolution clearly violated the free exercise clause found in Article I, Section 1(a) of the new Constitution of the Cheyenne and Arapaho Tribes.[285] Second, the court held, "it is clear the Court would not have jurisdiction over this matter" because the claim was about tribal members attempting to "conduct" a Sun Dance and Article VIII, Section 5(c) forbade the tribal courts from exercising jurisdiction "over traditional religious matters such as the conduct of ceremonies."[286] For these reasons, the Court vacated the injunction and refused to hear the contempt claims or otherwise exercise jurisdiction over the case.

Whether these holdings, and indeed the provisions of the constitution itself, are reconcilable is a difficult question. The trial court offered some reflections in dicta. First, it expressed deference to the "will of the Cheyenne-Arapaho people who overwhelmingly approved" the new constitution.[287] At the same time, the court was concerned about the free exercise clause:

> Whether you agree with Birdshead and Spottedwolf or agree with the manner in which they went about a Sun Dance is irrelevant under the new Constitution; the new Constitution protects them more than the Tribes. This law [the Business Council's resolution] does prohibit free exercise of religion and must be found unconstitutional. . . . Hopefully, the drafters of the new Constitution thought about all this and the possibilities when they put this before the people for a vote. Hopefully, the people of the Cheyenne-Arapaho Tribes thought about this before voting.

The court reiterated its position, now confirmed by the constitution, that it was not the place for such disputes. The court expressed its hope that any further proceedings would be handled by "others with the traditional power of judge and jury" and that their decisions would be respected. Such respect was critical, the court concluded, to save tradition and avoid "bad things and times coming upon the Tribes and its people."[288]

The case of *Redman v. Birdshead* is a poignant one.[289] It features many of the dynamics discussed in this chapter—an ancient and still vital tribal religion, a tribe and religion that have been persecuted by the United States, religious interference by outsiders (including an anthropologist), apparent attempts by some tribal members to revive a religious practice, and resistance by elders responsible for maintaining the traditional religion—all meeting in a legal proceeding where ICRA had been expressly adopted in the tribal constitution but where everyone knew that traditional custom remained a powerful force.[290] Faced with this confluence of religion and law, the Cheyenne-Arapaho tribal court tried to defer to traditional dispute resolution; it tried to use custom as an interpretive device; and it tried to respect tribal legislation and a constitutional reform process that took place in the middle of the case. Only members of the Northern and Southern Arapaho tribes will know if the resolution of *Redman v. Birdshead* was a satisfactory one, but it is clear from the case that the issues were of critical importance to everyone involved.

CONCLUSION

Many indigenous peoples believe that spirituality is the key to their survival as distinct peoples.[291] For this reason, the law must treat religious matters carefully. Today, religious freedoms cases arising on reservations will be decided by tribal courts applying tribal law, either exclusively or in conjunction with the ICRA. Tribal constitutions offer a number of different types of religious freedoms provisions, ranging from language that incorporates federal law to more culturally distinctive, tribal-specific protections. At the same time, scholars express concerns about the appearance of any individual rights in tribal constitutions. I agree that the assimilation critique of individual civil rights is applicable in the religious freedoms area and that it offers important cautions for tribal judges and lawmakers. Nevertheless, as I have suggested, tribes may have a variety of reasons for maintaining laws on individual religious freedoms and may be able to implement such laws in ways that reflect tribal values and enhance sovereignty. In such cases, individual rights may not trump collective interests as they would in the classic liberal tradition. Instead, in tribal communities, the relevant questions are often whether and how to reconcile individual and collective religious interests.[292] Given the importance of religion and spirituality to American Indian people, this area of law will likely see many developments in the coming years.

NOTES

This chapter is a revised and updated version of my article *Considering Individual Religious Freedoms under Tribal Constitutional Law,* 14 Kan. J.L. & Pub. Pol'y 561 (2005). With thanks to Samantha Greendeer and Kate Williams-Shuck for their research assistance.

    1.   *See* WILMA MANKILLER, EVERY DAY IS A GOOD DAY, REFLECTIONS BY CONTEMPORARY INDIGENOUS WOMEN 24 (2004) (quoting Gail Small, Northern Cheyenne).

2. *See generally* MATTHEW L.M. FLETCHER, AMERICAN INDIAN TRIBAL LAW (2011); JUSTIN B. RICHLAND & SARAH DEER, INTRODUCTION TO TRIBAL LEGAL STUDIES (2004). As of 2010, there were 565 federally recognized Indian tribes. *See* Department of the Interior, Bureau of Indian Affairs, Indian Entities Recognized and Eligible To Receive Services From the United States Bureau of Indian Affairs, Federal Register, Vol. 75, No. 190, Friday, Oct 1, 2010, *available at* http://www.bia.gov/idc/groups/xofa/documents/document/idc012038.pdf (listing 564) and Federal Register, Vol. 75, No. 207, Wed., Oct 3, 2010, *available at* http://www.bia.gov/idc/groups/xraca/documents/text/idc012025.pdf (adding the Shinnecock Tribe).

3. *See* Robert J. McCarthy, *Civil Rights in Tribal Courts: The Indian Bill of Rights at Thirty Years*, 34 IDAHO L. REV. 465 (1998) and sources cited *infra* notes 4–9.

4. *See generally* ERIC LEMONT, ED., AMERICAN INDIAN CONSTITUTIONAL REFORM AND THE REBUILDING OF NATIVE NATIONS (2006); *see also* Robert B. Porter, *Strengthening Tribal Sovereignty Through Government Reform: What Are the Issues?*, 7 KAN. J.L. & PUB. POL'Y 72 (1997).

5. *See, e.g.,* Nevada v. Hicks, 533 U.S. 353, 383–84 (2001) (Souter, J., Kennedy, J., and Thomas, J., concurring); Duro v. Reina, 495 U.S. 676, 692–94 (1990); Oliphant v. Suquamish Indian Tribe, 435 U.S. 191, 212 (1978).

6. *See, e.g.,* Robert B. Porter, *Strengthening Tribal Sovereignty through Peacemaking: How the Anglo-American Legal Tradition Destroys Indigenous Societies*, 28 COLUM. HUM. RTS. L. REV. 235, 277–79 (1997) (on individual versus community concerns in dispute resolution systems); Angela R. Riley, *Recovering Collectivity: Group Rights to Intellectual Property in Indigenous Communities*, 18 CARDOZO ARTS & ENT. L.J. 175 (2000) (discussing the tension between individual and collective rights in the protection of indigenous culture); DONNA J. GOLDSMITH, *Individual vs. Collective Rights: The Indian Child Welfare Act*, 13 HARV. WOMEN'S L.J. (1990) (on the tension between individual and collective rights in Indian child custody matters).

7. *See* VINE DELORIA, JR., WE TALK, YOU LISTEN: NEW TRIBES, NEW TURF 150–51 (1970) ("[T]he major complaints [by Indian people] have been that the United States has failed to protect treaty rights of the tribes and that individual Indians have suffered accordingly. Indian tribes have a vested interest in maintaining the Constitutional framework, because tribal rights derive from this document and individuals receive from tribal rights the identity and status they seek as individuals").

8. *See* Angela R. Riley, *(Tribal) Sovereignty and Illiberalism*, 95 CAL. L. REV. 799 (2007) (considering individual Indian rights vis à vis traditions of liberal democracy and tribal sovereignty).

9. Feminist legal scholars, for example, have engaged in robust conversation about women's individual rights to property, membership, and political participation in tribal communities. *See, e.g.,* Judith Resnik, *Dependent Sovereigns: Indian Tribes, States, and the Federal Courts*, 56 U. CHI. L. REV. 671 (1989) and Catharine MacKinnon, *Whose Culture? A Case Note on Martinez v. Santa Clara Pueblo* (1983), in FEMINISM UNMODIFIED 63 (1987); *see also* Gloria Valencia-Weber, *Three Stories in One: The Story of* Santa Clara Pueblo v. Martinez, in INDIAN LAW STORIES 451 (2011) (updating the debate from an indigenous perspective). Similarly, intellectual and cultural property scholars query whether the protection of American Indian cultural property will harm individual Indians' rights of expression and autonomy. *See, e.g.,* Madhavi Sunder, *Intellectual Property and Identity Politics: Playing With Fire*, 4 J. GENDER RACE & JUST. 69 (2000); William J. Hapiuk, Jr., Note, *Of Kitch and Kachinas: A Critical Analysis of the Indian Arts and Crafts Act of 1990*, 53 STAN. L. REV. 1009 (2001).

10. *See* Talton v. Mayes, 163 U.S. 376, 381–82 (1895) (right to grand jury under the Fifth Amendment inapplicable in capital case before Cherokee Nation court).

11. *See id.*; Santa Clara Pueblo v. Martinez, 436 U.S. 49 (1978) (rejecting individual equal protection claim against tribal government absent statutory provision of cause of action and waiver of sovereign immunity).

12. Indian Civil Rights Act of 1968, Pub. L. 90-284, Apr. 11, 1968, 82 Stat. 77–80, codified at 25 U.S.C. §§ 1301–1303.

13. *See, e.g.,* Angela R. Riley, *Good (Native) Governance*, 107 COLUM. L. REV. 1049 (2007) (considering individual and collective Indian rights in the context of tribal governing practices) and sources cited in notes 7–14).

14. *See* Carole E. Goldberg, *Individual Rights and Tribal Revitalization*, 35 ARIZ. ST. L.J. 889 (2003) (and sources cited therein that are described in greater detail below).

15. *See* DAVID H. GETCHES, ROBERT A. WILLIAMS, JR., CHARLES F. WILKINSON AND MATTHEW L.M. FLETCHER, CASES AND MATERIALS ON FEDERAL INDIAN LAW 141–152 (6th ed. 2011) (detailing federal statutes and policies comprising the allotment and assimilation era from 1871–1928).

16. *See, e.g.,* Kristen A. Carpenter, *Contextualizing the Losses of Allotment Through Literature,* 82 N. DAKOTA L. REV. 605 (2006); Allison M. Dussias, *Ghost Dance and Holy Ghost: The Echoes of Nineteenth-Century Christianization Policy in Twentieth-Century Native American Free Exercise Cases,* 49 STAN. L. REV. 773 (1997).

17. *See infra* notes 114–29.

18. *See* Goldberg, *supra* note 14, at 889–90.

19. *Id.* at 890.

20. *See* Riley, *supra* note 8, at 830–49.

21. *See* Bear Lodge Multiple Use Assn v. Babbit, 175 F.3d 814, 817 (10th Cir. 1999).

22. *See* 25 U.S.C. § 1302.

23. *See* Lyng v. Northwest Indian Cemetery Protective Ass'n, 485 U.S. 439, 448 (1988) ("the Free Exercise Clause 'affords an individual protection from certain forms of government compulsion. . . .'" (quoting Bowen v. Roy, 476 U. S. 693 (1986)).

24. *Lyng,* 485 U.S. at 459–60 (Brennan, J. dissenting) (internal quotations omitted). Brennan's complaint about the poor fit between the free exercise clause and Native American religions is, of course, a contested point. Some scholars claim that "non-Christian religious outsiders," including Jews, Muslims, and American Indians "have difficulty convincing the Court that their religious convictions are sincere and meaningful." Stephen M. Feldman, *Religious Minorities and the First Amendment: The History, the Doctrine, and the Future,* 6 U. PA. J. CONST. L. 222, 253 (2003). Still others argue that religious practitioners *in general* receive "very little Constitutional protection" from the modern Supreme Court. *See, e.g.,* Alan Brownstein, *Taking Free Exercise Rights Seriously,* 57 CASE W. L. REV. 55, 60 (2006).

25. By "traditional tribal religions," I refer to the spiritual and cultural practices arising out of indigenous communities (*e.g.,* the Cherokee Stomp Dance or Iroquois Longhouse Religion), as contrasted with religions that originated elsewhere (*e.g.,* Christianity). While commonly used among scholars and in Indian communities (*See, e.g.,* Vine Deloria, Jr., *Religion and the Modern American Indian,* in FOR THIS LAND: WRITINGS ON RELIGION IN AMERICA 123 (1999) (describing Indians who maintain a "traditional religious life"), the term *traditional* is imprecise and open to interpretation. *See, e.g.,* George Tinker, *Review Essay of James Treat, Around the Sacred Fire: Native Religious Activism in the Red Power Era: A Narrative Map of the Indian Ecumenical Conference* (2003), 20 WICAZO SA REVIEW 203, 204–05 (2005) (discussing the "contested" nature of the term *traditional* in Indian religious and other matters). Moreover, there are many examples of syncretic religions, such as the Native American Church, the Indian Shaker Church, the Handsome Lake Religion, and others that embrace "traditional" indigenous and "Christian" elements.

26. *See* VINE DELORIA, JR., GOD IS RED 194 (1992).

27. *Lyng,* 485 U.S. at 451.

28. Professor Goldberg describes a number of nuances and counterpoints to her argument, noting for example that scholars such as Will Kymlicka and Aviam Soifer "advance a creative vision of individual rights as a basis for supporting and protecting the sovereignty of Indian nations." *See* Goldberg, *supra* note 14, at 890.

29. For a series of works theorizing the connection between American Indian spirituality and political sovereignty, see GEORGE E. "TINK" TINKER, AMERICAN INDIAN LIBERATION: A THEOLOGY OF SOVEREIGNTY (2008); GEORGE E. "TINK" TINKER, SPIRIT AND RESISTANCE: POLITICAL THEOLOGY AND AMERICAN INDIAN LIBERATION (2004); and CLARA SUE KIDWELL, HOMER NOLEY, AND GEORGE E. "TINK" TINKER, A NATIVE AMERICAN THEOLOGY (2001).

30. Most of the cases discussed in this chapter involve an individual tribal member's religious freedoms claims vis à vis a tribal government. Of course, nonmembers may also bring lawsuits in tribal court. *See, e.g.* Bethany Berger, *Justice and the Outsider: Jurisdiction over Nonmembers in Tribal Legal Systems,* 37 AZ. ST. L. J. 1047, 1067 (2005) ("For many nonmember plaintiffs, tribal court is the only option"). Whether the plaintiff is a member or nonmember, the question of jurisdiction will depend on whether the tribal government has waived its sovereign immunity.

31. *See generally* Inés Hernandez-Avila, *Mediations of the Spirit: Native American Religious Traditions and the Ethics of Representation,* in NATIVE AMERICAN SPIRITUALITY 11–36 (2000).

32. MERRIAM WEBSTER'S COLLEGIATE DICTIONARY 988 (10th ed. 1998).

33. *Dikaneisdi (Word List),* CHEROKEE NATION, http://www.cherokee.org/Culture/Dikaneisdi.aspx?Tab=Culture (last visited March 2, 2011).

34. JACE WEAVER, OTHER WORDS: AMERICAN INDIAN LITERATURE, LAW, AND CULTURE 301 (2001). *See also* VIRGINIA M. SOBRAL AND HOWARD L. MEREDITH, EDS., *AJALAGI NUSDV NVGOHV ELOHI*: CHEROKEE VISION OF ELOHI (1997) (translated by Wesley Proctor) (book-length bilingual treatment of the Cherokee concept of "*elohi*").

35. *See* MANKILLER, *supra* note 1, at 11–16.

36. *See generally* Barre Toelken, *The Demands of Harmony*, in I BECOME A PART OF IT: SACRED DIMENSIONS IN NATIVE AMERICAN LIFE 59–71 (1989).

37. James W. Zion, *Navajo Therapeutic Jurisprudence*, 18 TOURO L. REV. 563, 603–04 (2002).

38. Henrietta Mann, *Earth Mother and Prayerful Children: Sacred Sites and Religious Freedom*, in NATIVE VOICES: AMERICAN INDIAN IDENTITY AND RESISTANCE 194–209 (2003).

39. *See* CHARLES E. LITTLE, SACRED LANDS OF INDIAN AMERICA 133 (2001).

40. MANKILLER, *supra* note 1, at 13.

41. *Compare* Marcy C. Churchill, *Purity and Pollution, Unearthing an Oppositional Paradigm in the Study of Cherokee Religious Traditions*, *supra* note 31, at 212–13 (describing some of the ways that scholars' inaccurate presumptions about Cherokee origins may lead to questionable conclusions about religious and cultural matters); TINKER, SPIRIT AND RESISTANCE, *supra* note 29, at 79–87 (criticizing book on Lakota spirituality).

42. *See* Christopher Ronwanien:te Jocks, *Spirituality for Sale, Sacred Knowledge in the Consumer Age*, *supra* note 31, at 61–77 (reflecting on "what is or not to be shared with outsiders, in relation to traditional thought and practice" with specific grounding in Iroquois Longhouse ceremonies and stories).

43. *See, e.g., Sweat lodge deaths investigated as homicides*, CNN.COM, October 15, 2009, http://www.cnn.com/2009/US/10/15/arizona.sweat.lodge/index.html and *'Sweatbox' victims were attending 'Spiritual Warrior' program*, CNN.COM, October 10, 2009, http://www.cnn.com/2009/US/10/10/sweat.box.deaths/index.html (news articles describing death of two individuals and injuries to dozens of others partaking in a "sweat lodge" led by non-Indian "self-help author" James Ray as part of a "spiritual warrior" program with apparent inspiration from "Native American" traditions).

44. *See* Dussias, *supra* note 16, at 787–805 (recounting various acts by federal government and religious institutions, often acting together, that suppressed Indian religions); John Rhodes, *An American Tradition: The Religious Persecution of Native Americans*, 52 MONT. L. REV. 13 (1991); GEORGE E. TINKER, MISSIONARY CONQUEST: THE GOSPEL AND NATIVE AMERICAN CULTURAL GENOCIDE (1993).

45. *See Bear Lodge*, 175 F.3d at 817 (internal quotations and citations omitted).

46. *See* American Indian Religious Freedom Act, Public Law 95–341, August 11, 1978, 92 Stat 469, codified at 42 U.S.C. § 1996 and 1996a.

47. *See Lyng*, 485 U.S. at 447–49 (federal government's decision to build a road and harvest timber on sacred site did not violate American Indians' free exercise clause rights because government action would not coerce belief and government had a right to use its lands). *See also* Employment Div., Dept. of Human Resources of Oregon v. Smith, 494 U.S. 872 (1990) (state statute denying unemployment benefits to employee and member of Native American Church terminated for sacramental peyote use did not violate his free exercise clause rights because the law was facially neutral and generally applicable).

48. *See* Navajo Nation v. United States Forest Service, 535 F.3d 1058 (9th Cir. en banc 2008), *cert. denied* 129 S.Ct. 2763 (2009).

49. Accordingly, much of my scholarship focuses on challenges to tribal religious freedom, especially in the sacred sites context. *See, e.g.,* Kristen A. Carpenter, *A Property Rights Approach to Sacred Sites Cases: Asserting a Place for Indians as Nonowners*, 52 UCLA L. REV. 1061 (2005); Kristen A. Carpenter, *Old Ground and New Directions at Sacred Sites on the Western Landscape*, 83 DENV. UNIV. L. REV. 981 (2006); Kristen A. Carpenter, *The Interests of "Peoples" in the Cooperative Management of Sacred Sites*, 42 TULSA L. REV. 37 (2006); Kristen A. Carpenter, *Real Property and Peoplehood*, 27 STAN. ENV. L. J. 313 (2008); Kristen A. Carpenter, *In Defense of Property*, 118 YALE L. J. 1022 (2009) (with S. Katyal & A. Riley). *See also* Rebecca Tsosie, *Reclaiming Native Stories: An Essay on Cultural Appropriation and Cultural Rights*, 34 ARIZ. ST. L.J. 299, 319–21 (2002) (on "claims aris[ing] from the acts of non-Indians who appropriate tribal rituals or songs for New-Age religions").

50. *See, e.g.,* Native American Church v. Navajo Tribal Council, 272 F.2d 131 (1959) (tribal religious practitioners who were members of the Native American Church sue tribal government to enjoin anti-peyote legislation); Toledo v. Pueblo de Jemez, 119 F.Supp. 429 (D.N.M. 1954) (tribal members who were Protestant

sued the tribal government for various acts allegedly violating their religious freedom).

51.　*See generally* LEMONT, *supra* note 4; Porter, *supra* note 4.

52.　*See, e.g.*, Michelene E. Pensatubbee, *Religious Studies on the Margins: Decolonizing our Minds*, *supra* note 38, at 209–22 (discussing the state of academic studies pertaining to Native religious traditions).

53.　*See, e.g.*, Richard A. Grounds, *Yuchi Travels: Up and Down the Academic "Road to Disappearance,"* *supra* note 38, 306–10 (noting that he would not publicly disclose certain Yuchi cultural or religious traditions).

54.　*See, e.g.*, THOMAS BIOLSI AND LARRY J. ZIMMERMAN, INDIANS AND ANTHROPOLOGISTS: VINE DELORIA, JR., AND THE CRITIQUE OF ANTHROPOLOGY (1997) (on the relationship between Indians and anthropologists).

55.　U.S. CONST. amend. I.

56.　*See* Robert Odawi Porter, *The Inapplicability of American Law to the Indian Nations,* 89 IOWA L. REV. 1596, 1596 (2004) ("It is a fundamental premise of American law dealing with the Indian nations in the United States that the U.S. Constitution does not apply to regulate the conduct of Indian tribal governments").

57.　Talton, 163 U.S. at 381–82 (the right to a grand jury under the Fifth Amendment is inapplicable in capital cases before the Cherokee Nation court).

58.　*See* Native American Church of North America v. Navajo Tribal Council, 272 F.2d 131 (10th Cir. 1959).

59.　OMER STEWART, PEYOTE RELIGION: A HISTORY 296 (1987).

60.　*See id.*

61.　*See Native American Church*, 272 F.2d at 132.

62.　*Id*. at 134.

63.　*Id.*

64.　*See* Ann E. Beeson, *Dances with Justice: Peyotism in the Courts*, 41 EMORY L.J. 1121, 1140 (1992). As Beeson has pointed out, "the irony of this set of events seems incredible given the . . . treatment of peyotism in the American courts."

65.　Toledo v. Pueblo de Jemez, 119 F.Supp. 429 (D.N.M. 1954).

66.　*Id*. at 430.

67.　*Id.*

68.　*Id.*

69.　*Id*. at 431 (citing 8 U.S.C.A. § 43 (later 42 U.S.C.A. § 1983). There were also "some general allegations" not directly addressed by the court, growing out of the First Amendment and Treaty of Guadalupe Hidalgo.

70.　*Id*. at 432.

71.　*See* Robert Berry, *Civil Liberties Restraints on Tribal Sovereignty after the Indian Civil Rights Act of 1968,* 1 J. L. & POL'Y 1, 16–17 (1993) (reviewing pre-ICRA cases).

72.　If Congress has the power to enact such legislation, it derives from its much critiqued but often-accepted "plenary power" over Indian nations. *See* Santa Clara Pueblo v. Martinez, 436 U.S. 49, 58 (1978) ("tribal sovereignty . . . is subject to the superior and plenary control of Congress"); United States v. Wheeler, 435 U.S. 313, 319 (1978) ("Congress has plenary authority to legislate for Indian tribes in all matters"). *Compare* Porter, *supra* note 56, at 1599 (critiquing the plenary power doctrine on grounds that "Indigenous nations and peoples are not subject to American law as a matter of their own law and that organic Indigenous laws and treaties should be fully incorporated into any analysis assessing the source and scope of tribal governmental powers").

73.　*See* Johnson v. Lower Elwha Tribal Community of Lower Elwha Indian Reservation, 484 F.2d 200, 203 (9th Cir. 1973) (describing ICRA as "patterned in part on" the Bill of Rights).

74.　*See* 25 U.S.C. §§ 1301–1303. *See also* Thomson v. State of New York, 487 F.Supp. 212, 229 (N.D.N.Y. 1979) (the purpose of ICRA is to prohibit tribal governments from violating the individual civil rights of tribal members).

75.　25 U.S.C. §§ 1302. The full list of protections is:

　　　No Indian tribe in exercising powers of self-government shall—

　　　(1) make or enforce any law prohibiting the free exercise of religion or abridging the free-

dom of speech, or of the press, or the right of the people peaceably to assemble and to petition for a redress of grievances;

(2) violate the right of the people to be secure in their persons, houses, papers, and effects against unreasonable search and seizures, nor issue warrants, but upon probable cause, supported by oath or affirmation, and particularly describing the place to be searched and the person or thing to be seized;

(3) subject any person for the same offense to be twice put in jeopardy;

(4) compel any person' in any criminal case to be a witness against himself;

(5) take any private property for a public use without just compensation;

(6) deny to any person in a criminal proceeding the right to a speedy and public trial, to be informed of the nature and cause of the accusation, to be confronted with the witnesses against him, to have compulsory process for obtaining witnesses in his favor, and at his own expense to have the assistance of counsel for his defense;

(7) require excessive bail, impose excessive fines, inflict cruel and unusual punishments, and in no event impose for conviction of any one offense any penalty or punishment greater than imprisonment for a term of one year and [or] a fine of $5,000, or both;

(8) deny to any person within its jurisdiction the equal protection of its laws or deprive any person of liberty or property without due process of law;

(9) pass any bill of attainder or ex post facto law; or

(10) deny to any person accused of an offense punishable by imprisonment the right, upon request, to a trial by jury of not less than six persons.

76. Carol Tebben, *Trifederalism in the Aftermath of Teague: The Interaction of State and Tribal Courts In Wisconsin*, 26 AM. INDIAN L. REV. 177, 188 (2001–2002).

77. RICHLAND & DEER, *supra* note 2, at 248. *See also* BRUCE ELLIOT JOHANSEN, ED., THE ENCYCLOPEDIA OF NATIVE AMERICAN LEGAL TRADITION, 260 (1998) (some Pueblos are governed by a religious leader). *See also* Janis v. Wilson, 385 F.Supp. 1143 (D.S.D. 1974), *remanded on other grounds* 521 F.2d 724 (by omitting certain clauses of Bill of Rights, and by modifying the clauses that were finally incorporated into the ICRA, Congress recognized as legitimate the tribal interest in maintaining traditional practices that conflict with constitutional concepts of personal freedom developed in a different social context).

78. *See* Santa Clara Pueblo v. Martinez, 436 U.S. 49 (1978).

79. 25 U.S.C. § 1303 ("The privilege of the writ of habeas corpus shall be available to any person, in a court of the United States, to test the legality of his detention by order of an Indian tribe").

80. *Compare* Poodry v. Tonawanda Band of Seneca Indians, 85 F.3d 874 (2nd Cir. 1996) (orders by tribal council members purporting to banish tribal members from reservation were "criminal sanctions" providing sufficient basis for jurisdiction under ICRA's habeas corpus provision), *with* Shenandoah v. Halbritter, 366 F.3d 89 (2nd Cir. 2004) (allegation that tribe's housing ordinance was used to retaliate against residents who resisted tribal leadership was insufficient for habeas jurisdiction under ICRA).

81. *Santa Clara*, 436 U.S. at 62. *See also* Means v. Wilson, 383 F.Supp. 378 (D.S.D. 1974) (purpose of ICRA is to "enhance civil liberties of individual Indians without unduly undermining Indian self-government and cultural automony"), *aff'd in part, rev'd in part on other grounds*, 533 F.2d 833 (8th Cir.(S.D.) 1975), *cert. denied*, 424 U.S. 958 (1976).

82. *See Martinez*, 436 U.S. at 72, n. 32 ("A tribe's right to define its own membership for tribal purposes has long been recognized as central to its existence as an independent political community. . . . Given the often vast gulf between tribal traditions and those with which federal courts are more intimately familiar, the judiciary should not rush to create causes of action that would intrude on these delicate matters").

83. *See* Tebben, *supra* note 76, at 188.

84. *See* Catherine T. Struve, *Tribal Immunity and Tribal Courts*, 36 ARIZ. ST. L.J. 137 (2004). *See also* RICHLAND & DEER, *supra* note 2, at 260. *Compare* Goldberg, *supra* note 14, at 899 (The highest court of the Hopi tribe "has taken the position that the Indian Civil Rights Act is not necessarily binding law").

85. *See* Struve, *supra* note 84, at 157.

86. For a broader survey of civil rights provisions appearing in 220 tribal constitutions, see Elmer R. Rusco, *Civil Liberties Guarantees Under Tribal Law: A Survey of Civil Rights Provisions in Tribal Constitutions*, 14

AM. INDIAN L. REV. 269, 276–78 (1990). In addition to Rusco's article, I reviewed roughly one hundred tribal constitutions available on the Web sites of some individual tribes and on the following online resources: *The National Indian Law Library's Online Collection of Tribal Codes and Constitutions*, NARF.ORG, http://www.narf.org/nill/triballaw/onlinedocs.htm; *Native American Constitution and Law Digitization Project*, U. OF OKLAHOMA, http://madison.law.ou.edu/const.html; *The Tribal Court Clearinghouse*, TRIBAL L. AND POL. INST., http://www.tribal-institute.org/lists/constitutions.htm. I did not review constitutions existing only in print nor attempt to find online tribal constitutions outside the databases listed above. Thus my chapter does not offer an exhaustive survey of tribal religious freedoms provisions nor does it offer any general conclusions supported by statistical data. Rather I discuss certain *examples* of tribal constitutional approaches to religious freedoms as potentially illuminating to what I see as a tribe-specific inquiry into the dynamics of assimilation and sovereignty vis à vis individual rights. A more complete survey would attempt to examine all of the available tribal constitutions and legislative codes, as well as customary, decisional, and regulatory law, on tribal religions freedoms.

87. CROW TRIBAL CONST., art. XI, § 4 (2002), *available at* http://www.tribalresourcecenter.org/ccfolder/crow_const.htm.

88. CONST. AND BYLAWS OF THE MISSISSIPPI BAND OF CHOCTAW INDIANS, art. X, § 1, *available at* http://www.tribalresourcecenter.org/ccfolder/mississippi_choctaw_const.htm.

89. CONST. OF THE SKOKOMISH INDIAN TRIBE, art. IX, *available at* http://doc.narf.org/nill/Constitutions/skoconst/skokomishconst.htm#const9.

90. CONST. OF THE MIAMI TRIBE OF OKLAHOMA, art. VII (1995), *available at* http://doc.narf.org/nill/Constitutions/miamiconst/miamiconst.htm#artvii.

91. CONST. OF THE BIG LAGOON RANCHERIA, art. IV (1985), *available at* http://doc.narf.org/nill/Constitutions/lagoonconst/biglagconst.htm#art4.

92. CONST. AND BY-LAWS OF THE UTE INDIAN TRIBE OF THE UINTAH AND OURAY RESERVATION, art. VII, § 3 (1937), *available at* http://doc.narf.org/nill/Constitutions/uteconst/uteconst.htm#Bill.

93. CONST. OF THE CHOCTAW NATION OF OKLAHOMA, art. IV, § 2 (1983), *available at* http://doc.narf.org/nill/Constitutions/choctawconst/choctawconst.htm#a4. *See infra* notes 111–128 for a discussion of similar language originating from the Indian Reorganization Act and federal models for tribal constitutions emerging in the 1930s.

94. CONST. OF THE MUSCOGEE CREEK NATION, art. IV, § 2 (1995), *available at* http://thorpe.ou.edu/constitution/muscogee/index.html

95. *Compare* CONST. OF THE WAMPANOAG TRIBE OF GAY HEAD (Aquinnah), art. III. § 3 (b) (1995), *available at* http://thorpe.ou.edu/constitution/wampanoag/index.html ("[T]he tribal council shall ... ensure that tribal members have free access to the clay in the cliffs on an equal basis provided that such access is subject to reasonable regulation in order to protect and preserve the resource"). *See also* Wampanoag Tribe of Gay Head Web site http://www.wampanoagtribe.net/Pages/Wampanoag_Way/aquinnah (on significance of The Aquinnah Cliffs) and http://www.wampanoagtribe.net/Pages/Wampanoag_Way/other (providing information for "visitors" including "It is prohibited to take clay from the Aquinnah Cliffs, climb on them, or otherwise disturb the Cliffs in any way").

96. CONST. OF THE IROQUOIS NATIONS, *available at* http://www.indigenouspeople.net/iroqcon.htm.

97. *See id.* at para. 1 ("I am Dekanawidah and with the Five Nations' Confederate Lords I plant the Tree of Great Peace. I plant it in your territory, Adodarhoh, and the Onondaga Nation, in the territory of you who are Firekeepers. I name the tree the Tree of the Great Long Leaves. Under the shade of this Tree of the Great Peace we spread the soft white feathery down of the globe thistle as seats for you, Adodarhoh, and your cousin Lords. We place you upon those seats, spread soft with the feathery down of the globe thistle, there beneath the shade of the spreading branches of the Tree of Peace. There shall you sit and watch the Council Fire of the Confederacy of the Five Nations, and all the affairs of the Five Nations shall be transacted at this place before you, Adodarhoh, and your cousin Lords, by the Confederate Lords of the Five Nations"). Sources commonly situate Dekanawidah between 1450 and 1525. Professor Porter indicates, in a substantial discussion of Iroquois or Haudenosaunee law, that the Iroquois Confederacy was formed through the Five Nations' acceptance of the Gayanashagowa "some time before Columbus." *See* Robert B. Porter, *Building a New Longhouse: The Case for Government Reform Within the Six Nations of the Haudenosaunee*, 46 BUFF. L. REV. 805, 810 (1998).

98. CONST. OF THE IROQUOIS NATIONS at para. 99–104.
99. Similarly Rusco's study describes:

> A number of provisions on religious freedom obviously were written specifically for the situation of the tribe. For example, several refer to traditional Native religious beliefs or practices. For example, the constitution of the Miccosukee Tribe states that "[t]he members of the tribe shall continue undisturbed in their religious beliefs and nothing in this constitution and bylaws will authorize either the General Council or the Business Council to interfere with these traditional religious practices according to their custom." While these two provisions dealing with religious freedom refer only to traditional tribal beliefs, several other specific provisions stating freedom of religion guarantee religious diversity. For example, the constitution of the Pueblo of Laguna states, "All religious denominations shall have freedom of worship in the Pueblo of Laguna, and each member of the Pueblo shall respect the other members' religious beliefs." The constitution of the Alabama-Quassarte Tribal Town states that "no member shall be treated differently because he does or does not believe in or take part in any religion or religious custom." The constitution of the Cocopah Tribe says that "the members of the tribe shall continue undisturbed in their religious beliefs and nothing in this Constitution will authorize the Tribal Council to interfere with religious practices."

Rusco, *supra* note 86, at 276–78.

100. *See* LAND POLICY AND CONSTITUTION OF THE PEOPLE OF BILL MOORE'S SLOUGH (1988), *available at* http://thorpe.ou.edu/constitution/billmoores/index.html. (This chapter follows the somewhat irregular use of possessives in the Bill Moores Slough Constitution.) While too long to reprint here, the Yurok Tribe's Constitution has extensive and detailed provisions on traditional religion and culture. *See Constitution of the Yurok Tribe* (1993), *available at* http://www.yuroktribe.org/government/councilsupport/documents/Constitution.pdf.

101. LAND POLICY AND CONSTITUTION OF THE PEOPLE OF BILL MOORE'S SLOUGH at Preamble.

102. *Id.* at Art I, II.

103. CONST. OF THE POARCH BAND OF CREEK INDIANS, pmbl. (Adopted June 1, 1985), *available at* http://doc.narf.org/nill/Constitutions/poarchconstitution/poarchconsttoc.htm.

104. *Id.* at art. II.

105. CONST. OF THE WHITE MOUNTAIN APACHE TRIBE OF THE FORT APACHE INDIAN RESERVATION ARIZONA, art.V (1993) *available at* http://thorpe.ou.edu/codes/wmtnapache/Constitution.html.

106. *See* WHITE MOUNTAIN APACHE GOV'T CODE, ch. 8, PRESERVATION OF RELIGIOUS SITES (1991) (designating religious sites within the White Mountain Apache Reservation for the use of practitioners of the traditional religion and providing civil and criminal penalties for desecration, including traditional Apache punishment), *available at* http://www.tribalresourcecenter.org/ccfolder/wht_mtn_apache_tribalcode_government.html.

107. RICHLAND & DEER, *supra* note 2, at 265 (citing Colville Tribal Civil Rights Act, Ch. 1–5 (adopted Feb. 4, 1988, resolution 1988–76, certified Feb. 16, 1988)).

108. *See, e.g.,* The Navajo Nation Bill of Rights, 1 N.N. C., Sec 4 (free exercise and establishment clauses), *available at* http://www.navajocourts.org/Harmonization/NavBillRights.htm; The Fundamental Law of the Dine (religion and spiritual provisions throughout), *available at* http://www.navajocourts.org/dine.htm.

109. Again, for a broader survey of constitutional civil rights provisions, including detailed analysis of religious freedoms, see Rusco, *supra* note 86, at 275–76.

110. *See* Goldberg, *supra* note 14, at 889.

111. *Id.* (citing Robert B. Porter, *Strengthening Tribal Sovereignty through Peacemaking: How the Anglo-American Legal Tradition Destroys Indigenous Societies*, 28 COLUM. HUM. RTS. L. REV. 235, 278 (1997)).

112. Goldberg, *supra* note 14, at 889 (citing VINE DELORIA, JR., & CLIFFORD M. LYTLE, THE NATIONS WITHIN: THE PAST AND FUTURE OF AMERICAN INDIAN SOVEREIGNTY 213 (1984) (internal quotations and changes omitted).

113. Goldberg, *supra* note 14, at 889 (citing Professor Kevin Washburn, Remarks at the Arizona State University College of Law Goldwater Lecture on American Institutions (Feb. 20, 2003)).

114. For an historical overview, *see* Goldberg, *supra* note 14, at 892–99.

115. *See* CHARLES WILKINSON, BLOOD STRUGGLE: THE RISE OF MODERN INDIAN NATIONS 60–62 (2005).

116. *See* GETCHES ET AL., *supra* note 15, at 189–194 (excerpting Comment, Tribal Self-Government and the Indian Reorganization Act of 1934, 70 MICH. L. REV. 955, 955–79 (1972). Initially 181 tribes voted to accept, and 71 tribes voted to reject, the IRA. At the end of twelve years, there were 161 tribes with constitutions and 131 with corporate charters.

117. *See* GETCHES ET AL., *supra* note, 15 at 195–97 (describing Hopi experiences with the IRA); *see also* Stephen Cornell and Joseph P. Kalt, *Where Does Economic Development Really Come From? Constitutional Rule Among the Contemporary Sioux and Apache,* 33 ECON. INQUIRY. 402 (1995); Joseph P. Kalt, *The Role of Constitutions in Native Nation Building: Laying a Firm Foundation, in* MIRIAM JORGENSEN, ED., REBUILDING NATIVE NATIONS: STRATEGIES FOR GOVERNANCE AND DEVESLOPMENT (2007).

118. *See* FELIX S. COHEN, ON THE DRAFTING OF TRIBAL CONSTITUTIONS (David E. Wilkins, ed., 2006); DALIA TSUK MITCHELL, ARCHITECT OF JUSTICE, FELIX S. COHEN AND THE FOUNDING OF AMERICAN LEGAL PLURALISM (2007).

119. COHEN *supra* note 118, at xxvi–xxvii.

120. *See id.* at xxvi–xxvii (Cohen was "opposed to sending out canned constitutions" to tribes and he made clear his view "that constitutions must be worked out in the first place by the Indians in the field").

121. *See id.* at 173–82.

122. *See id.* at 76–78.

123. *See* WILKINSON, *supra* note 115, at 60.

124. 25 U.S.C.A 476 (c).

125. 25 U.S.C.A 476 (c)(3).

126. 25 U.S.C.A 476(d).

127. *Compare* Kirsty Gover, *Comparative Tribal Constitutionalism: Membership Governance In Australia, Canada, New Zealand, And The United States,* 35 LAW & SOC. INQUIRY 689, 708 (2010) ("About half of US tribes are organized under the IRA and are required by the act to gain the approval of the secretary of the interior for new constitutions and constitutional amendments, but the review power is only rarely used. . . . The secretarial review power is controversial and its scope remains unclear").

128. *See* 25 U.S.C.A sec. 476(a)

> Any Indian tribe shall have the right to organize for its common welfare, and may adopt an appropriate constitution and bylaws, and any amendments thereto, which shall become effective when—
>
> (1) ratified by a majority vote of the adult members of the tribe or tribes at a special election authorized and called by the Secretary under such rules and regulations as the Secretary may prescribe; and
>
> (2) approved by the Secretary pursuant to subsection (d) of this section.

See also ROBERT T. ANDERSON, BETHANY BERGER, PHILIP P. TRICKEY & SARAH KRAKOFF, AMERICAN INDIAN LAW: CASES AND COMMENTARY 137–40 (2008) (reprinting the 1936 constitution and bylaws of the Hopi Tribe, including art. VI's provision that the Hopi Constitution shall be ratified by a majority of the adult voters of the tribe "at a referendum called for the purpose by the Secretary of the Interior" and then "submitted to the Secretary of the Interior, and if approved, shall take effect from the date of approval").

129. Goldberg, *supra* note 14, at 895.

130. *See, e.g., In re* Status of the 1999 Constitution, 9 Okla. Trib. 392 (Cherokee Sup. Ct. 2006) (describing the Cherokee Nation's 1975 Constitution requiring approval by the secretary of the Interior and its 1999 constitution not requiring such approval). This decision and the two Cherokee constitutions are described in greater detail below; *see infra* notes 249–56.

131. *See* Goldberg, *supra* note 14, at 892 ("A combination of heavy pressure from federal laws and administration, inculcation of non-Indian values through federally supported missionaries and boarding schools, and a desire by tribes to fend off jurisdictional challenges likely explains how these individual rights protections developed in tribal law").

132. *See Lyng,* 485 U.S. at 447–49. *See also* Amy Bowers and Kristen A. Carpenter, *The Story of Lyng v. Northwest Indian Cemetery Association: Challenging the Narrative of Conquest, in* INDIAN LAW STORIES (2010).

133. *Lyng,* 485 U.S. at 450–51.

134. *Id.* at 451.

135. *See Smith*, 494 U.S. at 890. *See also* GARRETT EPPS, TO AN UNKNOWN GOD, RELIGIOUS FREEDOM ON TRIAL (2001) and CAROLYN N. LONG, RELIGIOUS FREEDOM AND INDIAN RIGHTS: THE CASE OF OREGON V. SMITH (2000) (both analyzing the Smith case).

136. *See Smith*, 494 U.S. at 890.

137. *See* WEAVER, *supra* note 34, at 180.

138. *See infra* notes 226–48, 261–90 and accompanying text discussing tribal court cases interpreting individual religious freedoms laws.

139. *See* GETCHES ET AL., *supra* note 15, at 412 (describing that tribal courts face the task of "blending the old with the new").

140. *See generally* Russel Lawrence Barsh, *Putting the Tribe in Tribal Courts: Possible? Desirable?*, 8 KAN.J.L. & PUB. POL'Y 74 (1999); Goldberg, *supra* note 14, at 896–97 ("Despite the many differences among tribal cultures, and the assertions by tribal courts that they were not bound to mimic non-Indian law, tribal court interpretations of due process were remarkably similar to one another, as well as to non-Indian readings of the requirement"). Matthew Fletcher has theorized that tribal courts are likely to apply the internal, customary law of the tribe ("intratribal law") to matters involving tribal members, especially those matters growing out of an "indigenous legal construct"—and to apply law resembling or borrowed from state and federal sources ("intertribal law") to matters involving nonmembers, especially those matters growing out of an "Anglo-American legal construct." Matthew L.M. Fletcher, *Toward a Theory of Intertribal and Intratribal Common Law*, 43 HOUS. L. REV. 701, 718–32 (2006). It would be interesting, in a subsequent article, to evaluate this theory in the context of religious freedoms cases.

141. *See infra* notes 226–48 and accompanying text (discussing *Townsend* and *Garcia* cases).

142. *See* DELORIA, GOD IS RED, *supra* note 26, at 194 ("When we turn from Christian religious beliefs to Indian tribal beliefs . . . , the contrast is remarkable. [Indian] [r]eligion is not conceived as a personal relationship between the deity and each individual. It is rather a covenant between a particular god and a particular community").

143. Dean B. Suagee, *The Cultural Heritage of American Indian Tribes and the Preservation of Biological Diversity*, 31 ARIZ. ST. L. J. 483, 510 (1999).

144. *Id.*

145. *Compare* RICHLAND & DEER, *supra* note 2, at xviii ("We realize that . . . accounts [by non-Indian historian and anthropologists] may not always be consistent with the beliefs . . . of Native peoples. We include them as a starting point for discussing traditional [lawmaking]. We encourage readers . . . to read critically and form independent analysis of the passages").

146. RUTH M. UNDERHILL, RED MAN'S RELIGION 209–10 (1965). Ruth Underhill's methodology has been the subject of some critical commentary, including that of Native "informants" and "interpreters" who worked with her. *See, e.g.,* SUSAN BERRY BRILL DE RAMÍREZ, NATIVE AMERICAN LIFE-HISTORY NARRATIVES, COLONIAL AND POST-COLONIAL NAVAJO ETHNOGRAPHY 75 (2007).

147. UNDERHILL, *supra* note 146, at 116.

148. *Id.* at 142.

149. *See* Northwest Indian Cemetery Protective Ass'n v. Peterson, 565 F. Supp. 586, 591–92 (N.D. Cal. 1983).

150. *Id.* at 592.

151. *See Lyng*, 485 U.S. at 458.

152. MANKILLER, *supra* note 1, at 15.

153. *Id.* at 16–17.

154. Navajo Nation Council Resolution CD-107-94 (Dec. 13, 1994).

155. *See generally* Dussias, *supra* note 16. *See also Bear Lodge*, 175 F.3d at 819.

156. *See, e.g.,* Lorie M. Graham, *"The Past Never Vanishes": A Contextual Critique of the Existing Indian Family Doctrine*, 23 AM. INDIAN L. REV. 1, 10–18 (1998) (describing assimilationist programs).

157. *See, e.g.,* Mark A. Michaels, *Indigenous Ethics and Alien Laws: Native Traditions and the United States Legal System*, 66 FORDHAM L. REV. 1565, 1571 (1998) ("Because Native religions depend on the oral tradition for their transmission, the death of a language often means the death of a religion. Stories and ceremonies are at the core of most, if not all, Native religions, and these stories and ceremonies lose their context and meaning when translated"); *See* MANKILLER, *supra* note 1, at 37 ("You have to be able to speak Cherokee to be a

Cherokee medicine person. How can you say the right words if you can't speak Cherokee?") (quoting Florence Soap).

158. *See* RICHLAND & DEER, *supra* note 2, at 313–22 (on traditional dispute resolution forums).

159. *See infra* notes 244–48 and 261–90 (discussing the cases).

160. *Compare* Matthew L.M. Fletcher, *Rethinking Customary Law in Tribal Court Jurisprudence,* 13 MICH. J. RACE & L. 57, 82 (2007) (describing the challenges of utilizing customary law in tribal court decision making).

161. *See* Thlopthlocco Tribal Town v. Tomah, 8 Okla. Trib. 451, 2004 WL 5744828 (Muscogee 2004).

162. *Id. See also* Bowers and Carpenter, *supra* note 128 at 500 (describing role of Courts of Indian Offenses in late-nineteenth-century religious suppression).

163. *See* GETCHES ET AL., *supra* note 15, at 408–26.

164. *See generally* Porter, *supra* note 56 (on the incompatibility of adversarial Anglo-American legal institutions and with indigenous societies and traditions).

165. Compare RICHLAND & DEER, *supra* note 2, at 323–31 (describing how Navajo Peacemaker Court—while not necessarily a venue for bringing religious disputes—serves as an alternative to tribal courts, fostering Navajo values and the restoration of relationships).

166. Compare Eric Cheyfitz, *The Colonial Double Bind: Sovereignty and Civil Rights in Indian Country,* 5 U. PA. J. CONST. L. 223, 239–40 (2003) (tracing the "subversion of traditional sovereignty by a tribal sovereignty generated within the colonial context that leads grassroots groups such as the . . . Navajos in the *Manybeads* case to invoke a language of individual rights (in this case the right to freedom of religion) in order to assert their traditional sovereignty").

167. *Compare* Goldberg, *supra* note 14, at 910–29 (considering the contentions that (1) "individual rights are fully consistent with tribal cultures;" (2) "individual rights must be protected in order for tribal governments to secure economic growth and respect from non-Indian governments;" (3) "native nations need individual rights to protect them from congressional attacks on their sovereignty and culture").

168. RICHLAND & DEER, *supra* note 2, at 239.

169. *Id.*

170. *Id.* at 240 (quoting James W. Zion in *Civil Rights in Navajo Common Law,* 50 U. KAN. L. REV. 523 (2001), on the Navajo concept of "individualism").

171. *See, e.g.,* Kristen A. Carpenter and Ray Halbritter, *Beyond the Ethnic Umbrella and the Buffalo: Some Thoughts on American Indian Tribes and Gaming,* 5 GAMING LAW REVIEW 311 (2001).

172. Rebecca Tsosie, *Introduction: Symposium on Cultural Sovereignty,* 34 ARIZ. ST. L.J. 1, 7 (2002) (quoting Duane Champagne, *Challenges to Native Nation Building in the 21ˢᵗ Century,* 34 ARIZ. ST. L.J. 47, 50 (2002)).

173. KARL N. LLEWELLYN & E. ADAMSON HOEBEL, THE CHEYENNE WAY (1941). I acknowledge, as others have, that this source is somewhat problematic but try to draw useful points from it.

174. *Id.* at 9.

175. *Id.* at 10.

176. *Id.*

177. *Id.*

178. *See id.* at 11.

179. *Id.*

180. *Id.* at 11–12.

181. *Id.* at 12.

182. *See id.* at 9–12.

183. *Id.* at 12.

184. *See* ELLA CARA DELORIA, WATERLILY x (1988). Deloria wrote in the 1940s and *Waterlily* was published after her death.

185. *Id.* at 3.

186. *See id.* at 113.

187. *Id.* at 17.

188. *Id.*

189. *Id.* at 18.

190. *Id.*

191. Vine Deloria, Jr. (b. 1933) and Ella Cara Deloria (b. 1889) were members of the same prominent Dakota Family in which several members were leaders in traditional spirituality and Christianity. Their ancestor Saswe was a medicine man, while both of their fathers were clergymen in the Episcopal Church. Ella Deloria graduated from Colombia University and worked with the famed anthropologist Franz Boas. She published a number of books, in English and Dakota. Vine Deloria, Jr., graduated from Iowa State University, Lutheran School of Theology, University of Colorado School of Law. He directed the National Congress of American Indians and served as a professor of law, history, religious studies, and political science at the University of Colorado. *See* VINE DELORIA, JR., SINGING FOR A SPIRIT: A PORTRAIT OF THE DAKOTA SIOUX (2000) (on the family's spiritual experiences and legacy).

192. DELORIA , GOD IS RED, *supra* note 26, at 195.

193. *Id*. at 196.

194. *Id*. at 196–97. *Compare* Melissa A. Pflug, *Pimadaziwin: Contemporary Rituals in Odawa Community, in* Irwin, *supra* note 31, at 127 (suggesting a distinction between "personal prayer" and "communal ceremonies").

195. DELORIA, GOD IS RED, *supra* note 26, at 198.

196. *Id*. at 197.

197. See Robert B. Porter, *Decolonizing Indigenous Governance: Observations on Restoring Greater Faith and Legitimacy in the Government of the Seneca Nation*, 8 KAN. J.L. & PUB. POL'Y 97 (1999). Porter describes the major event in Seneca history when Handsome Lake, the half-brother of the Seneca War Chief Cornplanter, had in 1799 the first of a series of visions setting forth religious and secular solutions for problems in Seneca society at the time. Handsome Lake's subsequent visions eventually formed the basis of a social gospel and a new religion, the Gaiwiio. Porter argues that the Handsome Lake religion was itself an assimilationist force among Senecas, importing Quaker and federal values, and disrupting traditional kinship patterns.

198. A contemporaneous (though somewhat controversial by present-day standards) account can be found in JAMES MOONEY, THE GHOST-DANCE RELIGION AND THE SIOUX OUTBREAK OF 1890 (1896) (reprinted 1973).

199. *See generally* STEWART, *supra* note 59.

200. *See* DELORIA, GOD IS RED, *supra* note 26.

201. *See* MANKILLER, *supra* note 1, at 37 (quoting Florence Soap).

202. *Id*. at 26–27 (quoting LaDonna Harris).

203. *See id*. at 27.

204. *See id*. at 27 ("Some of the missionaries would come and preach in a way that was designed to make us question our identity. The message was that if we gave up music, dance, and our identity and then went to church, they might accept us. But they never accepted us") (quoting LaDonna Harris); *id*. at 30 ("Various Christian groups divided up the reservations . . . Christianity really disrupted the kinship unit") (quoting Beatrice Medicine).

205. *See id*. at 35 ("I realized my own culture had more [than Christianity] to offer me as a human being and as a woman. I learned that our Earth and all its elements are living entities to be celebrated and honored') (quoting Joanne Shenandoah).

206. *Id*.

207. *See id*. at 33 ("Spirituality is a very private matter" that need not be demonstrated outwardly to others). Navajo law recognizes property rights in one's religious materials. *See In re* Estate of Apachee, 4 Nav. R. 178 (Navajo 1983) ("The court classifies property as follows: A man is standing in an imaginary circle, and he has all his possessions—everything he calls life. They are (1) his wife and children, (2) his religion (including its paraphernalia, mountain dust, bundles, etc.) (3) his land, (4) his livestock and (5) his jewelry, including money").

208. *See* MANKILLER, *supra* note 1, at 33 ("The emphasis is on the collective, for no one medicine person could emit the power that the participating collective puts forth")

209. *See id*. at 26.

210. *See, e.g.,* James W. Zion, *Civil Rights in Navajo Common Law, in* RICHLAND & DEER, *supra* note 2, at 240 (on the Navajo concept of "individualism").

211. *See generally* NOAH FELDMAN, DIVIDED BY GOD: AMERICA'S CHURCH-STATE PROBLEM AND WHAT WE SHOULD DO ABOUT IT (2006) (situating current religious disputes in American religious freedoms history).

212. *See* G. Peter Jemison, *The Journey*, 7 ST. THOMAS L. REV. 433, 435 (1995) ("Our [Seneca] religion and

our government are entwined as one; we do not separate them and we do not call it religion. Rather it is an Indian way of life that encompasses everything that we do").

213. *Compare* Angela R. Riley, *"Straight Stealing":Towards an Indigenous System of Cultural Property Protection,* 80 WASH. L. REV. 69, 118–23 (2005) (urging tribes to protect cultural property by enacting tribal laws that reflect tribal custom in an act of "living sovereignty").

214. *See generally* RICHLAND & DEER, *supra* note 2, at 283–88 (on the challenges of making law meaningful in tribal communities today).

215. *See* Goldberg, *supra* note 14, at 934 ("The project of tribal revitalization cannot begin with denial of the cultural changes and growing expectations regarding individual rights that have taken place within Indian country").

216. *See* Sandra Day O'Connor, *Lessons From the Third Sovereign,* 33 TULSA L.J. 1, 2 (1997) ("To fulfill their role as an essential branch of tribal government, the tribal courts must provide a forum that commands the respect of both the tribal community and the non-tribal community including courts, governments, and litigants. To do so, tribal courts need to be perceived as both fair and principled").

217. *See, e.g.,* Nevada v. Hicks, 533 U.S. 353, 383–84 (2001) (Kennedy J., Souter, J., and Thomas, S. concurring) (discussing the "special nature" of tribal courts and potential effects on non-Indian parties).

218. *See* DELORIA, GOD IS RED, *supra* note 26, at 246 ("Traditional Indians of [the Navajo and Hopi] tribes are fighting desperately against any additional strip-mining of [reservation] lands. Tribal councils are continuing to lease the lands for development to encourage employment and to make possible more tribal programs for the rehabilitation of tribal members").

219. According to Ann Beeson, the Navajo tribal council's enactment of the anti-peyote legislation was an act of resistance against John Collier, the head of the Bureau of Indian Affairs at the time. Collier was pushing restrictions on sheep grazing, an unpopular position with the Navajos, and was also supportive of the peyote users. *See* Beeson, *supra* note 64, at 1139 (1992).Viewed in this light, the council's later decision to lift the peyote ban and provide religious freedom should be examined in a broad historical context, querying what kind of religious freedoms were available before, during, and after the peyote ban—rather than assuming freedom of religion is merely a modern "import."

220. *See* RICHLAND & DEER, *supra* note 2, at 286.

221. *See* Elizabeth E. Joh, *Custom, Tribal Court Practice, and Popular Justice,* 25 AM. INDIAN L. REV. 117, 120 (2001).

222. *See* Robert D. Cooter & Wolfgang Fikentscher, *Indian Common Law: The Role of Custom in American Indian Tribal Courts,* 46 AM. J. COMP. L. 287, 287 (1998) Joseph A. Myers & Elbridge Coochise, *Development of Tribal Courts: Past, Present, and Future,* 79 JUDICATURE 147, 147 (1995); Gloria Valencia-Weber, *Tribal Courts: Custom and Innovative Law,* 24 N. M. L. Rev. 225, 226 (1994).

223. *See* Matthew L.M. Fletcher, *Toward a Theory of Intertribal and Intratribal Common Law,* 43 HOUS. L. REV. 701 (2006); Matthew L.M. Fletcher, *Looking to the East: the Stories of Modern Indian People and the Development of Tribal Law,* 5 SEATTLE J. FOR SOC. JUST. 1 (2006); Matthew L.M. Fletcher, *Rethinking Customary Law in Tribal Court Jurisprudence,* 13 MICH. J. RACE & L. 57 (2007); Matthew L.M. Fletcher, *The Supreme Court's Legal Culture War Against Tribal Law,* 2 INTERCULTURAL HUM. RTS. L. REV. 93 (2006).

224. *See, e.g., In re* Validation of Marriage of Loretta Francisco, 6 NAV. REP. 134, 16 Indian L. Rep 6113 (1989).

225. *Id.*

226. Townsend v. Port Gamble S'Klallam Housing Authority, 6 NICS App. 179 (citing *Braunfield v. Brown,* 366 U.S. 599, 605 (1961) (state may prohibit retailers from operating on Sunday even if this disadvantages Jewish retailers whose religion also requires them to close on Saturday)).

227. *Id.*

228. *Id.*

229. *Id.*

230. Garcia v. Greendeer-Lee, 30 Indian L. Rep. 6097 (Ho-Chunk Sup. Ct. 2003).

231. Matthew L.M. Fletcher, *Resisting Congress: Free Speech and Tribal Law,* THE INDIAN CIVIL RIGHTS ACT AT FORTY (2012).

232. *See* THE CONSTITUTION OF THE HO-CHUNK NATION, Art. 10, Sec 1., *available at,* http://www.ho-chunknation.com/?PageId=294.

233. *See* Hoover v. Colville Confederated Tribes, 3 CTCR 43, 6 CCAR 16, (2002), *available at* http://www.tribal-institute.org/opinions/2002.NACC.0000004.htm. *See also* Hoopa Valley Tribe v. Bugenig, 5 NICS App. 37 (Hoopa Valley Tribal Court of Appeals 1998) (affirming tribe's authority to prohibit logging in an areas designated by the tribal council as a "buffer zone" around a sacred site). Additionally Justin Richland's recent book on Hopi jurisprudence describes various ways in which concepts like tradition and evidence about ceremonial obligations and clan relationships affect property disputes. *See* JUSTIN B. RICHLAND, ARGUING WITH TRADITION: THE LANGUAGE OF LAW IN HOPI TRIBAL COURT 56–57, 71–72 (2008).

234. *Hoover*, 3 CTCR 43 (2002).

235. *Id.* The question of tribal authority over nonmembers, though beyond the scope of this chapter, is largely governed by *Montana v. United States*, 450 U.S. 544, 565 (1981) ("A tribe may regulate . . . the activities of non-members who enter consensual relations with the tribe or its members, through commercial dealings, contracts, leases, or other arrangements . . . a tribe may . . . exercise civil authority over the conduct of non-Indians on fee lands within its reservation when that conduct threatens or has some direct effect on the political integrity, the economic security, or the health or welfare of the tribe").

236. *Hoover*, 3 CTCR 43 (2002) (citing Bugenig v. Hoopa Valley Tribe, 266 F.3d 1201 (9th Cir. 2001)).

237. *Id.*

238. *Id.*

239. *Id.*

240. *See Hoover*, 3 CTCR 43 (2002) (emphasis added).

241. *See id.*

242. *See* Mary Jo B. Hunter, *Tribal Court Opinions: Justice and Legitimacy*, 8-WTR KAN. J.L. & PUB. POL'Y 142 (1999). *See also Government*, HO-CHUNK NATION, http://www.ho-chunknation.com/?PageId=3 (describing tribal constitution, court system, and boards and committees of the nation).

243. Valencia-Weber, *supra* note 217, at 251–52.

244. *See* Elk Horn Society v. Red Hat, 3 Okla. Trib. 327 (1990).

245. *See id.*

246. *See In re* The Sacred Arrows, 3 Okla. Trib. 332 (1990). *See also* McCarthy, *supra* note 3, at 496–97 (describing the cases).

247. *In re* The Sacred Arrows, 3 Okla. Trib. at 338 (1990). I do not know the ultimate fate of the Sacred Arrows following this opinion.

248. *Compare* WILLIAM WAYNE RED HAT, JR. CHEYENNE KEEPER OF THE ARROWS (2008).

249. *See* RICHLAND & DEER, *supra* note 2, at 286 ("If, at a later time, members of the tribe come to power that have a more traditional outlook, they might change the law to reflect that interest. This, too, would be just another expression of the same sovereignty. Traditions themselves are not necessarily static; they evolve and change over time").

250. *See* Eric Lemont, *Overcoming the Politics of Reform: The Story of the Cherokee Nation of Oklahoma Constitutional Convention*, 28 AM. INDIAN L. REV. 1 (2003-2004); D. Jay Hannah, *The 1999 Constitution Convention of the Cherokee Nation*, 35 ARIZ. ST. L. J. 1 (2003).

251. CONST. OF THE CHEROKEE NATION OF OKLA. of 1975, *available at*, http://thorpe.ou.edu/constitution/cherokee/index.html.

252. CONST. OF THE CHEROKEE NATION (1999) (approved by the Cherokee citizens and Election Council in 2003, ruled effective and ordered implemented by the Cherokee Nation Judicial Appeals Tribunal in 2006), *available at* http://www.cherokee.org/Docs/TribalGovernment/Executive/CCC/2003_CN_CONSTITUTION.pdf.

253. There were some comments about religion submitted by tribal citizens in the "Pre-Convention" testimonial phase. *See, e.g.*, Letter of Robert McCoy Wood to Constitutional Convention Commission, Cherokee Nation (Nov. 4, 1998), *available at* http://www.cherokee.org/docs/tribalgovernment/executive/CCC/Written.htm (suggesting an elders' board be established in the new constitution to advise the principal chief on religious and cultural matters including repatriation). This suggestion does not appear to have been adopted.

254. Cherokee Nation Constitution Convention, Transcript of Proceedings, Volume 1 (February 27, 1999), *available at* http://www.cherokee.org/Docs/TribalGovernment/ Executive/CCC/vol2.htm (Comments of

Mr. Hoskin, Jr.) ("I'd like to stress that enumerating our own Bill of Rights as opposed to just by implication taking the Indian Civil Rights Act, will allow us to develop our own notions of due process and protection, which I think is important for any sovereign people who are concerned with individual rights"). This portion of the transcript contains substantive debate about various individual rights proposed in the new constitution.

255. CHEROKEE CONSTITUTION of 1827, art. VI, § 3 ("The free exercise of religious worship and serving God without distinction shall forever be allowed within this Nation, provided that this liberty of conscience, shall not be so construed, as to excuse acts of licentiousness, or Justify practices inconsistent with the peace and safety of this Nation") (note: sources vary for the 1827 constitution and in some, the enumeration of articles and sections differs); CONSTITUTION OF THE CHEROKEE NATION of 1839, Art. VI, § 2 (same). Of course many have argued that the Cherokees' 1827 constitution was enacted as a means of showing the outside world that the tribe was "civilized." For various views of "traditional" Cherokee religion, *see, e.g.*, JAMES MOONEY, MYTHS OF THE CHEROKEES AND SACRED FORMULAS OF THE CHEROKEES (reprinted in 2007); FRED GEARING, PRIESTS AND WARRIORS: SOCIAL STRUCTURES FOR CHEROKEE POLITICS IN THE 18TH CENTURY (1962); and JACK FREDERICK KILPATRICK AND ANNA GRITTS KILPATRICK, FRIENDS OF THUNDER: FOLKTALES OF THE OKLAHOMA CHEROKEES (1995). *See also* RENNARD STRICKLAND, FIRE AND THE SPIRITS: CHEROKEE LAW FROM CLAN TO COURT (1975) (discussing the evolution of Cherokee traditional laws).

256. *See In re* Status of the 1999 Constitution, 9 Okla. Trib. 392 (Cherokee Sup. Ct., 2006).

257. FORT MOJAVE CONST., art. V, § 2 (cited in RICHLAND & DEER, *supra* note 2, at 264).

258. *See* Rusco, *supra* note 86, at 277–78.

259. *See infra* note 286 (and accompanying text) (describing that the new constitution of the Cheyenne and Arapaho tribes prohibits tribal courts from exercising jurisdiction over traditional religious matters).

260. *Compare* Goldberg, *supra* note 14, at 914 ("As former Navajo Nation President Peterson Zah remarked, Indian peoples should be asked what an individual right is for them, and should have time to conduct a 'dialogue' regarding the meaning of such rights, so that each tribal community can mold individual rights to suit its own cultural framework").

261. Redman v. Birdshead, 9 Okla. Trib. 660 (Chey.-Arap. D.Ct., 2003).

262. *Id.*

263. For just one example of many historical works on the Arapaho people, *see, e.g.*, VIRGINIA COLE TRENHOLM, THE ARAPAHOS, OUR PEOPLE (1970).

264. *See* Cheyenne and Arapaho Tribes of Oklahoma Web site, *at* http://www.c-a-tribes.org/government.

265. *See* Northern Arapaho Tribe Web site, *at* http://www.northernarapaho.com *See also* United States v. Shoshone Tribe of Indians, 304 U.S. 111 (1938).

266. The Sun Dance is a religious activity often kept private from outsiders and scholarly research on it is controversial, as discussed below in the *Redman* case itself. *See also* THE ARAPAHO PROJECT, *available at* http://www.colorado.edu/csilw/arapahoproject/dancemusic/sacred1.htm.

267. *See* Redman v. Birdshead, 9 Okla. Trib. 660 (2003).

268. Redman v. Birdshead, 9 Okla. Trib. 114 (Chey.-Arap. D.Ct. 2005).

269. Redman v. Birdshead, 9 Okla. Trib 660 (2003). The court made a lengthy statement on this point vis à vis what it saw as the defendants' inconsistent use of "tradition" in the case:

> I agree this is a matter related to the centuries old spiritual ways of the Arapaho. Defendants have stated the same in their pleadings. So why does Defendant Spottedwolf state in a letter to the editor in the Watonga paper that Defendant Birdshead turned him on to the proper Arapaho ways in books written by a white anthropologist, George Dorsey, in the early 1900's? Traditions are usually passed down orally from generation to generation. We do not usually get our customs and traditions from white anthropologists. Why? Because custom and tradition, especially our spiritual ways, were to be protected from outsiders. So when white anthropologists came to our reservations we gave them stories to get rid of them. The stories we gave them rarely had the truth in them, and when they did they had selected truth in order to protect our ways. We see this even today as people, many times anthropologists, attempt to exploit tribal cultures for profit or some other benefit. This certainly makes Defendants' argument interesting that the tribal court cannot be involved in this matter, but a white anthropologist is the one who knows the Arapaho way.

Id.

270. *Id.*

271. *Id.*

272. *Id.*

273. Redman v. Birdshead, 9 Okla. Trib 660 (2003).

274. *Id.* ("The spiritual ways of the tribe are the very essence of the tribe. This deals with the ultimate judge, our Creator, and should not be taken lightly by anyone. Things occur when we do not follow 'our' ways and do things outside of the proper traditional ways. We must maintain balance and harmony").

275. Redman v. Birdshead, 9 Okla. Trib. 114 (2005).

276. *Id.*

277. *Id.* ("Sometimes the Court has no option but to decide a matter. The problem is that western legal law casts its shadow on what is traditional. In this particular case, there is no reason for the Court to decide anything with relation to the spiritual aspect of this case, because there are tribal governments which have taken action, and it is this action on which the Court can proceed").

278. *Id.*

279. *Id.*

280. Redman v. Birdshead, 9 Okla. Trib. 114 (2005).

281. *See* Redman v. Birdshead, 9 Okla. Trib. 495 (Chey.-Arap. Tr. Ct., 2006).

282. *Id.* (citing CONST. OF THE CHEYENNE-ARAPAHO TRIBES, art. I, § 1(a)).

283. *Id.* (citing CONST. OF THE CHEYENNE-ARAPAHO TRIBES, art. VIII, §5(c)).

284. *See Redman*, 9 Okla. Trib. 495 (2006).

285. *Id.*

286. *Id.*

287. *Id.*

288. *Id.*

289. For news coverage, see Anthony Lane, *Lengthy dispute underlies Sun Dance conflict*, CASPER STAR-TRIBUNE, July 15, 2006, *available at* http://trib.com/news/state-and-regional/article_36cd5fbc-9628-5004-b462-da2476ecba81.html.

290. While the Redman case was filed in the Cheyenne-Arapaho court system (in Oklahoma), the Northern Arapaho (in Wyoming) also have religious freedom legislation which amplifies some of these dynamics and makes particular note of the federal government's historic ban on the Sun Dance. *See* Tribal Codes, Northern Arapaho Tribe, Title 13 Religious Freedom, *available at* http://www.northernarapaho.com/code/religious-freedom.

291. *See, e.g.,* MANKILLER, *supra* note 1, at 27–28 ("Spirituality has sustained indigenous peoples since time immemorial. With the incursions into and eventual takeover of our traditional homelands by foreign interlopers, it has been the key to our very survival as a people").

292. *Compare* Mark Rosen, *Evaluating Tribal Courts' Interpretations of the Indian Civil Rights Act*, in THE INDIAN CIVIL RIGHTS ACT AT FORTY (2012) (exploring "cultural syncretism of Anglo and tribal values" in tribal court interpretations of ICRA).

PART IV
CRIMINAL LAW IN INDIAN COUNTRY

CHAPTER 10

Tightening the Perceived "Loophole": Reexamining ICRA's Limitation on Tribal Court Punishment Authority

ELIZABETH ANN KRONK

The Indian Civil Rights Act (ICRA) celebrated its fortieth anniversary in 2008.[1] When it passed the ICRA as a rider to the Civil Rights Act of 1968,[2] Congress intended to apply the protections of the US Constitution to Indian country in the hope of better protecting the civil rights of individual Indians.[3] After more than four decades, one may necessarily pause to consider whether the statute has in fact been effective and improved the status of Indian country.[4] This article concludes that the ICRA has not improved Indian country, and, instead, because of Section 1302(7) and its limitation on tribal court punishment authority, has actually played a contributing role in making Indian country less safe for those who reside there.[5] Accordingly, the limitation on tribal court punishment authority contained within ICRA should be reformed to increase tribal court punishment authority, and, in turn, to help counter the perception that Indian country lacks effective enforcement.[6]

Data overwhelmingly show that Indians generally face a higher incidence of violence than other racial groups. A Department of Justice Bureau of Justice Statistics Report (BJS Report)[7] concluded that "[t]he findings reveal a disturbing picture of the victimization of American Indians and Alaska Natives. The rate of violent crime estimated from self reported victimizations for American Indians is well above that of other U.S. racial or ethnic groups and is more than twice the national average."[8] The BJS Report is replete with startling statistics regarding violence and crime facing American Indians, Alaskan Natives, and Native Hawaiians. For example, "[o]n average, American Indians experience an estimated 1 violent crime for every 10 residents age 12 or older."[9] Furthermore, "[t]he violent crime rate in every age group below age 35 was significantly higher for American Indians than for all persons."[10] As a result of this high incidence of violence in Indian country, more than 80 percent of manslaughter cases, 60 percent of sexual abuse offense cases, and half of all murders and assaults cases tried in federal courts arise from crimes committed in Indian country.[11]

As explained below, the untenable criminal jurisdiction framework in place within Indian country and the perceived jurisdictional "loopholes" likely contribute to the increased incidence of crime facing American Indians and Alaskan Natives. Recently, troubling reports have emerged of criminals and abusers taking advantage of the perceived loopholes in criminal jurisdiction within Indian country.[12] Take, for example, the story of Jesus Martin Sagaste-Cruz.[13] Mr. Sagaste-Cruz developed a business plan for the expansion of methamphetamine (meth) sales, use, and addiction into Indian country.[14] Beginning in the late 1990s, Sagaste-Cruz, in conjunction with a Mexican drug cartel, led a meth ring targeting Indian reservations in Wyoming, South Dakota, and Nebraska.[15] Believing he could capitalize on jurisdictional loopholes and the lack of law enforcement in Indian country, Sagaste-Cruz moved his meth operations onto the Wind River Indian Reservation with a business plan to prey on the surrounding Indian community.[16] Sagaste-Cruz's associates initiated their plan by moving into the community and developing romantic relationships with Indian women.[17] The women were given free samples of meth, became addicted, and became meth dealers to feed their addictions.[18] The cycle of addiction was then passed along to the women's families and friends, and eventually to the larger community.[19] Sagaste-Cruz and his associates believed their plan was foolproof, as they blended into the community and felt Indians were easy targets for addiction.[20] Mr. Sagaste-Cruz is not alone in targeting Indian country for criminal activities, as other Mexican cartels have "set up shop" on Indian reservations under the assumption that "operating on tribal land shielded them from prosecution."[21]

The increased problem of crime in Indian country is not limited to drug offenses. In 2006, Amnesty International released a study highlighting the expansiveness of the problem of domestic violence in Indian country.[22] The report begins by spotlighting the scope of the problem:

> Data gathered by the US Department of Justice indicates that Native American and Alaska Native women are more than 2.5 times more likely to be raped or sexually assaulted than women in the USA in general. A US Department of Justice study on violence against women concluded that 34.1 per cent of American Indian and Alaska Native women—or more than one in three—will be raped during their lifetime; the comparable figure for the USA as a whole is less than one in five. Shocking though these statistics are, it is widely believed that they do not accurately portray the extent of sexual violence against Native American and Alaska Native women.[23]

As in the case of Sagaste-Cruz, Amnesty International found that perpetrators of sexual offenses are aware of and take advantage of the jurisdictional complexities associated with criminal enforcement in Indian country.

> Support workers told Amnesty International about the rapes of two Native American women in 2005 in Oklahoma. In both cases the

women were raped by three non–Native men. Other similarities between the crimes were reported: the alleged perpetrators, who wore condoms, blindfolded the victims and made them take a bath. Because the women were blindfolded, support workers were concerned that the women would be unable to say whether the rapes took place on federal, state or tribal land. There was concern that, because of the jurisdictional complexities in Oklahoma, uncertainty about exactly where these crimes took place might affect the ability of these women to obtain justice.[24]

Through its research, Amnesty International found that the lack of prosecution of many sexual offenses in Indian country has likely, in part, led to the increased incidence of sexual violence in Indian country because "[t]o a sexual predator, the failure to prosecute sex crimes against American Indian women is an invitation to prey with impunity."[25]

The Sagaste-Cruz business plan and the incidents of increased domestic violence reveal that criminals realize that potential benefits are to be gained by exploiting the insufficient criminal jurisdiction scheme applicable in Indian country. The combination of congressional actions, including passage of the ICRA, Section 1302(7), and a questionable Supreme Court decision create a jurisdictional labyrinth in Indian country. It was only a matter of time before sophisticated criminals would learn of and attempt to exploit the situation.

The current Congress is aware of the problems facing Indian country as a result of the existing criminal jurisdiction scheme. As introduced in the Senate, the pending Tribal Law and Order Act of 2009 summarized the situation as follows:

(11) the complicated jurisdictional scheme that exists in Indian country—
    (A) has a significant negative impact on the ability to provide public safety to Indian communities; and
    (B) has been increasingly exploited by criminals;
(12) the violent crime rate in Indian country is—
    (A) nearly twice the national average; and
    (B) more than 20 times the national average on some Indian reservations;
(13) (A) domestic and sexual violence against Indian and Alaska Native women has reached epidemic proportions;
    (B) 34 percent of Indian and Alaska Native women will be raped in their lifetimes; and
    (C) 39 percent of Indian and Alaska Native women will be subject to domestic violence. . . .
(17) the Department of Justice has reported that drug organizations have increasingly targeted Indian country to produce and distribute methamphetamine, citing the limited law enforcement presence and jurisdictional confusion as reasons for the increased activity.[26]

This chapter argues that ICRA, Section 1302(7), and its limitation on tribal court punishment authority is an important contributor to the flawed existing criminal jurisdictional framework in place, with the result being that Indians experience higher rates of violence than any other racial or ethnic group in Indian country. "The US federal government has created a complex interrelation ... that undermines equality before the law and often allows perpetrators to evade justice. In some cases this has created areas of effective lawlessness which encourages violence."[27] In other words, ICRA's limitations on tribal court enforcement authority, combined with the other elements of the current criminal jurisdictional scheme, have made Indian country less safe over the past four decades. The author does not purport that reforming ICRA will lead to a complete reversal of this troubling trend in Indian country. In fact, only a small group of individuals, member and nonmember Indians, facing rising crime and violence in Indian country, may directly benefit from the proposal articulated here; however, reversing the perception that tribal courts lack punishment authority by increasing the punishment authority available to tribal courts will likely have a positive impact. It is this author's assertion that if potential criminals perceive tribal courts as having effective enforcement authority within Indian country, they will be less likely to commit crimes there. It is a small but important step toward addressing the problem of increased crime in Indian country.

Accordingly, this chapter suggests that Congress can begin to address the problem it helped create by reducing or eliminating the restriction on tribal court enforcement authority. The first section introduces the existing criminal jurisdictional scheme within Indian country, followed by an examination of the relevant ICRA legislative history from 1961 to 1968 in an effort to ascertain why Congress enacted ICRA, Section 1302(7). The final section concludes that the concerns that occupied Congress in the 1960s and established the foundation for passage of the ICRA, Section 1302(7) have largely been ameliorated. Therefore, in order to begin to address the perception that tribal courts lack effective enforcement authority within Indian country, Congress should repeal ICRA, Section 1302(7) or, at the very least, substantially increase tribal court punishment authority.

A BRIEF EXAMINATION OF LAWS APPLICABLE TO CRIMES OCCURRING IN INDIAN COUNTRY

The unique nature of jurisdiction in Indian country developed from the sovereign status of Indian tribes. Beginning with the Constitution of the United States, the federal government has recognized the sovereign nature of Indian tribes.[28] As early as 1831, the United States Supreme Court acknowledged the separate, sovereign nature of Indian tribes.[29] Every administration since President Nixon's has acknowledged the sovereignty possessed by tribes[30] and, to this day, the Supreme Court continues to recognize the existence of tribal sovereignty.[31] Indeed, since 1975, Congress has also advocated and encouraged a policy of self-determination and recognized tribal sovereignty.[32]

Tribal sovereignty may be limited by the plenary power Congress asserts over tribes.[33] In the context of criminal jurisdiction in Indian country, Congress has acted on several occasions to limit tribal sovereignty, including through the enactment of the Indian Country Crimes Act,[34] Major Crimes Act,[35] and the Indian Civil Rights Act.[36][37]

Although ICRA is generally thought of as applying the protections of the Bill of Rights to Indian country, it has a substantial impact on the scope of tribal enforcement authority in criminal matters by limiting the sentences that may be applied by tribal courts. In language tracking the US Bill of Rights, ICRA grants individual Indians rights against tribal governments.[38] These rights include: the free exercise of religion and many of the protections of the federal criminal process.[39] ICRA also grants individual Indians the right to equal protection and due process, as well as the writ of habeas corpus.[40] Notable for the purpose of this article, however, the ICRA also limits penalties issued by tribal courts to a $5,000 fine and imprisonment for one year.[41] As a result of the ICRA, tribal courts are significantly restricted in the punishment they can administer.[42] Accordingly, the ICRA is a significant piece of the existing criminal jurisdictional framework limiting the effectiveness of law enforcement in Indian country.

In addition to these significant congressional limitations on tribal jurisdiction, the United States Supreme Court in *Oliphant v. Suquamish Indian Tribe*[43] placed a considerable limitation on tribal criminal jurisdiction when it held that tribes may not assert jurisdiction over non-Indians committing crimes in Indian country.[44] In reaching its decision, the Court relied on the domestic dependent status of tribes, finding such dependent status to be inconsistent with jurisdiction over non-Indians.[45] The Court referred to two hundred years of federal legislation that allegedly implied an absence of criminal jurisdiction over non-Indians.[46]

As a result of the existing criminal jurisdictional scheme in Indian country, the federal government plays a large role in law enforcement within Indian country; however, concerns regarding the effectiveness of federal prosecutions have arisen. "[T]ribal authorities often criticized enforcement of the Major Crimes Act (like that of the General Crimes Act) as being too lax. Overburdened U.S. attorneys have often been unenthusiastic about prosecuting the less serious of the major crimes."[47] There are a myriad of reasons why a US attorney may be unenthusiastic about prosecuting crimes arising in Indian country, such as jurisdictional complexities raised by such prosecutions[48] and the geographic isolation of many reservations.[49] The lack of enthusiasm from many US attorneys has seemingly resulted in a high declination rate for crimes occurring in Indian country.[50] Additionally, some have suggested that US attorneys who do focus on prosecuting crimes in Indian country are treated negatively as a result. For example, many of the US attorneys targeted by the Bush Administration were actively prosecuting crimes in Indian country.[51] Of the nine US attorneys ultimately fired, five served on the Native American issues subcommittee.[52] Moreover, even where the US Attorneys' office does prosecute a crime that occurred in Indian country, federal judges may not have the expertise to adequately adjudicate matters that transpired there[53] because such prosecutions raise issues normally not addressed in federal courts.[54]

Consequently, effective law enforcement is significantly handicapped in Indian country because of these statutes and the Court's decision in *Oliphant*. By enacting the MCA, ICCA, and ICRA, Congress not only limited the likelihood that tribes would assert jurisdiction over most major crimes in Indian country, but also further limited effective enforcement by capping the sentences tribal courts may levy. For example, "[t]he maximum prison sentence tribal courts can impose for crimes, including rape, is one year. The average prison sentence for rape handed down by state or federal courts is between eight years and eight months and 12 years and 10 months respectively."[55] *Oliphant* further compounded the problem by removing tribal criminal jurisdiction over non-Indians. Combined, these developments create a criminal jurisdictional scheme in Indian country that fails to address adequately the emerging problems in Indian country, as evidenced by the troubling statistics found in the BJS Report,[56] the example of Jesus Martin Sagaste-Cruz, and the high incidence of domestic violence in Indian country noted above. Congress's actions combine to make Indian country less safe.

Given that the ICRA's limitations on tribal court punishment authority presents one of the most significant obstacles to effective tribal court enforcement within Indian country, the section below focuses on legislative history relevant to Section 1302(7). In hindsight justifying such limitations is difficult, but by examining this legislative history, Congress's reasons for passing Section 1302(7) become more clear.

LEGISLATIVE HISTORY RELATED TO SECTION 1302(7) OF THE INDIAN CIVIL RIGHTS ACT

As explained above, Section 1302(7) of ICRA provides substantial limitations on the punishment authority of tribal courts. As originally passed, Section 1302(7) provided that:

> [n]o Indian tribe in exercising powers of self-government shall require excessive bail, impose excessive fines, inflict cruel and unusual punishments, and in no event impose for conviction of any one offense any penalty or punishment greater than imprisonment for a term of six months, a fine of $500, or both;[57]

Again, this limitation on the punishment authority of tribal courts significantly constrains the ability of tribal courts to deal effectively with increasing crime occurring within Indian country.

Although no explicit statement appears to exist explaining why Congress placed this substantial limitation on the punishment authority of tribal courts, several reasons are implicit from the available legislative history spanning from 1961 to 1968. First, it appears that Congress believed tribal courts were already substantially limited in their punishment authority. Second, it seems likely that Congress opted to restrict tribal court punishment authority in response to concerns that (1) individual Indians were being abused by tribal governments; (2) tribal courts were inadequate; and, (3) tribal court judges were uneducated and incapable of fulfilling the duties of a judge. This section explores the legislative history relevant to each of these assertions in order.

Existing Limitations on Tribal Court Punishment Authority

Based on the legislative history related to ICRA, Congress appears to have believed that tribal court punishment authority was already significantly restricted under existing law.[58] Accordingly, Congress may have intended to codify existing punishment limitations, making them applicable to all tribal courts through the enactment of ICRA, Section 1302(7). As noted, the legislative history on this point is sorely lacking.

However, some testimony on record indicates that during hearings before the Senate Subcommittee on Constitutional Rights of the Committee on the Judiciary ("Constitutional Rights Subcommittee" or "subcommittee"), several tribes testified that the punishment authority of their tribal courts had already been significantly restricted. For example, Judge Shirley Nelson, chief judge of the Hualapai court, and Senator Keating had the following exchange:

> Mrs. Nelson. We tried him for assault and battery.
> Senator Keating. But of course, the limit of your sentence is 1 year, isn't it?
> Mrs. Nelson. Six months is all we can give in our court. It is the highest sentence that comes in our court.[59]

Similarly, Alfred Sheck, councilman and tribal judge for the Zuni Tribe, testified accordingly:

> Mr. Creech.[60] When you try him what do you sentence him to? If I am tried for being drunk and disorderly and I say I am guilty, or if I am convicted, what kind of sentence do I get?
> Mr. Sheck. Well, so much fine usually.
> Mr. Creech. So much fine?
> Mr. Sheck. So much fine and so many days in jail.
> Mr. Creech. What is the greatest number of days in jail?
> Mr. Sheck. Like 30 days.
> Mr. Creech. Only 30 days. Can you give 3 months?
> Mr. Sheck. Ninety days.

> Mr. Creech. Did you ever give anybody 6 months?
> Mr. Sheck. No.
> Mr. Creech. Did you ever give anybody as much as a year?
> Mr. Sheck. No.
> Mr. Creech. The most sentence you can impose is 3 months?
> Mr. Sheck. Yes. But in major crimes we just have to depend on our agents.[61]

Preston Keevana from the San Juan Pueblo testified during the same hearings that the maximum sentence the San Juan Pueblo tribal court could apply was ninety days in the city jail of Santa Fe.[62] Governor Ernest Mirabal of the Nambe Pueblo Conference testified that the Nambe Pueblo court had never sentenced an individual to jail and that he was not aware of any sentencing authority that would allow the tribal court to do so.[63] As a result of the testimony given to the Constitutional Rights Subcommittee on November 25, 29 and December 1, 1961, it is plausible that the subcommittee was led to believe that tribal courts did not have substantial punishment authority beyond a few months of imprisonment.

The summary of these hearings prepared by the Constitutional Rights Sub-committee published in 1964 supports this conclusion.[64] In its summary of the hearings held between 1961 and 1963, the subcommittee concluded that "[t]ribal codes limit their courts to trying offenses committed by Indians on the reservation and imposing a maximum sentence of 6 months for punishment."[65] The subcommittee also stated that "[i]n both types of courts [tribal courts and courts of Indian offenses], sentences for criminal offenses range from a minimum of not more than 5 days for assault to a maximum of 6 months for offenses such as abduction, theft, fraud, forgery, malicious mischief, bribery, and perjury."[66] Based on its two-year study of civil rights in Indian country, the Constitutional Rights Subcommittee appears to have concluded that tribal courts did not incarcerate individuals for longer than six months.

Further evidence that the Constitutional Rights Subcommittee held this opinion is present in its Summary Report, published in 1966.[67] The Constitutional Rights Sub-committee continued its investigations into the civil rights of individual Indians through hearings in 1965.[68] In its Summary Report, the subcommittee again indicated its conclusion that tribal courts "usually impose sentences up to 6 months."[69]

Senator Sam Ervin, chairman of the Constitutional Rights Subcommittee and the champion of ICRA, maintained the view that tribal courts had no greater punishment authority than six months' incarceration. In his comments on House Bill 2516 and in reference to ICRA, Title II(7), Senator Ervin indicated that "[t]he penalty of a $500 fine or imprisonment for a term of 6 months or both would *remain* the maximum limitation as to punishment for any one offense."[70] By referring to the fact that a $500 fine or imprisonment up to six months would *remain* the maximum punishment that a tribal court could impose, Senator Ervin confirmed his understanding that the proposed ICRA would not bring significant change to the existing punishment authority of tribal courts.

The legislative history of ICRA shows that the Constitutional Rights Subcommittee received testimony indicating that tribal courts did not exercise punishment authority beyond incarcerating individuals for up to six months. The subcommittee apparently came to the conclusion that six months was the maximum sentence tribal courts could impose, as evidenced by statements to this effect published in the subcommittee's 1964 and 1966 Summary Reports. Finally, Senator Ervin, as late as 1968, indicated that the punishment authority in Section 1302(7) would remain at a fine of $500 and/or imprisonment of six months. It may therefore be inferred that Congress imposed the limitations on tribal court punishment authority through Section 1302(7) in part due to a belief that it was the maximum authority allowed tribal courts under existing law.

Congressional Concerns with Existing Tribal Courts

The legislative history of ICRA suggests that Congress may have imposed Section 1302(7) on tribal courts for reasons other than mere belief that the existing law limited tribal court punishment authority to a $500 fine and/or six months in jail. The ICRA legislative history is replete with instances where the Constitutional Rights Subcommittee expressed concerns about tribal courts. Although there is some overlap, these concerns can be broken down into three categories: (1) lack of protection from arbitrary tribal governmental actions; (2) general adequacy of tribal courts; and, (3) uneducated tribal judges. Each of these apparent congressional concerns will be examined in turn below.

Lack of protection from arbitrary tribal governmental actions

The Constitutional Rights Subcommittee received substantial testimony regarding the alleged interference of tribal legislative and executive branches in the workings of tribal courts. As previously indicated, the subcommittee began its investigations into the civil rights of Indians in 1961. The record of hearings from 1961 is full of testimony indicating that the subcommittee was concerned that individuals associated with the political "branches" of tribal government would interfere with tribal courts. In fact, the statement initiating the subcommittee's work on August 29, 1961 referenced this concern, as Senator Ervin stated that "it appears that a tribe may constitutionally deprive its members of property and liberty without due process of law and not come under the constitutional limitations applicable to Federal and State Governments as stated in the Bill of Rights."[71] Immediately after Senator Ervin finished this statement, Senator Keating added, "[i]t is very necessary, then, that we should not permit instances of large-scale injustice to go uncorrected within our own country."[72]

Representative Berry elaborated on the concerns expressed by Senators Ervin and Keating when he testified that:

> As presently established, Indian reservations in the United States are not only the world's best example of complete socialism, but they are the world's best example of a lack of law and authority. Government on

these reservations is strictly a government of men and not of law. There is no limitation upon the governing body. Most governing bodies serve both as the legislative, executive, and judicial functions of the government. The tribal council makes the law, they execute the laws they make and with practically no limitation as to what laws they can make, and they appoint the judges of the tribal courts with tenure of office limited to the whim of the council.[73]

Representative Berry explained further:

> the only court protection and court jurisdiction is in the hands of the tribal courts who are appointed in most instances by the tribal council in power, and apparently serve pretty much at the will of the council in power. There is no appeal from a tribal court decision except to the tribal council itself.[74]

Apparently, Representative Berry was not only concerned with tribal governments' abuse of powers, but also that tribal councils essentially controlled the actions of tribal courts through their appointment authority and their ability to review appeals from tribal courts.

Senator Burdick shared Representative Berry's concerns regarding the involvement of tribal councils in tribal courts. In particular, Senator Burdick questioned the wisdom of allowing tribal councils to appoint tribal judges. According to Senator Burdick, "[t]he appointment of the [tribal] judge is confirmed by a vote of the tribal council. This presents the problem of the judge maintaining good relations with the tribal council members. It is reasonable to assume that he will be very careful when dealing with relatives and friends of the tribal council."[75] Senator Burdick even went so far as to state, "in many cases the tribal courts are 'kangaroo courts.' One of the basic reasons for my statement is that the method of selecting tribal judges insures that an Indian appearing before tribal court, in too many cases, will not get fair treatment."[76]

The Constitutional Rights Subcommittee continued to hear testimony regarding the involvement of tribal governments within tribal courts. Mateo Aragon, a member of the Santa Domingo Pueblo, testified that the actual tribal council for the Santa Domingo Pueblo served as the Pueblo's tribal court.[77] Similarly, Preston Keevana, from the San Juan Pueblo, testified that the Pueblo's tribal court "consists of the governor, the lieutenant governor, and the sheriff."[78] Although the Mescalero Apache Tribe's tribal court was separate from its tribal council, R. A. Wardlaw, assistant to the president of the Mescalero Business Committee, testified that "[i]f [a litigant] is not satisfied with the decision from the lower court, they have got the right according to the constitution, to appeal it right to the business committee, which is the governing body of the tribe."[79] The subcommittee therefore received testimony from tribal representatives suggesting that tribal courts were, in fact, not separate and independent from tribal governments.

When introducing Senate bills S. 961 through S. 968 on May 23, 1967, Senator Ervin reaffirmed his concern regarding tribal governments, stating that "[t]he historical development of a unique relationship between the Indian communities and the United States has resulted in a situation in which there exists, unfortunately, both the potentiality and the actuality of deprivation of individual rights by tribal governments."[80] Moreover, in speaking about the Civil Rights Act of 1968, Senator Ervin stated that "Title II of the substitute bill would grant to the American Indians enumerated constitutional rights and protection from arbitrary action in their relationship with tribal governments, State governments, and the Federal government."[81] Senator Ervin's statements reflect his belief that tribal governments deprived Indians of their constitutional rights, a belief he apparently shared with Senators Keating and Burdick and Representative Berry.

The legislative history of the ICRA therefore shows evidence that several members of Congress believed that tribal governments deprived individual Indians of their rights. This pervasive belief, coupled with testimony from tribal representatives that tribal councils played a significant role in the functions of tribal courts and, in some instances, even served as tribal courts, may have been impetus for Congress to limit the punishment authority of tribal courts. If Congress believed that tribal governments were capable of depriving individuals of their rights and that tribal courts were not independent from tribal governments, a restriction on tribal court punishment authority would have been an effective mechanism for limiting the damage a tribal government could do to an individual through the tribal court. Accordingly, the opinions expressed by members of Congress in the legislative history of the ICRA strongly suggest that Congress supported a limitation on tribal court punishment authority to limit unfair or arbitrary actions by tribal governments.

Inadequate tribal courts. In addition to interference into tribal court affairs by less-than-fair tribal governments, the legislative history of the ICRA suggests that Congress was concerned about the adequacy of the tribal courts themselves. This concern, which predated the investigations of the Constitutional Rights Subcommittee, may also have prompted Congress to place limitations on tribal court punishment authority. On July 10, 1961, the Task Force on Indian Affairs presented a report to the secretary of the Interior, evaluating civil rights in Indian country.[82] Notably, the Task Force on Indian Affairs first raised the issue of tribal court adequacy when it found that:

> there are tribal courts established in Indian country where, due to inadequate tribal funds, there is only one judge, untrained, no police force, and an outworn building for detention purposes.... Under tribal courts, witnesses complained of all the above-mentioned inadequacies and recited numerous instances of favoritism, denial of civil rights, outmoded detention facilities, and absence of proper facilities for female and juvenile offenders.[83]

The Constitutional Rights Subcommittee received a copy of the task force's report and would have been aware of these concerns.[84] The subcommittee's awareness of these concerns is evidenced by the fact that the subcommittee began to address the adequacy of tribal courts early in its hearings in August 1961. Senator Keating expressed concern that tribal court procedures were not always written down: "For example, if you attempt to obtain up-to-date copies of these tribal codes or regulations you will find them difficult to obtain. In fact, you may well find that some tribes have no written laws or regulations governing their courts."[85] Representative Berry was not quite so kind, as he referred to tribal rules and regulations as "fearful, absolutely fearful."[86] Mr. Carver, assistant secretary of Indian Affairs, elaborated on the secretary of the Interior's concerns regarding the adequacy of tribal courts:

> Many Indian courts are unable for a variety of reasons to do an effective job in the overall administration of justice on the reservation. Some of those who are elected or appointed as Indian judges lack educational qualifications. In some instances tribes employ outside or nonmember Indians as judges and in some cases, they have employed attorneys or judges who reside near the reservation to preside over the Indian courts. The inadequacies of the facilities, services, and resources available to the Indian courts have become increasingly apparent in recent years. In the area of juvenile dependency and delinquency, for example, most Indian courts do not have available to them the same services available to State and Federal courts in the treatment and rehabilitation of juveniles.[87]

Similarly, the subcommittee heard testimony from Palmer King, regional solicitor of the Department of Interior for the Denver Region, suggesting that tribal courts were inadequate. Mr. King testified that "[a]lthough they [tribal courts] are limited to the misdemeanor type of case, a man can be released in one day and brought back in the next day. Through such a system he can be deprived of substantial liberty over and above what would be normal in misdemeanor-type cases."[88] Although he admitted that he did not have the facts to support this assertion, Mr. King provided the subcommittee with testimony that tribal courts were arbitrarily depriving individuals of their liberty. In a later statement on the same day from the counsel to the subcommittee, Mr. Creech suggested that the subcommittee possessed negative views of tribal courts.[89]

The subcommittee also received testimony from tribal representatives that subcommittee members apparently found troubling with regard to tribal court adequacy. Tribal representatives testified to a litany of problems with tribal courts; for example, several tribal representatives testified that their tribal courts did not have written codes or regulations.[90] Additionally, the subcommittee received substantial testimony and exhibits from the Standing Rock Sioux Tribe that tribal judges were asserting jurisdiction over individuals for whom the tribal court did not have jurisdiction and were sentencing individuals who had pled not guilty without factual basis.[91] Moreover, the subcommittee received testimony that individual Indians were being denied jury trials by tribal courts, despite requests for such trials.[92]

In its 1964 Summary Report, the Constitutional Rights Subcommittee expounded on another alleged inadequacy of tribal courts—this time in the appellate processes.

> One of the serious inadequacies of Indian courts is the absence of an appeal system similar to that of the Federal and State courts. An appeal from an Indian tribal court is heard by a three-member appellate tribunal, such a court seldom exists on the reservation. The usual appellate court consists of the trial judge who heard the original complaint and two tribal members, who usually have no judicial training, serving as appellate judges by appointment of the tribal council.[93]

Ultimately, the subcommittee concluded in its 1964 Summary Report that "the deficiencies in the Indian courts seriously curtail the effective administration of justice on reservations."[94] Again, in its 1966 Summary Report, the subcommittee reached a similar conclusion when it found that "[t]ypically ... the Indian's day in court is likely to be a haphazard, error-laden prospect at best."[95]

With the testimony and exhibits it had received, the subcommittee possessed substantial material suggesting that tribal courts were inadequate. Testimony included assertions that tribal courts did not have written regulations, lacked effective appellate courts, denied individuals jury trials, and acted outside of their jurisdiction. Based on the subcommittee's conclusions in the 1964 and 1966 Summary Reports, the subcommittee appears to have been convinced that tribal courts were inadequate and not effectively administering justice in Indian country. Accordingly, because of its low opinion of the effectiveness and fairness of tribal courts, the subcommittee likely would have welcomed the opportunity to restrict tribal court punishment authority as a way of minimizing the effects of tribal court inadequacies. Coupled with the subcommittee's view of existing tribal court sentencing authority and the unjust involvement of tribal governments in tribal court affairs, the subcommittee's conclusion that tribal courts were inadequate, as evidenced in its summary reports, would have provided additional justification for the restriction on tribal court punishment authority, as found in ICRA, Section 1302(7).

Uneducated tribal judges. Finally, the ICRA legislative history provides substantial evidence that Congress regarded tribal judges as uneducated and therefore incapable of effectively administering their duties as tribal judges. Based on this legislative history, it is possible to infer that Congress acted to limit the punishment authority of tribal courts through the enactment of ICRA, Section 1302(7), in part due to the belief that tribal court judges were uneducated.

The view that tribal judges were uneducated and therefore not capable emerged almost immediately in the initial hearings conducted by the Constitutional Rights Subcommittee. In a prepared statement, Senator Roman Hruska stated that "[t]ribal courts established on Indian reservations are presided over by judges who, in many instances, are not legally trained."[96] Royal Marks, an attorney in Phoenix, Arizona, also indicated that in his experience tribal judges were not legally trained, as he stated "[i]t is true our tribal judges need a little more education, perhaps on some of these reservations."[97] Ramon Roubideaux, an attorney in South Dakota, shared Mr. Marks's opinion regarding uneducated tribal judges, and elaborated that:

> Many of our Indian people, of course, are doing the best they can. They don't have enough education. They don't have enough experience in order to see to it that these defendants brought before them are adequately protected in their rights, and it results in a great many injustices. I think the qualified tribal court judges, appointed by the U.S. district court, and a method of appeal from determinations made by the tribal court—you see, we have no appeal now, and injustice is perpetrated through ignorance. I don't think it's done purposely. It results in a lot of these Indian people being deprived of constitutional rights.[98]

In fact, Mr. Roubideaux went so far as to compare a tribal judge to a five-year-old child.[99] As practicing attorneys in tribal courts, Mr. Marks and Mr. Roubideaux likely left a powerful impression with the subcommittee regarding the alleged lack of education of tribal judges.

Even individuals representing tribal interests testified that tribal judges were not formally trained to practice law. D'Arcy McNickle, representing American Indian Development, Inc., testified that "[t]he judges even now have not been trained in law, and in the beginning some judges had very little formal schooling of any kind."[100] Richard Cavanaugh, a member of the Fort Totten Reservation tribal council, explained that "[o]ne of the biggest problems that we have on Fort Totten Reservation is probably law and order. One in particular is the judge. This Indian judge is untrained as a judge. He shows favoritism, unreasonable sentencing, partiality and lack of education."[101]

After considering all of this testimony, the Constitutional Rights Subcommittee concluded in its 1964 Summary Report that "[t]he problem of inadequate judicial administration is further compounded by judges who are frequently untrained for their responsibilities.... Indian judges are too frequently untrained for their responsibilities in the administration of justice."[102] The subcommittee reached a similar conclusion in its 1966 Summary Report when it stated that:

> Indian citizen's rights are most seriously jeopardized by the tribal government's administration of justice. These denials occur, it is also apparent, not from malice or ill will, or from a desire to do injustice, but

from the tribal judges' inexperience, lack of training, and unfamiliarity with the traditions and forms of the American legal system.[103]

Based on these statements in the 1964 and 1966 Subcommittee Summary Reports, the subcommittee clearly concluded that tribal judges were generally uneducated. Accordingly, based on this conclusion, the subcommittee, investigating ways for protecting the civil rights of Indians, likely wanted to decrease the impact of uneducated tribal judges on individual Indians. Coupled with concerns about tribal governmental interference and inadequate tribal courts, the subcommittee likely looked to the lack of educated judges as reason to include the limitation on tribal court punishment authority in ICRA, Section 1302(7).

CONGRESS SHOULD INCREASE TRIBAL COURT ENFORCEMENT

Authority Under ICRA Section 1302(7)

As explained above, American Indians and Alaskan Natives face higher incidences of crime and violence than other populations in the United States. Although little data is available regarding the crime and violence facing American Indians and occurring within Indian country, one may infer from the general data that American Indians and Alaska Natives face higher incidences of crime and violence generally within the United States and are more likely to face increased crime and violence within Indian country itself. As demonstrated anecdotally above, the increased crime and violence that is likely occurring within Indian country may be attributed to a perception of ineffective law enforcement within Indian country and to a related dysfunctional criminal jurisdictional scheme.

One piece of this dysfunctional criminal jurisdictional scheme is the limitation on tribal court punishment authority under ICRA, Section 1302(7). As discussed above, Congress appears to have restricted tribal court punishment authority both because it believed that tribal court enforcement authority was already significantly restricted and in response to concerns about tribal courts overall. This section addresses these apparent congressional concerns. As explained below, the issues motivating Congress in the 1960s to restrict tribal court enforcement authority have, in part, been ameliorated over the intervening four decades. Congress has the authority to take steps to increase tribal court enforcement authority given that its concerns may have been addressed.

Congress has the authority either to remove the limitations in ICRA, Section 1302(7) entirely or to substantially increase these limitations.[104] Congress can restore tribal rights and has done so previously.[105] In 1990, the US Supreme Court held in *Duro v. Reina* that tribal sovereignty did not include criminal jurisdiction over nonmember Indians within the reservation.[106] Congress promptly acted to overturn the court's decision by passing legislation recognizing "the inherent power of Indian tribes, hereby recognized and affirmed, to exercise criminal jurisdiction over all

Indians."[107] Following this action, the US Supreme Court recognized Congress's right to affirm the preexisting rights of tribes.[108] Therefore, Congress has the authority to recognize the tribal rights that tribes have historically possessed. Given that tribes possessed complete punishment authority over all offenders before congressional and judicial interference, Congress has the authority essentially to reverse itself and remove such limitations on tribal court punishment authority.[109] Notably, Congress has already acted in other contexts to expand tribal court authority where appropriate.[110]

Moreover, some current members of Congress support an expansion of tribal punishment authority. On April 2, 2009, the Tribal Law and Order Act of 2009 was introduced in the Senate, cosponsored by Senators Dorgan, Barrasso, Baucus, Bingaman, Lieberman, Kyl, Wyden, Johnson, Cantwell, Murkowski, Thune, Tester, Begich, and Udall.[111] One purpose of the then-proposed bill was "to improve the prosecution of, and response to, crimes in Indian country."[112] Section 304 of the proposed bill would increase the punishment authority of tribal courts to a maximum of three years' imprisonment, a $15,000 fine, or both under certain conditions.[113] In response to the proposed increase in tribal court punishment authority, the Honorable Theresa M. Pouley, judge of the Tulalip Tribal Court and president of the Northwest Tribal Court Judges Association, stated that "[t]oward this end, we [the Tulalip Tribes, NICS and Northwest Tribal Court Judges Association] strongly support the extension of criminal sentencing authority as necessary in certain cases to protect the Reservation community from dangerous offenders."[114] The Honorable Theresa M. Pouley further stated:

> The Tulalip Tribes strongly supports the proposed legislation's extension of tribal court sentencing authority from one to three years. At Tulalip, the Tribal Court is the primary forum for criminal prosecutions on the Reservation involving Indian offenders. The effective administration of justice benefits the entire Reservation community, both Indian and non-Indian. The Tribe's criminal justice system is often the first and last line of defense in protecting the community from violent offenders. Many serious crimes, including those involving dangerous offenders, end up falling to the tribal justice system for prosecution. Since September 11, 2001, federal resources have been reallocated. According to data released by this Committee, federal criminal investigations on Indian lands in Washington State declined by 55 percent since 2001. This has left a gap not only in the prosecution of major crimes, but the serious crimes that fall into the gap between misdemeanors and Major Crimes Act felonies. The reality on the ground is that Tribal Courts are often responsible for prosecuting felony crimes. In sentencing serious criminal offenders, I have long been concerned that the one year sentencing limitation was placing the safety of the tribal community at risk. Although the need to impose longer sentences is not a common occurrence in my courtroom, in those situations where the

court is faced with prosecuting serious violent crimes, it is important for the Tribal Court to have appropriate sentencing authority.
During my tenure as a judge, I have presided over cases involving
charges of rape, child sexual assault, drug trafficking, aggravated
assault and serious domestic violence. Increasing sentencing to three
years will provide Tribal Courts with the authority necessary to protect the Reservation community.[115]

Moreover, Congress should repeal or expand the limitations found in ICRA Section 1302(7) because the concerns raised by Congress over four decades ago, which
were seemingly the underlying justification for such a restriction on tribal court
punishment authority, have been ameliorated over time.[116] Additionally, tribal courts
are the better entities to adjudicate matters arising in Indian country. Each of these
arguments is addressed below in turn.

Amelioration of Congressional Concerns

The concerns that plagued Congress between 1961 and 1968 regarding tribal courts,
including intrusion from tribal governments, inadequate tribal courts, and uneducated
tribal judges, have been addressed significantly over the subsequent four decades. In
essence, the concerns that motivated Congress in the 1960s to restrict tribal court
enforcement authority have substantially diminished in the intervening decades. Indeed,
Congress's actions in 1968 have likely contributed to an increase in crime, as discussed
above. Taken together, these developments strongly suggest that tribal court enforcement authority should be expanded.

The not-so-unfamiliar forum. As can be seen in the testimony and exhibits
received by the Constitutional Rights Subcommittee discussed above, many of those
who testified in front of the subcommittee expressed a fear of the "unfamiliarness"
of tribal courts. This fear of the unfamiliar seems to have motivated many of the subcommittee's considerations during that time. The US Supreme Court has "repeatedly
commented on the 'strange' or 'different' nature of tribal laws."[117] Although no state or
federal court would ever accept as convincing an argument from a party that the applicable law was too difficult to understand,[118] it is helpful to begin a discussion of the current status of tribal courts by illuminating the fact that tribal courts, although perhaps
once "alien" to the American-trained lawyer, are no longer unfamiliar.

Although many types of tribal courts exist,[119] a typical lawyer or party no longer
has any reason to fear or to feel uncomfortable in tribal court, as many tribal courts
model state courts, many apply laws adapted from state and federal law, and the
extent of tribal court jurisdiction is defined by the federal government.[120] This trend
is particularly true of gaming tribes that have substantial contacts with non–Indian
interests.[121] Not only are tribal courts increasingly modeling state courts, but also
tribal courts often apply state[122] and federal law[123] that is familiar to lawyers and

parties. In fact, because of the close relationship between the federal government and tribes, "[t]he extent of tribal court jurisdiction is a matter of federal as well as tribal law, involving as it does issues at the heart of the relationship between the federal government and Indian tribes."[124] Even when a tribal court applies customary or tribal law, the typical lawyer will likely find the resulting decision to be familiar.[125] Additionally, the cases typically found on a tribal court docket are similar to those found on a state or federal court docket.[126] "Tribal cultural differences are most obviously marked in property and family law cases."[127] This assertion is consistent, however, with the general policy of the federal government to leave issues related to tribal members solely within the inherent tribal sovereignty of tribal governments.[128]

In her comments on the then pending Tribal Law and Order Act of 2009, the Honorable Theresa Pouley clearly articulated the similarity between tribal courts and state and federal courts:

> At the hearing last month on the draft Tribal Law and Order Act, representatives from the Departments of Justice and Interior expressed concerns to this Committee regarding the extension of tribal court sentencing authority. DOJ and BIA expressed concerns as to whether tribal courts would adequately protect the rights of criminal defendants. DOI expressed similar concerns, and also raised issues regarding increased costs of longer detentions and possibly an increase in habeas petitions.
>
> With regard to the rights of the accused, I can personally attest that all of the tribal courts that I have served as a judge, or practiced in as an advocate, have a strong commitment to protecting the rights of criminal defendant that is equal to that of the state and federal courts. Although tribal courts may differ in size and scope (some tribal governments rely on state rather than tribal criminal law enforcement), an ITJA [Indian Tribal Justice Act] survey published in 2000 reported that the vast majority of participating tribes had formal justice systems similar to state or federal court systems, and virtually all provided for appellate review. Washington State courts have adopted court rules which provide full faith and credit for Tribal Court judgments....
>
> All NICS member tribes have developed tribal codes. The NICS member tribal codes are publicly available from court clerks and law libraries. Many are also available on-line. Most of these tribes have comprehensive civil court procedural rules like those at Tulalip. In addition, the other large tribes in Washington State including Colville, Lummi, Puyallup and Swinomish operate their own sophisticated court systems complete with indigent public defense services and all utilize comprehensive Tribal codes and court rules....
>
> Similarly, most Washington tribes have developed a court of appeals. NICS provides appellate services to all of its member tribes as well as to non-member tribes in Washington, Oregon and California.

The Colville Confederated Tribes has a constitutionally established Court of Appeals and appoints nine justices to serve six year terms. All the opinions are available and are maintained by the Court.[129]

Previously, tribal courts may have seemed alien and unfamiliar due in part to their inaccessibility. Dean Nell Jessup Newton explained that many lawyers lack knowledge about tribal courts in part because "most tribal court opinions are not widely distributed."[130] Recent publication developments may therefore have a significant impact on the accessibility and familiarity of tribal courts.[131] Notably, Westlaw recently developed databases for thirteen tribes and two more expansive tribal court reporters, West's American Tribal Law Reporter and Oklahoma Tribal Court Reports. Additionally, a new board of authors and editors is updating *Cohen's Handbook of Federal Indian Law*, the foremost treatise of federal Indian law, on a regular basis,[132] making recent developments in the field more accessible. Furthermore, many tribal judges are now actively participating in academic and public discourse regarding their decisions.[133] Developments that have made tribal court case law more accessible will likely also increase the familiarity of those outside of Indian country with tribal courts and the law they apply.

Limited tribal governmental intrusion on tribal courts. Though tribal legislative and executive branches of government may still attempt to influence tribal courts (the same is also true within state and federal governments), much has been done to alleviate unjust intrusions. In general, some tribal governments have developed over the years, limiting the possibility that a few individuals could jeopardize civil rights.[134] Some tribes have made strides in ensuring that tribal courts are politically independent from other branches of tribal government. First, the influence of any one branch of government on the selection of tribal judges is often limited.[135] Second, some tribal judiciaries are now politically independent.[136] Third, increasing evidence indicates that tribal governments generally are not violating the civil rights of individual Indians[137] or that, in instances where there are civil rights violations, tribal courts will find in favor of the petitioning party.[138] Moreover, "[t]he trend in tribal court development, clearly favored by the Congress and the Bureau of Indian Affairs, is to insulate tribal judges from reprisals through contracts for a term, terminable only for cause, and providing for judicial review of legislative acts."[139] Given that tribal governments have increasingly developed to preclude tyranny by the minority and that tribal judges are finding themselves increasingly independent from other branches of government, Congress need no longer be as concerned about the intrusion of unjust tribal governments into tribal court affairs as it was during the 1960s.

Adequacy of tribal courts and judges. The legislative history surrounding ICRA also suggests that Congress was concerned about the general inadequacy of tribal courts. Tribal courts have developed significantly since the 1960s. Congressional passage of the Indian Child Welfare Act (ICWA) of 1978 was perhaps the first indication that the adequacy of tribal courts and judges had improved. With the passage of ICWA, Congress expressed its clear intent to defer to tribal judgment on matters concerning the custody of tribal children and consequently gave tribal courts exclusive jurisdiction over child custody proceedings involving an Indian child who resides or is domiciled within the reservation of such tribe, except where such jurisdiction is otherwise vested in the state by existing federal law.[140] Congress also provided guidelines to ensure that any proceedings taking place in state court followed "strict procedures and [met] stringent requirements to justify any result in an individual case contrary to these preferences."[141] The 1978 BIA guidelines for state courts similarly reinforce a congressional trust and preference of having tribal courts adjudicate matters concerning Indian children.[142] Accordingly, the passage of ICWA in 1978 suggests that Congress believed that tribal courts were capable of handling matters related to Indian children, matters that had previously been handled by state courts.

More recently, a cornucopia of training opportunities has developed for tribal court staffs and judges, which further assists in the development of tribal courts. For example, the National Tribal Justice Resource Center was started on September 1, 2000 to assist in the development of tribal courts.[143] The National Tribal Justice Resource Center provides substantial assistance to the development of tribal courts, including providing a helpline and assistance in running a tribal court.[144] Numerous tribes and tribal judges have taken advantage of the resources provided by the National Tribal Justice Resource Center[145] and numerous other training opportunities.[146] Furthermore, some tribal courts have developed in a way that significantly resembles Anglo court systems, as discussed above.[147] Given the substantial development of tribal courts over the past forty years and the resources now available to tribal courts, Congress's fears regarding the adequacy of tribal courts should be allayed.

As discussed above, substantial testimony in the legislative history of the ICRA suggested that Congress viewed tribal judges as largely uneducated.[148] As with the adequacy of tribal courts, tribal judges have become increasingly law educated, as many tribal judges are either lawyers or have attended educational seminars and classes through organizations such as the National Judicial College or the National Indian Justice Center.[149] For example, both the tribal courts for the Little Traverse Bay Band of Odawa Indians (LTBB) and Sault Ste. Marie Tribe of Chippewa Indians of Michigan employ a substantial number of attorney judges, and non-attorney judges for these tribes are strongly encouraged to attend judicial training.[150]

Not only are tribal judges themselves becoming more law educated, but lawyers in general are also becoming more involved in tribal courts.[151] Therefore, Congress need no longer fear the uneducated tribal judge who acts like a "five-year-old child" presiding over a "kangaroo court," as tribal judges are now largely educated in the formalities of the Anglo-style legal system.

As suggested from the testimony discussed above, implicitly related to the "fear" of uneducated judges is the concern that these judges are biased against non-Indian parties; however, research demonstrates that tribal court judges are typically not biased.[152] Such findings are logical. For tribal judges to exhibit bias against non-Indian parties would be counter to tribal interests related to economic development and external legitimacy. Moreover, even if the occasional tribal court judge makes an error, tribal court judges may in fact be being held to a higher standard than their state and federal counterparts.

> A number of very high profile cases exist regarding the incompetence, bias, and/or criminality of state judges. Sol Wachtler, the Chief Judge of the State of New York, was convicted of harassing his mistress; David Lanier, a judge in Tennessee, was convicted of violating the civil rights of a number of women who worked for his court; numerous state judges have been convicted of bribery, and the list goes on. Even in the absence of misfeasance, state court judges sometimes flat get it wrong.[153]

Beyond the tribal judges themselves, the adequacy of tribal courts in general appears to be improving as determined by the federal government. The BIA Tribal Courts Assessment Program found in its 2009 report that only .01 percent of BIA-funded tribal judicial systems received an acceptable rating under the independent tribal judicial system reviews.[154] In the same 2009 report, however, the program found that the percent of BIA-funded tribal judicial systems receiving an acceptable rating dramatically increased in 2008, when 22 percent of these systems received an acceptable rating.[155]

Tribal Courts Do It Better

> *Difference does not always mean inferiority.*
> —Nell Jessup Newton[156]

As evidence of the general belief that tribal governments and some tribal courts in particular are now fully capable of increased enforcement authority,[157] some are calling for the restoration of full tribal court enforcement authority.[158] Those who support increased tribal court enforcement authority recognize that "[o]nly those tribes that have acquired meaningful control over their governing institutions have experienced improvements in local economic and social conditions."[159] This explicit support is implicitly supported by the general lack of cases challenging tribal court authority in federal court after the exhaustion of tribal court remedies, which suggests that those parties finding themselves subject to tribal court authority are content with tribal court decisions.[160]

Increased tribal court enforcement authority also promotes tribal self-determination, which is crucial given the unique cultural and historical aspects of Indian country.[161] Research shows that the "success" of tribal governments often rests on the ability of the tribes to exercise meaningful control.[162] One concern associated with the restoration of full tribal court enforcement authority is the lack of funding currently available for tribal law enforcement.[163]

> Statistics indicate that federal and state governments provide significantly fewer resources for policing in Indian Country and Alaska Native villages than are provided to comparable non-Native communities. According to the US Department of Justice, available data suggests that tribes have between 55 and 75 per cent of the law enforcement resources available to comparable non-Native rural communities.[164]

Some tribes believe that they would be in a better position to address the problems associated with the current criminal jurisdictional scheme if their funding needs were met.[165] For tribes that are currently willing and able, therefore, the best solution is to restore tribal sovereignty by allowing those tribes to increase their authority over law enforcement generally and to increase tribal court enforcement authority specifically.[166] As former US Attorney Janet Reno said:

> While the federal government has a significant responsibility for law enforcement in much of Indian country, tribal justice systems are ultimately the most appropriate institutions for maintaining order in tribal communities. They are local institutions, closest to the people they serve. With adequate resources and training, they are most capable of crime prevention and peace keeping. Fulfilling the federal government's trust responsibility to Indian nations means not only adequate federal law enforcement in Indian country, but enhancement of tribal justice systems as well.[167]

Some current senators agree with Reno. Under Section 2 of the then proposed Tribal Law and Order Act of 2009, the bill's sponsors reiterated former US Attorney Reno's sentiments, stating that "tribal justice systems are ultimately the most appropriate institutions for maintaining law and order in tribal communities."[168]

Moreover, as suggested previously, the federal government has struggled to effectively prosecute crimes arising in Indian country. The then pending Tribal Law and Order Act of 2009 also recognized this fact, stating that "a significant percentage of cases referred to Federal agencies for prosecution of crimes allegedly occurring in tribal communities are declined to be prosecuted."[169] In 2006, Dean Kevin Washburn published an article examining in-depth many of the factors contributing to ineffective federal enforcement.[170] Dean Washburn explained that effective federal enforcement is difficult because the crimes and their punishments are defined largely by federal officials and not by tribal officials, meaning that the tribal communities have not had an opportunity to actively engage in criminal enforcement.[171] Effective federal enforcement is further hampered by geographical constraints, as the sheer distance between the location of a crime committed in Indian country and the federal courthouse means that the Indian defendant may be the only Indian person present in the courtroom when tried. Geographic obstacles not only isolate an Indian defendant, but also usually mean that the federal prosecutor has no connection to the tribal community she is supposedly representing.[172] Because of the typical lack of connection between the federal prosecutor and the community, which also means that the prosecutor is not accountable to that community, "the fundamental criminal law justifications for broad prosecutorial discretion simply do not apply when a federal prosecutor is working in Indian country."[173] Additionally, "[t]he prosecution and imprisonment of an Indian for an on-reservation crime against another Indian is perhaps the single most aggressive use of federal power against an Indian that routinely occurs, at least in modern times, and thus may be one of the greatest existing intrusions on internal tribal affairs."[174] Ultimately, the existing scheme sends the message to tribal communities that they are inferior.[175]

Although Dean Washburn's article is specific to limitations in the existing federal scheme for prosecuting crimes occurring in Indian country, his findings are helpful in discussing the viability of increasing tribal court punishment authority. Based on Dean Washburn's conclusions, the current federal system is not working and change is necessary. Dean Washburn found that federal prosecution is in part ineffective because the federal prosecutors are physically and culturally removed from the tribal communities they are supposedly serving. Likewise, the tribal community that has been "injured" by the crime cannot participate fully in the trial because of physical and cultural distances. Many tribes have largely acquiesced to the federal prosecution of crimes because, given ICRA's limitations, tribal courts do not have broad enough sentencing authority to have a deterrent effect on offenders. However, this tendency of deferring to federal prosecutions may be curtailed if tribal courts and prosecutors felt emboldened by increased enforcement authority. Returning these prosecutions to the tribal communities would thereby limit and perhaps eradicate the physical and cultural distance that so significantly handicaps effective federal enforcement, the overall net effect being that increasing tribal court enforcement authority would likely contribute to more effective enforcement overall.

Increasing tribal court enforcement authority is a step in the right direction to restoring effective law and order on reservations. Moreover, "the authority to impose sentences commensurate with the crime" is "consistent with international human rights standards."[176] It is hoped that increased tribal court sentencing authority would also address the perception that tribal law enforcement is ineffective—or that a loophole exists within the criminal law enforcement scheme in place in Indian country. By helping to address such negative perceptions, increasing tribal court punishment will likely serve to decrease the disproportionate crime and violence facing American Indians in Indian country.

CONCLUSION

Accordingly, the concerns that plagued Congress regarding tribal courts seem to have been addressed in part over the intervening forty years. With the erosion of the historical concerns that originally justified passage of ICRA, Congress should act to repeal or substantially decrease the limitations on tribal court punishment authority under ICRA, Section 1302(7). To allow these limitations to remain in place merely encourages criminals such as Jesus Martin Sagaste-Cruz to target Indian country—as criminals are becoming increasingly aware of the limitations on tribal court punishment authority for crimes occurring in Indian country. Although only a small group of individuals facing rising crime and violence in Indian country may directly benefit from this proposal, reformation of the tribal court punishment limitation contained within the ICRA may go a long way toward remedying the perception that ineffective enforcement occurs within Indian country. Therefore, Congress must act to remedy the problem created by the passage of ICRA, Section 1302(7) to safeguard the very people that it originally sought to protect from a future that only promises increasing violence.[177]

NOTES

1. Indian Civil Rights Act, 25 U.S.C. §§ 1301–03 (2006).

2. Civil Rights Act of 1968, 82 Stat. 73 (codified in scattered sections of 18, 25, 42 U.S.C.).

3. See S. Rep. No. 721, 90th Cong., 2d Sess. 21 (1968) (Additional Views of Mr. Ervin, Title VII) ("The proposed Indian legislation … is an effort on the part of those who believe in constitutional rights for all Americans to give 'the forgotten Americans' basic rights which all other American enjoy. The measures … will be important steps in alleviating many inequities and injustices with which they are faced. These rights, fundamental to our system of constitutional freedoms, are not now secured by laws respecting the American Indian.").

4. "Indian country" is defined at 18 U.S.C. section 1151, which provides that "[e]xcept as otherwise provided in sections 1154 and 1156 of this title, the term 'Indian country', as used in this chapter, means (a) all land within the limits of any Indian reservation under the jurisdiction of the United States Government, notwithstanding the issuance of any patent, and, including rights-of-way running through the reservation, (b) all dependent Indian communities within the borders of the United States whether within the original or subsequently acquired territory thereof, and whether within or without the limits of a state, and (c) all Indian allotments, the Indian titles to which have not been extinguished, including rights-of-way running through the same."

5. 25 U.S.C. § 1302(7) (2006) ("No Indian tribe in exercising powers of self-government shall require excessive bail, impose excessive fines, inflict cruel and unusual punishments, and in no event impose for conviction of any one offense any penalty or punishment greater than imprisonment for a term of one year and a fine of $5,000, or both"). ICRA was amended in 1986 to increase the period of imprisonment from six months to one year and the maximum fine from $500 to $5,000. Pub. L. No. 99-570, § 4217, 100 Stat. 3207.

6. As exemplified by the recent passage of the Tribal Law and Order Act (TLOA), both Congress and the president recognize that increased tribal court punishment authority, as argued for in this chapter, is necessary. On July 29, 2010, President Obama signed into law TLOA, otherwise known as Public Law 111-211. Under Section 234 of the TLOA, a tribal court may now impose sentences of up to three years per count and up to nine years per case. Additionally, the same section increases the limit on fines to $15,000. This increased sentencing authority is conditioned on the tribe coming into compliance with certain requirements, such as making bar-licensed indigent defense counsel available, utilizing a bar-licensed judge, making tribal criminal laws available for public inspection, and recording court proceedings. Christopher B. Chaney,

The Promise of the Tribal Law & Order Act, 58-APR FED. LAW 44 (2011). Additionally, congressional passage of the TLOA is explicit recognition by Congress that it has the authority to remedy the problems of violence and crime in Indian country to which ICRA contributed.

7.   The findings of the BJS Report are startling. Yet, for purposes of this chapter, the BJS Report is overly broad in two regards. First, the BJS Report is based on Census 2000 information, which relied on self-identification to identify who is an Indian. Therefore, the BJS Report is not limited to federally and state-recognized tribes or actual tribal enrollment. Moreover, the figures are not limited to crimes that were actually committed in Indian country, where ICRA applies. STEVEN W. PERRY, BUREAU OF JUSTICE STATISTICS, U.S. DEP'T OF JUSTICE, AMERICAN INDIANS AND CRIME—A BJS STATISTICAL PROFILE 1992–2002, at 1–11 (Dec. 2004), *available at* http://www.ojp.usdoj.gov/bjs/pub/pdf/aic02.pdf. Therefore, while the BJS Report is helpful to understand the extent of the general problem of violence facing American Indians and Alaskan Natives throughout the United States, it should not be concluded that the proposed reformation of ICRA proposed in this chapter would resolve all of the problems articulated in the BJS Report.

8.   *Id*. at iii.

9.   *Id*. at iv.

10.   *Id*.

11.   *Report of the Native American Advisory Group*, 1–2, Nov. 4, 2003, *available at* http://www.ussc.gov/NAAG/NativeAmer.pdf.

12.   AMNESTY INT'L, MAZE OF INJUSTICE: THE FAILURE TO PROTECT INDIGENOUS WOMEN FROM SEXUAL VIOLENCE IN THE USA, 30 (2006) ("Reportedly, the apparent gap in jurisdiction or enforcement has encouraged non-Indian individuals to pursue criminal activities of various kinds in Indian Country"). For an in-depth discussion of the existing criminal jurisdiction scheme currently in place within Indian country, see the discussion starting at page 213.

13.   Jesus Martin Sagaste-Cruz is non-Indian and therefore not subject to tribal court jurisdiction under the existing criminal jurisdictional scheme currently in place. However, the story of Sagaste-Cruz is instructive regarding the overall problem of lawlessness that has been created as a result of the current ineffective criminal jurisdictional scheme. Although Sagaste-Cruz would not fall under the jurisdiction of tribal courts, it would be much less likely that an organization such as the one he developed would exist if enforcement were more effective within Indian country. This article argues that strengthening tribal court enforcement authority would be a step in the direction of addressing the overall perceived issue of lawlessness in Indian country.

14.   Sarah Kershaw, *Through Indians Lands, Drugs' Shadowy Trail*, N.Y. Times, Feb. 19, 2006, at 26 ("The recently convicted leader of a Mexican drug ring had a chilling strategy on five reservations in Wyoming and the Midwest, the authorities said: targeting tribes with high alcohol addiction rates and handing out free methamphetamine, recruiting the newly addicted Indians as dealers and orchestrating romantic relationships between gang members and Indian women").

15.   Brodie Farquhar, *Meth Ring Targeted Reservations*, Casper StarTribune.net, Aug. 21, 2005, *available at* http://http://trib.com/news/article_bd90d2a4-1fd1-5640-be55-b587522dd811.html; Press Release, Drug Enforcement Admin., *Drug Trafficker Who Preyed on Native Americans is Sentenced to Life in Prison*, July 7, 2005, *available at* http://www.dea.gov/pubs/states/newsrel/denver070705p.html; *Meth Dealer Gets Life Sentence*, Billingsgazette.com, July 8, 2005, *available at* http://www.billingsgazette.com/newdcx.php?display=rednews/2005/07/08/build/wyoming/60-dealer-sentence.inc.

16.   Farquhar, *supra* note 15.

17.   *Id*. *See also* Sarah Kershaw, *Through Indians Lands, Drugs' Shadowy Trail*, N.Y. Times, Feb. 19, 2006 ("And on a growing number of reservations, drug traffickers—particularly Mexican criminals—are marrying Indian women to establish themselves on reservations").

18.   *Id*.

19.   *Id*.

20.   *Id*. Non-Indians like Sagaste-Cruz and his associates are not the only individuals to take advantage of the perceived jurisdictional loopholes in Indian country. Indian drug-traffickers, such as John Oakes from the St. Regis Mohawk Reservation in New York, have also established lucrative operations in Indian country. Sarah Kershaw, *Through Indians Lands, Drugs' Shadowy Trail*, N.Y. Times, Feb. 19, 2006.

THE INDIAN CIVIL RIGHTS ACT AT FORTY

21.   Joel Millman, *Mexican Pot Gangs Infiltrate Indian Reservations in U.S.*, The Wall Street Journal, Nov. 5, 2009 (detailing how Mexican marijuana growing operations appear to be flourishing on Indian reservations in the Northwest).

22.   Amnesty International's report was based on research conducted in 2005 and 2006 by Amnesty International USA in three locations: the Standing Rock Sioux Reservation in North and South Dakota, the State of Oklahoma, and the State of Alaska. US Attorneys did not participate in this study. The report also does not reflect the experiences of American Indian women living away from reservation communities. AMNESTY INT'L, *supra* note 12, ii–iii (2006). Amnesty International's report does qualify its findings by pointing to the fact that "no statistics exist specifically on sexual violence in Indian Country and available data is more likely to represent urban than rural areas." However, the report goes on to conclude that "[w]hile the available data does not accurately portray the extent of sexual violence against Native American and Alaska Native women, it does indicate that Native American and Alaska Native women are particularly at risk of sexual violence." *Id.* at 4.

23.   *Id.* at 2 (citations omitted).

24.   *Id* at 27.

25.   *Id.* at 61 (citing Dr. David Lisak, Associate Professor of Psychology, University of Massachusetts (Sept. 29, 2003)).

26.   Tribal Law and Order Act of 2009, S. 797, 111th Cong., § 2(a) (11–13, 17) (April 2, 2009) (as introduced in the Senate).

27.   AMNESTY INT'L, *supra* note 12 at 8.

28.   *See* U.S. CONST. ART. I, § 8, CL. 3 & art. II, § 2.

29.   *See* Cherokee Nation v. Georgia, 30 U.S. (5 Pet.) 1, 2 (1831) (explaining that while tribal governments are dependent on the federal government they still remain separate entities outside of the complete control of the federal government and tribes are therefore "domestic dependent nations"). *See also* Worcester v. Georgia, 31 U.S. (6 Pet.) 515, 519 (1832) ("The Indian nations had always been considered as distinct, independent political communities, retaining their original natural rights, as the undisputed possessors of the soil, from time immemorial").

30.   *See, e.g.,* Memorandum from Barack Obama to Heads of Executive Departments and Agencies: Tribal Consultation (Nov. 5, 2009), 74 Fed. Reg. 57881 (Nov. 9, 2009); Memorandum from George W. Bush to Heads of Executive Departments and Agencies: Government-to-Government Relationship with Tribal Governments (Sept. 23, 2004), *available at* http://www.whitehouse.gov/news/releases/2004/09/print/20040923-4.html.

31.   *See* United States v. Lara, 541 U.S. 193, 210 (2004) ("[T]he Tribe acted in its capacity of a separate sovereign....").

32.   Indian Self-Determination and Education Assistance Act, 25 U.S.C. § 450 (2006).

33.   *See, e.g.*, United States v. Kagama, 118 U.S. 375, 383–85 (1886).

34.   Indian Country Crimes Act, 18 U.S.C. § 1152 (2006) [hereinafter ICCA]. Passed in 1817, the ICCA could be considered the first major intrusion by the federal government into tribal jurisdiction. Additionally, ICCA works to divest tribal criminal jurisdiction for crimes committed in Indian country where the crime committed is interracial in nature, meaning that either the victim or the perpetrator is Indian and the other is not. ICCA extends the general laws of the United States to Indian Country. *Id.*

35.   Major Crimes Act, 18 U.S.C. § 1153 [hereinafter MCA]. Reacting to a Supreme Court decision finding the federal government did not have jurisdiction over the murder of one Indian by another Indian, *Ex parte* Crow Dog, 109 U.S. 556 (1883), Congress enacted the MCA in 1885. The Supreme Court held that the MCA was constitutional in *U.S. v. Antelope*, 430 U.S. 641 (1977). The MCA grants jurisdiction to the federal government when certain enumerated crimes are committed by an Indian within Indian country. 18 U.S.C.A. § 1153(a) (2006). The federal government will generally have concurrent jurisdiction with the appropriate tribe when an Indian commits a crime in Indian country enumerated under the MCA. Referred to as "major crimes," the enumerated crimes include: murder; manslaughter; kidnapping; maiming; any felony under the sexual abuse statutes; incest; assault with intent to commit murder, assault with a dangerous weapon, resulting in serious bodily injury, or against a child under sixteen; felony child abuse or neglect; arson; burglary; robbery; and felony theft. *Id.*

36. Indian Civil Rights Act, 25 U.S.C. §§ 1301–03 (2006) [hereinafter ICRA]. For purposes of this article, it is not necessary to discuss the complexities of the criminal jurisdictional scheme applicable to Indian country, and, therefore, only a brief overview is provided. For a full discussion of these complex jurisdictional issues that arise in enforcement within Indian country, please see Kevin K. Washburn, *American Indians, Crime, and the Law*, 104 MICH. L. REV. 709 (2006).

37. For purposes of criminal jurisdiction, the analysis is limited to whether or not the individual is "Indian" and not whether the individual in question is a member of the affected tribe. In 1990, the Supreme Court held that tribal sovereignty did not include the authority to assert jurisdiction over nonmembers of the tribe, even if the individuals in question were members of other tribes. Duro v. Reina, 495 U.S. 676 (1990). Congress responded quickly to the Court's decision, and, in 1991, passed legislation essentially "overturning" the Supreme Court by recognizing "the inherent power of Indian tribes, hereby recognized and affirmed, to exercise criminal jurisdiction over all Indians." 25 U.S.C. § 1301(2). The Supreme Court reviewed the constitutionality of Congress's actions and ultimately held that Congress possessed the authority to recognize the inherent authority of Indian tribes over all Indians. United States v. Lara, 541 U.S. 193 (2004). Furthermore, the Ninth Circuit Court of Appeals recently addressed the question of who is an "Indian," finding that the question turns on two elements, a racial and a political element. In other words, an Indian is an individual who possesses a degree of Indian blood and has tribal or governmental recognition as an Indian. U.S. v. Bruce, 394 F.3d 1215 (9th Cir. 2005).

38. 25 U.S.C. §§ 1301–03 (2006).

39. *Id.*

40. *Id.*

41. The Indian Civil Rights Act of 1968 was amended in 1986 to increase the period of imprisonment to one year and the maximum fine to $5,000. Pub. L. No. 99-570, §4217, 100 Stat. 3207 (codified at 25 U.S.C. §1302(7)).

42. AMNESTY INT'L, *supra* note 12, at 29 (2006) ("The message sent by this law [ICRA] is that, in practice, tribal justice systems are only equipped to handle less serious crimes. As a result of this limitation on their custodial sentencing powers, some tribal courts are less likely to prosecute serious crimes, such as sexual violence").

43. Oliphant v. Suquamish Indian Tribe, 435 U.S. 191 (1978).

44. *Id.* at 212.

45. *Id.* at 206–12.

46. *Id.* at 201–06.

47. NATIONAL CONGRESS OF AMERICAN INDIANS, FACT SHEET: VIOLENCE AGAINST WOMEN IN INDIAN COUNTRY, 3, available at http://www.ncai.org/ncai/advocacy/hr/docs/dv-fact_sheet.pdf (last accessed July 22, 2009).

48. The Ninth Circuit Gender Bias Task Force, *The Effects of Gender in the Federal Courts: The Final Report of the Ninth Circuit Gender Bias Task Force* (pt. IX, Gender and Federal Indian Law), 67 S. CAL. L. REV. 745, 909 (1994) ("Due to the jurisdictional overlap among tribal, state, and federal courts, a cumbersome procedure is followed whenever a crime is committed in Indian country. The difficulties of prosecution in general, coupled with traditions of non-involvement by law enforcement officials in spousal abuse, may make federal enforcement more difficult"); AMNESTY INT'L, *supra* note 12, at 27–28 (2006) ("The jurisdiction of these different authorities often overlaps, resulting in confusion and uncertainty. In many areas there may be dual jurisdiction. The end result can sometimes be so confusing that no one intervenes, leaving victims without legal protection or redress and resulting in impunity for the perpetrators, especially non-Native offenders who commit crimes on tribal land"); *see also* Sarah Kershaw, *Through Indians Lands, Drugs' Shadowy Trail*, New York Times (Feb. 19, 2006) ("For traffickers of marijuana, cocaine, methamphetamine, painkillers and people, reservations offer many advantages. Law enforcement is spotty at best. Tribal sovereignty, varying state laws and inconsistent federal interest in prosecuting drug crimes create jurisdictional confusion and conflict").

49. *Id.* at 910 ("Tribes vary across a range of dimensions, and generalizations across differing tribes is inappropriate. Some tribal authorities may lack resources; further, the relative isolation of some Indian reservations means that federal actors, the FBI and the U.S. Attorneys, are sometimes located some distance away. While many FBI field offices are located on or near reservation lands, the wide dispersion of people in a vast area of land puts an extra burden on investigators who must speak to witnesses, confirm alibis, and gather other evidence" (citation omitted)).

50.   AMNESTY INT'L, *supra* note 12, at 66–67 (2006) ("Significantly, between 2000 and 2003, the BIA was consistently among the investigating agencies with the highest percentage of cases declined by federal prosecutors.... It appears that US prosecutors may be applying overly stringent criteria for selecting cases for prosecution. According to the Executive Office for US Attorneys, the rate of conviction in criminal cases filed by US Attorneys has been over 90 per cent since 2000. While prosecutors should select cases based on their merit, Amnesty International is concerned that the Executive Office of US Attorneys may have created a climate in which prosecutors are not encouraged to pursue more challenging cases... Federal government statistics show that there are few federal prosecutions of crimes in Indian Country, and the Department of Interior has recognized that this is a problem" (citations omitted)). *See also* Kevin K. Washburn, *American Indians, Crime, and the Law*, 104 MICH. L. REV. 709, 718 (2006) (arguing that prosecution of crimes committed in Indian country is likely not a priority for federal officials).

51.   *U.S. Attorneys Targeted for Indian Country Work*, Indianz.com, Sept. 30, 2008, http://64.28.12.138/News/2008/011122.asp ("The only complaint about Heffelfinger [US attorney for Minnesota] was his 'focus on Native American issues,' ... Chiara and Hagen were criticized for traveling far distances together for work affecting the Native issues subcommittee and Indian Country"); Amy Forliti, *Heffelfinger says something within DOJ is "Broken,"* Indian Country News, May 24, 2007, https://indiancountrynews.net/index2.php?option=com_content&task=view&id=573&pop=1&page=0 ("[F]ormer Justice Department White House liaison Monica Gooding told the Senate Judiciary Committee investigating the firings of U.S. attorneys that there was a concern Heffelfinger was spending too much time on American Indian issues"); U.S. Department of Justice, An Investigation into the Removal of Nine U.S. Attorneys in 2006, (2008) 21 n. 20, available at http://www.usdoj.gov/opr/us-att-firings-rpt092308.pdf (accessed July 22, 2009) ("Finally, Comey said he was concerned that Heffelfinger was overly focused on Indian affairs issues").

52.   *U.S. Attorneys Targeted, supra* note 51.

53.   *Gender and Federal Indian Law, supra* note 48, at 905 ("The Advisory Committee noted that federal judges have described themselves as lacking expertise and understanding in this area of the law [federal Indian law]. The Committee urged increased judicial attentiveness to this area of litigation and called for education about these issues for federal judges").

54.   *Id.* at 908 ("Federal Indian jurisdiction thus brings the federal courts into questions such as the admissibility of evidence of sexual conduct, the relevance of battering as a defense, and the manner in which child abuse victims should testify—issues not always thought to be within the federal criminal domain" (citations omitted)).

55.   AMNESTY INT'L, *supra* note 12, at 8 (2006).

56.   As previously mentioned, however, the impact of the BJS Report is mitigated by the fact that the BJS Report is overly inclusive in that it considers violence and crime impacting all American Indians and Alaskan Natives throughout the United States and relies on statistics based on those individuals who have self-identified, rather than on tribal enrollment.

57.   Pub. L. 90-284, Title II, § 202, Apr. 11, 1968, 82 Stat. 77. The limitations on tribal court punishment were subsequently increased to one year, a fine of $5,000 or both. 25 U.S.C. § 1302(7) (2006).

58.   This congressional belief likely stemmed from existing regulations governing Courts of Indian Offenses (also known as "CFR courts"). Courts of Indian Offenses predated the ICRA. *See* Casey Douma, *40th Anniversary of the Indian Civil Rights Act: Finding a Way Back to Indigenous Justice*, 55 FED. LAW 34, 34 (2008) ("The Western systems of justice to which most Native people were exposed at the end of the 19th century came from the Courts of Indian Offenses (C.F.R. Courts). These courts were set up by the secretary of interior in 1883 as a way to assimilate Native people by punishing them for practicing their traditional ways of life"). While relatively few CFR courts exist today, see 25 C.F.R. § 11.100 (2009); at their peak around 1900, these courts were operated in about two-thirds of the reservation districts served by the BIA. *See* WILLIAM THOMAS HAGAN, INDIAN POLICE AND JUDGES—EXPERIMENTS IN ACCULTURATION AND CONTROL 109 (1966). Congress never expressly authorized these CFR courts, but their legitimacy has been sustained through congressional ratification and acquiescence. *See* FELIX S. COHEN, HANDBOOK OF FEDERAL INDIAN LAW 333 (Michie Co. 1982). In the decades leading up to the passage of the ICRA, the punishment authority of CFR courts was governed by a revised Code of Indian Tribal Offenses, published in 1935. *Id.* Under the 1935 code, the maxi-

mum criminal penalty generally allowed was six months' labor or imprisonment or a $366 fine. *Id.* at 337 n. 42. Currently, the sentencing limitations for CFR courts are one year imprisonment, $5,000 fine, or both. 25 C.F.R. § 11.315 (2009). Although Congress' intent behind the sentencing limitations of the ICRA remains ambiguous, scholars have proposed several possible motives, including the possibility that the BIA desired to maintain a strong level of control over tribal courts and councils through such limitations. *See* Donald L. Burnett, *An Historical Analysis of the 1968 'Indian Civil Rights Act'*, 9 HARV. J. ON LEGIS. 557, 583 (1972).

59.   *Hearings Before the Subcomm. on Constitutional Rights of the Senate Comm. on the Judiciary*, 87th Cong. 384 (1961) (testimony of J. Shirley Nelson).

60.   Mr. Creech was counsel for the Constitutional Rights Subcommittee.

61.   *Hearings, supra* note 59, at 463 (testimony of Alfred Sheck).

62.   *Hearings, supra* note 59, at 484 (testimony of Preston Keevana).

63.   *Hearings, supra* note 59, at 465 (testimony of Governor Ernest Mirabal).

64.   *Summary Report of Hearings and Investigations by the Subcomm. on Constitutional Rights of the Senate Comm. on the Judiciary*, 88th Cong. Preface (1964) ("Initial hearings were begun in Washington during August 1961, and concluded there in March 1963. In addition to these hearings, field hearings and staff conferences were conducted in Arizona, California, Colorado, Idaho, Nevada, New Mexico, North Carolina, and North and South Dakota. These hearings and staff conferences were geographically scheduled in such a way that the subcommittee would receive the views of the largest number of tribes in each area. In all, the representatives of approximately 50 tribes appeared before the subcommittee.... This report summarizes the subcommittee's findings during its 2-year study and presents its recommendations for legislative action").

65.   *Id.* at 6. Interestingly, the Constitutional Rights Subcommittee seemed to recognize that such limitations on tribal court punishment authority would substantially impair the ability of tribal courts to effectively address crime within their jurisdiction. The subcommittee stated that "because of the limitations on the sentences imposed by a tribal court, the punishment may be entirely out of line with the crime." *Id.* at 7.

66.   *Id.* at 15–16.

67.   *Summary Report of Hearings and Investigations by the Subcomm. on Constitutional Rights of the Senate Comm. on the Judiciary*, 89th Cong. (1966).

68.   *Id.*

69.   *Id.* at 3.

70.   S. REP. NO. 90-721, 1968 U.S.C.C.A.N. 1837, 1865 (1967) (additional Views of Mr. Ervin (emphasis added)).

71.   *Hearings Before the Subcomm. on Constitutional Rights of the Senate Comm. on the Judiciary*, 87th Cong. 3 (1962) (statement of Sen. Ervin).

72.   *Id.* at 4 (statement of Sen. Keating).

73.   *Id.* at 40 (testimony of Representative E.Y. Berry).

74.   *Id.* at 46.

75.   *Id.* at 89 (testimony of Sen. Quentin Burdick).

76.   *Id.* at 88.

77.   *Hearings Before the Subcomm. on Constitutional Rights of the Senate Comm. on the Judiciary*, 87th Cong. 431 (1963) (testimony of Mateo Aragon).

78.   *Id.* at 482 (testimony of Preston Keevana).

79.   *Id.* at 487 (testimony of R.A. Wardlaw).

80.   Senator Ervin, *Legislation to Protect the Constitutional Rights of the American Indian*, 113 Cong. Rec. 13473 (May 23, 1967).

81.   S. REP. NO. 90-721, 1968 U.S.C.C.A.N. 1837, 1864 (1967) (additional Views of Mr. Ervin).

82.   REPORT TO THE SECRETARY OF THE INTERIOR BY THE TASK FORCE ON INDIAN AFFAIRS (July 10, 1961).

83.   *Id.* at 28. The "above-mentioned inadequacies" included "insufficient law enforcement officers, inadequately prepared judges, the absence of attorneys, non-use of the courts in civil actions, and inadequate appellate provisions." *Id.*

84.   *See Hearings Before the Subcomm. on Constitutional Rights of the Senate Comm. on the Judiciary*, 87th Cong. 60–85 (1962) (testimony of Philleo Nash).

85. *Id.* at 9 (statement of Sen. Keating).

86. *Id.* at 42 (testimony of E.Y. Berry).

87. *Id.* at 17 (statement of Mr. Carver, Assistant Secretary of Indian Affairs).

88. *Hearings Before the Subcomm. on Constitutional Rights of the Senate Comm. on the Judiciary Pursuant to S. Res. 260,* 87th Cong. 574 (1963) (testimony of Palmer King).

89. *Id.* at 579 (statement of Mr. Creech) ("Of course, the right to counsel is just one of the problems that has been brought to the subcommittee's attention. Another has been the allegation that in some instances the tribal courts have been trying Indians over whom they do not have jurisdiction. For instance, it has been alleged tribal police have arrested Indians who live off the reservation and brought them onto the reservation before the tribal court which had no jurisdiction over them. In fact these courts did try them. Many tribes have no provisions for an appellate court. The subcommittee hearings indicate that in some instances, the law and order code provides for an appellate court, but these have not been provided. Where tribal codes provide for a three-man court, maybe only one or two judges have been appointed. In other instances in the appellate court, the same judge presides, with a two- or three-judge court, as the judge of original jurisdiction").

90. *See Hearings Before the Subcomm. on Constitutional Rights of the Senate Comm. on the Judiciary,* 87th Cong. 460 (1963) (testimony of Alfred Sheck) (explaining that the Zuni Pueblo did not have written rules or regulations, because it utilized a traditional court); *Id.* at 465 (testimony of Ernest Mirabal) (stating that the Nambe Pueblo did not have a written constitution or law and order code).

91. *Hearings Before the Subcomm. on Constitutional Rights of the Senate Comm. on the Judiciary Pursuant to S. Res. 260,* 87th Cong. 747–48 (1963).

92. *Hearings Before the Subcomm. on Constitutional Rights of the Senate Comm. on the Judiciary Pursuant to S. Res. 260,* 87th Cong. 798 (1963) (testimony of George Peltier).

93. *Summary Report of Hearings and Investigations by the Subcomm. on Constitutional Rights of the Senate Comm. on the Judiciary,* 88th Cong. 16 (1964).

94. *Id.* at 17–18.

95. *Summary Report of Hearings and Investigations by the Subcomm. on Constitutional Rights of the Senate Comm. on the Judiciary Pursuant to S. Res. 194,* 89th Cong. 3 (1966).

96. *Hearings Before the Subcomm. on Constitutional Rights of the Senate Comm. on the Judiciary,* 87th Cong. 6 (1962) (statement of Senator Roman Hruska).

97. *Hearings Before the Subcomm. on Constitutional Rights of the Senate Comm. on the Judiciary,* 87th Cong. 378 (1963) (testimony of Royal Marks).

98. *Hearings Before the Subcomm. on Constitutional Rights of the Senate Comm. on the Judiciary Pursuant to S. Res. 260,* 87th Cong. 598 (1963) (testimony of Ramon Roubideaux). In a written statement to the subcommittee, Mr. Roubideaux added that "[o]n the few occasions I was allowed to represent an Indian defendant in tribal court, I found the courts were run by practically illiterate judges with little or no protection for the defendant." *Id.* at 608–09.

99. *Id.* at 600.

100. *Hearings Before the Subcomm. on Constitutional Rights of the Senate Comm. on the Judiciary Pursuant to S. Res. 260,* 87th Cong. 579 (1963) (testimony of D'Arcy McNickle).

101. *Hearings Before the Subcomm. on Constitutional Rights of the Senate Comm. on the Judiciary Pursuant to S. Res. 260,* 87th Cong. 775 (1963) (testimony of Richard Cavanaugh).

102. *Summary Report of Hearings and Investigations by the Subcomm. on Constitutional Rights of the Senate Comm. on the Judiciary,* 88th Cong. 17–18 (1964).

103. *Summary Report of Hearings and Investigations by the Subcomm. on Constitutional Rights of the Senate Comm. on the Judiciary Pursuant to S. Res. 194,* 89th Cong. 24 (1966).

104. *See supra* n. 6 (asserting that Congress has the authority to amend ICRA as demonstrated through the recent passage of TLOA). Moreover, the author recognizes that not all tribes may welcome an increase in tribal court punishment authority given the resource restrictions discussed in this article or for other reasons. Accordingly, such an increase in tribal court enforcement authority should be offered to tribes on an opt-in basis; that a tribe may choose to opt in to increased punishment authority should it feel it is in a position to accept additional enforcement authority. In choosing whether or not to opt in, one factor considered by a tribe should be whether it provides legal representation to indigent defendants. Some have suggested that tribal

court punishment authority was limited to no more than one year in prison because this is consistent with a felony, which is a crime that carries a potential sentence of more than one year in prison. In the Anglo-American system, indigent individuals charged with a felony are guaranteed legal representation. If tribal courts are to obtain enforcement authority beyond one year, they may also consider mandatory indigent representation for crimes where an individual could be sentenced to jail for longer than a year. *See* Melissa Tatum, *Tribal Courts: The Battle to Earn Respect Without Sacrificing Culture and Tradition* in HARMONIZING LAW IN AN ERA OF GLOBALIZATION: CONVERGENCE, DIVERGENCE AND RESISTANCE 81, 87 (Larry Cata Backer ed., 2007). However, there may be less of a need for attorney representation in tribal court because "[m]ost tribal courts operate under a less strict set of procedural rules, ones that are more forgiving to a litigant representing herself." *Id.* at 88.

105. COHEN'S HANDBOOK OF FEDERAL INDIAN LAW § 2.01[1] (2005), *available at* Lexisnexis COHEN ("Congress's primacy over the other branches of the federal government with respect to Indian law and policy is rooted in the text and structure of the Constitution, and has been recognized in numerous Supreme Court decisions" (citations omitted)).

106. Duro v. Reina, 495 U.S. 676 (1990).

107. 25 U.S.C. § 1301(2) (2006).

108. United States v. Lara, 541 U.S. 193 (2004).

109. *See supra* n. 6.

110. In 1978, Congress recognized that the historic bias of state courts harmed Indian children and mandated tribal court jurisdiction over such matters under the Indian Child Welfare Act. P.L. 95-608, 92 Stat. 3069 (1978) (codified at 25 USC §§ 1901–1963 (1994)).

111. *See supra* n. 6 (explaining that TLOA was signed into law on July 29, 2010).

112. Tribal Law and Order Act of 2009, S. 797, 111th Cong. (as introduced in the Senate, April 2, 2009).

113. *Id.* at Sec. 304.

114. Prepared Statement, Hon. Theresa M. Pouley, Judge, Tulalip Tribal Court; President, Northwest Tribal Court Judges Association, 28 (July 24, 2008).

115. *Id.* at 33.

116. Historically, Congress has not been alone in its criticism of tribal courts. In 1978, both the American Bar Foundation and National American Indian Court Judges Association released reports that were highly critical of tribal courts, with the American Bar Foundation going so far as to propose the elimination of tribal courts entirely. The concerns regarding tribal courts raised in these reports largely mirror congressional concerns discussed above as the concerns touched on unqualified judges, procedural irregularities, discrimination, and political partiality. *See* SAMUEL J. BRAKEL, AMERICAN INDIAN TRIBAL COURTS: THE COSTS OF SEPARATE JUSTICE (1978); THE NATIONAL AMERICAN INDIAN COURT JUDGES ASSOCIATION, INDIAN COURTS AND THE FUTURE (1978).

117. Tatum, *supra* note 1, at 86 (citing Oliphant v. Suquamish Tribe, 435 U.S. 191 (1978)).

118. *Id.* at 87. ("'[I]gnorance of the law is no excuse'. Our legal structure holds each person accountable for following the rules of conduct in the place where that person chooses to live").

119. *Id.* at 87 (explaining that "tribal courts are as diverse in structure and practice as the cultures they serve" as some tribes have retained traditional courts, some the CFR courts while others have chosen to mirror state and federal courts. There are over 300 tribal courts currently in existence).

120. Nell Jessup Newton, *Tribal Court Praxis: One Year in the Life of Twenty Indian Tribal Courts*, 22 AM. INDIAN L. REV. 285, 294 (1998) ("In conscious or unconscious anticipation to the possibility of federal interference with tribal authority, some tribal courts operate as nearly exact replicas of state courts").

121. *Id.*

122. *Id.* at 300–01 ("For many tribes, the application of state law to fill gaps may be regarded as appropriate in light of the tribe's assessment of the basic fairness of state common law doctrines and of the tribal interest in making tribal courts accessible for non-Indian parties").

123. *Id.* at 318 ("Federal law can influence a tribal court opinion because it is a necessary part of a multi-layered analysis, as when a difficult issue of tribal court jurisdiction over non-Indian parties or over particular subjects may begin with an examination of tribal law and end with an examination of federal law. Or, federal law can be a ready source of norms—especially procedural norms, but also norms concerning justiciability such as standing. In short, federal procedure, common law, constitutional law, or even statutory law may be applied as persuasive or mandatory authority in a case of first impression").

124. *Id.* at 320.

125. Gloria Valencia-Weber, *Tribal Courts: Custom and Innovative Law*, 24 N.M. L. REV. 225, 250 (1994) ("The legal reasoning based on custom can also result in outcomes facially indistinguishable from those based on federal or state law. One must distinguish external form from internal substance to appreciate how the outwardly similar is not so"). *See also* Newton, *supra* note 120, at 304–05 (discussing the Navajo Supreme Court's decision in *Castillo v. Charlie* and how the court's application of tribal law resulted in a decision that utilized fact-finding and decision-making methods similar to those employed in state court).

126. Nell Jessup Newton read eighty-five cases published in the *Indian Law Reporter* from 1996. Of the cases she read, she determined that the majority raised jurisdictional and procedural questions, although there were a few property, tort, and family law cases. Newton, *Tribal Court Praxis, supra* note 120, 298–99.

127. *Id.* at 308.

128. *See generally* Worcester v. Georgia, 31 U.S. 515 (1932) (holding that the laws of Georgia did not have any effect within the Cherokee Nation's territory); Santa Clara Pueblo v. Martinez, 436 U.S. 49 (1978) (holding that tribes have the power to determine tribal membership).

129. Prepared Statement, Hon. Theresa M. Pouley, Judge, Tulalip Tribal Court; President, Northwest Tribal Court Judges Association, 33–34 (July 24, 2008).

130. Newton, *supra* note 120, 289.

131. Tatum, *supra* note 104, at 92 ("Some tribal court decisions are available online in traditional legal databases, such as Westlaw and VersusLaw, or even posted on websites maintained by tribal courts themselves, and some tribes have also chosen to publish their decisions in book format. The Navajo Nation has long published its decisions in paper, and other tribes such as the Mashantucket Pequot and Muscogee (Creek) Nation are also opting for this approach").

132. A new edition was released in 2005 and supplements are released every two years.

133. Tatum, *supra* note 104, at 92 ("[T]ribal judges have begun actively speaking at conferences and publishing articles. Those speeches and articles cover topics ranging from how a particular court works to complex, theoretical analyses of specific legal issues. Tribal judges have also begun seeking out their state colleagues at meetings and conferences to put a public face on the tribal courts. Many states now have joint state/tribal court judicial conferences and training sessions").

134. Charles Wilkinson, *Indian Nations and the Federal Government: What will Justice Require in the Future? Claims Against the Sovereign 20th Judicial Conference of the United States Court of Federal Claims*, 17 FED. CIR. B.J. 235, 237 (2008) ("Today, there are more than 70 tribes, comprising well over 90 percent of all Indians, with tribal governments that have governmental staffs—excluding gaming operations—totaling 300 or more. Most of these tribal governments are larger than the nearby county governments. Even small tribes have elaborate operations").

135. *See, e.g.,* Chief Justice Tom Tso, *The Process of Decision Making in Tribal Courts*, 31 ARIZ. L. REV. 225, 228 (1989) ("Navajo judges and justices are chosen through a process designed to insulate them from politics. When a judge is to be selected, interested persons submit applications to the Judiciary Committee of the Navajo Tribal Council. The Judiciary Committee screens the applicants and draws up a list of the most highly qualified people according to the qualifications set forth in the Navajo Tribal Code. This list is then sent to the Tribal Chairman who appoints a judge from the list for a two year probationary period. Each appointment must be confirmed by the Tribal Council. During the probationary period, the judge receives training from carefully selected judicial education establishments which offer a quality legal-judicial education" (citations omitted)).

136. *See e.g.,* Little Traverse Bay Bands of Odawa Indians, Const. art. VI, § D, Separation of Functions ("No branch of government shall exercise the powers or duties or functions delegated to another branch"); *see also* Tso, *supra* note 135, at 231 ("Once a court makes a decision, that decision is subject to change only through judicial processes. No other part of the tribal government has the authority to overrule that decision.... The Tribal Code establishes the Judicial Branch as a separate branch of government" (citations omitted)).

137. *See* Angela R. Riley, *(Tribal) Sovereignty and Illiberalism*, 95 CAL. L. REV.. 799, 847 (2007) ("Despite heavy criticism fueled largely by *Santa Clara Pueblo*, evidence indicates that violations of civil liberties by tribal governments are, in fact, rare" (citations omitted)); Carole E. Goldberg, *Individual Rights and Tribal Revitalization*, 35 ARIZ. ST. L.J. 889, 893 (2003) (stating that work with tribes "suggests growing demand for the recognition and protection of such [individual] rights"); Alex Tallchief Skibine, *Respondent's Brief: Reargument*

of Santa Clara Pueblo v. Martinez, 14 KAN. J. L. & PUB. POL'Y 79, 86 (2004) ("all available evidence indicates that tribes have not violated the edicts of the ICRA").

138. Newton, *supra* note 120, 342–43 ("Of the eighty-five cases submitted to the *Indian Law Reporter*, twenty-two raised civil rights questions. In eleven cases the tribal courts agreed with the party raising a civil rights claim").

139. Newton, *supra* note 120, 347.

140. 25 U.S.C. § 1911(a) (2006).

141. Guidelines for State Courts; Indian Child Custody Proceedings, 44 Fed. Reg. 67, 584–6 (Nov. 26, 1979) ("notice pertain[ing] directly to implementation of the Indian Child Welfare Act of 1970").

142. *See id.* at 67, 584 (1978) ("State and tribal courts are fully capable of carrying out the responsibilities imposed on them by Congress without being under the direct supervision of this Department. Nothing in the legislative history indicates that Congress intended this Department to exercise supervisory control over state or tribal courts or to legislate for them with respect to Indian child custody matters").

143. NATIONAL TRIBAL JUSTICE RESOURCE CENTER, 2000–2001 ANNUAL REPORT at 1.

144. *Id.* at 3.

145. *Id.* at 2.

146. Tatum, *supra* note 104, at 88 ("More and more ... tribal judges receive some type of formal legal training, even if that is not an actual law degree. A wealth of training is available to tribal judges from a variety of sources.... Most tribes will send their judges to a wide variety of conferences to receive training on everything from general judicial skills to specialized topics such as issuing and enforcing protection orders").

147. *See, e.g.,* Tso, *supra* note 135, at 227–28 ("Today the Navajo courts are structured very much like those in the state and federal courts. We have seven judicial districts. The district courts are courts of general civil jurisdiction and of limited criminal jurisdiction.... The second tier of the Navajo court system is the Navajo Nation Supreme Court, composed of three justices. The Supreme Court hears appeals from final lower court decisions and from certain final administrative orders.... The tribal government is rapidly developing an extensive network of administrative bodies with quasi-judicial functions. The final decisions of bodies such as the Tax Commission and Board of Election Supervisors are appealable directly to the Native Supreme Court.... All opinions of the Navajo Supreme Court, and some of the opinions of the district courts, are published in the *Navajo Reporter*. Additionally, the Navajo courts have established rules of procedure for criminal, civil, probate and appellate matters").

148. The concern that tribal court judges are uneducated seems to be linked with the idea that most tribal court judges at the time of ICRA's passage were not legally trained. Notably, there is no requirement that US Supreme Court justices or federal court judges possess a law degree. Moreover, "[i]n approximately two thirds of the de novo court systems, judges need not be members of the bar. While statutes may require these lay judges to attend a basic training course or successfully complete an examination, they will nevertheless preside without the basic legal background required of the least experienced practitioner. Some systems require only a high school diploma for a person to be eligible for the bench. Thus, many lower court judges are marginally qualified to rule on complex legal issues, decide guilt and innocence, and pass sentence." David A. Harris, *Justice Rationed in the Pursuit of Efficiency: De Nova Trials in the Criminal Courts*, 24 CONN. L. REV. 381, 388 (1992) (citations omitted).

149. *See* Tso, *supra* note 135, at 229; *See also* Wilkinson, *supra* note 134, at 238 ("Tribal judges regularly take courses at the judicial colleges").

150. All the time of writing, LTBB employs five judges, two tribal court judges, and three tribal appellate court judges. Both tribal court judges and two of the three tribal appellate court judges have obtained their juris doctorates from accredited law schools within the United States. The Sault Ste. Marie Tribe of Chippewa Indians employs eight judges, one tribal court judge, and seven tribal appellate court judges (five full-time tribal appellate court judges and two reserve tribal appellate judges). The tribal court judge and three of the tribal court appellate judges have obtained their juris doctorates from accredited law schools within the United States. For both tribes, the chief tribal court judges and chief appellate court judges are attorneys.

151. Robert Odawi Porter, *The Inapplicability of American Law to the Indian Nations*, 89 IOWA L. REV. 1595, 1613 (2004) (explaining that more attorneys are becoming involved in Indian nations, serving as tribal general counsels, tribal prosecutors, tribal judges, defense counsel, and general private practitioners).

152. *See* Newton, *supra* note 120, at 323 ("The most controversial issue surrounding tribal courts involves the exercise of jurisdiction over non-Indians. The sampled cases indicate that the assumption of tribal court bias against non-Indians is simply not warranted").

153. Tatum, *supra* note 104, at 90.

154. OFFICE OF MGMT. & BUDGET, EXEC. OFFICE OF THE PRESIDENT, DETAILED INFORMATION ON THE BUREAU OF INDIAN AFFAIRS—TRIBAL COURTS ASSESSMENT (Jan. 9, 2009); *available at* http://www.whitehouse.gov/omb/expectmore/detail/10001091.2003.html.

155. *Id.*

156. *See* Newton, *supra* note 120, at 297.

157. *See supra* n. 6. Recent congressional passage of the TLOA and the president's subsequent act of signing TLOA into law suggests that both Congress and the president believe that tribal courts are capable of increased punishment authority.

158 AMNESTY INT'L, *supra* note 12, at 63 (2006) ("Congress should amend the Indian Civil Rights Act to recognize the authority of tribal courts to impose penalties proportionate to the offences they try").

159. WAKELING, ET AL., POLICING ON AMERICAN INDIAN RESERVATIONS: A REPORT TO THE NATIONAL INSTITUTE OF JUSTICE viii (July 2001).

160. *See* Newton, *supra* note 120, at 328.

161. WAKELING, POLICING ON AMERICAN INDIAN RESERVATIONS, *supra* note 159, at 4.

162. WAKELING, POLICING ON AMERICAN INDIAN RESERVATIONS, *supra* note 159, at 48 ("The Harvard Project's research shows that one indicator of a tribal government's ability to effectively make and implement decisions is whether or not it has increased control over its own institutions (seizing de facto sovereignty, and not merely de jure).... Only those tribes that have acquired meaningful control over their actual sovereignty—have experienced improved local economic and social conditions").

163. WAKELING, POLICING ON AMERICAN INDIAN RESERVATIONS, *supra* note 159, at vii ("Inadequate funding is an important obstacle to good policing in Indian Country. Existing data suggest that tribes have between 55 and 75 percent of the resource base available to non-Indian communities"). As further example of a lack of funding being a contributing factor to the problem of crime in Indian country, "Congress failed to provide additional funds to Public Law 280 states to support the law enforcement activities they had assumed. The BIA, however, reduced funding to tribal authorities as a result of the shift in jurisdiction. This has led to a situation where tribal and state authorities have not received sufficient funds to assume their respective law enforcement responsibilities, resulting in a sense of 'lawlessness' in some communities and difficult relations between tribal and state officials"). AMNESTY INT'L, *supra* note 12, at 29 (2006).

164. AMNESTY INT'L, *supra* note 12, at 42 (2006).

165. Kershaw, *supra* note 14 ("At the Mohawk Reservation, the tribe spends more than half the revenue from its casino and other enterprises—roughly $2 million annually—on border patrol and other law enforcement. Tribal leaders say they could fight the trafficking here better than outside law enforcement, given adequate resources. 'We feel like that's our responsibility,' says James W. Ransom, a Mohawk tribal chief. 'That's our goal'").

166. NCAI, *supra* note 47, at 2 ("A report of the Executive Committee for Indian Country Law Enforcement Improvements of the U.S. Department of Justice submitted in October 1997 concluded that one of the major problems of law enforcement in Indian Country is the poor coordination between law enforcement bodies caused by the fragmentation of the criminal justice system. The only solution would be, the report concluded, to consolidate services under one authority").

167. *A Federal Commitment to Tribal Justice System*, 79 JUDICATURE 113 (1995).

168. Tribal Law and Order Act of 2009, S. 797, Sec. 2(a)(3)(B), 111th Cong. (as introduced in the Senate, April 2, 2009).

169. *Id.* at Sec. 2(a)(10).

170. Washburn, *supra* note 36.

171. *Id.* at 718.

172. *Id.* at 729–30.

173. *Id.* at 734.

174. *Id.* at 725.

175. *Id.* at 738 ("Use of a federal prosecutor to address major crimes between Indians sends a clear message of inferiority about tribal law enforcement and tribal courts, that is, that tribes cannot handle felonies. And it robs the tribal community of leadership in one of the most important areas of governance: maintenance of public safety and criminal justice. In some respects, the system can create a vacuum of tribal leadership on public safety issues that can exacerbate crime problems by sidelining the people who might be best able to address these serious issues").

176. AMNESTY INT'L, *supra* note 12, at 12 (2006). Moreover, "[i]ndigenous people have the right to maintain and strengthen their distinct political, legal, economic, social and cultural institutions." *Id.* at 21 (citing UN DECLARATION ON THE RIGHTS OF INDIGENOUS PEOPLES art. 5).

177. Passage of TLOA is likely a step in the right direction (although some scholars have criticized TLOA for further enforcing an Anglo legal system on tribes). However, even if tribes come into compliance with the requirements for increased punishment authority articulated under TLOA, tribal court punishment authority is still limited to three years in prison and/or a $15,000 fine. Only time will tell whether this increase in tribal court punishment authority is enough to offset the perception of some criminals that a loophole in effective law enforcement exists within Indian country.

CHAPTER 11

Searching for an Exit:
The Indian Civil Rights Act and Public Law 280

CAROLE GOLDBERG AND DUANE CHAMPAGNE

T he Indian Civil Rights Act of 1968[1] (ICRA) gets most attention as a law protecting individuals—Indian and non-Indian—from unfair treatment by tribal governments. What this emphasis on rights against tribes overlooks, however, is another major component of ICRA—a section designed to protect Indians against discrimination and abuses by states.[2] In a law widely known as Public Law 280,[3] passed in 1953, Congress gave six states considerable civil and criminal jurisdiction on reservations, lifting a ban on state jurisdiction derived from the Constitution, federal statutes and treaties, and the very establishment of the reservations themselves. Under the terms of Public Law 280, tribal consent was neither required nor sought. Furthermore, all other states were allowed to opt into the same jurisdictional arrangement, also regardless of tribal consent.[4]

From the outset, tribes found Public Law 280 objectionable on numerous grounds.[5] As a matter of principle, the absence of tribal consent was unacceptable. On a more practical level, many tribes complained that their existing mix of tribal and federal law was working effectively, and that they were unprepared for subjection to a set of alien legal norms. But at least as important, tribal leaders in Public Law 280 jurisdictions voiced civil rights complaints about states' exercise of their Public Law 280 jurisdiction, including denial of police protection and discrimination or abuse by state law enforcement and criminal justice systems; and tribes potentially subject to Public Law 280 without their consent expressed fear that the mistreatment they were receiving from state officials in nearby off-reservation communities would spill onto their reservations.

Beginning in the early 1960s, as Congress held hearings on the Indian Civil Rights Act, Indian complaints about Public Law 280 attracted wide attention.[6] Congress eventually responded with provisions in ICRA, preventing future assertions of state jurisdiction without Indian consent, and allowing states to return (or retrocede) their Public Law 280 jurisdiction back to the federal government.[7] Notably, no tribe has consented to the extension of state jurisdiction under Public Law 280 since ICRA introduced this requirement. A striking gap in the congressional response, however, is the absence of any provision allowing tribes to initiate the retrocession process. The states were allowed to relieve themselves of unwanted responsibilities for Indian country;[8] but the existing Public Law 280 tribes got no relief from their concerns. All of the tribes subjected to Public Law 280 before ICRA remained in its thrall unless they could persuade their respective states to give up their power. Congress made a limited inroad into this situation ten years later, through the Indian Child Welfare Act of 1978, which allowed Public Law 280 tribes to "reassume" jurisdiction over child dependency and adoption matters whether their states agreed or not.[9]

Political and social theory concerned with "good governance" view the accountability of government agencies to their citizens as a key determinant of success, and the option to "exit" from control by particular government institutions as a valuable source of accountability.[10] This theory strongly suggests that the possibility of tribes consenting to state jurisdiction would be a valuable tool for ensuring the effectiveness of federal and tribal criminal justice in Indian country. Consent to state jurisdiction would represent a form of exit from the federal system. Likewise, tribally initiated retrocession, a form of exit from state authority, would be a valuable tool for ensuring the effectiveness of state jurisdiction under Public Law 280, as well as for preventing civil rights and other violations by state officials. Thus, the absence of tribally initiated retrocession represented a departure in ICRA from generally accepted principles of good governance.

This chapter revisits Indian charges of civil rights violations by state law enforcement and judicial systems, and examines why, in light of them, ICRA did not give tribes the power to initiate the retrocession process. We also compare those civil rights charges with the findings of our recent, national empirical study of law enforcement and criminal justice under Public Law 280. As this study demonstrates, in the absence of tribal authority to wrest jurisdiction away from the states, many of the same old civil rights complaints remain unaddressed. Although some tribes have been able to establish cooperative, cogovernance arrangements with state and local governments,[11] many tribes have not. In sum, while critics of tribal sovereignty focus on the failure of ICRA to protect individuals from tribal overreaching, state civil rights violations have gone unaddressed because of the wide latitude afforded Public Law 280 states. Only a further amendment to Public Law 280, similar to the provision already in place under the Indian Child Welfare Act, can correct this serious omission in ICRA.

STATE CIVIL RIGHTS VIOLATIONS AND THE INDIAN CIVIL RIGHTS ACT

President Eisenhower had doubts about Public Law 280, even as he signed the bill. Echoing others who had protested its passage, he questioned the absence of a tribal consent provision, and urged that one be inserted through later amendment.[12] Congress did nothing immediately, even as complaints mounted from the affected tribes, the

National Congress of American Indians (NCAI), and sympathetic organizations such as the Association on American Indian Affairs. Then, beginning in 1961, Senator Sam J. Ervin, chairman of the Subcommittee on Constitutional Rights of the Committee on the Judiciary, opened hearings, first as a general investigation of "The Constitutional Rights of the American Indian," and later to elicit comments on specific bills that emerged from the investigative findings. Among the provisions included in the bills were several amendments to Public Law 280, including provisions requiring Indian consent for new assertions of state jurisdiction and allowing state-initiated retrocession. Eventually the House Committee on Interior and Insular Affairs conducted its own hearings on similar measures.

Discrimination by states against Indians and tribal communities—through biased or abusive treatment and failure to provide law enforcement and justice services—was a key justification for the Indian consent provision. In May 1968, Harry Anderson, then assistant secretary of the Interior, wrote to the chairman of the House Committee on Interior and Insular Affairs that a new requirement of Indian consent to state jurisdiction

> is highly desirable. Our files are replete with resolutions and communications from many Indian groups urging this change. The change would do much to allay the fears, whether real or imagined, of the Indian people that they may be subjected to strange courts before they are ready, or before they are assured of fair and impartial treatment.[13]

Anderson's skeptical account of the Indians' concerns—describing them as "real or imagined"—flies in the face of repeated testimony to Congress over a period of seven years. The civil rights concerns can be divided into three broad categories: (1) complaints from Public Law 280 tribes that they were not receiving adequate or equal law enforcement services from state and local agencies (Type 1 Complaints); (2) complaints from Public Law 280 tribes that state and local officials handling on-reservation matters were actively treating Indians in a discriminatory or abusive fashion (Type 2 Complaints); and (3) complaints from non-Public Law 280 tribes about mistreatment by state and local officials in nearby off-reservation communities (Type 3 Complaints).

Type 1 Complaints: Inadequate and Discriminatory Provision Of Law Enforcement Services Under Public Law 280

Type 1 Complaints of inadequate provision of state law enforcement services clearly made an impression on the Senate subcommittee. In his opening comments at the 1965 hearings, Senator Ervin described what the subcommittee's investigations over the previous four years had revealed about Public Law 280. According to Ervin, "Public Law 280 . . . was found by the subcommittee's investigation to have resulted in a breakdown in the administration of justice to such a degree that Indians are being denied due process and equal protection of the law."[14]

An array of witnesses from Public Law 280 tribes hammered the point that they were not getting a proper level of service, or service comparable to that provided non-Indian communities. The testimony of Edward Cline, counselor and member of the Omaha Tribe of Nebraska, one of the mandatory Public Law 280 states, emphasized that the state was refusing to prosecute outsiders who engaged in theft of tribal resources, and that "often the State does not adequately service the tribal area because it does not contribute substantially to the State's treasury."[15] James Jackson, chairman of the Quinault Tribe of Washington, a state that had opted into Public Law 280 through a complex scheme, protested,

> During the period between 1958–64, the State exercised total jurisdiction over the Quinault Reservation. However, the State never did provide adequate law enforcement. There were no regular police patrols, and in fact the sheriff would not come on the reservation unless an Indian would drive to Ocean City, 25 miles away, and swear out a complaint. This amounted to no law and order at all for the everyday type of misdemeanor, which is 95 percent of what law and order means to a community.[16]

Senator Ervin observed, "The result of it is that, as you see it, the act of the State of Washington in assuming jurisdiction has in effect deprived the tribe of police protection which the tribe itself would have afforded had it had jurisdiction."[17] Chairman Jackson concurred. Eagle Seelatsee, chairman of the Confederated Bands and Tribes of the Yakima Indian Nation, another tribe in Washington state, echoed Jackson's concern, asserting, "The State will not provide funds for proper and adequate law and order enforcement."[18] Robert B. Jim, a member of the Yakima Tribal Council joined in, putting the complaint in constitutional terms: "We are appealing to you today because we feel that the Yakima Tribe has been deprived of due process of law."[19] To underscore his point about inadequate service, Yakima Chairman Seelatsee quoted a statement by Congressmember Arnold Olsen of Montana regarding the situation on the Omaha Reservation, mentioned above: "The counties in which the Omaha Reservation is located refused to assume this jurisdiction. The Federal Government and Omaha Tribe were deprived of jurisdiction by the act. A lawless area was created by act of Congress. Murdered men have, laid in the street within the Omaha Reservation for over 24 hours before police have investigated the crime."[20]

During the subcommittee's earlier hearings, Chief Counsel William A. Creech had posed questions about the adequacy of law enforcement under Public Law 280 to Philleo Nash, then commissioner-designate of Indian Affairs in the Department of the Interior, and a member of the Indian Task Force that the secretary had established in 1961 to investigate areas where policy changes were needed. According to Nash, this task force had interviewed spokespeople from two hundred tribal groups, federal and state government officials, and representatives of religious, educational, scientific, and public service organizations interested in Indian affairs.[21] Creech pointed out that this task force, as well as a separate study published by the Fund for the Republic, had "indicated that the administration is not adequate in certain States," especially Nebraska (a mandatory Public Law 280 state) and South Dakota (a state that had opted in solely for offenses occurring on highways within the state). Nash responded that the situation in Nebraska was especially egregious because the Omaha Tribe had been paying property taxes to the state under a federal statute, but the county still refused to assume financial responsibility for law enforcement after passage of Public Law 280. In 1961, the state finally passed a law to provide funding to the county, "but there was a long period in which there was very inferior law-and-order protection," and Nash wasn't even sure that the state funds had solved the problem.[22] Testimony of William A. Zimmerman, Jr., also a member of the Secretary's Task Force on Indian Affairs, and himself a former acting director of the BIA, went even further. Zimmerman observed, "We have had indications in some areas that the assumption of jurisdiction by the States and the local governmental units has not been entirely satisfactory. We have heard testimony from Indians in California, in Nevada, Washington, Minnesota, indicating that there is still a gap between effective enforcement by the State and the county and the prior administration by Federal officers."[23] Helen Peterson, executive director of NCAI, summarized the Nebraska problem:

> When Congress, under Public Law 280, transferred jurisdiction to Nebraska that State was obviously unable or unwilling to accept its new responsibility. The Omaha and Winnebago tribes were without law enforcement for almost 8 years. Recently, we are informed, those Indian citizens and their non-Indian neighbors, with professional help, including research, from the University of Nebraska have finally gotten the State to assume this responsibility. The denial to these people of protection of the law for some 8 years, the energies expended to get for themselves what other citizens take for granted, the time, travel and other resources spent on this that should have gone into more constructive development programs are shameful to contemplate, particularly in view of the fact that the lands of the Omahas and Winnebagos have been taxed all along, that these two small tribes constitute a very small fraction of the State's total population and it can hardly be claimed that this is a case where the State can't afford to furnish the protection of the law.[24]

Nebraska was not the only state singled out for Type 1 Complaints, however. In the subcommittee's field hearings in California, held in 1961, testimony from a variety of tribal leaders charged that law enforcement services were not up to the level found off reservation, and were certainly inadequate to meet community needs. When Senator John A. Carroll of Colorado tried to ignore testimony to this effect from leaders of the Morongo Band of Mission Indians, Chief Counsel Creech interjected,

> What the witness is saying that under Public Law 280 the county assumes jurisdiction for law and order enforcement in the area. The

witness does not feel that Indians are receiving it and the lack of police protection is perhaps a deprivation of constitutional rights. Under the 14th amendment, he and the other Indians living in the community are entitled to equal protection under the law and that they are not receiving the same amount that the other people are who reside in the rural communities.[25]

One of the witnesses from Morongo, Roy Waite, then chimed in that this problem "happens to almost all the reservations; almost all of them are in the same predicament as ours."[26] Senator Carroll tried to argue that the problem of inadequate patrolling at night arises in cities as well, but Waite held his ground, replying, "It is not as bad."[27] Max Mazzetti, of the Rincon Tribal Council in San Diego County, California, offered the graphic account of local government inattention to reservation needs:

> There were a few Indians who became intoxicated one evening, and the superintendent of the forests called to say that if we didn't get the sheriff up there that someone might be killed. So, someone called the sheriff down in San Diego, but they didn't come out; so they called again about 10:30 p.m. and said it was very serious and that they should be there right away. However, the sheriff didn't come until the next morning when I was going to work. One particular man came to my house and told my wife about 6:30 in the morning that one Indian girl was killed and another seriously bleeding to death. This was approximately at 6:30 in the morning, and at 9:30 an ambulance came out and took them to the county hospital. . . . My wife asked them why they didn't come out right away, and they said that they thought it was just another Indian party.[28]

Senator Carroll then suggested that the tribe approach the county sheriff and ask for several of its tribal members to be deputized to conduct patrols, presumably at tribal expense. A former attorney for the tribe, now sitting as a California Superior Court judge, objected, because that would be off-loading the sheriff's responsibilities onto the tribe. That would be unfair, Judge Lindsley noted, because the tribes are no more costly to patrol than other parts of the county that were receiving adequate services. According to Judge Lindsley, "[T]he reservations are not isolated from the areas of the county and there are people who live all around the area and are not on the reservations who have the services of the sheriff's office without the necessity of being locally deputized. . . . Why should the Indian on the reservation have to undertake to do that for themselves when the other citizens surrounding them are not called upon to do it?"[29] Robert Lovato of the Pala Band of Mission Indians, another San Diego County tribe, pointed out that the tribe's central location meant that it had to manage a large number of tourists, but because of infrequent patrolling by the sheriff's department, "we are handicapped because we don't have the policing we should have. . . . [W]e have patrolling that is all supposed to be under Public Law 280 and we think we should have the same rights as anybody else."[30] According to Lovato, "They don't come out unless somebody is in trouble," and that "takes them 2 or 3 hours."[31] Edwin Jackson, a member of the Business Committee of the Quechan Tribe of Arizona (non–Public Law 280) and California, likewise complained of inadequate patrolling and long delayed responses to calls for service.[32] The county was claiming that its jurisdiction was uncertain because the tribal land remained in trust, and meetings that the tribe arranged with county and state officials produced no real help. Asked to compare the service the tribe got with service to surrounding non–Indian areas, Jackson at first seemed hesitant to accuse the county of discriminatory treatment, and then stated the tribal service was "on a more lax basis, let's put it that way."[33]

Type 1 Complaints directed at South Dakota, which asserted jurisdiction over reservation highways, were mounted during the subcommittee's field hearing in that state. The state prosecutor responsible for Shannon County, site of the Pine Ridge Reservation, viewed the state law as invalid under Public Law 280, because it took jurisdiction only over one geographic part of the reservation. The federal government, on the other hand, saw the law as valid under Public Law 280, and refused to take responsibility for those highways. Gerald Reade, assistant attorney general for South Dakota, admitted that "there is not proper law enforcement . . . there is very little, if any, law enforcement at all on those highways."[34] Several witnesses, including William Whirlwind Horse, chairman of the Oglala Sioux Tribe, told the poignant story of three elderly women, tribal members, who went to the BIA and the local county police for protection after some teenagers and their father threatened them at an off-reservation site. The elders were fearful of being waylaid on their way home to the reservation. Both sets of authorities denied they had jurisdiction on the reservation roadways. The Oglala chairman added, "We, the Sioux Indians of South Dakota, recognized in our United States as citizens, feel very strongly that we are being denied equal rights because of the present jurisdiction question. We feel that a State, although they passed this law, has no intention of giving us law and order."[35] John B. Richards, member of the Oglala Sioux Tribe and chief judge of the Oglala Sioux Tribal Court, testified that once the South Dakota attorney general decided that the law should be enforced, the Shannon County prosecutor had instructed police "to pick up the drunken drivers only, and not to bother the minor offenders in the car that the driver was arrested from. These passengers are left free to continue to menace the public. The State refuses to take those offenders and the tribe cannot, due to lack of jurisdiction on the highways. The Indians again become the victims of discriminatory law."[36]

Hearings on similar legislation in the House Committee on Interior and Insular Affairs, held in 1968, yielded similar findings. A questionnaire that the Committee directed to the BIA asked whether any state that has assumed criminal jurisdiction under Public Law 280 has failed to provide law enforcement services comparable to those formerly furnished by the BIA and the tribe. The response from the Bureau acknowledged there was a problem:"Shortly after Public Law 280 became effective in 1953, a number of allegations were made by Indian leaders that law enforcement services by the States and local subdivisions were inadequate to the reservations' needs. We know that transfer of jurisdiction by Public Law 280 created additional financial burdens that local subdivisions were hard pressed to assume." Nebraska, Wisconsin, California, and Minnesota were all cited as mandatory Public Law 280 states, in which Indians have "complained then and have continued to complain of inadequate services."[37] Alaska, another mandatory Public Law 280 state, was also the object of Type 1 Complaints during the House hearings. The House committee received a letter from Henry S. Littlefield, Sr., council member from the Annette Islands Reserve in Alaska, pointing out that since Alaska became a Public Law 280 state in 1958, they have had to fly in a state trooper from Ketchikan, which is sixteen miles away by water, and sometimes also a magistrate. As Littlefield explained,

> They cannot answer our call sometimes because they have other areas to cover. Sometimes weather does not permit them to come in even when they are drastically needed. This way a lot of things lag. Witnesses sometimes don't show up or change their minds about a given case after some time has elapsed. . . . Misdemeanor—breaking windows, marking up posters, stealing bicycles, ignoring curfew, break-ins and pilfering, shoplifting, and the like has been hard to curtail and more or less rampant since Public Law 280. The State Police and Magistrate at Ketchikan do not want to, or do not have time for these cases.[38]

Summarizing the views expressed in the investigative hearings on Public Law 280, the Senate Subcommittee on Constitutional Rights pronounced, "after unilateral transfer of jurisdiction from Federal to State courts, the already overburdened law enforcement officials were given the added responsibility of patrolling and policing the Indian communities. The lax enforcement resulting from this has given rise to Indian allegations of denial of equal protection of the laws."[39] Whereas one BIA official testified that "services furnished by States under Public Law 280 have been adequate, and above and beyond what they [the Indians] had prior to Public Law 280,"[40] a member of the Secretary's Indian Task Force, William Zimmerman, contradicted that claim.[41] In other words, even the secretary of the Interior's fact-finding supported tribes' Type 1 Complaints of civil rights violations by states, strongly suggesting that those complaints should be credited.

Type 2 Complaints: Discrimination and Abuse Under Public Law 280

Type 2 Complaints—of discriminatory or abusive treatment by police and courts in Public Law 280 jurisdictions—also made an impact in the hearings leading up to the Indian Civil Rights Act. Omaha Tribe Counselor Edward Cline offered several examples.

We have knowledge of our tribal members who have been held in jail without charges against them in excess of the legal time limit, and so forth. I know in our county when an Indian goes to jail there for plain disorderly conduct, or some other misdemeanor, he is held in jail; say if he goes to jail on a Tuesday night, he is held there until the following Tuesday night or without the proper legal procedures for setting up bail, and so forth.[42]

In California, representatives of the Morongo Band of Mission Indians pointed out that the local county was trying to enforce building codes against tribal housing when non-Indians were allowed to violate the very same code provisions.[43] Edwin Jackson, representing the Quechan Tribe, straddling California and Arizona, complained that in an island in the middle of the Colorado River, where the two states contested jurisdiction, prosecutors in Imperial County, California went after Indians who committed crimes there, but did not bring charges against non-Indians.[44]

Type 2 Complaints also surfaced in South Dakota, where the state took jurisdiction over offenses occurring on state highways going through reservations. Robert Burnette, a Rosebud Sioux tribal member and executive director of the National Congress of American Indians asserted flatly, "[P]ractically every resolution on record in the Washington office of the National Congress of American Indians indicated, in 1953, that Public Law 280 would cause discrimination against the Indians, and I think it definitely has." Pointing to a newspaper article regarding the methods state police used to patrol reservation highways, he observed, "the system they use to charge Indians and sentence them. You can see the difference in sentencing of Indians and non-Indians within this one paper."[45] John B. Richards, member of the Oglala Sioux Tribe and chief judge of the Oglala Sioux Tribal Court, likewise asserted that the state law asserting jurisdiction over reservation highways "is discriminating against the Indians of South Dakota," largely because of selective underenforcement of the law on reservation roads.[46]

John L. Baker, minority counsel for the Senate subcommittee in 1965, asked Vine Deloria, Jr., executive director of NCAI, whether it would be advisable to call in more witnesses from tribes already subject to Public Law 280. Though he agreed it would be useful, Deloria cautioned Baker about the difficulty of eliciting such testimony. Deloria pointed out,

But, you see, even in many cases if you would have a tribe who has been under Public Law 280 for about 10 years, the people did not understand the law when it was passed. They do not understand what they have been going through for 10 years, and most of them would be scared to death to talk to you to tell you really their experiences under it, you see. So there is a big problem there.[47]

Thus, the Senate was aware that there might well be many more Type 1 and Type 2 Complaints from Public Law 280 tribes that they weren't hearing.

Type 3 Complaints: Off-Reservation Discrimination and Abuse

Type 3 Complaints of off-reservation discrimination and abuse by state officials appear throughout the hearings leading up to ICRA. Representatives of many of the non-Public Law 280 tribes, testifying in support of a tribal consent amendment to the statute, cited off-reservation conduct by state officials as their reason for resisting state jurisdiction. As Assistant Secretary of the Interior John A. Carver indicated in his testimony before the Senate subcommittee in 1961, Indian groups "vigorously resisted" the extension of state jurisdiction to their reservations under the opt-in provisions of Public Law 280 because they are "fearful of hostile local and State attitudes [and] discrimination."[48] Arthur J. Lazarus, general counsel for the Association on American Indian Affairs, made the same point:

> [T]ribal leaders protest that off the reservation Indians frequently are the victims of police brutality and that in the local courts their fellow tribesmen are not advised of their rights, are meted out unusually long sentences and are otherwise given more onerous, punishments than non–Indians, including substantial fines if funds for payment are known to be available. Just to make the picture more bleak, the complaint also is registered that non–Indians accused of crimes against Indians are let off without punishment or with only light punishment, and that no real effort is made even to apprehend them. With this background of past and present violations of their constitution rights . . . small wonder that the vast majority of Indians fear and oppose the unilateral extension of State jurisdiction on Indian reservations.[49]

The following examples, many of them from South Dakota, do not exhaust all the stories presented at the hearings. Alfreda Janis, an Oglala Sioux tribal member representing the Association on American Indian Affairs, provided a letter from the director of the Oglala Sioux Civil Liberties Committee to the local BIA area director, describing how off-reservation Indians have been unable to afford lawyers to represent them in state court, and explaining that the state has not provided them with free counsel. The letter concluded: "State law enforcement—the Pine Ridge people will not soften their attitude toward it as long as they cannot afford or find lawyers to represent them in off-reservation communities."[50] Robert Burnette, a Rosebud Sioux tribal member and executive director of NCAI, told several stories of arrests of Indians by off-reservation county police in South Dakota in which Indians were provided no explanation of their constitutional rights, and charges were eventually dropped because there were no witnesses. Burnette asserted that there may be a time when Indian people request state jurisdiction, but he did not "think that time will arrive unless and until the State courts show that they do not have any prejudice or discrimination against the Indian."[51] John B. Richards, chief judge of the Oglala Sioux Tribal Court, described several incidents of severe police brutality against tribal members by police in Martin, South Dakota, including unwarranted tear gassing, smashing a tribal member's fingers while closing a jail cell door, and pulling individuals by their hair and throat. According to Richards, the records in Martin and other towns neighboring the Pine Ridge Reservation, including Rapid City, "will reflect two systems of justice: one system for Indians; one of non-Indians. Comparing the sentences imposed between the Indian and non-Indian, published in our local newspaper, will substantiate this allegation."[52] Robert Philbrick, chairman of the Crow Creek Sioux Tribe, testified that he overheard a police commissioner in the city of Chamberlain, South Dakota tell his officers, "Well, I think the boys are going to have to get some more Indians in jail, because we need quite a lot of snow moved over there on the north side of town."[53] The city was apparently relying on Indian prisoners to get municipal work done. Philbrick also recounted an incident of police abuse, in which one young man had been hit over the head with a blackjack, without justification, and had become partially paralyzed.[54]

South Dakota was not the only state singled out for complaints. Theodore Jamerson, secretary for the Judicial Committee at the Standing Rock Sioux Tribe in North Dakota, reported that cases with Indian victims result in unusually light sentences. He also complained of police brutality directed at Indians, recounting the case of one young Indian man who was wrongfully chased and shot by the police and paralyzed for life.[55] R. Max Whittier, general counsel to the Shoshone-Bannock Tribes in Idaho, charged that "Indian constitutional rights are not being recognized in a good many instances in their treatment by State and local civil authorities and courts. . . . Many complaints were made by the Indians concerning their treatment, but no action was taken to cure the abuses."[56] He explained that when a tribal member successfully challenged the state's longtime exercise of jurisdiction on the reservation, jurisdiction that had not invoked the authority of Public Law 280, a backlash occurred in nearby non-Indian towns.

> Immediately certain State and municipal authorities started a newspaper campaign against the Indians, slandering their names and advising the public that Indians had no law enforcement. Groups were organized to openly oppose the tribal organization and promises were made by these State and county officials that Indians would be prosecuted vigorously if they were found in certain areas of the city of Pocatello and suspected of violating the law. Indians alone were singled out for this attack, although citizens of many races abound in this area. This act on the part of these groups has caused the decent law-abiding Indians to be subject to ridicule and contempt on a racial basis.[57]

Whittier also presented a list of 78 fatalities involving Indian victims on or near the reservation, none of which had been prosecuted, and another list of five Indians who were prosecuted for the deaths of non-Indians.[58] Finally, he told the story of a young Indian man who was picked up by county police after drinking a poisonous substance, and taken to jail rather than to the hospital. The young man died in jail. According to Whittier, the non-Indian authorities "justify the acts that at any time an Indian is picked up, they throw him in jail first, and then if they decide he is sick, they put him in the hospital, rather than doing what they should do by taking him to the hospital first."[59] William Wall, tribal council member of the Crow Tribe in Montana, testified that police harass any Indians who are drinking in Billings, angering them and prompting arguments and arrest. Wall asserted that Indian drinkers are arrested far more often than the more numerous non-Indians on skid row. In one case, an Indian who was "dead drunk" was picked up by the Billings police, put in a police car, and then found dead at the outskirts of the city the next day. Another Indian, arrested by police in Hardin, Montana, was left at the city limits bordering the reservation, rather than taken to jail. With the weather below zero, the Indian tried to walk to the first Indian home he could find, which was five miles away. By that time, he had lost all his fingers to frostbite, and they had to be amputated.[60] Cummins implored, "We again direct your special attention to this unfair treatment. . . ."[61]

THE ORIGINS OF RETROCESSION IN THE INDIAN CIVIL RIGHTS ACT

These three types of tribal complaints gave Congress strong reason to support a requirement of Indian consent before states could exercise Public Law 280 jurisdiction, augmenting more principled concerns about "consent of the governed." But Congress did not follow the concept of Indian consent through to its full logical implications. If state officials were sometimes discriminating against Indians or engaging in abusive conduct, then not only should tribes be able to block future state jurisdiction under Public Law 280, but they should also be able to undo state jurisdiction that arose under Public Law 280 before any tribal consent requirement existed. In other words, the logic of tribal consent dictated that Congress should allow tribes already subject to state jurisdiction under Public Law 280 to petition the secretary of the Interior for its removal, enabling them to reestablish exclusive jurisdiction over non-major crimes committed by Indians against other Indians.

Congress, of course, did no such thing in ICRA. It merely authorized states to rid themselves of their Public Law 280 jurisdiction if the federal government was willing to accept it back. At no point did any of the precursor bills provide otherwise. Why Congress failed to allow for tribally initiated retrocession is unclear, but there are some clues in the legislative record.

First, at least some tribes sought to promote retrocession at the behest of tribes already ensnared in Public Law 280. At the 1965 Senate subcommittee hearing, Edward Cline, a member and counselor of the Omaha Tribe in Nebraska, stated directly:

We feel that in all instances where tribes are under Public Law 280 if the State fails to adequately serve the tribe, that the tribe, as a matter of right, can then go to the Federal Government for assistance and it would be required to consider the problem. This would eliminate difficulties such as we have experienced where neither the State nor the Federal Government will accept jurisdiction with the result that we have no remedy. ... The second suggestion which we would like to make to the subcommittee is that while we had no option when the Omaha Tribe was placed under the provisions of Public Law 280, we feel strongly that Public Law 280 should be amended to include a "consent clause" which would enable the tribe affected to selectively accept or reject State jurisdiction according to its own needs.[62]

Cline contended that the prospect of tribally initiated retrocession would confer "bargaining leverage" on the tribes, enabling them to negotiate for more effective service from the states. Edmond Jackson, executive business manager and council member of the Quechan Tribe in California, submitted a resolution from his tribal council, which urged an amendment to the pending bill that would provide: "[t]he extent of such jurisdiction, either civil or criminal, shall be as agreed upon from time to time by the State and the tribe concerned, and may be extended or retracted by agreement of both the State and the particular tribe as experience proves practicable and planning may indicate to them advisable."[63] Jackson made his point even more directly when he added, "The Quechan Tribe would like to have a retrocession clause, amendment to S. 966 [the pending bill that addressed Public Law 280] to allow those tribes who are presently affected by Public Law 280. The tribe would like to be given the right to decide and consent to any legislation affecting American Indians. They were not given that right when Public Law 280 was passed."[64] Representing Hopland Rancheria, also in California, Chairman George Feliz insisted, "I feel it would be more just to the Indian people of a certain reservation if they would decide for themselves if they would want the State government to have governing power over their criminal actions or civil problems. I cannot imagine all of these Indians being so ill educated for not being able to decide for themselves."[65] Representatives of the Yakima Tribe concurred: "[P]rovision should be further made [in the proposed legislation] that tribes now within State jurisdiction, without their consent, should be allowed to withdraw by petition to the Governor."[66] Senator Ervin wanted to make sure he understood the Yakimas' position, and interjected, "You ask for the passage of a law which would give tribes the privilege of withdrawing from State jurisdiction when they have been made subject to State jurisdiction without their consent."[67] Robert Jim of the Yakima delegation confirmed that they meant exactly that. Frank George, secretary of the Washington State Indian Council, likewise insisted that a requirement of tribal consent "should be [imposed] in all cases, even in cases where tribes have been put under State jurisdiction without their consent."[68]

A few non–Public Law 280 tribes came out in favor of tribally initiated retrocession, but they were a distinct minority. Domingo Montoya, chairman of the All-Pueblo Council of New Mexico, a non–Public Law 280 state, criticized the bill that the Senate subcommittee addressed in its 1965 hearings, arguing that "in relation to the retrocession provision . . . the All-Pueblo Council believes that retrocession should be available upon the request of the particular tribe involved as well as by unilateral action of the States."[69] Similarly, the governor of Santa Clara Pueblo, also in New Mexico, protested during the 1968 hearings in the House that "there is no provision made for the retrocession of jurisdiction back to its true owner."[70]

Second, the national Indian organizations were not promoting the idea of retrocession at the behest of existing Public Law 280 tribes. They seemed far more concerned about the tribes that had not yet come under Public Law 280—tribes afraid that their states would opt in over their objections. During the 1961 Senate subcommittee hearings, Arthur Lazarus, Jr., counsel for the Association on American Indian Affairs, emphasized that "tribes throughout the country have concentrated their efforts on opposing the extension of State jurisdiction and on seeking the repeal of Public Law 280."[71] The limited scope of that agenda became clearer as Lazarus testified at the subcommittee's subsequent round of hearings four years later. Speaking in support of the consent requirement in the proposed legislation, Lazarus stated that the main purpose of the legislation "is to repeal Public Law 280 of the 83rd Congress—probably the most objectionable general legislation affecting Indians passed in the 20th century." In the next breath, however, he reassured the subcommittee that the legislation "would not change the status quo in any State which already had taken over jurisdiction on Indian reservations pursuant to Public Law 280," and that the states (but not the tribes) could decide if they had made a mistake in taking jurisdiction.[72] In other words, the proposed legislation would not fully "repeal" Public Law 280—it would only repeal the parts relating to states' opt-in jurisdiction.

Many representatives of non–Public Law 280 tribes proceeded to focus their efforts at amending the opt-in portion of Public Law 280 only. Attorney Marvin Sonosky, representing several different tribes, acknowledged that the legislative proposals requiring tribal consent under Public Law 280 would apply only "to those tribes where State jurisdiction has not already been lawfully extended." But, he asserted, "[t]he most objectionable provisions of Public Law 280 are those contained in sections 6 and 7 [the opt-in provisions]. These provisions were inserted in committee without an opportunity for the tribes affected by those sections to be heard."[73] Sonosky failed to mention that consent had not been obtained from the tribes in the six "mandatory" states either, and that several tribes had already been subjected to state jurisdiction without their consent through the opt-in part of Public Law 280. Other non–Public Law 280 tribes made the mistake of equating repeal of that opt-in portion with repeal of the entire law.[74] The exception was Wendell Chino, president of the Mescalero Apache Tribal Council, a non–Public Law 280 tribe, who made it clear that he favored a prospective tribal consent requirement, but also asserted that "[t]he complete repeal of Public Law 280 is not recommended." In contrast, when Public Law 280 tribes spoke of repealing Public Law

280, they meant undoing all of the state jurisdiction that had already been imposed upon them, at their own option.[75]

The National Congress of American Indians did not provide clear support for retrocession at the initiative of the previously nonconsenting Public Law 280 tribes. In its 1958 resolution on the subject, for example, NCAI resolved only that the opt-in portions of Public Law 280 be amended.[76] One year later, NCAI passed another resolution that went a bit further in the direction of tribally initiated retrocession, but not all the way. It advocated amendment of Public Law 280 "to provide that the assumption by States of jurisdiction in criminal and civil actions in Indian reservations be brought about only after negotiation between a State and an Indian tribe, and only to the extent, from time to time, agreed upon by the Indian tribe. . . . "[77] Helen Peterson, the NCAI executive director who testified before the Senate subcommittee in 1961, explained that NCAI's proposal would "permit the undoing of specific transfers, again provided that the tribe and the State agree this should be done."[78] By requiring state as well as tribal acquiescence, however, the NCAI position denied existing Public Law 280 tribes any control over the retrocession process. Eventually, NCAI directed its full support to the section of ICRA that addressed Public Law 280, even though it lacked a provision for undoing existing Public Law 280 jurisdiction at the tribes' behest.[79]

Third, resistance from the Bureau of Indian Affairs may also have prevented tribally initiated retrocession from achieving any legislative momentum. As discussed above, the BIA tried to convince Congress that Public Law 280 was working well in the six mandatory states.[80] Although William Zimmerman of the Secretary's Indian Task Force contradicted that statement, and the Senate subcommittee apparently concurred with Zimmerman's characterization, the BIA's position may have made denial of tribally initiated retrocession more comfortable. During the Senate subcommittee's 1965 hearings, Minority Counsel John L. Baker observed that in some areas, Public Law 280 had been working "quite well and in other areas it has been, I think at best, a miserable failure." He then asked Frank Barry, solicitor for the Department of the Interior, "Would it be an appropriate step, do you think, to allow those tribal areas now under Public Law 280 to elect either to remain under 280 or to fall under the provisions of S. 966 or a similar bill?"[81] Barry demurred, but Philleo Nash, commissioner of Indian Affairs, jumped in with a response:

> Well, you would have a very serious practical problem. In those States, in the Public Law 280 States, there are no secretarial courts and there are no tribal courts. . . . So if you were to bring them retroactively—I do not know if that is the right word—under this proposed law, you would have to reconstitute tribal courts. I do not know of any desire in Minnesota outside of the Red Lake Reservation to have this done. There are some problems as between the people of Minnesota in those tribes and the State of Minnesota with respect, let us say, to wild rice regulations. But that is not of the order that we are talking about.[82]

Three years later the House Interior and Insular Affairs Committee was holding its own hearings on constitutional rights of American Indians, and posed a question to the Assistant Secretary of the Interior Harry R. Anderson: "Do any tribes now subject to state jurisdiction want to terminate the jurisdiction?" Anderson's reply downplayed the need for attention to this problem:

> We know that the Quinault Tribe, one of the 13 in Washington that had originally requested the state to assume jurisdiction, has requested termination of the state's jurisdiction. We have had no formal expression of a desire by any other tribe to terminate state jurisdiction. Informal discussions from time to time with tribal leaders and individual Indians indicate some dissatisfaction with state jurisdiction.[83]

Fourth, some members of Congress themselves presented opposition to undoing states' Public Law 280 jurisdiction. Most notable were the statements of Senator John A. Carroll, Democrat of Colorado, a member of the Senate subcommittee who presided over its 1961 investigative field hearing in California. When a representative of the Morongo Band of Mission Indians asked whether it would be possible to return to the system of federal law enforcement that existed before Public Law 280, Carroll resisted: "I think that while this would help you ... it would also deny you some rights that you get. If you were to balance it, off, in my judgment, I believe that you are better off under Public Law 280 because under this if you are either on or off the reservations you are citizens like other people in the State of California, except for the fact that you apparently are not getting proper police protection; that is, adequate police protection."[84] Although the Morongo representatives stood their ground, insisting that they were state citizens even before Public Law 280, Carroll was unmoved. Moreover, Senator Carroll seemed to be under the misimpression that Congress was helpless to remedy the problem of Public Law 280 tribes receiving poor service from local policing authorities. At one point he told the representatives from Morongo: "If the county and State do not assume their responsibilities, I do not know of a single thing that the Federal Government can do about it. This is a point that I want to bring to you, and if I am wrong on this, I would like to be informed about it."[85] Unfortunately, no one corrected him on this point, because it was untrue. As Congress had demonstrated in its enactment of the Indian Child Welfare Act, the federal government has plenary authority to grant or to retract state jurisdiction if state officials are not properly carrying out their responsibilities.[86]

In the end, the official reports and floor debates on Public Law 280 offer no real insight into why Congress ignored the evidence of state civil rights violations and denied Public Law 280 tribes the initiative to undo state jurisdiction. A combination of tepid support from national Indian organizations, differences in the priorities of Public Law 280 and non-280 tribes, and resistance from the BIA and certain members of Congress can help us understand what happened. But neither the Senate nor the House bothered to explain itself. Most of the official statements on retrocession consist of rephrasings of the statutory language.[87]

If there was widespread state opposition to tribally initiated retrocession in the Public Law 280 states, it didn't emerge in the congressional hearings. It is possible, of course, that such opposition was operating in the background, making a prospective tribal consent provision the only politically feasible alternative. Or perhaps Congress felt that the tribes already subjected to state jurisdiction under Public Law 280 would be unable to undertake the exercise of criminal jurisdiction following retrocession. But if that were true, why Congress would allow *states* to initiate retrocession remains unclear. Certainly, if tribal incapacity were the real concern, Congress could have done what it did ten years later in the Indian Child Welfare Act—provided for Interior Department approval of any tribal reassumption of jurisdiction and mandatory technical assistance to tribes.[88]

CONTINUED CONCERNS ABOUT STATE JURISDICTION UNDER PUBLIC LAW 280

The full report of our Public Law 280 research is available online.[89] A summary of the research methods and a sampling of the results appear in an article in the *University of Connecticut Law Review*.[90] In brief, we conducted interviews and administered quantitative surveys at seventeen reservations—ten in mandatory Public Law 280 states, two in optional states, two in states that had retroceded jurisdiction back to the United States, one that had been excluded from Public Law 280 from the outset, two in non–Public Law 280 states, and one that straddled a Public Law 280 and a non–Public Law 280 state. More than 350 individuals were interviewed and surveyed, including reservation residents, law enforcement officials, and criminal justice personnel. Individuals were not chosen randomly, but rather on the basis of their familiarity and affiliation with the criminal justice system. All of the research sites and individual interviews were confidential.

The findings of this study include negative assessments by reservation residents of the fairness and quality of state law enforcement and criminal justice.[91] Several other results from our Public Law 280 research fill out the reasons for reservation residents' dissatisfaction with state jurisdiction. In particular, when asked to assess law enforcement and criminal justice, substantial numbers of reservation residents in Public Law 280 jurisdictions complained about abuse of authority, prejudicial treatment, and discrimination. Just under half complained that police overstep their authority through excessive use of force, arrests without proper warrants, and discrimination against Indian people.[92] Looking at the state criminal courts, more than half say that cases with Indian victims or defendants are not treated the same as other cases in the state system, with two-thirds of those going so far as to say that state and county courts are prejudiced against such Indian cases, especially courts with generally all-white juries.[93] In three out of four measures of fairness—rate of case dispositions, sentencing, and judge and jury responses—most Public Law 280 reservation residents said that they are experiencing unfairness in state court systems. Even Public Law 280 criminal justice workers agreed that judges and juries are responding negatively to Indian cases.[94] Here are some representative statements we obtained from reservation residents in Public Law 280 jurisdictions through our interviews:

> I know that there is a feeling in the community that the court is harder on Indian defendants. That they are not necessarily as fair as they should be, or, if there are two parallel cases, the white person gets off, but the Indian person gets prosecuted. I know that there is a very strong feeling within the community that once things get to that court atmosphere, that things are not equal.[95]

> I probably shouldn't say this, but there have been times I felt that our people have been discriminated against over there. Simply looking at the penalties applied. . . . They are not comparable very often. If you see the court results, it always seems like the poor Indian pays a heavier penalty.[96]

Reservation residents in non-Public Law 280 states view tribal courts as far less likely to treat Indian victims and defendants disadvantageously.[97] Not only do fairness concerns contribute to the problem of legitimacy of state criminal justice in Indian country, but state officials' insensitivity to tribal cultures can also aggravate the problem. Eighty percent of the reservation residents in Public Law 280 jurisdictions indicated that state or county police do not understand tribal cultures.[98] Approximately three-quarters of both the reservation resident and state/county criminal justice personnel respondents in Public Law 280 jurisdictions stated that state court officials do not understand tribal cultures.[99] Among the indicators of cultural insensitivity were disrespectful actions such as disruption of ceremonial activities and disregard for the position of elders.[100]

RETROCESSION: THE RECORD TO DATE

Given these widely held negative views of Public Law 280 in Indian country, has ICRA's provision for retrocession afforded tribes an effective exit? Retrocession reinstates the complex criminal jurisdiction regime that operates in those parts of Indian country that have never been subject to state jurisdiction under Public Law 280. That alternative regime entails exclusive tribal jurisdiction over non-major crimes between Indians and over victimless crimes by Indians; shared federal and tribal jurisdiction over major crimes committed by Indians and over non-major crimes committed by Indians against non-Indians; and a mix of federal and state jurisdiction over offenses by non-Indians.[101] ICRA's provision for retrocession is brief:

> The United States is authorized to accept a retrocession by any State of all or any measure of the criminal or civil jurisdiction or both, acquired by such State pursuant to [Public Law 280].[102]

As discussed above, ICRA provides for state-initiated retrocession, so that tribes seeking retrocession must first lobby and persuade their state governments.[103] Once state approval is secured, the process moves to the Department of the Interior (DOI) for review. No guidelines regulate how DOI should review retrocession petitions, other than a federal executive order specifying that the secretary of the interior shall consult first with the attorney general.[104]

Of the more than 150 tribes under Public Law 280 jurisdiction in the lower forty-eight states, only thirty-one have been the subject of retrocession since 1968, and only seven of those are from the five "mandatory" Public Law 280 states other than Alaska. There have been no retrocessions by the more than 235 tribes and Native villages in Alaska.

Retrocessions in Mandatory Public Law 280 States

Alaska	*None*
California	*None*
Minnesota	Bois Forte [40 FR 4026 (1975)]
Nebraska	Omaha [35 FR 16,598 (1970)]
	(except for motor vehicle offenses)
	Winnebago [51 FR 24,234 (1986)]
	Santee Sioux [71 FR 7994 (2006)]
Oregon	Burns Paiute [44 FR 26,129 (1979)]
	Umatilla [46 FR 2195 (1981)]
Wisconsin	Menominee [41 FR 8516 (1976)]

Retrocessions in Optional PL 280 States

Florida	*None*
Idaho	*None*
Montana	Salish Kootenai [60 FR 123 (1995)]
	(misdemeanors only)
Nevada	Battle Mountain Colony
	Carson Colony
	Dresslerville Colony
	Elko Colony
	Goshute Reservation
	Lovelock Colony
	Odger's Ranch
	Reno-Sparks Colony
	Ruby Valley Allotment
	South Fork Reservation
	Washoe Tribal Farms
	Washoe Pinenut Allotment
	Winnemucca Colony and
	Yomba Reservation [40 FR 27,501 (1975)]
	Ely Indian Colony [53 FR 5837 (1988)]

Retrocessions in Optional PL 280 States

Washington	Quinault [34 FR 14,288 (1969)]
	Port Madison [37 FR 7353 (1972)]
	Colville [52 FR 8372 (1987)]
	Chehalis, Quileute, and Swinomish [54 FR 19,959 (1989)]
	Tulalip [65 FR 75,948 (2000)]

As this list shows, in Nevada, fourteen tribes retroceded in one group and, in Washington, three in one group. So, if we count discrete retrocession campaigns, the number shrinks to sixteen retrocessions. This number is not large, especially given the considerable evidence of tribal dissatisfaction with state jurisdiction, amply documented in our Public Law 280 study.

Using published sources, our research includes five case studies of tribes that successfully navigated the retrocession process and one tribe that was unable to accomplish retrocession despite multiple efforts. From our confidential data, we were also able to analyze the views of reservation residents in two retroceded tribes, as well as the views about retrocession among respondents in the Public Law 280 tribes.[105]

The case studies reveal that tribes were driven to campaign for retrocession by the discriminatory practices—both neglectful and abusive—of state law enforcement and court officials.[106] The most serious obstacle to retrocession in those cases was resistance from local governments, followed by financial considerations. In the one case where retrocession did not go forward, the local sheriff was supportive, but other state and local officials (e.g., the prosecutor) were resistant, largely because they did not trust the tribe to deliver effective law enforcement. Interestingly, even where local governments do not have adequate resources to maintain effective law enforcement and criminal justice services on reservations, they have sometimes attempted to maintain their jurisdiction, often at the behest of non-Indians living on the reservation (who may be receiving more satisfactory services).

The successfully retroceding tribes in our five case studies deployed a variety of strategies to overcome state, local, and federal resistance to retrocession. The most common approach was to address the concerns of local communities, either through careful limitations on the scope of retrocession[107] or through cooperative agreements or contracts allowing county officials to participate in reservation law enforcement. Where local communities were more resistant, tribes turned to public relations campaigns and even, in one case, a boycott of local non-Indian businesses. Increased tribal political and economic power, as a result of gaming and other economic development ventures, has recently improved tribal prospects for securing state support of retrocession.

All of the successful retrocession cases seem to have a high level of tribal satisfaction with the results. Not only has tribal sovereignty been enhanced through more active involvement of tribal government in community affairs, but also law enforcement has been rendered more accountable to the community and is more trusted to address community concerns. Thus, more frequent police patrolling occurs, as does a higher level of community cooperation with law enforcement and criminal justice systems that more closely matches community values. The ultimate consequence has been a drop in crime in several of the case study tribes. In other words, where exit has been possible, government services have improved, as the good governance literature would predict.

Although they are useful in illustrating the common features of successfully retroceding tribes, the case studies do not examine tribes that have chosen not to retrocede or have been unable to do so. It's possible, for example, that the tribes for which retrocession has occurred had unusually bad experiences with Public Law 280 or were unusually well organized. Likewise, it's possible that the states that agreed to retrocession were atypical with respect to financial resources for the exercise of Indian country jurisdiction or other motives for returning jurisdiction to the federal government. Our Public Law 280 research project was designed to provide a systematic examination of retrocession using the comparative method to look at retrocession in a broader context.

Detailed presentation and analysis of the data can be found in the full research report.[108] Worth emphasizing here is that the reservation residents we interviewed from two retroceded tribes largely confirmed the findings from the case studies regarding reasons for seeking retrocession. We identified six themes that emerged from the interviews: poor services, prejudicial treatment, police brutality, sovereignty, high crime, and cultural insensitivity. By far, the most common complaint was prejudicial treatment. This prejudice manifested itself in a continuum of severity that included profiling tribal members, accusations of unfair detention practices, and use of excessive force.

The two tribes that experienced retrocession have been generally satisfied with the results. Retrocession has had a positive impact on crime on reservations through increased police presence, prosecutions, and reporting of crimes; but it also has had broad-ranging benefits to community well-being and has provided a sense of self-determination. For reservation residents, retrocession has imposed new costs and responsibilities relating to the administration of justice. Nonetheless, putting an end to discriminatory and culturally insensitive state criminal justice has been a key advance. As one interviewee explained about the post-retrocession experience:

> I think they have to think through their own vision for what they want as justice for their own tribal people . . . you need key people that see the pain and hurt of the tribe, but also see the vision of healing and working toward a just law system. We're not there yet. . . . That doesn't mean we can't be there, but we're a lot farther away from the devastating models we had in the past. . . . Look toward the point where they will get law enforcement officers, personnel, court personnel systems that are respectful to tribal and cultural mores. That are respectful to human beings. And that can understand and

maintain within diverse culturally traditional patterns. So, move along the steps in that way.[109]

Interviewees from jurisdictions still subject to Public Law 280 indicated whether they were interested in retrocession, and if so, why. A little over a quarter of the reservation residents from these tribes indicated that their tribe had discussed or initiated moves toward retrocession. Funding and infrastructure issues appear to be the main reason why efforts had not advanced further, with concern over the politicization of tribal justice being a minor theme.[110] Significantly, 70 percent of the reservation residents from these same tribes believed that retrocession was a good idea, or would be a good idea if certain conditions were fulfilled—usually augmented resources for law enforcement and criminal justice infrastructure at the tribal level.[111] The most common reason they gave for favoring retrocession is that they would receive better service under the tribal/federal non–Public Law 280 arrangement. Those reservation residents in Public Law 280 jurisdictions who approve of retrocession generally do so for the same reasons that retroceded tribes sought retrocession—to achieve enhanced, less biased service and fuller expression of sovereignty.

CONCLUSION

The various sessions of Congress that considered ICRA had plentiful evidence that state jurisdiction was not functioning properly for many of the Public Law 280 tribes, either because service was being denied, powers were being abused, or both. Had it followed the logical implications of the principle of tribal consent, Congress would have allowed tribes already subject to state jurisdiction to rid themselves of it through retrocession. This form of exit would have also enhanced good governance in Indian country. For a variety of reasons, including lack of support from national organizations and lobbying by the BIA, tribally initiated retrocession never became a part of ICRA.

ICRA failed Indian country by granting states the exclusive power to initiate retrocession. As our research demonstrates, problems of discrimination and abusive practices remain in some Public Law 280 jurisdictions. In 2008, the National Congress of American Indians finally passed a resolution urging Congress to complete the unfinished business of ICRA and to authorize tribes to take the initiative.[112] Though such a measure would impose new obligations on the federal government,[113] the United States can shoulder that burden more effectively than the states; and, unlike the states, the United States stands in a trust relationship to Indian nations. No tribe that is satisfied with state jurisdiction (or concerned about the federal government's attentiveness to its trust responsibilities) should be required to retrocede. Indeed, some Public Law 280 tribes have established stable, successful cooperative arrangements with their state and local governments; however, for those lacking prospects for such solutions, the power to initiate retrocession should be theirs. Any concerns about adequate tribal preparation to assume new law enforcement and criminal justice responsibilities could be allayed through federal financial support and technical assistance. As a back-up, Congress could insert a provision such as the one found in the Indian Child Welfare Act, which requires federal approval and assistance before state jurisdiciton is removed and tribal jurisdiction reinstated.[114] In that way, tribes and states alike could be assured that the removal of state jurisdiction will not result in a dangerous community-safety vacuum—the very problem the Indian Civil Rights Act failed to correct.

NOTES

1.   Pub. L. 90–284, 82 Stat. 77–80 (1968) (codified at 25 U.S.C. §§ 1301–03, 1311–12, 1321–26, 1331, 1341).

2.   *Id.* at Title IV, 82 Stat. 78–79 (codified at 25 U.S.C. §§ 1321–26).

3.   Pub. L. 83–280, 67 Stat. 588-90, (1953) (codified at 18 U.S.C. § 1162, 25 U.S.C. §§ 1321–26, and 28 U.S.C. § 1360).

4.   For a detailed analysis of Public Law 280, see NELL JESSUP NEWTON ET AL., COHEN'S HANDBOOK OF FEDERAL INDIAN LAW § 6.04[3] (2005 ed.) [hereinafter cited as COHEN'S HANDBOOK]; Carole E. Goldberg, *Public Law 280: The Limits of State Jurisdiction over Reservation Indians*, 22 UCLA L. REV. 535 (1975) [hereinafter cited as Goldberg]. Tribal jurisdiction remained concurrent with state jurisdiction, but the Department of the Interior refused to fund law enforcement and justice systems on Public Law 280 reservations. *See* CAROLE GOLDBERG & DUANE CHAMPAGNE, FINAL REPORT: LAW ENFORCEMENT AND CRIMINAL JUSTICE UNDER PUBLIC LAW 280, at ch. 11 (2007), *available at* http://cdn.law.ucla.edu/SiteCollectionDocuments/centers%20and%20programs/native%20nations/pl280%20study.pdf (last visited May 10, 2010) [hereinafter cited as FINAL PUBLIC LAW 280 REPORT].

5.   *See* Goldberg, *supra* note 4, at 544–51.

6.   For example, the Commission on the Rights, Liberties, and Responsibilities of the American Indian recommended amendment of Public Law 280 to include a tribal referendum or consent requirement. COMMISSION ON THE RIGHTS, LIBERTIES, AND RESPONSIBILITIES OF THE AMERICAN INDIAN, A PROGRAM FOR INDIAN CITIZENS 27 (1961).

7.   *See* Title IV, *supra* note 2.

8.   *See* Goldberg, *supra* note 4, at 558–62.

9.   25 U.S.C. § 1918. Under the petition procedure, the tribe must "present to the Secretary for approval a petition . . . which includes a suitable plan to exercise such jurisdiction." 25 U.S.C. § 1918(a). The secretary then considers the feasibility of the plan, and in doing so may take into account matters such as the existence of a membership roll for the tribe, the size of the reservation and the tribe's population, and whether multiple tribes occupy the same reservation. 25 U.S.C. § 1918(b)(1)(i)–(iv). The secretary may approve only a partial reassumption of jurisdiction. 25 U.S.C. § 1918(b)(2). If the secretary rejects the petition, the secretary must provide technical assistance to the tribe to assist in the correction of any deficiencies in the petition. 25 U.S.C. § 1918(c).

10.   For the "exit, voice and loyalty" literature and some contemporary developments *see, e.g.*, ALBERT O. HIRSCHMAN, EXIT, VOICE, AND LOYALTY: RESPONSES TO DECLINES IN FIRMS, ORGANIZATIONS, AND STATES (1970); Soo-Young Lee and Andress B. Whitford, *Exit, Voice, Loyalty and Pay; Evidence from the Public Workforce*, 18 J. PUB. ADMIN. RES. & THEORY 647 (2007); Marco Goli, *The Voice of Exit: Toward a Theory of Democratic Inconsistency*, 3 J. SOC. SCI. 60 (2007).

11.   *See* GOLDBERG & CHAMPAGNE, FINAL PUBLIC LAW 280 REPORT, *supra* note 4, ch. 12.

12.   Dwight D. Eisenhower, 166—Statement by the President Upon Signing Bill Relating to State Jurisdiction Over Cases Arising on Indian Reservations, THE AMERICAN PRESIDENCY PROJECT, *available at* http://www.presidency.ucsb.edu/ws/?pid=9674 (last visited May 10, 2010). Eisenhower claimed that the Indians in the original five states covered by Public Law 280 (Alaska was added when it became a state in 1958) "enthusiastically endorsed" the legislation. But there is no documentation to that effect from the affected tribes. It is likely that the BIA provided this information.

13. *Rights of Members of Indian Tribes: Hearing on H.R. 15419 and Related Bills Before the Subcomm. on Indian Affairs of the House Comm. on Interior and Insular Affairs*, 90th Cong., 2nd Sess. 25 (1968) (letter from Harry R. Anderson, Assistant Secretary of the Interior, to Hon. Wayne N. Aspinall, Chairman, Committee on Interior and Insular Affairs, House of Representatives, [Mar. 27, 1968]) [hereinafter cited as 1968 House Hearing].

14. *Constitutional Rights of the American Indian: Hearing on S. 961, S. 962, S. 963, S. 964, S. 965, S. 966, S. 967, S. 968, and S.J. Res. 40 Before the Senate Subcomm. on Constitutional Rights of the Comm. on the Judiciary*, 89th Cong., 1st Sess. 4 (1965) [hereinafter cited as 1965 Senate Hearing].

15. *Id.* at 124.

16. *Id.* at 102. Washington did not assume full Public Law 280 jurisdiction over every reservation in the state, only over those that consented. The Quinault Tribe had consented to such jurisdiction in 1958, but withdrew its consent in 1965. *See* State v. Pink, 144 Wn. App. 945, 951–52 (Wash. Ct. App. 2008). Following passage of the Indian Civil Rights Act, the secretary of the Interior accepted retrocession of most of Washington's Public Law 280 jurisdiction at Quinault. 34 Fed. Reg. 14, 288 (1969). Arguably, the federal government retained concurrent criminal jurisdiction in the optional Public Law 280 states. *See* COHEN'S HANDBOOK, *supra* note 4, § 6.04[3][d][i]. However, no evidence exists that the federal government exercised such jurisdiction during the period when Washington enjoyed full Public Law 280 jurisdiction at Quinault.

17. *Id.* at 102–03.

18. *Id.* at 245.

19. *Id.* at 246.

20. *Id.* at 245.

21. *Constitutional Rights of the American Indian: Hearings Before the Senate Subcomm. on Constitutional Rights of the Comm. on the Judiciary*, 87th Cong., 1st Sess., Pursuant to S. Res. 53, Parts 1–3 at 60 (1961–62) [hereinafter cited as 1961–62 Senate Hearings].

22. *Id.* at 75.

23. *Id.* at 99.

24. *Id.* at 201.

25. *Id.* at 329.

26. *Id.*

27. *Id.* at 332.

28. *Id.* at 298.

29. *Id.* at 300.

30. *Id.* at 348–49.

31. *Id.* at 350.

32. *Id.* at 406–14.

33. *Id.* at 414.

34. *Id* at 627–28.

35. *Id.* at 684. *See also id.* at 690 (statement of John B. Richards, Oglala Sioux and chief judge of the Oglala Sioux Tribal Court).

36. *Id.* at 690.

37. 1968 House Hearing at 29.

38. *Id.* at 126.

39. *Constitutional Rights of the American Indian: Summary Report of Hearings and Investigations by the Senate Subcomm. on Constitutional Rights of the Comm. on the Judiciary*, 88th Cong., 2nd Sess., pursuant to S. Res. 265 at 13 (1964) [hereinafter cited as 1964 Summary Report].

40. *Id.* at 10.

41. *See* 1961–62 Senate Hearings *supra* note 23, and accompanying text.

42. 1965 Senate Hearing at 126.

43. 1961–62 Senate Hearings at 337.

44. *Id.* at 407–08.

45. 1961–62 Senate Hearings at 634.

46. *Id.* at 690.

47. 1965 Hearing at 200.

48. 1961–62 Hearings at 15–16.
49. *Id.* at 224.
50. *Id.* at 612.
51. *Id.* at 634.
52. *Id.* at 689–90.
53. *Id.* at 898.
54. *Id.* at 890.
55. *Id.* at 740.
56. *Id.* at 819.
57. *Id.* at 820.
58. *Id.*
59. *Id.* at 821–22.
60. *Id.* at 882–83.
61. *Id.* at 883.
62. 1965 Senate Hearing at 124.
63. *Id.* at 193.
64. *Id.*
65. *Id.* at 338.
66. *Id.* at 245.
67. *Id.* at 254.
68. *Id.* at 246.
69. *Id.* at 191.
70. 1968 House Hearing, *supra* note 13, at 66.
71. 1961–62 Senate Hearings, *supra* note 21, at 220.
72. 1965 Senate Hearing, *supra* note 14, at 67.
73. 1968 House Hearing at 109.
74. "As we read Senate bill 966, it essentially amounts to a repeal of Public law 280, and a reenactment of that law with the added condition that tribal consent be secured prior to assumption of jurisdiction by the State." 1965 Senate Hearing at 356 (statement of Ziontz, Pirtle & Fulle, counsel for the Makah Indian Tribe). *Also see Resolution of the Salt River-Pima Maricopa Tribe,* 1965 Senate Hearing at 81.
75. *See id.* at 205 (statement of Albert L. Whitebird, chairman of the Bad River Band of the Lake Superior Tribe of Chippewa Indians of the State of Wisconsin).
76. NCAI Resolution 21, 1958, *quoted in* 1961–62 Senate Hearings at 198.
77. 1961–62 Senate Hearings at 199. NCAI reiterated this position in resolutions adopted in 1966 and 1967. 1968 House Hearing at 120.
78. 1961–62 Senate Hearings at 200.
79. 1968 House Hearing at 120. NCAI submitted statements from a variety of tribes offering support for Title III, later incorporated into the final legislation as Title IV, as well. *Id.* at 123.
80. *See* 1961–62 Senate Hearings, *supra* note 23, 1965 Senate Hearing at 126, *supra* notes 40–41 and accompanying text.
81. 1965 Hearing at 57.
82. *Id.*
83. 1968 House Hearing at 29.
84. 1961–62 Senate Hearings at 327.
85. *Id.* at 329.
86. *See* 25 U.S.C. § 1918, *supra* note 9 and accompanying text.
87. *See, e.g.,* 1964 Summary Report, *supra* note 39 at 23; *Constitutional Rights of the American Indian: Summary Report of Hearings and Investigations by the Senate Subcomm. on Constitutional Rights of the Comm. on the Judiciary,* 89th Cong., 2nd Sess., pursuant to S. Res. 194 at 6 (1966) [hereinafter cited as 1966 Summary Report].
88. *See* 25 U.S.C. § 1918, discussed at note 9 *supra*, and accompanying text.
89. GOLDBERG & CHAMPAGNE, FINAL PUBLIC LAW 280 REPORT, *supra* note 4, ch. 12.

90. Carole Goldberg & Duane Champagne, *Is Public Law 280 Fit for the Twenty-First Century? Some Data at Last*, 38 CONN. L. REV. 697 (2006) [hereinafter cited as *Is Public Law 280 Fit*].

91. In fact, across a number of issues, state law enforcement and criminal justice officials believe they are doing a far better job than reservation residents do. These issues include thoroughness of crime investigation, effective communication with tribal communities, and cultural sensitivity. By contrast, in the non-Public Law 280 jurisdictions studied (including the retroceded, excluded, straddler, and non-Public Law 280 tribes), there is far greater convergence between the views of reservation residents and the federal officials who are responsible for some of the law enforcement and criminal justice on those reservations. These non-Public Law 280 ratings converge at a point that is just above the ratings that reservation residents give state officials operating under Public Law 280, and far below the ratings that those state officials give themselves. A reasonable inference from this pattern is that the state officials are rating themselves unusually highly. The reservation residents in Public Law 280 jurisdictions do not appear to be unusually harsh in their assessments. *Is Public Law 280 Fit* at 711–23.

92. GOLDBERG & CHAMPAGNE, FINAL PUBLIC LAW 280 REPORT, *supra* note 4, at 144.

93. *Id.* at 198–99.

94. *Id.* at 204.

95. *Id.* at 183.

96. *Id.* at 188. For additional statements, see *id.*, ch. 7.

97. *Id.* at 190, 196.

98. *Id.* at 157–58.

99. *Id.* at 218.

100. *Id.* at 160.

101. This regime is described in COHEN'S HANDBOOK, *supra* note 4, ch. 9.

102. 25 U.S.C. § 1323.

103. *See* pages 13–19 *supra*.

104. Lyndon B. Johnson, Exec. Order No. 11,345, 33 Fed. Reg. 17,339 (Nov. 21, 1968).

105. *See* GOLDBERG & CHAMPAGNE, FINAL PUBLIC LAW 280 REPORT, *supra* note 4, .ch. 13. Project Director Heather Valdez Singleton contributed significantly to the writing of this chapter. We have no comprehensive count of tribes that have requested retrocession from their state governments and failed. The unsuccessful effort of the Shoshone-Bannock Tribes of the Fort Hall Reservation in Idaho, an optional state, is presented in *id.* at 421–26.

106. *Id.* at 412–40.

107. PL 280 provides that retrocession can apply to less than a state's full jurisdiction under the act. 25 U.S.C. § 1323.

108. GOLDBERG & CHAMPAGNE, FINAL PUBLIC LAW 280 REPORT, *supra* note 4, at 440–72.

109. *Id.* at 459.

110. *Id.* at 461–62.

111. *Id.* at 463–69. In contrast, only 30 percent of the law enforcement personnel interviewees held that view.

112. *See* National Congress of American Indians, Resolution #PHX-08-049 (2008), *available at* https://www.ncai.org/ncai/resolutions/doc/PHX-08-049FINAL.pdf (last visited April 16, 2010).

113. Congress recently paved the way for the federal government's post-retrocession role by passing a provision in the Tribal Law and Order Act that allows the United States to reassume concurrent jurisdiction in Public Law 280 states. The tribe must request the federal jurisdiction, and the United States is not required to accept. Tribal Law and Order Act of 2010, PL 111-211, § 221 (July 29, 2010). If the United States has already assumed jurisdiction pre-retrocession, its burden upon retrocession will not be so great.

114. 25 U.S.C. § 1918.

PART V

THE POWER AND LIMITS OF THE INDIAN CIVIL RIGHTS ACT

CHAPTER 12

Evaluating Tribal Courts' Interpretations of the Indian Civil Rights Act

MARK D. ROSEN

The United States Constitution does not apply to tribal governments.[1] Concerned with potential abuses of power by the tribes, Congress imposed statutory obligations on tribal governments in the Indian Civil Rights Act (ICRA) in 1968 that track almost verbatim the language of the Bill of Rights by guaranteeing (for example) the "free exercise of religion" and "freedom of speech."[2]

Although the ICRA is federal law, tribal courts—not federal courts—have exclusive subject matter jurisdiction over virtually all ICRA claims.[3] Moreover, the United States Supreme Court has ruled that tribal courts need not interpret the ICRA's provisions as the United States Supreme Court has interpreted ICRA's sister terms in the Bill of Rights.[4] Instead, tribal courts may interpret the ICRA in light of tribal needs, values, customs, and traditions. More than this, each tribe is allowed to craft its own interpretation of the ICRA in light of its own tribe's unique needs, values, customs, and traditions.

In short, there are multiple authoritative interpreters of the Indian Civil Rights Act. Due process means one thing in Manhattan, something else on the Navajo Reservation according to Navajo tribal courts, and yet another thing within the Ho-Chunk nation according to the Ho-Chunk tribal courts.

How well—or poorly—does this regime of multiple authoritative interpreters operate? This chapter provides a set of tools and a framework for assessing ICRA's operation. The tools permit an assessment of the nature and extent of tribal court deviations from federal constitutional doctrines. The framework identifies the potential benefits and costs of ICRA's regime of multiple authoritative interpreters. The chapter then applies its tools and framework to a study I have undertaken of every tribal court decision interpreting ICRA that was reported in the *Indian Law Reporter* over a thirteen-year period.

The principal potential cost of ICRA's regime is the risk of undermining the very protections the ICRA was intended to provide. This chapter's analysis suggests that this danger has not materialized; rather, tribal courts for the most part have interpreted the ICRA in good faith, often requiring significant changes in tribal governmental practices and announcing extensive individual rights.

The primary benefit of ICRA's highly decentralized system of authoritative legal interpretation is the promise of allowing the diverse Native American communities the opportunity to maintain their distinctive cultures. Ample evidence indicates that this goal has been realized. Further, even though tribal courts provide independent interpretations of the ICRA, the courts have deeply assimilated many Anglo constitutional values. The tribal assimilation of Anglo values has not resulted in the displacement of Indian values, but rather in a cultural syncretism of Anglo and tribal values.

More generally, allowing diverse communities the opportunity to authoritatively construe a shared text holds out the possibility of creating commonality without commanding homogeneity. It is a method for simultaneously coordinating a diverse citizenry and championing heterogeneity. The reported tribal case law suggests that the ICRA has accomplished these ends to a considerable degree.

The first part of this chapter presents the tools and framework for evaluating the ICRA's regime of multiple authoritative interpreters. The second part details the study's methodology. The third part applies the tools and framework to the reported cases. The final part provides a brief conclusion.

A TOOL AND A FRAMEWORK

The Tool

A tribal court can take five possible approaches in its interpretation of ICRA's terms. Clarifying each approach is important for several reasons. Recognizing the five possible approaches helps to identify patterns that can bring order to the tribal case law. Further, each approach is capable of producing a distinctive range of variations from ordinary federal doctrine. Finally, each approach presents distinctive benefits and potential risks.

A simple model for describing constitutional doctrine. The five approaches to past Supreme Court pronouncements can best be appreciated in relation to a simple model I've developed that describes constitutional doctrine. Understanding the model, in turn, requires appreciation of the well-known jurisprudential distinction between "rules" and "standards."[5] Standards are legal edicts that "describe a triggering event in abstract terms that refer to the ultimate policy or goal animating the law," whereas rules are legal edicts that "describe the triggering event with factual particulars or other language that is determinate within a community."[6]

For example, "drive safely" is a standard, whereas "maximum speed 55 miles per hour" is a rule.

Now to the model. All ICRA provisions take the form of standards that require active interpretation to identify concretely the actions that are required, permitted, or proscribed in particular circumstances. The interpretive process can be usefully conceptualized as involving three steps.

The first step is identifying the provision with a larger "goal," that is, a broad-stroke description of what the provision attempts to accomplish. For example, the goal of the Fourth Amendment has been identified as protecting various "personal and societal values," including a "right to privacy."[7] It is easy to forget that the goal is almost always a nonaxiomatic translation of the constitutional provision, and instead to view the contemporarily understood goal as inevitable. But this is not so. Indeed, Supreme Court justices frequently disagree as to what a particular constitutional provision aims to accomplish, and doctrinal changes as to what is the goal of a constitutional provision are not at all unusual.[8] Understanding that the goal is part of the process of doctrinal development is vital to appreciating the respects in which a tribal court's ICRA holding may deviate from ordinary constitutional doctrine.

The second step in the interpretive process is the creation of a "legal test" to determine whether the identified goal is met.[9] This second step occurs because the goal is inevitably too abstract and consequently unworkable for the judiciary's institutional need to have a shorthand method for decision-making that identifies as legally relevant only a subset of the infinite facts that characterize any given circumstance. The test almost always includes one or more standards. For example, the Supreme Court has translated the aforementioned Fourth Amendment goal into a legal test composed of several standards that ask whether "the individual manifested a subjective expectation of privacy in the object of the challenged search," and whether society is "willing to recognize that expectation as reasonable."[10] This legal test helps to particularize the goal but, by deploying standards such as "reasonable" and "expectation of privacy," still leaves ample uncertainties as to what concretely satisfies the test.

Step three describes what occurs to the legal test's standard over time. As it is applied over a series of cases, the standard almost always becomes increasingly rule-like. This change occurs because cases, by their very nature, are disputes that involve particular facts, and as the cases are decided they become showcases of what as a concrete matter the standard means.[11] I dub this process the "rulification of the standard," and will call step three's product a "rulified standard." For example, do people have a "subjective expectation of privacy" in open fields? The Supreme Court has said no.[12] In curtilage surrounded by a high double fence? Not from a naked-eye observation taken from an aircraft, said the Court.[13]

This simple model of interpretation can be graphically depicted as follows:

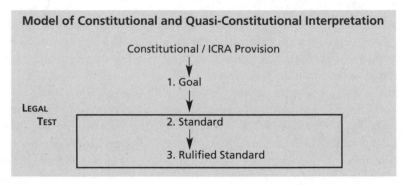

Model of Constitutional and Quasi-Constitutional Interpretation

Constitutional / ICRA Provision

1. Goal

LEGAL
TEST

2. Standard

3. Rulified Standard

Five possible approaches to case law. The model of doctrinal development permits us to see that tribal courts can take five possible approaches when they construe the ICRA. First, a tribal court can ignore altogether the federal case law and proceed to construe the provision wholly on its own.[14] Call this the "tabula rasa" approach.[15] In *Navajo Nation v. Crockett*,[16] for example, the tribal court looked to Navajo common law rather than to American case law to define the contours of free speech. The court noted that a Navajo has a "fundamental right to express his or her mind by way of the spoken work and/or actions." But this right is limited insofar as there is "freedom with responsibility." The Navajo concept of responsibility can impose permissible content limitations. For example, "on some occasions, a person is prohibited from making certain statements, and some statements of reciting oral traditions are prohibited during specific times of the year."[17] Responsibility can also impose limits with respect to style of presentation; thus "speech should be delivered with respect and honesty."[18] Finally, Navajo responsibility can impose "another limitation on speech, which is that a disgruntled person must speak directly with the person's relative about his or her concerns before seeking other avenues of redress with strangers."[19] In the employment context, for example, the *Crockett* court held that an employee dissatisfied with his supervisor "should not seek to correct the person by summoning the coercive powers of a powerful person or entity," but instead first must engage in the process of "talking things out" with his superior.[20] As *Crockett* shows, and as intuition would suggest, tabula rasa can create doctrines that are virtually unrecognizable to students of American constitutional law.[21]

The remaining four approaches (that is, approaches two through five) involve varying degrees of engagement with, and adoption of, the federal case law.

The second approach is the polar opposite of tabula rasa: the tribal court completely adopts the federal doctrine. Call this "incorporation." Does a tribal court's decision to incorporate federal law mean that the tribal court was superfluous? Sometimes yes, but generally no. As to the sometimes yes: tribal courts sometimes adopt federal case law without explanation or reason[22]—what I'll label "stock incorporation." Stock incorporation is the mode of interpretation under which tribal courts provide the least "value added"[23] insofar as they appear to act just as a federal court would. More frequently, however, tribal courts actively fit the federal doctrine to the tribal context—what I call "fitted incorporation." This mode can take several forms. First, incorporation frequently occurs only after the tribal court has established that the federal approach fits well within the tribal context, a determination that an ordinary federal court might not be capable of making.[24] Second, the tribal court that incorporates a federal doctrine that is not developed far beyond a standard still has to apply the standard to the tribal context, and the tribal court likely is far better suited to undertake this central part of legal interpretation than is a general federal court. Third, tribal courts that incorporate may conceptualize the federal approach as consistent with or derivable from tribal culture and values, and this may have important social meaning to the tribal community, which would be lost if the adjudication had taken place in a federal court.[25] Although the federal legal test is adopted in all three instances of fitted incorporation, the tribal court plays an important role in bringing together tribal and Anglo traditions.

The remaining three approaches (approaches three through five) reject (to varying degrees) federal doctrine as ill-suited to the tribal context. Under the third approach, the tribal court adopts the federal standard but disregards the rulification of the standard.[26] Instead, the tribal court applies the standard in a manner that is closely tailored to the context-at-hand. Call this "tailoring." This approach is well illustrated by the case of *Colville Confederated Tribes v. Bray*,[27] which concerned due process protections enjoyed by persons who had been arrested without a warrant. Federal case law had established that constitutional due process requires that defendants arrested without a warrant be brought "promptly" before a judge, which meant forty-eight hours absent exceptional circumstances.[28] The tribal court accepted the Supreme Court's goal and standard, but not its rulified standard. It invoked the standard that there be a "reasonable accommodation of the competing interests,"[29] but ruled that the tribal ordinance's seventy-two hour requirement satisfied the "promptly" requirement. The tribe's requirement obviated the need to hold weekend court for Friday night arrestees, and "[t]he cost to the Tribes for this procedure would seem to outweigh the extra 24 hours for a defendant."[30]

The fourth interpretive technique is to adopt the federal courts' description of the goal but to reject the federal courts' standard. Call this method "restandardizing." For example, in *Hopi Tribe v. Lonewolf Scott*, the Hopi tribal court accepted that the goal of due process's void for vagueness doctrine is to ensure that persons have fair notice of what conduct is criminally sanctionable. But instead of deploying the ordinary standard—an objective test that looks to the mere "possibility of discriminatory enforcement" and lack of notice[31]—the court applied a subjective test and analyzed how the Native American community in question understood the ordinance and how the tribal authorities had applied it.[32]

The fifth (and last!) approach is to replace the goal identified by the Supreme Court. Call this "retargeting." An example of retargeting can be seen in *Downey v.*

Bigman,[33] where the Navajo Supreme Court decided that the goal of the jury right was not only to preserve litigants' rights but also to advance the tribal community's interest in "participatory democracy," that is, to participate in law making and law application. This example provides an instance of retargeting because the United States Supreme Court's stated goal behind Sixth and Seventh Amendment jury rights concerns the rights of the litigant and the integrity of the legal system, not the rights of jurors to participate in government.[34] Retargeting of the jury right led the tribal court to create a new jury procedure whereby the jury was empowered to direct questions to witnesses.[35]

All that remains is the definition of a few more terms that cut across the five approaches. Under all approaches except for tabula rasa, the tribal court *adopts* federal case law, and under fitted incorporation, tailoring, restandardizing, retargeting, the tribal court also *adapts* the federal law to the tribal context. I will refer to the last set of interpretive approaches collectively as "adapted adoption." Finally, because tribal courts sometimes cite other tribal court opinions as precedent, distinguishing between "subjective" and "objective" adapted adoption is important. "Subjective adoption" refers to cases where the tribal court itself looks to federal case law and either tailors, restandardizes, retargets, or incorporates. "Objective adoption" refers to a tribal court's *de facto* adoption of the federal doctrine without its having cited to federal law (as, for instance, when the tribal court cites to tribal case law as precedent that itself utilized subjective adoption).

To summarize, the five approaches that a multiple authoritative interpreter can take can be mapped onto the model of intrpretation as follows:

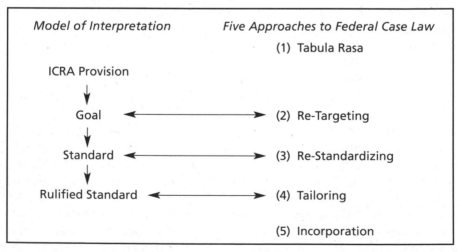

Comparing the five approaches. Of the five approaches, tabula rasa and retargeting afford the potential for most radically departing from constitutional doctrines. After all, incorporation, tailoring, and restandardizing accept the goal identified by the Supreme Court as the principle behind the ICRA provision; what drives tailoring and restandardizing is simply the view that realizing the goal in the context-at-hand requires a deviation from what ordinarily is constitutionally required in federal courts, permitted or proscribed. By contrast, retargeting recasts the goal. Tabula rasa allows for this recasting as well. Incorporation self-evidently leads to the smallest deviation—none—from the ordinary federal case law.

The differences between tabula rasa and retargeting vis-à-vis deviating from constitutional doctrine are subtle. Formally, retargeting provides the same opportunity to alter the goal as does tabula rasa. In practice, however, tabula rasa may allow greater opportunity for deviation than does retargeting. Because retargeting is performed in relation to the federal case law, the goal identified by the Supreme Court, even though it is rejected by the tribal court that retargets, may circumscribe the range of imagined alternatives.[36] To the extent that a tribal court could really approach an ICRA provision without preconceived notions provided by federal case law—an uncertain possibility, to be sure, and something increasingly less certain as tribal courts are increasingly populated by people who have received law degrees from American schools—the tabula rasa approach is not so limited. But it still is possible, of course, particularly where tribal judges are religious leaders rather than lawyers.

Though more limited than retargeting and tabula rasa with regard to creating deviations, tailoring and restandardizing still can create significant departures from the ordinary requirements in federal courts. This can be most dramatically illustrated by considering tailoring, the more limited of the two methods (given that it accepts more of the teachings of federal case law as compared to restandardizing). Tailoring can create immense deviations from what is ordinarily permitted or proscribed. The magnitude of the departure depends on the standard and on how community-specific the court is willing to tailor. For example, tailoring has been utilized to uphold prior restraints in select places in the United States.[37]

The Framework

We can now proceed to generating a framework for evaluating tribal courts' interpretations of the Indian Civil Rights Act.

Potential benefits. There are three core benefits to the ICRA's regime of multiple authoritative interpreters. First, it increases tribes' powers of self-governance. Second, it permits variations in governmental structures and accordingly extends the possible range of institutional diversity. Third, the ICRA's regime of multiple authoritative interpreters may enable communities to flourish that otherwise might not be able to insofar as some tribal communities' self-definition may turn on their government's having the power to govern themselves in a manner that would not be compatible with federal constitutional requirements.

Potential costs. The principal potential cost is that permitting tribal courts to construe the ICRA's provisions independently might subvert the very protections that the ICRA was intended to provide in the first place. Call this the cost of "under-protection."

It is difficult as an *a priori* matter to identify, however, what substantive interpretations constitute under-protection. The most obvious candidate—that any variation from what is constitutionally required in general society—is insupportable on both doctrinal and normative grounds. Doctrinally, more than thirty years ago the Supreme Court expressly held that the ICRA's provisions need not have the same substantive meanings as their sister terms in the Bill of Rights.[38] The logic behind this determination is that the ICRA was intended to accomplish two goals that are in tension with one another: protecting the rights of persons who enter Indian country by imposing limits on tribal governments, on the one hand, while preserving "Indian self-government" and the "tribe's ability to maintain itself as a culturally and politically distinct entity,"[39] on the other. Over the past thirty years Congress has considered amending the ICRA many times to respond to the *Martinez* decision, but at no point has it suggested that this aspect of the case should be statutorily overruled. So, as a doctrinal matter, tribal court deviations from Bill of Rights jurisprudence do not on their own mean that the ICRA provisions have been under-protected.

As a normative matter, rather than undermining the protections that the ICRA's quasi-constitutional provisions are intended to provide, tribal courts' doctrinal variations may actually be necessary to fully realize the foundational liberal commitments memorialized in the ICRA. Elsewhere I have argued at length that foundational liberal commitments found in liberal constitutions may demand the accommodation of (some) communities that have what may be termed "illiberal" values.[40]

In the end, identifying what variants from ordinary constitutional doctrines are normatively acceptable requires recourse to such "thick" political theory. Nonetheless, this chapter will not draw directly on this thick theory, but instead will review tribal court deviations on an intuitive, inductive level. Why? First, as is the case with all thick theories, the particular theory I have propounded rests on nonaxiomatic grounds that not everyone would accept.[41] Because this chapter's empirical findings are relevant even to those who do not accept my thick political theory, I think it preferable to present my findings in a manner that does not presume the reader's agreement with it.

Second, the inductive approach alone can, at the very least, defeat a potentially devastating threshold objection that can be leveled at the ICRA's regime of multiple authoritative interpreters. One may think that ICRA's protections will be undermined by granting authoritative interpretive power to the very institutions (i.e., tribal governments) that ICRA aims to constrain. Buttressing such skepticism is the fact that the tribal governments in the main strongly opposed ICRA's enactment.[42]

Yet this chapter's analysis disposes of this challenge by showing that tribal courts have engaged in what might be termed "good faith" interpretation of the ICRA. Such good-faith efforts admittedly are a necessary, but not sufficient, condition to ensure acceptable under-protection costs. But establishing tribal courts' good-faith interpretation of ICRA is a sufficiently significant demonstration in the course of a single book chapter. Once again, fully establishing the extent to which ICRA has been under-protected requires recourse to a thick political theory, something beyond the scope of a single chapter.

METHODOLOGICAL CONSIDERATIONS

This part provides background information that is essential to understanding the third part's empirical review of the ICRA case law. The first section, on tribal courts, explains important information about tribal courts. Subsections on the structure of tribal courts and the role of the tribal judiciary discuss the data relied upon and the study's methodology.

Tribal Courts

Because tribal courts are the institutions that construe and apply the bulk of the ICRA's provisions, understanding ICRA's implementation requires an understanding of the tribal courts themselves.

Structure of tribal courts. Adjudication in Indian country takes place in either tribal courts or Courts of Indian Offenses. Courts of Indian Offenses, frequently called "CFR Courts," are established and run by the Bureau of Indian Affairs. Tribal courts are adjudicatory bodies created either by tribal constitutions or by tribal legislative bodies.

Lacking constitutionally mandated structure and forms, tribal court systems are extraordinarily diverse, with approximately 130 entities in the United States.[43] The Navajo Nation, for example, has seven district courts, a children's court, a peacemaker court within each district,[44] and an appellate court called the Navajo Nation Supreme Court. Some tribes, such as the Chickasaw Nation, the Choctaw Nation, the Pueblo of Sandia, and the Pueblo of Taos, do not have appellate courts. In some tribes, the tribal council—the body that enacts tribal legislation—functions as the appellate forum. In many of the pueblos in New Mexico, the tribal leader functions as tribal judge. Finally, many tribes belong to intertribal court and appellate systems. For example, the Intertribal Court of Appeals consists of the Crow Creek Sioux Tribe, the Sisseton-Wahpeton Sioux Tribe, the Rosebud Sioux Tribe, the Three Affiliated Tribes, and the Omaha Tribe.[45] Tribal courts also vary according to the sizes of the tribes, their reservations' general populations, their caseloads, their wealth and resources, their traditions, and the tribunals' longevity."[46]

The role of the tribal judiciary. Notwithstanding the differences among tribal courts, an important commonality is that they are institutions that independently review the limits on tribal government imposed by the Indian Civil Rights Act.[47] Indeed, assumption of this function is a mandate of federal law. When it ruled in *Martinez* that federal courts were generally unavailable to hear ICRA claims, the Supreme Court also stated that tribes must provide forums "to vindicate rights created by the ICRA."[48] Consistent with this assertion, tribal courts have almost unswervingly found that efforts by tribal council members to exert "undue influence" on them would violate the ICRA's due process guarantees.[49]

A potential doctrinal obstacle to tribal courts vindicating ICRA rights is the doctrine of tribal sovereign immunity. *Martinez* specifically found that the ICRA did not waive tribal sovereign immunity.[50] Although this at first might seem to be odds with *Martinez's* other holding that tribal courts must provide forums to vindicate ICRA rights, it should be recalled that the most commonly employed claims asserted against federal and state governments to vindicate civil rights claims—*Bivens* and Section 1983 claims—also assume that governments have not waived sovereign immunity.[51] These federal claims typically yield prospective injunctive relief or damages against individual government officials who have acted beyond the scope of their duties.[52] Even though damage claims against the federal and state governments themselves typically are unavailable on account of sovereign immunity, *Bivens* and Section 1983 claims are widely viewed as providing effective checks on governmental power.

So, too, with Native American tribes. Many tribal courts have held that the ICRA does not waive tribal sovereign immunity[53] but have allowed prospective injunctive relief or damages where tribal officials act beyond the scope of their duties.[54] The success of *Bivens* and Section 1983 claims in checking governmental abuses means that the ICRA's same structure of remedies need not interfere with the deployment of ICRA to protect rights in keeping with *Martinez's* charge.[55]

Data

The study's greatest limitation is the incomplete body of reported case law from which it was able to draw. Most tribes do not publish their tribal court opinions, and the most comprehensive reporter of tribal court decisions, the *Indian Law Reporter*, typically publishes no more than one hundred decisions per year that come from about twenty-five tribes. Further, the *Indian Law Reporter* does not publish all cases that are submitted to it by tribes. For these reasons, the reported case law is selective, rendering impossible any effort to generalize about what is happening in Indian country. At the very least, though, the data provides a concrete understanding of what is possible within the ICRA regime. To the extent that favorable patterns emerge from the limited data set available, it is advisable to institute information-gathering changes in the law (like funding and requiring the publication of tribal court decisions) that illuminate what really is occurring across tribal courts rather than to draw negative conclusions on the basis of anecdotal evidence.

Methodology

Eschewing reliance on indices, this study examined every published tribal court decision reported in the *Indian Law Reporter* over the thirteen-year period, from 1986 to 1998 (along with five reported cases from 1999). The study only takes into account cases in which some substantive provision of the Indian Civil Rights Act or analogous provisions in tribal constitution was construed. Thus, the study does not include the many opinions that dealt exclusively with important nonsubstantive background legal issues such as sovereign immunity, the nature of the relief (injunctions as opposed to damages, for example), and the like; nor does the study consider cases where the ICRA is simply mentioned but not substantially analyzed.[56] In total, there were 193 reported cases, in which 248 claims were pressed.[57]

The study does not distinguish between cases interpreting ICRA provisions or tribal constitutional provisions. This method merits some explanation. Nearly all tribes have tribal constitutions with provisions that verbatim track the ICRA and the Bill of Rights, and these tribal constitutional provisions frequently are relied upon by litigants in tribal courts in conjunction with ICRA and, sometimes, are the only provisions invoked by litigants. Though important technical differences exist between claims based on ICRA and on a tribal constitution,[58] these differences are not relevant for purposes of this article's study. The legal claims analyzed in this chapter all originate from the Anglo world, regardless of whether their source is ICRA or the federally drafted tribal constitutions. Further, what a claim under either ICRA or a tribal constitution means is determined solely by tribal courts, and neither is reviewable by a federal court. A tribal court's interpretation of due process under the tribal constitution accordingly sheds much light on how tribal courts interpret Anglo jurisprudential concepts. Consequently, this article does not differentiate between claims based on the ICRA and those based on tribal constitutions.

EMPIRICAL STUDY OF INDIAN CIVIL RIGHTS ACT CASE LAW

At last, the empirical study. The first part examines the ICRA case law from the vantage point of determining whether the ICRA has achieved the potential benefits associated with a regime of multiple authoritative interpreters. The second part analyzes the case law to assess if tribal courts have under-protected the ICRA.

Testing the Framework's First Criteria: Potential Benefits

The framework's first set of criteria aims to assess whether ICRA has achieved its potential benefits of extending possibilities for self-governance, expanding the range of legal and institutional options, enabling idiosyncratic but valuable communities to flourish, and firing the legal imagination. Ample evidence points to the affirmative, on the basis both of the interpretive canons regularly used by tribal courts and the courts' substantive holdings.

Tribal interpretive canons. Consistent with the license provided by the Supreme Court in *Martinez*, tribal courts have recognized that the ICRA's provisions need not be interpreted as having their sister terms in the Bill of Rights. As one tribal court has put it, "[w]hen analyzing due process claims, it is important to note that the Indian nations have formulated their own notions of due process and equal protection in compliance with both aboriginal and modern tribal law. Indian Tribes, whose legal traditions are rooted in more informal traditions and customs, are markedly different from English common law, upon which the United States' notions of due process are founded."[59] The tribal court in *Plummer v. Plummer*[60] similarly noted that "due process protections are a product of moral principles, and our own morality and tribal customs frame such principles in the Navajo way." And the court in *Ponca Tribal Election Board v. Snake*[61] observed that "[w]hen entering the arena of due process in the context of an Indian tribe, courts should not simply rely on ideas of due process rooted in the Anglo-American system and then attempt to apply these concepts to tribal governments as if they were states or the federal government."[62] At the same time, tribal courts are not unwilling to consult federal case law. For example, the very next sentence in the *Snake* opinion states, "[t]hat is not to say that the general concepts of due process analysis with regard to state and federal governments are wholly inapplicable to Indian governments."[63]

Identical outcomes. Achieving the benefits of community-building and self-governance does not mean that tribal courts must interpret the ICRA differently than federal courts have understood the Bill of Rights. Self-governance requires that the tribe has the power to self-govern, but on its own implies nothing about the substance of the governing policies. Likewise, community-building can be advanced by tribal court decisions that deploy tribe-specific values and approaches that, at the end of the day, arrive at the same outcomes that a federal court likely would have come to.

In relation to these ideas, consider the case of *Atcitty v. District Court or the Judicial District of Window Rock*.[64] At issue was whether applicants for housing services on the Navajo Reservation had sufficient property interest to assert due process claims that the housing services department's procedures were inadequate. The tribal court engaged in tailoring, adopting the federal standard that a claimant must have a "legitimate claim, rather than a mere unilateral expectation to the benefit." But instead of using the legal test developed by federal courts—which required an examination of the statutes and policy guidelines to determine whether a claimant has the requisite legitimate claim to the benefit—the tribal court defined "legitimate claim" by way of reference to the Navajo concept of *k'e*. The court explained that *k'e* concerns "one's unique, reciprocal relationships to the community and the universe." *K'e* "frames the Navajo perception of moral right, and therefore this court's interpretation of due process rights."[65] *K'e*:

> promotes respect, solidarity, compassion and cooperation so that people may live in hozho, or harmony. *K'e* stresses the duties and obligations of individuals relative to their community. The importance of *k'e* to maintaining social order cannot be overstated. In light of *k'e*, due process can be understood as a means to ensure that individuals who are living in a state of disorder or disharmony are brought back into the community so that order for the entire community can be reestablished.

K'e therefore required the court to examine the Navajo doctrine of "distributive justice:"

> Distributive justice is concerned with the well-being of everyone in a community. For instance, if I see a hungry person, it does not matter whether I am responsible for the hunger. If someone is injured, it is irrelevant that I did not hurt that person. I have a responsibility, as a Navajo, to treat everyone as if he or she were my relative and therefore to help that hungry person. I am responsible for all my relatives. This value which translates itself into law under the Navajo system of justice is that everyone is part of a community, and the resources of the community must be shared with all. . . . Distributive justice requires sharing of Navajo Nation resources among eligible applicants.

Applying these principles to due process, the court then ruled that "[i]f the respondents are eligible for receiving governmental benefits, and although they are mere applicants, they have a sufficient property interest under Navajo common law to assert due process claims."[66]

Even though a federal court would likely have reached the same conclusion had it applied federal doctrines,[67] that the tribal court concluded as it did by reference to its tribe's particular cultural values is significant vis à-vis both self-governance and community-building. Tribal court independence in interpreting the ICRA affords tribes the opportunity to treat the narratives that reflect their self-understandings (such as *k'e* and Navajo distributive justice) as law, thereby gaining for their communities the socializing and other benefits that law peculiarly affords.[68]

Variant outcomes. Frequently, community-building is viewed as requiring outcomes that vary from what would have been obtained in ordinary federal courts under ordinary federal doctrines. Here are some examples.

(1) Due process and respect for tribal leadership. At issue in *Colville Confederated Tribes v. Bray*[69] was whether due process requires the probable cause determination following a nonwarrant arrest to be made by a judge, or whether it could be made by the prosecutor. Federal law requires that such determinations be made by a judge.[70] Tailoring, the tribal court ruled that tribal prosecutors also could make probable cause determinations.[71] *Bray*'s conclusion rested on the traditional Indian value of trust in leadership. "[L]eaders were chosen because of the respect others had for their decision-making ability in a particular area. . . . Traditionally, when a tribal leader made a decision, it was followed because of the respect and trust the tribal community had for him."[72] The trust deemed integral to tribal government, concluded the court, would be undermined by the type of checks and balances required by Anglo due process. Trust is consistent with self-rule, continued the court, because when the community no longer trusted the decision-making ability of the leader, they just stopped following him.[73]

These traditional principles carried over, the *Bray* court held, to the issue at hand: "It is incumbent upon the tribal judges and justices to sustain the attitude of trust and respect in their leadership role in the Indian community in order to maintain the community's confidence in the court system. . . . [The tribe must] trust that the prosecutor will, in fact, truly and faithfully carry out his duties."[74]

(2) Search and seizure and checking after members' welfare. A man named Kahe had not been seen by his Hopi neighbors for more than a day. Concerned about Kahe's well-being, a neighbor asked the police to look out for him. Pursuant to this request, tribal police stopped Kahe's vehicle for what was known on the Hopi Reservation as a "welfare check." Though the stop had not been prompted by concerns of criminal conduct, the police requested to see Kahe's license and to search his car.

At issue in *Hopi Tribe v. Kahe*[75] was whether this search and seizure was unreasonable under ICRA. The court employed fitted incorporation, adopting the federal doctrinal rubric of "probable cause," but determining its meaning by reference to considerations unique to the Hopi Tribe. Probable cause had to take "into consideration customary and traditional ways of the Hopi people. Because of the extended family system, Hopi people look out for and take care of each other. It is Hopi to be concerned about the welfare of your family and neighbors and to make sure that they are okay."[76]

The *Kahe* court concluded that the welfare check was lawful but that the requests to see the driver's license and search the car were not. There was probable cause to stop the vehicle because "when someone makes a request of the police to check on the well-being of a person it is expected that police officers have the responsibility and obligation to make the welfare check."[77] But concern for not undermining Hopi values led to the court's second holding that the tribal police's request to see the defendant's license and to search his car was unlawful. "[T]his court wants to encourage the principle behind welfare stops. It does not want to discourage calls from concerned family members with the threat that those individuals will immediately be subject to arrest."[78]

(3) Void for vagueness, honesty, and the integration of wrongdoers back into the community. A man named Stepetin had driven his truck at high speed on a gravel road close to pedestrians, injuring no people, but killing a dog. A tribal ordinance provided that "[w]here state law . . . does not conflict with the Tribal Code, the Tribal Court may resort to and enforce any state statute within tribal jurisdiction." No provisions of the tribal code directly governed Stepetin's actions, but state law criminalized them.

The question before the tribal court in *Stepetin v. Nisqually Indian Community*[79] was whether the ordinance's incorporation of state law was void for vagueness under ICRA's due process guarantee. A majority of the tribal court answered in the affirmative. Deploying stock incorporation, the tribal court held that "[t]he principle underlying the vagueness doctrine is that no one is to be held criminally responsible for conduct which he or she could not reasonably understand to be proscribed." Even though "[a]ny reasonable person should know this type of conduct is prohibited in any community . . . the issue is not whether [defendant] knew this conduct was wrong, but whether he knew it was a crime."[80] The incorporation provision did not meet this test.[81]

The dissent in *Stepetin* spotlights the connection between variations from ordinary doctrines and community well-being. The dissent criticized the majority for "ignoring the internal dynamics of the tribal community." Rather than importing the ordinary federal legal test, the dissent restandardized. Criticizing the majority's conclusion that criminal prohibitions had to appear in written statutes, the dissent argued that "traditionally, for a member of what is now the Nisqually Indian Community, there was no difference between wrongful conduct and that which was societally sanctioned." Further, it did not matter whether the source of the tribal member's knowledge was a written prohibition or an oral tradition. Accordingly, the rule for ICRA due process purposes should follow the traditional Nisqually approach, for the ICRA is to be construed "in the context of tribal traditions" and in view of the "cultural expectations and the dynamics of the tribal community."[82] Applying the restandardized rule in the context-at-hand, the dissent concluded that the defendant had the requisite actual knowledge that his behavior was wrong.[83]

Moreover, the dissent forcefully argued that the majority's approach harmed the community's well-being. The majority's rule rewarded a defendant's factually false claim that he lacked notice, thereby interfering with the "high value on telling the truth, and on the admission of fault by a wrongdoer" valued by the tribal community. Moreover, the majority's rule hindered the "correction of the wrongful conduct and/or recompense for its consequences" that is "necessary in order for the wrongdoer to be taken back into the fold of the tribal community. To allow an offender to go unpunished for obvious wrongdoing is destructive to the social health of the tribal community."[84]

(4) Novel doctrines and the value of self-governance. Several tribal courts have designed novel legal doctrines to advance the tribal value of self-governance. Utilizing the jury right, the case of *Downey v. Bigman*[85] developed limitations on the

powers of tribal judges to disregard jury findings. The court grounded its holding in tribal customs concerning not only the defendant's rights but also the community's interest in participating in government. In so doing, the tribal court engaged in retargeting insofar as the goal behind the jury right in American constitutional law is to protect the defendant and the integrity of the judiciary, not to provide a forum for self-government.[86]

Consulting tribal tradition, the *Bigman* court first noted that juries are a "modern expression of our longstanding legacy of participatory democracy," that is, "the ability of the people as a whole to make law":

> Navajo participatory democracy guarantees participants their fundamental right to speak on an issue, and discussion continues until the participants reach consensus. In this sense, decisions are a product of agreement among the community rather than a select few. Status, wealth and age are not determinants of whether a person may participate in the decision-making process. Furthermore, no one is pressured to agree to a certain solution, and persuasion, not coercion, is the vehicle for prompting decisions.

Juries, said the court, are a continuation of the tradition of "community participation in the resolution of disputes through deliberation and consensus."[87] Participation as a juror is a part of community self-governance by interpreting and executing community laws. These tradition-based principles led the *Bigman* court to adopt strict limits on a trial court's ability to overturn a jury verdict.[88] They also led the court to create a wholly novel jury procedure under which jurors may "ask questions of the witnesses during trial," so that the jury would be "more reflective of Navajo participatory democracy."[89]

The tribal court in *Rough Rock Community School v. Navajo Nation*[90] similarly relied on both tailoring and restandardizing to advance the value of self-governance. It struck down on due process grounds a tribal ordinance that limited school board candidates to persons who had a "demonstrated interest, experience and ability in Educational Management."[91] The tribal court first held that there exists a Navajo "higher law," akin to "the Anglo concept of natural law," that can be found in "Navajo customs and traditions that are fundamental and basic to Navajo life and society." Determining that Navajo higher law guarantees Navajos the "political liberty" to participate in government, the tribal court then tailored when it ruled that participation is a protected liberty under the ICRA's due process clause. The court then restandardized, looking to tribal traditions and concluding that laws affecting liberties derived from "higher law" must have "ascertainable standards."[92] The court's novel standard reflected fundamental Navajo values: the absence of "objective" standards "delegate[s] unregulated discretion which could lead to manipulation and abuses of authority. Navajo thought deplores abuses of authority because of the consensual and egalitarian principles of governance."[93]

(5) Variations across tribes. Finally, tribal courts create non-uniformities vis-à-vis not only federal law but also other tribes. Thus, although tribes sometimes cite to the opinions of the courts of other tribes,[94] most frequently they cite only to case law from their own tribe's courts. When citing to other tribes' courts, moreover, they recognize that these opinions are not binding authority[95] and that they can take into account the "custom, history and tradition" of their own tribes in construing the ICRA.[96] Another factor justifying different constructions is the unique "composition and territory" of the tribe.[97] As one court has noted, "[i]n many cases, large tribes with large reservations have adopted the Federal Rules of Procedure and/or have incorporated state substantive laws into their codes. Case law from these tribal courts does not necessarily fit smaller reservations with strongly integrated communities, tribes with a different economic base and practices, or tribes with more relaxed procedures or simplified law and order codes."[98]

Testing the Framework's Second Set of Criteria: Potential Costs

The framework's second set of criteria seeks to evaluate whether tribal court interpretations have led to under-protection of the ICRA. My empirical study of the ICRA case law provides strong preliminary evidence that the costs of ICRA's regime of multiple authoritative interpreters have been minimal. Tribal courts have developed substantive ICRA doctrines with real bite and in the process have effectuated significant changes in tribal government practices. Additional evidence of good-faith interpretation by the tribal courts is their attentiveness to federal court precedents, construing ICRA's sister terms in the Bill of Rights. Further, tribes typically depart from federal interpretations only after explaining that there are good reasons to do so. Moreover, as will be explained, the case law reveals that tribal courts have deeply assimilated many Anglo constitutional values even as they have given the provisions varying applications. Additional important evidence is that tribal courts appear to have dealt fairly with non-Indians and nonmembers who have raised ICRA claims. As discussed above, however, a full evaluation of whether ICRA has been under-protected requires a thick political theory.

Protecting rights and reshaping tribal practices. The costs of under-protection would be prohibitively high if tribal courts did not take their charge of interpreting the ICRA seriously. This response has not happened. As will be seen more fully below, tribal courts have created doctrines that impose significant limitations on tribal governments. To offer just a few examples, tribal courts have used ICRA to close a tribal jail;[99] enjoin tribal elections pending the implementation of changes in voter qualifications;[100] strike down ordinances that prescribed qualifications for public office;[101] reverse the removal of tribal council members;[102] reverse tribal banishment decrees;[103] impose obligations on tribal governments to provide information to tribal members;[104] require that terminated employees be provided representation at termination hearings;[105] dismiss criminal cases for the failure to prosecute in a timely fashion;[106] exclude from introduction into evidence information obtained pursuant to unlawful searches and seizures;[107] strike down or enjoin enforcement of ordinances for violating equal protection,[108] due process,[109] and the right to free exercise of religion;[110] and reverse countless determinations by tribal administrative bodies for due process violations.[111]

The respect accorded to federal precedent by tribal courts. A necessary (though not sufficient) condition to containing under-protection costs is that the tribal courts engage in good-faith efforts of interpretation. A strong indication that tribal courts take seriously their responsibility to construe the ICRA is the respect they give to federal case law construing the Bill of Rights. Although federal case law is not binding, federal case law is cited in nearly every tribal court opinion and, in fact, plays an important role in tribal court construction of the ICRA.[112] Tribal courts only occasionally engage in tabula rasa or retargeting, and almost always deploy some form of adapted adoption: tribal courts most frequently employ tailoring and fitted incorporation, commonly restandardize, and occasionally engage in stock incorporation.

The distribution of interpretive approaches suggests that tribal courts are not averse to consciously adopting Anglo law that they believe to be consistent with their tribe's values. This attention is a strong sign that the tribal courts do not irresponsibly interpret the ICRA, nor does tribal court reliance on federal case law mean that tribal courts lack legal imagination or that tribal court autonomy is a waste of resources. The significant tribal court deviations from ordinary federal doctrines documented in this chapter belie this suggestion. Though tribal courts virtually always look to federal case law for guidance, they neither reflexively reject nor parrot federal approaches.

Assimilation and syncretism. The reported ICRA decisions indicate that tribal courts have deeply assimilated the Anglo jurisprudential concepts that appear in the ICRA's substantive provisions even as they have given them applications that reflect tribal values. In the words of one tribal court, "[a]lthough tribal due process may differ when it comes to its application to customary and traditional laws, many of the principles embodied in the Bill of Rights have become key ingredients in the Indian legal processes."[113] The result is a syncretism of Anglo and tribal values and, in the process, a deep assimilation of many Anglo constitutional values. This integration constitutes further evidence that tribal courts have engaged in good-faith efforts to interpret the ICRA seriously, for such syncretism and assimilation likely would not have occurred absent good-faith attempts to construe the statute.

Importantly, assimilation is present not only when a holding wholly adopts federal law, but also as tribal courts advance unique constructions of the ICRA provisions. Consider, for example, the role that Anglo jurisprudential concepts play even as tribal courts define ICRA provisions by reference to tribal customs. The tribal custom must be fitted within an Anglo term, which leads tribal courts to assimilate

Anglo judicial concepts into their lexicon and way of thinking.[114] This regard may lead tribal courts to adopt the larger gestalt of the system of which the Anglo term is a part; for example, due process is part of a jurisprudential system that emphasizes the rights of individuals rather than, say, the duties of individuals or the rights of the government.[115] Interpreting an Anglo term by reference to tribal customs thus may affect a tribal court's understanding of its own tribe's customs, enacting a particularly deep form of assimilation and cultural syncretism.

These phenomena are well illustrated in *Begay v. Navajo Nation*.[116] The tribal court held that "[t]he concept of due process was not brought to the Navajo Nation by the Indian Civil Rights Act.... The Navajo people have an established custom of notifying all involved parties in a controversy and allowing them ... an opportunity to present and defend their positions."[117] To support this assertion, the court pointed to the tribe's customary approach to dispute resolution:

> When conflicts arise, involved parties will go to an elder statesman, a medicine man, or a well-respected member of the community for advice on the problem and to ask that person to speak with the one they see as the cause of the conflict. The advisor will warn the accused of the action being contemplated and give notice of the upcoming group gathering. At the gathering, all parties directly or indirectly involved will be allowed to speak, after which a collective decision will be made.

From this narrative of customary practices, the tribal court derived the content of what the court dubbed "Navajo customary due process:" "The heart of Navajo due process, thus, is notice and an opportunity to present and defend a position."[118]

The degree of deep assimilation in *Begay* extends far beyond attaching an Anglo label to customary tribal practices but, it seems, to the court's understanding of the practices themselves. The narrative was intended to identify the content of due process, but rather than yielding what the court found—that due process requires notice and a hearing—the narrative revealed that there were six components of customary dispute resolution: parties [1] *voluntarily* went to a [2] *respected elder* who gave [2] *notice* to the party believed to have done wrong of an [3] *upcoming group gathering* at which [4] *all parties directly or indirectly involved* were allowed to [5] *speak*, after which a [6] *collective decision* was made. Yet *Begay* concluded that only two of these components—"notice and an opportunity to present and defend a position"—constituted the "heart of Navajo due process."[119] Why? Surely the court could have concluded that due process requires that the aggrieved party choose an elder statesman as arbiter, participate in a group gathering, and then obtain a collective decision. It seems plausible to suggest that the Navajo Supreme Court's understanding of its tribe's customary practices was influenced by the court's understanding of what (Anglo) due process requires.

Another gauge of deep tribal court assimilation of Anglo jurisprudence is evidence of tribal courts' progressive fluency with the ICRA provisions. A large number of tribal cases employ terms such as *due process, fundamental rights, equal protection, warrant, probable cause,* and so forth, without citing to any statutory or tribal constitutional sources.[120] Similarly, many recent tribal court decisions that cite to an ICRA provision will then articulate the provision's legal test without citing to case law,[121] even where other parts of the decision cite to legal authority to establish legal propositions.[122] Ready invocation of the ICRA's terminology and doctrine without statutory and case citation suggests that the Anglo concepts have worked their ways into tribal judges' basic professional vocabularies and ways of thinking.[123]

Other signs indicate that the ICRA has led to a deep tribal assimilation of Anglo values. For one, tribal courts sometimes attribute the legislative purposes of advancing due process and other Anglo values to tribal ordinances, and accordingly construe the ordinances in ways that reflect those doctrines.[124] Also, tribal courts sometimes adopt federal doctrines without apparently recognizing that there are plausible alternatives.[125] For example, in *In the Matter of D.N.*[126] the Hopi Children's Court decided that a teacher's search inside a student's waistband violated the ICRA's guarantee against unreasonable searches. The court recognized that federal case law was not binding upon the court but consulted federal law for guidance in determining the merits of whether the teacher's search had, indeed, been unlawful. Upon finding a violation, the court immediately concluded that the evidence was to be excluded. The court did not cite to a single federal case to substantiate its decision to apply the exclusionary remedy, nor did it consider whether the exclusionary remedy fit the tribal context.[127] The court's reflexive adoption of the Anglo approach suggests deep assimilation insofar as the court did not even appear to appreciate that it had made a nonaxiomatic election.

Review of ICRA case law. This subsection examines tribal court interpretation of the ICRA. It provides a rich sense of the nature of the questions that have been presented to tribal courts, the substantive holdings of the decided ICRA cases, and the methodologies of interpretation that the tribal courts deploy. Rather than provide a case-by-case analysis of roughly 250 claims reported in 193 cases,[128] the subsection proceeds serially through the major ICRA guarantees and provides an overview of the most frequently litigated issues and outcomes. In the process, I point out the courts' methodologies of interpretation and identify the "hard cases," that is, the cases with results or reasoning that likely would be troubling to enthusiasts of American constitutional law (even if, in the end, they are not problematic when analyzed under a deep political theory).

The overview provides several useful vantage points to assess whether allowing tribal courts the autonomy to interpret the ICRA independently has imposed underprotection costs. The methodologies and substantive holdings suggest that the tribal courts have taken seriously their responsibilities to construe the ICRA. The case law also reflects deep assimilation of Anglo constitutional principles and an intriguing jurisprudential syncretism, further indicia of good-faith interpretations of the ICRA. Even without invoking deep political theory, the cases' substantive holdings support the inductive conclusion that the ICRA regime has not imposed significant under-protection costs; the cases are strongly rights-protective, even if the actual doctrines vary somewhat from ordinary federal case law.

Due Process

Due process was the most heavily litigated provision in the reported cases, accounting for 135 of the 248 litigated claims. Sixty-six of these claims were resolved in favor of the complainants and sixty-nine in favor of the government. Analysis of this case law reveals significant degrees of adapted adoption; tribal courts have engaged in a significant amount of tailoring and fitted incorporation and some restandardizing to accommodate unique tribal values and needs. The decisions almost without exception are strongly rights protecting; only a few qualify as hard cases.

(1) *Doctrinal overview of due process case law.* Most due process claims concerned notice and hearing requirements. Most decisions engage in either tailoring or incorporation, and most of the cases have found violations of the complaining party's ICRA rights. Many of the cases presented the question of whether particular arms of tribal government were required to provide notice and hearing to potentially affected persons in particular instances.[129] For example, one court utilized fitted incorporation when it held that due process was violated when the challenger of a tribal election was not given notice as to the date and time of a post-election hearing conducted by the election commission.[130] Another court deployed stock incorporation when it held that notices of suspension from a public employer must give employees "a sufficient understanding of the facts behind the suspension so that they can consider whether to grieve the suspension."[131] Many cases—both criminal and civil—have held ordinances void for vagueness because they provided inadequate notice of the required or proscribed behavior.[132] In the civil cases, one tribal court restandardized so as to provide tribal members greater protections than are afforded under federal law.[133] There were many cases in which courts applied fitted or stock incorporation to reverse government officials' run-of-the-mill neglect to afford affected parties a hearing[134] or the government's failure to abide by its own procedures and regulations.[135]

Though the study uncovered no tribal courts that rejected the federal rule that due process requires hearing and notice, the tribal courts frequently engaged in tailoring and fitted incorporation to accommodate tribal customs, values, and needs. For example, to determine whether an "ordinary" person can understand a statute for purposes of void-for-vagueness analysis, one court looked to the "ordinary Navajo person, who very often will be bilingual, with English as a second language."[136] Similarly, several tribal courts have held that notice is satisfied by posting and other methods of public announcement that, given the realities of tribal life, are reasonably calculated to inform interested parties.[137] Another set of cases utilizing subjective tailoring ruled on the basis of tribal custom that due process requires that virtually any nonparty be provided an opportunity to have her views heard in court.[138]

Tribal courts have used due process to impose obligations on various arms of tribal government to proactively provide information to tribal members. In *Simplot v. Ho-Chunk Nation Department of Health*,[139] the tribal court held that a tribal agency violated due process when it failed to inform an employee that he had a right under personnel procedures to displace less senior workers. The tribal court in *Knudson v. Ho-Chunk Nation Treasury Department* ruled that due process requires that terminated public employees be given the identical data relied upon by their supervisors so the employees can adequately represent themselves during the administrative review process.[140] Illustrative of a deep assimilation of Anglo values, the *Knudson* court cited neither to case law nor to statutory provision. One tribal court held that due process requires judges to inform persons jailed for contempt that they are entitled to a hearing of indigence after which, if they demonstrate poverty, they will be freed from jail,[141] and the court in *Hopi Tribe v. Mahkewa* determined that tribal police must inform persons stopped for drunk driving that they have a right to obtain an independent blood-alcohol test.[142] The *Mahkewa* court engaged in restandardizing, ruling that due process "include[s] and require[s] that defendants have a fair chance to obtain potentially exculpatory evidence to prepare their defense."[143] Neglecting to inform people of their right to an independent test, continued the court, "would in effect suppress evidence favorable to the defendant and would be violative of due process of law."[144]

By relying on due process, tribal courts have generated many other protections and relief. One court concluded that due process imposes a litany of requirements on the tribal police with respect to arrestees.[145] Another court held that due process requires that public employees have a right to representation at termination hearings.[146] Yet another court restandardized and reversed a trial court's order excluding several members from the reservation.[147] The court adopted a novel rule—that due process is violated where a court fails in the course of its opinion to give consideration to a liberty interest—and determined that family relationships implicate the liberty interest of "intimate associations."[148] The lower court had violated due process, said the tribal appellate court, because the excluded members had wives and children on the reservation and the trial court had failed to "consider[] these relationships and the serious, resulting breakup of the appellants' families and the effect on the tribal community."[149]

(2) "Hard cases" involving due process. One set of potential "hard cases" spotlights the tribal court tendency to avoid highly formalistic interpretations of the law and instead to consult what they understand to be the likely real-world consequences of the legal edict at issue. In *Hopi Tribe v. Lonewolf Scott*,[150] a tribal court restandardized when it rejected a void-for-vagueness challenge to a tribal ordinance.

Eschewing the federal standard under which statutes may be void for vagueness where there is the mere "possibility of discriminatory enforcement" and lack of notice,[151] the tribal court undertook a pragmatic, contextualized analysis of how the affected community understood the ordinance that was the subject of the challenge:

> It seems theoretic conjecture that the defendants claim that they did not understand the plain language of the statute.... The Hopi courts have properly limited the application of this statute so as to not overstate the criminal sanctions imposed on a defendant. Its meaning and application is clear to the police, prosecutors, and the reservation communities. There have been no episodes of capricious or arbitrary arrests based on [the ordinance] and the Hopi courts have applied this criminal statute in a uniform, consistent, and limited manner.[152]

This scenario probably qualifies as a hard case insofar as the court upheld an ambiguous criminal ordinance because there had not yet been discriminatory enforcement.

Another hard case is the tribal appellate court's decision in *Moore v. Hoopa Valley Tribe*,[153] which held that a trial court's poorly worded (and therefore objectively ambiguous) order for a defendant to appear at a contempt hearing did not violate due process because the defendant had actual notice of the hearing.[154]

How problematic from the vantage point of under-protection are these cases of subjective, realistic interpretation? Not very, for a subjective approach does not necessarily under-protect the ICRA. The federal case law's embrace of an objective approach is not necessarily tantamount to a rejection of the validity of a subjective approach in all circumstances. Indeed, federal courts' objective approach may be wise on account of the difficulties that would attend trying to identify subjective understandings across this country's large and diverse national citizenry. In the context of a small, homogeneous community, by contrast, a common subjective understanding may exist—notwithstanding "objective" ambiguity.[155] Consistent with this theory, the United States Supreme Court has utilized subjective analysis to uphold criminal provisions "[n]otwithstanding the[ir] apparent indeterminateness" in the military context because the provisions are applicable to a discrete community within which "what those crimes are, and how they are to be punished" was "well known."[156]

Interestingly, the challenges of securing justice for indigent parties have spurred many tribal court procedural innovations under the rubric of ICRA's due process provision. For example, although the ICRA's guarantee to the right of counsel does not include a requirement that tribes provide counsel to indigents,[157] one tribal court has held that due process requires counsel where charges are serious and defendants have limited education and understanding.[158]

Many other cases have held that due process imposes significant duties on judges to act to achieve substantive justice. One tribal appellate court ruled that trial judges must inform *pro se* defendants of the lesser included offense doctrine and must rule *sua sponte* on the sufficiency of the prosecution's evidence at the end of the prosecution's case.[159] The tribal appellate court in *Teeman v. Burns Paiute Indian Tribe*[160] imposed a duty on trial judges to research certain questions of law for *pro se* defendants. The trial court had refused to recognize the defense of self-defense because the defendant had not found a legal source for it. In response, the appellate court in *Teeman* court held that "[w]hen all the resources, training and background knowledge in law repose within the government, it is basically unfair to shift to the presumptively innocent defendant the burden of proving the law." The law instead "plac[es] responsibility on the trial court judge to rule upon the questions of law presented at the trial. . . . An unbelievably unfair result obtains when the guilt or innocence of a *pro se* defendant is decided upon his or her ability to research law."[161]

Many other cases have relied on due process to place other affirmative duties on trial judges. One tribal court concluded that where parties are indigent, not represented by council, and untutored in the law, tribal court judges should take an active role akin to judges in Germany's inquisitorial system. The judge's role may include propounding legal theories and developing the facts.[162] Another tribal court has indicated that judges may lead the questioning at legal hearings,[163] and yet another stated that judges may have *ex parte* communications with potential witnesses if the court then informs the parties of the substance of the communications and permits the parties to respond.[164]

Although these cases nobly intended to assist the impecunious, one may also think that they constitute hard cases due to the significant powers they grant to judges. But further reflection deflates this concern. Similar proactive and discretionary powers are exercised by administrative law and bankruptcy judges, who "share many characteristics with the inquisitorial model of dispute resolution."[165] In any event, to the extent that tribal judges exercise greater discretion than do Article III judges, such differences are not necessarily problematic. Tribal judges likely have greater political accountability to tribal communities than federal judges have over the people whose disputes they hear because tribal judges typically do not enjoy life tenure and socially interact more directly with the people over whom they exercise power. Such accountability makes discretion more palatable, for the possibility of meaningfully registering community dissatisfaction likely serves as a check on the tribal judges.

The most troubling hard cases are those instances in which tribal courts give what might be deemed as excessive weight to the community's interests in the due process calculus. In *Ben v. Burbank*,[166] for instance, the court upheld a tribal ordinance that gave appellate courts the power to refuse to hear appeals where "substantial justice" had been done between the parties. The appellant had refused to pay for construction that had been performed by a relative. After years of informal efforts to collect the debt, the relative sued successfully in court. The appellant appealed, arguing that the trial court had applied the incorrect statute of limitations and that the case should have been dismissed. The appellate court dismissed the appeal, refusing to even hear the appellant's argument on the ground that there could not be appellate review because there had been "substantive justice." In upholding the ordinance limiting appellate jurisdiction, the appellate court ruled that due process rights are "fundamental, but they are not absolute, limitless or unrestricted" and held that the tribe's interests outweighed the appellant's interest in seeking to "hide behind her statute of limitations claim in order to avoid paying for the work."[167] The tribe's interests were to achieve substantive justice, which furthers the "concept of community good and moral right," as well as tribal members' "deep feeling for responsibilities to others and the duty to live in harmony with them."[168]

Even more troubling is the case of *Helgeson v. Lac Du Flambeau Bank of Lake Superior Chippewa Indians*,[169] where the tribal appellate court upheld a trial court's finding that the defendants had violated a noncriminal ordinance that barred the possession of certain gambling devices notwithstanding the presence of a fundamental trial court error. In a trial whose "whole purpose . . . was to determine if the devices were contraband," the lower court had prematurely ruled that the devices indeed were to be considered gambling devices. The appellate court analyzed the due process issue by means of a balancing test drawn from federal law, but deployed tailoring to ascertain the appropriate weight to accord to the community's interest. Unusual for ICRA case law, the tribal court harshly criticized the ICRA, stating that "[p]rior to European influence, it was a well accepted belief throughout Indian Country that individual rights lie subordinate to the rights of the tribe" and describing the ICRA as a Western "imposition" that "infringe[d] on the rights of Indians to govern themselves."[170] The court proceeded to balance the costs imposed on the individuals of a monetary fine and forfeiture of the seized devices against the potential costs on the tribe of loss of the right to regulate gaming activity insofar as the illegal devices violated the tribal-state gaming compact pursuant to which the tribe was permitted to run its casino. Because the tribe's gaming operations was "one of the most precious economic resources [the tribe has] ever had," the court upheld the conviction.

The *Ben* and *Hegelson* cases are the types of due process decisions that most threaten to impose under-protection costs. Even so, it is not clear that the cases are, in the end, normatively problematic. The balancing that occurs in tribal court opinions is different in degree rather than kind from what occurs in federal decisions inasmuch as constitutional due process rights also typically involve *de facto* if not *de jure* balancing.[171] Monetary considerations are deemed a relevant factor in quantifying the government's interest in federal due process case law,[172] and the tribal interest in securing gaming is particularly strong insofar as most tribal communities were impoverished and incapable of providing basic essentials to their members before the income streams from gambling began to flow. Moreover, consider *Ben* and

Hegelson in the context of federal habeas case law, which similarly disallows habeas review for procedural defaults unless defendants can "demonstrate that the failure to consider the claim will result in a fundamental miscarriage of justice;"[173] in other words, substantive review in both the federal habeas case and the tribal court cases thus is tied to substantive fairness.[174] Finally, even if the *Ben* and *Hegelson* courts had accorded the community's interests greater weight than would federal doctrine, this consideration would not necessarily mean that they had under-protected the ICRA. Determining whether the cases under-protected the ICRA's rights would require a normative theory to identify the quantum of weight allocated to governmental interests that are problematic. Elsewhere I have argued that these cases' holdings are not problematically under-protective from this perspective,[175] though *Hegelson's* reasoning is troublesome insofar as it admits of virtually no limits.

Equal Protection

There were thirty-five published opinions concerning ICRA's equal protection guarantee. Courts ruled against the tribe in twelve cases, though two of these were later reversed by the case that most threatens to under-protect ICRA. The equal protection case law continues the twin trends of adapted adoption and assimilation that appear in the due process jurisprudence.[176]

(1) Doctrinal overview of equal protection case law. *Bennett v. Navajo Board of Election Supervisors*[177] is a strong rights-protecting equal protection decision that showcases both tailoring and assimilation. The case struck down an ordinance placing requirements on who could run for public office. The court invoked the federal doctrine of "fundamental rights" without citing to federal case law,[178] reflecting yet another instance of deep tribal assimilation of Anglo values. The court then tailored, looking to tribal traditions and deciding that the "political liberty" to run for office, "a part of the concept of republican participatory democracy [that is] grounded in Navajo tradition," constituted a "fundamental right" that was infringed upon by the ordinance in question.[179]

Like federal courts, tribal courts sometimes rely on ICRA provisions as guides for construing tribal ordinances. At issue in *Griffith v. Wilkie*[180] was whether an ordinance providing that "[t]he mother of an illegitimate unmarried child is entitled to its custody" meant that fathers could not be awarded custody.[181] Engaging in tabula rasa analysis, the tribal court concluded that if the ordinance were "interpreted as eliminating a father of an illegitimate child as a potential custodial parent, he is denied equal protection of the law."[182] It then interpreted the ordinance as establishing a presumption of maternal custody if paternity were undeterminable, but a "best interest of the child" test if the father were known.

Several cases have addressed allegations of the selective enforcement of tribal law. The most aggressive deployments of equal protection can be seen in two cases, each of which was a consolidation of numerous criminal cases. Mark Fox, a tribal council member who sat on the judicial committee, had been charged with assault in December of 1996, but had delayed his prosecution for more than a year by transferring the prosecutor originally assigned to him and not appointing a replacement. Fifteen tribal members who had been charged with various crimes around the same time as Fox, but whose prosecutions had gone forward, brought equal protection challenges. Without identifying a legal test, the tribal court accepted the fifteen defendants' arguments and dismissed the criminal cases against them.[183] Similarly, the tribal court in *Conroy v. Bear Runner* court found that an ordinance imposing an occupation tax had been selectively applied in violation of equal protection. *Conroy* held that equal protection is violated "where the statute or ordinance, although valid on its face, is enforced so as to discriminate against certain persons, occupations, or privileges of the same class."[184]

Other tribal courts have erected a higher burden, adopting legal tests almost identical to the federal standards.[185] The tribal court in *Southern Ute Tribe v. Baca*[186] ruled against the claim that inconsistent prosecutorial practice necessarily violates equal protection. Engaging in fitted incorporation, the court cited to federal case law to hold that "aberrational implementation of proper criminal procedures does not give rise to an equal protection claim absent a showing of intentional or purposeful discrimination."[187] The court explained the rule by reference to tribal circumstances: "courts publish few written opinions identifying particular court practices [and] a strict equal protection rule on procedural matters which would continually elevate particular variations in court practices to the level of equal protection claims would be unwise."[188]

Similarly, the tribal court in *Burns Paiute Indian Tribe v. Dick*[189] ruled that inconsistent enforcement of a tribal exclusion ordinance violates equal protection only where the tribe "has not excluded others similarly situated for similar conduct and the decision to exclude was based upon bad faith, or on impermissible grounds, as, for example, race, religion or the exercise of other constitutional rights."[190] Tribal courts have adopted similar legal tests in response to equal protection challenges to the distribution of tribal resources.[191]

(2) Hard cases in the equal protection context. Another set of cases in the selective enforcement context displays tribal equal protection at its most and least rights-protecting. Two cases decided on the same day by the same judge ruled that charging only males under a gender-neutral statutory rape ordinance violates equal protection[192]— equal protection at its most protective. This ruling was overturned, however, in *Winnebago Tribe of Nebraska v. Bigfire*,[193] the tribal court opinion of all the 193 reported cases that most threaten to impose under-protection costs. Setting the stage for its analysis, the *Bigfire* court stated that, "[l]ike most tribes, the Winnebago Tribe of Nebraska agreed to removal from their ancestral homelands and to the acceptance of new reservation lands precisely to preserve their separate cultural and political identity as a people."[194] Accordingly, the "tribal court is free to interpret the tribal constitution independently of the meaning afforded similar language in federal law."[195] It explained that "[t]his independence is not only a logical result of the sovereignty of the tribe as a separate

political community within the United States, but also a necessary option to protect the separate and different cultural heritage of the tribe and to adapt the meaning of legal concepts derived from Anglo-American roots to the unique cultural context of communal tribal life." Thus, there must be "sensitive adaptation of such legal concepts to the precise tribal community served by tribal law."[196] The *Bigfire* tribal court then restandardized and tailored, adopting the compelling interest test rather than the inter-mediate scrutiny test for gender discrimination under federal law and finding a compelling governmental interest in gender-differentiated application of the statutory rape ordinance.[197]

The bulk of the *Bigfire* opinion sought to explain why gender differentiations constituted a compelling government interest in the tribal context. "[I]n determining what constitutes a compelling governmental interest, this Court must always look to the preservation of tribal culture, traditions, and sovereignty and to the promotion of the health and welfare of tribal members as the most compelling reasons for the formation and operation of tribal government."[198] The court continued, the "traditional differentiations, commonly accepted and practiced by the Tribe without pejorative or discriminatory implications . . . must be sustained as involving the compelling tribal governmental interest of preserving tribal traditions and culture." The court then cited to evidence suggesting that, under tribal customs and tradition, "gender role differentiation and gender differences in legal or customary treatment related to" roles deemed to be "natural and expected" and that such "gender differences or disparities in treatment do not signal hierarchy, lack or respect or invidious discrimination." The court upheld the gender-differentiated application of the statutory rape ordinance because "within the Winnebago culture, the male clearly is assigned the obligation of protecting the women. The areas of sexual misconduct and domestic abuse were specifically singled out as areas in which the Winnebago tradition and customary law assigned roles and responsibilities based on gender."[199]

Most troublesome about the *Bigfire* opinion from the perspective of underprotection is that the court articulated virtually no limits external to tribal tradition on what types of gender-based differential treatment is unacceptable; only traditional practices with "pejorative or discriminatory implications" as determined by tribal standards would be struck down. On the other hand, whose standards should govern? The *Bigfire* court surely is correct that the role of women in many Native American communities "is not analogous to the roles of females in the Anglo-American cultures," and concluded that Native American (rather than contemporary American) values ought to be determinative under the ICRA. Those who take issue with *Bigfire* must explain why contemporary American sensibilities concerning gender should displace Winnebago sensibilities. Answering the question requires a full-fledged normative theory of what types of variations from ordinary doctrine are acceptable within a liberal polity as ours. Under the thick political theory I've put forward elsewhere, the gender differentiation upheld in *Bigfire* would be acceptable,[200] though the court's reasoning does not adequately cabin tribal discretion.[201]

Search and Seizure

Thirteen cases concerned search and seizure. Four found in favor of the parties claiming rights against tribal governments, whereas most of the others were circumstances in which the tribal court found probable cause or reasonable suspicion that upheld the challenged search.[202] In several cases, courts were interpreting not the ICRA or a tribal constitution but instead tribal criminal codes, several of which have adopted verbatim (or nearly so) the federal doctrines. These latter cases are germane for present purposes for the same reason that tribal case law construing tribal constitutions is instructive.[203]

The search and seizure case law continues the trend of adapted adoption found elsewhere in the ICRA jurisprudence. Without exception, the doctrines found in the thirteen cases closely track federal case law. Indeed, tribal courts in all cases utilized either incorporation or tailoring, suggesting a strong degree of assimilation. This conclusion is further buttressed by the tribal courts' tendency to recite the federal rules without citing to case law and, in one instance, the court's adoption of the federal exclusionary rule without appearing to have considered alternative remedies. Finally, there are few if any "hard cases" here; the reported search and seizure cases adopt legal tests that are at least as rights-protecting as federal law, and two cases used legal tests that are even more rights-protecting.

The case of *Winnebago Tribe of Nebraska v. Pretends Eagle*[204] is representative of the interpretive approaches found in the ICRA search and seizure case law. A tribal member had placed a call to the police, in which she stated, "Tom Pretends Eagle just almost side-swiped me. I think he is drunk." Police located Pretends Eagle's car and observed him, during which time they saw neither traffic violations nor erratic driving, but they still arrested him for driving under the influence. At issue was whether this warrantless arrest satisfied the "reasonable cause" requirement that appeared in the Winnebago Criminal Procedure Code. Though it recognized that federal case law was not binding,[205] the tribal court engaged in stock incorporation by adopting the definition of "probable cause" in Black's *Law Dictionary*. Looking to the "facts and circumstances within an officers' knowledge" that might lead "a person of reasonable caution in the belief that an offense has been, is being or will be committed," the tribal court held that the information provided to the tribal police "did not establish facts sufficient to show that the defendant was driving under the influence."[206] Tribal police accordingly were without authority to conduct a stop and frisk, for there is a higher tribal "standard for a stop and frisk than the Supreme Court set out in *Terry v. Ohio*."[207]

The tribal courts typically engage in careful, rights-protecting applications of the search and seizure standards. In *Hopi Tribe v. Dawahoya*,[208] for example, the court was asked whether an anonymous tip that the defendant was transporting an unknown quantity of alcohol in a truck on a certain road gave police "reasonable suspicion" to stop him. Engaging in stock incorporation, the tribal court answered in the negative because the tip did not contain sufficient indicia of reliability that could be corroborated independently by the police and could "lead to the inference that the informant had reliable access to inside information." Similarly, in *In the Matter of D. N.*,[209] which involved a school official's search of a student, the tribal court determined that although asking a student to empty his pockets and thereafter administering a pat-down search was reasonable, it was not reasonable for a teacher to have reached under the waistband of a student's underwear. A "search will be permissible only when the measures adopted in the search are reasonably related to the objectives of the search and are not excessively intrusive in light of the age and sex of the student and the nature of the infraction."[210] Finally, the appellate court in *Randolph v. Hopi Tribe*[211] reversed a conviction as it clarified the burdens of proof and persuasion in suppression of evidence hearings by means of fitted incorporation. The court canvassed non-Indian case law, found two general approaches, and then considered "which allocation of the burden of proof comports with Hopi public policy."[212] It concluded that the prosecution bore the burden of proof by a preponderance of the evidence.

In search and seizure—far more than elsewhere—tribal courts have adopted federal doctrine by means of incorporation.[213] One result is that tribal search and seizure jurisprudence is completely familiar to anyone acquainted with federal criminal law, as indicated by the presence of concepts of "reasonable suspicion,"[214] "probable cause,"[215] "stop and frisk,"[216] and the like. As discussed earlier, several reasons elucidate why this influence does not undercut the significance that it is tribal rather than federal courts that are interpreting the law. First, tribal courts sometimes conceptualize the legal test as being consistent with and advancing tribal culture. For example, after noting that federal decisions "are not binding upon this court," the tribal court in *In the Matter of D.N.*[217] adopted the federal rule that a "school official may conduct a search of a student's person if the official has a reasonable suspicion that a crime has been committed or that the student is in the process of committing an offense."[218] The tribal court engaged in fitted incorporation, partly attributing the rule to the "Hopi tradition and the Hopi's strong belief in the extended family [insofar as] a Hopi person who sends their child to school expects the school and its officials to act *in loco parentis*."[219] Conceptualizing the legal test as consistent with tribal culture facilitates both the assimilation of Anglo jurisprudence as well as cultural syncretism.

Second, tribal courts typically are assiduous in fitting the capacious federal standards they adopt to the tribal context, a task non-Indian courts may not be suited to accomplishing. Examined earlier in detail was the *Kahe* case, for example, in which the tribal court took account of the Hopi concept of the "welfare check" in upholding an officer's stop as reasonable.[220] Similarly, after adopting the federal rule that driveways are only "semi-private," such that the reasonableness of a driveway search turned on the possessor's expectation of privacy and the officer's reasons for being in the driveway, the tribal court in *Hopi Tribe v. Mahape*[221] found "the attitude of the Hopi people to be concerned about the safety and welfare of others"[222] to be relevant in upholding an officer's search of a vehicle containing human occupants that had been parked on a driveway for a long period of time during the winter; Hopi concern for others led to the conclusion that it was reasonable for the officer to respond to a tribal member's "concern for the safety and welfare of her family and neighbors."[223] The last two cases—*Kahe* and *Mahape*—are the search and seizure holdings that most threaten to under-protect ICRA insofar as they sanction the most expansive searches in all the case law, though they may not strike many readers as being particularly hard cases.

With respect to remedies, all the reported tribal court decisions have engaged in incorporation and prescribed the exclusionary rule upon finding search and seizure violations.[224] The *Pretends Eagle* court deployed fitted incorporation, taking tribe-specific considerations into account when it adopted the exclusionary rule. It expressly stated that its holding was provisional because "neither party brought to the attention of the Court any tribal customs or traditions which would help the Court in interpreting the Constitution," explaining that its holding "may be subject to review and revision by the court in the future upon submission of evidence as to tribal traditions and customs."[225] Another tribal court, in a testimonial to deep assimilation, did not appear to appreciate that adopting the exclusionary rule involved a choice. The *D.N.* court viewed exclusion of evidence obtained outside of a lawful search or seizure to be the natural outcome.[226]

It is interesting to consider why tribal courts have so fully adopted federal search and seizure jurisprudence, rather than developing independent doctrines as they have done with most of the other ICRA provisions. There are several possible explanations. First, federal search and seizure case law employs particularly capacious broad standards—like "probable cause" and "reasonable suspicion"—that allow themselves to be fitted to the Indian context. Second, the Anglo jurisprudence of search and seizure may fit particularly well with traditional tribal customs. Third, it is possible that the federal doctrine approach is sound at the levels of goal and standard and may even be largely transcultural.[227]

First Amendment Analogues

There were fourteen reported tribal court decisions construing the ICRA's First Amendment analogues of freedom of speech, the right to petition the government, assembly, and the free exercise of religion.[228] Though too small a sample to make any but preliminary conclusions, some patterns do emerge. Here, more than in any other ICRA provisions, the tribal courts have struck out on their own to develop ICRA doctrines independent of the federal case law. This response may be the case because American First Amendment protections are more reflective of a particular Western, liberal tradition and both shape and reflect societal values more than any other constitutional protections. It also might be a product of the complexity of much First

Amendment law, particularly free speech, which makes recourse to the federal approach a time-consuming and difficult project. Even so, several cases make use of incorporation, and where there is adapted adoption one still finds that the core First Amendment values have been assimilated, even if the Anglo values are refracted more sharply through the Indian cultural prism here than with other ICRA provisions. Also present are several cases where tribal courts engaging in tabula rasa assert that a given circumstance violates the ICRA provision without making any effort to develop a rule.[229]

(1) Free speech case law. In one of the seven cases concerning free speech, a trial court found that a newspaper had libeled an individual and then ordered that the newspaper print a retraction. Engaging in stock incorporation, the tribal supreme court reversed the retraction order due to the "right of the press to be free of governmental intervention." Continued the court, "[t]he choice of material to be printed is a protected exercise of editorial control and judgment and the government is prevented from regulating this process. A responsible press is desirable, but it cannot be legislated by the Navajo Tribal Council or mandated by the Navajo courts."[230] Although "[t]his does not mean that the press is free to print libelous material, because the government does have a legitimate interest in protecting an individual's good name,"[231] a court can only assess damages.

Another case provides an interesting example of tabula rasa *ipse dixit* reasoning.[232] A petition had garnered sufficient signatures to trigger a so-called "recall election" to summon school board members from office. A tribal ordinance provided that other candidates could run in the recall election. The tribal court concluded that the ordinance transformed the recall election into a *de facto* general election, thereby "harm[ing the school board members'] First Amendment rights." The court accordingly enjoined application of the tribal ordinance, limiting the election to the question of whether the board member should be recalled. The tribal court apparently thought that allowing new candidates to run burdened existing board members' ability to defend themselves against the recall petition, but the court did not provide an explanation as to why.

One of the issues in *Navajo Nation v. Crockett*[233] was whether a tribal agency's "interest in promoting the efficiency of the public services it performs through its employees" outweighed employees' free speech rights to "disclose demoralizing or disruptive" but true information about possible mismanagement and misconduct. The court ruled for the employee. *In dicta*, though, the court provided very different rules governing employee dissatisfactions that were not matters of "public concern," and which subordinated the disgruntled employee's interests to the community interests in encouraging negotiated solutions over litigation. The court did not cite to federal case law, but instead proceeded via tabula rasa.[234]

Another case considered whether an ordinance prohibiting the damaging of public property interfered with free speech when applied to protesters who had unearthed part of the Hopi-Navajo fence. Engaging in stock incorporation, the court decided in the negative, holding that the defendants' acts "constituted civil disobedience that resulted in physical damage and was not . . . protected speech and conduct. . . . [The] activities were not speech oriented, but were physical and allegedly destructive."[235]

(2) Free exercise. The one reported free exercise decision exemplifies tabula rasa in service of helping to preserve distinctive tribal institutions. The Hopi Tribe's constitution provided that villages could alter their political organization by means of a village-wide referendum if 25 percent of the "voting members" of the village signed a petition. *Kavena v. Hamilton*[236] and a companion case[237] concerned a referendum in "traditional villages," where "Hopi religion and village organization . . . is virtually inseparable [and m]embership in a village is in part religious as well as civil." The advocates of change expressly hoped to break the linkage between village membership and religion.

The specific question before the tribal court in *Kavena* was whether a petition containing 269 valid signatures satisfied the 25 percent voting-members requirement. An official of the federal Bureau of Indian Affairs who, under the Hopi constitution was responsible for "see[ing] that there [was] a fair vote," had determined the total number of voting members by counting the number of village residents who had voted in a previous tribal election. The tribal court found that this method of counting understated the number of voting members because "[m]any village members . . . do not reside in the village of their membership." Nonresidents still could qualify as members because "[v]illage membership in a [traditional] village . . . with the traditional Hopi organization, is a concept with much deeper meaning than mere physical presence or residence." Membership "involves the maintenance of religious and cultural ties and relationships with the village and its ceremonies" such that village membership is "virtually inseparable" from the practice of their religion.[238] Denying the franchise to nonresident members of traditional villages accordingly infringed nonresidents' "religious freedom."[239] The court permanently enjoined the election because less than 25 percent of the voting members had petitioned for the referendum, taking into account the larger number of village members.[240]

(3) Other First Amendment analogues. Only limited case law has construed the rest of the ICRA's First Amendment analogues, but they have almost uniformly been rights-protecting. One court confronted a claim that a tribe's "one person/one caucus rule," which allowed tribal members to attend the caucus of only one candidate for tribal council, violated the "right of the people peaceably to assemble." Engaging in fitted incorporation, the tribal court adopted the federal legal test and struck down the tribal rule.[241]

Several reported cases involved the right to petition for redress of grievances. One court, under the impression that it was engaging in stock incorporation, held that the right to petition "extends to all departments of the government," including "access to the courts," with the result that the right to petition waived the tribe's sovereign immunity for wrongful termination actions.[242] Another tribal court ruled that although the right to petition did not mandate judicial review of community council actions to remove council members, it did require that there be some "appropriate forum" to which grievances could be brought.[243] Yet another tribal court confronted the question of whether allowing counterclaims by governmental agencies for abuse of process unlawfully burdened the right to petition for redress of grievances.[244] The tribal court looked to federal and state decisions but restandardized, synthesizing its own legal test from several approaches that had been taken by lower federal courts and state courts.[245] Interestingly, this example appears to be a rare instance of restandardizing not to create doctrine fitted to tribal needs, but instead to create (what the tribal court believed to be) a better rule. The tribal court explained what plaintiffs would have to establish at trial to prevail and then remanded the case back to the trial court.[246]

(4) Hard cases. There is one hard case concerning freedom of expression. The tribal court in *Brandon v. Tribal Council for the Confederated Tribes of the Grand Ronde Community of Oregon* restandardized and tailored to uphold the suspension of a tribal councilman for making a vulgar statement to his cousin that violated an ordinance prohibiting council members from using vulgar speech in public. From the federal case law allowing the regulation of obscenity and fighting words, the tribal court restandardized when it formulated free speech's applicable legal test as requiring a "valid and compelling reason . . . to ban certain expressions or conduct upon the part of its citizens."[247] The court then tailored this test to the tribal context, concluding that

> the tribe has the right to expect its council members to conduct themselves in public with dignity and respect, and refrain from using words or phrases that a normal tribal member is privileged to use. [Moreover,] the type of language used by Mr. Brandon was arguably "fighting words" that were likely to create a violent or hostile situation. . . . Finally, the Grand Ronde Tribe has a vested interest in protecting its reputation throughout the community. It thus has a compelling reason to have enacted a provision in its tribal code prohibiting tribal members from involving themselves in actions or activities that may bring discredit or disrespect upon the tribe.[248]

To be sure, it is unlikely that a provision such as the tribe's would be found to fall within the "fighting words" exception under ordinary federal doctrine.[249] On the other hand, the *Brandon* court repeatedly stressed that "council members should be expected to conduct themselves at a higher level of restraint than other tribal members," and there is a well-established branch of free speech doctrine that provides relaxed standards for regulating the speech of government employees.[250] It could be argued that the Grand Ronde ordinance is analogous insofar as maintaining respect for political leaders could be said to be a precondition for effective public service. In any event, a tribal court's conclusion does under-protect simply because it deviates from what would have been the likely outcome in federal court. Once again, if and to what extent *Brandon* imposes under-protection costs has to be determined on the basis of a thick political theory.[251]

Sixth Amendment Analogues

There were twenty-nine claims based on the ICRA's Sixth Amendment analogues. Ten cases involved the right to a jury trial, eight cases addressed the right to counsel, nine involved speedy trial claims, one case construed the nature and cause of accusation clause, and one case concerned the guarantee of compulsory process. The pattern of adapted adoption continues, although there are significant deviations in right to jury and counsel cases because ICRA's language is different from the Sixth Amendment's insofar as ICRA enumerates conditions precedent to the vesting of jury and counsel rights. The tribal case law throughout the Sixth Amendment analogues is consistently quite protective of rights; there are virtually no hard cases here.

(1) ICRA's jury right. Three cases presented threshold questions concerning the applicability of the ICRA's jury right. One considered whether the jury right extends to civil matters.[252] Relying on straightforward statutory interpretation—the ICRA provision grants the jury right only to persons "accused of an offense punishable by imprisonment" —the tribal court held in the negative. In *Nisqually Indian Community v. J.S.K.*,[253] a tribal court engaged in stock incorporation and held that juvenile defendants who were in juvenile court proceedings for conduct that would be criminal for adults were not entitled to a jury trial. The *Nisqually* court relied on federal Supreme Court precedent that distinguished the punitive purposes of criminal proceedings from juvenile proceedings' goal of rehabilitation. Finally, the tribal court in Pueblo of *Pojoaque v. Jagles*[254] concluded that an adult defendant accused of theft was not entitled to a jury. The court reasoned that there was no jury right because the tribe's limited resources precluded imprisonment, and ICRA required juries only for offenses "punishable by imprisonment." This example might qualify as a hard case. On the one hand, the *Jagles* opinion fits the pattern observed above of the practical prevailing over the hypertechnical; the case might not be problematic for the reasons discussed there.[255] On the other hand, the *Jagles* court did not consider the possibility that "imprisonment" may be a statutory proxy for crimes with social consequences that are of sufficient magnitude to demand the jury guarantee. Under this view, the mere fact that the defendant could not have been imprisoned would not eliminate the need for a jury trial.

Another threshold question frequently litigated relates to the conditions under which the jury right can be waived. In contrast to the Sixth Amendment, ICRA by its terms contains a condition precedent: the criminal defendant must "request" a jury to trigger the tribe's obligation of not "deny[ing]" the request.[256] Though not explicit in the statute, all tribal courts I surveyed concluded that there must be a knowing and voluntary waiver of ICRA's conditional jury right. The court in *Confederated Salish and Kootenai Tribes v. Peone*, for example, held that "the failure of the accused to make a request for a jury trial constitutes a valid waiver only when that failure to request a jury trial is made knowingly and intentionally, and the accused is aware that s/he is giving up his/her right to a trial by jury."[257]

Similarly, in *Laramie v. Colville Confederated Tribes*,[258] the tribal court struck down an ordinance that required parties who had requested a jury trial at the start of litigation to confirm their desire to have a jury ten days before trial.[259] The court rejected the tribe's concern that the "difficulties of bringing in jurors over long distances and the efficient administration of justice" required confirmation. "While we are sympathetic to the concerns of the tribe, the fundamental right to a trial by jury cannot be diluted because of administrative difficulties."[260] Illustrative of the rights-protecting character of this opinion is that the tribal court rejected the tribe's argument that any burden on the right was cured by the defendant's option to move to continue the trial and then renew her demand for a jury trial, a procedural motion that both the tribe and the defendant agreed was "routinely granted." The tribal court then reversed the defendant's nonjury conviction and remanded the case to the lower court for a jury trial.

Other tribal courts have more readily found that the jury right had been waived. In *Squaxin Island Tribe v. Johns*,[261] the tribal court held that although the defendant had made a timely request for a jury, he subsequently waived it by "knowingly and voluntarily failing to appear on two occasions without justification after assurances of appearance were made to the court." The court noted that "[a]rranging and preparing for the trial and summoning the jurors was done at considerable expense to the court, its staff, and the tribe," and that the defendant accordingly had "waived or forfeited his opportunity for a jury trial."[262] In *Hummingbird v. Southern Ute Indian Tribe*,[263] a tribal appellate court acknowledged that the "right to a jury trial is a fundamental right" under the ICRA, but noted that, "in order to take advantage of this fundamental right certain procedures need to be followed. "The appellate court upheld the lower court's determination that the defendant had waived her jury right because the defendant had been informed of the applicable procedures—a written jury request and payment of a $25 jury fee—but had not followed them.[264] Though they are less rights-protecting than *Laramie* and *Peone*, *Johns* and *Hummingbird* likely do not qualify as hard cases. After all, though federal Sixth Amendment rights must be knowingly waived,[265] the bulk of federal constitutional rights are waivable without showing that the waiver was knowingly undertaken.[266] Further, as the courts in both *Jones* and *Hummingbird* pointed out, the defendants had actual knowledge of the procedural requirements.

Interestingly, one tribal court conceptualized ICRA's jury right as reflecting Indian values. The court in *Downey v. Bigman*[267] held that, with only a few exceptions, a judge's overturning of a jury's verdict violates the jury right.[268] As explained earlier,[269] the *Downey* court grounded its decision in tribal traditions of "participatory democracy." Conceptualizing juries as Anglo forms of tribal consensus-building and democracy likely facilitates the absorption of Anglo trial values insofar as the novel Anglo procedure is characterized as a traditional Indian commitment. At the same time, such a conceptualization allows the Anglo values to be reshaped in accordance with tribal values and needs, leading to cultural syncretism. The tribal court came to its conclusion by means of retargeting, identifying community participation in decision-making as the jury right's goal. It then created a novel procedure to implement the goal, allowing juries to propound questions to witnesses during trial.[270]

(2) ICRA's right to counsel. Consistent with what is implicit in the language of the ICRA, which prohibits tribes only from "deny[ing] to any person in a criminal proceeding the right . . . at his own expense to have the assistance of counsel for his defense,"[271] tribal case law is unanimous that the right to counsel can be waived. But tribal courts have required knowing waiver. Seven of the nine reported cases concerning the right to counsel presented the question of whether a particular defendant had knowingly waived the right to counsel. In two cases where tribal courts found waiver, explicit evidence existed that the defendant had been "fully informed" of his right to assistance of counsel, but that he "willingly chose" to represent himself.[272] In two cases the defendants' insufficient effort to obtain counsel was the basis for finding waiver: One defendant had been informed of his right to counsel, but "made no effort to contact spokespersons who appear before the Suquamish Tribal Court to assist indigent tribal members"[273] over a period of fifteen months, and another defendant "was advised at arraignment of his right to counsel throughout the proceedings but failed to exercise that right until a few days before trial," which was eighteen months after first having been informed of the right to counsel.[274]

All three cases finding that defendants had not made informed waivers were from the Hopi courts. This circumstance is due to the extensive requirements that have been judicially created in Hopi jurisprudence for ensuring "knowing[] and intelligent[]" waiver. The requirements were first articulated in the case of *Hopi Tribe v. Consolidated Cases of Emerson AMI*,[275] which tailored federal case law to the Hopi context. Speaking of the right to counsel as a "fundamental right" because it "protect[s] the defendant against the power of the Tribe," the court proceeded to construe a Hopi ordinance that required "knowing" waiver of counsel. Because the term "knowing" was not defined in the ordinance, the court looked to federal and state case law, noting that "[a]lthough federal law is not necessarily binding in Hopi courts, a review of federal law will provide an example of a standard that this Court can modify to meet the needs of the Hopi Tribe."

The tribal court in *AMI* ultimately held that defendants "must have knowledge about the dangers associated with proceeding *pro se* . . . , the charges against them, the range of allowable punishment, possible defenses to the charges, and factors in mitigation of the charge."As is true of the due process cases that seek to protect the indigent,[276] the *AMI* court charged the trial judge with the duty of bringing this information to defendants.The judge is also required to consider the defendant's "education and mental condition."The *AMI* court then mandated changes to a form given to defendants to inform them of their rights.The court also held that a defendant's signature on the form is not sufficient to constitute a waiver. Notwithstanding such a signature, the judge must make an "active inquiry."That step was necessary, the court held, because many defendants have limited command of English, because the "novel, frightening and stressful situation" of having been arrested might further compromise comprehension, because the original form provided so much information it is "probably overwhelming to most defendants," and because "[m]any defendants may be too embarrassed or frightened to admit that they do not understand something."[277] The *AMI* court then reversed three convictions,[278] whereas two subsequent cases each reversed additional convictions on the ground that there had been an invalid waiver of the right to counsel.[279]

None of the seven reported decisions concerning waiver qualifies as a hard case. Though the Hopi requirements are the most stringent, the less formalized approaches taken by the four courts that found valid waivers show no indications of being problematic. Finally, the fact that *all* tribal courts have some form of a knowing waiver requirement is a testimonial to their having taken the right to counsel seriously insofar as the ICRA does not expressly prescribe such a requirement.

(3) Ineffective assistance of counsel. Two reported cases rejected claims of ineffective assistance of counsel, and neither is a hard case. The tribal court's analysis in *Navajo Nation v. MacDonald, Sr.*[280] is a fine example of cultural syncretism.The decision began by conceptualizing tribal customs in Anglo terms, stating that the "Navajo common law" includes the "right to effective assistance of counsel."The court then engaged in fitted incorporation, adopting the federal approach but looking to tribal custom to guide its application.[281] It concluded that the defendant "received some very aggressive and competent representation," and that counsel "spoke for [the defendant] wisely, and with knowledge, consistent with a traditional Navajo 'talking things out' session." The second effective assistance of counsel case cited to the *MacDonald* opinion for the proposition that the federal case law provided the applicable rules and determined that the defendant had received an "excellent defense."[282]

(4) Speedy trial. Six cases raised speedy trial claims. All adopted the federal standard, which instructs courts to consider the length of delay, reason for the delay, whether and when the defendant asserted his speedy trial right, and prejudice in determining if there has been a speedy trial violation.[283] One tribal appellate court remanded the case back to the trial court to determine whether the defendant's speedy trial right had been violated.[284] The second reported case clarified when the clock for speedy trial purposes begins and upheld a tribal ordinance that provided that no delay of less than six months could be considered unreasonable for purposes of the speedy trial right.[285]

Four cases found that the speedy trial right had not been violated,[286] and in none of the cases do the facts suggest under-protection. In none of the cases did the defendants allege prejudice by virtue of the delays.[287] In two cases the delay had been caused largely or exclusively by the defendant.[288] In the third case the defendant appeared to have behaved strategically, asserting his speedy trial objection only three working days prior to a trial that had been scheduled six weeks before and relying on the theory that the rescheduled trial, which was due to occur ninety-one days after his arraignment, violated his rights because of a Washington state court rule requiring that no more than ninety days elapse between arraignment and trial.[289] In the fourth case, the delay of six-and-a-half months between arraignment and trial was due to the complexity of the case, which involved twenty-three counts of conspiracy, aiding and abetting bribery, and violations of the Navajo Ethics in Government Act that were brought against a former Navajo counsel member.[290]

The speedy trial cases exhibit tribal courts' readiness to consult federal case law in the absence of definite tribal customs. In *Komalestewa v. Hopi Tribe*,[291] the tribal court engaged in fitted incorporation in a manner that encouraged immediate integration of the Anglo values behind the provision. The court stated that "Hopi custom speaks to fairness, but it does not provide specific guidance for defining when the right to a speedy trial has been violated. Therefore, we will consider foreign law and apply it to the extent it is consistent with our customs, traditions and culture."[292] Identifying the speedy trial right as part of the tribe's cultural ethos of fairness is a fast track toward assimilation of the Anglo value. The tribal court in *Sisseton-Wahpeton Dakota Nation v. Cloud*[293] similarly was unable to locate tribal custom bearing on speedy trial and determined that "this court [therefore] is permitted to look at other decisions that define and clarify what speedy trial is."[294] The court identified four factors looked to by federal courts and remanded the case back to the trial judge.

(5) Nature and cause of accusation. Only two cases construed ICRA's nature and cause of accusation clause. The tribal court in *Walker River Paiute Tribe v. Jake*[295] held that the requirements of ICRA's nature and cause of accusation clause were not waivable. The *Jake* court deployed tabula rasa, most likely because it viewed the legal question as having a very simple answer,[296] and dismissed the criminal complaint. The tribal appellate court in *Hopi Tribe v. Consolidated Cases of Emerson AMI*[297] deployed fitted incorporation in its conclusion that the nature and cause of accusation clause requires a knowing, intelligent, and voluntary guilty plea.

(6) Compulsory process. The one reported case applying the ICRA's guarantee of compulsory process was decided in the plaintiff's favor. The defendant in *Sisseton-Wahpeton Sioux Tribe v. Seaboy*[298] had been arraigned in court on May 18, 1998, and the trial was set three weeks later, for June 8. Two days before trial, the defendant applied for and was granted a continuance. No new trial date was set. At the end of August, the defendant was informed that his trial would take place in four days. After the defendant's conviction for theft, the tribal appellate court reversed on

the ground that only four days' notice of the trial date deprived him of the right "to have compulsory process for obtaining witnesses in his favor."[299] In a sophisticated analysis, the tribal court deployed tabula rasa and reasoned analogically from the notice for trials required under federal civil rules.

Fifth Amendment Analogues (excluding due process)

There were fifteen reported decisions construing the ICRA's guarantees against double jeopardy, self-incrimination, and uncompensated takings. The cases were uniformly rights-protecting; there are no hard cases here.

(1) Right against self-incrimination. Three of the eight reported cases addressing the right against self-incrimination found violations or possible violations of the right. Nearly all reported cases deployed either stock or fitted incorporation. Two cases concerned interpretation of tribal ordinances that either mirrored the ICRA provision or incorporated more detailed doctrinal formulations found in federal case law.[300]

The right against self-incrimination has been assiduously guarded by the tribal courts. The appellate court in *MacDonald v. Navajo Nation*,[301] for example, raised self-incrimination concerns *sua sponte*, observing that although "[t]his court will not normally address errors which are not raised by an appellant, . . . [w]here it is not clear that an individual has made a knowing and intelligent choice between claiming or waiving a fundamental privilege, and where this court sees errors to which no exception has been taken and they would seriously affect the fairness, integrity or public reputation of judicial proceedings, we will act." The appellate court then analyzed a lower court order that the defendant produce personal diaries and other personal documents, directing the trial court to conduct a hearing to ensure that the requested documents did not run afoul of the standards the appellate tribal court had adopted via stock incorporation.[302]

Another illuminating decision is *Hopi Tribe v. Consolidated Cases of Emerson AMI*, where the tribal court explained at length why the right against self-incrimination is a "fundamental right[]" of defendants. It

> protect[s] the defendant against the power of the Tribe. . . . It forces the Tribe to prove the case against the defendant and not coerce a guilty plea from an innocent defendant. When a defendant enters a guilty plea, he waives many of his other rights including the right to a trial, the right to confront witnesses against him, and the right to have his own witnesses testify. This reduces the burden on the Tribe and makes it much easier for the Tribe to impose punishments.[303]

This may be a tabula rasa interpretation of the right, as the court did not cite to federal or state case law discussing the right against self-incrimination, though it did look to federal case law to clarify other ICRA provisions during its opinion. On the other hand, this formulation is sufficiently similar to the federal understanding that the decision more likely is an instance of deep assimilation where the values were sufficiently obvious to the court as not to require citation. Relying also on due process, the *AMI* court ultimately reversed the defendant's guilty plea and imposed a set of requirements on trial judges designed to ensure that defendants knowingly and voluntarily plead guilty.

Relevant to assimilation, two of the tribal courts conceptualized the right against self-incrimination as reflecting tribal values. After explaining the core of the "fundamental" right against self-incrimination—that "an individual must not give information to be used for his or her own punishment unless there is a knowing and voluntary decision to do so"—the tribal court in *Navajo Nation v. MacDonald Jr.*[304] explained,

> [t]his is also a Navajo principle. Navajo common law rejects coercion, including coercing people to talk. Others may "talk" about a Navajo, but that does not mean coercion can be used to make that person admit guilt or the facts leading to a conclusion of guilt. Navajos often admit guilt, because honesty is another high value, but even after admitting guilt, defendants in Navajo courts are reluctant to speak.

Similarly, in *Lower Elwha Klallam Indian Tribe v. Bolstrom*[305] the tribal court adopted the exclusionary rule as the remedy for violations of the right against self-incrimination, justifying it on the basis of tribal values: "While there is no Lower Elwha Klallam statutory or case law (this being a case of first impression) prescribing a remedy for failing to give *Miranda* rights in a timely fashion, this court finds that the exclusionary rule conforms to the spirit of fundamental fairness inherent in Lower Elwha Klallam law."[306]

None of the three decisions finding no violation is a hard case. One found no violation because neither of the defendants had made any statements to the officer and there accordingly had been no harm from the officer's failure to advise defendants of their right to remain silent.[307] In the second case, the defendant had been charged with fishing in restricted waters. The tribal court carefully canvassed federal and state law and engaged in stock incorporation in concluding that the right against self-incrimination does not apply to noncriminal proceedings.[308] The last case employed stock incorporation to define "in custody," finding no custody when the police asked the defendant questions at the scene of an automobile accident and in a hospital emergency room.[309]

(2) Double jeopardy. Four cases concerned double jeopardy. All four ruled in favor of the defendants, and the cases were at least as protective of double jeopardy rights as is federal case law. Three tribal courts engaged in fitted or stock incorporation. In an opinion reflecting assimilation, one court utilized the concept of double jeopardy to flesh out the meaning of a reasonableness inquiry in the context of administrative law. There are no hard cases here.

Three cases considered whether double jeopardy precludes the prosecution from appealing an acquittal. All answered affirmatively. Deploying stock incorporation, one of the three cases concerned a tribe's attempt to prosecute defendants under a tribal regulation that was distinct from the regulation the defendant had been tried for violating in a prior trial, but whose elements to be proven were "identical under the facts of this case" to what the tribe unsuccessfully had tried to prove in the earlier prosecution.[310] Another tribal appellate court determined *sua sponte* that the double jeopardy provision barred the prosecution from appealing the trial court's interpretation of the tribal ordinance the defendant had been accused of violating after the defendant had been acquitted.[311] Although the court did not cite to any case law, the legal test it used is identical to the federal approach, suggesting that the case is an example of deep assimilation and incorporation rather than tabula rasa. In the third case, *Hopi Tribe v. Huma*,[312] the trial judge had ruled *sua sponte* after a full trial that a police officer did not have an articulable suspicion of wrongdoing prior to making a stop and for that reason had acquitted the defendant. The prosecution appealed, arguing *inter alia* that the trial court did not have the power to ignore evidence to which the defendant had not objected. The tribal appellate court relied on fitted incorporation and dismissed the appeal on the ground that it violated double jeopardy.

The *Huma* court showcases tribal openness to embracing admittedly foreign jurisprudential values that the tribal courts predict will have salubrious effects on tribal life. The court noted that double jeopardy "is an elemental principle of the United States criminal law," and acknowledged that the tribe itself had neither "created a provision for the Tribe to appeal an acquittal [n]or expressly rejected the doctrine." Canvassing the purposes behind double jeopardy identified in federal case law, the tribal court concluded that double jeopardy "serves goals that will protect the Hopi people and increase the Hopi confidence in the courts."[313]

In the last case, a tribal administrative agency had suspended Mr. Rave's gaming license for a period of one year on the basis of an alleged noncriminal violation. Rave appealed, and a tribal court found that the agency had violated its own procedures and accordingly ordered the agency to correct its errors and award Mr. Rave relief. On remand, the agency denied Rave any relief and *sua sponte* levied a new penalty without providing him notice or hearing. Rave appealed again. Noting that "[i]t is a well-settled tenet of administrative law that agency decision must prove reasonable under the circumstances," the tribal appellate court concluded that the agency's action was "without foundation in law," "arbitrary," "capricious," and an "abuse of discretion." Continued the court, "[i]t is contrary to law. *This is the administrative equivalent of double jeopardy or to be twice punished for the same transgression*."[314] This case is probably best read as an importation of double jeopardy concepts in the service of defining reasonableness," illustrating deep tribal assimilation of Anglo jurisprudential values insofar as the court equated double jeopardy with fundamental concepts of reasonableness and fairness.[315]

(3) Uncompensated takings. Three decisions concerned the guarantee against

uncompensated takings. In one,[316] a tribal court engaged in tabula rasa interpretation when it held that the tribal housing authority's removal of "an abandoned vehicle hulk" that had not been moved for three years and that had been deemed by the government to be a "danger to inquisitive children and an eyesore to the community" was a taking that accordingly required compensation.[317] In the two other decisions, tribal courts engaged in fitted incorporation and held that the appointment of counsel to represent indigents is not an uncompensated taking because the practice of law is a privilege that can be conditioned on the performance of pro bono representation.[318]

Other miscellaneous ICRA rights. There also were several reported cases construing ICRA's protections against cruel and unusual punishment, bills of attainders, and *ex post facto* laws.

(1) Cruel and unusual punishment. Five decisions interpreted ICRA's ban against cruel and unusual punishment. Three upheld sentences against challenges. In *Colville Confederated Tribes v. Sam*,[319] a tribal court engaged in objective incorporation as it cited to an earlier tribal court decision that had adopted the federal standard that cruel and unusual punishment is violated by a punishment "arbitrary and shocking to the sense of justice." Relying also on the federal rule that the trial court's sentencing will be overturned only for abuse of discretion, the tribal appellate court upheld a sentence of 720 days for multiple offenses of driving while intoxicated in light of the defendant's "lengthy criminal history, failed attempts at rehabilitation" and the fact that the sentence fell far short of the statutory maximum.[320]

In the second case, *Navajo Nation v. MacDonald, Sr.*,[321] the tribal appellate court employed tailoring when it adjudged the magnitude of the offense by reference to tribal values. The defendant was a former chairman of the Navajo Nation who had been convicted of accepting bribes while in public office. Upholding a sentence of 2,160 days imprisonment and 1,800 days of labor pursuant to the applicable tribal ordinances, the appellate court explained that "[o]fficial corruption in public office is a serious offense, because it robs the Navajo people of their property. Even more seriously, using Navajo culture, it robs the Navajo people of their dignity."[322] Continued the court, "corruption in public office through bribes, kickbacks, and violations of ethical standards results in poor goods or services, favoritism to non-Navajos, and a host of other injuries to the public good." Finally, the parties who paid the bribes were non-Navajos, and "[w]e are not blind to past exploitations of the Navajo people, and the Navajo Nation Council was not blind to them when it enacted both a revised criminal code and an ethics code."[323] In a subsequent case the Navajo Supreme Court relied on *MacDonald, Sr.* to uphold a similar sentence against another defendant in the same public corruption case.[324]

In *In the Matter of A.W., a Minor*,[325] the court held that the ban against cruel and unusual punishment requires that a juvenile detention area "be provided with a padded area to lie on, a blanket, and food to eat."[326] The court ordered that the detention center be closed until it was in compliance with the court's understanding of what the ban on cruel and unusual punishment requires. The tribal court in *McDonald v. Colville Confederated Tribes*[327] similarly ordered the closure of a tribal jail on grounds that the jail had an inadequate ventilation system, a faulty and outdated electrical system, and conditions that presented a danger to the health and safety of the inmates.

(2) Bills of attainder and *ex post facto* laws. Five cases addressed claims that tribal legislation violated the ICRA's ban on bills of attainder or *ex post facto* laws.[328] Two cases entertained bill of attainder claims. One considered whether placing a tribal leader on administrative leave pending the results of a public corruption investigation qualified as a prohibited bill of attainder.[329] After noting that "[a] bill of attainder is apparently unknown to traditional Navajo culture," the tribal appellate court engaged in stock incorporation. The appellate court directed the trial court to apply the ordinary federal standard to the administrative leave, but stressed that the trial court should tailor the standard to the tribal context; in determining whether the leave constituted a "punishment," the trial court was instructed to consider not only "what historically has been regarded as punishment for purposes of bills of attainder and bills of pains under the law of England and the United States," but also "what historically has been regarded as punishment under Navajo common law."[330]

In *MacDonald, Sr. v. Redhouse*,[331] a later appeal in the case discussed immediately above, the appellant argued that amendments to the Navajo election statutes disqualifying from office people convicted of public corruption violated the ICRA's ban on bills of attainder. The tribal appellate court engaged in stock incorporation and dismissed the appellant's arguments. The court took judicial notice of other would-be candidates for public office who were disqualified under the amendments to conclude that the amendments did not "target" the appellant, one of the legal tests under federal law for identifying a bill of attainder. Three cases addressed *ex post facto* claims. Though none of the cases granted relief, none is a hard case. In one case, the tribal court engaged in stock incorporation in holding that legislation prohibiting convicted criminals from public office had a valid legislative purpose and accordingly did not constitute an *ex post facto* law.[332] In the second case, *Frost v. Southern Ute Tribal Council*,[333] the tribal court appears to have deployed tabula rasa. The chairman of the tribal council decided to conduct an investigation of the plaintiff, who was an elected member of the tribal council. A provision of the Southern Ute Constitution provided that the council should establish procedures and regulations for the conduct of removal proceedings, and the tribal council enacted such regulations only a few days after the plaintiff had been served with notice of the removal proceedings. The tribal court rejected the argument that such proceedings qualified as an *ex post facto* law because another constitutional provision granted the council investigatory jurisdiction.[334] The tribal court cited no federal case law to identify the applicable legal test. Also suggestive of tabula rasa is the existence of federal case law that squarely addresses the issue raised in the case and that would have decided the issue in the same way the tribal court did.[335]

The final case denying relief was *Colville Confederated Tribes v. Stead.*[336] Some background is necessary. The United States Supreme Court in the 1990 case of *Duro v. Reina*[337] had held that tribal courts did not have criminal misdemeanor jurisdiction over Indians who were not members of their tribes (known as "nonmembers"). This conclusion was contrary to two hundred years of settled law, and Congress soon thereafter enacted temporary, and ultimately permanent, legislation that reversed *Duro.* The temporary legislation was enacted on November 5, 1990, and by its own terms was set to expire on September 30, 1991. Defendant Stead, a member of the Rosebud Sioux Tribe, was arrested for driving without a valid driver's license on the Colville Indian Reservation during the time that Congress' temporary legislation was in effect. His trial took place, however, on September 8, 1991, eight days after the temporary legislation expired and one day before Congress enacted a second piece of temporary legislation.[338]

The question before the tribal court in *Stead* was whether the trial court had erred in denying Stead's motion to dismiss for want of jurisdiction on the day of the trial. The tribal appellate court decided that the trial court had jurisdiction. The appellate court canvassed the federal case law and engaged in stock incorporation, but the crux of the tribal court's reasoning did not turn on the niceties of *ex post facto* doctrine but rather on the proposition that the Supreme Court decision in *Duro* was incorrect *ab initio* and accordingly could not have extinguished the tribe's inherent authority over nonmembers. The tribal court buttressed its reasoning by quoting the legislative history for the permanent legislation, which stated that Congress intended to "[c]larify and reaffirm the inherent authority of tribal government to exercise criminal jurisdiction over all Indians on their reservations," not to delegate new powers to the tribes.[339] The tribal court also quoted a federal court decision that similarly had decided that tribes' jurisdiction over nonmembers "had always existed and . . . continued uninterrupted, despite the *Duro* decision." This example is the decision in the *ex post facto*/bill of attainder context that comes closest to imposing under-protection costs, yet it is difficult to say that the tribal court's decision is problematic.

The treatment of outsiders. Relevant to under-protection is how tribal courts have functioned when a party is either a nonmember of the tribe or a non-Indian (hereinafter an "outsider"). After all, the temptation always exists to favor one's own, and resisting it would be a sign of commitment to the rule of law. More cynically, one might attribute a well-behaved tribal judiciary to political accountability or cultural affiliation with affected parties rather than commitment to the ICRA. Because these factors are absent when an outsider's interests are involved, outsiders constitute a control group from which inferences can be drawn as to whether commitment to the ICRA or other considerations drives tribal judges.

Unfortunately, generalizing is difficult because there is only a small sample of reported cases—ten—where outsiders have been parties. This sample is explicable in no small part because tribal powers vis-à-vis outsiders are governed largely by non-ICRA doctrines for which there is federal court review. In any event, most of the tribal cases represent good-faith interpretations of the ICRA, and none involves patently outrageous reasoning or outcomes. However, two cases, though readily explicable on innocent grounds, may be instances where the reasoning and outcomes were affected by the presence of outsiders. One of the ten reported cases was resolved in favor of the outsider, five of the remaining nine are wholly unproblematic, and two other cases resulted in arguably harsh outcomes but do not signal tribal court unreliability. This subsection reviews the cases from least to most problematic.

Shohone Business Council v. Skillings[340] is the one reported decision that found in favor of a person who was, technically at least, an outsider. After Mr. Skillings had been adjudged to be a member of the Shohone tribe in a trial, the tribal council passed an act stating that Skillings was *not* a tribal member. The tribal court struck this down on the ground that revoking membership rights following a full litigation violated due process. The facts of *Skillings*, however, make it unrepresentative *vis-à-vis* outsiders, for the plaintiff had obvious and significant ties to the tribe.

Five of the cases that ruled against the outsiders are not even arguably troublesome. In one case,[341] the tribal court approved of the plaintiff's service by mail on the outsider notwithstanding written tribal rules that appeared to require personal service. Due process was not violated because the defendants had actual notice and the "well-established procedures of this Court provide the option of service by mail for all papers, including the initial petition."[342] In another case,[343] the tribal court engaged in stock incorporation when it used rational basis to review an equal protection challenge that the appellant, "as a nonmember Indian, is placed in the classification 'Indian' for criminal prosecution, along with [member] Navajos, when non-Indians are not."[344] The tribal court found strong reasons to permit the prosecution of nonmember Indians, including the fact that about 6.39 percent of the population of the Navajo Reservation was composed of nonmember Indians.[345] The court's holding is consistent with longstanding federal Indian law that permits tribes to exercise misdemeanor criminal jurisdiction over nonmember Indians but not non-Indians,[346] further evidence of the reasonableness of the tribal court's decision.

The other three unproblematic cases raised equal protection and due process challenges to tribes' exertions of power over nonmembers on grounds that nonmembers did not have political representation within the tribe. Two challenges were in the jury context. Tribal courts rejected arguments in *Sanders v. Royal Associates Management, Inc.*[347] and in *Hopi Tribe v. Lonewolf Scott*[348] that tribal juries were inherently unfair because only tribal members could be jurors. Both courts observed that this method was the only way to ensure that juries constitute a representative cross-sample of the population, a legitimate governmental interest.[349] The *Sanders* court also noted that the tribe has "no enforceable authority to order non-members to appear for jury duty and serve on" juries.[350] These are reasonable holdings that reflect the same logic that leads states to exclude non-domiciliaries from jury service.[351]

Similarly, the tribal court in *Iron Cloud v. Meckle*[352] rejected the argument that tribal laws violated equal protection and due process because nonmembers could not vote in tribal elections or hold office. This holding resonates with longstanding federal policy permitting tribes to exercise jurisdiction over nonmembers for misdemeanor criminal offenses committed on the reservation. Such tribal powers are a product not of consent, but of the inherent nature of tribal sovereignty.[353] For similar reasons, states are permitted to exercise criminal jurisdiction over noncitizens who commit crimes in the state, and the federal government can exercise criminal jurisdiction over aliens when they are in the United States.[354]

We now move to two cases that resulted in arguably harsh outcomes but that likely do not signal tribal court disregard of outsiders. In one, the tribal court upheld against a due process challenge a $6,000 tax penalty assessed against an outsider for failing to post a bond.[355] The court held that due process did not require that the tax penalty be proportionate to the actual damage incurred by a party (indeed, the tribe admitted that it had suffered no loss or harm). Though the outcome might be deemed harsh, the applicable ordinance did not by its terms apply only to outsiders, and there was no basis for believing that the outcome had anything to do with the fact that the appellant was an outsider. The same is true in the other case, where the guardian of a non-Indian's security interest lost the interest because he failed to perfect the interest in accordance with tribal law. [356] Though the tribal court noted that the guardian had been the victim of "sharp dealing," the tribal appellate court showed that the outsider had not been treated under tribal law any differently than an insider would have been.[357]

The next case did not create any harsh results—in fact the outcome seems quite fair—but there is room to wonder whether the court would have been less activist had no outsider been involved. At issue in *Thorstenson v. Culmore*[358] was how to construe a bylaw in the tribal constitution providing that tribal courts have jurisdiction over "disputes or lawsuits . . . between Indians and non-Indians when such cases are brought before it by stipulation of both parties."[359] The outsider argued that the tribal court did not have jurisdiction because his written contract with a member Indian did not contain a provision explicitly stipulating to the tribal court's jurisdiction. The tribal court held that the contract on its own satisfied the "stipulation" requirement. The court relied upon the ICRA's due process provision, reasoning that to require an express stipulation would "contravene[] fundamental Lakota cultural notions of fair play that allow people the opportunity to be heard, which includes the right to have 'their day in court.'"[360] To understand the stipulation requirement otherwise would

> offend[] basic notions of due process in that it potentially creates
> situations in which the tribe affirmatively regulates the (civil) con-
> duct of private parties (both Indian and non-Indian) on the reser-
> vation but permits or condones the inability of injured parties to
> seek to enforce or to vindicate (through civil litigation) the very

> legal norms the tribe expects them to comply with. You cannot,
> it seems to this court, establish legal norms to regulate civil con-
> duct, but then effectively place the opportunity to pursue reme-
> dial redress in the hands of the alleged "wrongdoer." If due process
> means anything, it must, at its most fundamental level, mean that
> the duty to obey the civil law carries with it the necessary cor-
> relative of access to the appropriate (tribal) forum to be heard.[361]

These arguments are all reasonable, but the fact remains that the *Cudmore* court
adopted quite an activist approach. One can only speculate as to whether the tribal
court's analysis was affected by the fact that an outsider was involved. On the other
hand, as shown by the numerous tribal court cases surveyed above that deployed
activist reasoning when the parties were insiders, the mere fact of judicial activism
is not unusual.

The most problematic case, *Public Service Co. of New Mexico v. Tax Protest Panel*,[362]
resulted in a harsh outcome for the outsider, but it once again is unclear whether
the court's holding was due to the fact that the losing party was an outsider. The
tribal court determined that a 7 percent possessory interest tax assessed against the
value of property owned by a public utility that passed through a reservation did not
violate equal protection.[363] The court engaged in stock incorporation, adopting the
rule that equal protection precludes classification of taxpayers based on residence.
The court determined that the tax at issue classified property on the basis of usage,
which under federal law is subject to only rational basis scrutiny, and the tribal court
was able to identify rationales that justified exemptions for retail businesses and
homes.

The problem not recognized by the court was that the rationales turned on considerations virtually metonymic with residency. For example, the court explained that
the retail business and home exemption "seems to be intended to facilitate (or at least
not penalize) the building of homes, renovation of existing homes, and location of jobs
on the reservation" and justified the exemptions for consumer businesses as methods
to "preserve the existing services for the community as well as to encourage location
of new services into the community."[364] On this reasoning, virtually no possessory
interest tax that in effect differentiated between insiders and outsiders would be struck
down. Nevertheless, the near-toothless standard adopted by the tribal court may have
been a good-faith determination that high deference is appropriate in the area of local
taxation.[365] Indeed, as the tribal court correctly noted, the United States Supreme Court
has adopted a highly deferential approach in the context of local taxation.[366]

To conclude quickly, although there is only limited case law concerning outsiders, the bulk, if not the entirety, of the cases conforms to the pattern of responsible and good-faith interpretation of the ICRA observed with respect to insiders.
Two cases may be instances when tribal court dispositions were affected by the
presence of outsiders, and for this reason the treatment of outsiders, though not

demonstrably problematic, merits further attention as case law develops over time. The fact that the bulk of the case law concerning outsiders appears to be well-functioning constitutes provisional additional evidence that tribal courts have worked well insofar as there is no indication that tribal courts have succumbed to the temptation to disadvantage the outsider. Further, outsider jurisprudence suggests that factors aside from political accountability and cultural affiliation have led tribal courts to engage in good-faith attempts to apply the ICRA.

CONCLUSIONS

Strong preliminary evidence indicates that the ICRA is a well-functioning regime of multiple authoritative interpreters, though a definitive determination requires access to more case law than currently is publicly available. The ICRA regime has realized the potential benefits of institutional diversity and sustaining valuable idiosyncratic communities, as it has allowed for the creation of doctrines and institutions that reflect the distinctive needs and values of Native Americans. The regime also has let the tribes transform their community narratives and self-understandings from mere literature to law, lending these narratives and self-understandings the weight, socializing power, and coercive potential that characterize law. All this effort supports tribal culture. The ICRA has provided extraordinary opportunities for self-governance, even as it has constrained tribal autonomy by imposing Anglo political values.

Leaving ICRA's interpretation and enforcement in the hands of tribal courts does not seem to have created significant under-protection costs. The legal doctrines that tribal courts have created, as well as their methods of interpretation, suggest that tribal courts have interpreted the ICRA in good faith, a necessary though not sufficient condition to guard against under-protection. The ICRA has been deployed to require significant changes in tribal governmental practices and to create extensive rights for individuals. Tribal courts take federal case law seriously and tend to deviate from it only for good reasons. Moreover, tribal courts have deeply assimilated many Anglo constitutional values.

This chapter's findings also clarify several important issues in the field of American Indian law. Two of the issues have arisen in the context of the limited matters over which federal courts have subject-matter jurisdiction over ICRA claims. First, some federal courts have not understood that legal rights such as due process may look different in Indian country.[367] For example, in response to the argument that due process protections of Native Americans against tribal governments are different from the due process protections of non-Indians in general American society, the United States Court of Appeals for the Second Circuit has replied, "there is simply no room in our constitutional order for the definition of basic rights on the basis of cultural affiliations."[368] This chapter's empirical study corrects this severe misconception.

Second, even among those federal courts that have not made the Second Circuit's error, some have held that variations from federal doctrines are permissible only when the Indian practice being challenged "differ[s] significantly from those commonly employed in Anglo-Saxon society."[369] But when tribes adopt procedures akin to those found in general society, these courts have held, the tribes are subject to the ordinary federal requirements imposed by due process, equal protection, and so forth.[370] The federal courts that have adopted this approach have not offered a theoretical justification for it, and this article's analysis suggests several notable problems with it. Insofar as it is premised on the view that only gross variations from Anglo approaches are of importance to Indian tribes, the approach is premised on a misconception; tailoring can be very important insofar as it can create significant doctrinal variations. Further, these federal courts' approach provides an incentive for tribes to avoid procedures akin to Anglo procedures, threatening to interfere with the assimilation and valuable cultural syncretism that otherwise occurs. Finally, requiring tribes to adopt federal approaches undermines the assimilation and syncretism that ordinarily accompany the deployment of fitted incorporation.

Third, and perhaps most importantly, this chapter's findings counsel strongly against the proposals advanced by some commentators and members of Congress that federal court jurisdiction over the ICRA be expanded, or that tribal court jurisdiction be curtailed, because tribal courts have not responsibly interpreted the ICRA.[371] The concerns purportedly prompting these proposals have been based on anecdotal evidence.[372] Close examination of the tribal case law suggests that they are grossly overstated if not misplaced.[373] This chapter's study suggests that the ICRA's regime of multiple authoritative interpreters has worked well. To be sure, the study's conclusions in this regard are limited due to the restricted sample of available tribal case law to analyze. At the very least, however, the study's preliminary findings suggest that additional research be done, or that changes like requiring publication of tribal court decisions be implemented, before drastically limiting tribal court jurisdiction.[374]

NOTES

I would like to thank Kathy Baker, Anita Bernstein, Jacob Corre, David P. Currie, Howard Eglit, Jack L. Goldsmith, Sarah K. Harding, Dan M. Kahan, Hal Krent, John Parry, Dean Henry Perritt, Jr., Jeff Sherman, Dina Warner, Richard Wright, and the participants in a Chicago-Kent Roundtable for providing exceedingly helpful comments and questions. This chapter largely draws from Mark D. Rosen, *Multiple Authoritative Interpreters of Quasi-Constitutional Federal Law: Of Tribal Courts and the Indian Civil Rights Act*, 69 FORDHAM L. REV. 479 (2000).

1. *See* Oliphant v. Suquamish Indian Tribe, 435 U.S. 191, 210 (1978); Talton v. Mayes, 163 U.S. 376 (1896).

2. The only express remedy provided in the ICRA is a habeas provision in 25 U.S.C. § 1303, which states that "[t]he privilege of habeas corpus shall be available to any person, in a court of the United States, to test the legality of his detention by order of an Indian tribe." 25 U.S.C. § 1303 (2006). Based on legislative history and an assessment of the Act's "distinct competing purposes" of guaranteeing the rights of individual members of the tribe and encouraging Indian self-government, the Supreme Court has held that habeas corpus review is the *exclusive* path for federal court review of allegations of tribal violations of the Act. *See* Santa Clara Pueblo v. Martinez, 436 U.S. 49, 72 (1978).

3.   The federal courts of appeals are without jurisdiction by virtue of the fact that lower federal courts generally are without subject matter jurisdiction under the *Martinez* decision and there is no special appellate statute granting jurisdiction. *See* 28 U.S.C. § 1291 (2006). Despite the fact that the ICRA is federal law, no jurisdictional statutes would appear to grant the Supreme Court jurisdiction to review tribal court opinions that are not already subject to federal appellate court review. *See* 28 U.S.C. § 1253, 1254, 1257, 1258 (2006). The question of whether the Supreme Court can review such tribal court decisions has never been presented, and after *Martinez* the Court has not heard any challenges to tribal court interpretations of ICRA's substantive provisions.

4.   *See Martinez*, 436 U.S. at 55 ("recognizing that standards of analysis developed under the Fourteenth Amendment's Equal Protection Clause [are] not necessarily controlling in the interpretation of this statute [the ICRA]").

5.   A long line of scholarly literature discusses rules and standards. *See, e.g.,* FREDERICK SCHAUER, PLAYING BY THE RULES: A PHILOSOPHICAL EXAMINATION OF RULE-BASED DECISION-MAKING IN LAW AND IN LIFE (1991); Kathleen M. Sullivan, *The Supreme Court, 1991 Term—Foreword: The Justices of Rules and Standards*, 106 HARV. L. REV. 24, 57–69 (1992); Mark D. Rosen, *What Has Happened to the Common Law? Recent American Codifications, and Their Impact on Judicial Practice and the Law's Subsequent Development*, 1994 WIS. L. REV. 1119, 1162–63 [hereinafter Rosen, *Recent American Codifications*].

6.   Mark D. Rosen, *Nonformalistic Law in Time and Space*, 66 U. CHI. L. REV. 622, 623 (1999).

7.   Oliver v. United States, 466 U.S. 170, 177, 181–83 (1984).

8.   For example, early case law understood that the goal of the free speech clause was to preclude prior restraints, with the result that publishers could be punished after publication if their works were deemed to harm the public welfare. *See, generally,* DAVID M. RABBAN, FREE SPEECH IN ITS FORGOTTEN YEARS 132 (1997). The contemporary understanding of the free speech clause's goal is considerably broader. *See, e.g.,* R.A.V. v. City of St. Paul, 505 U.S. 377 (1992) (holding that an ordinance banning hate speech violates the First Amendment).

9.   It is frequently the case that the identified goal implies a limited set of possible legal tests, but it also frequently is the case that two or more possible goals could lead to an identical legal test, the significance of which is that the chosen goal is reflected only in the legal test's application.

10.   California v. Ciraolo, 476 U.S. 207, 211 (1986).

11.   Over time, the facts of decided cases frequently crowd out the standard, as can be seen when courts reason analogically from the facts of previously decided cases.

12.   *See Oliver*, 466 U.S. at 177.

13.   *See Ciraolo*, 476 U.S. at 213–14.

14.   The mere fact that a tribal court does not cite to federal case law does not mean it is engaging in tabula rasa. Federal standards sometimes become so ingrained that courts invoke the formula (for example, due process requires notice and hearing) without bothering to cite to federal case law. Such courts do not ignore the federal case law but rather have deeply assimilated it. *See* discussion *infra* at 29. Sometimes it can be difficult to distinguish tabula rasa from this type of deep assimilation. *See* discussion *infra* at 59.

15.   To be sure, tabula rasa represents an idealization insofar as it is unlikely that a tribal court justice would be completely unaware of at least some of the Supreme Court precedent and hence could not be said to construe the provision without reference to the federal case law, even if federal cases are not mentioned. Even so, the mere effort to take a tabula rasa approach to interpreting a provision is significant for purposes of understanding the nature of the resulting jurisprudence.

16.   Navajo Nation v. Crockett, 24 Indian L. Rep. 6027 (Nav. Sup. Ct. 1996).

17.   *Id.* at 6028.

18.   *Id.* at 6029.

19.   *Id.* at 6029.

20.   *Id.* Unless the employee's dissatisfactions concern matters of "public concern." *Id.*

21.   More frequently, the first time it proceeds to construe a provision via the tabula rasa approach, a court does not create "doctrines," but instead produces an *ipse dixit* opinion that tautologically identifies a set of facts as violative of an ICRA provision without attempting to formulate a legal test. *See, e.g.,* Rave v. Ho-Chunk Nation Gaming Commission, 25 Indian L. Rep. 6042 (Ho-Chunk Nat. Tr. Ct. 1997). This parallels the reasoning found in the early opinions of the United States Supreme Court. *See, e.g.,* DAVID P. CURRIE, THE CON-

STITUTION IN THE SUPREME COURT: THE FIRST HUNDRED YEARS 443 (1985) (noting that the Supreme Court's analysis in its first First Amendment case was "wholly conclusory"). Such a pattern of *ipse dixit* decision-making followed by rule-generation is not surprising, but instead is consistent with the common law method of lawmaking that characterizes the constitutional interpretation undertaken by courts.

22. *See, e.g.*, MacDonald v. Navajo Nation, 18 Indian L. Rep. 6003, 6007–08 (Nav. Sup. Ct. 1990) (undertaking close analysis of federal self-incrimination case law to determine whether the protection applies to personal diaries; "[w]hile the thrust of Supreme Court decisions appears to be approaching such a holding, we are not prepared to conclude that such is the actual state of the law").

23. Even in these circumstances, tribal courts are not wholly superfluous insofar as incorporation is *their* decision, thereby advancing the value of self-government.

24. In *Cheyenne River Sioux Tribe v. Williams*, for example, the tribal court adopted the federal "open fields" search and seizure rule, under which an "open field is neither a house nor an effect, and therefore the government's entrance upon open fields in not an unreasonable search within the meaning of the fourth amendment"—only after determining that the federal doctrine was the "most appropriate and just doctrine to apply in the tribal context." 19 Indian L. Rep. 6001, 6002–3 (Chy. R. Sx. Ct. App. 1991) (citing to Oliver v. United States, 466 U.S. 170 (1984)).

25. I develop this point in greater detail *infra* at 19.

26. In practice, it can be difficult to distinguish between tailoring and fitted incorporation because it is not always clear whether a standard has become a rulified standard. Though the precise characterization may be a close call, the model is useful because locating an interpretation on the border between tailoring and incorporation still communicates much about the nature of the court's reasoning and the deviation from ordinary doctrine.

27. 26 Indian L. Rep. 6061 (CCT Tribal Ct. 1999).

28. *Id.* at 6061 (citing Gerstein v. Pugh, 420 U.S. 103 (1975)).

29. *Id.* at 6061.

30. *Id.* at 6061.

31. *See, e.g.*, Gentile v. State Bar of Nevada, 501 U.S. 1030, 1082 (1991) (O'Connor. J., concurring).

32. 14 Indian L. Rep. 6001, 6005 (Hopi Tr. Ct. 1986).

33. 22 6145 (Nav. Sup. Ct. 1995).

34. *See, e.g.*, Lewis v. United States, 518 U.S. 322, 334 (Kennedy, J., concurring) ("The primary purpose of the jury in our legal system is to stand between the accused and the powers of the State"); Colgrove v. Battin, 413 U.S. 149, 157 (1973) ("the purpose of the jury trial in criminal cases [is] to prevent government oppression and, in criminal and civil cases, to assure a fair and equitable resolution of factual issues") (internal citations omitted). Only occasionally has the Court alluded to the benefit to the community of participating in law making, *See, e.g.*, J.E.B. v. Alabama *ex rel.* T.B., 511 U.S. 127, 140 (1994).

35. *Downey*, at 6146–7.

36. *Cf.* Rosen, *Recent American Codifications, supra* note 5, at 1217–52 (observing a similar phenomenon that results from codifying common law).

37. *See* Mark D. Rosen, *Our Nonuniform Constitution*, 77 TEXAS REV. 1129, 1148–49 (1999).

38. *See Martinez*, 436 U.S. at 55. For an example of a pre-*Martinez* appellate court decision that held the same, *see* Tom v. Sutton, 533 F.2d 1101, 1104 n. 5 (9th Cir. 1976).

39. *Martinez*, 436 U.S. at 72.

40. For a full exposition of this, *see* Mark D. Rosen, *The Outer Limits of Community Self-Governance in Residential Associations, Municipalities, and Indian Country: A Liberal Theory*, 84 VA. L. REV. 1053, 1136, at 1089–1106 (1998) (arguing that commitments to due process and equal protection require that certain "illiberal" communities be given significant powers to govern themselves). In addition, the normative strength of Native Americans' claims to variations that facilitate the flourishing of their communities surely are strengthened by virtue of the history of their displacement by the early Americans.

41. Mine builds on John Rawls. For a prominent alternative, *see* AMARTYA SEN, THE IDEA OF JUSTICE 52–74 (2009).

42. *See* Rosen, *The Outer Limits of Community Self-Governance, supra* note 40, at 1136 (1998).

43. THE INDIAN CIVIL RIGHTS ACT: A REPORT OF THE UNITED STATES COMMISSION ON CIVIL RIGHTS

29 (1991) [hereinafter *Commission Report*].

44. The peacemaker court "integrate[s] traditional Navajo dispute resolution methods with traditional Anglo-American judicial methods."Tom Tso, *The Process of Decision Making in Tribal Courts*, 31 ARIZ. L. REV. 225, 227 n.3 (1989). *See also* James W. Zion, *The Navajo Peacemaker Court: Deference to the Old and Accommodation to the New*, 11 AM. INDIAN L. REV. 89 (1983).

45. *Commission Report, supra* note 43, at 32–35.

46. *Id*. at 32. For example, whereas the Navajo Tribal Courts handled more than 40,000 cases in 1983, the Las Vegas Paiute Tribal Court heard only fourteen. *Id*.

47. I have found only one reported case in which a tribal court has held that it is without the power of judicial review. *See* Lane-Oreiro et al. v. Lummi Indian Business Council, 21 Indian L. Rep. 6143 (Lum. Tr. Ct. 1994). The case grounds its decision in the tribal tradition of deference to elders, who obtained their leadership position as tribal council members through a lifetime of wisdom and garnering respect.

48. *Martinez*, 436 U.S. at 65. Most tribal courts accordingly have held that even though there is not a general separation of powers requirement, there is a specific requirement for there to be an independent tribal judicial forum to hear ICRA claims. *See, e.g.*, Good Iron v. Hall, 26 Indian L. Rep. 6029, 6030 (Dist. Ct. of Three Affiliated Tribes of the Fort Berthold Reservation).

49. *See, e.g.*, Cheyenne River Sioux Tribe v. Dupree American Legion Club, 19 Indian L. Rep. 6097, 6101 (Chy. R. Sx. Ct. App. 1992) (noting that overreaching by tribal council that impedes judicial autonomy would "raise fundamental question of due process" in violation of the ICRA).

50. *Martinez*, 436 U.S. at 59.

51. *See* McCollum v. Bolger, 794 F.2d 602, 608 (11th Cir. 1986) (cert. denied, 107 S. Ct. 883 (1987)) (Bivens action cannot be brought against federal government because there is no waiver of sovereign immunity); Will v. Michigan Department of State Police, 491 U.S. 58, 67 (1989) (holding that 28 U.S.C. section 1983 did not override state sovereign immunity).

52. *See, e.g.*, Bivens v. Six Unknown Named Agents of the Federal Bureau of Narcotics, 403 U.S. 388 (1971) (monetary relief against federal agents in their individual capacity).

53. *See, e.g.*, TBI Contractors, Inc. v. Navajo Tribe, 16 Indian L. Rep. 6017 (Nav. Sup. Ct. 1988). On the other hand, many tribal courts have held otherwise and found that ICRA waived tribal immunity. *See, e.g.*, Davis v. Keplin, 18 Indian L. Rep. 6148, 6149 (Turt. Mt. Tr. Ct. 1991); Oglala Sioux Tribal Personnel Board v. Red Shirt, 16 Indian L. Rep. 6052–3 (Ogl. Sx. Tr. Ct. App. 1983); LeCompte v. Jewett, 12 Indian L. Rep. 6025 (Chy. R. Sx. Ct. App. 1985).

54. *See, e.g.*, Committee for Better Tribal Government, 17 Indian L. Rep. at 6097 ("Although sovereign immunity bars Indian Civil Rights Act suits against tribes, this tribal immunity only extends to tribal officials acting in their representative capacity and within the scope of their authority.") Further, as is true of states, many tribes have elected to waive sovereign immunity in particular contexts.

55. Whereas the case law analyzed *infra* in the empirical study shows that tribal sovereign immunity has not precluded meaningful utilization of the ICRA to bring about changes in tribal government, the limited case law available for this study does not permit the broader conclusion that tribal sovereign immunity has not been problematic. For a study concluding that tribal sovereign immunity sometimes has proven to be problematic, *see Commission Report, supra* note 43, at 72.

56. *See, e.g.*, Brehmer v. White Wolf, 23 6073, 6074 (Chy. R. Sx. Ct. App., Nov. 5, 1993) ("Such a summary procedure might raise some question of due process under [ICRA]. Given its ruling that it lacks jurisdiction over this appear under the tribal equivalent of 28 U.S.C. § 1292(a), however, the court need not resolve such due process questions").

57. For a full list of the cases, see Rosen, *Multiple Authoritative Interpretors, supra* unnumbered note, at 585–91.

58. For example, only the former is a federal claim and only the ICRA provides a basis for federal court jurisdiction under § 1303's habeas provision.

59. Kinslow v. Business Committee of the Citizen Band of Potawatomi Tribe of Oklahoma, 15 Indian L. Rep. at 6007 (C.B. Potawatomi Sup. Ct. 1988); *see also* Ponca Tribal Election Board, 17 Indian L. Rep. 6085, 6088 (Ct. Ind. App., Ponca 1988).

60. 17 Indian L. Rep. 6151 (Nav. Sup. Ct. 1990).

61. 17 Indian L. Rep. 6085 (Ct. Ind. App., Ponca 1988).

62. *Id.*

63. *Id.* Another court has put the matter succinctly: "Under the Indian Civil Rights Act, parties . . . should be cautious in evaluating due process in Anglo terms." Colville Confederated Tribes v. Wiley, 23 Indian L. Rep. 6037, 6037 n.4 (Colv. Tr. Ct. 1996).

64. 24 Indian L. Rep. 6013 (Nav. Sup. Ct. 1996).

65. 24 Indian L. Rep. at 6014.

66. 24 Indian L. Rep. at 6014.

67. *See* Board of Regents of State Colleges v. Roth, 408 U.S. 564, 577 (1972) (noting that "welfare recipients in Goldberg v. Kelly had a claim of entitlement to welfare payments that was grounded in the statute defining eligibility for them. The recipients had not yet shown that they were, in fact, within the statutory terms of eligibility. But we held that they had a right to a hearing at which they might attempt to do so").

68. *See The Outer Limits of Self-Governance, supra* note 40, at 1064–68 (discussing significant socializing effect of law).

69. 26 Indian Law. Rep. 6061 (CCT Tribal Ct. 1999).

70. Gerstein v. Pugh, 420 U.S. 103, 112–13 (1975).

71. For a tribal court that has held otherwise, see Walker River Paiute Tribe v. Jake, Indian L. Rep. 6204 (Walk. Riv. Tr. Ct. 1996) (noting that the probable cause determination following a warrantless arrest must be "made by a neutral tribal court judge").

72. *Id.* at 6062.

73. *Id.* at 6062.

74. *Id.* at 6062.

75. 21 Indian L. Rep. 6079 (Hopi Tr. Ct. 1994).

76. *Id.* at 6079.

77. *Id.* at 6079.

78. *Id.*

79. 20 Indian Law. Rep. 6049 (Nisq. Ct. App. 1993).

80. *Id.* at 6051.

81. *Id.* at 6051.

82. *Id.* at 6053 (internal quotation omitted).

83. The defendant "knew that the type of behavior he engaged in could result in tribally imposed sanctions" by virtue of his having lived in the "close-knit society" of the Nisqually Indian community all his life. His "knowledge of those common social duties imposed by traditional tribal mores constituted adequate notice that his conduct could trigger tribal sanctions." Furthermore, continued the dissent, the defendant "also had actual notice that the reckless driving statute and other state motor vehicle offenses were being enforced on the Nisqually Reservation, and that his conduct could or would be punished. . . . [W]ord travels very fast [on the reservation]. To discount its existence and effectiveness in providing notice . . . would be to deny reality." *Id.* at 6051–3.

84. *Id.* at 6055. Why did the majority rule as it did? After all, the majority agreed with the dissent's description of the "realities" of tribal life. *See, e.g., id.* at 6051 ("We are aware that on the Nisqually Reservation word may travel quickly throughout the reservation"), and does not explain why it believes the dissent's reliance on the Nisqually cultural context to be mistaken. The majority simply asserts that written ordinances are the "proper" way to publicize what is illegal. *Id.* The majority's adoption of a writing requirement perhaps can best be explained as an instance of the assimilation of Anglo values.

85. 22 Indian L. Rep. 6145 (Nav. Sup. Ct. 1995).

86. *See supra* note 34.

87. *Id.* at 6146–47.

88. *Id.* at 6146.

89. *Id.* at 6146. The court also decided that "[t]o maintain impartiality, all the questions will be channeled through the judge, whose authority to permit or forbid the question is discretionary." *Id.*

90. 22 Indian L. Rep. 6162 (Nav. Sup. Ct. 1995).

91. *Id.* at 6165.

92. This is a wholly new substantive rule. Under federal law, the doctrine most similar to it, void for vagueness, voids civil statutes only if a statute is "so vague and indefinite as really to be no rule or standard at

all." Boutilier v. INS, 387 U.S. 118, 123 (1967). Legislation affecting "fundamental rights" under substantive due process—the other analogous doctrine—are reviewed under strict scrutiny. *See, e.g.,* Planned Parenthood v. Casey, 505 U.S. 833, 847 (1992), a legal test that also is different from the requirement of "objective" and "ascertainable standards."

93. *Id.* at 6165.

94. *See, e.g.,* Kinslow v. Business Committee of the Citizen Bank Potawatomi Indian Tribe of Oklahoma, 15 Indian L. Rep. 6007, 6009 (C. B. Pot. Sup. Ct. 1988) (citing to Navajo opinions); Office of Navajo Labor Relations v. West World, 21 Indian L. Rep. 6070 (Nav. Sup. Ct. 1994) (citing to many other tribes' opinions).

95. *See, e.g.,* Rave v. Reynolds, 22 Indian L. Rep. 6137, 6139 (Winn. Tr. Ct. 1995) (noting that other tribes' holdings are "not binding on this court").

96. *Rave,* 22 Indian L. Rep. at 6139.

97. Stepetin v. Nisqually Indian Community, 20 Indian L. Rep. 6049 (Nisq. Ct. App. 1993).

98. *Id.* at 6053 (Irving, J., partial dissent).

99. McDonald v. Colville Confederated Tribes, 17 Indian L. Rep. 6030 (Colv. Tr. Ct. 1990) (ordering closure of tribal jail facility on grounds that the jail has an inadequate ventilation system, a faulty and outdated electrical system, and that the conditions of the jail present a danger to the health and safety of the inmates).

100. Kavena v. Hamilton, 16 Indian L. Rep. 6061 (Hopi Tr. Ct. 1988), *aff'd,* 16 Indian L. Rep. 6063 (Hopi Tr. App. Ct. 1989).

101. *See, e.g.,* Bennett v. Navajo Board of Election Supervisors, 18 Indian L. Rep. 6009 (Nav. Sup. Ct. 1990).

102. Coalition for Fair Government II v. Lowe, Jr., 23 Indian L. Rep. 6181 (Ho-Chunk Tr. Ct. 1996).

103. Burns Paiute Indian Tribe v. Dick, 22 Indian L. Rep. 6016, 6017 (Burns Paiute Ct. App. 1994).

104. *See, e.g.,* In the Matter of Consolidated Small Claims Cases, 24 6109 (Chy. Riv. Sx, Tr. Ct. 1996) (due process requires the court to give notice to persons that they are entitled to a hearing of indigence after which, if they demonstrate poverty, they will be freed from being jailed for contempt of court); Hopi Tribe v. Consolidated Cases of Donald Mahkewa, 25 Indian L. Rep. 6144 (Hopi App. Ct. 1995) (due process requires that defendants arrested for DUIs be informed of the right to arrange to have an independent blood alcohol test); Hopi Tribe v. Consolidated Cases of Emerson AMI, 25 Indian L. Rep. 6163 (Hopi App. Ct. 1996) (before defendants waive their right to counsel, the court must tell them that lawyers understand law and procedure better than lay people, that they will be at a disadvantage without counsel, disclose the maximum consequences of the plea, and inform defendants of the availability of public defenders).

105. *See* Johnson v. Mashantucket Pequot Gaming Enterprise, 25 Indian L. Rep. 6011 (MPCA 1996).

106. Suquamish Indian Tribe v. Purser, 21 Indian L. Rep. 6090 (Suq. Ct. App. 1992).

107. In the Matter of D.N., 22 Indian L. Rep. 6071 (Hopi Child. Ct. 1995).

108. *See, e.g.,* Conroy v. Bear Runner, 16 Indian L. Rep. 6037 (Oglala Tr. Ct. App. 1984).

109. *See, e.g.,* Rough Rock Community School v. Navajo Nation, 22 Indian L. Rep. 6162 (Nav. Sup. Ct. 1995).

110. *Kavena,* 16 Indian L. Rep. at 6062.

111. *See, e.g.,* One Feather v. Oglala Sioux Tribal Public Safety Commission, 16 Indian L. Rep. 6042 (Oglala Tr. Ct. App. 1986).

112. *Id; see also* Hoopa Valley Indian Housing Authority v. Gerstner, 22 Indian L. Rep. 6002, 6005 (Hoopa Ct. App. 1993) ("Even though the decisions of federal courts are not controlling in this court, such decisions can be used as guidance . . .").

113. *See, e.g.,* Teeman v. Burns Paiute Indian Tribe, 25 Indian L. Rep. 6197, 6199 (Burns Paiute Ct. App. 1997).

114. *See, e.g.,* Navajo Nation v. Platero, 19 Indian L. Rep. 6049, 6049 (Nav. Sup. Ct. 1991) (tribal court uses Anglo terms of "due process," "fundamental fairness," and "common law" to describe traditional and distinctive Navajo law: "Navajo due process, which is fundamental fairness in a Navajo cultural context," can be found in "Navajo common law").

115. Cf. Helgeson v. Lac Du Flambeau Bank of Lake Superior Chippewa Indians, 25 Indian L. Rep. 6045, 6053 (Lac Du Flambeau Trib. App. Ct. 1998)("Prior to European influence, it was a well accepted belief throughout Indian Country that individual rights lie subordinate to the rights of the tribe. . . . The notion of individual rights was foreign to Indian people and the imposition of the Indian Civil Rights Act is looked upon as an infringement on the rights of Indians to govern themselves").

116. 15 Indian L. Rep. 6032 (Nav. Sup. Ct. 1988).

117. *Id.* at 6034.

118. *Id.* at 6034.

119. *Id.* at 6034.

120. *See, e.g.,* Carmeneoros v. Southern Ute Indian Tribe, 18 Indian L. Rep. 6147 (S.W. Intertr. Ct. App. 1991) ("due process"); Hopi Tribe v. Kahe, 21 Indian L. Rep. 6079 (Hopi Tr. Ct. 1994) (discussing "warrant" and "probable cause" but not citing to ICRA's Fourth Amendment analogue); Williams v. Cheyenne River Sioux Tribe, 18 Indian L. Rep. 6091 (Chy. R. Sx. Ct. App. 1991) (same); George v. Shoshone Bannock Tribes, 16 Indian L. Rep. 6084 (Sho.-Ban. Tr. Ct. 1989) ("due process" and "equal protection"); Palmer v. Millard, 23 Indian L. Rep. 6094 (Colv. Ct. App. 1996) ("due process").

121. *See, e.g.,* Murphy v. Standing Rock Sioux Election Commission, 17 Indian L. Rep. 6069 (St. Rk. Sx, Tr. Ct. 1990) (holding that due process requires notice and hearing without citing to case law); In re the Matter of B.F.C., a minor child, 21 Indian L. Rep. 6035 (Nook. Ct. App. 1990) (same); Confederated Salish and Kootenai Tribes v. Peone, 16 Indian L. Rep. 6136, 6137 (C.S. & K. Tr. Ct. 1989) (waiver of trial right is valid when it is "made knowingly and intentionally").

122. *See, e.g.,* Muscogee (Creek) Nation v. American Tobacco Co., 25 Indian L. Rep. 6054 (Musc. Nat. D. Ct. 1998) (enumerating requirements of due process without case law citation while citing to statutory language from other pieces of legislation in the course of the court's opinion).

123. The sort of deep assimilation discussed in this chapter lends support to the critiques propounded by some that ICRA imposes Anglo values notwithstanding tribes' power to construe their terms. *See, e.g.,* Robert N. Clinton, *Redressing the Legacy of Conquest: A Vision Quest for a Decolonized Federal Indian Law,* 46 ARK. L. REV. 77, 124 (1993).

124. Johnson v. Belgarde, 25, Indian L. Rep. 6183, 6184 (Hopi App. Ct. 1996) (defining tribal ordinance term of "good cause" as requiring "reasonable notice of a hearing and an opportunity to be heard"); Martin v. Hopi Tribe, 25 Indian L. Rep. 6185, 6186 (Hopi App. Ct. 1996) (explaining policy behind a tribal ordinance as being the protection of due process rights; the duty "of the Tribal Courts to hear and determine all cases before it in a fair and impartial manner [is] rooted in sound public policy and in statutes designed to protect a litigant's right to constitutional due process").

125. This is consistent with the point made earlier in the chapter—that precedent can blunt imagination.

126. 22 Indian L. Rep. 6071 (Hop. Chil. Ct. 1995).

127. *See also* Winnebago Tribe of Nebraska v. Pretends Eagle, 24 ILR 6240, 6244 (Winnebago Tr. Ct. 1997) (same; adopting exclusionary rule "without deciding the policy reasons for this action" or pointing to tribal custom).

128. *See* Rosen, *Multiple Authoritative Interpreters, supra* unnumbered note, at 585–91.

129. *See, e.g.,* Tulalip Housing Authority v. Alcombrack, 22 Indian L. Rep. 6119 (Tul. Ct. App. 1994) (applying due process notice and hearing requirements against tribal housing authority); Lezard v. Colville Confederated Tribes, 22 Indian L. Rep. 6135 (Colv. Ct. App. 1995) (tribal court must provide notice and the right to a hearing before holding a party in criminal contempt).

130. Murphy v. Standing Rock Sioux Election Commission, 17 Indian L. Rep. 6069, 6072 (St. Rk. Sx. Tr. Ct. 1990).

131. White v. Ho-Chunk Nation Dept of Personnel, 24 Indian L. Rep. 6182, 6185–86 (Ho-Chunk Nat. Tr. Ct. 1996) (pointing to federal case law for the proposition that the employee had a protectable due process interest in her employment that accordingly triggered notice and hearing requirements).

132. *See, e.g.,* Burns Paiute Indian Tribe v. Dick, 22 Indian L. Rep. 6016, 6017–18 (Burns Paiute Ct. App. 1994) (civil); Stepetin v. Nisqually Indian Community, 20 Indian L. Rep. 6049, 6050–51 (Nisq. Ct. App. 1993) (criminal).

133. *See* text *supra* at notes 90–93.

134. *See, e.g.,* In re the Matter of B.F.C., 21 Indian L. Rep. 6035 (Nook. Ct. App. 1990) (reversing the trial court's summary dismissal of a case after the trial court had refused to allow the party to be heard on a motion to continue; objective incorporation); McKinney v. Business Council of the Shoshone-Paiute Tribes, 20 Indian L. Rep. 6020 (Duck Valley Tr. Ct. 1993) (reinstating judge of tribal court dismissed by the council without a hearing; subjective incorporation).

135. *See, e.g.,* Pioche v. Navajo Board of Election Supervisors, 18 Indian L. Rep. 6071, 6073 (Nav. Sup. Ct. 1991); Carmenoros v. Southern Ute Indian Tribe, 18 Indian L. Rep. 6147 (S.W. Intert. Ct. App. 1991); One Feather v. Oglala Sioux Tribal Public Safety Commission, 16 Indian L. Rep. 6042 (Oglala Tr. Ct. App. 1986).

136. Bennett v. Navajo Board of Election Supervisors, 18 6009, 6012 (Nav. Sup. Ct. 1990) (deploying subjective tailoring).

137. *See, e.g.,* Rave v. Reynolds, 23 Indian L. Rep. 6150, 6169 (Winn. Sup. Ct. 1996) (subjective tailoring); Baldy v. Hoopa Valley Tribal Council, 22 Indian L. Rep. 6015, 6016 (Hoopa V. Ct. App. 1994) (subjective tailoring).

138. *See* Johns v. Leupp Schools, Inc., 22 Indian L. Rep. 6039, 6039 (Nav Sup. Ct. 1995) (a "broad scope of inquiry is in keeping with the general Navajo common law rule of due process. . . . The Navajo people have an established custom of notifying all involved parties in a controversy and allowing them, and even other interested parties, an opportunity to present and defend their positions. . . . All perspectives are important for a court to hear when making discretionary rulings"); In the Matter of the Estate of Tasunke Witko v. Heileman Brewing Co., 23 Indian L. Rep. 6104, 6108 (Rbd. Sx. Sup. Ct. 1996) (*en banc*) (referring to "traditional Lakota notions of due process that provide everyone the opportunity to be heard before making a decision").

139. 23 Indian L. Rep. 6235, 6241 (Ho-Chunk Tr. Ct. 1996).

140. 26 Indian L. Rep. 6011 (Ho-Chunk Sup. Ct. 1998).

141. In the Matter of Consolidated Small Claims Cases, 24 Indian L. Rep. 6109 (Chy. Riv. Sx. Tr. Ct. 1996).

142. 21 Indian L. Rep. 6139, 6140 (Hopi Tr. Ct. 1992).

143. *Id.,* *aff'd* in 25 Indian L. Rep. 6144 (Hopi App. Ct. 1995).

144. *Id.,* *aff'd* in 25 Indian L. Rep. 6144 (Hopi App. Ct. 1995).

145. *See* Drags Wolf v. Tribal Business Council of the Three Affiliated Tribes, 17 Indian L. Rep. 6051, 6052 (Ft. Bert. Tr. Ct. 1990) ("1. Each defendant will be given a written, verified complaint following his arrest. 2. Each defendant will be provided with a copy of such complaint at his arraignment, if not in possession of a copy at that time. 3. Each defendant shall be read and contemporaneously given a detailed explanation of his rights and written acknowledgment of such by each defendant shall be filed with the clerk of court. 4. That in addition to advising each defendant as to the alleged violations of tribal law, a meaningful explanation by the judge-magistrate with a layman's explanation as to the specific elements of the alleged crime in order that a defendant having never previously appeared in court and unschooled in legal jargon could reasonably be expected to ascertain if his conduct did in fact violate tribal law").

146. Johnson v. Mashantucket Pequot Gaming Enterprise, 25 Indian L. Rep. 6011 (MPCA 1996) (due process violated where an administrative law judge disallowed an attorney from representing an employee).

147. Burns Paiute Indian Tribe v. Dick 22 Indian L. Rep. 6016 (Burns Paiute Ct. App. 1994).

148. *Id.* at 6017.

149. *Id.* at 6017. The appellate court concluded that these relationships implicated the liberty to "associate with persons of one's choice," which is the "the right of intimate association." *Id.*

150. 14 Indian L. Rep. 6001, 6005 (Hopi Tr. Ct. 1986).

151. Gentile v. State Bar of Nevada, 501 U.S. 1030, 1082 (1991) (O'Connor, J., concurring).

152. *Lonewolf,* 14 at 6005.

153. 26 Indian L. Rep. 6013 (Northwest Regional Tribal App. Ct. 1998).

154. This tendency toward subjective rather than objective interpretation is found outside the due process context. *See, e.g.,* Pueblo of Pojoaque v. Jagles 24 Indian L. Rep. 6137 (Poaque Pueblo Tr. Ct. 1997) (trial by jury), discussed *infra* at 52.

155. This observation may not hold in respect of the case of Lonewolf insofar as the defendants there were not members of the Hopi Tribe. See *Lonewolf,* 14 Indian L. Rep. at 6001. On the other hand, the defendants belonged to a tribe that shared the Hopi border and may have had shared cultural understandings, as the tribal court suggested when it spoke of the ordinance's clear understanding to the "reservation communities." *Id.* at 6005 (emphasis supplied).

156. *See* Dynes v. Hoover, 61 U.S. 65, 82 (1857) (military law), quoted approvingly in Parker v. Levy, 417 U.S. 733, 747 (1974). The Court in Parker also upheld a void-for-vagueness challenge to two articles in the Uniform Code of Military Justice that the Court acknowledged would not have passed constitutional muster "as measured by contemporary standards of vagueness applicable to statutes and ordinances governing civilians." The military code provisions were upheld because, *inter alia,* the "content" of the provisions "may be sup-

plied . . . by less formalized custom and usage" within the military community. *Id.* at 741, 754. For a discussion of the role played in Parker by the presence of a discrete community, *see* Rosen, *Our Nonuniform Constitution, supra* note 37, at 1175–9.

157. 25 U.S.C. § 1302(10).

158. Colville Confederated Tribes v. Thomas, 18 Indian L. Rep. 6126 (Colv. Ct. App. 1990).

159. Southern Ute Tribe v. Baca 17 Indian L. Rep. 6010 (S. Ute Tr. Ct. App. 1989).

160. 25 Indian L. Rep. 6197 (Burns Paiute Ct. App. 1997).

161. *Id.* at 6199.

162. Butler v. Siletz Tribal Council 16 Indian L. Rep. 6044 (Siletz Tr. Ct. 1989).

163. Clown v. Coast to Coast, 23 Indian L. Rep. 6055, 6057–59 (Chy. R. Sx. Ct. App. 1993). To prevent judges from acting in an "authoritarian manner," however, the *Clown* court also provided extensive guidelines with regard to *pro se* trials that included, for example, instructions to the court to expressly give parties the choice to either question the opposing party themselves or have the court do it. *Id.*

164. Miner v. Banley, 22 Indian L. Rep. 6044 (Chy. R. Sx. Ct. App. 1995).

165. Rosen, *Recent American Codifications, supra* note 5, at 1210–11. Moreover, even ordinary federal trial court judges "may appoint an expert witness, examine such a witness himself." *Id.*

166. 24 Indian L. Rep. 6001 (Nav. Nat. Sup. Ct. 1996).

167. *Id.* at 6001.

168. In the end, it is difficult to explain analytically at what point "too much" weight has been accorded to the tribal interest in the due process calculation. The line between plausible and problematic in many cases will be contestable and controversial. For present purposes I aim only to bring potentially problematic instances to the reader's attention.

169. 25 Indian L. Rep. 6045, 6053 (Lac Du Flambeau Trib. App. Ct. 1998).

170. I have made a similar argument. See Rosen, *The Outer Limits of Community Self-Governance, supra* note 40, at 1136.

171. *See, e.g.,* Goldberg v. Kelly, 397 U.S. 254, 263 (1970) (balancing a welfare recipient's interest versus the government's interest to determine the nature of the hearing required by due process; *de jure* balancing).

172. *See, e.g., id.*

173. *See* Coleman v. Thompson, 501 U.S. 722, 750 (1991).

174. To be sure, there remains an important difference between federal habeas doctrine and the *Coleman* and the *Ben* court's holdings insofar as the unavailability of habeas does not impair the availability of an initial appeal.

175. *See* Rosen, *Multiple Authoritative Interpreters, supra* unnumbered note, at 538–39.

176. A series of equal protection cases were brought by non-Indians and nonmember Indians, claiming that the differential treatment they received as "outsiders" of the tribe violated equal protection. I examine these cases below in subsection entitled "The Treatment of Outsiders."

177. 18 Indian L. Rep. 6009 (Nav. Sup. Ct. 1990).

178. An alternative explanation for the reference to "fundamental rights" without case law citation is that the court consulted the federal case law but for some reason simply did not cite to it. This explanation seems unlikely, however, because the court cited to numerous federal cases elsewhere in its opinion. *See Bennett,* 18 Indian L. Rep. at 6011–12.

179. *Id.* at 6011.

180. 18 Indian L. Rep. 6058 (N. Plns. Intert. Ct. App. 1991).

181. *Id.* at 6058.

182. *Id.*

183. *See id.*

184. 16 Indian L. Rep. 6037 (Oglala Tr. Ct. App. 1984).

185. For an example of the federal rule, *see* United States v. Armstrong, 517 U.S. 456, 464–65 (1996).

186. 17 Indian L. Rep. 6010 (S. Ute. Tr. Ct. App. 1989).

187. *Id.* at 6011 (quoting United States v. Doe, 401F. Supp. 63, 65 (E.D. Wis. 1975)).

188. *Baca,* 17 Indian L. Rep. at 6011; *see also* Frost v. Southern Ute Tribal Council, 23 Indian L. Rep. 6135, 6136 (S. Ute. Tr. Ct., June 25, 1996) (failure of the tribe to prosecute similar allegations in the past does not in

and of itself violate equal protection).

189. 22 Indian L. Rep. 6016 (Burns Paiute Ct.App.1994).This is virtually identical to the federal rule. *See Armstrong*, 517 U.S. at 464 (observing that "the decision whether to prosecute may not be based on an unjustifiable standard such as race, religion, or other arbitrary classification"). Interestingly, the *Dick* court did not cite to any federal case law for the proposition of law, though it cited to federal case law elsewhere in its opinion. *See Dick*, 22 Indian L. Rep. at 6017. *Dick* accordingly is either an example of deep assimilation or of tabula rasa where the tribal court intuited the federal rule.

190. *Id.* at 6017.

191. *See, e.g.*, Badgley v. Hoopa Forest Industries, 19 Indian L. Rep. 6009, 6009 (Hoopa Ct. App. 1990) (claim for failure to hire as log hauler; equal protection violated only where person "treated differently from other persons similarly situated on account of her marital status to a non-Indian, her race, sex or any other category . . ."); Day v. Hopi Election Board, 16 Indian L. Rep. 6057, 6058 (Hopi Tr. Ct. 1988) (The fact that the Hopi fluency requirement for candidates for public office was not enforced in past elections does not mean that its enforcement as to several candidates in the present election violates equal protection; the question is whether at any point in time there is unequal treatment rising to the level of "unreasonabl[e] discriminat[ion]").

192. *See* Winnebago Tribe of Nebraska v. Frazier, 25 Indian L. Rep. 6021 (Winn.Tr. Ct. 1997); Winnebago Tribe of Nebraska v. Levering, 25 Indian L. Rep. 6022 (Winn.Tr. Ct. 1997).There had been four prosecutions under the ordinance, and only males had been charged. See *Frazier*, 25 Indian L. Rep. at 6021.

193. 25 Indian L. Rep. 6229 (Winnebago Sup. Ct. 1998).

194. *Id.* at 6230.

195. *Id.*

196. *Id.*

197. The *Bigfire* court correctly cited to Craig v. Boren, 429 U.S. 190 (1976), for the proposition that federal courts utilize intermediate scrutiny to analyze gender discrimination claims and expressly and explicitly adopted instead strict scrutiny. *See Bigfire*, 25 Indian L. Rep. at 6231.

198. *Id.* at 6231.

199. *Bigfire*, 25 Indian L. Rep. at 6231–34.

200. See Rosen, *Multiple Authoritative Interpreters, supra* unnumbered note, at 544.

201. For example, it could uphold an educational system that deprived girls of education. *See id.* at 544–45, explaining why this would be problematic).

202. *See, e.g.*, Southern Ute Tribe v. Williams, 18 Indian L. Rep. 6049 (S. Ute.Tr. Ct. 1990) (slow and erratic driving provides probable cause to initially stop a vehicle); Southern Ute Tribe v. Price, 18 Indian L. Rep. 6117 (S. Ute.Tr. Ct. 1991) (driving a car backwards on a major road provides probable cause for a stop).

203. *See* discussion *supra* at 11.

204. 24 Indian L. Rep. 6240 (Winnebago Tr. Ct. 1997).

205. *Id.* at 6241.

206. *Id.* at 6243.

207. *Id.* at 6244.The tribal court noted that Terry allowed stop and frisk when a "police officer observes unusual conduct which leads him reasonably to conclude in light of his experiences that criminal activity may be afoot," *id.* (quoting Terry v. Ohio, 392 U.S. 30 (emphasis added by trial court)), whereas the tribal ordinance requires the officer to have "probable cause." *Id.* at 6244.This is arguably in tension with, though not flatly inconsistent with, the tribal court's earlier analysis, where it equated reasonable and probable cause. *Id.* at 6243.

208. 25 Indian L. Rep. 6107 (Hopi App. Ct. 1995).

209. 22 Indian L. Rep. 6071 (Hop Child. Ct. 1995).

210. *Id.* at 6071.

211. 26 Indian L. Rep. 6015 (Hopi App. Ct. 1997).

212. *Id.* at 6017.

213. *See, e.g.*, Southern Ute Tribe v. Scott, 18 Indian L. Rep. 6105, 6106 (S. Ute.Tr. Ct. 1991) (deciding two search and seizure issues by means of incorporation; intoxication does not per se negate consent to a search and roadside sobriety tests are not incident to lawful arrest); Southern Ute Tribe v. Price, 18 Indian L. Rep. 6117 (S. Ute.Tr. Ct. 1991) (similar); In the Matter of D.N., 22 Indian L. Rep. 6071 (Hopi Child. Ct. 1995).

214. *See, e.g.* Hopi Tribe v. Dawahoya, 25 Indian L. Rep.6107, 6107 (Hopi App. Ct. 1995).

215. *See, e.g.,* In the Matter of D.N., 22 Indian L. Rep. 6071, 6071 (Hop Child. Ct. 1995).

216. Winnebago Tribe of Nebraska v. Pretends Eagle, 24 Indian L. Rep. 6240, 6244 (Winnebago Tr. Ct. 1997).

217. 22 Indian L. Rep. 6071 (Hopi Child. Ct. 1995).

218. *Id.*

219. *Id.* at 6071.

220. *See supra* at text surrounding notes 75–78.

221. 21 Indian L. Rep. 6138 (Hopi Tr. Ct. 1994).

222. *Id.* at 6139.

223. *Id.*

224. *See, e.g., Matter of D.N.*, 22 Indian L. Rep. at 6072; *Pretends Eagle*, 24 Indian L. Rep. at 6244.

225. *Id.* at 6244.

226. *D.N.*, 22 Indian L. Rep. at 6072. In fact, the exclusionary rule is by no means the only logically plausible remedy. *See, e.g.,* L. Timothy Perrin et al., *If It's Broken, Fix it: Moving Beyond the Exclusionary Rule*, 83 IOWA L. REV. 669, 736–55 (1999) (proposing numerous alternatives).

227. Another reason is that search and seizures legal tests have been codified in many tribal ordinances or tribal constitutions; of course, this is not an independent explanation, but instead it pushes the inquiry back one step as to why tribal law codified the federal approach.

228. The ICRA does not have any provisions paralleling the First Amendment's establishment clause.

229. *See supra* note 21 (describing "tabula rasa" aproach).

230. Chavez v. Tome, 14 Indian L. Rep. 6029, 6032 (Nav. Sup. Ct. 1987).

231. *Id.*

232. Gwin v. Bolman, 25 Indian L. Rep. 6121 (Three Aff. Tribes of Fort Berthold Reserv. Dist. Ct. 1998).

233. 24 Indian L. Rep. 6027 (Nav. Sup. Ct. 1996).

234. *See supra* at 4.

235. Hopi Tribe v. Lonewolf Scott, 14 Indian L. Rep. 6001, 6005 (Hopi Tr. Ct. 1986) (citing to federal case law for the proposition).

236. 16 Indian L. Rep. 6061 (Hopi Tr. Ct. 1988).

237. Kavena v. Hopi Indian Tribal Court, 16 Indian L. Rep. 6063 (Hopi Tribal App. Ct. 1989).

238. *Id.* at 6065.

239. *Id.* at 6061.

240. *Id.* at 6066.

241. *See* Rave v. Reynolds, 23 Indian L. Rep. 6150, 6165 (Winn. Sup. Ct. 1996).

242. Hudson v. Hoh Indian Tribe, 21 Indian L. Rep. 6045 (Hoh Ct. App. 1992). The *Hudson* case was unusual because it required interpretation of a tribal constitution that by its terms appeared to require that its provisions be construed no differently than its sister terms in the United States Constitution. *See id.* at 6045, 6046. The *Hudson* court accordingly sought to engage in stock incorporation, citing to federal precedent to identify the appropriate legal tests. *See id.* at 6046. In concluding that the right to petition "must be read as a limitation upon any sovereign immunity that the Hoh Tribe may possess," however, the tribal court appeared to misconstrue the federal case law insofar as the right to petition has not meant the end of federal sovereign immunity. *See, e.g.,* United States v. King, 395 U.S. 1, 4 (1969).

243. Kowalski v. Elofson, 22 Indian L. Rep. 6007 (L. Elwha. Ct. App. 1993).

244. Souther Ute Public Housing Authority v. Pinnecoose, 18 Indian L. Rep. 6115 (S. Ute. Tr. Ct. 1991).

245. *Id.* at 6117.

246. *See id.*

247. 18 Indian L. Rep. 6139, 6141 (Grand Ronde Tr. Ct. 1991). The tribal court's formulation qualifies as restandardizing because the federal legal test is not a compelling interest standard, which would permit the creation of new exceptions, but instead treats fighting words and obscenity as the only discrete exception into which new factual scenarios must fall if they are to be immunized from ordinary First Amendment constraints. *See, e.g.,* R.A.V. v. City of St. Paul, 505 U.S. 377, 382–83 (1992).

248. Brandon, 18 Indian L. Rep. at 6141.

249. In fact, the Supreme Court has not upheld a conviction on the basis of the fighting words doctrine since Chaplinsky, the case that created the doctrine. *See* GEOFFREY R. STONE, LOUIS M. SEIDMAN, CASS R. SUNSTEIN, AND MARK V. TUSHNET, THE FIRST AMENDMENT 83 (1999).

250. *See, e.g.,* U.S. Civil Service Comm'n v. National Ass'n of Letter Carrier, 413 U.S. 548 (1973).

251. Elsewhere I've argued this holding is not normatively problematic. See Rosen, *Multiple Authoritative Interpreters, supra* unnumbered note, at 554.

252. Shippentower v. Confederated Tribes of the Umatilla Indian Reservation of Oregon, 20 Indian L. Rep. 6026 (Uma. Tr. Ct. 1993).

253. 20 Indian L. Rep. 6049 (Nisq. Tr. Ct. 1986).

254. 24 Indian L. Rep. 6137 (Pojoaque Pueblo Tr. Ct. 1997).

255. *See supra* at 22–23.

256. 25 U.S.C. § 1302(10) (emphasis supplied).

257. 16 Indian L. Rep. 6136, 6137 (C.S.&.K. Tr. Ct. 1989).

258. 22 Indian L. Rep. 6072 (Colv. Ct. App. 1995).

259. The court's reasoning technically cannot be analyzed under the model developed earlier in this chapter because there is no constitutional analogue to the ICRA language it was construing. Nonetheless, the court's approach can be analogized to stock incorporation because it looked to federal case law concerning waiver in other constitutional contexts.

260. *Id.* at 6074.

261. 15 Indian L. Rep. 6010 (Sq. I. Tr. Ct. 1987).

262. The court also held that disallowing a jury trial under these circumstances did not violate due process. *See id.* at 6011.

263. 19 Indian L. Rep. 6067 (S. W. Intertr. Ct. App. 1991).

264. The Hummingbird court did not expressly hold that the procedures were compatible with the ICRA. The appellant did not argue that the procedures violated the ICRA and the tribal court only upheld the trial court's finding that the procedures had not been followed.

265. *See* Godinez v. Moran, 509 U.S. 389, 396–99 (1993).

266. *See, e.g.,* Daigle v. Maine Medical Center, 14.F3d. 684, 687 (1st Cir. 1994) (refusing to consider the constitutional claim that jury right was violated because the plaintiff failed to raise it at the trial level; no showing that such waiver was knowing); Cohen v. President & Fellows of Harvard Coll., 729 F.2d 59, 60–61 (1st Cir.), *cert. denied,* 469 U.S. 874 (1984) (rejecting assorted constitutional claims because they were not raised at trial).

267. 22 Indian L. Rep. 6145 (Nav. Sup. Ct. 1995).

268. Namely, where "the evidence is insufficient, as a matter of law, to support the finding . . . or when the jury is confused." *Id.* at 6146–47.

269. *See supra* at text surrounding notes 85–89.

270. *See* 22 Indian L. Rep. at 6146.

271. 25 U.S.C. § 1302(6).

272. Lummi Indian Nation v. Solomon, 21 Indian L. Rep. 6085, 6085 (Lum. Ct. App. 1992); see also Hoh Idaho Tribe v. Penn, 15 Indian L. Rep. 6029, 6030 (Hoh Ct. App. 1988).

273. Suquamish Indian Tribe v. Mills, Sr, 21 Indian L. Rep. 6053, 6054 (Suq. Ct. App. 1991).

274. Lummi Indian Tribe v. Edwards, 16 Indian L. Rep. 6005 (Lummi Tr. Ct. App. 1988).

275. 25 Indian L. Rep. 6163 (Hopi App. Ct. 1996).

276. *See supra* text surrounding notes 159–164.

277. *Id.* at 6165.

278. *Id.* at 6167–68.

279. Harvey v. Hopi Tribe, 25 Indian L. Rep. 6212 (Hopi App. Ct. 1997); Poleahla v. Hopi Tribe, 25 Indian L. Rep. 6224 (Hopi App. Ct. 1997).

280. 19 Indian L. Rep. 6053 (Nav. Sup. Ct. 1991).

281. *See* MacDonald, 19 Indian L. Rep. at 6055 ("The traditional Navajo 'trial' involved affected individuals 'talking' about the offense and offender to resolve the problem. The alleged offender had the right to have someone speak for him. The effectiveness of a speaker (and there could be more than one) was measured by

what the speaker said. If the speaker spoke wisely and with knowledge while persuading others in their search for consensus, that indicated effectiveness. If the speaker hesitated, was unsure, or failed to move the others, that person was not a good speaker and thus was ineffective").

282. *See* Navajo Nation v. MacDonald, Jr., 19 Indian L. Rep. 6079, 6082 (Nav. Sup. Ct. 1992).

283. *See* Barker v. Wingo, 407 U.S. 514 (1972).

284. *See* Sisseton–Wahpeton Dakota Nation v. Cloud, 21 Indian L. Rep. 6115 (N. Plns. Intertr. Ct. App. 1994).

285. *See* Cheyenne River Sioux Tribe v. Cook, 22 Indian L. Rep. 6037 (Cy. R. Sx. Ct. App., Feb. 17, 1995) (*in dicta*).

286. *See* Komalestewa v. Hopi Tribe, 25 Indian L. Rep. 6213, 6214–15 (Hopi App. Ct. 1996); Stepetin v. Nisqually Indian Community, 20 Indian L. Rep. 6049, 6050 (Nisq. Ct. App. 1993); Navajo Nation v. MacDonald Jr., 19 Indian L. Rep. 6079, 6083 (Nav. Sup. Ct. 1992); Lummi Indian Tribe v. Edwards, 16 Indian L. Rep. 6005, 6007 (Lummi Tr. Ct. App. 1988).

287. *See Komalestewa*, 25 Indian L. Rep. at 6215 ("Appellant does not allege any prejudice caused him by the delay in prosecution"); *Stepetin*, 20 Indian L. Rep. at 6050 ("no prejudice occurred to the defendant"); *MacDonald*, 19 Indian L. Rep. at 6083 ("there is no indication that evidence was lost, memories were dimmed, defense witnesses disappeared or the defense was impaired").

288. *See Edwards*, 16 Indian L. Rep. at 6006 (defendant caused the eighteen-month gap between arraignment and trial by twice requesting continuances and then failing to appear at trial); *Komalestewa*, 25 Indian L. Rep. at 6215 (three-and-a-half month delay attributable to appellant's "own requests for delays and stipulations to continuances" and five weeks of the delay attributable to government).

289. *Stepetin*, 20 Indian L. Rep. at 6050.

290. *MacDonald*, 19 Indian L. Rep. at 6083.

291. 25 Indian L. Rep. 6213 (Hopi App. Ct. 1996).

292. *Id*. at 6214.

293. 21 Indian L. Rep. 6115 (N. Plns. Intertr. Ct. App. 1994).

294. *Id*. at 6116.

295. 23 Indian L. Rep. 6204 (Walk. Riv. Tr. Ct. 1996).

296. This is suggested by the *Jake* court's one-sentence analysis of the question ("This court specifically rejects any concept or notion that a criminal complaint passes muster even though the information required by . . . the ICRA is omitted") and the fact that elsewhere in the opinion the court looked to federal law to construe other ICRA provisions. *See id*. at 6205–06.

297. 25 Indian L. Rep. 6163, 6166 (Hopi App. Ct. 1996).

298. 17 Indian L. Rep. 6027 (Intertr. Ct. App. 1989).

299. *Id*. at 6028.

300. *See* Lower Elwha Klallam Indian Tribe v. Bolstrom 19 Indian L. Rep. 6026, 6027 (L. Elwha Ct. App. 1991) (noting that the ordinance "is essentially a statutory list of the decision of Miranda v. Arizona, 384 U.S. 436 (1966)"); Southern Ute Tribe v. Lansing, 19 Indian L. Rep. 6091, 6092 (S. Ute. Tr. Ct. 1992) (ordinance required police to inform person of rights "[b]efore any person who is in custody is questioned or in any manner interrogated concerning any possible criminal activity by that person").

301. 18 Indian L. Rep. 6003, 6007 (Nav. Sup. Ct. 1990).

302. *See id*. at 6007–08. In a subsequent case the same court engaged in fitted incorporation, explaining that the right against self-incrimination is identical to a longstanding tribal custom. *See* Navajo Nation v. MacDonald Jr., 19 Indian L. Rep. 6079, 6084 (Nav. Sup. Ct. 1992), discussed *infra* at 59.

303. 25 Indian L. Rep. 6163, 6164 (Hopi App. Ct. 1996).

304. 19 Indian L. Rep. 6079 (Nav. Sup. Ct. 1992).

305. 19 Indian L. Rep. 6026 (L. Elwha Ct. App. 1991).

306. *Id*. at 6027.

307. *Id*.

308. Chippewa-Ottawa Tribes v. Payment, 18 Indian L. Rep. 6141, 6141–42 (Chip.-Ott. Cons. Ct. 1991).

309. Southern Ute Tribe v. Lansing, 19 Indian L. Rep. 6091 (S. Ute. Tr. Ct. 1992).

310. Lummi Indian Tribe v. Kinley, 19 Indian L. Rep. 6027, 6029 (Lummi Tr. Ct., App. Div. 1991).

311. Winnebago Tribe of Nebraska v. Bigfire, 25 Indian L. Rep. 6229, 6234 (Winnebago Sup. Ct. 1998).

312. 25 Indian L. Rep. 6108 (Hopi Tr. App. Ct. 1995).

313. *Id.* at 6108.

314. Rave v. Ho-Chunk Nation Gaming Commission, 25 Indian L. Rep. 6042 (Ho-Chunk Nat. Tr. Ct. 1997).

315. Alternatively, the case could be understood as a retargeting of double jeopardy insofar as it applies the protection outside the criminal context. *See* Helvering v. Mitchell, 303 U.S. 391 (1938) (double jeopardy applies only to criminal assessments).

316. Kanzleiter v. Colville Indian Housing Authority 25 Indian L. Rep. 6181 (Colville Tr. Ct. 1998).

317. *Id.* at 6183.

318. Boos v. Yazzie, 17 Indian L. Rep. 6115 (Nav. Sup. Ct. 1990); Navajo Nation v. MacDonald, Sr., 17 Indian L. Rev. 6124 (1990). A takings claim was raised in one other case; *see* St. Regis Mohawk Tribe v. Basil Cook Enterprises, 23 Indian L. Rep. 6172 (St. Regis. Tr. Ct. 1996). The tribal court did not address the merits of a takings claim because the tribe had not waived its sovereign immunity. *Id.* at 6174.

319. 21 Indian L. Rep. 6040 (Colv. Ct. App. 1994).

320. *Id.* at 6043.

321. 19 Indian L. Rep. 6053 (Nav. Sup. Ct. 1991).

322. *Id.* at 6059.

323. *Id.* at 6059–60.

324. *See* Navajo Nation v. MacDonald, Jr., 19 Indian L. Rep. 6079, 6084 (Nav. Sup. Ct. 1992).

325. 15 Indian L. Rep. 6041 (Nav. Sup. Ct. 1988).

326. *Id.* at 6042.

327. 17 Indian L. Rep. 6030 (Colv. Tr. Ct. 1990). Although the tribal court did not identify any legal provisions in the course of its laconic opinion, the source of its authority may well have been the ICRA's ban on cruel and unusual punishment.

328. I treat bills of attainder and *ex post facto* laws together because they are frequently overlapping claims. Both involve the "denunciation and condemnation by an individual" by a legislature, "often act[ing] to impose retroactive punishment." Nixon v. Administrator of General Services, 433 U.S. 425, 468 n. 30 (1977), quoted in MacDonald, Sr. v. Redhouse, 18 Indian L. Rep. 6045, 6047 (Nav. Sup. Ct. 1991).

329. *In re* Certified Question II: Navajo Nation v. MacDonald, 16 Indian L. Rep. 6086 (Nav. Sup. Ct. 1989).

330. *Id.* at 6093.

331. 18 Indian L. Rep. 6045 (Nav. Sup. Ct. 1991).

332. *See id.* 6046–47 (citing to De Veau v. Braisted, 363 U.S. 144 (1960) for this principle).

333. 23 Indian L. Rep. 6135 (S. Ute. Tr. Ct. 1996).

334. *Id.* at 6136.

335. *See* Duncan v. Missouri, 152 U.S. 377, 382–83 (1894) (Procedural changes in the adjudication of criminal cases may violate *ex post facto* if they deprive the defendant of substantial protections of law that were in effect when the crime was committed).

336. 21 Indian L. Rep. 6005 (Colv. Ct. App. 1993).

337. 495 U.S. 676 (1990).

338. Congress ultimately enacted final legislation overturning *Duro* on October 28, 1991.

339. *Id.* at 6009.

340. 22 Indian L. Rep. 6050 (Sho.-Arap. Ct. A pp. 1994).

341. Muscogee (Creek) Nation v. American Tobacco Co., 25 Indian L. Rep. 6054 (Musc. Nat. D. Ct. 1998).

342. *Id.* at 6059.

343. Means v. District Court of the Chinle Judicial District, 26 Indian L. Rep. 6083 (Nav. Sup. Ct. 1999).

344. *Id.* at 6084.

345. *Id.* at 6084, 6088.

346. Rosen, *Multiple Authoritative Interpreters, supra* unnumbered note, at 488–89.

347. 24 Indian L. Rep. 6068 (Chitimacha Ct. App. 1997).

348. 14 Indian L. Rep. 6001, 6003–4 (Hopi Tr. Ct. 1986). The *Lonewolf* court also was presented with void-for-vagueness and free speech claims. Though the court ruled against the outsider in respect of these arguments as well, the court's reasoning was sound, as explained elsewhere in this chapter.

349. *See Sanders*, 24 Indian L. Rep. at 6070; *Lonewolf*, 14 Indian L. Rep. at 6004–05.

350. Sanders, 24 Indian L. Rep. at 6070.

351. *See, e.g.,* Cal. Civ. Pro. § 203(3).

352. 24 Indian L. Rep. 6229 (Standing Rock Sioux Nat. Sup. Ct. 1996).

353. In other words, it is widely accepted that non citizens who physically enter a polity may be subjected to that polity's laws even though the non citizen self-evidently played no role in selecting the polity's lawmakers.

354. Cf. Duro v. Reina, 495 U.S. 676, 707 (Brennan J., dissenting) ("we have never held that participation in the political process is a prerequisite to the exercise of criminal jurisdiction by a sovereign. If such were the case, a state could not prosecute nonresidents, and this country could not prosecute aliens who violate our laws").

355. Gould v. Southern Ute Indian Tribe, 19 Indian L. Rep. 6129 (S. Ute. Tr. Ct. 1992).

356. Guardianship of Jack J. Schumacher v. Menominee Indian Tribe of Wisconsin, 24 Indian L. Rep. 6084 (Men. Sup. Ct. 1997).

357. *Id.* at 6087.

358. 18 Indian L. Rep. 6051 (Chy. R. Sx. Ct. App. 1991).

359. *Id.* at 6052.

360. *Id.* at 6053.

361. *Id.* at 6054. The court also noted that although the bylaw was part of the tribal constitution, the constitution had been prepared "almost in boilerplate fashion" by the Bureau of Indian Affairs "without any meaningful input or discussion at the local tribal level." *Id.* at 6053.

362. 18 Indian L. Rep. 6097 (Jic. Ap. Tr. Ct. 1991).

363. The tribal court also rejected a second set of due process and equal protection arguments, but these holdings appear to be wholly unproblematic. Plaintiff outsiders sought to challenge the tribe's 1988 and 1989 tax assessments but failed to meet procedural requirements for challenging the 1989 payments. The plaintiff argued that enforcing the tribe's procedural deadlines would violate due process and equal protection because they never before had been enforced. The tribal court noted that the tax code and its administrative procedures for challenging assessments was "relatively new" and that circumstances that "result[] in a taxpayer becoming the first to run afoul of a clear requirement is not a cause to excuse the breach." *Id.* at 6099–6100.

364. *Id.* at 6101.

365. *See, e.g.,* Lehnhausen v. Lake Shore Auto Parts Co., 410 U.S. 356 (1973) ("[u]nless a classification abridges fundamental personal rights or is based on inherently suspect distinctions such as race, religion or alienage, the statutory distinction is valid if it is rationally related to a legitimate governmental interest").

366. *See id.*

367. "Indian country" is a statutory term denoting places of tribal jurisdiction. *See* 18 U.S.C. § 1151(a).

368. Poodry v. Tonawanda Band of Seneca Indians. 85 F.3d 874, 900–01 (2d Cir. 1996).

369. Randall v. Yakima Nation Tribal Court, 841 F.2d 897, 900 (9th Cir. 1988) (internal quotation omitted).

370. *Id.* (due process); Howlett v. Salish and Kootenal Tribes of the Flathead Reservation, 529 F.2d 233, 238 (9th Cir. 1976) (equal protection).

371. *See, e.g.,* S. 1691, "The American Indian Equal Justice Act," 105th Cong. § 7 (1998), reprinted in 144 Cong. Rec. S. 1155–56 (daily ed. Feb. 27, 1998) (bill introduced by Senator Gorton to grant federal district courts jurisdiction to hear all ICRA claims); 134 Cong. Rec. S11, 656 (daily ed. Aug. 11, 1988) (statement of Senator Hatch regarding proposed bill to grant federal courts jurisdiction over ICRA claims); Carla Christofferson, Note, *Tribal Courts' Failure to Protect Native American Women: A Reevaluation of the Indian Civil Rights Act,* 101 YALE L.J. 169, 181 (1991) (advancing proposal to expand federal court jurisdiction over ICRA claims).

372. *See* Nell Jessup Newton, *Tribal Court Praxis: One Year in the Life of Twenty Indian Tribal Courts,* 22 Am. Indian L. Rep.. 285, 285–88 (1998) (making this point); *Tribal Courts' Failure, supra* note 371, at 170, 178–79 (relying entirely on the statement of one woman to conclude that tribal court application of the ICRA has not adequately protected Native American women).

373. For similar conclusions, see Robert J. McCarthy, *Civil Rights in Tribal Courts: The Indian Bill of Rights at Thirty Years,* 34 IDAHO L. REV. 465, 513 (1998); Newton, *Tribal Court Praxis, supra* note 372, at 353.

374. Cf. Commission Report, *supra* note 43 at 72–73 (making a similar suggestion).

About the Contributors

Lawrence R. Baca served as senior trial attorney in the Civil Rights Division, United States Department of Justice, for thirty-two years. At the time of his retirement he was the deputy director of the Office of Tribal Justice. He was the senior and longest-serving American Indian attorney in the history of the Department of Justice. He has been an adjunct professor of federal Indian law at the American University Washington College of Law and Howard University School of Law, national president of the National Native American Bar Association three times, and national president of the Federal Bar Association. His scholarly work has appeared in the *Howard Law Journal*, the *University of Illinois Law Review*, and the Smithsonian Institution's *Handbook of North American Indians*.

Kristen A. Carpenter is associate dean for faculty development and associate professor at the University of Colorado Law School where she teaches property, cultural property, and American Indian law. Her research on those topics has been published in the *Yale Law Journal, UCLA Law Review, Stanford Environmental Law Journal, American Indian Law Review,* and other venues. Professor Carpenter is a graduate of Dartmouth College and Harvard Law School, and is active in the Colorado Indian Bar Association and Federal Bar Association's Indian Law Section. She lives in Boulder, Colorado with her husband and two small children.

Duane Champagne is a member of the Turtle Mountain Band of Chippewa from North Dakota. He is professor of sociology and American Indian studies, a faculty adviser for the UCLA Native Nations Law and Policy Center, a member of the Tribal Learning Community and Educational Exchange Working Group, and contributor of the education chapter to the United Nation's *State of the World's Indigenous Peoples Report*. Professor Champagne was director of the UCLA American Indian Studies Center from 1991 to 2002 and editor of the *American Indian Culture and Research Journal* from 1986 to 2003. He has written or edited more than 125 publications including *Social Change and Cultural Continuity Among Native Nations; The Native North American Almanac;* and *Captured Justice: Native Nations Under Public Law 280*. Professor Champagne's research and writings focus on social and cultural change in historical and contemporary Native American communities and the study of justice institutions in contemporary reservations.

Matthew L. M. Fletcher is professor of law at Michigan State University College of Law and director of the Indigenous Law and Policy Center. He is the chief justice of the Poarch Band of Creek Indians Supreme Court and also sits as an appellate judge for the Pokagon Band of Potawatomi Indians, the Hoopa Valley Tribe, and the Nottawaseppi Huron Band of Potawatomi Indians. He is a member of the Grand Traverse Band of Ottawa and Chippewa Indians, located in Peshawbestown, Michigan. In 2010, Professor Fletcher was elected to the American Law Institute. Professor Fletcher graduated from the University of Michigan Law School in 1997 and the University of Michigan in 1994. He recently published *American Indian Tribal Law* (Aspen 2011).

Carole Goldberg is the Jonathan D. Varat Distinguished Professor of Law and vice chancellor, Academic Personnel, at UCLA. She also serves as a justice of the Court of Appeals of the Hualapai Tribe. She has published articles and books on a wide range of subjects in federal Indian law and tribal law, including *Defying the Odds: The Tule River Tribe's Struggle for Sovereignty in Three Centuries* (Yale University Press, 2010, with Gelya Frank) and *Indian Law Stories* (Foundation Press, 2010, coedited with Kevin Washburn and Philip Frickey). She is also coeditor and coauthor of *Cohen's Handbook of Federal Indian Law* (1982 and 2005 editions). In 2011, President Barack Obama appointed her to the Indian Law and Order Commission.

Elizabeth Kronk is an assistant professor at Texas Tech University School of Law. She teaches in the areas of property, environmental and natural resources, and federal Indian law. In 2010, Professor Kronk was selected to serve as an Environmental Justice Young Fellow through the Woodrow Wilson International Center for Scholars and U.S.–China Partnership for Environmental Law at Vermont Law School. Professor Kronk currently serves as chair of the Federal Bar Association's (FBA) Indian Law Section, as well as on the editorial board for the FBA's *The Federal Lawyer*. Professor Kronk currently serves as a director on the Federal Bar Association's (FBA) board of directors, as well as on the editorial board. Additionally, she serves as chief judge of the Sault Ste. Marie Tribe of Chippewa Indians Court of Appeals, and is also a tribal citizen of the Sault Ste. Marie Tribe of Chippewa Indians.

Catharine A. MacKinnon is Elizabeth A. Long Professor of Law at the University of Michigan, long-term James Barr Ames Visiting Professor at the Harvard Law School, and Special Gender Adviser to the Prosecutor of the International Criminal Court, the Hague. She created the legal claim for sexual harassment, the civil rights ordinances against pornography (with Andrea Dworkin), the legal claim for rape as genocide, and the concept of gender crime internationally. The Supreme Court of Canada has largely adopted her approach to equality. Her legal writings are empirically documented as among the most widely cited in the English language. She is a teacher, writer, lawyer, and activist for equality around the world.

Kevin Noble Maillard is associate professor of law at Syracuse University. He is the author of the forthcoming book, *Loving v. Virginia in a Post-Racial World* (with Rose Villazor, Cambridge 2011). Professor Maillard's research focuses on civil liberties within the family and popular culture. His interests include nontraditional families, racial intermixture, and the role of marriage in America. His work has been published in the *Car-*

dozo Law Review, SMU Law Review, Fordham Law Review, and *Law & Inequality.* Professor Maillard received his BA in Public Policy from Duke University, his law degree from Penn Law School, and his PhD in political science from the University of Michigan. Originally from Oklahoma, he is a member of the Seminole Nation, Mekesukey Band.

Eva L. Petoskey, MS, is a member of the Grand Traverse Band of Ottawa and Chippewa Indians and served on the Tribal Council of the Grand Traverse Band for six years, four years as the vice-chairperson. She has more than thirty years of experience working with tribal communities throughout the Great Lakes region on issues related to wellness, education, evaluation, and culture. She currently serves as the program director for the Inter-Tribal Council of Michigan's Anishnaabek Healing Circle Access to Recovery, a large statewide collaborative involving the twelve federally recognized tribes in Michigan. Ms. Petoskey has a reputation for finding creative, culturally based solutions to complex problems. She has a longstanding commitment to living her life based on Anishnaabek values.

Frank Pommersheim is professor of law at the University of South Dakota. Prior to joining the faculty in 1984, he lived and worked on the Rosebud Sioux Reservation for ten years. He currently serves on a number of tribal appellate courts throughout Indian country, including as chief justice for the Cheyenne River Sioux Tribal Court of Appeals and the Rosebud Sioux Supreme Court. Professor Pommersheim is the author of *Braid of Feathers: American Indian Law and Contemporary Tribal Life* and *Broken Landscape: Indians, Indian Tribes, and the Constitution,* as well as numerous scholarly articles. He is also a poet. His most recent book of poetry is *East of the River: Poems Ancient and New.* A chapbook entitled *Small is Beautiful: The Buddha Correspondence* came out this spring.

Angela R. Riley is professor of law at the UCLA School of Law and director of the UCLA American Indian Studies Center. Her work has been published in some of the top legal journals in the country, including the *Yale Law Journal, Columbia Law Review,* and *California Law Review,* among others. She is a graduate of the University of Oklahoma and Harvard Law School. In 2003, she was selected to serve on her tribe's Supreme Court, becoming the first woman and youngest justice of the Supreme Court of the Citizen Potawatomi Nation of Oklahoma. In 2010, she was elected as chief justice. She is also an evidentiary hearing officer for the Morongo Band of Mission Indians. She lives in Los Angeles with her husband and her two daughters.

Mark D. Rosen is a professor of law at the Chicago-Kent College of Law (Illinois Institute of Technology). His expertise is in constitutional law, conflicts-of-law, state and local government law, federal Indian law, and election law. Professor Rosen's writings have appeared in the *Harvard Law Review,* the *University of Pennsylvania Law Review,* the *Minnesota Law Review,* the *University of Chicago Law Review,* the *Northwestern University Law Review,* the *Notre Dame Law Review,* the *William & Mary Law Review,* the *Emory Law Journal,* and *Constitutional Commentary,* among others. Professor Rosen has testified before Congress concerning the constitutionality of pending legislation, and has consulted to all levels of government in the United States as well as many private corporations. He graduated from Yale College and Harvard Law School.

Paul Spruhan is assistant attorney general for Human Services and Government at the Navajo Nation Department of Justice in Window Rock, Arizona. He received his AB in 1995 and his AM in 1996 from the University of Chicago. He received his JD in 2000 from the University of New Mexico. He graduated Order of the Coif and received an Indian law certificate. He and his wife, Bidtah Becker, also an attorney for the Navajo Nation Department of Justice, have two children and live in Fort Defiance, Arizona.

Rina Swentzell has a PhD in American Studies from the University of New Mexico and a master's degree in architecture. She has written an architectural history of Santa Clara Pueblo, a comparison of educational philosophies between the Western and Pueblo worlds, and various articles on culture and philosophy as well as a novel about pre-European Pueblo people in Northern New Mexico. She lives in Santa Clara Pueblo and is part of a community movement to address the seventy-year-old gender discrimination issue which states that the children of women who marry outside the Pueblo cannot become recognized members, while the same is not true for men. Her passion is to understand the values, lifestyles, and thoughts of her ancestors who lived in the southwest for thousands of years.

Ann Tweedy is an assistant professor at the Hamline University School of Law. She was previously a fellow at California Western School of Law and a visiting assistant professor at Michigan State University College of Law. After clerking for Judge Gould of the Ninth Circuit Court of Appeals and Judge Armstrong of the Oregon Court of Appeals, she worked for several years representing Indian tribes, first as in-house counsel for the Swinomish Indian Tribal Community and then as an associate at Kanji & Katzen, PLLC. She has written extensively on tribal sovereignty under federal law and also writes on tribal law and sexuality and the law. In addition to her work as a scholar, she is also a poet.

Gloria Valencia-Weber is a professor at the University of New Mexico (UNM) School of Law. A graduate of Harvard Law School, Valencia-Weber completed federal clerkships in Indian country for the Oklahoma Western District Court and for the chief judge of the Tenth Circuit. She established and served as director of the first Indian Law Certificate programs at the University of Tulsa, then at UNM. She recently completed a chapter on the Santa Clara Pueblo case for *Indian Law Stories* (2011). President Obama appointed Valencia-Weber to the board of directors for the Legal Services Corporation, which provides legal representation to poor individuals in the United States. Her honors include being selected for the American Law Institute. She also serves as a judge in the Southwest Intertribal Court of Appeals.

Index

prisoners, 68
procedure for civil lawsuits, 6
property interest, 122
Public Law 280, 249–258
Public Service Co. of New Mexico v. Tax Protest Panel, 322

R

race discrimination
    in criminal jurisdiction, 1978, 152
    in employment, 64
    inequality of Indians 3–7, 20, 21, 257–258, 301
    intermixing of African and Native Seminoles, 91–100
    police brutality statute, 18 U.S.C § 242, 11–15, 20, 21
    tribal nondiscrimination rules, 66–68
Randolph v. Hopi Tribe, 304
rape and sexual assault, 29, 33–34
Rave v. Reynolds, 141–142
Rave v. Reynolds (Rave II), 144
Redman v. Birdshead, 189–193
referendum, 106–108
religious freedom
    American Indian Religious Freedom Act of 1978, 164
    Brennan, US Supreme Court Justice William J., 161–162
    Cherokee religious ceremonies, 177–178
    Comanche family's experiences, 182–183
    First Amendment, 165–167
    Indian sacred sites, 162, 165
    individuals, 175
    legal sources on, 165–172
    Religious Freedom Restoration Act, 165
    tribal constitutions and religion, 175–177
    variation among Native cultures, 163–164
    writing about, 163–165
Religious Freedom Restoration Act, 165
Reno, Janet, 232
retrocession, 258–268
Reynolds, William Bradford, 8
Richards, John B., 253, 255, 257
Richland, Justin, 184
rights, civil
    assimilation critique, 160–163
    Convention on the Elimination of All Forms of Discrimination Against Women, 32
    Convention on the Elimination of All Forms of Racial Discrimination, 32
    egalitarian philosophy in Anishnaabek community, 47–50
    ICRA case law, empirical study of, 285–323
    individual rights, Navajo approach to, 124–126
    individual v. collective, 5, 29–31, 41, 50, 136–137
    individual women's rights and equality, 27–38